MONTANA
HANDBOOK

MONTANA
HANDBOOK

W.C. McRAE AND JUDY JEWELL

MOON
PUBLICATIONS INC.

MONTANA HANDBOOK

Please send all comments,
corrections, additions, amendments,
and critiques to:

**W.C. McRae and Judy Jewell
c/o Moon Publications Inc.
722 Wall Street
Chico, CA 95928, USA**

Published by
    Moon Publications, Inc.
    722 Wall Street
    Chico, California 95928, USA

Printed by
    Colorcraft Ltd., Hong Kong

PRINTING HISTORY
1st edition, March 1992
Reprinted August 1992

Library of Congress Cataloging in Publication Data
McRae, W.C., 1956-
    Montana Handbook / W.C. McRae & Judy Jewell. — 1st ed.
        p.   cm.
    Includes bibliographical references and index.
    ISBN 0-918373-76-X : $13.95
    1. Montana—Description and travel—1981—Guide-books.
I. Jewell, Judy, 1957-   . II. Title.
F729.3.M38   1992
917.8604'33—dc20   91-44030
                                                                            CIP

Printed in Hong Kong

To our parents,
Frank and Betty, and Charley and Hazel.

ACKNOWLEDGEMENTS

A heart-felt thank you to editor Anne-Marie Nicoara, who managed to unwind our sentences and to endure both our zeal and petulance. Thanks too to Mark Morris, Moon's ambassador to Portland, who did double duty as neighbor and copy editor. And thanks to Mary Orr for sharing the grumbling and hot gossip. We owe everyone at Moon for taking our enthusiasm and turning it into a book.

Montana Handbook would not have been possible without the use of Michael Powell's guidebook library on Pioneer Courthouse Square. Thank you, Michael and Ann Smith, for the encouragement and the opportunity to write this book while still employed. Tack Goodell taught our laptops to write this book; for this, and his friendship, we are grateful.

Thanks most of all to our friends and family who have stood by us through the project. To the staff at Powell's Travel Store, we owe a huge thank you for your support, your complicity, and in general for covering our rears. Thank you Steve for your great phone manner; and thanks to John for the phone calls and info on natural resources. Allison and Mike, we owe a debt of gratitude for the dinners, drinks and the haven during hard times. And thanks to Kim, Susan, and Tom for insisting on a hand of bridge even if there wasn't any time in the schedule.

Montana-side, thanks to Richard and Liz for the lodging and Helena tips. To George, Neva, and the folks at the BDAR, thank you for your generous hospitality, your insights and opinions, the loan of books and photos, and for putting up with frazzled authors.

IS THIS BOOK OUT OF DATE?

Between the time we tooled around the Great Plains, traded jokes and cold brews with as many Montana folks as possible, wrote it all down and put it on the shelf, a few things have probably changed. The grass is taller. That yellow dog might've wandered off. Heck, even a hotel or two may have changed hands. We'll be keeping track of things, but between editions you can help out.

Found a restaurant too good to pass up? Let us know. A local craftsman who deserves national attention? We'd be glad to hear about it. Please alert us to mistakes and changes. That's what we're here for.

Scribble notes directly into the book as you travel; all information sent to us will be checked and considered for use in the next edition.

If you just want to sound off about this book, or about Montana in general, please drop us a line: we'd love to hear from you.

W.C. McRae/Judy Jewell
c/o Moon Publications Inc.
722 Wall Street
Chico, CA 95928
USA

CONTENTS

LIST OF MAPS

MAP SYMBOLS

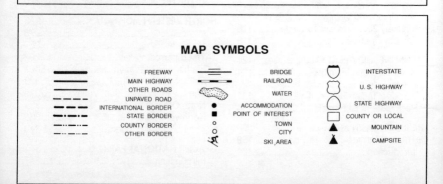

LIST OF CHARTS

ABBREVIATIONS

4WD—four wheel drive
B&B—bed and breakfast
d—double occupancy
F—fahrenheit
km—kilometer
Mt.—mount
OW—one way

p.o.—post office
pp—per person
RT—roundtrip
RV—recreational vehicle
s—single occupancy
WPA—Works Projects' Administration

PREFACE

$\mathcal{M}$ontana has been a traveler's destination for centuries. During summers, Indian hunting parties journeyed into Montana, returning west to their mountain homes with stories of a rich, mysterious land full of buffalo and holy sites. Cattle drovers, following the seasons northward, summered in Montana and returned south with tales of abundant game, endless grasslands, and high adventure. Immigrant farmers and ranchers were drawn to the expanses of Montana, and brought the newcomer's conviction of fresh beginnings. Nowadays, Montana attracts writers and artists who find in the state a "sense of place" both nurturing and hostile to the people who endure there.

Montana is often described as if it were two states, an eastern prairie and a western mountain range. But more than a common government links these regions. A visitor first notices the space: a sense of monumentality unites Montana, whether it's the glaciered peaks of the west or the corroded badlands of the east. It's called the Big Sky Country; here nature limbers up, stretches out past the horizons, takes up room.

But as much as space, it's the people. Today's Montanans derive from many strains: immigrant farmer, sheepherder, Indian, miner, logger, shopkeeper, rancher. They were all people who came to a hard land and stayed, making from Montana a living only of sorts, but always a home. Montanans are self-reliant, quick to see humor, with personalities so expansive that so few really *do* fill the state. History is not very old here. Montanans are still experiencing their past, not as Western history, but as Western Ethic.

Montana only recently adopted a daytime speed limit. It's observed only intermittently by the locals who have miles to go before they shop, visit, feed, or do much of anything in this huge state. However this guidebook recommends that the traveler take it slow. Stop to investigate Montana's towns and cities, its streams and parks. Follow a hunch, dawdle along a side road: the land fairly explodes with small epiphanies of beauty. Take the long way around to a spot where a moment of history can be relived, where a lazy picnic can be shared, or where the obscure and the out of the way can be found for its own sake.

BOB RACE

INTRODUCTION

THE LAND

Montana's borders rope in just over 147,000 square miles, making it the fourth-largest state behind Alaska, Texas, and California. The northern edge of the state spans the Canadian province of Alberta, and catches two-thirds of Saskatchewan and the eastern part of British Columbia to boot. North and South Dakota lie off to the east, Wyoming flanks much of the south, and the Idaho state line rims the Bitterroot Mountains at the western and southwestern borders. Central Montana is particularly varied, with high plateaus and isolated mountain ranges running in no set direction. The Continental Divide enters from Canada in Glacier National Park, twists through the western mountains, and exits on a high, flat stretch of land just west of Yellowstone Park. The eastern part of the state, renowned for its dryness, is coursed by the Missouri and the Yellowstone rivers and a host of smaller valleys. Contorted badlands, eroded terraces, and steep rimrocks fringe river valleys and dot the plains. Minerals, coal, and oil are concealed throughout the state, giving rise to the nickname, the "Treasure State."

GEOLOGY

Precambrian sand and mud deposits blanketed western Montana over 570 million years ago, before the supercontinent of Pangaea broke up into Europe, Africa, and the Americas. Traces of blue-green algae are the only fossils found in Precambrian rocks, which can still be seen in western and central Montana where later movements forced them to the surface. Glacier National Park is almost entirely Precambrian in origin.

Toward the end of the Mesozoic era, tectonic plates were scudding all over the world. According to plate-tectonics theory, as the Atlantic Ocean widened, the North American Plate was shoved into the Pacific Ocean Plate, which slipped under the western edge of the continent. The crust of western Montana crumpled, cracked, and faulted, then lifted way up above sea level. About 70 million years ago, the Rocky Mountains were produced by this upheaval.

Sedimentary layers were scrambled during these crustal movements, and in some places, old rocks slipped on top of younger ones. This is especially apparent in Glacier National Park. When the Rockies lifted, layers of rocks skidded eastward from what are now the Flathead and North Fork valleys, ending up as the Lewis Overthrust on the eastern front of the Rockies. Volcanic intrusions further developed the Rockies and formed separate mountain ranges to the east of them.

As western Montana lifted, ancient seas rolled back off the eastern part of the state for the final time. Swamps and floodplains stretched across eastern Montana by the end of the Mesozoic. Plants and animals lived on these sedimentary flats, and their remains go into our gas tanks today. Big peat swamps flourished along the floodplains; eventually they crumbled and rotted into thick veins of coal.

Volcanoes began erupting in present-day Yellowstone Park about 50 million years ago. A monumental eruption 600,000 years ago shot magma over the West, leaving a large crater, or caldera. Recurrent outpourings of lava formed the high plateau that's there now.

Alternating wet and dry periods over the past 40 million years modified terrain all over the state. During dry spells, river valleys filled with sediments, threatening to completely bury mountain peaks. When the climate dampened, rivers washed away the fill to re-expose underlying structures. This deposit-erosion cycle has made eastern Montana a paleontologist's dream. The largest complete Tyrannosaurous rex skeleton on record was unearthed in remote Garfield County.

Cenozoic glaciers advanced south, covering much of northwestern Montana. East of the di-

vide, glaciers plowed the land flat as far south as the Missouri. The Beartooth Plateau, just north of Yellowstone Park, was glacier-covered at much the same time lava was flowing over it. An ice dam in Idaho backed up the Clark Fork River until most of the valleys in western Montana were covered by glacial Lake Missoula. When the ice dam gave way, which it did time and time again, torrents of water barreled across the Northwest, scouring topsoil and carving river gorges all the way to the Pacific coast.

East of the Rockies, glacial Lake Great Falls formed at the southern edge of the glacier and reached from Great Falls to Cut Bank. Glacial ice forced the Missouri River, which originally emptied into Hudson's Bay, to alter its course southward to the Mississippi; the Milk River now flows in a section of the Missouri's original bed.

PHYSICAL FEATURES

The Plains
Erosion and uplifts formed the prairie landscape. Water, frost, and wind have cut gullies and gulches into the plains and sculpted benches or terraces along river valleys.

Montana's badlands, desolate and without vegetation, tend to be found south of the Missouri, where glaciers never deposited thick layers of good soil. Soft bedrock just beneath the surface of bare ground is easily eroded by rain; gullies form, sediment outwashes spreading from their mouths. The bare, rain-pounded soil develops a hard crust, which exacerbates the runoff and makes it all the more difficult for any

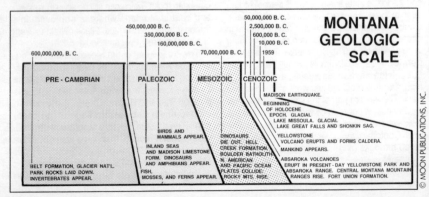

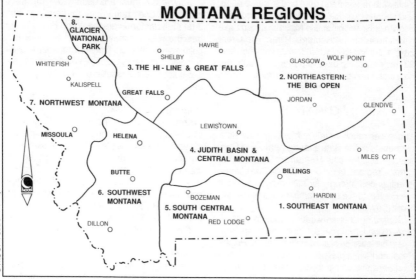

MONTANA REGIONS

8. GLACIER NATIONAL PARK
WHITEFISH
KALISPELL
HAVRE
SHELBY
3. THE HI-LINE & GREAT FALLS
GLASGOW   WOLF POINT
2. NORTHEASTERN: THE BIG OPEN
GREAT FALLS
7. NORTHWEST MONTANA
JORDAN
GLENDIVE
MISSOULA
HELENA
LEWISTOWN
4. JUDITH BASIN & CENTRAL MONTANA
MILES CITY
BUTTE
6. SOUTHWEST MONTANA
BILLINGS
BOZEMAN
5. SOUTH CENTRAL MONTANA
HARDIN
1. SOUTHEAST MONTANA
DILLON
RED LODGE

© MOON PUBLICATIONS, INC.

vegetation to take hold. The barrenness of the badlands perpetuates itself.

Northeastern Montana prairie is broad, flat, and underlain by gravel beds. These high plains were formed 3-15 million years ago in a dry climate. The gravel layer allows efficient surface drainage, avoiding erosion and the channels and gullies of the badlands. Glacial debris has further enriched the soil, making this some of the state's best agricultural land.

The Mountains

The ranges of the Rockies have different geologic histories. The Boulder batholith, a mass of intrusive granite between Butte and Helena, is filled with mineral veins, especially copper. The Absarokas and the Gallatin Range are blanketed with volcanic rocks from eruptions in and around Yellowstone Park. Many mountains carried glaciers, and some still do. In the far northwest part of the state, glaciers shrouded the mountains, leaving them relatively small and softly shaped. Where glaciers ran down from high cirques into mountain valleys, there is a characteristic straightening of the valley's path and a U-shape to its floor, unlike the V-shaped river valleys. Glaciers also pushed along gravel and soil, left in big hills called moraines when the glaciers retreated.

The isolated mountain ranges of central Montana are not part of the Rockies. Many of them were formed at the end of the Mesozoic era, about 20 million years after the Rockies, when molten granite shot up from the depths of the earth and bowed up the sedimentary formations. Other areas of central Montana were lifted along faults to form high plateaus and buttes.

Rivers

Coursing across the eastern part of the state, the Missouri and the Yellowstone rivers look on the map like a big crab's pincer, joined to the leg just over the North Dakota border. Western rivers, notably the Clark Fork of the Columbia and the Kootenai, are tucked into mountain valleys. Rivers provided the way into Montana for the first white explorers, who were hoping to sail out on the Columbia. Trappers and traders also used the rivers as thoroughfares. Steamboats made the difficult trip up the Missouri through sandbars, rapids, and fallen trees to Fort Benton until railroads took over the transportation business. Towns sprung up in the river valleys, and highways were built on their banks.

The dams that now harness water power and create reservoirs across the state have altered Montana's geography. Every large river but the

Yellowstone has been dammed at some point, and millions of gallons of water are backed up in Fort Peck Reservoir on the Missouri and in Lake Koocanusa on the Kootenai River. The Great Falls of the Missouri, which took Lewis and Clark 22 back-breaking days to portage in 1805, are now just a series of hydroelectric dams.

CLIMATE

There's as much variety in Montana's weather as there is in the state's topography. The Continental Divide splits Montana into two broad climatic regions. West of the Divide, the climate is influenced strongly by mild marine air from the Pacific; to the east, harsher continental patterns prevail.

Stories of extreme weather abound in Montana. Indeed, it can get *cold;* the lowest temperature in the lower 48 states was recorded at Rogers Pass, northwest of Helena, in 1954: -70° F. Hot summers are common, with temperatures of 117° recorded in both Glendive and Medicine Lake.

Pacific fronts are often almost spent out after passing over the Olympic, Coast, and Cascade mountains. By the time they reach Montana, little moisture is left for the western slopes of the Rockies.

During the spring, the winds shift, and moisture comes up from the Gulf of Mexico. These storms sweep through the Midwest and hit the east slopes of the Rockies. May and June are the wettest months over most of the state; the exception is the northwest, which gets most of its moisture from winter Pacific storms.

July and August are usually the warmest months. It does rain during the summer, but brief thunderstorms are the norm. By September, the weather may start to change for the colder and wetter, but there is frequently a lovely Indian summer in October. Winter storms can begin anytime, but roads are often clear through early November.

Chinooks

Warm, dry winter winds coming off the east slopes of the Rockies and across the plains are called "chinooks." As the Pacific air passes over the mountains, it unloads its moisture and is warmed on its eastern downslope run. Chinook winds carry an almost mythological force. They can bring incredibly rapid relief from frigid weather; in Great Falls, the temperature once rose from -32° to 15° in seven minutes, almost seven degrees a minute.

Droughts

Montana's dry spells can be as striking as its extremes in heat and cold. Average rainfall for the western part of the state is 18 inches a year, 13 inches for the east. Studies of almost 300 years' worth of tree rings have shown that, every 20-some years, the western U.S. experiences a drought. A five-year drought that started in 1917 in eastern Montana drove many homesteaders away from agriculture. This drought was coupled with particularly harsh winters. The 1930s saw not only economic depression, but (according to tree rings) the most severe drought since 1700. When it's too dry for prairie grasses to survive, ranchers are forced to buy expensive feed, or sell their herds and wait for rain.

FLORA AND FAUNA

Montana's geography dictates its habitats, and the flora and fauna can be considered in two broad categories: prairie and mountain. Precipitation and elevation are the major factors determining what grows where.

Since Lewis and Clark began recording their observations of Montana's plants and animals, a number of species have been exterminated, but both variety and abundance remain. Montana hosts some 107 species of mammals, 382 kinds of birds, 86 sorts of fish, 2,400 types of vascular plants, 17 varieties each of reptiles and amphibians, and 315 different mollusks and crustaceans.

PRAIRIE

Nineteenth-century atlases called the plains the Great American Desert, an undeserved name that ignores both the subtle variety of the grasses and the wild proliferation of animals.

Flora

The savannahs of eastern Montana offer more than sagebrush and prickly pear landscapes. Lewis and Clark noted a "scattering of pine and cedar" on the hills, and prickly pear, chokecherries and currants on lower ground. The cottonwoods that grew near riverbottoms were prized for firewood and for dugout canoes.

Eastern Montana is mostly shortgrass prairie—that is, a dry grassland supporting perennial grasses such as bluestem, bluejoint, and June, wheat, and pine grass. Cheat grass grows in overgrazed areas; it starts strong but can't last through the summer. Other "nuisances" are feather grass and needle grass, which irritate the skin and eyes of sheep. Russian thistle, or tumbleweed, arrived with European immigrants and is almost universally reviled.

blue gramma

Prairie flowers include the buttercup, yellow-bell, crocus, shooting star, bluebell, blanketflower, golden aster, and daisy. Blue camas and death camas grow in moist areas. Prickly pear and three other species of cactus still dog those who try to walk across the prairie. Milkweed, a common roadside "weed," was variously used as eye medicine, gravy stock, and chewing gum by the Cheyenne. The deep, thick roots of the Indian breadroot plant were an important food for eastern Montana Indians.

Chokecherry bushes are widespread on the northern plains and into the Rockies. Chokecherries were pounded, dried, and stored for the winter by Plains Indians. Indians also brewed a tea from the bark to relieve stomach ailments; unripe chokecherry puree was used by both Indians and white settlers to treat diarrhea. Chokecherries, normally bitter, were traditionally harvested after the first freeze, which sweetened them.

Prairie sage is a traditional sacred and medicinal plant to many Montana Indians.

While the prairie is not known for its trees, lodgepole pine does grow on some hillsides, and deciduous trees, especially willows and cottonwoods, take root in the river valleys.

Fauna

Lewis and Clark found the plains fairly swarming with wildlife, and not just with "musquetoes," either. Just upstream from the confluence of the Missouri and Yellowstone rivers, Lewis noted:

> The whole face of the country was covered with herds of Buffaloe, Elk & Antelopes; deer are also abundant, but keep themselves more concealed in the woodland. the buffaloe Elk and Antelope are so gentle that we pass near them while feeding, without appearing to excite any alarm among them; and when we attract their attention, they frequently approach us more nearly to discover what we are, and in some instances pursue us to a considerable distance apparently with that view.

They also reported encounters with rattlesnakes, wolves, black bears, grizzlies, beaver (one of

BEARS

Grizzly bears are huge: adults commonly weigh 600-800 pounds and stand four feet high at their muscular shoulder humps. A grizzly's dish-shaped profile contrasts with the black bear's straight Roman nose. Smaller size and the lack of a shoulder hump further distinguish the black bear from the grizzly; black bears weigh about 200 pounds and stand about three feet tall.

Color is not a reliable distinguishing trait—no shade of brown is unusual for either bear. Black bears can be honey-colored and are commonly cinnamon; grizzlies are not always silver-tipped and grizzled looking.

But perhaps the ability to tell bears apart is not the most important thing to know when confronted by any ursine species.

Safety Considerations

Find out where bears, especially grizzlies, live, and take precautions. In Montana, grizzlies live in Glacier and Yellowstone national parks, and in wilderness areas throughout the Rockies. Rangers will usually know if bears have been spotted locally, and trails are sometimes closed due to bear activity.

Try not to surprise a bear. Stay alert and make some noise while hiking—many hikers wear bells. Keep strong odors down. Don't wear a fragrance; don't cook strong-smelling foods (freeze-dried foods are almost odor-free). At night,

keep food and smelly clothing inside a car or strung high in a tree. Sleep well away from the cooking area. Women are frequently cautioned to avoid bear country while menstruating.

If you do see a bear, give it plenty of room. Try to stay upwind of the bear so it can get your scent. If the bear becomes aggressive, drop something that may absorb its attention and climb the nearest tall tree. If this isn't possible, the next best bet is probably to curl up into a ball, clasp your hands behind your neck, and play dead, even if the bear begins to bat you around.

Bears can, and occasionally do, kill people, but most people who enter bear country never have any problem. In fact, it is a special thing to see a grizzly; they are as impressive as they are rare. Precautions and respect for bears will ensure not only your continued survival, but theirs as well.

grizzly, Ursus horribilus   MIKE WELLINS

which gave Lewis's dog a nasty bite), bighorn sheep (whose meat was reportedly a delicacy), a "polecat" (skunk), mule deer, and prairie dogs. On their trip up the Missouri, Lewis provided the first descriptions of the sage grouse, the western meadowlark, and the cutthroat trout.

The buffalo, bears, and wolves may be gone from the prairies, but what Lewis called "our trio of pests"—mosquitoes, gnats, and prickly pear—remain. Add to that rattlesnakes and grasshoppers, and you'll have a picture of what homesteaders faced on the savannah.

Many plains animals dig burrows. Witness the prairie dog. It can metabolize its own waste water and survive for years without drinking. The black-tailed prairie dogs of Montana live in "towns" of burrows, which are occasionally sublet by burrowing owls.

Another burrowing animal is the pocket gopher, a long-clawed, small-eyed rodent that comes aboveground only for quick passes at mating. Pocket gophers get their nutrition—both food and water—from plants they suck, roots first, into their burrows.

While burrows may provide defense for many rodents and birds, the pronghorn relies on fleetness. Individuals have been clocked at 70 mph. The prong is part of a sheath composed of keratin (a fingernail-like protein) and fused hairs covering a core of bone. Pronghorns (which despite the common appellation, are not antelopes) shed their horn sheaths annually and pass the winter and spring sporting the bare, bony horn core. They are the only mammals that shed horns (as opposed to antlers, which are, as a rule, dropped annually).

Deer, both white-tailed and the large-eared mule deer, roam the breaks of the big eastern Montana rivers. Coyotes still prey on both wild and stock animals.

Rattlesnakes can turn up just about anywhere in eastern Montana, and it pays to watch where you put your hands and feet. Wear sturdy shoes for hiking. Though healthy adults rarely die from a rattlesnake's venom, a bite does warrant prompt medical attention.

There's no dearth of insect life on the prairie. Most everyone who's read a Western can talk of grasshoppers scouring the grasslands and swarming around cattle, cowboys, and horses.

The sharp-tailed grouse, mourning dove, killdeer, bob-o-link, long-billed curlew, horned lark, magpie, western meadowlark, goldfinch, Brewer's blackbird, and sparrow hawk can all be spotted on the eastern Montana plains.

Warm-water species of fish, such as paddlefish, walleye, northern pike, ling, and channel catfish inhabit the Yellowstone and the Missouri where they cross the plains.

CONIFEROUS FORESTS

Most of western Montana supports lush growth, dominated by coniferous trees. Though there are some western Montana prairies (especially around the Mission Valley), timbered hillsides are the rule. This category is usually broken down into at least two separate habitats: lower montane and higher subalpine. The highest peaks of Montana also support small areas of alpine tundra.

Flora

Forests of conifers with shrubby undergrowth cover mountainous western Montana. Ponderosa pine predominates low on the slopes. A little higher, Douglas fir takes over and, above that, lodgepole pine, a species that depends on fire for its propagation, may form dense stands. Western larch, western red cedar, western white pine, grand fir, aspen, and birch can also be found. Willows and alders sprout up along streambeds, and kinnikinnick, Oregon grape, and serviceberries are common elements of the understory.

Subalpine forests are rooted in subalpine fir and Engelmann spruce. Alpine larch is another hardy, high-elevation conifer. An autumn hillside of reddish-gold "evergreens" doesn't necessarily mean a lot of dead trees. Rather, it's probably a stand of larch, one of the few conifer species that drops its needles in the winter. Huckleberries are perhaps the best-loved subalpine understory shrub.

Wildflower meadows of glacier lilies, alpine poppies, columbine, Indian paintbrush, asters, arnica, globeflowers, white dryads, and bear grass color the midsummer hillsides. Dogtooth violets and mariposa lilies grow a little farther down the slopes. In the valleys and low on the hills, the state flower, the bitterroot, blossoms in early June. Serviceberry bushes turn white with flowers early in May and bear purplish berries late in July. This member of the rose family grows on the slopes and canyons of the Rocky Mountains.

Fauna

There are bears here, mostly black bears but some grizzlies. Elk live high in the summer, low in the winter. They're sometimes called wapiti, and they grow their antlers fresh every summer and shed them in the winter. Moose are common, but private. Mule deer negotiate rough forest terrain; white-tailed deer run across more open areas. Transition areas between two types of habitat (such as the edges of a meadow or clearcut) are usually good places to look for wildlife. Bighorn sheep, mountain goats, and grizzly bears are all more likely to be seen high on the slopes of the Rockies.

Mountain lions have been showing up in some unlikely places, like the streets of Columbia Falls, the parks of Missoula, and the campgrounds of Glacier National Park. Big people can usually frighten them off with shouting and menacing gestures, but children and small adults have been attacked. Youngsters should hike within sight of adults.

Labeled a dangerous predator, the wolf has been trapped, hunted, and poisoned to nearextinction. Since receiving protection as an endangered species, wolf populations have made a slight comeback, mostly in Glacier and Yellowstone national parks. The wolf's smaller relative, the coyote, has managed not only to survive the abuses given to predator species but to actually thrive in human-inhabited areas.

Dippers, Clark's nutcrackers, spruce grouse, owls, woodpeckers, jays, chickadees, wrens, sparrows, flycatchers, mountain bluebirds, western tanagers, warblers, rufous hummingbirds, waterfowl, bald eagles, osprey, and hawks all find niches in the varied habitats provided by western Montana's forests.

Westslope cutthroat trout, the state fish, is native to Montana's streams and lakes. First described by Meriwether Lewis, its Latin name, *Salmo clarki* , remembers William Clark. The name cutthroat is just as revealing: these black-specked fish sport two red slashes under their jaws. Because of their tendency to hybridize with rainbow trout, cutthroat are becoming rarer.

Bull trout, more euphonically called Dolly Vardens, live mostly in northwest Montana, especially in their native Clark Fork and Flathead drainages. They're olive green with orange or yellow spots on their sides, and can run up to 30 pounds.

Brown trout were imported from Europe in the 1880s and their numbers have now surpassed many native species. Browns have a reputation for being wily and tough to hook. Another introduced species, the brook trout, comes from the eastern U.S. The backs of these fish have light-colored "worm tracks" on their otherwise dark olive backs.

Whitefish are silver-sided with olive-green backs and small mouths. They are usually five pounds or less, and live in the western part of the state.

Arctic grayling are not common, but can be caught in southwest and south-central Montana. They are small copper-colored or bluish fish, usually less than a foot long, with large dorsal fins.

Until recently, kokanee salmon thrived in Flathead Lake, where they'd been planted in the 1920s. Although changes in the lake's ecology have not favored the Flathead kokanee, they are still abundant in other parts of northwest Montana. Kokanee are landlocked salmon with small dark spots on a blue-tinted body.

ALPINE TUNDRA

Alpine conditions exist in a few places in Montana. Above the timberline (9,000-10,000 feet) the gray-green ground cover includes small, low-lying vegetation: grasses, mosses, lichens, sedges, and krummholz (small, twisted trees pruned by the wind) of whitebark pine.

Plants and animals pack as much as possible into the short, cool summers of the high country. Hoary marmots, ground squirrels, pikas, and mountain goats are commonly spotted around Logan Pass, one of Glacier Park's alpine communities. The white-tailed ptarmigan is the only bird living year-round on the tundra, though other species, such as water pipits and finches, summer here.

cutthroat trout, Salmo clarki
BOB RACE

HISTORY

The First Settlers

Proto-Indians first arrived in Montana from Asia about 10,000-15,000 years ago. After crossing the Bering Sea causeway, they traveled along the Great North Trail, the rift that opened up along the east face of the Rocky Mountains when the ice fields of the last ice age retreated into the mountains. These people hunted big game and used tools made of chipped stone. Between 8000-6000 B.C., these early Indians lived principally on the plains and foothills. Around 5000 B.C. a desert climate developed, and Indians left the state.

Buffalo again spread across the region as a more moderate climate developed about A.D. 500. The hunters returned, probably from the south and west, bringing with them new techniques and cultural practices. These early dwellers of Montana were probably the ancestors of the Salish Indians. Prior to the introduction of horses, new hunting techniques, such as using a buffalo jump, or *pishkun,* were developed. Entire herds of buffalo would be stampeded off precipices, and then slaughtered for meat. The use of the tepee, or moveable skin tent, was introduced. Pictographs and petroglyphs, rock paintings and carvings, date from this period.

Historic Indian Tribes

When white traders and settlers arrived in the region in the early 1800s, they did not find a land peopled with indigenous native tribes. Instead, the Indians of Montana were themselves only recent immigrants, attempting to establish homelands and work out the cultural changes that their recent uprooting had set loose.

Some of the tribes that migrated to Montana during this period were not traditionally nomadic. Most came from woodlands in the Great Lakes-Mississippi basin region, where they were sedentary, sometimes agricultural people who lived in permanent earthen dwellings. During the process of dislocation to the west, agriculture was lost, and a hunting culture developed. The earth lodge was abandoned for the tepee. For these people, the buffalo became more than a food source: it was the central assumption upon which their entire cultural life was predicated.

Social organization was structured by warrior societies, and in some cases, by clan. Women were responsible for most of the daily work, save hunting and fighting. The Plains Indians shared an animistic religion.

The first tribe to enter Montana during the historic period was the Shoshone, who began to move into the southwestern corner of the state from the Great Basin area about 1600. They drove the resident Salish tribes farther north into the mountains. The Shoshone were fearsome warriors and the first Montana tribe to ride horses.

The Crow Indians arrived in Montana shortly thereafter, and settled along the Yellowstone River drainages, the first tribe to actually settle on the Montana prairies. The Blackfeet entered Montana from the north and east about a century later, around 1730, and brought with them the rifle. The Blackfeet, and their allies the Gros Ventre and the Assiniboine, soon established dominance over the northern Montana plains.

Further pressure from white settlement forced the Sioux and Northern Cheyenne into eastern Montana. The Cree and Chippewa tribes entered Montana in the 1870s as they were displaced from the Canadian prairies. As more and more tribes were squeezed into the area that would later become Montana, intertribal rivalries intensified. The Crow were hated enemies of the Blackfeet. The Blackfeet slaughtered the Salish or Kootenai Indians who dared to leave the safety of the mountains. As the Sioux entered Montana, they too became enemies of the Crow.

The Salish and Kootenai retained some traditions of the Northwest Indian tribes. Although these tribes once traveled over the Rockies to hunt buffalo, the presence of the fierce Blackfeet confederation on the prairies soon made these hunting expeditions too dangerous.

The Corps Of Discovery

In 1803 President Thomas Jefferson purchased the Louisiana Territory from France for $11,250,000. The territory was understood to be the land west of the Mississippi to its Missouri headwaters, and north of the Arkansas

Meriwether Lewis

By July 25, they were at the Three Forks of the Missouri and were heartened by Sacajawea's claim that they were near her homeland. Nineteen days later, near Lemhi Pass, Lewis encountered the expedition's first Montana Indian (a Shoshone, who led them to Sacajawea's brother). They traded for horses and proceeded down the Bitterroot Valley. On September 13, they crossed Lolo Pass out of Montana toward the Pacific Coast.

After a hungry and flea-ridden winter on the Oregon coast, the Corps started back up the Columbia. They backtracked to Lolo Pass and crossed into Montana on June 27, 1806. At the point where Lolo Creek meets the Bitterroot River, the expedition divided, on July 1. Clark took part of the Corps and retraced the previous journey to the Missouri headwaters, but this time followed the Gallatin River over the Bozeman Pass in order to explore the Yellowstone River Valley. Lewis took the rest of the men and followed old Indian trails up the Blackfoot River and thence over the Rockies to the Great Falls in order to scout a more direct passage over the Continental Divide. While Clark had an uneventful journey down the Yellowstone, Lewis had a confrontation with a group of Blackfeet that left two Indian warriors dead.

River to the 49th parallel. Jefferson engaged his personal secretary, Meriwether Lewis, to head an expedition to explore this new American territory, and to search for a passage from the Missouri River to the headwaters of the mighty Columbia. Lewis in turn chose William Clark to be the co-commander of what Jefferson called the Corps of Discovery.

The two captains, three sergeants, 23 enlisted men, and Clark's black slave, York, left St. Louis in May of 1804. In North Dakota, they made the acquaintance of the French trader Toussaint Charbonneau. Charbonneau had traveled widely on the upper Missouri, and he spoke several Indian languages. One of his wives, a 15-year-old Shoshone girl named Sacajawea, gave birth during the spring. Lewis and Clark hired Charbonneau as interpreter, and allowed the young mother and baby to accompany the Corps, as they later expected to travel through Shoshone territory.

The Corps entered Montana on April 26, 1805, passing the confluence of the Missouri and the Yellowstone rivers. They wound their way up the Missouri, traveling in canoes and pirogues.

William Clark

They met according to schedule at the confluence of the Yellowstone and the Missouri on August 12. By Sept. 23, 1806, they were in St. Louis. This amazing journey had an almost immediate effect on the history of Montana. Members of the Corps retold stories of vast amounts of wildlife, especially pelt-bearing mammals. Within a year, the first trading fort was built in Montana.

Trading Posts

The first fur-trading post, Fort Remon, was founded in 1807 by Manuel Lisa, at the confluence of the Bighorn and Yellowstone rivers. Beaver, much sought after in European fashions, was the major item of trade. Some Indian tribes, notably the Salish and Crow, maintained friendly relations with the white traders and trappers. The Blackfeet, who controlled the Missouri River area, were a marked exception.

John Jacob Astor's American Fur Company built Fort Union at the confluence of the Yellowstone and Missouri in 1829, and finally induced the Blackfeet to trade peacefully by dispatching a Blackfoot-speaking trapper to bring them to the fort for a conference. The Blackfeet complied. In 1838, 4,000 beaver pelts were taken from the heart of the dreaded Blackfeet territory by Astor's trappers.

Fort Union, and the American Fur Company, soon ruled the Montana fur trade. As beaver were increasingly trapped out (and European fashion changed), trade continued in buffalo hides. By 1840, the era of the trapper and mountain man was over; almost three dozen trading forts had been built in Montana before the beaver was trapped to near extinction.

The Black Robes

Iroquois Indians accompanied French trappers to western Montana in the early years of the 19th century. While the Iroquois were to teach the local Flathead and Nez Percé how to trap, they also passed on information about Christianity. The Montana Indians heard of "Black Robes" who possessed a Book of Heaven, whose "medicine" or power was great. The Flathead were greatly intrigued, and sent four delegations to St. Louis to ask for a Black Robe to come and visit the tribe.

Finally, in 1840, Father Pierre deSmet, a Belgian-born Jesuit, came west. Although the Indi-

ans' spiritual demands had more to do with the search for powerful medicine to protect them from the hostile Blackfeet than with traditional salvation, the Flathead and Nez Percé seemed genuinely friendly and anxious to learn the way of the Catholic fathers.

In 1841, St. Mary's Mission was established in the Bitterroot Valley, near Stevensville. Here, the Jesuits taught the Indians agriculture, music, milling, and, of course, religion. The original mission was abandoned in 1850, after deSmet made the mistake of starting missionary work with the Blackfeet. The Flathead were not anxious to share their "medicine" with their enemies, and lost interest in deSmet's projects. Another influential early church, St. Ignatius Mission, was established in 1854 in the Mission Valley amongst the Pend d'Oreille Indians.

Little attempt was made to bring Christianity to the Plains Indians until they were on reservations. Most of the early missionary work was done by the Catholic Church. Protestant missionaries entered the state only after white settlement had begun, and gold ore and high living induced the kind of bad doings best corrected by regular churchgoing.

Gold

The trappers and traders of the early part of the 19th century left little behind them, except endangered species. There were no roads, no communications networks, and almost no settlements (only Fort Benton still exists as a community).

James and Granville Stuart discovered gold on Gold Creek near Deer Lodge in 1860. In 1862, gold was found on Grasshopper Creek near Bannack, and the next year saw prospecting along Alder Gulch near Virginia City. Last Chance Gulch, which was to become Helena, boomed in 1864.

These large strikes, and many smaller mines, attracted people of varied character to Montana. There were fewer than 100 whites in the state in 1860. By 1870, there were over 20,000. Some men came to Montana to prospect for gold and get rich; others came to get rich by stealing and killing. Travel between the settlements of Virginia City, Bannack, and other mining camps became increasingly dangerous as "road agents" preyed on stagecoaches and miners.

For its protection, Virginia City elected as Sheriff Henry Plummer. Plummer, however, doubled as leader of the principal gang of road agents, called the "Innocents." Over 100 people were killed by the Innocents during 1862-63. In response, committees of vigilantes formed, and after reaching summary judgment, the Innocents were hanged.

By 1870, approximately $100 million in gold had been extracted from Montana claims. The advent of great wealth and property soon made firm government and community lawfulness imperative. In 1864, Montana became a territory, with Bannack its capital. Schools, churches, and other civic institutions were established in Virginia City. The miners began to bring their families out to the frontier to settle.

Treaties Made And Broken

While the Indians of the western mountains accommodated the arrival of white miners, trappers, and missionaries, the Plains Indians largely maintained their traditional ways during the first years of white ingress.

The first trail across the northern U.S. was the Oregon Trail. To protect travelers along its passage through Wyoming, the U.S. government produced the Fort Laramie Treaty in 1851, which was signed by the Crow, Gros Ventre, and Assiniboine. These tribes were assigned reservations in eastern Montana, along with the Blackfeet, who did not attend the meeting and who did not sign the treaty, but were in absentia assigned a reservation.

The discovery of gold in the western mountains increased the demand for transportation routes across treatied Indian country. The Bozeman Trail, blazed during the 1860s, led to the gold fields of Montana across Sioux tribal land. Three military forts were built to protect the trail. Gold was discovered in the Black Hills of South Dakota, country considered sacred by the Sioux, and prospectors flooded in.

These infractions by the whites infuriated the Indians. The American government responded by unilaterally diminishing the size of the original reservations. The Sioux and Cheyenne, among the last of the tribes to be forced into Montana by white western expansion, were especially angry at the ongoing incursions. After the gold rush in the Black Hills, the Sioux quit the reservation completely and resumed their traditional plains life-style on the prairies of eastern Montana.

Army Vs. Indian

The U.S. government in 1876 ordered the Sioux and the Cheyenne back onto the reservation. The Indians refused, and the Army was dispatched to compel them back. Three columns of infantry set out. The first column to arrive in Indian country divided, sending General George Custer and the Seventh Cavalry on ahead to seek the hostiles. They found the combined Cheyenne and Sioux force (perhaps 5,000 warriors) on June 26, 1876. Custer rashly decided to do battle alone, and his entire command (265 men) was destroyed.

The next year the Nez Percé under Chief Joseph fled from their Oregon reservation across Montana, attempting to reach sanctuary in Canada. After a battle at the Big Hole in western Montana, the Nez Percé struggled south to the Yellowstone Park area, and then veered north, hoping to escape into Canada near Havre. Thirty miles from the border, General Nelson Miles overtook the fleeing tribe. The Nez Percé, of Northwest origins, were sent to reservations in Oklahoma.

Custer's annihilation notwithstanding, by 1877 all the Indians in Montana were incarcerated on reservations. In fact, many forces besides the Army had worked to weaken, and inevitably subjugate the Indian. Diseases introduced from white settlements decimated Indian populations; an outbreak of smallpox amongst the Blackfeet in 1837 is reckoned to have killed three-quarters of the tribe. Alcohol was illegally traded to the Indians, which corrupted and debilitated the traditional warrior societies.

As trade evolved from peltry to buffalo robes, the Indians were unwittingly involved in exterminating the animal which provided the cornerstone of their entire traditional culture. Before white settlers reached the plains, 60 million buffalo lived in North America. By 1870, that number was down to 10-20 million. By 1883, after railroads crossed the West and settlers were streaming in after the Civil War, there were only 100-200 buffalo left in the U.S.

With the buffalo largely exterminated, Native Americans were reduced to complete dependence on handouts from the government's Indian agent. By the mid-1880s, the federal government spent $7 a year per Indian on a reservation, while it spent $1000 a year on a soldier stationed in Montana's Indian land.

The Railroad Arrives

Riverboats were the only form of transportation linking Montana and the rest of the nation until the 1880s. Boats could reach as far inland as Fort Benton on the Missouri and to Pompey's Pillar on the Yellowstone. But real economic growth and settlement awaited the coming of the railroad.

The Union Pacific built a spur line north from Utah to Butte in 1881. The Northern Pacific crossed the length of Montana, linking Portland and Chicago in 1883. In return for opening the northern transcontinental line, the Northern Pacific was given a land grant: for every mile of track laid, the railroad received forty sections (40 square miles) of land. In Montana alone, this amounted to 17 million acres.

The Great Northern stretched its service along the Montana/Canada border, joining Minneapolis and Seattle in 1893. The Milwaukee Road crossed central Montana on its way to Seattle in 1909. With access to coastal markets, Montana opened up to further development and immigration.

Cattle Country

Montana had had a cattle trade in the western valleys and foothills since the 1860s as ranches grew up to feed the mining camps, and Texas longhorns had been trailed into Montana as early as 1866. But the era of the cattleman didn't really begin until the 1880s, when longhorn cattle were trailed north from Texas in great numbers.

Typically, the large "outfits" that brought cattle into Montana at this time were owned by a group of investors, who bought shares in herds often numbering in the tens of thousands. Cowboys would herd these longhorns north from Texas, summer them free on the grassy unfenced prairies of Montana, and then round them up, sort them by brand, and sell them to eastern markets. This get-rich-quick scheme worked for many, because with a small investment in the start-up animal, low labor costs with the cowboys, and no feed bills to pay, the profitability was great.

Initially, the fattened steers were trailed south into Wyoming to railheads on the Union Pacific. With the construction of the Northern Pacific along the course of the Yellowstone River in 1881-82, railheads such as Wibaux, Miles City, and Billings became centers for the livestock trade, and full-blooded Old West cattle towns. In 1870, there were 48,000 head of cattle in Montana. By 1886, the height of the open range period, there were 675,000 head.

Butte

In 1864, two miners staked a claim for gold on a lonely bluff near the Continental Divide at the headwaters of the Clark Fork River. The gold soon played out, but miners discovered something else: silver.

As a source of wealth, silver was as good as gold. But the mining techniques were quite different. Gold can be panned from streams by individuals working alone, and sold as powder or lumps. Silver, however, required underground mining to extract the ore, which then had to be refined by smelters. As mining at Butte developed in the 1870s, the era of the independent prospector passed and corporate mining began. Then, as silver ran out, copper became the lodestone of Butte mining.

The transcontinental railroads vied for lucrative contracts to take the refined metal to world markets. The railroads also brought in immigrants to work the deep veins. Railroads were built between Butte and Anaconda, and between Butte and Great Falls, to take the ore to smelters.

Butte, soon to be known as the "richest hill on earth," was dominated by smokestacks, peopled by immigrants, and undercut with 10,000 miles of mineshafts. It quickly became Montana's largest and wealthiest city. The city never slept: miners worked the veins 24 hours a day, and bars, restaurants, and other businesses were always open to serve their customers. The huge influx of immigrants that poured into Butte during this period from Central Europe, Italy, Cornwall, Ireland, and China, in particular, gave Butte its cosmopolitan flavor and its ethnic neighborhoods.

Other factors were not so positive. Butte was an environmental disaster. The pollution from the smelters soon killed all the vegetation within a 20-mile radius. The trees that weren't killed by smoke were cut for mine supports or to fuel the smelters. Smelting also used vast amounts of water, which was simply returned to streams laden with toxic chemicals and minerals. The mining process produced mountains of tailings, some of which were radioactive. Entire communities were built on these tailings.

THE COPPER KINGS

During the boom years of copper and silver mining in Butte in the 1870s and '80s, the mines, the city, and indeed the whole state were dominated by three men, called the Copper Kings. William Clark made his first fortune mining and smelting silver, and extended his empire into banking and politics. Marcus Daly cannily bought up depleted silver mines in order to exploit the mines' rich veins of copper (electrical power created a market for copper wire which turned copper from a junk metal to one of Montana's most precious commodities). Daly also had large business holdings in the lumber industry; his Butte-area mines used 40,000 board feet of timber a day. Fritz Augustus Heinze was the third and last of the Copper Kings. He cleverly manipulated the "Apex Law," which states that if a vein of ore surfaces on one person's claim, then that person has the right to the rest of the vein, no matter where it goes when underground. Because he owned the apex of mines owned by large mining interests (increasing-

William Andrews Clark

Marcus Daly

The End Of The Open Range

While Butte was booming during the 1880s and '90s, events conspired to end the Old West cattle days on the eastern prairies. The winter of 1886-87 has been made most famous by the grim drawing of the "Last of the 5,000" by artist Charley Russell. A very dry summer led to a long, extremely cold winter. The warm-weather longhorn, summered on the drought-stricken plains, died in huge numbers as temperatures remained below zero for weeks. One-half to three-quarters of the cattle in Montana reportedly froze or starved to death. A single winter ended the era of the great cattle drives.

Sheep had played a part in Montana agriculture since the days of deSmet's St. Mary's Mission, but now the number of sheep on the plains increased considerably as ranchers realized that the hardy sheep were a good hedge against losses of the more temperate cattle. In 1870, there were 2,000 head of sheep in the state, one for every 10 settlers; by 1900, with six million head, sheep outnumbered people 24 to one.

Also, while the railroads opened up the growth of the cattle trade in Montana, they also brought in settlements. The open range was increasingly privately owned. The various homesteading acts of the late 1800s and early 1900s opened public

THE COPPER KINGS, cont.

ly, Butte was controlled by national corporations), Heinze was able to thumb his nose at big business while becoming very wealthy.

Each of these men led almost raucously public lives. Heinze's wealth and reputation had less to do with his mining knowledge than with his control of the courtrooms. He courted public affection by publicly taking on the giant companies, such as Standard Oil, that were swallowing up Butte mining. Daly and Clark engaged in a fiercely contested rivalry involv-

Fritz Augustus Heinze

ing wealth, political influence, and popular opinion. Each controlled newspapers, bought judges, and paid off legislators. A classic battle was fought in 1889 as Montana became a state. Daly favored Anaconda as state capitol, while Clark lobbied for and triumphed with his choice of Helena. Daly got revenge by denying Clark a long-sought-after seat in the U.S. Senate. These and other battles were chronicled in the state press, and were the stuff of public gossip and debate.

Butte was not the only area influenced by the era of the Copper Kings. Missoula and Hamilton were largely built by the Daly logging empire. Anaconda was essentially a Daly company town, built around his Washoe smelter, but with great pretensions. The growth of Great Falls was assured when smelters were built on the banks of the Missouri to refine Butte ore.

The political complexion of early Montana was largely established by events centered in Butte. Many of the early miners and prospectors who were attracted to the gold strikes of the 1860s, and the boom in growth of the 1870s, were Southerners dislocated by the Civil War. They brought to Montana a strong hatred of Yankee Republicanism; most Irish immigrants were dependably Democratic. Both Daly and Clark fought their political battles from within the Democratic party. Butte was the largest city in the state by far, and its population of workers, when unionized, voted unswervingly Democratic. To this day, Montana has a stronger Democratic Party than many western states.

land for settlement. With the hegemony of the big cattle outfits broken after 1886, homesteaders set up along the fertile valley bottoms, fencing some of the best range and water access.

Homesteaders

Rail entrepreneurs like James Hill of the Great Northern quickly realized the benefits of establishing settlements all along his rail lines. Huge advertising campaigns were launched to tempt the homesteader to the plains of Montana. Rural European communities received advice from experts regarding the fertility of the Great Plains,

and immigrants were pamphleted as they disembarked onto U.S. soil.

Much of the promotional material presented by the railroads was fanciful, and some of it was flat wrong. It promised, for example, plenty of rain, fertile soil, and opportunities for all. Nonetheless, the advertising worked. The population of Montana grew 60% during the first decade of this century, and the number of farms doubled.

While homesteading acts allotted 320 acres of "free land" per individual (a husband and wife qualified for two allotments), even this quantity of land was insufficient to make a living in Montana. During good years with plenty of rain, the prairies provided adequate grazing. But most new settlers did not come to raise livestock (stockmen were seen as anachronisms). Farmers represented progress and the evolution of the West: they came to turn the soil over and raise grain.

Communities sprung up along the rail lines, particularly along the Great Northern near the Hi-Line and along the Milwaukee Road through central Montana. Towns were established along the rail sidings, and usually consisted of a grain elevator, a bank, a hotel and bar. Farms were "improved on" according to Homestead Act requirements, but were often little more than a tar paper or shod shack with ad hoc outbuildings for livestock. Eastern Montana has never been more populated than it was in 1918, with at least one homestead per square mile of arable land.

The Company

In the first years of this century, the Copper Kings Heinze, Daly, and Clark, largely to spite each other, each sold out to the buyer least likely to benefit the others. In each case it was Standard Oil. By 1906, Standard Oil, soon to reconfigure its holdings as the Anaconda Company, controlled almost everything in Butte. It became known simply as The Company. Then, in the 1910s, when the Anaconda Company became yoked with the Montana Power Company, these two corporations practically controlled the whole state.

The Copper Kings had been largely beneficent to their workers, and even suffered the unions gladly. Not so The Company. During the 1910s, Butte was a battlefield of labor/management disputes. Conditions in the mines worsened. The presence of Wobblies during World War I led to the Anaconda Company targeting "communist" influences that resulted in lynchings. The Great Depression further darkened conditions in Butte as the world price of copper fell 80%. Production of copper in 1933 was 10% of what it had been in 1929. The Company shifted much of its operations to Chile and Mexico, where copper was mined in open pits, involving fewer labor costs. Butte, once one of the richest towns in the West, now faced unemployment problems.

The Dust Bowl Years

For a time the weather cooperated with the homesteaders in eastern Montana. Then, from the late 1910s to the mid-'20s, nature shifted gears. In 1916, Shelby, on the Hi-Line, received over 15 inches of rain; in 1919, the third year of intense drought, the town received less than seven inches. Drought continued, coupled with high winds and grasshoppers. Range fires ruined crops and destroyed communities. By 1925, 60,000 people had left Montana, representing 11,000 abandoned farms; 214 state banks failed and Montana led the nation in bankruptcies. A few years later, disaster struck again. The stock market crash, combined with a second severe drought during the Dust Bowl years of the 1930s, eliminated many more farmers and ranchers.

Federal Spending

As elsewhere in the U.S., in Montana the Depression of the 1930s was followed by the spending programs of the New Deal. The works projects had great impact on the state. Not only did programs like the Civilian Conservation Corps (CCC) and the Works Projects Administration give employment and training to people out of jobs, they produced monumental results. One of the largest public works projects in the country was Fort Peck Dam, completed in 1940 to dam the Missouri. Going-to-the-Sun Highway in Glacier Park was a CCC project.

After the end of the New Deal era, government spending in Montana ceased to be a civilian affair and was given over to the military. Malmstrom Air Force Base was built in Great Falls in 1942 as a transit base for war materiel shipped to the United States's then-ally the Soviet Union. By the 1950s, it became a strategic air base assigned fighter jets to defend against then-enemy the Soviet Union. In the 1960s, Malmstrom became the first center for the Minuteman Missile system. By 1970, 200 Minutemen were buried in silos under 23,000 acres of central Montana prairie, pointed at equivalent missiles in Russia. The Glasgow Air Force Base brought population and business to that eastern Montana town until the base was closed in 1969.

Decline Of The West

While the 19th century saw the buildup of wealth and influence in western Montana, the 20th century brought decline to the mining and logging industries that had fueled early growth.

Butte struggled on until 1955, when open-pit mining began. Open-pit mining diminished overhead and overburden at the same time. The old Butte communities were ripped apart as steam shovels tore into the soil. The huge Berkeley Pit swallowed up Meaderville, which was once a lively Italian neighborhood sitting on a vein of low-grade copper ore. Although Berkeley Pit revived industry in Butte for about 20 years, by the 1980s Anaconda Company had sold all its holdings in Butte. A mile high and a mile deep, Butte contained just a century's worth of riches.

Likewise, centralized ownership and overproduction has crippled the timber-products industry. Huge companies control much of the timber production in Montana and have put local lumber mills and logging companies out of business. Much of the good timber in easily accessible private and state lands has already been harvested. With the old-growth trees gone, local loggers and mills have had to bear the expense of retooling machinery to accommodate smaller trees. Even though the loss of jobs and revenue in logging towns is a result of market forces, environmentalists usually receive the blame.

Coal And Oil

The 20th century saw other mineral development come to the eastern prairies. Coal had been mined in Montana since the early days of settlement, but large-scale exploitation of the incredible reserves of fossil fuels waited until the railroads arrived. The Northern Pacific developed Red Lodge, and later Colstrip, as sources of fuel for its steam trains, and the Milwaukee built up Roundup as its source. After trains were converted to electricity, coal mining ceased for a number of years. However, as machinery and technology more finely developed the techniques of strip-mining, the vast reserves of coal in the Fort Union Formation in southeastern Montana became more attractive.

In the 1970s energy companies proposed building four electric generators in Colstrip, with the power to be sold to markets on the West Coast. Battles erupted in courtrooms and communities as the breadth of the mining and environmental damage became clear. The issues surrounding development sundered many communities as the benefits of conservation and economic opportunity were debated. Despite grass-roots opposition from ranchers, Indians, and environmentalists, the generators went in.

Oil and gas exploration also brought wealth to some eastern Montana communities. Refineries helped Billings boom during the 1970s, and towns such as Sidney, Broadus, and Baker escaped the worst of recent agricultural downturns because of the presence of large nearby oil reserves.

Farming And Ranching

Bad years still follow good in Montana agriculture. A series of good years in the 1960s and early '70s brought prosperity and high land prices. The family ranch and farm began to modernize after borrowing against the inflated real estate values of the land. Then drought hit again, and land values fell. Farmers and ranchers found themselves with unsecured loans. The drought, bad markets, and financial breakdown of the 1970s and '80s became known as the Farm-Ranch Crisis, an echo of earlier times and of an ongoing cycle.

Government programs in the 1970s and '80s were designed to help the family farm and ranch, but were too easily manipulated by unscrupulous investors. Huge tracts of cheap drought-stricken grazing land were bought up solely for the government payments available for plowing it. The broken land, plowed but not planted, simply drifted on the wind across the prairies while the investment "farmers" pocketed the payments.

Farms and ranches are large and far between in Montana. Those that remain have long histories and many experiences of lean times. Most are still operated as family businesses, with the work and pleasures shared by several generations living together on one farm or ranch site. While during much of the 20th century, agriculture became more specialized and reliant on production of only one commodity (usually cattle or wheat), rural Montana is entering the 1990s with its eyes cast backward. A ranch that raises cattle, sheep, hay, wheat, and keeps chickens and a milk cow not only has a diversified product to sell but also goes a long way toward being self-sufficient. The repeated cycle of boom and bust, rain and drought, will continue. But after surviving three generations in eastern Montana, farmers and ranchers don't pretend to be in it for the money.

GOVERNMENT

Montana became a territory in 1864, and a state in 1889. The original state constitution of 1889 reflected the mining and timber interests that dominated the early days of the state. Due in part to that document's datedness, and to the climate of political reform in the late 1960s, Montanans voted to draft a new constitution. The results of the second Constitutional Convention in 1972 were a reformist, populist set of laws that affirms that the state government exists by consent of the people and for their benefit. The privileges of business and industry were diminished accordingly.

Montana granted women's suffrage in 1916, four years before the passage of the 19th Amendment. Jeannette Rankin, the first woman representative in the U.S. Congress, was elected from Montana in the same year.

Jeanette Rankin, the first woman representative in the U.S. Congress

The Montana Legislature is a bicameral, biennial body. There are 56 counties. Since the 1990 census, there is only one federal House member (down from two). One particularity of the Montana primary system is its open ballot. Voters are not asked to identify party affiliation to receive a primary ballot; instead, they receive a voting form from both parties. In the voting booth, the voter marks only one form, and both are deposited in the ballot box. The system has been both hailed as the truest form of democratic voting and denounced as the most open to political hanky-panky.

Reservation Self-government

Indian reservations are recognized by the federal government as independent political units. Legal jurisdiction is therefore something of a puzzle on reservations.

Tribes have certain inherent sovereign governmental rights. Tribes can run their own schools, regulate transport and trade, and have their own constitution, legislative councils, and tribal court and police systems. The state cannot tax reservation land or transactions that occur on reservations. While such legal considerations may not seem crucial to the traveler, Montana has in effect seven independent political entities within its borders. Visitors need to be aware that certain state laws do not apply on reservations.

Those cheap gas stations advertising cheap cigarettes aren't found just inside reservations by accident. State fuel and cigarette taxes aren't levied on those products sold by tribal members within reservations. Some local roads on reservation land are maintained by the tribes. Do not automatically assume that there is public access; sometimes individuals will deny use to non-tribe members. For instance, some of the Crow Reservation is off-limits to non-Indians.

Not all areas are open for recreation. The state does not have authority to regulate hunting, fishing, and recreation on reservations. Tribes can issue their own licenses for hunting and fishing, and may levy a user fee for hikers and campers. If you are not a tribe member, always check with tribal authorities before crossing reservation land.

ECONOMY

Montana is a rural state. Agriculture, mining, and the timber industry were among the founding trades of Montana and remain among its most important. Tourism is increasingly lucrative, and service industries like trucking and medical-treatment centers are major employers. Because it is so far from coastal markets or other significant population centers, it is unlikely that Montana will quickly become anything but a source for raw materials. Transport costs make industry unprofitable in so remote a state.

Agriculture

Montanans make strict differentiations between farms and ranches. Farms raise grain; ranches raise livestock. To the purist, any amount of cultivation degrades a ranch to a farm. Even though most people think of Montana as primarily an agricultural state, less than 10% of the population makes a living from farming and ranching. Still, recent census figures indicate that the number of farms and ranches in Montana is increasing slightly (there are more than 15,000); however, their average income has declined over the last decade. Beef cattle production is the most common form of ranching, with sheep production remaining a steady alternative. Spring and winter wheat are by far the most common crops, with barley a significant third. Along the Yellowstone River, corn, soybeans, and sugar beets grow in irrigated fields. In the Flathead Lake region, sweet cherry orchards augment the local tourist economy.

Mining

The state of Montana was born of prospecting and mining camps. However, the copper, silver, and gold that established the Montana econ-

LIVESTOCK

Montana is one of the largest livestock producers in the nation, with 65% of its land in agricultural production (although only eight percent of the population is engaged in ranching and farming.) Different breeds of livestock have been developed for different needs and different environments, and ranchers put a lot of thought into the types of animals they raise. And for Montanans, livestock breeds are another coded system of meanings that serve to characterize individuals: just as there are Ford or Chevy families, there are Black Angus or Targhee families, and each means something else in the system.

Cattle

Black Angus are probably the most prevalent cattle breed in the state. Ranchers prize these all-black cattle for their milking ability on the shortgrass prairie, and their hardy disposition. These qualities make Angus cows the preferred mother stock in many herds, especially for ranchers who choose to cross-breed.

Hereford cattle come either horned or polled (that is, naturally unhorned), and are distinguished by their red bodies and white heads and legs. Herefords are as traditional a breed as Angus and share many of the same attributes, but they are somewhat less popular nowadays because of the horns on the larger and more vigorous variety, and because the udders of white-fleshed Herefords can easily sunburn, causing the mothers to reject the hungry advances of newborn calves.

So-called exotic breeds were brought to the U.S. in the 1960s from Europe to introduce larger bone structures into local Hereford and Angus cattle. Federal livestock laws forbade the direct importation of live breeding stock, but not the importation of semen. Exotic cattle made artificial insemination of cows an everyday occurrence on Montana ranches. Because exotic breeds (most are named for the European region where they originated, like Maine-Anjou or Charolais) are much larger than the Angus or Hereford, they produce larger calves. But larger cattle demand more food and range; the economic benefit of exotic cattle depends largely on the condition of the range.

The number of dairy cattle has fallen as transportation costs and centralization of processing has made Montana herds uncompetitive. It is cheaper to ship in milk from out of state than to ship in the feed to support a dairy cow.

Longhorn cattle established Montana cowtowns like Miles City. But these cattle from Texas proved to be too delicate for Montana winters. Longhorn cattle are raised today mostly for rodeo stock.

LIVESTOCK, cont.

Sheep

The war between sheep raisers and cattlemen was never as fierce in Montana as in other Western states, because in harsh and unpredictable climates, sheep have proved to be a sensible livestock adjunct to cattle ranching. As a commodity, sheep have two basic values: in wool and meat. Sheep that are best for wool production are not the best for meat production, however. In fact, the qualities exist inverse proportion to each other. The larger and meatier the sheep, the coarser the wool. While all sheep produce wool, the staples that can be spun into suit wool fetch the highest prices; in a bad year, the cost of shearing the sheep may be greater than the fleece price of poor-quality wool.

Black-face sheep produce the most desirable carcass (the most meat per pound of grain), but the wool is almost worthless. White-faced, polled sheep like Columbias and Targhees are the sheepman's choice for mid-quality fleece and good-quality carcasses. If it's wool you're after, then Rambouillet, with their large curving horns and fine fleece, is Montana's best wool breed. If the wool market isn't good, however, you can't expect top price for the comparatively small-framed lambs.

Horses

Most jobs on most Montana ranches could be done by various machines or vehicles, but many Montanans persist in using horses for everyday work. It's part of the heritage, and, besides, grain is cheaper than gasoline. Most stock horses are quarter horses, known for their endurance and speed in short distances. Appaloosas are the horses with the spots on their hindquarters. Draft horses appear on farms and ranches occasionally, as fuel prices and whimsy dictate. Driving a team and wagon to feed stock is not common, but certainly not rare.

Hogs

Pigs are the single livestock commodity that has no Old West antecedent. But they are prevalent. Most farmers keep pigs, simply because the ratio of feed to profit is lower than with other livestock: put simply, pigs can utilize food disdained by sheep or cattle. Compare it to a diversified investment portfolio: like sheep, hogs can serve as a hedge against bad grain or cattle markets.

MIKE WELLINS

omy are largely depleted. Traditional centers of mining, such as Butte and Anaconda, have fallen on hard times as the world market has moved elsewhere to find cheaper, more easily mined minerals. But it's not that Montana has given up mining; copper, silver, and gold are still produced, but with modern techniques that don't demand an entire city's work force.

Montana remains rich in other mineral wealth: from the unpronounceable molybdenum to the sublime Yogo sapphire to ordinary talcum powder. Mining in Montana has moved to the rich coal and oil fields of eastern Montana and the palladium mines on the Stillwater River. Thirty-foot thick veins of bituminous coal lie under much of southeastern Montana and are unearthed by modern strip-mining techniques at places like Colstrip. The Stillwater Mine is the only U.S. source for valuable platinum. Oil and gas wells dot the eastern prairies.

Lumber

About half of Montana is forested. However, early overcutting and slow regrowth have limited the state's competitiveness in the world timber market. Locally owned mills have been forced to close when they can't compete against large corporate "timber-product" conglomerates, whose efficient automated factories have transformed logging from a life-style to a job. The forests still provide a living for enterprising Montanans, though: Christmas tree farms are found in northwest Montana, and log-home manufacturers have moved Montana into the first ranks of home-kit producers in the nation. More log homes are shipped to Japan than remain in Montana.

PEOPLE

The first residents of Montana arrived from Asia via the Bering Land Bridge about 10,000 years ago, after the last ice age. These prehistoric people were the ancestors of the North American Indians. However, the Indians who now live in Montana were not native to the area: they were forced westward after being displaced by other tribes and white settlers from the east.

Montana was one of the last states to be settled by whites. Railroads and the Homestead Act made Montana's free acreage very tempting to the thousands of immigrants who poured into the United States in the early 20th century. Many communities still retain their strong European heritage.

NATIVE AMERICANS

There are approximately 50,000 Native Americans living in Montana today (16% of the state's total population), representing 10 different tribes. The majority live on reservations, which make up nine percent of Montana's total land area.

Native Americans are often lumped together as "Indians," with the assumption that one culture, language, and history link these people. However, the tribes that now live in Montana come from very different traditions, speak different languages, and have not always been friendly toward each other.

Kootenai
The Kootenai tribe had settled in the Kootenai River area by 1500. Their original range included the northwest corner of Montana and adjacent areas of Alberta and British Columbia. As a people, the Kootenai are closely related to Indians of the Columbia Basin, although they speak a language seemingly unrelated to other languages of the area.

The Kootenai share the Flathead Reservation with the Flathead and Pend d'Oreille Indians. Approximately 1,500 Kootenai Indians presently live on the reservation.

Pend d'Oreille
These Salish-speaking people are closely related to tribes of the Pacific coast, but moved up the Columbia drainages into Montana many thousands of years ago.

The Salish tribes were the first to welcome white missionaries to Montana, and St. Ignatius Mission was built in 1854 to minister to the Pend d'Oreille tribe's spiritual needs. The Pend d'Oreille largely retained the culture of Northwest coast Indians, although Plains Indians' influence was evident in some aspects.

The Flathead
There is no satisfactory explanation for the term "Flathead," for these Salish-speaking people never practiced head flattening (though other Salish tribes did). The Flathead also differed from other Salish kinsmen by leaving the river valleys of the Columbia drainage and moving onto the plains of central Montana. Here they evolved a culture based largely on the buffalo while maintaining the religious and social traditions of the Northwest coast.

Like other Salish tribes, the Flathead were generally friendly to whites as they entered Montana. The tribe was moved from the Bitterroot Valley and settled on the Flathead Reservation in the Mission Valley.

The Crow
The Crow were the first of the contemporary Indian residents to enter Montana from the east, arriving as early as 1600 in response to dislocations farther to the east. The Crow, or the Absarokee, originally lived in the Great Lakes region, where they lived in earthen lodges and practiced agriculture.

Having arrived first onto the Montana plains, the Crow had the most to lose as other tribes crowded into the state. They became sworn enemies of the Blackfeet and later the Sioux.

The Blackfeet
Like other Plains tribes, the Blackfeet originally lived farther east, in the forests north of the Great Lakes. As they drifted westward across the Canadian prairies, the various Blackfeet tribes evolved into a loose confederation of entities sharing a common language (an Algonquian dialect) and mutual defense of their hunt-

ing lands. These groups, later known as the Piegan, the Blood, and the Northern Blackfeet, combined to form the Blackfeet Nation, one of the largest and most feared of Indian tribes.

The Piegan ventured farthest south, taking control of much of northern Montana by 1800. The Blackfeet were celebrated horsemen and warriors, and their social order was structured by membership in military societies. Men who were not militarily inclined were treated as women; first reported by French trappers, this cultural practice, called the *berdache,* was later found to be common in aboriginal societies. Religious practice centered on the ritual Sun Dance, and shamanistic powers derived from dreams and visions.

Gros Ventre
Meaning literally "Big Belly," Gros Ventre is a misnomer for a tribe more properly known as the Atsina. The Gros Ventre represent the northernmost tribe of the Arapaho, and belong to the Algonquian linguistic family. After moving to the Montana plains from their Minnesota homeland in the late 1700s, they allied themselves with the Blackfeet, sharing in their dominance over the prairies. The Fort Belknap Reservation was established in 1888 for the Gros Ventre and Assiniboine. The Gros Ventre tribe now claims about 2,500 members.

Assiniboine
The Assiniboine are a Siouan-speaking people who historically represented the most northerly of the Yanktonai Sioux in their original homeland north of Lake Superior. They were traditionally allied with the Cree against their common enemy, the Blackfeet. By the 1700s the Assiniboine had crossed into the present-day U.S., where they established a territory in the northern corner of Montana where the state meets North Dakota. The 2,000-member tribe is today divided between two reservations, Fort Belknap and Fort Peck.

Sioux
The Sioux represent one of the largest Indian nations in North America, which divides into three large linguistic groups: the Dakota, the Lakota, and the Nakota. All originally came from Canada and were pushed westward as white settlements displaced other tribes along the eastern seaboard. They arrived on the northern plains comparatively late, around 1800, when they settled in the Dakotas, southern Saskatchewan, and eastern Montana. They were regarded as a noble but fearsome people, skilled in battle and famed hunters of buffalo.

The Yanktonai Sioux settled around Fort Peck and, along with some Assiniboine kinsmen, be-

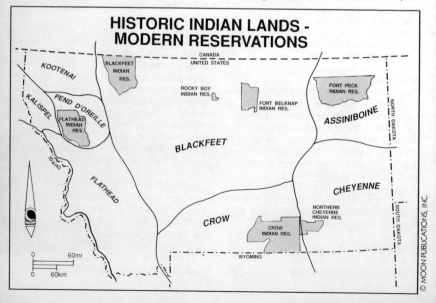

HISTORIC INDIAN LANDS -
MODERN RESERVATIONS

KOOTENAI

BLACKFEET INDIAN RES.

CANADA
UNITED STATES

ROCKY BOY INDIAN RES.

FORT PECK INDIAN RES.

KALISPEL

PEND D'OREILLE

FLATHEAD INDIAN RES.

FORT BELKNAP INDIAN RES.

ASSINIBOINE

NORTH DAKOTA

IDAHO

BLACKFEET

FLATHEAD

CHEYENNE

CROW

NORTHERN CHEYENNE INDIAN RES.

CROW INDIAN RES.

SOUTH DAKOTA

WYOMING

0   60mi
0   60km

© MOON PUBLICATIONS, INC.

NATURAL FEATURES

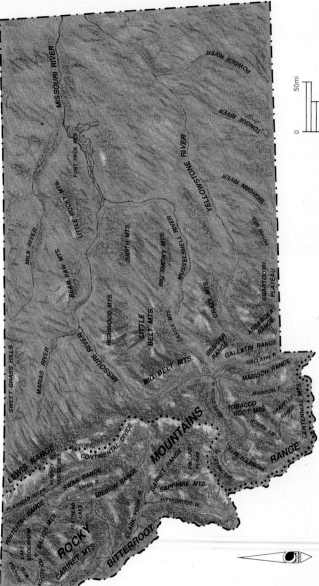

(top) the Rocky Mountain Front, west of Augusta (Judy Jewell); (bottom) Nevada City (W.C. McRae)

Cheyenne Indians

came residents of that reservation when it was created in 1888. Today, almost 10,000 individuals belong to the tribe.

Northern Cheyenne

The Cheyenne are a tribe of Algonquian linguistic ancestry, who lived largely agrarian lives in the Minnesota area. Pressures from other tribes forced the Cheyenne westward, and in about a 25-year period they evolved from a people who cultivated corn and other grains and made pottery to a nomadic Plains culture predicated on buffalo hunting. About 1830, after reaching the Black Hills, the tribe divided, with one group moving south to Colorado and the other moving farther westward into traditional Crow territory. Today, there are about 5,300 members of the Northern Cheyenne tribe.

Chippewa and Cree

The Chippewa and Cree originally lived in northern Michigan and southern Manitoba. On these northern prairies, the tribes lived in close proximity to French trappers and settlers. Intermarriage produced a culture and a people known as Metis. Like so many other Native peoples around this time, they moved west in the mid-1700s in response to displacement in the east.

By 1818, when the U.S. border was established, there were estimated to be about 10,000-12,000 Metis people living on the prairies. A Metis leader named Louis Riel in 1868 declared the Metis land a separate province of Canada. His rebellion against English Canadian authorities failed, and the Chippewa under their chief Rocky Boy along with some of the Metis moved south to Spring Creek, near Lewistown, Montana. In the following years, as the U.S. evacuated the Metis to Canada and the Canadians deported them back south, they were part of the "landless Indians" (Indians without a reservation) who wandered the West after the U.S. decided to forego its policy of reservation granting.

The Metis, Chippewa, and Cree were given a part of old Fort Assinniboine as a reservation in 1910.

SETTLERS

The first settlements in the state were trading posts and forts. Generally, men were attracted to trapping and trading for quick profit and did not settle in Montana any longer than necessary to make (or realize the futility of trying to make) money. Of all the forts built by traders in the early 1800s, only Fort Benton still exists as a town.

Only after gold was discovered in the 1860s did people start to build communities and settle in the state permanently. In addition to the gold diggers from other western states, like California, where gold had already played out, the first towns were peopled by Southerners who had been displaced by the Civil War.

The Immigrants

The establishment of the huge silver and copper mines in western Montana in the 1880s called for a large and stable work force, supplied mostly by immigrants. As Butte and Anaconda demanded workers, Europe had workers to spare. Irish laborers emigrated in huge numbers, and "Cousin Jack" miners from Cornwall found easy employment. The population of Montana grew 365% from 1880 to 1890, largely due to immigration.

By the 1890s large numbers of Germans, Slavs, Italians, Finns, and Eastern Europeans poured into Butte to work the mines. These foreign workers settled into separate ethnic neighborhoods, where traditional food, customs, and languages prevailed. A number of Jewish immigrants moved to the thriving mining centers and set up retail establishments. In 1910 black settlers in Montana numbered almost 2,000, most of whom lived in mining towns. Only after the establishment of Air Force bases near Glasgow and Great Falls in the 1960s were there more black residents in the state. Chinese immigrants were also attracted to Butte, where they set up laundries and restaurants. Although Butte's preeminence in Montana has dimmed, the early growth of immigrant population in the mining communities served to establish Roman Catholicism as the state's dominant religion, and Butte set a standard of openness to immigrants still observed by Montanans.

The railroads brought settlers to the plains of eastern Montana. Ambitious campaigns by the Great Northern and the Milwaukee Railroad succeeded in luring thousands of farmers to cultivate the dry prairie. Between 1900 and 1910 the number of farms and ranches in Montana doubled, and while many American-born homesteaders settled in Montana during this time, immigrants had an especially strong influence in eastern Montana. By 1910, one-quarter of all Montanans were foreign-born. Entire communities of Germans, Russians, and Scandinavians were founded as farms and towns sprung up alongside rail sidings, with a telltale Lutheran church. Scots and Irish continued to settle the plains as ranchers and herdsmen. Today, in

BRAND LORE

Contrary to popular belief, brands are not a cowman's vanity plate. Brands rarely represent something else; since there are 60,000 brands registered in Montana, brands are more often assigned than chosen.

Not all characters are equally effective as brands. Certain characters or symbols brand more cleanly than others; for instance, Bs and 8s are notoriously hard to apply, since the hot iron will simply singe an indistinguishable blotch on the animal's flesh. Letters like Y or N are preferred, since the clean lines are easily read. Other letters are easily altered: a hot iron can change an I to an E, for example.

Generally speaking, two-figured brands are preferred over three-figure brands: to a cattleman, it's one less iron to apply. The same brand can be registered to different people if it is applied to different parts of the animal. Cattle have six brand areas: the hips, ribs, and shoulders on both the left and right side. "HS-" on the right shoulder is a different brand from "HS-" on the left hip. The same rules apply to horses, except that they are branded on the jaw.

Montana law allows brands to be registered also for sheep, buffalo, elk, deer, hogs, and mules.

Brands must be reregistered every 10 years, for a $50 fee. Brands that aren't reregistered become available to newcomers. When applying for a brand, one specifies what letters are preferred, and the registrar sends a selection of brands not already taken that use those characters (most obvious combinations are already taken.) Two-figure brands have cachet, since they are more authentic. But the Brand Commision no longer issues them; the only two-figure brands available are those established brands that have been allowed to lapse. In the back of Montana livestock newspapers are ads for two-figure brands. A good brand with some history can bring $1500.

Recently, ranchers have experimented with freeze branding. Instead of hot irons searing the flesh, extremely cold irons, dipped in liquid nitrogen, freeze the animal's hair follicles, causing the hair in the brand to grow in white. The brand then shows up in contrast. Obviously, this method works best on dark animals.

northern and central Montana, the names in small-town phone books read like similar directories in Norway, Sweden, or Scotland.

Even though droughts and the Depression worked to depopulate the Montana plains, the foreign character remains in communities founded by immigrant farmers and ranchers. Many eastern Montanans are only first-generation Americans. From 1900 to 1920, 50,000 foreign-born settlers moved to the state, while 120,000 American-born settlers did so. But during the droughts and bad markets of the 1920s, 10 times as many American-born homesteaders gave up and moved on, as immigrants. By 1930, people of foreign birth or first-generation Montanans made up 45% of the population.

Some foreign settlers moved to Montana expressly to form communities. Mennonite groups settled in Montana during the homesteading years, but many left after the state Legislature, urged on by an organization called the Montana Council of Defense, drafted laws during World War I forbidding the German language. Hutterites maintain 22 communities in Montana and currently number over 2,000 adherents.

War policies have not always driven Montanans from the state. During World War II, Japanese internees from California were shipped to the state to work in sugar beet fields. Some found Montana to their liking; farming communities along the Yellowstone are still home to Japanese families.

Although not an ethnic minority, Mormons have established communities in Montana whose solidarity rivals that of old European enclaves. The Bitterroot Valley (and southwestern Montana in general) and the Great Falls area each have large Mormon communities. The Mormon Church is now the fourth-largest church in Montana.

THE ARTS AND CULTURE

If there is a Western culture, a lack of snobbery lies at its heart. Even in the literature it shows: a rancher's memoirs share a bookshelf with poems that don't rhyme. Both writers are from Montana, and natives brag on them both. Rural cafés often sell local arts and crafts, whether it's homemade pottery or country scenes painted on old saws. And locals will buy both. Montanans respect people who are creative; rare is the rural community that doesn't have a resident poet, painter, or musician. L'art naif or kitsch? In Montana, as often as not, it's the urge to express that's admired; it's not polite to question the quality of the expression.

From pioneers who kept journals and sent letters back east, to fourth-generation ranchers to established novelists who have found a home in the state, Montana's literary tradition is a source of pride to Montanans, who generally read a lot and who positively devour the regional. It's not surprising that Montana should harbor such a dynamic writing community. It's a small step to go from respecting the work of a local rhymester to welcoming a nationally known author to the farm next door.

LITERATURE

Any state that can fill a 1,150-page anthology with its literature is impressive. To have that become a regional bestseller points to a phenomenon. The Last Best Place chronicles the literary history of Montana, from Native American stories to modern cowboy poetry. Those unfamiliar with Montana's place in the literary firmament will be surprised at the number of writers who have had Montana addresses.

Early Writers
Montana literary history begins with the diaries and memoirs of early settlers and the transliteration of Indian tales. Teddy Blue Abbott trailed cattle up from Texas to Montana during the 1870s and '80s, and wrote We Pointed Them North. Andrew Garcia was a novice mountain man when he married a Nez Percé woman who just escaped following Chief Joseph's surrender at Bear Paw. In Tough Trip Through Paradise, Garcia gives his version of the Nez Percé flight in the 1870s and of what it was like for him to be an innocent among mountain men and Indians.

Frank Bird Linderman got to know Crow chief Plenty Coups and Pretty Shield, a Crow medicine woman, and recorded their stories. *Indian Why Stories* and *How It Came About Stories* are his versions of Indian fireside tales.

Frontier photographer L.A. Huffman brought his camera to early eastern Montana; *Before Barbed Wire* by Mark Brown and W.R. Felton features his photographs and recounts Huffman's life. Evelyn Cameron was an English immigrant whose passion for photographing the early settlement of remote Terry, Montana, resulted in the book *Photographing Montana: 1894-1928* by Donna Lucey. Charley Russell, whose greatest fame derives from his paintings of frontier Montana, also wrote books. His life straddled the open range and the homesteading eras; his book, *Trails Plowed Under,* recounts this period. Will James had a ranch south of Billings. Books like *Cow country* were popular adolescent reading during the '30s.

The Missoula School

The University of Montana at Missoula has had a seminal effect on serious writing in the state. In 1919, a writing program was established by Professor H.G. Merriam at the university, only the second in the nation. Merriam, who had left Colorado to attend Oxford, returned west determined to promote regional Montana writing. He began the literary journal *Frontier and Midland.* His writing program flourished, soon growing to offer a Master of Fine Arts degree. Students have included A.B. Guthrie Jr., author of *The Big Sky,* and Dorothy Johnson, author of *The Man Who Shot Liberty Valance* and other popular western stories.

The program has attracted many talented students, as well as nationally recognized faculty. Poet Richard Hugo inherited the writing program from Leslie Fielder in 1964, and remained until his death in 1982. Hugo had a tremendous influence on the development of Northwest regional literature. His poems speak of disappointment and abandonment in both life and the physical world, sometimes ending with a wry glimmer of hope. Joining Hugo at the U of M at one time or another were Madeline De-Frees, Patricia Goedicke, William Kittredge (who with Annick Smith edited *The Last Best Place,*) William Pitt Root, and Tess Gallagher.

MONTANA HISTORICAL SOCIETY

Andrew Garcia's Tough Trips Through Paradise *was found years after his death.*

Missoula has also attracted writers whose connections with the writing program are more tenuous. Rick deMarinis *(Under the Wheat)* did a stint as a mathematician before becoming a full-time writer. James Crumley, whose hardboiled detective novels are frequently placed in the Northwest, still lives in Missoula. Norman Maclean, who wrote *A River Runs Through It,* an idyll to fly-fishing and the spirit, grew up in Missoula. James Welch, who spent his youth on the Blackfoot and Fort Belknap reservations, studied with Hugo and now lives in Missoula. Welch has written several fine contemporary and historic novels of Indian life, including *Winter in the Blood.* Another Missoulian by way of the Hi-Line is Deirdre McNamer, whose recent novel *Rima in the Weeds* is set amongst the missile silos of northern Montana.

Natives And Newcomers

Although there are writers scattered across the expanse of Montana, a principality of established authors has grown up around the town of Livingston, north of Yellowstone Park. Thomas McGuane's novels, including *Keep the Change*, are Westerns filled with modern neuroses. McGuane lives in the area, as has Richard Ford (*Rock Springs*). Ford's *Wildlife* is set in Great Falls, and many of his stories are set in small Montana towns. Richard Brautigan, famous for *Trout Fishing in America*, was also a resident.

Not all Montana authors are imported. Joseph Kinsey Howard, a journalist and lightning rod for progessive politics in the 1940s, wrote a classic Montana history in *Montana: High, Wide and Handsome*. Ivan Doig's memoirs of his Montana boyhood (*This House of Sky*) and his fictional trilogy about Scottish ranchers in Montana (*Dancing at the Rascal Fair, English Creek,* and *Ride with Me Mariah Montana*) have garnered a wide readership.

Wallace Stegner, though not stricty a Montana writer, spent part of his boyhood in Montana and has written good regional books such as *Big Rock Candy Mountain*. Wally McRae, eastern Montana rancher and conservationist, is admired on the cowboy-poet ciruit. Another rancher-writer was Spike Van Cleve, who wrote with wit of the changing West in *A Day Late and a Dollar Short*.

ART

Montana was visited in its earliest days of settlement by noted artists, who left a rich legacy of landscape and wildlife art. Early artist-explorers Karl Bodmer and John James Audubon passed through Fort Union and up the Missouri; their journals and paintings portray Montana before settlement.

Charley Russell is the quintessential Montana painter. He knew the West from the inside, having lived the life of a cowhand for many years. A native of St. Louis, Russell came west during the days of the great cattle ranches, and lived in the Judith Basin area of central Montana. He began by sketching in bars and around campfires; the lives of the Indians and cowboys that he encountered daily became his subject matter. Often he traded his sketches for drinks, and until recently some of the best collections of his works were in bars. His studio in Great Falls is now the Charley Russell Memorial Museum. His works are also on display in the Montana Historical Society Museum in Helena.

The regional and Western tradition is still strong in Montana art. Ace Powell of Great Falls inherited the mantle of Charley Russell and painted fine tableaus of the emerging West. A contemporary master of reproducing the light and shade of the Montana landscape is Russell Chatham. His carefully balanced scenes capture the expanse and intimacy of the Montana countryside. Gary Carter paints wildlife and Western scenes, while Clyde Aspevig concentrates on landscapes.

The Montana arts scene doesn't end with Western-themed painting and sculpture. The universities and the Montana Arts Council foster more experimental artists. In Missoula, Rudy Autio produces nationally recognized ceramic sculpture. Another former U of M professor was Walter Hook, a math-professor-turned-painter. Hook developed a wry syntax of images, including buffalo, kites, and Easter eggs, that recur like visitants across his canvases.

John Buck and Debbie Butterfield are Bozeman-area artists whose work flirts with West-

Artist Charley Russell spent his youth as a range cowboy.

ern icons. Butterfield sculpts horses out of old signs or commercial media to achieve a haunting dissonance. Buck confounds Western art images and ready-mades—such as whittling—by incorporating them in aggressively modern constructions.

While the mountains allure writers, the prairies seem to attract—and inspire—visual artists. Far-flung ranches and small towns in eastern Montana harbor conceptual artists. Pat Zentz and Dennis Voss are ranchers who each employ quirky and experimental sculpture and assemblages to convey a sense of Montanan ritual and whimsy. Ted Waddell employs modern expressionistic techniques to paint the cows on his ranch, imbuing them with near-totemic presence. Gary Hornick's installations juxtapose isolation and a rich historicity.

A Missoulian who garnered fame as a poster illustrator is Monte Dollack. His movie and commercial poster paintings are immediately recognizable and avidly collected. Dollack has recently opened a gallery in Missoula to market his stylish and whimsical fine-art prints.

THEATER

While the most vital theaters in Montana are associated with the universities in Missoula and Bozeman, other community theaters are of note. Billings has two theater venues, and the Missoula Children's Theater has an excellent reputation throughout the Northwest.

Summer-stock theater is especially good in Montana. Bigfork's summer theater recruits many of its actors from the University of Montana. The Fort Peck summer theater also draws heavily from the Montana universities; the theater building itself is a lovely relic from the CCC days of the 1930s. Virginia City presents summer melodramas in a frontier opera house; West Yellowstone also has a summer family theater.

Montana State University presents an ambitious Shakespeare in the Parks series. During summers, the troupe tours the entire state, including remote towns in eastern Montana, with its productions.

OUTDOOR RECREATION

HIKING, BACKPACKING, AND CAMPING

Montana operates about 40 state parks focusing on both recreation and history. Many of the parks include campgrounds, which are open from mid-May to mid-September. Day-use fees are $3 at most state parks, with an additional $5 for overnight campers. For a pamphlet detailing all the state parks, write to the **Parks Division, Montana Department of Fish, Wildlife, and Parks**, 1420 E. Sixth Ave., Helena, MT 59620.

Public lands (state and national forests and BLM land) comprise roughly 35% of the state. Forest Service maps are good for spotting hiking trails and campsites. Forest Service campgrounds are widespread in western Montana. Fees range from free to $7, depending on the amenities (free campgrounds are those with a pit toilet and no running water—they're usually remote and rarely crowded).

Wilderness Areas

Montana has 12 federally managed wilderness areas, roadless and closed to mechanized use, including mountain bikes. Designated wilderness areas are sometimes more heavily used than remote, non-wilderness areas. Stop in at a ranger station and ask which local trails they favor. In addition to the wilderness areas that fall under the jurisdiction of the Forest Service, there are several tribal wilderness areas in Montana. Before hiking or fishing on tribal land, be sure that you have the necessary permits.

National Parks

Glacier National Park falls entirely within Montana, and its Canadian counterpart, Waterton Lakes National Park, is directly above the border. Though the bulk of Yellowstone National Park is in Wyoming, three of the park's entrances, as well as its northern edge, are in Montana. Entrance fees are $5 for Glacier and $10 for Yellowstone. This pays for a week's unlimited entrance into the specified park. An extra fee is charged to camp in park campgrounds.

HUNTING AND FISHING

Hunters flock to Montana in the fall for elk, deer, bear, and the occasional mountain lion or bighorn sheep. Anglers come in the summer for the plentiful but wily trout. The basic fee for a fishing license is $9.50 for Montana residents, $36 for nonresidents (or $8 for a two-day license). A basic hunting license, which includes fishing, is $45.50 for Montanans, $200-450 for nonresidents. Those who come from out of state should contact the Montana Department of Fish, Wildlife, and Parks, 1420 E. Sixth Ave., Helena, MT 59620, tel. (406) 444-2535, for up-to-date information on licensing and season dates. They can also provide a list of licensed outfitters.

Falcon Press publishes comprehensive guidebooks on hunting and fishing in Montana (see Booklist), well worth reading to become familiar with local conditions.

SKIING

Big Mountain, just outside of Whitefish, and Big Sky, some 30 miles south of Bozeman, are Montana's two big "destination" ski resorts. If you'd rather avoid the development but still can't resist the thrills of downhill, try one of the smaller ski areas outside Libby, Missoula, Bozeman, Anaconda, Darby, Dillon, Neihart, Red Lodge, or Choteau.

Once the back roads of national forests are covered with snow, many of them become cross-country ski trails. The Forest Service distributes a list of ski trails, and local ranger stations have specific maps for their areas. Trails groomed for both standard cross-country skiing and "freestyle," or "skating," are maintained by lodges, such as the Izaak Walton Inn in Essex, and by individual communities, like the Rendezvous Trails in West Yellowstone. There may be a fee to ski on groomed trails.

For an overview of downhill and cross-country ski areas, contact **Travel Montana**, Room 996, Deer Lodge, MT 59722, and request the

Montana Winter Guide. They also publish a snowmobiling guide, which surveys Montana's nearly 3,000 miles of snowmobile trails.

OTHER ACTIVITIES

Water Sports
River trips are offered by a number of guide services, and boats can be rented in most river towns. For a list of guides, contact the **Montana Outfitters and Guides Association**, Box 1339, Townsend, MT 59644, tel. (406) 266-5625 or 449-3578, or the Montana Board of Outfitters, Department of Commerce, 1424 Ninth Ave., Helena, MT 59620, tel. 444-3738.

Windsurfing hasn't been particularly developed in Montana, but occasionally a sail goes up on Flathead Lake. Strong winds on the Blackfoot Reservation and around Livingston have generated talk, if not actual windsurfing sites.

Bicycling
There are plenty of opportunities for both touring and mountain biking, from Glacier Park to the Pryor Mountains. Missoula is home to **Bikecentennial**, a tour-

JIM MASTERSON

ing organization and advocacy group for cyclists. They lead rides across the state and across the nation, and can answer questions regarding routes and conditions. Contact Bikecentennial at P.O. Box 8308, Missoula, MT 59807, tel. 721-1776. Visit their offices at 113 W. Main in Missoula.

Horseback Riding
Outfitters, resorts, and guest ranches all generally offer horseback riding. Guided trail rides are the usual, and cattle drives are becoming increasingly popular. A listing of the Montana Outfitters and Guides Association is available from Travel Montana, tel. (800) 541-1447. Contact **Montana Trail Drives**, P.O. Box 18, Roberts, MT, tel. (800) 535-3802, for information on cattle drives.

Rockhounding And Prospecting
Explore the Treasure State with a pan or a bucket. Prospect for gold near Libby, or buy a bucket of dirt outside of Helena or Philipsburg and pick through it in search of sapphires. Hunt for garnets in southwestern Montana, agates along the Yellowstone, and petrified wood in the Gallatin National Forest. The *Rockhound's Guide to Montana* contains detailed information on sites and facilities throughout the state.

ACCOMMODATIONS AND FOOD

ACCOMMODATIONS

Traditional Lodging

The development of the freeway system has led to the clustering of chain motels around the offramps on the edges of town. Often better deals on lodgings are found away from these developments along the old arterials. Also, don't dismiss staying at old downtown hotels. Some are renovated and reflect the splendor of yore; others, for the more daring, have survived as residential hotels. Chances are you'll have a unique experience.

Only a few fancy resorts have sprung up across the state, but guest ranches and hot-springs resorts, many with a lengthy pedigree, abound. Some small guest ranches enjoy a quiet fame with a long-standing blue-chip clientele; hot-springs resorts vary from the

full-blown convention-sized facilities, such as Fairmont Hot Springs, to modest mom-and-pop affairs. Some ski resorts like Big Sky have reputations that precede them; they are open year-round for hiking, fishing, and other summer activities.

Almost every rural community in Montana now boasts a "working guest ranch," a real ranch that welcomes the occasional tenderfoot to participate in normal ranch activities. Amenities vary, but good food, exercise, and horseback riding are usually *de rigueur*.

Bed and breakfasts have become a trend across the U.S., and Montana's not bucking it. B&Bs range from extra rooms in somebody's house to relatively large bed and breakfast inns. Rooms generally run $40-60, depending on season and pretension. **B&B Western Adventure** is a reservation service that will book you into almost any bed and breakfast in Montana or Wyoming. Reach them at P.O. Box 20972, Billings, MT 59104, tel. (406) 259-7993.

Camping And RV Parks

If you're at all inclined toward camping, bring along your gear and head out to the wilds of Montana. Western Montana is especially well endowed with public campgrounds in national forests and state parks. Tent campers need to plan ahead in other parts of the state if they want formal campsites, as public campgrounds thin out on the prairies. Ask to camp in town parks; the locals will be glad to have their parks appreciated. RV campers will find campgrounds in most towns. Fees in public campgrounds are usually $3-6; privately owned campgrounds charge $8-15 a night (most have rudimentary facilities for tent campers).

FOOD AND DRINK

Here's the stereotype, mostly true: Steaks are standard, and usually good. Vegetarians manage to make do with the pervasive salad bars.

BOB RACE

FASHION DOS AND DON'TS

While fashion in Montana may not look like much, even this style has its system. Here are a few clues to understanding the dictates of Montana chic.

In general, fashion is dictated by function. Ranchers dress the way they do because it's effective. Levi's are eschewed in favor of Wrangler jeans; one cowboy claimed that Wranglers fit better over boot tops. Another reason is the seam: on Wrangler jeans the seam runs down the outside of the leg, but the seam running along the inside of a pair of Levi's can get pretty uncomfortable for most cowpokes on horseback.

Boots are still mandatory footwear. Not only are they necessary protection for the feet and calves while horseback riding, their high tops also are prophylactic against snake bite. Bootmaking is still a custom trade in most Montana towns. Neck scarves are not just colorful accessories: they insulate against cold drafts in winter and dust and chaff the rest of the year.

Cowboy hats are still a popular hedge against the sun and wind, straw for summer and felt for winter. The cowboy hat's hegemony has been somewhat shaken by the baseball cap, although no one in Montana would consider calling a head covering by that name. Rather, net caps are known by the brand names they feature: call them a "Cat Cap" or a "King Rope Cap" and they are both identified and justified within Montana fashion. The prevalence of pearl snaps over buttons is as real as it is inexplicable.

It is unfortunate to report that, as in certain ornithological species, the male's attire is more engaging than the female's. Women's hair fashion suffers particularly. Very long hair is the norm, at least until marriage, at which time shorter, grown-out perms are considered the mode. In marked differentiation from the men's, women's clothing tends to be made of manmade fibers. Wardrobes are put together with a sense of proportion and coordination more like abandon than intention. It is probably a judgment on Western culture that women's fashion generally reaches its apex in the menswear department. Women often look their best when they dress in the same clothes as men: jeans, plaid shirts, and boots.

There is some regional variation in dress. West of the Divide, flannel shirts and Birkenstocks are common, particularly among college students. Cross-country ski boots are considered year-round footwear, donned when not wearing hiking boots. Plaid flannel faux-logger shirts are omnipresent.

Warning: Do not try to duplicate Montana fashion. Most attempts look staged: full western gear is probably not going to win you any extra points. While in Montana, dress comfortably. If you want to win the confidence or friendship of native Montanans, there are, however, a few rules to observe. Don't wear anything really trendy or goofy that will put an extra barrier between you and the residents. Hot summer weather doesn't necessarily mean shorts for men. Shirtlessness is almost taboo. Err on the side of comfortable modesty: in Montana, it is considered a factor of stylishness.

Plenty of thin, and often bitter, coffee is drunk, laden with sugar and Cremora.

There really isn't anything to justify the label "Montana cuisine." Dishes peculiar to the region usually ring changes on established entrées. Buffalo burgers are simply hamburgers made with ground buffalo meat; promoters claim buffalo is a leaner, more flavorful alternative to beef. Indian tacos load taco ingredients onto fry bread. Rocky Mountain oysters are more often threatened than served; served correctly, lamb or calf testicles are the quintessential offal meat, and surprisingly palatable.

But even when restaurant fare seems unimaginative compared to cuisine on the coasts, the general quality of the food is quite good. Home cooking sets the standard, and simple, unprepossessing food is often the best.

There are happy exceptions to the rule, however. Chefs have mastered sauces in some pretty out-of-the-way places: when you least expect it—Chico, Willow Creek, Essex—isolated but enterprising cooks have established restaurants with sophisticated dining. In cities, most notably Butte, there is *great* ethnic food.

Montanans like to eat out. Cafés and restaurants are social centers, and eating out is a way of combating isolation. The bar is the other meeting place, and not just for adults. Entire families meet up at bars, where it's perfectly normal to stick to soft drinks.

INFORMATION AND SERVICES

WOMEN TRAVELERS

Though it's not really the expected thing, there's little reason for a woman to feel uneasy about traveling alone around Montana. If you're not up to being outgoing, people will generally leave you alone. But if you get to feeling chatty or flirtatious, you're in real luck. You'll be a curiosity, and men and women alike will sit you down and spin tales, feed you, and make you grin. Of course, you have to look out for weirdos, but they're usually about as much of a threat as grizzly bears, and much easier to deflect. If a place makes you nervous, do the smart thing and leave. On the whole, travel in Montana is, for a woman on her own, exhilarating and ego-boosting.

PRECAUTIONS

Montana is not a particularly menacing place; however, a few considerations may save the traveler unpleasant experiences.

Animals

Grizzly bears are found in Glacier and Yellowstone national parks, and in smaller populations in wilderness areas in much of the Rockies. When provoked—and it doesn't always take much to rile them—grizzlies are vicious. Several people are mauled each year by grizzlies, with deaths not infrequent. If you are planning a trip through grizzly country, check with local rangers for bear updates; areas in Glacier are often closed to hikers due to grizzly problems. Make noise as you hike to forewarn nearby bears; small "bear bells" hooked on packs are common noisemakers. Don't sleep near smelly food, like bacon; hang food from branches away from tents.

Mountain lions are not as aggressive as grizzlies, but as their territory is whittled away, there is more lion-human contact. Mountain lions live in most of the Rocky Mountain region. While adults are in little danger from mountain lions, small children, especially if unattended, can attract them.

Not all threats come from carnivores. Moose are great hulking animals given to spontaneous charges if surprised. Buffalo, either at Yellowstone Park or on private land, can be short-tempered if provoked. These animals are not vicious, but are territorial and easily surprised. Be careful.

Rattlesnakes are common over the eastern two-thirds of the state. While a rattlesnake bite is rarely fatal these days, it's no fun either. If you are hiking anywhere in eastern Montana, it is imperative to wear strong boots with high tops. Watch where you step. Be especially careful around rocky promontories: snakes like to sun themselves on exposed rocks. It's probably not a good idea to hike by yourself.

Rattlesnakes are not aggressive to humans; given their druthers, they will slink away, rattling. If you have never heard a rattlesnake rattle, don't worry that you might mistake it for something else. It is a vestigial human trait to leap backward and shriek when you hear the rattle. When angered, however, rattlesnakes will coil and strike. If bitten, immobilize the affected area and seek immediate medical attention.

If you have insect bite allergies, don't mislead yourself into thinking that Montana's dry climate might be bug-free. It's not. An abundance of fierce insects await. Mosquito repellant is definitely recommended. Be suspicious of overly friendly small mammals. Rabies is, as elsewhere, a real problem. If you are hiking in the vicinity of stock animals, especially cattle, it is wise to remember that bulls can be threatened by the presence of humans. Give them a wide berth.

Weather

Weather extremes are common in Montana. When outdoors in high temperatures, remember to drink plenty of water; native Montanans often take salt pills to prevent dehydration. Listen for weather forecasts—sudden storms can blow in, causing rapid changes in temperature and wind conditions. Certain parts of Montana are known for their windiness: Great Falls ("the Windy City"), Livingston, and Cut Bank each deserves its reputation. If you are driving a high-profile vehicle, listen for wind warnings.

Winter cold is the greatest weather concern. Roads can be treacherous if snow-covered, and incremental melting leaves small, invisible patches of ice on the road. If you travel by automobile in Montana in the winter, make sure you have blankets or a sleeping bag, plenty of warm clothing, including gloves, a flashlight (days aren't long in the winter), and maybe even a paraffin heater. Again, pay attention to weather and road reports, and don't take chances.

SIX REGIONS OF MONTANA	
Charley Russell Country:	761-5036 or (800) 527-5348
Custer Country:	665-1671
Glacier Country:	756-7128 or (800) 338-5072
Gold West Country:	846-1943
Missouri River Country:	525-3410
Yellowstone Country:	446-1005 or (800) 736-5276

Crossing To Canada

Of the 15 roads that cross from Montana into Canada, only three are open around the clock. Highways 93 and 15 and Road 16 (in the far northeastern corner of the state) have 24-hour ports of entry. U.S. citizens need only show a driver's license or proof of citizenship to cross back and forth; the same goes for Canadians. Citizens of any other nation should be prepared to show a passport and the appropriate visas.

MAPS

The state highway department puts out a free road map that will suffice if you stick to paved roads. Request a copy from the Montana Promotion Division, Department of Commerce, 1424 N. Roberts, Helena, MT 59620, tel. (800) 548-3390.

For a more detailed look, Western Geo-Graphics puts out recreation maps of eastern and western Montana. They include lots of non-paved roads and some topographic detail. Pick them up for $2.95 at bookstores or order from Western GeoGraphics, P.O. Box 1984, Canon City, CO 81215, tel. (719) 275-8948.

National forest maps are invaluable for off-the-beaten-path travel in the western part of the state. Day-hikers sticking to established trails will usually be able to navigate nicely with these maps, available at local ranger stations or from the U.S. Forest Service Northern Region Headquarters, Box 7669, Missoula, MT 59807, tel. (406) 329-3511; they're $2 from the government, a bit more if you buy them from a bookstore.

Serious backpackers and hunters will want U.S. Geological Survey quadrangle maps. Many sporting-goods stores carry these maps for the more popular areas; they can also be ordered directly from the USGS, Federal Center, Box 25286, Denver, CO 80225, tel. (303) 236-7477. It pays to do a little library research before contacting the USGS; they'll want to know the exact names of the maps you're ordering.

WHAT TO TAKE ALONG

Montana is capable of extreme weather. Winter travel especially demands appropriate cold-weather gear.

Summer weather can be capricious, but it is usually hot, with afternoon temperatures in the 90s. Evenings can bring thunderstorms and much cooler temperatures. A jacket will make the evenings more comfortable. Few occasions demand formal clothing; besides, what passes for dress-up in Montana won't intimidate casually and comfortably dressed visitors.

Hikers and wilderness campers will need to augment their regular gear with bear bells (to warn bears of their approach). Take along a rope to hang food items from trees. Sunscreen and insect repellent are the premier emollients of summer.

While Montana is not backward, small trading towns exist to serve the needs of local farmers and ranchers, not out-of-state tourists. Black-and-white film and even color slide film can be hard to find outside the cities. If you have special dietary needs, don't assume that small towns will stock items beyond the most basic of food stuffs.

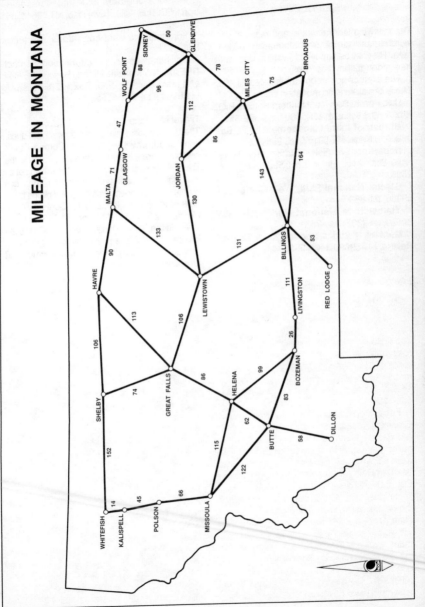

MILEAGE IN MONTANA

© MOON PUBLICATIONS, INC.

SERVICES

The following federal, state, and regional services can provide detailed information on Montana. They will be happy to fill your mailbox with free informational brochures.

The **area code** throughout the state is **406.** The entire state is on mountain time.

U.S. Forest Service, Northern Region, P.O. Box 7669, Missoula, MT 59807, tel. 329-3511.

Bureau of Land Management, P.O. Box 36800, Billings, MT 59107, tel. 255-2882.

Department of Fish, Wildlife, and Parks, 1420 Sixth Ave., Helena, MT 59620, tel. 444-2535.

Glacier National Park, West Glacier, MT 59936, tel. 888-5441.

Yellowstone National Park, YNP, WY 82190, tel. (307) 344-7381.

Montana Historical Society, 225 N. Roberts, Helena, MT 59620, tel. 444-2694.

Montana Outfitters and Guides Association, P.O. Box 1339, Townsend, MT 59644, tel. 266-5625.

For statewide **road conditions**, call (800) 332-6171.

For handicap-access information, contact **DREAM**, NW Montana Human Resources, First and Main Building, P.O. Box 1058, Kalispell, MT 59903, tel. 752-6565.

Travel Montana

The state's tourism bureau can answer most questions about travel in Montana. Some of their brochures are invaluable. Be sure to ask for the Travel Planner. It contains a complete listing of all the lodgings, campgrounds, outfitters, resorts, golf courses, and pertinent addresses and phone numbers of institutions in the state. Contact Travel Montana at (800) 541-1447, or 444-2654 in state.

In addition, Travel Montana has divided the state into six regions. (see p. 34) Each local unit also produces brochures about sites, history, and amenities.

TRANSPORTATION

Montana is a long way from just about anywhere, and even once you get there, it's a long way between stops. Although Montana has fine airline and bus service, and Amtrak's *Empire Builder* rolls along Montana's 550-mile border with Canada, the best way to visit the state is with your own vehicle. With so much territory to move around in, you'll want to wander freely.

DRIVING AND CAR CARE

A few considerations apply when you are planning a road trip to Montana. It's not that there are any real tricks involved in driving Montana, but those used to city and freeway driving may need some reassurance and a pointer or two.

Just about any regular car will serve you fine most of the time, but some remote dirt roads get pretty dodgy without a high-clearance vehicle. Likewise, two-wheel drive will handle most situations, but it's not a bad idea to throw a tow rope on the back seat and, except in the dead of summer, it makes sense to carry tire chains.

Distances are great in Montana: fill your tank frequently, especially in eastern Montana. Along Hwy. 200, hundreds of miles separate gas stations. Plan ahead. Don't assume every little dot on the map will have gas; many are merely pioneer post offices that mapmakers haven't bothered to delete. Ask gas station attendants how far the next gas station is, if you are in doubt.

Because distances are great, make sure your vehicle is in reasonable shape. Check tires, oil, and radiator water. Carry extra oil and water.

A less apparent consideration involves foreign cars. By and large, Montana is Ford and Chevy country. If, by Montana standards, you are driving a moderately obscure foreign vehicle, don't anticipate that parts will be readily available should a breakdown occur. If you know that the alternator is failing on your foreign-built car, don't head into rural Montana assuming that repairs will be easy.

If cattle are in the road, just drive slowly toward them and they'll grudgingly move out of the way. Sheep will rarely give way in any logical fashion.

Logging trucks rule the roads in the western forests. Don't be stubborn about keeping your piece of the roadbed when one bears down on you.

When the federal government demanded that states set speed limits, they didn't mandate specific penalties for violators. Montana thumbed its nose at the whole idea by setting the normal fee for a speeding ticket at five dollars.

The white crosses along state highways do, indeed, mark the sites of fatal automobile accidents.

The state highway information number is (800) 332-6171. Recordings are updated two to three times daily.

By Car

Montana's most traveled roads cross the state east to west. It's no coincidence that these roads parallel early explorer routes; then as now, most travelers come to Montana to get across it as expeditiously as possible. The I-94/I-90 corridor follows the Yellowstone and Clark Fork rivers, and is the most perfunctory route across the state. Dawdlers will prefer to cross the state along more northerly routes. Highway 12 follows the old Milwaukee rail line across central Montana; Highway 2 parallels the Canadian border on Montana's Hi-Line, along the old Great Northern rail line. Highway 200 connects the dots between the two. The only major highway

DRIVING MONTANA

The day is a woman who loves you. Open.
Deer drink close to the road and magpies
spray from your car. Miles from any town
your radio comes in strong, unlikely
Mozart from Belgrade, rock and roll
from Butte. Whatever the next number,
you want to hear it. Never has your Buick
found this forward a gear. Even
the tuna salad in Reedpoint is good.

Towns arrive ahead of imagined schedule.
Absorakee at one. Or arrive so late—
Silesia at nine—you recreate the day.
Where did you stop along the road
and have fun? Was there a runaway horse?
Did you park at that house, the one
alone in a void of grain, white with green
trim and red fence, where you know you lived
once? You remembered the ringing creek,
the soft brown forms of far off bison.
You must have stayed hours, then drove on.
In the motel you know you'd never seen it before.

Tomorrow will open again, the sky wide
as the mouth of a wild girl, friable
clouds you lose yourself to. You are lost
in miles of land without people, without
one fear of being found, in the dash
of rabbits, soar of antelope, swirl
merge and clatter of streams.

—Richard Hugo

By Air

Billings is the major air hub in Montana, and is served by most major western airlines. Missoula, Bozeman, Butte, Helena, Kalispell, and Great Falls are also serviced by major carriers. A regional airline, Big Sky Airlines, tel. (800) 882-4475, offers connections to smaller Montana population centers.

By Rail

Amtrak's *Empire Builder* crosses Montana's northern extreme along the old Great Northern rail line. By doing so, it offers service to none of Montana's major population centers. Unless you simply want to traverse Montana, or have friends or rental cars lined up to ferry you southward (and links at Havre and Whitefish aren't designed to meet the train), Amtrak isn't a very meaningful way to visit the state: you can't get there from here. The good news is that the *Empire Builder* skirts the southern edge of Glacier National Park and is reckoned to be one of the most scenic Amtrak routes. The independent traveler bent on kicking loose in Montana is best advised to hop off the train at either Spokane, WA, or Williston, ND, and rent a car.

By Bus

Greyhound buses hurtle along I-94 and I-90, traveling between Montana's major cities as the interstates parallel the state's southern boundary. The Evergreen Stage, Rimrock Buslines, Intermountain Busline, and Karst Buses are local carriers that link smaller towns to the Greyhound corridor in the south and to Amtrak's bailiwick in the north. Local Greyhound stations provide schedule information for the regional lines.

cutting north to south is I-15, which links Canada with Great Falls, Helena, and Butte, and extends to Salt Lake City.

CALENDAR OF EVENTS

Month	When	Event	Location
January	last weekend	Montana Winter Fair	Bozeman
February	mid-February	Race to the Sky	Dogsled race from Helena to Holland Lake and back
March	early March	Rendezvous cross-country ski race and Winter Festival	West Yellowstone
	mid-March	C.M. Russell Western Art Auction	Great Falls
	March 17	St. Patrick's Day Parade	Butte
April	early April	International Wildlife Film Festival	Missoula
May	third weekend	Jaycee Bucking Horse Sale	Miles City
June	second weekend	Virginia City Days	
	mid-June	College National Rodeo Finals	Bozeman
	third weekend	Battle of Little Bighorn Reenactment	Little Bighorn Battlefield
	late June	Lewis and Clark Festival	Great Falls
July	July 4 weekend	Arlee Powwow	
	July 4	Northern Cheyenne Powwow	Lame Deer
	July 4	Terry Rodeo	
	mid-July	International Choral Festival	Missoula
	mid-July	Logger Days	Libby
	mid-July	Yellowstone Boat Float	Livingston to Columbus
	third weekend	Crow Fair	Crow Reservation
	third weekend	North American Indian Days	Browning
	third weekend	Standing Arrow Powwow	Elmo
	last weekend	Cutting Horse Show	Big Timber
August	first week	Montana State Fair	Great Falls
	first weekend	Sweet Pea Festival	Bozeman
	second week	Festival of Nations	Red Lodge
	mid-month	Montana Cowboy Poetry Gathering	Lewistown
	third week	Montana Fair	Billings
	third week	Northwestern Montana Fair	Missoula
	third weekend	Eastern Montana Fair	Miles City
September	Labor Day	Ashland Powwow	
	first Saturday	big game bowhunting/gamebird season opens	
	third Sunday	backcountry big game season opens	
	third weekend	Nordicfest	Libby

CALENDAR OF EVENTS, cont.

October	first weekend	Fort Belknap Powwow	
	third weekend	Northern Invitational Livestock Exposition	Billings
	fourth Sunday	general big game season opens	
November	November 8	Anniversary of Montana's statehood (1889)	
December	mid-month	Christmas home tour	Butte
	all month	Christmas lights and decorations	Bigfork

BOB RACE

SOUTHEASTERN MONTANA
INTRODUCTION

INDIANS, CAVALRY,
AND COWBOYS

Southeastern Montana is the most "West"-erly of Montana's regions. Historically it is the West of the early trapper, and of the clash between Indian and infantry. It was the Montana of the cattle drover and the great cattle barons. Today, it is still home to thousands of American Indians, and it is still unembarrassedly cowboy country.

The Yellowstone River is the locus of the entire region. As the principal avenue of entree and exit in Montana, the Yellowstone took out the region's wealth of furs, brought in infantry soldiers, and transported cattle and sheep to eastern markets. Towns like Miles City, Glendive, and Billings grew up on its banks as railroads extended up the valley. Within memory, ranchers on the "North Side," up to Jordan country, and on the "South Side," down the Powder River,

trailed livestock to the "Valley." In these river towns, they partied, visited, and stocked up on groceries before heading out to their far-flung ranches.

The dominant social unit in southeastern Montana today is still the working ranch and family farm, and the same Yellowstone Valley towns are still the center of trade, shopping, and social life. This is about as real as the West gets, but it's not a Western theme park. Today, cowboys are stockmen, Indians are Native Americans, and the spirit of the Wild West has grown up into agribusiness.

Southeastern Montana is a region of rolling prairies, low mountains, and tree-lined rivers. Its wealth of recreational sites and wildlife make it a great destination for lovers of nature and solitude. It's rich in historic sites and memories of bygone times. It's not, however, a highly developed tourist destination. But for the traveler with patience, a sense of humor, and an interest in

BUFFALO

The buffalo, or the American bison as it is properly known, once ranged over most of the North American continent. Between Pennsylvania and the Continental Divide, and from the lower Mississippi and the Arkansas River north to the northern Alberta border, these shaggy members of the cattle family roamed over 40% of the continent in herds of up to a million animals. They were migratory creatures, following the seasons north to south.

Eastern Montana was ideal buffalo country, no matter the season. Huge herds that summered on the Canadian plains moved south to winter on the Montana prairies, while equally numerous herds from the grasslands of Colorado and Wyoming migrated north to summer on the plains of Montana. Perhaps as many as 60 million of these animals once roamed the continent, and as many as four million lived in Montana alone.

As previously agricultural Indians entered Montana from the east, the vast herds of buffalo soon changed the life-style of the Native Americans. American bison had always been an element of the culture of the Indian, but when the Indians were forced onto the plains, the buffalo's importance altered.

In ways that are difficult to imagine today, the buffalo provided the means of life for the early Plains Indians. The hide provided tepee coverings and leather for moccasins; the flesh was eaten fresh in season and also preserved for later consumption (steaks from the hump were delicacies). The bones were used to create a number of tools, from bone-splinter awls (with buffalo sinew for thread) to shoulder-blade hoes. Dried manure was used in campfires. Even the dried tail was used as a flyswatter.

Before the introduction of horses and firearms, the Indians hunted buffalo with bow and arrow, often using buffalo jumps, or pishkuns. The unsuspecting animals were stampeded off cliffs in large herds, after which the tribe harvested the dead and wounded buffalo. When the rifle from the north and east, and the horse from the south and west, met on the plains of Montana, the decimation of the vast herds began.

The development of new tanning techniques in the East allowed tanners to turn dried buffalo hides into soft marketable leather, changing forever the lives of the prairie Indians. In the 1840s, most of the fur-bearing mammals of the West were trapped out—by the 1860s and '70s, the great buffalo hunt was on. Waves of new white settlers (many displaced by the Civil War) moved west and joined the slaughter. Entire herds were completely wiped out in the course of a summer, as sharpshooters picked off the animals as they grazed. The animals were skinned, the hides shipped east by steamboat or rail, and the carcasses left to rot. Areas of the northern plains were white with bleached bones where the large herds had been slaughtered, and as the buffalo became scarce, a trade developed in dried buffalo bones (for fertilizers).

By 1884, the buffalo was effectively extinct in the United States. In 1908, when the government created the National Bison Range near Moiese, in northwestern Montana, it was mostly stocked with animals from Canada.

As the buffalo passed, so passed the life of the Plains Indian founded on the buffalo. The basis for a nomadic, warrior society was gone, leaving the Indian no source of food, shelter, or support, except the U.S. government.

BOB RACE

buffalo, Bison bison

wildlife, pristine landscapes, Native America, and the lore of the West, southeastern Montana has few equals.

THE LAND

Southeastern Montana is characterized by prairies, rough forested sandstone bluffs, and broad river valleys. The Yellowstone River flows through the entire region and the river and its valley are at its heart. As the Yellowstone moves eastward through the prairies, it picks up the waters of three major southerly tributaries: the Bighorn, the Tongue, and the Powder. As it debouches into the Missouri, the Yellowstone is the largest free-flowing river in the U.S.

It's hard to believe, looking at the dry and dusty buttes and rolling prairies of southeastern Montana, that amphibious dinosaurs and palm trees were once native to this area. For millions of years this area was the shoreline of vast inland seas. Southeastern Montana's most distinctive geologic formations—badlands, prairies, and sandstone bluffs, as well as the coal and oil they mask—all date from eastern Montana's maritime past.

The seas left deposits of sand, mud, and peat thousands of feet thick. Because exposed sedimentary formations were soft and easily eroded by wind and water, much of the terrain has relaxed into a uniform flatness. More resistant sandstone or clinker (coal-fire hardened sandstone) provided protection from erosion, and now tops buttes and caprocks, protecting softer subsoil from erosion. In other areas, the sedimentary uplands have been carved into deep canyons and sharp bluffs, called badlands (the distinctive barren gray soil is locally called "gumbo.")

Vast coal deposits, in veins up to 40 feet thick, underlie most of southeastern Montana. Strip-mining the coal has meant displacement of traditional agricultural interests. One person's overburden is another person's ranchland. Large strip mines, such as the aptly named Colstrip, have brought forth some of the New West's keenest legal sharpshooting, when ranching and environmental interests vie with the onslaught of corporate mining.

Climate

Southeastern Montana has a climate of extremes. The highest and one of the lowest temperatures in the state are recorded here (117° at Glendive, and -65° at Fort Keogh). The short-grass prairies of the region bake in mid- and late summer; Miles City annually registers some of the highest temperatures in the state. Expect temperatures in the 90s and 100s, and feel lucky if you find cooler weather. You can expect sunshine most of the summer, with frequent and spectacular thunderstorms. Evenings should be cool enough for a light jacket.

Winters are uniformly cold. Winter travel in eastern Montana is not for the faint of heart. Even though the snow and frost often lend the area a unique beauty, frequent contact with the road conditions phone line is recommended, tel. (800) 332-8553. Ideal travel seasons are the late spring and early fall, when warm days and cool evenings can be expected.

FLORA AND FAUNA

Flora

Ubiquitous plants of the high prairies include: blue gramma grass; the prickly pear cactus, with beautiful yellow/pink flowers in June; the prairie coneflower, with a few yellow petals around a central column of tiny flowers, which provided the makings for a hot beverage for the Indians; and sunflowers that grow along the broken soil of roadways, alongside several varieties of thistle.

Gullies are the home to shrubs whose fruit would be disdained in more generous climates. However, the chokecherry and buffalo berry possess virtues which have made them a food source for both Native Americans and early settlers. While the prairies are virtually free of trees, other parts of southeastern Montana are well forested. River bottoms are home to graceful cottonwood trees and willow. Juniper and ponderosa pines grow along the bluffs of sandstone uplands.

purple coneflower, Echinacea pallida

Fauna

With the exception of free-ranging buffalo, the wildlife of Western lore still thrive in southeastern Montana. Coyotes, foxes, and rattlesnakes live in the hills, and large populations of pronghorn, mule, and white-tailed deer make the region one of the state's premier hunting areas. The Pryor Mountains Wild Horse Range boasts Montana's only remaining herds of wild horses.

The region is especially of interest to bird-watchers. Golden eagles and the occasional bald eagle are seen, floating on updrafts, watching for their prey of cottontail rabbits and mice. Many other raptors, such as merlins, prairie falcons, red-tailed hawks and great horned owls, are also easily spotted.

The Central Flyway crosses southeastern Montana, making it both a great bird-watching and bird-hunting region. Teal, canvasback, wood, and mallard ducks are frequently seen, as are Canada geese. Blue herons are common sights. During the migration season, sandhill cranes, swans, and pelicans make short appearances.

Somewhere near Billings, the Yellowstone ceases being an oversized trout stream and becomes a prairie river. Although rainbow and brown trout are still found as far south as Miles City, sport species such as northern pike, walleye, and channel catfish are more common as the river slows and warms up.

The lower Yellowstone also yields one of the West's oddest fish. The paddlefish is an ancient species, related to the sturgeon, which has somehow survived in the Yellowstone. Its trademark long flat snout is useful for nosing around the river bottom in search of plankton.

HISTORY

One prominent Montana historian has claimed that the history of Montana is the history of its exploitation. Southeastern Montana's corollary to this truth is that the history of this lonesome corner of the state is the history of the avenue of its exploitation, the Yellowstone River. The Yellowstone was the avenue that brought in explorers, soldiers, and settlers, and the corridor that took out the furs, cattle, and coal.

Before the white man, however, the Yellowstone Valley was the ancient hunting grounds for Native Americans, especially the Crow Na-

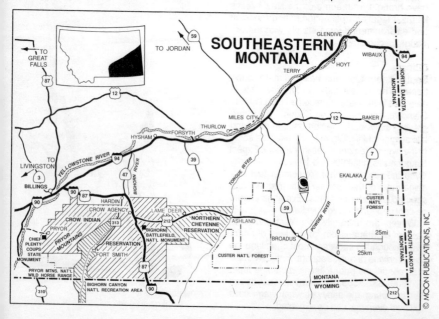

tion. The valleys of the Yellowstone and the rivers that feed it were rich with game and furs, and the prairies that adjoined the rivers teemed with buffalo.

The Yellowstone was not explored until 1806, during Lewis and Clark's return voyage. Clark floated most of the way down the river in dugout canoes. Upon reaching the confluence of the Missouri, he noted that, due to the enormous abundance of game along the rivers, the location would be advantageous for a trading fort. By the next year, Fort Remon was established at the mouth of the Bighorn, and trade with the Indians flourished. White settlers moved in to exploit the rich Yellowstone country, and others, with gold prospecting in western Montana on their minds, followed the Bozeman Trail north to the Yellowstone Valley across tribal land. The resulting conflicts with the Native Americans generated some of the most famous battles of the western Indian Wars, including the Battle of the Little Bighorn.

The eradication of the buffalo and the incarceration of the Indians left the prairies empty, but by 1880 huge herds of Texas cattle filled the "open range." The Northern Pacific Railroad pressed up the Yellowstone Valley at the same time, bringing in settlers and establishing trade centers like Billings and Miles City. Homesteaders replaced cattle barons, but they made only a tentative impact on this vast and arid, almost hostile and ungiving land. The coal and oil development of the last 20 years has done as much to change the landscape and character of southeastern Montana as a century of agriculture.

RECREATION

Hunting And Fishing

Southeastern Montana is a hunter's dream. Trophy-size mule deer haunt brushy coulees, and game birds such as pheasant and wild turkey are abundant. Obtaining hunting access is relatively easy. The Dept. of Fish, Wildlife, and Parks' Region 7, which encompasses most of southeastern Montana, has the state's highest number of landowners signed up in the Block Management Program. The program opens and maintains access to private land for recreation purposes. Ninety-five landowners have signed up;

almost two million acres of private land are guaranteed open for hunting. (A list of participating farmers and ranchers is available from the Dept. of Fish, Wildlife and Parks.) An increasing number of ranchers run outfitting and guide services.

As the Yellowstone River winds through its wooded valley in southeastern Montana, it attracts anglers with its wealth of walleye, northern pike, smallmouth bass, ling, channel catfish, the occasional trout, and sauger. The lower reaches of the river, especially near Glendive and Sidney, are home to the paddlefish. Public fishing sites on the Yellowstone are plentiful, as the Dept. of Fish and Wildlife is in the process of locating access areas every 12 miles along the river.

For trout fishers, the Bighorn River is the real news in southeastern Montana; below Yellowtail Dam, the Bighorn becomes one of the state's best fishing areas for trout, and Yellowtail Dam itself in the Bighorn Canyon has got to be one of the most awe-inspiring brown trout and walleye holes in the West. Because much of the Bighorn flows through the Crow Reservation, access is limited. The upper reaches of the Tongue River also provide good trout fishing.

Agate Hunting

The moss agates of the Yellowstone Valley are known around the world for their quality. Starting at the mouth of the Bighorn and continuing to its confluence with the Missouri, the Yellowstone passes through gravel beds rich with the semiprecious stones. It takes a trained eye to spot the matte, yellowish exterior of an agate in the rough, but often the jostling of the river will have chipped the surface, and its translucent interior will be visible. Stop at a fishing-access area, or along a bridge, to search for agates. The **Glendive Chamber of Commerce** also offers guided boat tours on the Yellowstone specifically tailored for agate hunters.

INFORMATION

For general information on southeastern Montana, write for the **Custer Country Regional Tour Guide**, Rte. 1, Box 1206, Hardin, MT 59034. The guide is a helpful free resource of addresses, travel information, and things to do.

The best map of the region is the Recreational Map of Eastern Montana, available from good map stores or from Western GeoGraphics, Box 1984, Canon City, CO 81215, tel. (719) 275-8948. Bureau of Land Management maps are available from the regional office, Box 36800, Billings, MT 59107, tel. (406) 255-2885.

The **Custer National Forest offices** can be reached at Box 2556, Billings, MT 59103, tel. 657-6361. The regional **Dept. of Fish, Wildlife, and Parks** office is at Rte. 1, Box 2004, Miles City, MT 59301, tel. 232-4365.

Getting Around

Greyhound runs along I-90 and I-94. Two flights daily link Miles City and Glendive with Billings.

BILLINGS

Billings (elev. 3,117 feet) is Montana's largest city, with a population of 100,000 in the greater urban area. Billings's physical setting is striking: the Rimrocks, sandstone cliffs several hundred feet high, ring the city; from them, five mountain ranges are visible. The Yellowstone Valley here is wide and green. Billings is primarily a sales and trade center, with some oil refining and energy generation enlivening its economy.

Billings makes much of being the largest city in the vector north of Denver and between Spokane and Minneapolis, and boasts of being the capital of the "Midland Empire," a vague principality consisting of eastern Montana, northern Wyoming, the western Dakotas, and on an expansive day, maybe even some of the prairie provinces. Certainly, to judge by the license plates at the stockyards or at one of the shopping malls, Billings is the service center for much of the northern plains. It's a city that is proud of its wealth and growth, and as the center of a vast agricultural area it has a sense of purpose and vitality that can almost seem like urban bustle.

HISTORY

The Yellowstone Valley at Billings has been at the crossroads of inter-Indian trade and warfare for years. Prehistoric Indians lived in this area beginning about 10,000 years ago, as the valley's abundant game and fertility made this a rich homeland, and caves in the Rimrocks gave shelter. Later, mountain tribes from the west, like the Shoshone, ventured down the Yellowstone on hunting trips to the buffalo-laden prairies. The Crow Indians moved into Montana in the 17th century and settled just south and east of Billings. A century later, when the Blackfeet moved in from the north and west and the Sioux moved in from the east, this part of the Yellowstone Valley became a contested hunting ground.

The first white settlement in this area was Coulson, a trade center and ferry crossing founded in 1877. When Frederick Billings brought the Northern Pacific Railroad to the Yellowstone Valley in 1882, the early settlers of Coulson were ready. These enterprising citizens assumed that the railroad would want (and pay amply for) access to the booming hamlet. Not so. Coulson wanted too much money for the right of way to the town, and the railroad bypassed them and established Billings a few miles north as its railhead. By 1884 Coulson was a ghost town, outpaced by prosperous Billings.

The history of Billings thereafter is the story of its growth as a regional trade and agricultural center. The wide valley above and below the city was developed into irrigated fields, and sugar beet cultivation was so successful that a refinery was built here in 1906. The energy boom of the 1960s and '70s brought further wealth to Billings, as both oil and coal reserves in eastern Montana were tapped increasingly.

Billings recently propelled itself into the news with the great Montana Centennial Cattle Drive of 1989. As part of the Montana Centennial celebrations, an "old-fashioned" cattle drive wended its way south from Roundup to Billings, a distance of about 60 miles. The 3,000 longhorn cattle brought in for the event were outnumbered by the 3,500 riders from all over the world. The five-day drive and concurrent media fair occasioned such festivities that even Billings, which has seen a party or two, stood up and noticed.

SIGHTS

Downtown Billings
The Western Heritage Center, 2822 Montana Ave., tel. 256-6809, is housed in the old Parmly Library, built in 1901 by Frederick Billings in honor of his brother Parmly. The center is a museum of the history and culture of the Yellowstone Valley. Historical photos, period clothing, art, Western crafts, historic artifacts, and interpretive exhibits are featured. The center is open Tues.-Sat. 10-5, and Sun. 1-5.

The **Yellowstone Art Center,** 401 N. 27th Ave., tel. 256-6804, located in the old county jail, mounts up to 20 exhibits a year in its five galleries. The center is devoted to securing and displaying contemporary regional and Western art, though it also houses international and historic pieces as well. There's also a museum

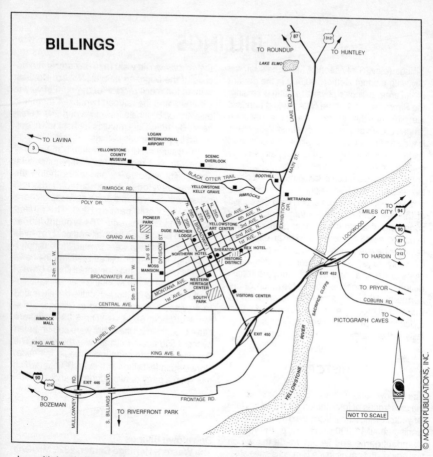

BILLINGS

shop with local gifts and books. The center is open Tues.-Sat. 11-5, and Thurs. until 8. Between Memorial Day and Labor Day, it opens an hour earlier, at 10 a.m.

Just west of the downtown area is a district of beautiful old homes. Only one of these is open to the public, but for anyone interested in turn-of-the-century architecture, a walk along these streets (between Division and Third streets, and Lewis and Yellowstone streets) is a pleasant diversion.

The **Moss Mansion**, at 914 Division, was built by an early Billings bank president, who engaged Henry Hardenberg, the architect of the Waldorf-Astoria Hotel in New York, to design his Billings

home. Completed in 1903, the three-story sandstone mansion has pronounced European touches. In fact, each room seems to be designed to reflect a different European country, from the Moorish entry hall to the Tudor dining room. Most of the original furniture and fixtures remain. Guided tours are offered on the hour, 11 a.m. to 3 p.m., $3 admission, tel. 256-5100.

The **Billings Historic District** stretches along Montana Ave. from 23rd to 26th streets. Here, paralleling the old Northern Pacific tracks, is the heart of old Billings. Turn-of-the-century hotels and commercial buildings crowd in around themselves, though the entire area has gone pretty seedy. The Rex Hotel, once frequented by Buffalo Bill Cody, is one of the sole islands of gentrification, though galleries and a good art supply store are also making a stand.

Trolleys once ran between new Billings and old Coulson. The "two-bit" fare included two glasses of beer at the Coulson brewery. The **Old Billings Trolley,** a replica of these old trolleys, now runs on downtown Billings streets. The 20-minute ride is enlivened by guides detailing history and telling stories of old Montana. The trolley leaves from the Northern Hotel, at the corner of Broadway and First Ave., on the half-hour; $2 adults, $1 for children, and the under-six crowd gets on for a quarter. Available Memorial Day to Labor Day, noon-7 p.m.

The Rimrocks
The Rimrocks are worth a visit, if only for the views from the top. From **Black Otter Trail** off

---

THE LEGEND OF SACRIFICE CLIFF

As told to Mark Brown by Old Coyote, a Crow storyteller.

Two brothers, both warriors, returned to their village to find it ravaged with smallpox. Old Coyote recounted:

They saw the dead on scaffolds. These brothers were courting two sisters. They saw many scaffolds on a cliff and climbed up there. One said to the other, "Take a look at these dead. What if they were the girls we were courting?" They recognized the sisters.

Their oldest brother was one of the chiefs. He was dead. There was no one to care for the people. They dug into their parfleches. They took out their best clothes and put them on. One had a grey horse. This was his best horse. They got on this horse, rode double. They rode through the camp and sang songs just like when there was no sickness, some lodge songs, and lastly their brothers' songs. After this ride, they went up to the cliff and rode along the rimrock singing their own songs. Then they blindfolded the horse and turned toward the edge of the cliff singing the Crazy Dog Lodge song. They were still singing when the horse went over the cliff.

—*The Plainsmen of the Yellowstone*

Airport Rd., five mountain ranges are visible. To the southeast are the Bighorns, farther west are the Pryors, to the southwest are the Beartooths, and northwest are the Crazies and Snowies. Across the Yellowstone from Black Otter Trail are the **Sacrifice Cliffs**. These 200-foot escarpments figure in a Crow legend (see sidebar).

On the Rimrocks along Black Otter Trail is **Yellowstone Kelly's Grave**, placed here at his request at a site overlooking the Yellowstone River. Luther Kelly was an adventurer of an old-fashioned sort, better suited to fiction than reality. He came west after the Civil War and found the rough and ready life here to his liking, despite his cultivated Eastern background. He knew both the Crow and Sioux languages, and campaigned with General Miles when the Army forced the Indians onto reservations following the Battle at Little Bighorn. Kelly later ventured to Alaska, and later still became a provincial governor in the Philippines. Back on this continent, he became an Indian agent in Nevada, where he also mined for gold. He died in California, and his body was returned to this site in 1928.

Follow Black Otter Trail to the eastern base of the Rimrocks to find **Boothill Cemetery,** one of the only reminders of the old town of Coulson. Fifty-two early residents are at rest here, many after meeting violent ends. Coulson's sheriff, "Muggins" Taylor, is buried here, as is Henry Lump, the man who killed him. Taylor was the Army scout who brought news of the Custer Massacre to the world, via Fort Ellis, in 1876.

Also on the Rimrocks, near the airport, is the **Peter Yegen Jr. Museum,** commonly known as the Yellowstone County Museum. This community museum features an old steam engine from the Northern Pacific, a sheepherder's wagon, a roundup wagon, and homesteader and Indian artifacts. Diorama fans will be uplifted by its display of life in the early years of Yellowstone settlement, and outdoors near the picnic tables is a telescope for viewing Billings and vicinity. Open Tues.-Sat. 10:30-5, Sun. 2-5, free admission, tel. 256-6811.

The most unusual of Billings's Rimrock attractions is the **Pictograph Caves State Monument.** Located southeast of Billings on the south side of the Yellowstone, the caves were inhabited for about 10,000 years. A succession of cultures have lived here, beginning with a tribe of prehistoric hunters. Excavations have yielded almost 30,000 cultural artifacts of early Paleo-Indians, making this one of the richest archeological sites in Montana.

The road into the monument passes by spectacular cliffs and ponderosa pine forests. At the site, three caves have been cut into the sandstone by water erosion. The best-preserved cave paintings are in Pictograph Cave. Here, buffalo, elk, prehistoric animals, and figurative and abstract designs are just visible on the sandstone walls of the cave. That the paintings have survived at all is amazing, especially after repeated assaults by vandals with spray paint. However, nature has eventually washed off the spray paint, and the colors of the painting, made from plant resins, cherry juice, animal fat, charcoal, and soil, once again show through. The other two caves, Ghost Cave and Middle Cave, were also inhabited by prehistoric Indians.

A hard-surface, 1,000-foot trail links all the caves from a central parking lot. A very nice picnic area (no camping sites, though), water, and toilets make this a great place to stop and explore. The abundance of birdlife along the rims and presence of typical prairie flora make the monument grounds a mini nature hike. To find Pictograph Caves State Monument, take exit 452, and follow the signs south along Coburg Road for five miles. The monument is open daily 8-8, April 15 to October 15.

ACCOMMODATIONS

Billings offers a wide selection of lodging options. If the deprivations of the prairies have you hankering for room service, then Billings has the hotels to pamper you. The **Radisson Northern Hotel** is the lodging doyen in Billings. Established in 1904 by banking magnate P.B. Moss, the Northern was conceived as the finest hotel north of Denver and west of Minneapolis. It's still a great hotel, and offers some of the best food in Billings at the Golden Belle Restaurant. The Northern is at Broadway and 1st Ave., tel. 245-5121, $63 s, $72 d.

A block up is the **Billings Sheraton.** The Sheraton offers the service and amenities you'd expect, but with the added privilege of doing so in Montana's tallest building (19 stories). The Sheraton is located at 27 N. 27th St., tel. 252-7400, with both single and double rooms starting at $50.

HOTELS IN BILLINGS

Hotel	Address	Phone	Rates	Features
Motel 6	5400 Midland Rd. (exit 446)	252-0093	$23 s, $29 d	pool
Super 8	5400 Southgate Dr. (exit 446)	248-8842	$32 s, $40 d	
Elliot Inn	1345 Mullowney Dr. (Exit 446)	252-2548	$30 s, $34-41 d	laundry, senior discount
Regal Inn	5353 Midland Rd. (exit 446)	248-7551	$25 s, $30 d	indoor pool, playground
Esquire Motor Inn	3314 1st Ave. N	259-4551	$25 s, $32 d	pool
Billings Inn	880 N. 29th	252-6800	$31 s, $35 d	continental breakfast, laundry, refrigerators
Econolodge	2601 4th Ave. N	245-6646	$27 s, $34 d	pool, senior discount
Best Western Ponderosa Inn	2511 1st Ave. N	259-5511	$40 s, $45 d	pool, sauna, exercise room, senior discount
Radisson Northern Hotel	Broadway and First	245-5121	$63 s, $72 d	
Billings Sheraton	27 N. 27th St.	252-7400	$50 s/d	
Dude Rancher	415 N. 29th St.	259-5561	$29 s, $31 d	coffee shop

Sacrifice Cliff rises east of Billings.

A charming alternative to these large downtown hotels is the **Dude Rancher**, a small and venerable motel with a pronounced Western atmosphere. Rooms are from $29 s, $31 d. The coffee shop here is a popular place for breakfast. The Dude Rancher is at 415 N. 29th St., tel. 259-5561.

Campgrounds

The **Billings Metro KOA** has 115 RV sites, 60 tent-camping sites, and a pool, all right next to the Yellowstone. The KOA is located off exit 450 at 3087 Garden Ave. (follow the signs), tel. 252-3104. The Billings KOA has the honor of being the first KOA in North America. The **Big Sky Campground** is located north off exit 446 at 5516 Laurel Rd., tel. 259-4110, and accommodates 100 RVs and 40 tent campers.

FOOD

The Billings restaurant scene is diverse, featuring several ethnic cuisines. But don't fool yourself. This is really red meat country. The **Cattle Company** has exceptional steaks and prime rib. It's located near the main entrance to Rimrock Mall (24th and Central Ave.), tel. 656-9090. Also on the west end of Billings is the **Black Angus Steak House**, 2685 Grand Ave., tel. 656-4949, with good steaks at good prices in an intimate atmosphere. Closer to downtown is the **Granary**, 1500 Poly Dr., tel. 259-3488, a light and airy restaurant in an old mill with good beef, a selection of chicken dishes, and seafood.

Steaks share top billing with gourmet fare at several downtown restaurants. At the **Golden Belle** at the Northern Hotel, 1st Ave. N and Broadway, tel. 245-2232, there's a varied menu of beef, lamb, and fresh seafood in an Old Montana atmosphere. The **Rex Hotel**, 2401 Montana Ave., tel. 245-7477, combines steaks with Italian dishes in a refurbished old hotel in the downtown historic district. Another historic building turned good restaurant is **George Henry's**, 404 N. 30th, tel. 245-4570. The 1882 home is now in the business of serving tasty steaks, salads, and light meals. **Jake's**, 2701 1st Ave. N, tel. 259-9375, combines a lively bar with tasty eclectic cuisine.

If you're looking for a break from steaks, Billings is also the place to be. Excellent Greek food is available at **The Athenian**, 18 N. 29th tel. 248-5681. In addition to familiar Greek specialties, leg of lamb is featured on the weekends.

Billings is blessed with an abundance of good Oriental food. **Wong Village**, 4061 Lockwood Flats, tel. 248-6015, has been around forever and still turns out good-quality, comfortably familiar Chinese food. The **Great Wall of China**, 13th and Grand Ave.; tel. 245-8601, features good Chinese food at the right price. Near to the hotels off exit 446 is **Jade Palace**, 2021 Overland, tel. 656-8888, which mixes Cantonese and Szechuan in an attractive setting.

Even nearer the same hotel strip is **Miyajima Gardens**, 5364 Midland Rd., tel. 245-8240, a superior Japanese restaurant. There are three dining rooms. The Teppan Yaki Room features brazier cooking. The Garden Room is less animated, with a fountain and pool. For the more traditional and limber there are also private tatami rooms.

Less formal dining is of course available, with Grand Avenue being the "strip" where all the fast-food places huddle. For sandwiches check out **Bert and Ernie's,** a popular watering hole where Montana-brewed beer is offered on tap, 2824 2nd Ave. N, tel. 248-4313.

Bars And Nightlife

Like any other Montana community, Billings has a nightlife centered on bars and restaurants. The **Rex Hotel**, 2401 Montana Ave., tel. 245-7477, began as an experiment in urban renewal through drink. By putting a trendy bar in an old hotel in the dilapidated historic district along the tracks, the developers began a process of refining both the building and the menu. It is still one of the most pleasant places in Billings for a drink, but it was more charming when there was still an element of raffishness to it.

Jake's, 2701 1st Ave. N, tel. 259-9375, is a waterhole much frequented by those who wish to be seen there. It's one of the liveliest bar scenes downtown. Jake's is the kind of bar where, after a couple drinks, everyone seems single. In a city, this would seem threatening. In Billings, it seems endearing.

Other nightspots of note include: the **Monte Carlo**, a horseshoe bar with piano entertainment; The **Golden Pheasant**, 109 N. Broadway, a handsome old bar that now features live jazz; **The Western**, a rowdy watering hole on the "wrong" side of the tracks that starts early and goes late. With live country music and live cowboys, **The Spur**, 1203 1st Ave., provides the wildest Western party scene in Billings.

EVENTS

MetraPark is the major venue in Billings for concerts, rodeos, fairs, and just about any other event that requires extensive seating and exhibition space. The **Midland Empire Fair** is a large agricultural affair, with a rodeo, carnival, and horse racing; it's held during the middle of August. The **Northern International Livestock Exposition** (NILE) is a large and prestigious livestock show held in October, featuring five nights of rodeo. For exact dates contact the chamber of commerce or call MetraPark at 256-

2400, and check the local newspaper for concert dates or sports engagements.

Live theater is presented in a number of venues in Billings. The **Alberta Blair Theatre**, 103 N. Broadway, tel. 256-6052, hosts a number of performance events, including theater by the Fox Committee for the Performing Arts, the Billings Symphony, and events featuring visiting artists. **Billings Studio Theatre**, 1500 Rimrock Rd., tel. 248-1141, is a local community theater featuring old and new favorites of the popular stage.

RECREATION

The **Billings Mustangs,** the Cincinnati Reds Farm team, trains in Billings and provides just about the only organized spectator sport besides rodeo. City parks cater to the casual athlete. **Pioneer Park**, between 3rd and 5th on Grand Ave., is a beautiful old park near the downtown area, and features tennis courts, jogging paths, and plenty of picnic space. The swimming pool is at **Athletic Park**, N. 27th at 9th Ave. North. **Riverside Park**, located along the Yellowstone River just off I-90, has picnic tables, jogging paths, fishing access, boat access for nonmotorized boats, and lots of room to romp. No overnight camping. Take exit 446 north to King Ave., and follow it to S. Billings Ave., and follow S. Billings Ave. to the park. **Lake Elmo State Recreation Area**, 2400 Lake Elmo Rd. in Billings Heights, offers swimming, fishing, nonmotorized boating, and picnic areas. Boat rentals are available. There's a $1 entry fee. No overnight camping.

There are several public golf courses in Billings. **Briarwood Country Club**, 3429 Briarwood Blvd., tel. 248-2702, has 18 holes and is south of Billings along Blue Creek. The **Par Three Golf Course** has 18 holes and is on Central Ave. at 19th St. W, tel. 652-2553. The **Lake Hills Golf Course** is near Lake Elmo State Park in Billings Heights. Follow Lake Elmo Rd. past Lake Elmo, and turn at Wickes Ln., tel. 252-9244.

SHOPPING

The downtown area of Billings hasn't fared so well, as shoppers have deserted older businesses in favor of new shopping centers on the city's fringes. A few older businesses persist in their original locations.

Billings is a good place to get "outfitted" with Western goods. **Lou Taubert Ranch Outfitters,** 114 N. Broadway, tel. 245-2248, is an established Western store with a wide selection of boots, hats, and gear. **Al's Bootery,** 1820 1st. Ave. N, tel. 245-4827, offers a wide selection of boots, and also silver jewelry. **Connolly's Western Wear,** 2911 Montana Ave., tel. 245-3859, is one of the area's original saddleries, having served southeastern Montana ranchers since 1912.

Indian art and crafts are available at a couple of local galleries, though oddly these shops seem to feature more Southwest Indian art than local Indian products. **Sundance Gallery,** 117 N. Broadway, tel. 256-9225, offers a wide selection of Native arts and crafts from a number of tribal traditions. **Buffalo Chips Indian Trading Post,** located in the Rimrock Mall, tel. 656-8954, seems to specialize in Southwestern artifacts.

Shopping in a flea market atmosphere for products ranging from Indian artifacts to bee pollen can be found at the **Great American Bazaar Shopping Mall,** 1600 Main in Billings Heights, tel. 259-6490.

Several art galleries in Billings emphasize Western and Montana art. The **Crumbacher Gallery,** 2814 2nd Ave. N, tel. 248-5014, Mon.-Fri. 9:30-5:30, Sat. 9:30-3:30, features limited-edition prints and some original Western-theme art. **Toucan Gallery,** 2505 Montana Ave., tel. 252-0112, Mon.-Sat. 10 a.m.-5 p.m., is located in the historic district of Billings and features contemporary local art and crafts. **Castle Gallery,** 622 29th N., tel. 259-6458, Tues.-Fri. 10-5:30, Sat. 10-4, is notable for its location in a historic home built in 1903. It also displays local contemporary arts and crafts.

INFORMATION

The **chamber of commerce** is at 815 S. 27th, P.O. Box 31177, Billings, MT 59107, tel. 245-4111. The main **post office** is directly behind the chamber of commerce at 26th Ave. S and 9th Ave. South. The downtown branch is at 2602 1st Ave. North.

Speedy Wash is downtown at 2505 6th Ave. N, tel. 248-4177; open daily 6 a.m.-11 p.m. **The Laundry Room** is near exit 446 at 3189 King Ave. W, tel. 652-2993; open daily 7 a.m.-9 p.m.

For a **local forecast** call 652-2000. For road conditions information, call 252-2806.

The **Fish, Wildlife, and Parks** office is at 2300 Lake Elmo Dr., Billings, MT 59105, tel. 252-4654. The **Custer National Forest headquarters** is at 2602 1st Ave. N, tel. 657-6600. The **BLM** office can be reached at Box 36800, Billings, MT 59107, tel. 255-2885.

Deaconess Medical Center is at 9th Ave. N and Broadway, tel. 657-4000. **St. Vincent's Hospital** is at 1233 N. 30th, tel. 657-7000.

TRANSPORTATION

Billings is the largest airlink in Montana. Horizon, Continental, Western, United, and Northwest Orient each fly into **Logan Field** several times daily. In addition, Big Sky Airlines connects Billings to smaller centers within the state. Logan Field sits atop the Rimrocks at the junction of Airport Rd. and N. 27th. **Hertz, Avis,** and **National** all operate car rental agencies at the airport.

Greyhound, 2502 1st Ave. N, tel. 245-5116, is the only form of public ground transportation in and out of Billings. **MET** is the city's public transport system.

THE UPPER YELLOWSTONE— FORSYTH AND COLSTRIP

Between Billings and Miles City lies an area of rich farm and pasture land, fed by the waters of the Yellowstone and shaded by cottonwoods. Irrigated farming is the mainstay of local economies, with corn, sugar beets, and soybeans the most prevalent crops. Feed lots, where cattle are wintered or fattened, are also common.

Past the steep sandstone bluffs that rise out of the valley floor, beyond the reach of the center-pivot sprinklers, the badlands and prairies begin. Out here, it's suddenly sagebrush and cactus, dusty roads and cattle country. After a drive across these unrelenting plains the traveler realizes the real value of the Yellowstone Valley to the natives: water, and a green thought in a green shade.

When traveling the Yellowstone Valley, one is always following in someone's footsteps. The wide, fertile valley cut by the river has been used for centuries as a thoroughfare, first by foot and horseback, then later by steamboat, railroad, and, most recently, by automobile along I-94.

History

Initially, it was the wildlife that brought people to the valley. Archaeological remains indicate that prehistoric Indians have lived here for thousands of years. Following Lewis and Clark, trappers exploited the region's abundance of fur-bearing animals and established trading forts at favorable points. By the end of the century, the range was being settled by big cattle and sheep outfits, then the valley itself began to fall to the plow.

Coal-fired electricity-generating plants built at Colstrip by the Montana Power Company in the 1970s sparked a huge debate in the state, as ranches sitting atop coal reserves were tempted and coerced to sell their mineral rights. Ecologists found allies in Indians and cowboys alike as the effects of the coal-fired plants on the environment became known. In the end, the plants went in. But not before families and neighbors divided over the issues surrounding economic growth, environmental damage, and rapid change in traditional communities.

POMPEY'S PILLAR

Pompey's Pillar has always been a landmark. Indians used it as a lookout and for sending smoke signals. But it was the Corps of Discovery that put Pompey's Pillar on the map. In July 1806, William Clark and his party were paddling down the Yellowstone when they sighted this 200-foot-high sandstone outcropping in the middle of the wide valley. Clark named the formation after Jean Baptiste, the son of Sacajawea and Charbonneau, the French trapper and adventurer who accompanied the Corps. Clark had nicknamed Jean Baptiste Little Pomp, meaning Little Chief. Clark wrote:

> July 25th, 1806 at 4 P M arived at a remarkable rock situated in an extensive bottom. this rock I ascended and from its top had a most extensive view in every direction. This rock which I shall call Pompy's Tower is 200 feet high and 400 paces in secumpherance and only axcessable on one Side. The nativs have ingraved on the face of this rock the figures of animals &c near which I marked my name and the day of the month and year. From the top of this Tower I could discover two low Mountains and the Rocky Mts covered with Snow one of them appeared to be extencive.

Some of the Pillar's petroglyphs still remain, and are reckoned to be the work of the Shoshone Indians who lived in this area before the current Plains tribes moved west. But the real curiosity here is Clark's signature, carved in the rock and still legible after almost 200 years. Clark was not the last to sign Pompey's Pillar. A pair of crossed hatchets, insignia medallions worn by members of the Corps, were probably carved by an enterprising Corpsman while Clark finished his signature. Captain Grant Marsh, pilot of the steamship *Josephine,* added his graffiti in 1875.

(top) the solitary life of a Montana sheepherder (Hazel McRae); (bottom) sheep ranching has declined in recent years (W.C. McRae)

(top) the solitary life of a Montana sheepherder (Montana Bureau of Tourism); (bottom) sheep ranching has declined in recent years (W.C. McRae)

Pompey's Pillar is on private property. The state is attempting to buy the site from the current landowner in order to turn it into a park. It is open to the public between Memorial Day and Labor Day, from dawn to dusk. There is a steep trail up its back side, and from the top there is a good vista of the Yellowstone Valley and the surrounding mountains. There are picnic tables near the car park, but no overnight camping is allowed.

The closest facilities are in Ballantine, where the **Longbranch,** alongside the freeway, has a good reputation with the locals for good, inexpensive food. The closest motel is either in Billings or Custer.

I-94 BETWEEN POMPEY'S PILLAR AND FORSYTH

Between Pompey's Pillar and Forsyth, I-94 parallels the Yellowstone River through a region of farms, ranches, and, near Hysham, badlands. The valley here is wide and where not under cultivation, forested with cottonwoods. At the edge of the river valley, steep sandstone cliffs rise, fringed with pine and juniper trees.

Although little remains to indicate it, this stretch of the Yellowstone saw much of the early history of Montana. At the mouth of the Bighorn,

JEAN BAPTISTE CHARBONNEAU

The child that William Clark knew as Pompey was born to a destiny usually reserved to heroes of fiction. He was born to Toussaint Charbonneau, a French trader living with the Mandan Indians in North Dakota, and one of his three wives, the 15-year-old Sacajawea, a Shoshone girl who had been stolen away from her tribe in Montana. His birth was difficult; after many hours of labor, the delivery was hastened by giving Sacajawea a potion of rattlesnake rattle and river water. Ten minutes later she delivered young Jean Baptiste. The Corps of Discovery, with the papoose Pompey, set out for the Pacific two months later.

Captain Clark grew very fond of the young child during the course of the journey. After the successful completion of the trip, the Corps once again reached the Mandan villages that were home to the Charbonneaus. Clark urged them to allow him to take the young Baptiste to rear as his own. They declined. Later the same year, Clark wrote Charbonneau to repeat his offer, that "if you bring your son Baptiste to me, I will educate him and treat his as my own child." This time it worked. Charbonneau, Sacajawea, and Baptiste moved to St. Louis, where Clark educated the boy in a Catholic academy.

When Baptiste was 18 years old, he met Prince Paul of Wurttemberg, a German aristocrat-cum-scientist intent on exploring Montana. The prince was intrigued by the well-educated half-breed (Baptiste already spoke three languages), and after ascending the Missouri in his company, asked Clark if Baptiste might accompany him back to Germany.

Baptiste spent the next six years living with the prince in his castle near Stuttgart and accompanying him on his travels to England, France, and North Africa. His education continued, and he learned two more languages. When the prince returned to America in 1829, Baptiste returned as well. This time, however, after journeying to the headwaters of the Missouri and back down the Yellowstone, Baptiste remained in the West.

Thereafter, he renounced the refinements of European court life for the rigors and adventure of the American frontier. He earned a living as a trapper for the American Fur Company until the fur trade declined in the early 1830s. By the 1840s, Baptiste was working as a guide for traders, explorers, and foreign visitors. He consorted with such famous mountain men as Solomon and Andrew Sublette, Jim Bridger, and Joe Meek. He led more hunting trips for European noblemen, including a well-documented expedition by the Scot Sir William Drummond Stewart in 1843. A contemporary judged him to be "the best man on foot on the Plains or in the Rocky Mountains."

In 1847, Baptiste was in California, after guiding a battalion of Mormons across the southwest deserts during the Mexican War. He was appointed *alcade* for the mission at San Luis Rey, until he resigned after being accused of "favoring the Indians more than he should," according to contemporary legal documents. The lure of gold drew Baptiste northward to prospecting country near Sacramento in 1848, where he lived for 18 years. Stories of gold strikes in Montana excited the old trapper, and he set out to revisit the scenes of his youth. However, he made it no farther than the Owyhee Valley in eastern Oregon before he died in 1866. Jean Baptiste Charbonneau is buried near Danner, Oregon.

near present-day Custer, traders erected the first structures in the state. Beginning with Fort Remon, established by Manuel Lisa in 1807 and named after his infant son, and soon followed by other forts, this location drew adventurers and frontiersmen who came to trade, trap, and to explore the wilderness.

The list of those who passed through these forts reads like a who's who of the early West: Jim Bridger, Father deSmet, John Bozeman. The mouth of the Bighorn River was traditionally the head of navigation for steamboats on the Yellowstone River. It is also the beginning of the agate-rich Yellowstone gravel that stretches downstream to the Missouri.

Nothing remains of the various trading forts along the Yellowstone, but from the fishing-access site at the mouth of the Bighorn River (exit 49), appropriately called Manuel Lisa, you can see where the forts must have stood, and imagine this deserted riverbank as one of the hotbeds of activity west of St. Louis.

For back-road enthusiasts, or anyone who wants a break from the freeway, there is a nice side road alternative to I-94 beginning at the little community of Bighorn and continuing to Forsyth. The road, gravel at first, then paved, passes through the small farming and ranching communities of Myers, Hysham, and Sanders. The road keeps much closer to the Yellowstone than the freeway does, and offers more interesting scenery.

There are limited but completely adequate tourist facilities. In Custer, the **D & L Cafe and Motel**, 311 Second Ave., tel. 856-4128, offers inexpensive rooms and good food. Call ahead in winter months; it closes during the off-season. In Hysham, the **Hysham Motel**, 514 Seventh, tel. 342-5627, is the place to stay.

Western juniper, Juniperus occidentalis

BOB RACE

COLSTRIP

South of the bluffs of Yellowstone Valley proper, the underlying sandstone changes from Eagle Formation to Fort Union Formation sandstone. While there are no visual differences between the two, there is a vast difference in mineral wealth. In the intervening 15 million years between the two sandstone-making periods, alongside the ancient seas and riverbanks, tropical forests laid down vast deposits of peat. When the climate changed, these deposits in turn were covered by others, and the peat slowly turned to coal.

The coal in this part of Montana is highly prized. It is covered by a modest layer of overburden (rock and soil on top of the coal) and makes for easy strip mining. Strip mining removes the overburden by levels, revealing the coal seam which is then gouged out by enormous power shovels. The coal itself is low-sulfur bituminous, which burns cleaner and at a higher temperature than soft coal from other parts of the country.

These considerations have made Colstrip, astride huge coal deposits, appealing to mining and energy interests. When Montana Power began to build coal-fired generators at Colstrip in the 1970s, Montanans were galvanized around the issues of progress, ecology, and heritage.

History

Colstrip (pop. 3,000, elev. 2,540 feet) began in 1924 as a source of coal for the engines of the Northern Pacific. Having depleted its original source of coal at Red Lodge, the Northern Pacific began to extract cheaper, more efficient coal from the eastern plains.

The Northern Pacific was one of the last major railroads to switch from coal- to diesel-fueled engines. After it did, in the 1950s, it sold its coal leases at Colstrip to a subsidiary of the Montana Power Company, called the Western Energy Company. Equipment was updated and coal development was expanded. In 1969, a coal-fired electric generator was built in Billings, operated by the Montana Power Company and fueled by Colstrip coal.

The success of the plant fueled plans for more electric generators. In tandem with the oil crunch of the 1970s, the Western Energy Company revealed plans to build four more huge generators. The power was to be sold to out-of-state markets in the Pacific Northwest and Midwest. But rather than ship the coal to generators near the markets, the Western Energy Company planned to build all four generators in Colstrip.

The amount of coal to be mined was enormous. Entire ranches would be devoured by the strip mines. The generators would pollute the air, which in almost the entire eastern part of Montana is pristine. However, the plants would bring economic growth to some of the most marginally successful agricultural communities in the state.

Instantly, battle lines were drawn. Environmentalists concerned with air quality joined with ranchers worried about wells and the lowering of the water table (coal seams function as aquifers, as coal is porous, and the water table in this part of Montana is often the shallow layer of coal underlying almost everything in the eastern third of the state). Other farmers and ranchers, who had struggled for decades against the weather, insects, and bad markets, were understandably excited by the prospect of finally earning a living from the land, albeit by a troubling method.

Even the Indian tribes divided: The Cheyenne fought to cancel coal leases on the reservation, and filed to have the reservation reclassified as an area with Class 1 air standards, usually granted only to wilderness areas. The Crow, on the other hand, sold mineral rights and watched strip mines operate on the reservation.

Grass-roots opposition found its focus in the Northern Plains Resource Council, and its leaders in articulate farmers and ranchers who feared the changes in environment and community that the growth of large-scale mining would entail. Development at Colstrip was a deeply divisive issue to rural Montanans. As traditional "leave me alone" libertarians who resented environmentalists as cowardly predator-lovers, these farmers and ranchers found the same mistrusted environmentalists to be allies against the juggernauts of big business and big development.

In the end, Colstrip 1 through 4 went in, after many delays and courtroom battles. However, the state instituted tough reclamation laws and levied a severance tax on coal sold out of state. The generators have left as many scars on rural Montana culture as they have on the plains near Colstrip.

Sights

After crossing Montana, the approach to Colstrip is a bit of a shock. The 29-mile drive south from I-94 crosses a countryside of barren, dry valleys and rocky buttes. It seems a marginal, rough piece of real estate. Then the land, without really changing, becomes a bit too smooth, too manicured, as if it had recently been mowed, revealing the good work of the reclaimers. Suddenly smokestacks fill the air. At 692 feet high, they are the tallest structures in Montana. Pipelines and rail lines converge at mammoth generators spewing out smoke. Piles of overburden rise above gashes in the earth, where man and machine render coal from flat fields of black and place it in rail cars.

Tours are available to the curious showing the workings of a modern strip mine and coal-fired generators. The Rosebud open-pit mine tour takes the visitor to the bottom of a working strip mine. The power shovels have to be seen to be believed. The second part of the tour goes to the generating plants. Three tours are offered Mon.-Fri. at 10, 1, and 2:45, and are free. Reserve a seat by calling 748-3746.

Almost as interesting is the town itself. Built almost totally from scratch since the 1970s (remnants of '20s-era buildings are labeled the "historic district"), Colstrip is what other Montana prairie towns might look like if they had money. Bike paths, manicured lawns around new homes, artificial lakes, lots of parks and sports facilities, even an ice-skating rink, all in a setting of rocky gumbo, make Colstrip seem almost surreal.

Practicalities

The visitor may as well make use of the facilities that money can buy. **Override Park** on Water Ave. offers basketball courts, tennis courts, a swimming pool, and a playground. There are also picnic tables at the visitor center just off Hwy. 39.

KAREN WHITE

Merlin, Falco columbarious

There is one hotel, the The **Fort Union Inn**, 5 Dogwood, tel. 748-2553. Camping is available from **Colstrip Community Services**, tel. 748-2375. **Bob's Place**, 17 Cherry, tel. 748-2566, is the locals' favorite for steak and seafood.

The **visitor center** is open Mon.-Fri. 8-5, Memorial Day-Labor Day, and from 10-3 the rest of the year at 6200 Main St., tel. 748-3746.

Civilization has its merits. **National Public Radio** is heard at 88.5 FM.

FORSYTH

Forsyth (pop. 3,000, elev. 2,515 feet), nestled beneath a rim of rough gumbo badlands along the banks of the Yellowstone, is a pretty little town with lots of trees and Western character. The presence of Colstrip to the south has elevated Forsyth above the general economic malaise assailing other small Montana towns, without developing it into an affluent parody of its historic self. For the traveler, Forsyth offers recreational opportunities and a friendly place to spend the night.

History

Forsyth is named for General James Forsyth, a U.S. Army officer who first landed here in 1875, before the town existed. Steamers stopped here to refuel their engines from the abundant stands of cottonwood. The town was established in 1880 and earned its own post office when the Northern Pacific arrived in 1882. The elaborate buildings along Main Street, including the imposing Rosebud County Courthouse, indicate the wealth of the young community during the early years of this century.

Forsyth grew into its own as a trading hub after the Milwaukee Road extended north from Forsyth into the Musselshell and Judith Basin country in 1910, opening up a vast new territory for settlement.

The railroads still fuel the Forsyth economy. Much of the coal that Burlington Northern ships out of state from Colstrip and other mines south of Forsyth pass through the rail yards here.

Sights

The Rosebud County Pioneer Museum, 1300 Main, tel. 356-7547, houses artifacts from the area's early years of settlement and photographs of pioneer days. Open Mon.-Sat. 9-7, Sun. 1-7, May-September.

Recreation

Forsyth is well placed to serve as a center for hunters, as it is the hub of many country roads that quickly take the outdoorsman into prime big-game territory. Pronghorn, mule, and white-tailed deer are the usual quarry. Also, with the fields that line the river and the river itself both serving as a temptation, bird hunters are rewarded with ample prey.

With fishing-access sites practically within city limits, Forsyth also welcomes anglers. The **Rosebud State Recreation Areas**, directly east and west of the city, offer fishing and boating access and camping. If you stop for a picnic, don't forget to look for agates.

The **Forsyth Golf and Country Club**, three miles west of Forsyth, exit 93 (Frontage Rd.), tel. 356-7710, has nine holes, rentals, and a clubhouse. The course winds up a steep gumbo canyon in the badlands just outside of town. There is also an indoor Olympic-size swimming pool in Forsyth.

Accommodations

Best Western Sundowner Inn, 1018 Front St., tel. 356-2115, $35 s, $41 d, is the premier motel in Forsyth and offers free passes to the city's indoor pool. **Westwind Motor Inn**, W. Main at Hwy. 12, tel. 356-2038, $32 s, $35 d, has a pretty location near fishing access along the Yellowstone. The **Restwel**, 810 Front St., tel. 356-2771, $22 s, $27 d, is a good value, as is the **Rail Inn**, tel. 356-2242. The **Econo Lodge**, 659 Front St., tel. 356-7947, is convenient to the freeway.

There are campsites at both the **Rosebud Recreation Areas** on the east and west ends of town. **Wagon Wheel Campsites**, exit 95, tel. 356-7982, welcomes both tent and RV campers.

Food

The **Blue Spruce**, 109 S. 10th St., tel 356-7955, is a family restaurant offering good beef from the owner's own herd. **B&L Big Sky Café**, 410 Front, tel. 356-7955, offers sandwiches and light meals. For a steak house atmosphere, try **J-C's**, 1001 Main, tel. 356-7352.

Services

The **Rosebud Health Care Center** is at 383 W. 17th St., tel 356-2161. **Emergency** is 911. The **chamber of commerce** can be contacted at Box 448, Forsyth, MT 59327, tel. 356-2233.

MILES CITY

Miles City (elev. 2,371 feet) is an attractive town located at the confluence of the Tongue River and the Yellowstone. Gumbo buttes vaguely fringed with juniper ring the town. Miles City is the second-largest city in southeastern Montana, with almost 8,500 inhabitants. It's a major trade center for farmers and ranchers who, in their pickup trucks, converge on the city for livestock sale days, during harvest for parts, or as often as an excuse can be found to "go to Miles."

HISTORY

Miles City was born in the aftermath of the Battle of the Little Bighorn. After the defeat of Custer's Seventh Cavalry, the Army decided to establish a permanent military presence in eastern Montana to protect settlers and to drive the Sioux back onto reservations. In the fall of 1876, six companies of the Fifth Cavalry under the command of General Nelson Miles established a military cantonment at the mouth of the Tongue River, and arranged for the building of Fort Keogh. The civilian settlement that grew up downriver was initially known as Milestown. Fort Keogh, the largest military fort built in Montana, was finished in 1878, and Miles City reestablished itself on the Tongue River's opposite shore.

Miles City quickly became important as a trade center. The military payroll made for a relatively affluent citizenry, encouraging a stable base for the trades and mercantile. Steamboats were the vehicle for almost all transportation in the early days, and Miles City was an important port. The steamboats brought up goods for Fort Keogh and the young community of Miles City, and took out a wealth of buffalo bones and hides.

After the Army had subdued the Sioux in 1877, and after the buffalo hunters had completed their own decimation, the vast prairies along the lower Yellowstone drainage were opened up for grazing. The first of the huge trail drives north from Texas was in 1879, and for the next 10 years Miles City was the center of a grazing region that summered tens of thousands of southern cattle. The Northern Pacific Railroad arrived in 1881, providing a railhead to eastern slaughterhouses and markets. These boom years in the 1880s justified Miles City's swaggering boast of being the "Cow Capital of the West," for as its population and wealth grew, so did its reputation as a hard-drinking, rough and tough cowtown.

Miles City Today

The old downtown, or what is left of it (the town has been victim to a suspicious number of arson fires in the last 10 years), contains remnants of

JIM MASTERSON

Western boomtown architecture. Elements of the town, especially the bars, rail stations, and Main Street, have changed little since they were built.

Fort Keogh still exists, at least in name. Indian hostilities on the northern plains ended in 1877, after General Miles defeated both the Sioux in southeastern Montana and Chief Joseph in the north-central part of the state. Fort Keogh remained an Army post until 1900, at which time it became a remount station where horses were trained for the U.S. Army. In 1924, the fort was transferred to the control of the Department of Agriculture, and an agricultural test station was established. The Livestock and Range Research Station at Fort Keogh is known primarily for its role in developing the purebred "Line One" of the Hereford cattle breed. But it is not known for its sensitivity to historic monuments. The original buildings of Fort Keogh fell into decrepitude, and many were simply burned. The only remaining building open for viewing, an officers' duplex, is at the Range Riders Museum.

SIGHTS

Range Riders Museum

Every community in eastern Montana has a local museum. If you see only one, make it the Range Riders Museum in Miles City. Located at the western edge of the city, near the confluence of the Tongue and Yellowstone rivers, it contains enough items to impress even the most jaundiced of museum-goers.

A one-room school, a frontier cabin, tepees, and a sheep wagon have been moved onto the grounds and maintained in period condition with authentic furnishings. A building from Fort Keogh, an officers' quarters, is open to visitors. Although only half of it is open, it is a vivid reminder of how civilized life on the Yellowstone was in 1878.

Inside the museum is an excellent gun and weapon collection, artifacts and memorabilia from the settling of the West, Indian artifacts, old photos, a southeastern Montana settler's "hall of fame," fossils, and more. There's also a reproduction of an 1890s Miles City street.

The best display also harkens back to Fort Keogh. In 1990, curator Bob Barthelmess presented his labor of love: a complete reconstruction of Fort Keogh at 1:80 scale. Housed in

a room with an artfully painted *trompe l'oeil* landscape of the valley, the fort is recreated with painstaking detail and accuracy. It's really amazing, both the model and (what must have been) the original. The Range Riders Museum is open daily 8 a.m.-8 p.m., April 1-Oct. 31, or by appointment, tel. 232-4483. Entry is $3.

Custer County Art Center

The Custer County Art Center is next door at the historic Miles City Water Works building. The gallery is housed in a 1924 building designed to filter and hold the city's water, and the galleries themselves are in the water-holding tanks. The center emphasizes Western art, not surprisingly, along with frequent talks, readings, and a "quick draw" contest. There's also a nice picnic ground around the museum, under some ancient cottonwoods. Turn north at the Fish and Wildlife office off Hwy. 10 just west of the Tongue River Bridge. The art center is open Tues.-Sat. 1-5 p.m., tel. 232-0635. Admission is free.

Downtown

Downtown Miles City is still intact enough, despite the efforts of arsonists, to look like the cattle trading capital it once was. There's an undeniably western flavor to the city, with its old bars, saddleries, cafés, and the clientele to appreciate them. Most of the downtown area is now listed on the National Register of Historic Places.

PRACTICALITIES

Accommodations

Most of the chain hotels are located at the Broadus exit (exit 138) off I-94. The **Super 8** is south of the interchange on Hwy. 59, tel. (800) 848-8888, 232-5261 in the area. Single rooms are $29, doubles run $29-32. **Motel 6** is north toward town, 1314 S. Haynes, tel. 232-7040; rates here are $23 s, $29 d. The **Best Western War Bonnet Inn** is the city's premium at 1015 S. Haynes, tel. (800) 528-1234, or 232-4560 locally. Single rooms start at $38, doubles at $42.

The city's cheapest lodgings are located along the old route Hwy. 12. The **Sagebrush**, 308 N. Custer, 232-1875, is a dependable, good value at $19 s, $21 d. The Hwy. 12 cluster is most easily reached by taking the Baker exit toward Miles City on Hwy. 12.

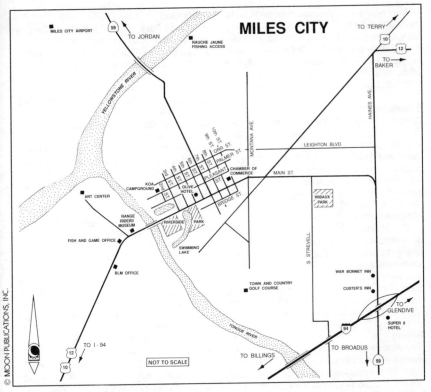

Downtown is the **Olive Hotel**, 502 Main, tel. 232-2450, $28 s, $35-38 d, the only old original Miles City hotel in operation. The Olive is so well established that even fictional characters (such as Gus McCrae of *Lonesome Dove*) stay there. You can choose to lodge in the old hotel or in the more modern motel to the side. Either way, you are staying at a Montana institution and are seconds away from a very good steak and Chinese food restaurant in the main hotel. The Olive's 1899 lobby is listed in the National Register of Historic Places.

For camping, the **Miles City KOA** is near the Tongue/Yellowstone juncture at 1 Palmer St., tel. 232-3991. It features a pool, tent sites, laundry, and hot showers from May to November. The **Big Sky Campground**, tel. 232-9894, is just off the Baker interchange (exit 141) and is open to both RVs and tents from May to November. Not much shade, though.

Food

There's a large concentration of fast-food restaurants, a truck stop, and a dependable 24-hour **4-Bs**, tel. 232-5771, at the Broadus exit off I-94. At the Baker interchange, there's the **Flying J Husky Truck Stop**, whose café, Li'l Darlin's, tel. 232-4121, has a good local reputation. There are no surprises on the menu, but the food is top-notch. The coffee is made from their own well water.

There's more character and probably better food uptown. Here, amongst the easily recognized fast-food and sandwich joints, are more authentic Miles City eating experiences. The **Olive Hotel Dining Room**, 502 Main, tel. 232-2450, has great steaks, and if eastern Montana has you glutted on good beef, the Olive also serves Chinese food. Another landmark is the **600 Café**, 600 Main, tel. 232-3860, full of character and characters, both local. It's a great place to catch the pulse of this old cow town.

Right next door is the more upscale **Hole in the Wall**, 602 Main, tel. 232-9887, featuring fairly intentional Western decor and steaks cooked in the 600's kitchen. The newest addition to Miles City's cuisine scene is **Club 519**, 519 Main, tel. 232-5133, featuring steaks in the historic First National Bank building (1910).

Entertainment

A night out in Miles City is a great way to experience one of the legacies of the Old West. Miles City started as a watering hole for thirsty soldiers, and it still is a major meeting place for stockmen and ranch hands. Miles City is a city exceptionally blessed with great old bars, and some of them have not changed appreciably (except for the addition of the ubiquitous gambling machines).

The **Montana Bar** is probably one of the greatest bars in the state, remarkably unchanged since it opened in 1902. You can imagine the many tall tales told and livestock trading that went on here at 612 Main Street. Other good bars are the **Range Riders**, 605 Main, the **Bison**, 618 Main, the **Log Cabin**, 710 Main, and the bar at the **Olive Hotel**, 501 Main.

Events

The **Jaycee Bucking Horse Sale** is the one event that Miles City is known for throughout the West. On the third weekend of May, rodeo stock contractors and bacchants from just about everywhere gather in Miles City to watch young untamed horses buck. The most promising of these mounts are then sold at auction as rodeo broncs.

The Bucking Horse Sale is one of the biggest parties in the state, though the actual rodeo is now the central event in a weekend's worth of events including horse racing, a street dance, a barbecue, cowboy poetry readings, and the like. Don't let these more civilized pursuits fool you: this is a flat-out celebration of the Dionysian element of the Old West. Admission to the rodeo is $10 a head for reserved seats; general-admission seats are $7; children under 12 get in $2 cheaper in either section.

The third weekend of June is set aside for the **Balloon Roundup**, Montana's largest hot-air balloon rally. Events include balloon races and games, a barbecue, a parade, and parties. The Balloon Roundup is held on S. Haynes Ave., near the Broadus interchange.

Recreation

Riverside Park, on W. Main at the Tongue River Bridge, has tennis courts and swimming in a natural lake. **Wibaux Park** has a good playground for kids and is easy to find from the freeway by following S. Haynes Ave. from the Broadus exit toward town and turning south two blocks at Strevell. The **Town and Country Golf Course** is a private nine-hole club open to the public at Montana and S. 4th Street. Call (406) 232-1600 for information.

There's hiking amongst the gumbo hills southeast of town. At **Strawberry Hill Recreation Area**, five miles east on Hwy. 12 from I-94, undeveloped trails lead up the Pine Buttes. **Woodruff Park** has picnic sites in grassy swales and pine trees. Although there are no formal trails, a nice wander along the ridges is enjoyable. Overnight camping is also allowed, although no water is provided, and garbage has to be carried out. Cross-country skiers make use of the park in winter.

The Yellowstone River provides good fishing for walleye, sauger, bass, and channel catfish from several local fishing-access areas. Canoes can be rented from **Yellowstone Canoe Rental**, 1015 N. 1st, tel. 232-1015. The Yellowstone has strong currents when high; inquire locally about conditions before boating.

White-tailed and mule deer are abundant in the countryside around Miles City, making it a good headquarters for hunters. Consider an outfitter if you are new to the area. **Blue Rock Outfitters** runs big-game and seasonal turkey hunts, c/o Kurt Hughes, Tongue River Stage, Miles City, MT 59301, tel. 232-5250. **Ray Perkins Outfitters Service** offers gamebird and big-game outfitting, 1906 Main, Miles City, MT 59301, tel. 232-4283.

Shopping

Where better to buy your Western togs than in the Cow Capital of the West? The **Miles City Saddlery** will outfit you (and the horse you rode in on) with quality Western gear. From boots, cowboy hats, spurs, and pearl snap shirts, to handmade saddles, it's all here, 808 Main, tel. 232-2512. In a happier era, Main Street was lined with shops, each peddling its own handmade boots and saddles. Wilson brand boots were once the local's boot of choice. Although the boots are now made elsewhere, **Wilson Saddlery** is still in operation, 616 Main, tel. 232-2800.

In the back of every saddlery was once a grandfatherly man making saddles for local ranchers and cowhands. Nowadays, if you hanker after a custom-made saddle, be prepared to pay a small fortune. **T-Bone Saddlery**, tel. 232-5176, is one of the few saddle-makers left in Miles City, and operates out of an unprepossessing shop on N. Haynes Ave. past Pine Hills School. Custom saddles begin at $1400.

Services
The **Post Office** is at 106 N. Seventh. The **Holy Rosary Hospital** is at 2102 Clark St., tel. 232-2540.

If the sky is threatening, call the **weather service** for an update, tel. 232-2099, and check the **road conditions** by dialing (800) 332-6171.

National Public Radio is heard locally on KEEC 90.7 FM.

Information
The Miles City **Chamber of Commerce** is located at 901 Main St., Miles City, MT 59301, tel. (406) 232-2890.

The **Dept. of Fish, Wildlife, and Parks** can be reached by mail at Rte. 1, Box 2004, Miles City, MT 59301, and is found just west of the Tongue River Bridge at 3 N.W. Main, tel. 232-1280.

The **BLM** office is across from the Miles City Sales Yards, about a mile west of the Tongue River Bridge. The mailing address is P.O. Box 940, Miles City, MT 59301, tel. 232-4331.

Getting There
Frank Wiley Field has daily flights into Miles City via Big Sky Airlines. A roundtrip flight from Billings is about $70. The **Greyhound** station, tel. 232-3900, is at 18 S. Sixth.

THE LOWER YELLOWSTONE

Between Miles City and its confluence with the Missouri, the Yellowstone becomes a languid prairie river flowing through increasingly arid badlands. The trees and the small towns thin out, and a kind of sullen barrenness grips the landscape.

This is ranch country, rugged and desolate. Since the days of the big cattle drives in the 1880s, the plains along the lower Yellowstone have been home to large holdings of livestock. Towns such as Terry, Glendive, and Wibaux had their beginnings as trade and rail centers in the early days of the West. Their economies are still largely tied to agriculture, although oil and gas production have bolstered them somewhat in the recent years of poor cattle, sheep, and grain markets.

This area is also home to curious opportunities for the traveler. Makoshika Park near Glendive offers startlingly rugged badlands filled with fossils, hiking trails, and wildlife. It also offers the chance to pull into old towns like Terry and Wibaux and experience the life of the modern stockmen on their own turf.

HISTORY

Until the end of the Indian Wars of 1876-77, this was Indian country, with the Sioux harassing travelers on the Yellowstone as they passed through. When the Northern Pacific was surveyed, hundreds of Army soldiers were needed to protect the engineers from the Indians. At this time, the only whites living in this part of Montana were rough-hewn loners who cut cottonwood for steamer fuel by summer and shot buffalo by winter.

By 1877 the Indians were mostly incarcerated on reservations and the land open to exploitation. One of the last great herds of buffalo on the open range were slaughtered in the Terry area, just in time to be shipped east on the first trains running east and west in the early 1880s on the Northern Pacific.

The prairie was soon overrun with herds of Texas longhorns. Glendive and Wibaux were major railheads for the shipment of the cattle to eastern markets, and were rough-and-ready "cow towns" in their day. After the hard winter of 1886, when vast herds of "free range" cattle died, the cattle industry was reborn in areas like Wibaux, where the cattle barons of the open range then founded ranches.

The Cedar Creek Anticline, which lifts the Makoshika Badlands above the plains, also traps natural gas and oil in domes beneath the prairies.

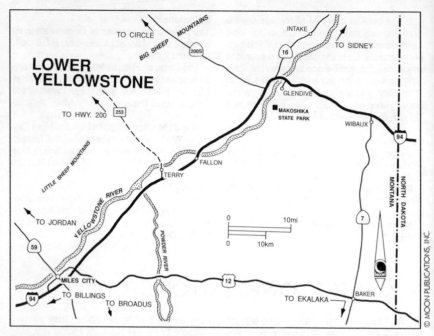

Development of these fuels prompted a boom in Glendive in the 1970s.

TERRY

This little ranch town sits along the Yellowstone, with prairies to the south and rugged badlands to the north. If you are traveling east, it's time to realize that you're well and truly on the plains of Montana. At Miles City, the Yellowstone is a wide green valley with irrigated pastures and fields. At Terry, 40 miles downstream, only a fringe of green isolates the river from the encroaching prairies.

Terry (pop. 659, elev. 2,244 feet) is a friendly town where ranchers meet to drink coffee or a beer and talk. The Sheep Mountains, gumbo breaks to the north, provide a scenic vista over badlands and river valley, and offer wildlife viewing. As ever, the Yellowstone is good fishing and boating.

Terry has a tradition of producing rodeo stars. Terry-born rodeo rider and showman Bernie Kempton toured the world in Wild West shows. In Australia he drew local attention by roping not one but two kangaroos per loop. Kempton retired to the Terry area where he ran a popular guest ranch. The Fourth of July Terry Rodeo is considered one of the best rodeos in the state.

History
The mouth of the Powder River, five miles upstream from Terry, is one of those locations that everyone noted when passing through. William Clark camped across the Yellowstone from the Powder on the last night of July, 1806. Sir George Gore made camp here on his big-game safari of 1856. General Custer passed through here on his way to destiny in 1876.

Terry began as a refueling station for the steamers bringing soldiers and supplies up the Yellowstone during the Indian Wars of the 1870s. The rough life during these early years is illustrated by a tombstone epithet at a small pioneer cemetery on the Powder River: "Killed in a quarrel at Top Foley's Roadhouse, 1880."

Sights
The **Sheep Mountains** directly north of Terry are not mountains at all. Rather, they are rugged

gumbo badlands that form the watershed between the Yellowstone and the Missouri river drainages. Especially in spring and early summer, when the striations are moist and highly colored, and the wildflowers in bloom, they seem almost forlornly beautiful.

Although the Sheep Mountains are not developed as a destination, Hwy. 253, a semi-improved road, continues on to Brockway and Hwy. 200. It passes through some very wild land, with deeply gashed ravines in the gumbo slopes and fringed with low-growing juniper, which the locals call creeping cedar. This heavily eroded land, with its jumble of rocks, scrub vegetation, and precipitous coulees, seems almost too primordial to evoke the West.

From a turnout high in the Sheep Mountains, two miles north and six miles west off Hwy. 253, a scenic viewpoint overlooks the Yellowstone. Called the **Terry Badlands**, this is a designated wildlife-viewing area. The usual big-game animals are here, as well as predators, golden eagles, and songbirds. Both look for and watch out for snakes. Informal hikes are possible along livestock trails or dirt roads. Highway 253 continues on through the "breaks," as these rugged landscapes are called locally, until you drop into the Missouri drainage and its fertile grain fields.

Several historic sites are commemorated near the mouth of the Powder River. A small **pioneer graveyard** sits on the west bank of the river at the Hwy. 10 bridge. A roadside sign describes the graveyard and its three headstones, which lie about 100 feet off the road. Another sign describes the old **Terry Supply Station** which stood on the Yellowstone and furnished fuel to steamers as they brought soldiers into Montana during the Indian Wars. Two soldiers of Custer's Seventh Cavalry are buried here. A road, suitable for high-clearance vehicles, leads to the site.

The **Prairie County Museum,** 105 Logan, is housed in an elegant turn-of-the-century bank building. Its exhibits include horse-drawn car-

YELLOWSTONE MOSS AGATES

Agates and sapphires are Montana's two official gemstones. Although agates occur worldwide, dendritic agates from the Yellowstone Valley are highly valued for their unusual figurations. Often called moss agates, the interiors of these stones reveal startlingly realistic mini-landscapes when correctly cut and polished.

Agates are made when gases form bubbles within cooling igneous strata. These cavities in the rock are slowly filled with water carrying a silica solution tinted with mineral traces (usually iron). As the silica hardens, it forms regular bands of color of varying intensity. Successive layers of colored silica are laid down within the cavity. As the overlying rock is eroded, the nodes of agate are freed from their setting.

Moss agates are different from banded, or riband, agates because of the presence of plume-like formations within the stone. Small fractures allow the penetration of minute amounts of water-borne minerals into the silica node, which, as it hardens, forms indicative tree- or feather-like apparitions in the translucent stone. Combined with bands of color within the agate, these formations make landscape images of trees and sunsets, or trees along a lakeside. The verisimilitude of moss agates can be uncanny.

These agates, often called picture agates, occur almost exclusively in the Yellowstone Valley between the mouth of the Bighorn River and the Missouri. Why this should be so is a matter of speculation. As the Bighorn, Tongue, and Powder rivers drain a common area of Wyoming, some theories propose that the agates formed in volcanic ash and lava beds near the watersheds of these rivers, and later washed downstream to the Yellowstone. This explanation seems rational, but no appropriate igneous formations have been found in Wyoming.

If you know what you are looking for, agates are not hard to find, but it takes a trained eye to spot agates in the rough. Only if they are scuffed or broken do they reveal their translucent interior; otherwise they are a dirty yellow-white.

Agate hunting is a favorite pastime for many locals, and many shops carry a basket of cut agates or agate jewelry for those not willing to hunt for their own. The same locals and shopkeepers are usually willing to lend advice to novice agate hunters. The best agate-hunting seasons are early spring and mid-summer, when snowpack runoff scours out the gravel beds. Inquire at the local chamber of commerce to find out if there are guided agate hunting tours. Just be sure not to cross private property without permission.

PADDLEFISH

Paddlefish occur in only two places on earth: in the upper Missouri drainage and in the Yangtze River in China. No paddlefish had been seen in the U.S. since 1912, and they were feared extinct. Then, in 1962, a fisherman near Intake landed a grotesque-looking specimen weighing 28 pounds, with no scales, and a very prominent snout. Since then, the sport of paddlefishing has become a popular early summer recreation in eastern Montana.

The paddlefish is a member of a primitive family that includes the sturgeon. Among its peculiarities are a three-chambered heart, a skeleton of cartilage instead of bone, a very long life span (up to 30 years) and, of course, its snout, which can be up to two feet long on an adult. It eats only plankton, which it strains out of river water flowing through its gills.

This means that the paddlefish won't rise to bait. Instead, it can only be snagged from the river depths where it lurks.

And thus, the *sport*, not art, of paddlefishing. Anglers use heavy rods and line, and heavy weights (or even spark plugs) to drop the line to the bottom of the river. The line is jerked along the bottom, with the hopes of snagging a paddlefish from its muddy lair. Once on the hook, a tremendous battle ensues, as paddlefish frequently weigh upwards of 80 pounds (the record paddlefish, apprehended in the Missouri, weighed 142 1/2 pounds).

While not all the flesh is edible, a large paddlefish yields an abundance of delicate white meat, which tastes something like lobster. Since 1989, the Glendive Chamber of Commerce has been authorized to collect paddlefish roe to make into commercially available caviar.

KAREN WHITE

riages, rebuilt offices and businesses, and historical photographs. The museum staff can direct the traveler to several Indian tepee rings and buffalo jumps in the hills around Terry.

Accommodations
One of Terry's original old hotels, the **Kempton Hotel**, 204 Spring St., tel. 637-5543, $19 s, $25 d, is still in operation and makes a stopover in Terry more intriguing. Except for the neon sign, the Kempton has changed little for decades, with its white clapboard exterior and second-floor balcony. The **Diamond Motel**, just off I-94, tel. 637-5407, is a more modern alternative, with some RV hookups. Doubles start at $27.

Fort General Terry, off Hwy. 253, tel. 637-9955, is principally an RV park, nicely situated right on the river. **Roy's Campground**, just off exit 176, tel. 637-5829, has tent camping and is closer to the freeway.

Food
Goplens, downtown, tel. 637-9922, is a Western bar that also serves simple lunches and suppers. On Sundays there's a buffet.

Outfitters
Big-game and gamebird hunting is famous in the Terry area. For guide service, contact **Robert Dolatta Outfitters**, HC 77, Terry, MT 59349, tel. 486-5736.

Services
The **chamber of commerce** can be reached at P.O. Box 667, Terry, MT 59349, tel. 637-5479. The **sheriff** can be reached at 637-5738.

GLENDIVE

Like other towns on the Yellowstone, Glendive (pop. 4,802, elev. 2,069 feet) seems like an oasis of green and trees after crossing the sere plains that surround it. Although agates are common all along the Yellowstone, Glendive probably has the best agate hunting in the state. One of the best collections of this beautiful stone can be found here, and organized float trips on the river are available to the would-be collector. And although the paddlefish lives in much of the lower Yellowstone, the Glendive area is the paddlefish capital of Montana. Makoshika State Park, a preserve of colorful and austere badlands at the southeastern edge of town, offers camping, hiking, wildlife viewing and fossil hunting.

History

Glendive began as Fort Canby, a military camp built to protect railroad workers as they laid the track for the Northern Pacific up the Yellowstone Valley in the late 1870s. The train actually arrived in the settlement on July 4, 1881. The name Glendive is apparently a corruption of "Glendale," the name given to a nearby creek by Sir George Gore on his hunting trip in 1854. (A more colorful story maintains that the name is a reference to a particularly earthy bar on the site named Glen's.)

Glendive was a division headquarters for the Northern Pacific. The grazing land around Glendive made it a railhead for cattle and, as the land fell to the plow, for grain and sugar beets as well.

Glendive is at the northern end of the Cedar Creek Anticline, whose rich oil and gas fields brought sporadic wealth and development to the area. Most recently, during the 1970s, oil exploration brought a quick boom in growth.

Makoshika State Park

Makoshika contains 8,800 acres of heavily eroded badlands, whose rugged beauty and facilities make it the premier attraction in the area. The same geologic buckling that formed the Cedar Creek Anticline raised these badlands hundreds of feet above the prairie. As water eroded the exposed land, it cut through the layers of the Fort Union Formation and revealed a lower, and earlier stratum, the Hell Creek Formation. Imbedded in the Fort Union Formation is a rich record of fossil life, including the enormous remains of such beasts as Triceratops and Tyrannosaurus rex.

Today, in Makoshika Park, deep ravines have been cut from ridgetops into box canyons whose walls contain these remains. Although fossil hunting is not encouraged in park lands, the park offers stunning overlooks onto the badlands, and many opportunities for recreation.

As the road leaves Glendive, it quickly climbs up a series of steep switchbacks onto a plateau. From here, the road continues 12 miles along steep ridges and barren canyons with frequent view points and picnic areas. Two maintained trails allow hikers access to the steep canyon

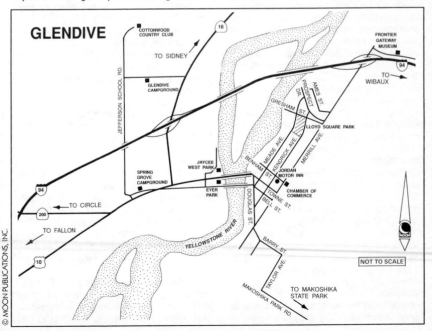

walls and valley floors and to the fantastically sculpted formations carved by erosion.

The **Cap Rock Nature Trail** is an interpreted trail that drops 160 feet onto the canyon walls. It passes a short natural bridge, pedestal rocks, fossil beds, and a gumbo sinkhole. A brochure available at the trailhead relates geological history and explains how the formations occurred. About half a mile farther in, the **Kinney Coulee Hiking Trail** winds down a canyon through juniper trees and eroded formations which take on fanciful shapes. This steep trail is about a mile long, and puts you onto the valley floor. A brochure identifies common plants and animals along the path.

Makoshika Park is also a good wildlife-viewing area. Most noteworthy is a summer population of turkey vultures. Golden eagles are common, as are hawks. Coyotes can be heard howling at night. Mule deer hide out here by day and descend to the valley floor by night.

At most overlooks there are picnic tables. Overnight camping is allowed at the campsite one mile inside the park. Drinking water is available. Trailers are not allowed past the campground, as the road becomes quite steep. A road guide to the park is available at the chamber of commerce or park entrance for $1. Entry fee is $2 per vehicle.

To reach Makoshika State Park, follow Merrill Ave. south from downtown and turn under the railroad tracks on Barry Street. Follow the signs right on Taylor Ave., until the park access road. For more information, contact the Park Manager at P.O. Box 1242, Glendive, MT 59330, tel. 365-8596. The park is open all year; heavy rain or snow may make the roads impassable.

Other Sights

The **Frontier Gateway Museum**, Belle Prairie Rd., tel. 365-8168, has several interesting exhibits. In addition to artifacts of local history, seven historic buildings have been moved to the site, as well as a collection of old fire engines. The museum basement houses a replica of old downtown Glendive. A unique exhibit here is a display of evidence from the area's past murder trials. Hours are Mon.-Sat. 9-12 and 1-5, June-Aug.; Sun. and holidays 1-5, May and September.

Agate lovers will want to see the **Klapmeier Agate Collection** in the lobby of the Holiday Lodge, 223 Kendrick. Moss agates are sometimes called "scenic agates" and this collection shows why. The eye is tempted to see land- and seascapes in the thinly cut slices of stone. Many of the agates are made into handsome Western jewelry. Peak into the hotel bar to see the mounted paddlefish.

Downtown Glendive has a number of interesting old buildings. A brochure with a walking tour of Glendive is available from the chamber of commerce.

Glendive also has attractive parks. **Lloyd Square Park**, a block and a half south of Merrill on Gresham St., has an outdoor pool and tennis courts. On the west end of the Bell Street Bridge is **Eyer Park**, with a playground and picnic grounds. On the other side of the road is **Jaycee West Park** with more tennis courts.

Recreation

Intake, an irrigation diversion 16 miles northeast of Glendive, is the center for paddlefishing, although paddlefish are found south to Miles City and in the Missouri as well. The State Dept. of Fish, Wildlife, and Parks closely supervises paddlefishing areas to limit abuses and over fishing. The season begins in May and ends July 15, and a special permit, beyond the usual fishing license, is necessary.

Another reason to take to the river is to hunt for agates. From March to October, **guided agate float trips** are offered by Montana Agate Adventures, P.O. Box 741, Glendive, MT 59330, tel. 365-5655.

The **Cottonwood Country Club**, north after Hwy. 16 exit to Highland Park Rd., tel. 365-8797, is a challenging nine-hole course.

Accommodations

The **Holiday Lodge**, 223 N. Kendrick, tel. 365-5655, $36 s, $41 d, is the local Best Western motel, and shares a lobby with Glendive's landmark hotel, the **Jordan**, 221 N. Merrill, tel. 365-3371, $28 s, $33 d. The **El Centro**, 112 S. Kendrick, tel. 365-5211, $19 s, $24 d, is downtown on a quiet street. At exit 215 are the **Super 8**, tel. 365-5671, $28 s, $34 d, and the **Days Inn**, tel. 365-6011, $28 s, $31 d.

The **Glendive Campground**, 206 First St., Highland Park, tel. 365-6721, has both RV and tent facilities. The **Green Valley Campground**, a half mile north on Hwy. 16, tel. 365-4156, has its own fishing pond. **Spring Grove Trailer Court and Campground,** 1720 Crisafulli Dr., tel. 365-2018, is convenient to travelers coming in on Hwy. 200.

Food
The best food in Glendive is at the **Blue Room Steak House** in the Holiday Lodge, 223 N. Kendrick. The dining room features murals of a cattle drive by J.K. Ralstron, and great steaks and prime rib. For more basic fare, try the **Jordan Coffee Shop** at 221 N. Merrill, tel. 365-2122, or **CC's Family Café,** 1902 N. Merrill, tel. 365-8926. If travel across Montana has made you really hungry, then the **Montana Inn,** at the Hwy. 200 exit, tel. 365-2024, might be the answer. Its "all you can eat" smorgasbord is only $3.75 for lunch and $4.95 for supper.

Shopping
This is prime agate country. Good places to shop for cut stones or agate jewelry are the **Jordan Gift Shop,** 223 N. Merrill, tel. 365-2207; **Big Sky Agates,** 817 Jefferson School Rd., tel. 365-3888; and **Kolstad Jewelers,** 107 W. Bell, tel. 365-2830.

Services
The **Glendive Community Hospital** is located at Prospect Ave. and Ames, tel. 365-3306. **Emergency** is 911. **Econo Wash,** 1212 W. Towne, is open seven days a week, 6 a.m.-10 p.m.

The **chamber of commerce** is at 200 N. Merrill, tel. 365-5601.

Getting There
Glendive is 35 miles west of the North Dakota border on I-94. Glendive has **Greyhound** bus service, and daily air service on Big Sky Airlines.

WIBAUX

Wibaux, pronounced WEE-boh, is a quintessential cattle town (pop. 628, elev. 2,634.) This small eastern Montana community has seen some of the West's most colorful characters, such as Teddy Roosevelt, and was an actor in some of the West's most colorful periods. Today, it is a comfortable corner of Montana whose past feels relatively recent.

History
The Northern Pacific passed through this area in 1881, spawning a tiny community called Mingusville. It became the railhead for the huge cattle ranches that grew up along the North Dakota/Montana border (and the local party town, since neighboring Dakota counties were "dry"). This area was coveted grazing land in the days of the open range, but the disastrous winter of 1886 spelled the end of the trail-drive days.

Among the investors who made a successful change to rancher was a Frenchman, Pierre Wibaux, who arrived in Montana in 1883. He is rumored to have made it through 1886 by feeding his cattle cottonwood branches, and, with an influx of French capital, was able to buy up livestock at low prices from desperate fellow cattlemen. By the mid-1890s, 65,000 head of cattle bore his brand, the W Bar.

So it was no mere act of hubris when Wibaux in 1894 presented the Northern Pacific authorities a petition asking that Mingusville, Wibaux's ranch's principal railhead, be changed to Wibaux. The authorities sensibly complied.

In this corner of the U.S., these were the days of colorful characters. Just over the border in North Dakota, the Marquis de Mores established the town of Medora. This French nobleman founded a huge cattle ranch and meatpacking plant in the middle of nowhere, built a manor house for his wife, and waited for fortune to come visit. Instead, he welcomed such visitors as Teddy Roosevelt, who had established a cattle ranch nearby after the deaths of both his mother and wife. Wibaux was another fixture in this stylish set.

Wibaux spent his final years in Miles City. Wibaux's original ranch, with its elaborate home and outbuildings, burned some years ago. Other original ranches still stand; all are privately held. Ask at the tourist office for information about touring the old ranching country.

Sights
Pierre Wibaux left a legacy in Wibaux which, for such a small town, seems very rich.

In 1884, Wibaux's father sent him money to build a church. **Saint Peter's Catholic Church** was built the next summer out of native stone and lava rock. Saint Peter's reveals its French background: its quiet rootedness recalls a Normandy churchyard more than a pioneer parish eight miles from North Dakota. It is an imposing structure on the prairies, in summer covered with green ivy, rising above the town that Wibaux built. Consider that when this handsome church was built, places like Glendive and Billings were little more than rail sidings. Beyond the church is a statue of Pierre Wibaux, looking north toward the location of his old ranch.

Wibaux's W Bar Ranch was 14 miles north of the present town. To conduct business in town he built an office and bunkhouse. This small clapboard "town house" now houses the **Wibaux County Museum,** Orgain and Wibaux streets, tel. 795-8112; tours are conducted daily at 1, 2, and 3 p.m., Memorial Day-Labor Day. The town house has been returned to its original 1892 condition, including the grounds, which French gardeners had designed with a pond, flower beds, and a grotto. The museum houses personal belongings and furniture as well as items typical of the days of open range.

In 1964, during the New York City World's Fair, Montana sent a rail car containing promotional exhibits about the state, as it was in the same year celebrating its centennial as a territory. Today, the rail car contains the **Centennial Car Museum,** East Orgain Ave., tel. 795-2289, open 9:30-5:30 Memorial Day-Labor Day.

Inside are Indian and pioneer relics, including the museum's pride, a human vertebrae with an arrowhead imbedded in it, which has been unofficially dated to a period at least 2,000 years ago. The Centennial Car also contains the **Wibaux Visitor's Center.** Admission is free.

A small private museum, the **Gateway Museum,** 310 Beaver St., tel. 795-8207, is housed in the Heidt home. On display is the family collection of Indian relics and fossils. Both the attractive gardens outside the home and the museum are free.

Accommodations

The **Wibaux Motel,** 400 Second Ave., tel. 795-2666, charges $20 s, $25 d; the **W-V Motel,** 106 Second Ave., tel. 795-2446, is $15 s, $20 d. The **Valley Motel and Trailer Court,** tel. 795-2522, is a half mile south of Hwy. 7.

Food

Wibaux's best dining is at **Jack's Club,** just east of town, tel. 795-2960. There is a restaurant in the **Palace Hotel** on Main St., tel. 795-2426.

Information

The **chamber of commerce** can be reached at P.O. Box 159, Wibaux, MT 59353, tel. 795-2412.

THE SOUTHEASTERN CORNER

While the Hi-Line could boast of being Montana's breadbasket, the "South Side" can stake claim to being its cattle range. Initially, this most southeasterly of Montana regions was Indian country; the line between Crow and Sioux territory fell somewhere between the Tongue and Powder rivers, and made for hard feelings. The tribes, competing for access to the rich buffalo-hunting grounds, became rivals.

The buffalo were here because of the rich grasses that grew during good years. Once a market was established for buffalo hides, and later for buffalo bones, days were numbered for these enormous animals. But any country good for buffalo was good country for cattle. When the Indians were safely sequestered on reservations and the buffalo were all slaughtered, the rich prairies were open to cattle.

The first cattle drives arrived in the 1870s. Ten years later, the first of the big ranches were in full swing. Miles City was the railhead for the region's livestock. The entire area was thought of as Miles City's "South Side," meaning the rich agricultural area south of the Yellowstone and east of the reservations where livestock grew fat and cowboys and ranchers grew restless for the temptations of a night in town.

Today, this once-vibrant region of the West has its horns tucked in due to years of drought and economic hardship. However, the underlying wealth of its oil and gas reserves has helped to keep these communities stable.

Southeastern Montana is one of the premier hunting areas of Montana. Pronghorn, mule deer, and white-tailed deer range across the entire area; it's also rich in game birds.

BAKER

Located 81 miles from Miles City and only 12 miles from North Dakota, Baker (pop. 1,818, elev. 2,929 feet) is a bustling commercial center with good recreational facilities. Baker first boomed during the early years of its founding, when the railroad came across Montana in the 1900s. Most of the downtown was built during

this time. In the 1960s and '70s nearby oil and gas exploration brought a new spate of civic building. Even though the oil boom has gone a bit bust, Baker has experienced enough prosperity to distance it from its roots as an agricultural trade center.

History

Originally a camping place on the Custer Trail between Wibaux and Camp Crook, Baker took off with the arrival of the Milwaukee Railroad in 1906, bringing homesteaders in its wake. The locals showed their gratitude by changing the name of the old settlement of Lorraine to Baker, to honor the construction engineer of the Milwaukee line. Due to the enormous railroad ad campaigns, which promised "free land" and great futures to immigrants, these Baker-area farmers and ranchers expected rich returns. But they could not have had any idea just how rich.

A driller exploring for water in 1915 instead struck natural gas; the well ignited and burned for six years. Drilling in earnest commenced, and soon Baker was at the center of extensive oil and gas fields. Baker's stable economy has allowed it to develop civic amenities (good schools, parks, athletic complexes) that most urban dwellers consider a necessity of life, but which are rare in poor, rural Montana.

Sights

The **O'Fallon Historical Museum,** Second St. at Fallon, tel. 778-3265, contains artifacts from the area's Indian past and early settlement. The real highlight here is an enormous stuffed steer, at almost 4,000 pounds one of the world's largest.

Recreation

While Baker does not have the Western character of some of its southeast Montana neighbors, it does offer the traveler sports and leisure facilities notably absent elsewhere in the region. **Baker Lake** is a reservoir in the center of town that's the focus of summer water sports. At Triangle Park, at the lake's south end, there is a swimming area, a picnic shelter, and a playground. There's fishing access on the lake at the Iron Horse Park. **South Sandstone Lake State Recreation Area,** 13 miles west of Baker on Hwy. 12 and then seven miles south, offers free camping and fishing access.

Baker Recreation Complex, 1015 S. Third W, tel. 778-3210, open Mon.-Fri. 6:30-8 a.m., 4-9 p.m., Sat. and Sun. 1-5, is a modern facility open to the public on the high school grounds. There are racquetball courts, an Olympic-size pool, and a weight room. The city tennis courts are also located near the high school. The **Lake-**view **Golf Course,** south on Hwy. 7, tel. 778-3166, has nine holes and a clubhouse.

This entire area is very popular for hunting deer, pronghorn, and game birds, including wild turkey.

Accommodations

The **Sagebrush Inn,** 518 W. Montana, tel. 778-3341, $29 s, $33 d, has an older extension with rooms for $6 less. **Roy's Motel,** 327 W. Montana, tel. 778-3321, is $18 s, $19 d.

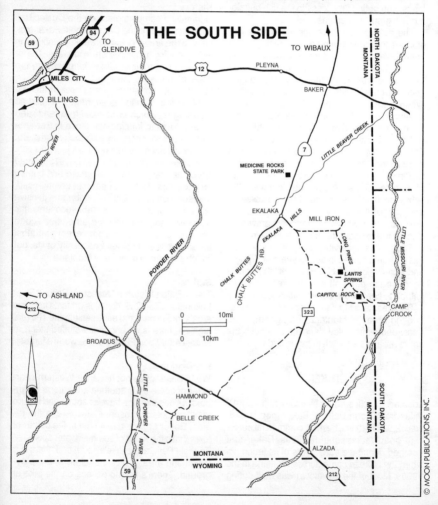

THE SOUTH SIDE

© MOON PUBLICATIONS, INC.

Claude Carter

Baker makes tourists welcome with free camping. Tent campers are encouraged to throw up a tent in **McClain Memorial Park**, Hwy. 12 at Third St. West. In the same complex is **Walt's RV Memorial Park**, which offers free RV camping with hookups.

Food
Good homestyle food is available at **Sakelaris's Kitchen** in the Lakeside Shopping Center, tel. 778-2202. If you want a drink with your steak, go to the **Loft**, 19 S. Main, tel. 778-3557.

Services
The **Fallon County Hospital** is at 320 Hospital Dr., tel. 778-3331. Call the **sheriff's office**, tel. 778-2879, in case of emergency.

The **Ken-Con Laundry** is in the Lake City Shopping Center and is open daily 7 a.m-10 p.m. The **chamber of commerce** can be reached at P.O. Box 849, Baker, MT 58313, tel. 778-2418.

EKALAKA

Ekalaka (pop. 439, elev. 3,457 feet) is known affectionately as "the town at the end of the road," for there is only one paved road to it. It is reached by first going to Baker (not exactly the center of the world itself) and turning south for an additional 35 miles. No one just turns up in Ekalaka by mistake, but there are ample reasons to make the trip in.

The Medicine Rocks, an Indian holy site, are 11 miles north of town. Three units of the Sioux Division of the Custer National Forest are within an hour of the town limits. Carter County Museum is nationally known for its collection of local dinosaur skeletons. The town buildings don't bother to hide their age or history.

But the real pleasures of Ekalaka are highly subjective and understated, almost ineffable. Ekalaka is for the connoisseur of Western towns. Ekalaka is for the traveler who will smile to see a main street on which original stone buildings house bars and museums, and street benches on which natives sit and chat; for a traveler who finds pleasure in a forest of scattered pines atop limestone cliffs; for a traveler content to watch the sun set at the site of ancient Indian rites; for the traveler who enjoys a quiet drink listening to the conversations of ranchers in old bars. Anybody beguiled by the languors of the West will find Ekalaka fascinating.

History
While other cities have founding fathers, Ekalaka has a founding bartender. Claude Carter, a Nebraska buffalo hunter who knew the weaknesses of his fellow settlers, was intending to establish a bar along Russell Creek when his wagon of logs bogged down several miles short of his destination. "Hell," Carter was reported as saying, "any place in Montana is a good place to build a saloon." His bar, the Old Stand, was the founding business of Ekalaka, and tradition places the date in the 1860s. In those days, Ekalaka was known as "Pup Town," for a nearby prairie dog town.

David Russell, the first white homesteader in the area, moved to the Old Stand settlement in 1881. His wife was a Sioux woman, named Ijkalaka ("Swift One" in Siouan), and a niece of Sitting Bull. When the post office came in 1885, it was named for her.

Time, if not prosperity, has been kind to Ekalaka; the town is much as the 1930s left it, for better or worse. Old stone buildings line the street, and an impressive old courthouse stands witness at the end of Main Street. Like Jordan to the northwest, this is still a Western town little affected by the trends and happenings of the outside world.

Sights
The **Carter Country Museum**, on Main St., open Tues.-Sun. 1-4, tel. 775-6886, is worth a detour. For any fan of dinosaur remains this is

probably the best museum in Montana, as its collection, and curator Marshall Lambert, are nationally known. Ekalaka country is particularly rich in fossil remains, and Lambert, a science teacher at the local high school, was a keen amateur paleontologist. His discoveries of entire dinosaur skeletons, including the only remains of the *Pachycephalosaurus* found in the world, allow the Carter County Museum to boast a collection of bones to rival the best museums in the country. There's also a good selection of Indian artifacts and minerals.

"One road in" is Ekalaka's motto. However, for the recreationist who has no fear of a gravel road, this corner of Montana offers little gems of beauty and adventure, and other ways out. **The Medicine Rocks State Park**, 11 miles north of Ekalaka on Hwy. 7, contains a series of sandstone outcroppings carved by the wind into weird and mysterious shapes. Some of the buttes tower 80 feet above the pine-clad prairie, and others wind along the hilltops like trains. The Sioux called the area Inyan-oka-la-ka, or "Rock With Hole In It" for the strange holes and tunnels in the stone. Legend maintains that the Indians used the area for vision quests and other rituals, and considered the rocks to be sacred and full of "medicine," or spirit power. Sitting Bull and his Sioux and Cheyenne warriors reportedly camped just before the Battle of the Little Bighorn, waiting for guidance from their medicine men. The mile-square park welcomes picnickers, campers, and sightseers. At the entrance to the park is a hand pump with good water; tables, fire pits, and latrines are also provided. A word of caution: beware of snakes.

Three sections of the **Sioux Division of the Custer National Forest** lie within easy striking range of Ekalaka. South of town, along a well-traveled gravel road, are the **Chalk Buttes**. These stark white cliffs sit atop rocky, forested buttes, and can be seen for miles. The Chalk Buttes have long served as landmarks for travelers and stockmen. Fighting Butte, or Starvation Rock, is the most northerly of the Chalk Buttes. Its flat top is inaccessible but for a treacherous, single-track path. According to Indian legend, members of one tribe, seeking to escape pursuers of another tribe, fled up the precipitous path leading to the summit. Once there, the pursuing Indians simply guarded the single-file access to the butte and waited for their foes to die of thirst and starvation.

According to a BLM official, there are species of grass that grow on the top of Fighting Butte that occur nowhere else in the Ekalaka area. One local sheep rancher grazed sheep on these unusual grasses, to his eventual chagrin. A windy storm blew up, and the entire herd of 600 drifted with the wind to fall off the sheer sides to their deaths.

Recreational opportunities are more numerous in the other sections of the Sioux Division of the Custer National Forest. In the **Ekalaka Hills**, southeast of Ekalaka, there are two camping areas. **Macnab Pond** is located in piney hills seven miles southeast of town on Hwy. 323 and one mile east on a gravel road. Watch for signs. Trout have been planted in the pond.

Ekalaka Park is more remote. Follow signs for **Camp Needmore**, three miles southeast on Hwy. 323, and after arriving at Camp Needmore, follow Forest Service Rd. 104 (Rimrock Carter Rd.) five miles. Although there are no official trails, hiking among the ponderosa pines and sandstone outcroppings is easy and interesting. Wildlife is abundant, and during the spring there is a good display of wildflowers.

If you like this kind of lonely, open country sprinkled with buttes and pines, and if you feel adventurous, then a day-trip to **Long Pines** the third section of the Sioux Division, is well worth it. Follow Prairie Dale Rd. (to Milliron) off Hwy. 323 (three miles south of Ekalaka) for about 10 miles, and turn south on Forest Service Rd. 107, Snow Creek Road. This gravel road follows the main spine of the Long Pines. Wildlife viewing is especially good.

Raptors love the sandstone bluffs (this is the nation's primary breeding range for merlin falcons), as do deer, coyotes, and wild turkeys. Just short of the North Dakota border lies Capitol Rock, a huge deposit of volcanic ash eroded into the shape of the nation's capitol. Again, hiking is informal, as there are no maintained trails. Camp at Lantis Spring Campground, about 15 miles into the national forest, where water is available. If you camp informally, make sure you heed fire restrictions, and carry garbage out.

If you follow Snow Creek Rd. out, you end up in Camp Crook, South Dakota, on the Little Missouri. Camp Crook was a station on the Deadwood Stage.

Accommodations

The **Midway Motel** is on Hwy. 7 as it enters Ekalaka, tel. 775-6619, $21 s, $31 d. The Guest House is an updated hotel on Main St., tel. 775-6337, $24 s, $34 d. **Cline Camper Court**, west of town, tel. 775-6231, is open April-Dec., but has no tent sites; **Ekalaka Park** is a Forest Service campground. Go three miles south on Hwy. 323, then follow signs on improved road for another six miles; it's open May-November. **Macnab Pond**, another Forest Service facility, is seven miles south on Hwy. 323, one mile east on improved road; both sites have toilets and water, and Macnab has fishing.

Food

The **Old Stand** is on Main St., tel. 775-6661, and still offers steaks and cocktails. The **Wagon Wheel Café**, just up the street, tel. 775-6639, is a friendly place for a lighter meal.

Outfitters

This area offers some of the best deer and antelope hunting in the state. The following guide services offer to make a hunting trip a successful and pleasurable experience. **J & J Guide Service**, Mill Iron, MT, tel. 775-8891, leads hunts for mule deer, whitetail, and pronghorn; **Mon-Dak Outfitters**, Alvin Cordell, Box 135 Montana Rte., Camp Crook, ND 57724, tel. (605) 797-4539, leads trips into southeastern Montana.

Services

Dahl Memorial Hospital is at 110 Hospital St., tel. 775-8730. The **sheriff** can be reached at tel. 775-8743.

There's a **swimming pool** in Ekalaka Park, just behind Main Street.

The **Custer National Forest Office** can be reached at tel. 775-6342.

BROADUS

There's something about the Powder River that excites the phrasemaker. "A mile wide, an inch deep," "Too thin to plow, too thick to drink," the sayings go. There is some truth: when the Yellowstone discharges into the Missouri, the Powder River has contributed only five percent of the flow, but 50% of the silt. The broad grassy valleys of the Powder River and the Little Powder

River have been home first to vast herds of wildlife and later to equally vast herds of cattle.

Nestled in the cottonwoods along the river, Broadus (pop. 572, elev. 3,030 feet) is an attractive ranching town. Oil revenue allows the town extras like a good school system and new county offices.

History

The early Indians spent summers hunting here, where buffalo, prairie elk, deer, pronghorn, and game birds were abundant. Later, after westward Indian migration began, these hunting grounds were at the heart of bitter disputes between the Crows, who claimed it as a homeland, and just about everyone else.

A sad presaging of the great buffalo decimation came in 1855, when Sir George Gore, an Irish sportsman, came to hunt the Powder River country. Gore was no rugged survivalist: his entourage included several guides, 20 servants, 112 horses, 12 yoke oxen, six wagons, and 21 carts for ammunition. After spending the winter at the mouth of the Tongue River, Gore killed local game in such numbers that finally the Crow protested.

After the Sioux were corralled and the buffalo eliminated from their range, the rich Powder River country became the avenue into Montana for Texas cattle drives. The cattle boom lasted barely 10 years, but survived long enough to form much of the iconography of the Old West.

Market forces, a disastrous winter, and the influx of homesteaders all contributed to the decline of the cattle drover and the establishment of the cattle rancher. By the 1890s, ranches and settlements were springing up along the Powder and its tributaries. Broadus, and euphonious crossroads like Sonette, Olive, Epsie, Liscom, Quietus, Mizpah, and other "South Side" outposts, began as trading centers and post offices.

Located near the confluence of the Powder and the Little Powder rivers, Broadus became the dominant trading center for the southeastern corner of Montana. Oil was discovered in Belle Creek, south of Broadus, in 1967. Within six years, the field had produced over a billion dollars' worth of oil alone; Belle Creek also produces significant amounts of natural gas.

Sights

The **Powder River Historical Museum** has a collection of artifacts illustrating local history,

W.C. McRAE

Medicine Rocks were an important ceremonial site for Native Americans.

along with old cars, an old buggy, and the old Powder River County Jail. **Mac's Museum**, in the high school, brings together Indian artifacts and sea shells.

Recreation
Rolling Hills Golf Course, at the junction of Hwy. 212 and Hwy. 59, is a public course with nine holes. The **swimming pool** is at 202 S. Wilbur, tel. 436-2822. In **Broadus City Park**, there're tennis courts, picnic grounds, and a playground.

Accommodations
The **Homestead Inn**, 701 S. Park, tel. 436-2615, $25 s, $31 d, has a restaurant and lounge. **C-J Motel**, 311 W. Holt, tel. 436-2576, $25 s, $33 d, offers kitchenettes for an extra $4. The **Quarterhorse Motor Inn** is at 101 N. Park, tel. 436-2626, $25 s, $33 d.

Another lodging alternative is to stay at a guest ranch. **Wagons West**, Box 483, Broadus, MT 59317, tel. 436-2350, is a 1920s-era ranch, where guests share ranch chores with the host family.

Town and Country Trailer Village, one block west of Hwy. 212 E; tel. 436-2595, open April-Nov., and **Wayside Park**, just south of the junctions of Hwys. 212 and 59, tel. 436-2252, both offer tent and RV camping.

Food
There's a restaurant associated with the **Homesteader Inn** on Hwy. 212, tel. 436-2615; the **Montana Bar and Cafe**, 111 E. Wilson, tel. 436-2454, serves three meals a day, with homemade pies a favorite.

Outfitters
The Powder River country is home to an abundance of outfitters. **Powder River Outfitters**, Box 678, Broadus, MT 59317, offers archery, deer, pronghorn, and game-bird hunting; call 427-5497 for Ken, call 427-5721 for Doug. **Golden Sedge Drifters**, Greg Childress, Box 342, Broadus, MT 59317, tel. 554-3464, offers float trips and fishing. **Doonan Gulch Outfitters**, Russell and Carol Greenwood, Box 501, S. Pumpkin Creek Rd., Broadus, MT 59317, tel. 427-5474, offers big game hunting, rockhounding, and hiking. **Cowboy Outfitters**, Gib Lloyd, Box 245, Broadus, MT 59317, tel. 436-2216, offers both big-game hunting and a guest ranch.

Services
Powder River Medical Service is at 507 N. Lincoln, tel. 436-2651.

Contact the **sheriff** at 436-2333.

The **chamber of commerce** is at Box 484, Broadus, MT 59317, tel. 436-2611.

THE CROW AND NORTHERN CHEYENNE RESERVATIONS

The Crow and Northern Cheyenne Reservations are basically the drainages of the Tongue and Bighorn rivers. The landscape combines the lyricism of rough sandstone bluffs and uplands covered with ponderosa pine forest with the austerity of the high, barren prairies. And underlying everything here are the vast coal deposits of the Fort Union Formation.

Except for the river valleys and small reservation towns, there is scarcely any development. Like the Custer National Forest to the east, the reservation lands seem to be maintained in a kind of ad hoc trust. While this has preserved the beauty and integrity of the area, it has hindered the economic development of the tribes.

This region has always been Indian land, first by tradition, later by decree. The Crow settled here 300 years ago. Later, other tribes vied for room on these rich hunting grounds south of the Yellowstone. When traders first came to barter with the Indians for furs, they came here; when the Army came to subdue the Indians, they came here as well. Some of the most stirring events of Western history took place on these plains and in these open forests. And something more than history, as well. The mixed prairies and forests of these reservations have themselves a cultural weight, their openness and limitlessness a statement of animistic potency.

HARDIN

Even though Hardin (pop. 2,940, elev. 2,966 feet) is not on the Crow Reservation, it serves as the primary trading center for residents of the reservation and the ranches to the north and west.

The confluence of the Little Bighorn and Bighorn rivers was a strategic outpost during the Indian Wars. The steamboat *Far West* maneuvered up the Bighorn to the mouth of the Little Bighorn in June 1876 to pick up wounded soldiers after the Reno-Benteen battle. In 1877 the year after the Custer battle, Bighorn Post was built on the cliffs above the confluence. Renamed Fort Custer, it was apparently rather a grand fort, in the manner of Fort Keogh; it was abandoned in 1898.

By 1906, the Dawes Act opened the area to white settlement. The next year, only nine years after Fort Custer ceased its patrol of the Crows, the Chicago, Burlington and Quincy Railroad built a spur line down to the present site of Hardin, both to bring in new settlers and to service their needs.

During World War II, almost 2,000 Japanese-American internees were brought into Montana to work sugar beet fields, as farmers were experiencing a labor shortage. A large number worked in the Hardin area; some settled here after the war.

Sights

The **Bighorn County Historical Museum**, just off exit 497, has several old restored buildings open for viewing, including a handsome 1917 German Lutheran church, an old post office and store, and old farm buildings. The museum contains displays on Crow Indians, Fort Custer, the Custer battle, and a good selection of books on local history and lore. The museum is open Mon.-Sat. 8-8, Sun. 8-6, June-Aug.; in Sept. daily 9-6; Tues.-Sat. 9-5, Oct.-May; tel. 665-1671.

The museum also has picnic tables and bathrooms. **Custer Park** has a playground and picnic tables. Take exit 495 south on Crawford St., but resist the urge to veer off to Yellowtail Dam and follow Crawford until Fourth Avenue.

Accommodations

The American Inn, 1324 Crawford, tel. 665-1870, $30 s, $35 d, has a guest laundromat. **The Western Inn**, 830 W. Third, tel. 665-2296, $30 s, $38 d, allows pets. **The Lariat**, 709 N. Custer, tel. 665-2683, $32.50 s, $42.50 d, has the honor of being right next to Margaret's Chat and Chew Café.

The **KOA** is one mile north of Hardin on Hwy. 47, tel. 665-1635. **Grandview Campground** is south of Hardin on Hwy. 313, tel. 665-2489.

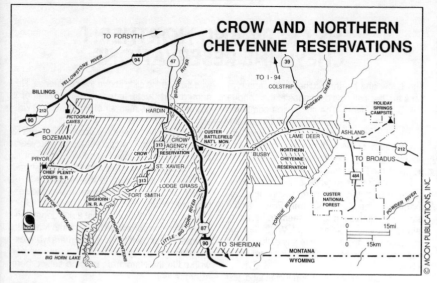

CROW AND NORTHERN CHEYENNE RESERVATIONS

© MOON PUBLICATIONS, INC.

Food
Besides the truck stops along the interstate, there are a couple of local favorites. **The Brown Cow**, just north of I-90 on Hwy. 47, is a vintage roadside diner. Downtown, **Simon's Chinese and American Café**, 412 N. Center, is a reminder that Hardin was home to several Asian settlers. Any restaurant named the **Chat and Chew**, 721 N. Center, deserves a stop, but since it makes its own doughnuts, it demands a visit.

Events
The Hardin Chamber of Commerce yearly sponsors **Little Bighorn Days**, whose main feature is the **Reenactment of Custer's Last Stand**. The event is held on the weekend closest to the anniversary of the battle on June 26. In addition to the battle itself, the actors stage the events that led up to the conflict. It's a huge swirl of horses, tepees, and warriors, and the drama is matched by the dust. The reenactment is held six miles west of Hardin, not at the battle site. Other events during Little Bighorn Days include a rodeo, Indian dancing, and special tours of the Custer Battlefield.

Hardin has proclaimed itself the Zucchini Capital of the World. Every August at the **Zucchini Festival**, the public gathers to honor and ponder this prolific vegetable.

Information
The **chamber of commerce** can be reached at 200 N. Center, Hardin, MT 59034, tel. 665-1672. The **post office** is at 406 N. Cheyenne. The **Bighorn County Memorial Hospital** is at 17 N. Miles, tel. 665-2310.

National Public Radio is KEMC at 91.7 FM.

THE CROW INDIAN RESERVATION

Before The White Man
The present-day Crow Indians derive from Hidatsa tribes who originally lived along the Mississippi headwaters. Of Siouan linguistic stock, they were an agrarian people who lived in earth lodges and made pottery. Sometime during the 1600s, the Crow left the larger Hidatsa tribe and began to move westward, first settling in the Black Hills area. Increasingly, lands as far west as the Powder, Tongue, and Bighorn river drainages were added to their hunting grounds, and by the 1770s the tribe had settled onto its historic homelands south of the Yellowstone.

When William Clark first traveled through Crow territory in 1806, the Crow were a wandering tribe of hunters living in tepees along the Bighorn. The horse had been introduced to the Crow only about 50 years before, and even though only 3,500 members belonged to the tribe, they already owned about 10,000 horses. The Crow had almost totally given up agriculture (though they continued to raise tobacco) and were nomadic within their hunting grounds. Crow women were famous for their bead and quill work, and Crow men were great horsemen and hunters. They were also proud of their long hair, and may have been "les beaux hommes," ("the handsome men") recorded by the French explorers, the Verendryes. The tribe was organized first by family, then by matrilineal clan. Known as the *Absaroka* in Hidatsan, or "Children of the Large-beaked Bird," they were considered to be crafty and enterprising as the raven, hence the English name Crow.

Friendly Relations

From their first contact with white explorers and traders, the Crow have maintained mostly friendly relations with European settlers. The first trading post in Montana, Fort Remon, was built in 1807 at the juncture of the Bighorn and Yellowstone to service beaver-pelt trade with the Crow. Although the Indians were initially not exactly willing partners in the beaver trade (they chafed at trapping and trading pelts for more goods

Crow braves

L.A. HUFFMAN/MONTANA HISTORICAL SOCIETY

than they had need for), the presence of white traders in Crow territory led to a long-standing and important alliance between the Europeans and the Crow.

In 1833, Fort Cass was built on the same ground as the abandoned Fort Remon. By this time, the main article of trade was buffalo hide, and this time the Crow were interested. A complex relationship between the Indians and whites emerged: the traders provided tobacco, food, guns, manufactured goods, clothing, and liquor, while the Crow provided pelts and hides, and protection from the hostile Blackfeet to the north. The whites and Indians hunted together, sharing knowledge and cultures.

But the Crow became economically dependent upon trade with the whites, a dependency serviced by plundering the riches of their homeland. While Indians like the Crow were instrumental in exterminating the vast herds of buffalo in the West, the buffalo remained their source of food and shelter. By the 1880s, the buffalo had disappeared from its range on the Yellowstone.

The alliance with the agents of the United States was also strategic for the Crows in their ongoing warfare with rival Indian tribes. The warlike Blackfeet to the north endangered their lucrative trade with the whites, while the Sioux and Cheyenne to the east threatened traditional Crow hunting grounds. The treaties of Fort Laramie in 1851 and 1868 guaranteed the Crow homelands against incursions by whites and by other Indian tribes, especially the hostile Sioux confederacy.

It wasn't just geopolitical concerns that provided the bond between the Crow and the white settlers. Their friendship lasted several generations and weathered many altercations. And while the U.S. government was not especially solicitous to the Crow (though the Crow were treated somewhat less abjectly by the U.S. than some other tribes), the Crow were faithful allies.

The Reservation Today

In 1965, the Bighorn River was dammed near the site of Fort Smith. This beautiful, rugged landscape became the Bighorn National Recreation Area in 1968. The Bighorn River below the dam changed from being a slow-moving catfish river to a crystal-clear blue-ribbon trout stream, one of the best fisheries for trophy-size trout in the country.

This once-remote corner of the Crow Reservation suddenly became popular with hunters, anglers, and tourists. But the Crow considered the Bighorn Canyon and the adjacent Pryor and Bighorn mountains to be sacred lands. In 1973, the tribe voted to close all hunting and fishing on the reservation to non-Indians, citing its rights to the Bighorn under the Fort Laramie treaties. The state of Montana took the tribe to court in order to open public access to the river. The case, known as the Battle of the Bighorn, went all the way to the U.S. Supreme Court, which in 1981 found for the state. There are now four fishing-access sites along the river within the boundaries of the reservation.

The present Crow Reservation, much reduced from the 1868 land grant, contains 37,000 square miles of rolling prairie and rugged foothills drained by the Bighorn River, making it Montana's largest reservation. There are about 7,000 tribal members, with a majority living on the reservation. The Crow language, a cousin to Siouan and Assiniboine, is spoken by more than 80% of the tribe. The retention of their native language is a combination of tradition (no Crow addresses another Crow in English), and the fact that the federal government never mandated English-only boarding schools on the Crow Reservation.

Sights
Chief Plenty Coups State Park: Chief Plenty Coups, the last of the great Crow war chiefs, is credited for advocating peaceful relations with the whites and for being the first Crow leader to recognize the need to adapt to the new life of the reservation. When the U.S. government opened the Crow Reservation to individual allotments in 1887, the young chief applied for his 320 acres, and began building and cultivating. The location of his allotment, just west of Pryor off Hwy. 416, is along a pretty stretch of Pryor Creek. It had been revealed to Chief Plenty Coups in a vision quest almost 30 years before that he would live out his life there, "where the plums grow."

Chief Plenty Coups attempted to set an example of how the Crow might coexist with the white settlers. He stressed education and mediated conflicts between his tribesmen and the whites. He cultivated his holding and built a two-story log home and a store, symbolically forsaking the tepee and the hunting life-style of the prairie nomad. He and his wife lived there until his death in 1932.

A stirring orator, Plenty Coups became a sort of celebrity, traveling to Washington, D.C. frequently to represent his people. While he was staying in Washington he visited Mt. Vernon, home of the first president. He then conceived of dedicating his land on the reservation as a memorial to the Crow Nation. Chief Plenty Coups Monument was dedicated in 1928 as a "token of my friendship for all people, both red and white." It is now a Montana state park.

The 40-acre park houses a museum of Crow culture, Plenty Coups' home and store, his grave, and a gift shop featuring Crow crafts. The spacious grounds allow plenty of room to stretch your legs, and there is a well-developed picnic area (but no overnight camping). The park is open 9-9 daily, and the museum is open 9-5 May 1-Sept. 30. There is a 50-cent admission charge to the park.

Events
The **Crow Fair** is the biggest event of the year and is perhaps the largest Native American gathering in North America. During the third weekend of August, the tribal campgrounds near Crow Agency become a sea of tepees, pickup trucks, and RVs as thousands of tribe members and visitors rendezvous to celebrate the Crow heritage. Traditional games are played, including innocent-seeming "hand games," where money is gambled in a variation of the shell game. A number of the Crow dress in traditional garb, which shows off their complex and colorful beadwork. The costumes largely come off during the dance contests. There is also a parade, an all-Indian rodeo, and horse racing. Visitors are welcome, and bead goods and Indian food are for sale. Bring sunscreen and a hat, and be prepared to get dusty. For more information, contact the Crow Tribal Council.

Recreation
The Bighorn River below Yellowtail Dam has become one of the most famous trout fisheries in the country. By trapping sediment, cooling the water, and maintaining a steady flow, the dam changed what was once a sluggish haven of catfish to an environment suited to trophy-size brown and rainbow trout.

The new-found popularity of the Bighorn has concerned the Crow, who object to the influx of people onto reservation land along the river. The state now maintains four fishing-access sites within the reservation. Do not attempt to fish on private land without getting permission. Anglers should stay within high-water marks, or in or on the river, to avoid trespassing on Indian land. A number of outfitters in the Fort Smith area rent boats and offer guide services.

Information
The **Crow Tribal Council** can be contacted at P.O. Box 159, Crow Agency, MT 59022, tel. (406) 638-2601.

Contact the **Bighorn National Recreation Area** at P.O. Box 458, Fort Smith, MT 59035, tel. 666-2412.

CUSTER BATTLEFIELD NATIONAL MONUMENT

The Battle of the Little Bighorn was one of those epochal historical moments when individual strands of fate, personality, and history wove a whole larger and more meaningful than any sum of its parts. Upon hearing the story of Custer and Sitting Bull, an elemental part of the psyche either rejoices at the victory of the American Natives or condemns the triumph of savagery. To stand on the sere slopes of the Wolf Mountains and ponder the events of 1876 is to sense that something much more than a battle between armies and cultures took place. The issues at stake continue to resonate as the historical march of culture confronting culture goes on.

George Armstrong Custer
However hackneyed the observation, George Armstrong Custer was, and remains, an enigma. He graduated last in his class at West Point. He served the Union in the Civil War. He became the youngest general in the history of the Army after General Lee surrendered to him; he was later court-martialed for ordering the shooting of Army deserters in Kansas.

Once reinstated, Custer became commander of the Seventh Cavalry. His exploits made him and his wife colorful and frequent guests at New York society functions. He fell afoul of the Grant administration for allegations made in Congressional hearings about corruption involving the president's brother and Indian trading licenses. He was arrested again.

George A. Custer   Sitting Bull, Sioux leader

A New York newspaper publisher who championed Custer as a future presidential candidate used his presses to mold opinion in Custer's favor. Rereleased, the 36-year-old Custer led 265 men to death on the Little Bighorn when he went on the offensive against a united war party with upwards of 3,000 Sioux and Cheyenne warriors.

The Sioux And Cheyenne

This butterfly of a man confronted representatives of an ancient, almost chthonic culture. The Sioux and Cheyenne were settled into one reservation in eastern Wyoming and the western Dakotas by the conditions of the Fort Laramie Treaty of 1868. However, the discovery of gold in 1874 in the Black Hills immediately caused the treaty to be broken by gold hunters. Sioux and Cheyenne warriors, responding to these incursions onto their reservation and to the age-old need to migrate to hunt buffalo, began to leave their reservation. Under the leadership of such warriors as Sitting Bull and Crazy Horse, they camped in the drainages of the Powder, Tongue, and Rosebud rivers, their numbers growing as more and more natives became disenchanted with their treatment. Here, for one last reprise, they practiced the centuries-old culture of the Plains Indian.

From here they also raided settlements and harassed travelers. The Commissioner of Indian Affairs ordered the Indians back onto the reservation, threatening military action if they did not comply by January 31, 1875.

The Sioux and Cheyenne did not respond, and the Army was sent to force the Indians to return to the reservation.

The Battle Of The Little Bighorn

Three separate expeditions were sent out to campaign against the hostiles. These troops were to move from three different directions into the southeastern corner of Montana, where the Indian forces were known to be encamped. Custer's Seventh Cavalry followed the course of the Rosebud River up to its divide with the Little Bighorn, where he was to wait for the two other columns. Instead, he divided his own command into thirds, and on June 26, 1876, took the offensive against one of the largest Indian forces ever gathered.

The details of the engagement at the Little Bighorn are best left for the traveler to discover at the battle site. What actually happened is quite complex and far from certain. It is also very compelling.

Perhaps we learn of Custer and the Sioux too early in life, when complex issues seem too simple. The Custer Battlefield is not merely a place for boys of all ages to gloat in the memory of battle. It is as chilling as Civil War battle sites, where you sense the ghosts of the past and somehow recognize the end of a culture and an epoch with a tightened and hollow gut. This is Montana's most haunted ground.

Sights

The battle site is 15 miles south of Hardin, a mile east off Hwy. 90. The visitor center is situated below the crest of the hill where the last stand took place. It contains some very interesting exhibits, and should be visited before going on to the battlefields. Exhibits explain the Indian background to the conflict, the military strategies, the contemporary life-styles of both cultures, and display artifacts of the battle. Probably the most arresting of the exhibits is a raised-relief map of the entire battle area, which uses colored lights (indicating soldiers and Indians) to show the ebb and flow of the battle. There is also a good bookshop where you'll want to pick up further reading. Also interesting is a plaque placed in 1988 by Indian activists on Last Stand Hill Monument demanding recognition of the Indian lives lost in the battle to preserve their homelands. The National Park Service has pledged to erect a memorial to Indian lives and perspectives on the conflict. Downhill from the visitor center is Custer National Cemetery, where some war dead from this and other conflicts are buried.

A quarter mile up the hill is Last Stand Monument, where the last of the Seventh Cavalry died. Grave markers now stand where the bodies of soldiers were found. They were interred in a common grave under the monument which bears the names of all the dead. Custer is buried at West Point.

To look down the grassy hillside at the markers, some standing alone, others huddled together, many clumped together around the swale where Custer's own body was found, is to vividly experience the full horror of the battle.

The paved road winds past the monument on a seven-mile loop road to the **Reno-Benteen Battlefield**. Major Marcus Reno and three of the Seventh Cavalry's companies were ordered by Custer to lead the first offensive against the Sioux and Cheyenne village on the Little Bighorn River. They were immediately routed and retreated up to this ridge, where they took up defensible positions. During the melee, the main thrust of the Indian attack was directed north to Custer's command. Reno was joined by Captain Frederick Benteen and the cavalry's pack train, the last third of Custer's original unit. On this hill, behind the bodies of slaughtered pack horses, these soldiers withstood 48 hours of attack by the victorious Sioux and Cheyenne before the Indians, almost inexplicably, retreated. A self-guided walking tour of the battlefield begins at the parking lot.

The visitor center is open Memorial Day to Labor Day, 8-7:45; Sept.-Oct., 8-5; and November to Memorial Day 8-4:30. There is a $3 fee. In addition, park rangers and Native Americans give free tours and programs on various matters relating to the battle. For information on special programs and on publications sold at the monument write Custer Battlefield National Monument, P. O. Box 39, Crow Agency, MT 59022, tel. (406) 638-2621.

Personalized tours of the battlefield are available by the half or full day. Contact **Custer Battlefield Tours**, 416 N. Cody, Hardin, MT 59034, tel. 665-1580.

Practicalities

The Custer Battlefield is about as lonely and forlorn a place as you can imagine. However, some amenities have grown up nearby, and Hardin is only 15 miles away.

Lodgings: The closest motel is **Little Big Horn Camp**, at the Custer Battlefield exit off I-90, tel. 638-2232, $18 s, $25 d. Twenty miles south toward Wyoming is the **Cottage Inn**, 22 Hester, tel. 639-2453, in the community of Lodge Grass.

Food: At the freeway interchange there's a good restaurant/gift shop, the **Custer Battlefield Trading Post and Café**, tel. 638-2270. Indian tacos, actually a variety of fried bread, are featured. The gift shop has a nice selection of Indian crafts and books.

THE NORTHERN CHEYENNE RESERVATION

Located between the Crow Reservation and the Tongue River, the Northern Cheyenne Reservation was granted to the Cheyenne Indians after a period of wandering and incarceration following the Battle of the Little Bighorn. The land is characterized by patches of dry prairie ringed in by sandstone uplands covered with ponderosa pines. The area is rich in prairie wildlife and game birds, and the Tongue River affords the angler opportunities for walleye, smallmouth bass, and, south near the Tongue River Reservoir, trout.

Onto The Plains

French traders first encountered the Cheyenne Indians in 1680, when they were living in present-day Minnesota. At that time they were an agricultural people who lived in earth and log cabins. The pressure of settlements to the east forced all Indian tribes to migrate west. The Cheyenne, however, were not pushed west by white settlers but by the hostile Sioux, who had themselves been displaced. Driven onto the plains, the Cheyenne lost their agricultural arts and divided into two federations, the Northern Cheyenne in Montana and the Dakotas, and the Southern Cheyenne in Colorado. By the time Lewis and Clark encountered them in 1804, the Northern Cheyenne tribe was living near the Black Hills. They lived in tepees and existed almost totally off the largesse of the buffalo. Their agricultural past had faded into tribal myth.

The increasing encroachment of American settlers and cavalry on the plains caused the tribe to divide into two groups, one that ranged farther north and west into Montana and Wyoming, and another that moved south into Colorado. The Northern Cheyenne soon were expeditiously allied with the Sioux due to the presence of two common enemies, the settlers and soldiers, and their traditional rivals the Crow, on whose hunting grounds the two tribes were increasingly interloping.

The Conflicts

When gold was discovered in the Black Hills in the 1870s, treaties barring non-Indians in the area were promptly ignored, and the resulting gold rush and cavalry action forced the Cheyenne (and other Plains tribes) into greater confrontation with the whites. In 1875, when all western tribes were ordered onto reservations, the Northern Cheyenne refused, choosing to live their traditional life on the prairies. The next year, part of the American cavalry under Lieutenant Colonel George Custer was sent to subdue the recalcitrant Sioux and Northern Cheyenne in southeastern Montana.

The victory of the Indians over the American forces earned the Cheyenne only momentary freedom. Within a year of the Battle of the Little Bighorn, all tribe members had been forced onto reservations, with the majority incarcerated in Oklahoma with the Southern Cheyenne. During the winter of 1878-79, about 300 of the Northern Cheyenne fled the Indian Territory and attempted to make their way back to rejoin their brethren then sequestered on the Tongue River. After many battles and skirmishes with the cavalry, only 60 of the original Northern Cheyenne lived to be reunited with the tribe remaining in Montana. In 1884, the government granted the tribe its own reservation.

Development

Like other Indian tribes who were once settled on what were considered marginal lands, the Northern Cheyenne have had to fight to resist the development of their lands by outside interests. The reservation sits on the vast coal fields of the Fort Union Formation. In the 1970s, coal companies sought to open up the area for stripmining. The tribe faced a painful decision: whether to allow the mining and reap the economic benefits which would bring jobs to the area and allow the building of needed public facilities, or to maintain the integrity of the land in its natural state.

By 1972, energy companies were poised to open up 70% of the reservation to exploration and development. But the following year, the tribe voted to cancel the leases. After protracted legal maneuvering, the U.S. government upheld the Cheyenne's wishes. During the same period, the Northern Cheyenne sought and finally obtained the first redesignation of air quality (to "pristine") ever granted to a reservation, thereby inhibiting development of coal-fired generators in close proximity to the reservation (the enormous generators at Colstrip are 20 miles north). The tribe did decide to allow oil exploration in the 1980s. However, no economically viable reserves were found.

The Northern Cheyenne Reservation contains 444,500 acres (almost 90% of which is controlled by tribal members). About 3,500 Cheyenne live on the reservation.

Sights

The St. Labre Indian School was established in 1884, after a Catholic soldier stationed at Fort Keogh contacted his bishop to tell him of the woeful state of the Cheyenne, who were wandering, starving and homeless, on the Tongue River. The bishop bought land on the river, and in 1884 four nuns from Toledo, Ohio, established the school and mission.

The Mission remains a center of Cheyenne cultural and educational life, currently schooling 750 students. The Mission also operates alcohol treatment, employment counseling, and other social services. Its modern chapel, built from local stone in the shape of an enormous tepee, dominates the campus. Tours are available. The St. Labre Visitor's Center contains the **Cheyenne Indian Museum**, which displays examples of the tribe's fabulous beadwork, open Mon.-Fri. 8:30-4:30, tel. 784-2200. Indian crafts are available next door at **Little Coyote Gallery**.

Practicalities

Lodging: Although the tribal headquarters for the Northern Cheyenne are located at Lame Deer, Ashland is the reservation's primary trading town and has the reservation's only motel, **The Western 8,** tel. 784-2400, $20 s, $32 d. Camping is available next door in the Custer National Forest.

Food: Dining opportunities are rather perfunctory. In Ashland, there's the **Justice Inn**, which features a full menu. Snacks and Cheyenne handicrafts are available at the tribe-owned **Cheyenne Depot** in Lame Deer.

Events

There are two powwows, one in Lame Deer on July 4, and another in Ashland over Labor Day. Cheyenne powwows feature dancing contests, Indian singing, and lots of food.

Chief Two Moons was a Cheyenne leader who fought at the Little Bighorn. In his honor, the tribe conducts The **Two Moons Annual World Peace Gathering**, a meeting featuring traditional prayer ceremonies and discussions of issues and events pertinent to contemporary Indians. The gathering is held the last weekend of June. Contact the tribal secretary for details, tel. (406) 477-6248.

Information
The Northern Cheyenne Tribal Council can be reached by writing Lame Deer, MT 59043, tel. 477-6248.

CUSTER NATIONAL FOREST, ASHLAND DIVISION

Across the Tongue River from the Cheyenne Reservation is eastern Montana's largest block of national forest. Like other isolated islands of woodland within the vast archipelago of the Custer National Forest, the Ashland Division is largely overlooked by travelers, save the hunters who come to stalk trophy mule deer and wild turkeys.

As in the other forests of southeastern Montana, here ponderosa pine savannahs are interspersed with shortgrass prairie, and isolated sandstone bluffs rise up spookily from the plains. The entire area is rich in wildlife, especially birds.

And like the other Custer forests, this is largely an undeveloped destination for the visitor.

But before dismissing these remote areas, the adventurous traveler should consider stopping to enjoy the vast and lonely expanses of these high-prairie grass- and woodlands.

Three areas of the Ashland Division have been designated as riding and hiking areas. They're off-limits to motorized vehicles, making them ideal for nature study and wildlife viewing. While the Forest Service had horses in mind when they called it a riding area, the rough but open landscape is also ideal for mountain-bike exploration. There are no maintained hiking trails, but the nature of the landscape allows for considerable ambling and scrambling.

Red Shale Campground is six miles east of Ashland and has 16 units. Other campsites are more remote. The **Holiday Springs** campsite is of interest not only because it serves as a campground but because the Forest Service maintains a rental cabin there. Whitetail Cabin sleeps four, and has electrical power (though no water), $15 a day. The cabin and campsite are about 18 miles east of Ashland, up the East Fork of Otter Creek.

While cross-country skiing is possible almost everywhere in the area when there's enough snow, the Forest Service has developed two loop trails near Camp's Pass, 20 miles east of Ashland. This area, near the defile where the highway enters the national forest from the east, contains some of the roughest land in this section of the Custer national forest.

For more information, write Ashland Ranger District, Box 297, Ashland, MT 59003, or call (406) 784-2344.

BIGHORN CANYON AND THE PRYOR MOUNTAINS

Nothing in the prairies and valleys of the Crow Reservation prepares the traveler for the magnitude and sheer drama of the Bighorn Canyon and the Pryor Mountains. The Bighorn River follows a wide, wooded valley from St. Xavier upstream to Fort Smith along Hwy. 313, where suddenly the land ends in upheaval, with bright red clinker stone topping gravel bluffs. The road climbs four miles up a series of steep switchbacks onto a plateau. At the base of the eroded face of the Pryors, an enormous canyon opens up, with the waters of Yellowtail Reservoir a ribbon of blue below thousand-foot cliffs.

The Bighorn Canyon isn't particularly on the way to anywhere: you have to really want to be there to get there at all. Much of the land around the canyon is Crow Reservation land and off-limits to most visitors. You cannot get from the dam at Fort Smith on the northern end of the canyon to the recreational access areas to the south (a distance of only 25 miles) unless you have a boat or want to drive a couple hundred miles around and about and down and through Wyoming and back up into Montana, since the Crow do not allow non-tribe members to cross tribal land. This inaccessibility isn't a problem for the locals, who tend to use the reservoir for boating. But a traveler on a schedule will need to make plans to see the entire canyon.

The Land

The Bighorn Canyon cuts through walls of limestone between the Pryor Mountains and the rugged Bighorn Mountains in Wyoming, revealing 500 million years of geologic history. Both the Pryors and the Bighorns were formed when Paleozoic-era sedimentary rock was shoved eastward by the rising Rocky Mountains and upward by a bulwark of rising igneous magma. Limestone that had been laid down 300 million years ago was forced to the surface, forming first the Bighorn Mountains in Wyoming and, trailing behind in Montana, the Pryors.

The Bighorn River rises in Wyoming and flows north uneventfully until it comes to the limestone plateau just east of the Pryors. Here the river has cut into the fault line between the two mountain ranges and has carved out one of the deepest and most dramatic canyons in the northern U.S.

HISTORY

Early Inhabitants

The Bighorn Canyon and the Pryor Mountains were home to many early Indians. Although the Crow were to adopt this land as their own many centuries later, prehistoric nomadic Indians lived here, where the prairies meet mountains, and where limestone caves provided easy shelter. Crow tradition describes the indigenous people of the Bighorn as "dwarfish," strong, and without fire. Bad Pass Trail, which skirts the rim of the Bighorn Canyon, led these early Indians from the grassy plains of Montana to the Great Basin country of Wyoming.

The tortured landscape seems to have induced a sense of awe or wonder in these early residents, for several sites appear to have been places of worship (such as the Medicine Wheel in the Bighorn Mountains of Wyoming). The stone remains of vision quest structures are found along rocky cliffs in the Pryors.

The area became the homeland of the Crow when they arrived here in the 17th century. The land around the canyon and the Pryors was considered especially sacred. Because Bad Pass Trail led through their territory, incursions by other tribes often led to skirmishes and feuds.

White Settlement

Early adventurers operating out of the various trading forts at the juncture of the Yellowstone and Bighorn rivers trapped the Bighorn country. John Colter, who "discovered" Yellowstone Park, was the first white to explore the Pryors, and Jim Bridger, tale spinner and backwoodsman, claimed to have been the first to float the Bighorn River. Frontier missionary Father deSmet said the first Catholic mass in the state under a large cottonwood tree near Fort Smith in 1840.

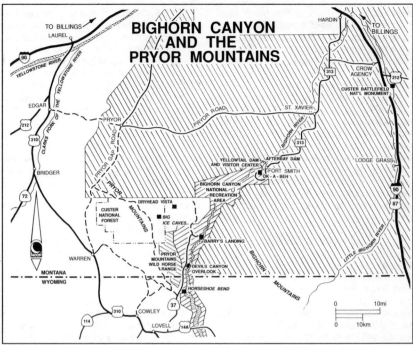

The first white settlement resulted from the Bozeman Trail. Established by John Bozeman in 1864, it cut off from the Oregon Trail and veered north up to the Yellowstone Valley and thence to the gold fields of western Montana.

The Bozeman Trail crossed into Montana near Decker and crossed the Bighorn River at the northern end of the canyon. In Wyoming the trail crossed Sioux land, which was greatly resented by them (the Crow tolerated the whites as long as they moved across their land without settling). A series of forts were built by the military to protect settlers and miners from the Sioux as they passed through the prairies. The most northerly of these, Fort C.F. Smith, was located at the crossing of the Bighorn in 1866.

The hostility of the Sioux, however, was to prove greater than the military's endurance, as the forts were perpetually under siege. After the Hayfield Fight in 1868 near Fort Smith, and the second Fort Laramie Treaty, the Bozeman Trail was closed and the fort left deserted; the entire area was ceded to the Crow.

A second, more peculiar adjunct to the local history came at the turn of the century, when the area was given over to guest or "dude" ranches and celebrity homesteaders. Writers like Will James and Carolyn Lockhart both ran ranches in the Bighorn and Pryor country. The buildings at Hillsboro Dude Ranch along the Bighorn Canyon are now open to visitors.

THE BIGHORN CANYON NATIONAL RECREATION AREA

The Bighorn Canyon National Recreation Area was designated in 1968 after the completion of Yellowtail Dam. The resulting 71-mile-long Bighorn Lake extends the full length of dramatic Bighorn Canyon.

The recreation area also divides the Crow Reservation. The Crow consider the land around the canyon to be sacred; they guard it as a de facto wilderness and do not allow access to non-tribe members. This means that the recreation area has a North District at Fort Smith, Montana, and a South District at Lovell, Wyoming. No direct land route connects the two districts. Lacking a boat, the visitor who wishes to see both halves of the recreation area will have to skirt the Crow Reservation by public highway, a journey of at least three hours by car.

While tourists may enjoy the scenery and the history of the Bighorn Canyon, it is the recreational opportunities that make the canyon a favorite with locals. Fishing and boating are very popular, and with good reason. Boats are without any doubt the conveyance of choice, since exploring the canyon by any other method is either impossible or illegal. Hiking opportunities also exist on unmaintained trails or old roads. More experienced travelers might be tempted to explore the area's many caves.

THE NORTH DISTRICT

Sights

The North District has its headquarters at **The Fort Smith Visitor Center**. There's information on the canyon and its history, exhibits about life in the canyon are displayed, and a film, "The Land of the Bighorn" is shown. The rangers are friendly and knowledgeable, and they offer informational and recreational activities, including campfire programs at Afterbay Campground. Check information boards at the visitor center for details. The center is open daily 9 a.m.-6 p.m. Memorial Day to Labor Day, and 9 a.m.-4:30 p.m. the remainder of the year; tel. 666-2339.

Fort C.F. Smith is located on private land; it can only be visited during a ranger-led tour. Prior arrangements are suggested; contact the Fort Smith Visitor Center. The tour involves a quarter-mile hike. Ask about the **deSmet Tree**, where in 1840 Father deSmet said the first Catholic Mass in Montana.

The **Yellowtail Visitor Center** offers tours of Yellowtail Dam, the tallest dam in the Missouri River drainage, built in 1968. Visitors can view the hydroelectric generators and peer off the 525-foot dam. In addition, there is a good museum exhibit of traditional Crow life in Bighorn Canyon. Open daily 9 a.m.-6 p.m. Memorial Day to Labor Day, tel. 666-2358.

Recreation

To reach **Ok-A-Beh Boat Landing** turn south at Fort Smith and ascend the steep face of the Bighorn Plateau, here burned to bright red clinker by the intense heat of ancient, smoldering underground coal seams. The road will deposit you at just about the same elevation you started, but on the other side of Yellowtail Reservoir in Bighorn Canyon. Think twice about making this 11-mile trip if your brakes are poor or your vehicle pulls hard on hills. Otherwise, the road to Ok-A-Beh is a great vantage point from which to overlook the canyon, the Crow Reservation, and the Pryor and Bighorn Mountains.

Boat facilities at Ok-A-Beh include a landing, a fish-cleaning area, and a marina with gas, oil, and boating supplies. On summer weekends tour boats leave from Ok-A-Beh for tours of the

the Bozeman Trail

Bighorn Canyon. Contact Bighorn Charters, P. O. Box 796, Hardin, MT 59035, tel. 248-6651. Shore fishing is almost impossible at public-access sites in the North District of Yellowtail Reservoir, but fishing by boat is good for brown trout and walleye. Boat rentals are available at the Ok-A-Beh Marina. Remember to have the appropriate state fishing license, as the reservoir spans both Montana and Wyoming and there is no license reciprocity. If you happen to have your scuba gear along, you'll find the area's best diving off the northern end of the reservoir, around Ok-A-Beh landing.

Fishing below the reservoir, however, is a different story. The Bighorn River downstream (north) of the dam is a world-class fishery for trophy-size brown and rainbow trout. Much of the access to the river falls under the jurisdiction of the Crow, who do not allow trespassing by non-tribe members. In the immediate area of Fort Smith, however, there are two public-access sites. Afterbay Dam just below Yellowtail Reservoir provides a boat launch and fishing access. From here, the Park Service offers free scenic (no fishing allowed) float trips three miles down the Bighorn River. Contact the visitor center for details.

No motorized vehicles are allowed on the Bighorn River below Afterbay Dam. Boat rentals are available from the many outfitters and fishing gear stores at Fort Smith.

As the Bighorn is both heavily fished and carefully monitored for access, anyone uncertain of the area and its conditions should consider a professional outfitter to guarantee fishing success and compliance with trespass laws.

The same laws that limit fishing access limit the amount of maintained hiking trails in the area. One very short jaunt, the **Beaver Pond Nature Trail**, leaves from the parking lot of the visitor center to overlooks onto beaver ponds in Lime Kiln Creek. For the more ambitious, **Om-Ne-A Trail** leads from Yellowtail Dam to the Ok-A-Beh boat launch. This three-mile hike is initially steep, but is worth it when the trail skirts the canyon rim.

Practicalities

The little community of Fort Smith offers some motel space, though lodgings are geared to anglers on package fishing trips. All of the following are found along Hwy. 313. The **Bighorn Anglers Motel**, tel. 666-2233, and the **Bighorn Trout Shop Motel**, $25 s, $40 d, tel. 666-2375, both offer gear and bait in addition to motel rooms. **Polly's Place**, $28 s, $30 d, tel. 666-2255, promises home cooking to serious anglers. Many of the outfitters will offer room and board to their angler guests.

Camping is a more economical means of spending the night in Fort Smith. The National Park Service maintains a free 30-site campground at **Afterbay. Cottonwood Camp**, tel. 666-2391, offers all the usual niceties, plus boat rentals and shuttle service to fishing-access sites. On Yellowtail Reservoir itself, the Park Service maintains a boat-in-only campsite with minimal facilities at the head of **Black Canyon**, five miles south of Ok-A-Beh by boat.

A larger selection of lodgings is available in Hardin, 42 miles north on Hwy. 313.

Outfitters

The Bighorn River below Yellowtail Dam is blue-ribbon trout fishing. Many outfitters offer fishing, floating, and hunting packages. If it's the trout luring you to the Bighorn, then the following outfitters are serious about fishing and promise results.

Quill Gordon Fly Fishers offers boat rentals, accommodations, and of course sage advice with its guide service, P.O. Box 597, Fort Smith, MT 59035, tel. 666-2253. **Bighorn Angler** offers boat rentals, accommodations, a tackle shop, and a full guide service, Fort Smith, MT 59035, tel. 666-2233. **Big Horn Charters and Outfitters** offers fishing on the Bighorn and also game and bird hunting throughout the region, P.O. Box 796, Hardin, MT 59035, tel. 248-6651.

THE SOUTH DISTRICT

Sights

The South District has its headquarters at **The Bighorn Canyon Visitor Center**, at the junction of Hwy. 14A and Hwy. 310 in Lovell, Wyoming. In this solar-heated building the traveler will find information on the wildlife, geology, and history of Bighorn Canyon. There is also a large raised-relief map of the recreation area that reduces a monumental landscape to a comprehensible scale. Self-guided cassette tours of the history and geology of the area are available. The rangers lead special activities, including campfire programs at Horseshoe Bend Campground.

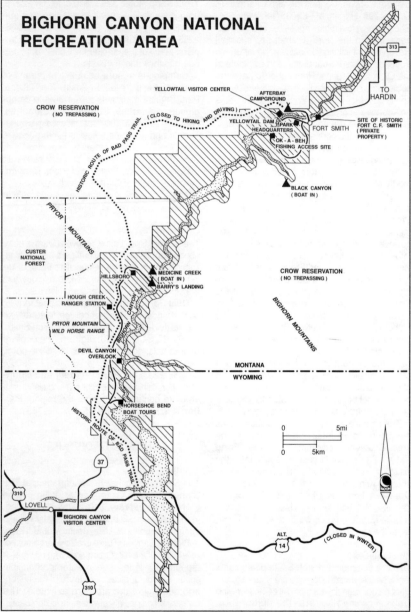

BIGHORN CANYON NATIONAL RECREATION AREA

CROW RESERVATION
(NO TREPASSING)

HISTORIC ROUTE OF BAD PASS TRAIL   (CLOSED TO HIKING AND DRIVING)

YELLOWTAIL VISITOR CENTER

AFTERBAY CAMPGROUND

YELLOWTAIL DAM
PARK HEADQUARTERS

OK - A - BEH
FISHING ACCESS SITE

FORT SMITH

TO HARDIN

313

SITE OF HISTORIC FORT C.F. SMITH (PRIVATE PROPERTY)

BLACK CANYON (BOAT IN)

PRYOR   MOUNTAINS

CUSTER NATIONAL FOREST

HILLSBORO

MEDICINE CREEK (BOAT IN)
BARRY'S LANDING

HOUGH CREEK RANGER STATION

PRYOR MOUNTAIN WILD HORSE RANGE

DEVIL CANYON OVERLOOK

BIGHORN   CANYON

CROW RESERVATION
(NO TREPASSING)

BIGHORN MOUNTAINS

MONTANA

WYOMING

HISTORIC   ROUTE OF BAD PASS TRAIL

HORSESHOE BEND
BOAT TOURS

0   5mi

0   5km

37

310

LOVELL

BIGHORN CANYON VISITOR CENTER

ALT.
14   (CLOSED IN WINTER)

310

© MOON PUBLICATIONS, INC.

Check the information board at the visitor center for details. Open 8 a.m.-6 p.m. daily Memorial Day to Labor Day, and 8 a.m.-5 p.m. the remainder of the year, tel. (307) 548-2251.

The South District contains the best access to dramatic views onto the canyon. As Hwy. 37 leaves the Lovell area, it climbs onto a plateau with strangely desert-like features such as thorn bushes and barren, rocky slopes. This almost lunar landscape is broken as the road drops onto **Horseshoe Bend**, where a wide expanse of the lake passes into the Bighorn Canyon to the north.

Highway 37 (misleadingly known as the Trans-Park Highway; no road connects both parks) then passes into the **Pryor Mountain Wild Horse Range**, where one of America's last herds of wild mustangs run free. The Wild Horse Range was established in 1968 and now contains 44,000 acres.

Within the boundaries of the Wild Horse Range is the most spectacular view onto Bighorn Canyon. Where Devil Canyon meets the Bighorn Canyon, sheer, 1,000-foot-high cliffs tower above the waters of the lake. From **Devil Canyon Overlook** atop one of these cliffs, the views are literally breathtaking, and vertigo-inducing. Informational signs explain the precipitous landscape.

A short hike off the highway near the campsite at Barry's Landing leads to the remains of **Hillsboro**, a ghost town originally built by an early white settler, G.W. Barry. After several financially unsuccessful attempts at mining and horse ranching in the first decade of this century, Barry converted his settlement into Cedarville Dude Ranch, a guest ranch for tourists. Most of the original buildings are still standing. Highway 37 ends at **Barry's Landing,** a boat launch established by Barry, who offered boat tours of the canyon. Barry's Landing is now maintained as a boat launch and campsite by the Park Service.

After crossing the Montana line, Hwy. 37 parallels the path of the ancient **Bad Pass Trail**, the path used for centuries by Indians as they passed from the plains and valleys of Montana to the great basin land of Wyoming. Travois trails and stone cairns are still visible along the trail. You can get a feel for the Bad Pass Trail if you hike or drive up Dryhead Road (an unimproved road that begins where the paved portion of Hwy. 37 dead-ends at the turnoff for Barry's Landing) into the **Lockhart Ranch**.

Carolyn Lockhart was a successful journalist who left the *Boston Post* for the life of a Bighorn Canyon homesteader and Western novelist. Lockhart and her companion weathered the Depression years only to fight the government for the title to the land when it claimed that the two women had not improved on the homestead. Lockhart was awarded the title to her land in 1936. The original structures still stand at her ranch. Dryhead Road continues to parallel Bad Pass Trail for another 12 miles beyond the Lockhart Ranch, but is passable only to high-clearance vehicles or hardy hikers.

Practicalities

Lovell, Wyoming, is 12 miles south of the recreation area, and is the closest community to the Southern District. The **Super 8 Motel**, at the east end of Main St., tel. (307) 548-2725, $28 s, $36 d, offers a restaurant and RV park. The **Cattlemen Motel**, 470 Montana Ave., tel. (307) 548-2296, $25 s, $30 d, is comfortable and quiet. The **Horseshoe Bend Motel**, 375 E. Main, tel. (307) 548-2221, $24 s, $27 d, is on the main road going to Bighorn Canyon.

Campgrounds are available in the recreation area. At **Horseshoe Bend Campground** there are 126 sites, with most modern facilities. Seventeen miles downriver is **Barry's Landing Campground** with 14 sites, but bring your own water. **Medicine Creek Campsite** is a hike- or boat-in-only area two miles north of Barry's Landing, with primitive facilities.

Recreation

While fishing is certainly a popular pastime on Yellowtail Reservoir, water-skiing, swimming, nautical sightseeing, and even scuba diving are the order of the day. **Horseshoe Bend Campground and Boat Launch** is located on the northern end of Bighorn Lake, just before it disappears northward into the defiles of the canyon. Besides its role as a boat-in area, Horseshoe Bend serves as a hub of other recreational activities, including supervised swimming. Free canoe trips into the canyon are offered by rangers, as are evening campfire programs. Check the information boards at the visitor center in Lovell for details.

Privately operated Bighorn Canyon boat tours are also offered from Horseshoe Bend. For information on the two-hour tours, contact S-S Enter-

Bighorn Canyon exposes millions of years of geologic history.

prises, P.O. Box 717, Cowley, WY 82420, tel. (307) 548-6418. Boat rentals are available from the Horseshoe Bend Marina. A second boat launch is located 17 miles farther north, at Barry's Landing.

From Horseshoe Bend Campground **Crooked Creek Nature Trail** wends a quarter mile through the arid landscape. Self-guiding brochures identify plant and animal life. **Medicine Creek Trail** follows the rim of the Bighorn Canyon for almost two miles from Barry's Landing to Medicine Creek Campground. In addition to these maintained trails, options for hiking in the Bighorn Canyon area are dictated only by the energy and forethought necessary to strike out on your own. The area is full of old mining, logging, and ranching roads. With the help of a ranger and a Forest Service map, much of the area is open for exploration.

Spelunking is another activity offered to the adventurous in the Bighorn region. The entire area is a huge uplift of limestone which has eroded for millions of years. The results are networks of caves, filled not simply with mineral formations but also with the archaeological remains of early Indians. The Park Service and the

BLM limit access to many of the caves, but most (such as the Bighorn Caverns) are open to experienced spelunkers upon request. Ask at the visitor center, or at the Cody, Wyoming BLM office for permission, keys, and information on specific dangers. Most will require a four-wheel-drive vehicle for access.

THE PRYOR MOUNTAINS

Rising to the west of the Bighorn Canyon are the low, greatly eroded plateaus of the Pryor Mountains. Although these mountains are not very high in the Montana scale of things, they form a very curious destination for the traveler. The Pryors are so extraordinarily rich in Indian tradition and sites that the parts of the range that fall in the Crow Reservation are considered sacred and treated as wilderness. The area is rich in limestone caves, noted both for their mineral formations and archaeological interest.

The Pryors are surrounded by the Crow Reservation and the Bighorn National Recreational Area. They are therefore not easily accessible. But the difficulty of getting in is more than made up for by the reward of being there. This is really remote country, with tepee rings and ice caves, bighorn sheep and mustangs, views over holy land, all amply served by Forest Service roads. Although a high-clearance vehicle is a good idea, the Pryors cry out for exploration by mountain bikes.

Sights
In the mid-1960s, public concern became focused on about 200 wild horses living in the Pryors, remnants of larger herds that roamed the remote areas of the West. In 1968 the BLM established the **Pryor Mountain Wild Horse Range** on a 44,000-acre site on the Montana-Wyoming border. The ancestry of these animals is mixed. Some horses are merely escapees from ranch herds; others derive from Indian pony stock, which in turn was generated from imported Spanish horse lines. "Tiger stripes" on the legs or back are characteristics derived from Spanish breeds. A dominant stud, his harem of mares, and their foals form common mustang social units.

Wild horse viewing is easiest along Hwy. 37 coming north from Wyoming into the Bighorn Recreation Area. For the more adventurous, the meadows and box canyons of the Pryors are a more memorable place to see the herds.

Bighorn sheep, for which this entire area was named, have been restocked in the Pryors. Deer and elk are common, and the area is popular in the fall for hunting.

The remoteness of the Pryors makes them tempting destinations for a certain kind of adventurer. Mountain bikers will find this a compelling challenge, because of the flora and fauna (where else can one pedal amongst wild horses?) and also because of the archaeological wealth of the area. Most importantly, there are many deserted roads from the days when these mountains were mined and logged.

The Forest Service map of the Custer National Forest indicates a great number of caves, many open to public access. **Big Ice Cave** was once a popular picnic spot for day-trips in the early years of the century. It was closed for many years except to guided tours by the Forest Service, but now is open for informal exploration. There are picnic grounds and wilderness camping opportunities nearby. Big Ice Cave is found at the top of the Pryors, along Forest Service Road 3093. Spelunkers are advised to check with the BLM or Forest Service for details of access to other caves, since some are locked in order to prevent vandalism and to protect the unsuspecting from specific dangers.

Almost the best reason to venture into the Pryors is the last one reached, at least by civilized routes. Past Big Ice Cave, on Forest Service Road 849, is **Dry Head Vista**, a panoramic viewpoint with the Bighorn Canyon dropping away 4,000 feet below.

Campgrounds

Within the bounds of the **Custer National Forest** are a couple of camping areas. **Sage Creek Campground** is the first encountered, and it has a spring (bringing water is a good idea for the squeamish, even though there are several natural springs with potable water). **Crooked Creek Campground** is farther in and more rudimentary, and requires a more energetic motor vehicle.

Getting There

This isn't as simple as it looks. Maps show a road south from the little town of Pryor. Called Pryor Gap Road, it is in fact the old roadbed of an abandoned rail spur line. It is not in very good shape, but it is the shortest way into the Pryors from southeastern Montana. It also crosses Crow land, and sometimes access has been denied. It's best to check on road conditions and access before starting up the gap. The standard but somewhat indirect way into the area is from the west, via Hwy. 310, onto Pryor Mountain Rd. two miles south of Bridger, or north and east from Warren, Wyoming, along Sage Creek. About 20 miles of gravel road later you will arrive in the canyons of the Pryors.

From the Wyoming side, if you have a four-wheel-drive vehicle, there are several rough and scenic routes into the Pryors. Cowley Airport Rd. turns into a four-wheel-drive road called Crooked Creek Road. In its rough-and-ready fashion it leads past tepee rings and the two highest peaks in the Pryors before reaching Crooked Creek Campground. For the very hardy, a road leads up to (or more prudently, down from) Dry Head Vista, along Sykes Ridge Road. Before attempting either route, ask locals for directions and cautionary tales.

INFORMATION

For details on the Wild Horse Range and other destinations, the **Bighorn Canyon Visitor Center** can be reached at P.O. Box 487, Lovell, WY 82431, tel. (307) 548-2551. It's at the junction of Hwys. 310 and 14A at the east end of Lovell.

The **Fort Smith Visitor Center** can be reached at P.O. Box 458, Fort Smith, MT 59035, tel. 666-2339, at the junction of Hwy. 313 and Afterbay Road.

Yellowtail Visitor Center is at the end of Hwy. 313, at Fort Smith, MT 59035, tel. 666-2358.

The **Beartooth Division of the Custer National Forest** has jurisdiction over the national forest in the Pryor Mountains, and can be reached at Rte. 2, Box 3420, Red Lodge, MT 59068, tel. 446-2103. The **Custer National Forest Supervisor's Office** is in Billings at 2602 First Ave. N, Billings, MT 59103, tel. 657-6361.

The **BLM office** in Cody, Wyoming has the keys to many of the caves in the Bighorn Canyon area. Reach them at (307) 587-2216.

The Lovell, Wyoming **Chamber of Commerce** can be reached at P.O. Box 322, Lovell, WY 82431, tel. (307) 548-7552.

CRISIS

Get the coal out, with a tumult and shout.
Yes, tear it out of the ground.
There's a crisis to smite and cities to light.
There's billions of tons to be found.
And when coal is burned great wheels will be turned.
And a shaft from the wheels turns the earth.
It's simple you see (or so they tell me)
As they ravage the land of my birth.

Damn pristine air! There's water to spare!
We'll lower your taxes for you.
We'll pave all your roads. Help shoulder your loads.
Their cajoling beats a tatoo.
We'll build swimming pools and public schools—
Build an empire upon your Plains.
Just climb in with us, on our omnibus.
Eat our truffles and drink our champagnes.

Don't fret for the grass. If our plans come to pass,
You'll have more than you've ever seen.
For we can "reclaim." (At least that's our aim.)
We'll improve what once was pristine.
But if you feel doubt, then we'll buy you out
For more money than you've ever seen!
Enjoy wealth to the hilt. To assuage your guilt,
Wash in dollars if you still feel unclean.

In times such as these, in our energy squeeze,
You must try the "big picture" to see.
If untempted by booty, then think of your duty.
If you're selfless, then you must agree:
Our country must grow or the grey faceless foe
will surely stalk o'er our grave.
For Growth made us great. It must not abate.
It's no monster, you see, Growth's our slave.

We'll win in a rout, if we get the coal out.
We'll all be the winners, you see.
We'll not freeze in the dark. We'll continue our lark.
And coal—good black coal—holds the key.

On their shrill voices go. Drifting, sifting like snow.
I resist them with all of my might.
For their cloying sweet song is grievously wrong.
Deep within me, I know that I am right.

—Wallace McRae

BOB RACE

NORTHEASTERN MONTANA AND THE BIG OPEN

One of the least-visited areas in the state, northeastern Montana is usually dismissed as an unwieldy piece of real estate that has to be crossed to get to more verdant or populated destinations. But this vast region contains enormous reserves of wildlife, the homelands of three Indian tribes, and some of the best hunting and fishing in the state. History is not very old here: some of the wildest rodeos in the state are permitted out here; at Fort Union, would-be frontiersmen in buckskins gather to shoot muskets; and local Indians look for new reasons to throw powwows. Memories of the Old West of the open range, cattle rustlers, and the homestead movement drift in and out of conversations.

Even though you probably won't plan your vacation around it, what you're likely to remember about this part of the state is the people. In some kind of contrast to the rugged terrain and remorseless weather, the inhabitants of this lonesome corner of Montana are genuinely friendly, if haughtily independent, and are probably some of the most inveterate socializers you'll ever meet.

THE LAND

In few places is the dinosaur fossil record so easily read as in northeastern Montana. Once tropical seacoast, these prairies sprouted exotic vegetation, and dinosaurs of every size and description crowded in hoping to eat and not be eaten. Some still-unknown event curtailed these exuberant life forms about 70 million years ago; sediments continued to accumulate along the marshes, burying the remains of these ancient plants and animals.

After a prolonged altercation with ice-age glaciers, the Missouri River cut a new channel across the prairies, revealing hundreds of feet of fossil-rich sediment in the deep, gorge-like

Missouri Breaks. The formation, named for Hell Creek near Jordan, where extensive fossil excavations have taken place, continues to yield up its ancient secrets.

The ice sheets of the last ice age did more than divert the Missouri. They ground down the prairies north of the Missouri River's present channel to a uniform flatness.

Climate

In a word, extreme. Winter winds find nothing between the Arctic Circle and here to halt their chilling advance. While winters are not particularly snowy, cold temperatures—Glasgow's average reading in January is 10° F—combine with these winds to produce even more intense chill factors. Summer is very hot, with daytime temperatures usually in the 90s, though Medicine Lake once matched the state record of 117°. Hot parching winds often blow throughout the month of August. Although one of the most arid parts of Montana, summer thunderstorms sometimes bring late evening showers. Probably the best time to travel is the fall, when clear, crisp, and dry weather can be expected through mid-November.

Flora

The shortgrass prairie here is rarely interrupted by trees, and only the occasional resilient chokecherries and red-stemmed willows break up the hegemony of the grasslands. Along the Missouri, however, substantial cottonwood groves sway above the river; in the bluffs above Fort Peck Dam, ponderosa pine and juniper cling to a baleful existence.

Fauna

The state's largest wildlife refuge, the Charles M. Russell National Wildlife Refuge sustains populations of elk and bighorn sheep no longer found on the plains. Smaller but important wetland refuges shelter migrating waterfowl.

Much of the rest of this region might as well be a refuge. Wildlife is common. Mule and white-tailed deer abound, as do pronghorn; even the most casual observer can see dozens of each along the roads. Waterfowl, pheasants, and grouse are equally pervasive. It's no surprise that this is paradise for hunters.

HISTORY

The Sioux, Assiniboine, and Blackfoot Indians shared these buffalo-rich plains in shifting, suspicious alliances. The development of transportation corridors across Montana's northern tier—first with steamboats on the Missouri River

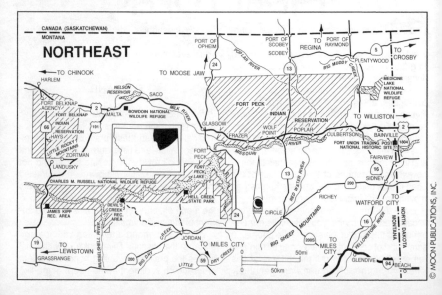

SHEEPHERDERS' MONUMENTS

You'll notice them on the tops of gumbo buttes in eastern and central Montana: steep piles of rock rising like parapets against the skyline. Known as sheepherders' monuments, they are the work of Scottish and Irish herders whose sheep-tending jobs gave them lots of free time on hilltops.

In many ways, the open range lasted longer for sheep ranchers than for cattlemen. Before the proliferation of stock reservoirs, sheepherders (Montanans never use the term "shepherd") trailed sheep from pastures near "camp" to water every day; the range may have been fenced, but sheep needed the herder's extra inducement to behave sensibly. While at camp, herders typically kept watch over their flocks from nearby hills, mindful of predators and wayward sheep. Most ranches still had herders, typically of Basque, Irish, or Scottish origin, throughout the 1950s.

Sheepherders always claim that they began to build cairns on the tops of high hills as windbreaks. but something more than utility went into it. Herders took pride in building the highest, or the most tightly fitted, monument; old-timers can still tell you which herder built every monument on the skyline.

Unfortunately, few ranches employ herders anymore, so remaining monuments have begun to slump a bit in their advanced age. Tragically, vandals derive pleasure from toppling over those sheepherder's monuments convenient to the highway. Please respect their age, and the isolation, work, and pride that went into their construction.

in the 1830s, then with the Great Northern Railway up the Milk River Valley in the 1880s— set the stage for the Indians' removal to reservations.

The homestead era brought the greatest changes to northeastern Montana. With a farm family on every half-section, these arid plains were forced momentarily to yield up a bounty of grain. Scandinavians and other northern Euro-

peans were especially attracted to this unsettled area, and many small villages, dominated by a Lutheran or Methodist chuch spire, were settled with vague, utopian aspirations. The profoundly varying climate, leagued with Depression-era drought and insect infestations, brought the end to most homesteads.

Many of the unemployed farmers and tradesmen did find local work, however. The greatest of all Public Works Administration projects was Fort Peck Dam on the Missouri River. Employing tens of thousands of workers and flooding 250,000 acres of riverbottom, Fort Peck is one of the world's largest dams and an important source of hydroelectricity.

INFORMATION

Travel Montana's **Missouri River Country** region covers much of northeastern Montana. Write for their free travel information at P.O. Box 11990, Wolf Point, MT 59201, or call (406) 525-3410.

TRANSPORTATION

Amtrak's *Empire Builder* traverses northern Montana, with service east from Portland and Seattle and west from Chicago. There are daily stops at Wolf Point, Glasgow, and Malta. Call (800) 872-7245 for information and reservations.

Big Sky Airlines flies into Wolf Point and Glasgow from Billings, and into Sidney from Williston, North Dakota. Call (800) 882-4475 for schedule information.

Automobile travelers need to be aware that parts of northeastern Montana are very remote: not every dot on the map has a gas station; nor in fact does every dot exist in a form helpful to travelers. Along Hwys. 2 and 200, gas up frequently. Don't count on 24-hour service stations to help you cross the area at night.

THE LITTLE ROCKY MOUNTAINS AND THE FORT BELKNAP RESERVATION

The Little Rockies are the easternmost of the volcanic outlier mountains of central Montana. The core of the range, blanketed by displaced, tilted layers of limestone, contains significant deposits of gold. The usual mix of prospectors, ne'er-do-wells, and colorful characters rushed in during the 1890s, founding Zortman and Landusky. Outlaws from the Missouri badlands, a kind of resort community for rapscallions, made these mining camps their local watering holes. Such criminals as Kid Curry and Butch Cassidy were habitués of the remote and lawless Little Rockies.

THE FORT BELKNAP INDIAN RESERVATION

From the Little Rockies north to the Milk River lies the 645,000-acre Fort Belknap Reservation, home to the Gros Ventre and Assiniboine Indians. These two tribes were rivals in the complex intertribal politics characteristic of the 1800s. The Assiniboine are a Siouan people that drifted west as settlement to the east displaced them from their traditional home near Lake Winnipeg. After arriving on the plains, the Assiniboine became fierce rivals of the Blackfoot Indians. After smallpox decimated their numbers in the 1830s, the tribe settled along the Milk River to hunt the fast-disappearing buffalo.

How the Gros Ventre (French for "Big Belly") came by their name is something of a mystery; not only the French but the Blackfeet and Shoshone referred to the tribe as the "belly" people. One theory holds that in sign language the tribe was indicated by gesturing to the ribs, where early Gros Ventre tattooed symbols.

The Gros Ventre were allied with the powerful Blackfoot Nation. This Indian cartel roamed freely across northern Montana, terrorizing Indian and white settler alike. But increasing trade with the whites, especially for whiskey, demoralized the tribes. Old alliances were scrapped, and the Blackfeet and Gros Ventre fell to fighting. The Gros Ventre soon found themselves siding with their old enemies, the Assiniboine and the U.S. Army, against the marauding Black-

feet. The Gros Ventre settled on the northern slopes of the Little Rockies. The U.S. government built Fort Belknap to protect the tribes in 1871, and in 1887 created the reservation.

Sights
At Hays, along the flanks of the Little Rockies, Jesuit F.H. Eberschweiler founded **St. Paul's Mission** in 1886 to instruct the Gros Ventre. The early church was built of logs and contained instructional paintings; it burned during the 1930s, and was rebuilt in stone. Some original log outbuildings (1890s) remain.

Behind Hays, leading up People's Creek into the Little Rockies, is **Mission Canyon**. A gravel road passes beneath steep limestone cliffs riddled with caves. After two miles the road leads to a **natural bridge**, where water has carved through the limestone, leaving an arch 60 feet above the valley floor.

Events
Milk River Indian Days, held in Fort Belknap the last weekend of July, features contest dancing, a marathon run, and a giveaway; in mid-June, the **Hays Mission Canyon Dance** is held in the canyon behind the town. The public is welcome to attend these celebrations.

Information
Contact the Tribal Offices, Fort Belknap Agency, Rt. 1 Box 66, Harlem, MT 59526, tel. (406) 353-2205, for information on tribal activities.

THE LITTLE ROCKY MOUNTAINS

On the map, the southern border of the Fort Belknap Reservation looks as if someone took a bite out of it. In fact, that's about what happened. Prospectors found gold in the Little Rockies in 1884; by the 1890s, in contravention of treaties, miners overran the narrow gulches of these low mountains. The federal Indian agent for the reservation was unable to stop the influx, and he urged the Assiniboine and Gros Ventre tribes to sell a strip of land four miles wide and seven miles long to the BLM. The tribes received $350,000 for the land in 1895; the mines there are currently producing $25 million a year in gold and silver.

History

Although rumors of gold in the Little Rockies were abroad as early as the 1860s, the Blackfeet discouraged exploration. Development awaited Pike Landusky, a grizzled veteran of past gold rushes, Indian fights, and whiskey trading. He and a companion found gold in 1894 near the town that now bears his name; within months hundreds of miners streamed in. The next year the government bought the land from the reservation, and within a decade, placer mining was replaced by more efficient, but environmentally damaging, cyanide stamp mills.

Even for mining camps, the towns of Landusky and Zortman drew more than their quota of rough characters. Pike Landusky himself was no milquetoast: in 1868, he went to the mouth of the Musselshell to trap and trade with the Indians; instead, he was ambushed by a party of Sioux. The irascible Landusky seized his frying pan and started beating one of the warriors with it; startled, the Sioux braves ceased their advance, and Landusky jerked the breechcloth off another and commenced lashing him in the face with it. Sensing a demonic presence, the Indians withdrew, leaving this dervish two ponies as an offering.

In an altercation with the Blackfeet, Landusky was shot in the jaw. The bullet shattered the bone and teeth; Landusky simply fished the fragments out of his mouth, discarded them, and went on fighting.

Landusky was representative of other rough-and-tough characters in this neighborhood: this was not a delicate society. Jew Jake was the local barkeeper; his leg had been shot off by a lawman in Great Falls, and he used a Winchester rifle for a crutch. The Curry Gang, three brothers who skirted civility and the law, owned a ranch just south of town. Pike Landusky fell afoul of the Curry Gang when he objected to the youngest Curry, Lonnie, wooing his daughter. Sensing a slight, Kid (Curry eldest) rode to town and shot Landusky dead at Jew Jake's bar. As a final humiliation, the other Curry brother, Johnny, moved in with Mrs. Landusky.

The Currys gained national prominence after they formed the Wild Bunch with Butch Cassidy and the Sundance Kid, and went on a spree of bank and train robberies.

Mining in Landusky and Zortman peaked in the 1910s; the second-largest cyanide mill in the world was erected in Zortman to leach gold out of quartz ore. By 1940, almost all activity had ceased, but in the 1980s the price of gold was high enough to justify reopening the mines at Zortman. Currently, about 300 people work at the mines.

Sights

The facilities of the **Zortman Mining Company** are open for tours during summer months, on Tuesdays and Thursdays at 10 a.m. and 1 p.m. The tours start at the Pegasus Mining Corp. offices. Call 673-3252 to reserve a space.

Both **Zortman** and **Landusky** have preserved the flavor of old gold camps and are protected as national historic sites. Although nominally considered ghost towns, neither has really developed its old buildings as a tourist attraction. In Zortman, the original jail still stands, and the Buckhorn Store and Bar and the Miners Café still minister to the hungry and thirsty. The trailers and campers of today's miners contrast oddly with the rough log cabins of yesteryear. Landusky shows even fewer signs of life: a mining town is probably in extremis when its bar has closed.

Ten miles south of the Little Rockies lie the Missouri River Breaks. This province of rough badlands and river frontage has been included in the Charles M. Russell National Wildlife Refuge. Just about the only easily accessible part of the refuge is reached by a **self-guided auto tour** off Hwy. 191 a mile north of the Robinson Missouri River Bridge. This 20-mile drive along good gravel roads passes great wildlife viewing and scenic landmarks.

Practicalities

In Zortman, the **Buckhorn Store,** tel. 673-3162, offers cabins ($30), campsites, and groceries. The **Zortman Garage,** tel. 673-3160, also offers RV hookups and cabins for $30. The **Miner's Café,** tel. 673-3325, open 6 a.m.-10 p.m., welcomes miner and tourist alike with simple, tasty food. One mile north of Zortman, the BLM maintains **Camp Creek,** a streamside campground.

Another BLM campsite, **Montana Gulch,** is one-half mile west of Landusky. From the campground, it's a short hike to the natural bridge in Mission Canyon.

THE MILK RIVER VALLEY

Between Malta and Glasgow, Hwy. 2 unrolls between cottonwoods and willows and the green thread of the Milk River. The prairies of northern Montana continue their expansive, monotonal rhythm. Occasionally a ridge of uplands, outriders from the wild Missouri Breaks just south, infringes, causing the horizon to hike up its skirts.

Ice-age glaciers covered this part of Montana, homogenizing the prairie surface and obstructing the old Missouri River course. When the ice sheets retreated, about 10,000 years ago, the Missouri found a more southerly valley to its liking. The sluggish and inconsiderable Milk River, so named by Lewis and Clark who thought its waters resembled "a cup of tea with the admixture of a tablespoonful of milk," has borrowed the old channel.

Eastern Montana's only hot springs resorts, a wildlife refuge dense with birdlife, and some of the state's best big-game hunting make a virtue out of these implacable prairies.

HISTORY

The Bad Old Days
First the Plains Indians and the buffalo, then open-range cowboys and cattle claimed this rich rangeland. Just as the Indians entered remote areas of Montana after being displaced by homesteaders elsewhere, so settlement in the Judith Basin during the 1890s pushed untamed cowboys, desperados, and loners north into the Milk River Valley.

The Missouri Breaks and the Little Rockies were a villainous no-man's land. From rugged hideouts, rustlers trailed stolen cattle to Canada and back, across the law-free expanses of Milk River country. The Hole-In-The-Wall Gang, led by Kid Curry, found cattle and horse theft too facile. In 1901, they held up the westbound Great Northern train five miles west of Malta. After stopping the train and blowing up the safe, the gang fled with worthless unfranked bank notes.

Painter Charley Russell rode with other cowboys along the Milk River. One of his most famous paintings re-created a 1904 episode that occurred just south of Saco. Early-rising cowpunchers found that 40 horses were missing from the remuda. A quick search revealed that a grizzly bear had entered camp, charged the horse covey, and was chasing the frightened horses across the prairie. The cowboys gave chase, and, within seconds, lassoed the furious bear. Russell's *Loops and Swift Horses Are Surer Than Lead* commemorates the event.

successful paddlefish hunters

BRENT McRAE

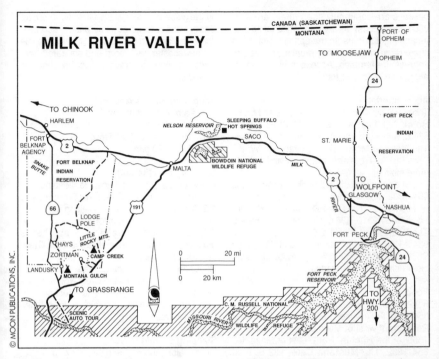

Settlement

The Great Northern Railway pushed up the Milk River Valley in 1887. Initially, it brought little settlement to this part of the state, except for villages where cowboys loaded cattle onto railcars. The seclusion of northern Montana ended in the 1910s, when the homestead land rush brought in thousands of dryland farmers. Throughout the Milk Valley, homesteads sprang up every 320 acres. The Great Northern actively promoted the cheap land of northern Montana in Central and Eastern Europe; these immigrants founded ethnically homogeneous enclaves. Amongst the most resilient are the Hutterites, who maintain several communities in the area.

MALTA AND VICINITY

Yes, Malta (pop. 2,340, elev. 2,254 feet) was named for the Mediterranean island. No, Malta was not named for or by Maltese immigrants. As the Great Northern built across unpopulated north-

ern Montana in 1887, enterprising employees spun the globe and then stopped it with a jab of the finger. Thus were deserted sidings along the Great Northern saddled with exotic names.

The siding at Malta jump-started. Ranchers whose herds of cattle ranged the unfenced prairies needed a railhead, and thirsty cowboys needed a town to carouse in. Irrigated farms along the Milk River notwithstanding, this is still cattle country: Malta is a rancher's, not a farmer's town.

Sights

Housed in the old Carnegie library is the **Phillips County Museum,** 133 S. First St. W, tel. 654-1037, open Tues.-Sat. 10 a.m.-noon and 1-5 p.m., Memorial day-Labor Day. With displays of cowboy gear, Indian beadwork, and homesteader-era artifacts, it commemorates the area's history.

Just two miles east of Malta is the **Bowdoin National Wildlife Refuge,** tel. 654-2863. Founded in 1936, this marshy lake is a major stopover for both migrating and nesting waterfowl. White pelicans are commonly seen (there are over 800 nesting pairs), as are rarer white-faced ibises and night herons. In the spring watch male sharp-tailed grouse as they drum their chests to impress the females. Access is by canoe, or along a six-mile auto tour.

Accommodations

The nicest place to stay in Malta is the **GN Motel Hotel**, 2 S. First Ave. E, tel. (406) 654-2100, $36 d, with a bar, restaurant, and steak house. The **Maltana Motel**, 138 S. First Ave. W, tel. 654-2610, $30 d, is also downtown, and a shade more modest.

Out on Hwy. 2, the **Edge Water Motel**, tel. 654-1302, $38 d, has an indoor pool, sauna, and campsites. The **Riverside Motel**, 8 N. Central, tel. 654-2310, $36 d, also rents RV spaces. The **Sportsman Motel**, 231 N. First St. E, tel. 654-2300, $31 d, and **Mann's Motel**, 17 N. First St. E, tel. 654-1150, $28 d, are comfortable older units with kitchenettes.

Food

For steaks, try the **GN**, 2 S. First Ave. E, tel. 654-2100. For a lighter meal, go to the **Westside Restaurant** west of Malta on Hwy. 2, tel. 654-1555, or the **Hitchin' Post**, east of Malta, tel. 654-1882. The **Mustang Café**, 122 S. First St./Ave., tel. 654-1510, is a good locals' kind of eatery; if you need a stretch, you can bowl a few strikes in the adjacent bowling alley while you wait for lunch; open 10 a.m.-11 p.m. Pizza heads the bill at **Long X Corral** south of town, tel. 654-1578, but there are also evening buffets.

Information And Services

Contact the **Malta Chamber of Commerce** at Box GG, Malta, MT 59538, tel. (406) 654-1776.

The **Phillips County Hospital** is at 417 S. Fourth St./Ave. E, tel. 654-1100. For emergencies, call the **sheriff**, tel. 654-1211.

For a local **road report**, call 265-1416.

SACO AND VICINITY

Saco (pop. 2,612, elev. 2,184 feet) is a little agricultural trading center named, like Malta, by the globe-spinners at the Great Northern for Saco, Maine. In its cowboy past, Saco also shares history with Malta. Chet Huntley, the late TV newscaster, was born and educated near Saco; the country grade school he attended now stands in a city park.

Accommodations And Food

There's one motel in town, **O'Brien's**, at 203 Taylor, tel. 527-3373, $26 d. **O'Brien's Café** is down the street at 507 Taylor, tel. 527-9968, open 6 a.m.-10 p.m.

Camping And Fishing

A mile off Hwy. 2 and adjacent to Sleeping Buffalo Resort is **Nelson Reservoir State Park**, a 4,500-acre lake with camping along its banks. Locals use the reservoir for water-skiing and fishing (northern pike and walleye). There's more good fishing at more attractive **Coal Gravel Pits Lakes** about five miles past Nelson Reservoir along the same road. Here, in six deep gravel pits dug by the Great Northern, are lakes up to eight acres in size; stocked with pike, largemouth bass, and rainbow trout, these lakes also make for a good picnic spot.

Sleeping Buffalo Resort

Unique along the northern tier, this popular hot springs spa combines modern accommodations, water-skiing, and aqua-therapy. Named for large glacial rocks half-buried in the prairies, the hot springs were tapped in 1924 when oil drillers struck a pool of hot, highly mineralized water at 3,200 feet. When the water reached the surface, the mineral gases ignited. The spring burned for six years.

Initially developed as an old-fashioned health spa, the hot springs at Sleeping Buffalo have been modernized and developed into a family recreational facility. Presently, the resort includes both indoor and outdoor hot pools (106°), a water slide, two bars, a restaurant, a golf course, and rooms in venerable cabins ($29 d) or modern motel units ($34 d).

Sleeping Buffalo Resort, Star Rte. 3, Box 13, Saco, MT 59621, tel. (406) 527-3370, is 10 miles west of Saco on Hwy. 2, then about four miles north along a good gravel road.

GLASGOW AND FORT PECK

The largest Public Works project of the 1930s' New Deal era, and holding one of the largest reservoirs in the world, Fort Peck Dam is an enormous tribute to the spirit that overcame the Great Depression. The old rail town of Glasgow, now the largest city in northeastern Montana, was the stepping-off point for the dam project and is now the livestock trade center of the region. Vivid history, unparalleled recreational opportunities, as well as tours of the enormous hydroelectric facilities make this northeastern Montana's most enticing stopover.

HISTORY

Early traders built the orignal Fort Peck as an Indian trading post in 1867. Located right on the banks of the Missouri River for ease in loading and unloading steamboats, the trading post did a bang-up business with the Sioux and Assiniboine. The Great Northern Railroad in 1887 chose to build through the gentle Milk River Valley rather than traverse the intemperate badlands of the Missouri River, thereby bypassing the old fort.

Glasgow began as a rail siding on the Great Northern. It took off as a regional hub after the Army Corps of Engineers built Fort Peck Dam, the largest on the Missouri River system, in the 1930s. Little shanty towns sprang up to serve the needs of the 10,000-strong labor force.

GLASGOW

The Great Northern established a wide spot along the rails called Siding 45 in 1887. The town, originally just a series of tents, became Glasgow in 1889. Glasgow (pop. 3,572, elev. 2,216 feet) grew fitfully as homesteaders and ranchers made use of the rail connections.

During the 1930s, Glasgow boomed as it became the primary trade and transport center for the shifting population of workers at Fort Peck Lake. This period of growth lasted only 10 years, and although few dam workers permanently settled in the area, Glasgow remains the focus for anglers and holidaymakers at the reservoir.

More problematic for the city was the Glasgow Air Force Base. During the mid-1960s, the population of Valley County nearly doubled with Air Force personnel and their families. Glasgow built new schools, redesigned the old downtown for more traffic, and prepared for sustained growth. When the Air Force pulled out in 1969, the city planners were left with a facility, unlike Fort Peck, that had no apparent afterlife. Currently, Boeing rents the base for flight training and equipment testing. The 1,200 living units on the base are being marketed as St. Marie's, a retirement community for military personnel.

Sights
The **Valley County Pioneer Museum,** Hwy. 2 at Eighth Ave. N, tel. 228-8692, is one of eastern Montana's best museums. Diorama fans should prepare to be giddy, as the museum utilizes a number of these well-done displays to present local history. An authentic tepee is the focus of the Indian exhibit, a sheepwagon and chuckwagon commemorate the life of the early stockman, and there's also a re-creation of a frontier town.

Food
If you like a good steak and you like a Western bar atmosphere, then you'll treasure **Sam's Supper Club**, 307 First Ave. N, tel. 228-4614. The clientele, a mix of cowboys, anglers, and businessmen, converge here for the outstanding beef. Another Glasgow institution is **Johnnie Café**, 433 First Ave. S, tel. 228-4222, an old 24-hour downtown diner where Glasgowans gather. The dining room at the **Cottonwood Inn**, east on Hwy. 2, tel. 228-8213, is open from 6 a.m.-10 p.m., and offers chicken and pork dishes in addition to the compulsory steaks.

Eugene's Pizza, 193 Klein, tel. 228-8552, open 4 p.m.-midnight, serves Glasgow's best pizza. If you've ever wondered what goes on in fraternal organizations, plan to eat at the **Glasgow Elks Club Dining Room**, 309 Second Ave. S, tel. 228-2233; the lodge dining room is now open to the public for lunch and dinner from 9 a.m.-9 p.m.

FORT PECK FACTS

Construction crews at Fort Peck moved 130 million cubic yards of dirt and replaced it with four million cubic yards of gravel and 1.6 million cubic yards of riprap. The reservoir has the capacity to store 19 million acre-feet of water (the runoff from one-third of Montana), although recently the Corps of Engineers has chosen to keep the level of upstream Missouri dams like Fort Peck far below historic water levels. The maximum depth of the lake is 220 feet.

The construction technique that built Fort Peck Dam is called "hydraulic fill." The sediment from the Missouri River bottom was pumped to the dam face as slurry, where it was drained into rock structures that trapped the mud and let the water drain away. More rock was then layered on top of this earth embankment. The dam stretches from bluff to bluff across the Missouri, a distance of 3 1/2 miles.

Information
Contact the **Glasgow Chamber of Commerce** at 110 Fifth St. S, Glasgow, MT 59230, tel. (406) 228-2222.

The **Dept. of Fish, Wildlife, and Parks** is at Hwy. 2 W, Glasgow, MT 59230, tel. 228-9347.

The **BLM** office is west on Hwy. 2, tel. 228-4316.

Transportation
Amtrak passes through Glasgow twice a day, once going east, once going west. Call (800) 872-7245 for information; the depot, at 424 First Ave. S, is operated by the Burlington Northern and endures Amtrak traffic without promoting it. Three flights a day link Glasgow to Billings on **Big Sky Air**, tel. (800) 882-4475. **Budget Rent-A-Car** is at 626 Second Ave. S, tel. 228-9595.

FORT PECK

History
In the fall of 1933, workers began to clear brush in preparation for the building of Fort Peck Dam. The largest and most ambitious of Franklin Roosevelt's Public Works projects, construction of the dam created jobs for tens of thousands of people during the Great Depression and altered the face of Montana. At the time of its completion, Fort Peck was the largest reservoir in the world. Fifty years later, 150 miles long, with a shoreline longer than California's, it is still the planet's second-largest earth-fill reservoir.

The Army Corps of Engineers justified the expense of Fort Peck ($150 million) by promising better river navigation, flood control, hydroelectric generation, and irrigation possibilities. But Fort Peck's biggest impact on Montana was the amount of jobs it provided. During the seven years of construction, at one time or another, 50,000 people worked at the dam.

The Corps of Engineers built a showpiece town to house its personnel and serve as the dam headquarters. Named after the old trading post, Fort Peck also contained an enormous theater and a grand hotel, each built in the arts-and-crafts style characteristic of New Deal architecture.

But handsome, well-planned Fort Peck was not where the workers lived or played. The towns that grew up to service this largely young, energetic, and migratory work force quickly accrued reputations for wild times that would have made Bannack jealous. Shanty boomtowns like Wheeler, New Deal, and Park Grove shot up, invigorated with government cash and hard-won

Fort Peck was the nation's largest Public Works project.

GLASGOW ACCOMMODATIONS

Name	Address	Phone	Rates	Features
Cottonwood Inn	Hwy. 2 E	228-8213, (800) 321-8213	38, $4 d	Glasgow's newest
Koski's Motel	Hwy. 2 E	228-8282	$31 s, $36 d	
Campbell Lodge	534 Third Ave. S	228-9328	$26 s, $31 d	downtown and venerable
Rustic Lodge	700 First Ave. N	228-2451	$30 s, $41 d	
Roosevelt Hotel	412 Third Ave. S	228-4341	$21 s, $25 d	the old downtown hotel
Star Lodge Motel	Hwy. 2 W	228-2494	$21 s, $32 d	
La Casa Motel	238 First Ave. N	228-9311	$23 s, $32 d	

1930's *jouissance*. For its first issue (Nov. 23, 1936), *Life* magazine sent Margaret Bourke-White to Fort Peck to chronicle life on this new frontier. Little remains of this short and incandescent moment of Montana's development except derelict buildings and memories of landmarks like the Buckhorn Bar, destroyed by fire in 1983.

Sights
The **Fort Peck Power Plants** near the junction of Hwys. 24 and 117, tel. 526-3411, offer tours of the turbines and electrical-generation facilities. Call ahead for times; the facilities sometimes close for repairs. The main power plant also houses the **Fort Peck Museum**, which contains an excellent collection of prehistoric fossils and Indian relics discovered while building the dam.

While the town of Fort Peck will not overwhelm the visitor with sheer size, some of the old Public Works buildings are astonishing relics. The **Fort Peck Theater** on Main St., tel. 526-9943, was built in 1934 as a cinema in an imposing and somewhat squatty chalet style, all the better to accommodate its 1,100-patron capacity. It's hard to imagine a grander example of New Deal architecture. For over 20 years, the theater has been home to one of the state's best summer theater companies. The shows run June through August; call (800) 828-2259 for details. The **Fort Peck Hotel** on Missouri Ave. and the dam's **administration building** on Kansas Ave. were built at the same time, and share the 1930s' grandiose architectural vision.

Fort Peck Theater

BOB RACE

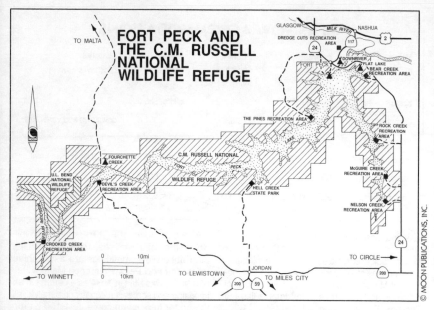

There's excellent wildlife viewing just downstream from the dam. Starting at the Downstream Campground, the **Beaver Creek Nature Trail** winds along brushy streams and ponds; interpretive signs point out habitat and help identify species. Larger mammals, like deer, pronghorn, and buffalo can be seen along an auto trail at the **Leo B. Coleman Wildlife Exhibit**, which begins just across from the C.M.R. refuge headquarters on Hwy. 117.

If there's any question in your mind about the meaning of the term "badlands," then continue south of Fort Peck on Hwy. 24 toward Hwy. 200. Like a boat cresting waves, the road peaks and troughs through sandstone uplands and spectacular badland ridges and valleys. This land is adjacent to the C.M.R. and offers opportunities for viewing pronghorn, mule deer, coyote, and other prairie residents.

Accommodations

The **Fort Peck Hotel**, on Missouri Ave., tel. (406) 526-3266, is one of Montana's most unusual lodgings. This venerable three-story log hotel contains 47 rooms, a bar, and a dining room. Little has changed at this clean and efficient hotel since the '30s, but that is all the more

draw for anyone who hankers for a taste of bygone days; doubles begin at $28. If charm isn't necessary, there are also cabins at the **Lakeridge Motel and Conoco**, just west of Fort Peck on Hwy. 24, tel. 526-3597, $26 d.

Camping

There are numerous campgrounds around Fort Peck Dam, all with access to fishing. Just under the bluff from Fort Peck Town on Hwy. 117 is the **Downstream Campground**; it's a great site, but bring the insect repellent. Likewise, the **Dredge Cut Campground** is three miles north of Fort Peck on Hwy. 117, where there's good fishing for walleye and northern pike. On the lake itself is **West End Campground**, three miles west of Fort Peck off Hwy. 24.

Food

The **Fort Peck Hotel**, tel. 526-3266, offers tasty and sometimes imaginative food in a great dining room reminiscent of summer camp; open 6:30 a.m.-9 p.m. For a short-order meal with cocktails, try the **Gateway Inn**, ("The best dam bar by a dam site"), west of Fort Peck on Hwy. 24, tel. 526-9988.

Recreation

The Fort Peck area offers the best recreational opportunities in eastern Montana. The 245,000-acre reservoir contains sturgeon, northern pike, walleye, paddlefish, sauger, channel catfish, and lake trout. Locals also use the lake for water-skiing, sailing, parasailing, and windsurfing. There are six recreation areas within four miles of the dam itself and a dozen others farther afield. The best and most accessible fishing areas are south along Hwy. 24, along the Big Dry Arm.

From the mouth of the Musselshell on, the Missouri River has cut down through the Hell Creek Formation; it contains one of the richest records of prehistoric life in the world. No angler or boater goes to Fort Peck Lake without keeping an eye open for fossils, and others, taken more by the Cretaceous-era outcroppings than the jet sailing, come to the lake expressly to hunt fossils. Although fossil excavation isn't al-

lowed on the C.M. R. Wildlife Refuge itself, often banks of sandstone and shale offer up fossils for viewing, particularly petrified fish, mollusks, and leaf imprints.

A word of warning: if you are exploring Fort Peck environs on back roads, head back to pavement at *the first sign* of rain; the gumbo hills quickly become impassably slick. Also, boaters need to pay attention to storm and wind warnings. Intense thunderstorms build quickly along the prairies; high winds can cause waves high enough to be a hazard for small boats.

Information

For more information on Fort Peck Dam, contact the **Corps of Engineers**, E. Kansas St., Fort Peck, MT 59223, tel. (406) 526-3411.

The Fort Peck office for the **C.M. Russell National Wildlife Refuge** is north along Hwy. 117, tel. 526-3464.

THE NORTHEAST CORNER

In Montana's northeast corner, the center does not hold. Up here the locals keep one eye on Canada, one on North Dakota, and their back to the rest of Montana.

Saskatchewan is at least as important to Plentywood and Scobey as is, say, western Montana. Canadians pour over the border by the thousands, both to shop and to carouse. Considering that goods are already significantly cheaper in the U.S. than in Canada, and that Montana doesn't even *have* a sales tax, for many Canadians shopping in northern Montana isn't a weekend's amusement but an economic necessity.

Montana too has some of the most relaxed liquor laws in the nation, while Saskatchewan has some of Canada's most restrictive. Montana allows gambling in many forms; Saskatchewan doesn't. Add up this equation and you have, in the middle of these arid unpopulated prairies, a couple of the most unlikely holiday towns in the country.

But this corner of Montana isn't just festivities and holidaymaking on the northern plains. Surrounding Plentywood and Scobey is rich farmland, pressed flat as table linen by ancient glaciers, with an occasional divot carved out for small farm ponds. Medicine Lake Wildlife Refuge

is one of the state's foremost areas for viewing migratory waterfowl and other prairie species. Both Scobey and Plentywood offer fine museums that commemorate the homesteaders who helped tame the Wild West.

SCOBEY

With sufficient rain, Scobey (pop. 1,154, elev. 2,450 feet) is at the center of some of the most productive wheat-growing land in the state. As in Saskatchewan, the growing season is too short to depend on the grain to ripen for combining. When the seed heads are fully grown but not yet dried and golden-colored, farmers cut the grain into windrows. The wind and sun quickly dry the plants into straw and ripened kernels, and the grain is then combined off the ground.

Scobey, like many other towns along the Great Northern Railroad, was settled principally by Scandinavians; it's now a trading town for local farmers and ranchers, as well as visiting Canadians. Only 17 miles from Saskatchewan, the Canadian influence is strong. Canadian radio is pervasive on the airwaves, the occasional "Eh?" sneaks into conversations, and—

most damning—Montana's only curling rink is found in Scobey.

Sights

Pioneer Town, a project of the Daniels County Museum, is one of the state's best walk-through museums. Basically a re-creation of an early homesteader town, the 20-acre site contains 40 buildings, some with period furnishings. Included are a restored schoolhouse, barber shop, blacksmith shop, and undertaker's office, a two-story hotel, two churches, and vintage automobiles and farm equipment. The historical archives for the county are also kept here.

Pioneer Town is just west of town, off Second Avenue. It's open daily 1-5, Memorial Day-Labor Day, or by appointment the rest of the year. Call the Daniels County Museum at 487-5965 for details.

Accommodations And Food

Scobey's newest motel is the **Cattle King Motor Inn** on the south edge of town on Hwy. 13, tel. (406) 487-5332, $40 d. The **Juel Motel**, 514 Main, tel. 487-2765, $27 d, and the **J.O. Motor Inn**, 9 Main, tel. 487-5408, $32 d, are downtown and a bit more lived-in.

The **Cozy Café**, 15 Main, tel. 487-5370, is a family-style diner with light meals. The **Ponderosa**, 102 Main, tel. 487-5001, is a bar and grill that also serves pizza. The **Silver Slipper** is the local supper club.

Information And Services

Contact the **Scobey Chamber of Commerce** at P.O. Box 91, 59263, tel. (406) 487-5961.

The **Daniels Memorial Hospital** is at 105 Fifth Ave. E, tel. 487-2296. Contact the **sheriff** at 487-2691. Reach the **border patrol** at the Port of Scobey, tel. 487-2621.

PLENTYWOOD

Located just about as far as it could get from the centers of Montana trade and power, Plentywood (pop. 2,136, elev. 2,024 feet) is closer to Winnipeg than to Helena; Minneapolis is closer than Dillon. But Plentywood isn't any the less Montana-like for it. In fact, Canadians love to visit Plentywood precisely because it is so much more Wild and Western—that is, Montanan—than their prairie provinces.

By the way, only on a vast and treeless plain would a cowboy be reduced to calling a place Plentywood simply (so the story goes) because he found enough wood to build a fire.

History

For such a far-flung locality, Plentywood is in the mainstream of Montana history. The Sioux chief Sitting Bull and his followers passed through this area after the Battle of the Little Bighorn in 1876. After living for five years safely in southern Saskatchewan, they moved south and surrendered to U.S. Army officials at the present site of Plentywood.

After the military evacuated the Indians, the plains of northern Montana became rangeland. However, the presence of valuable cattle and horses, combined with the absence of any effective law enforcement, made the area popular with rustlers. The Outlaw Trail, so named by Butch Cassidy, crossed the Canadian line just north of Plentywood. Gangs of rustlers drove stolen Canadian cattle across the border here and followed Cassidy's trail across the most lawless and inaccessible parts of Montana on their way to markets in the Southwest.

During the early 1900s, a number of shady characters lived in the gulches north of Plentywood. Unembarrassed to smuggle whiskey, to alter brands after ferrying livestock back and forth across the border, or to rob a train, these denim-collared criminals earned the area a reputation, according to an early brand inspector, as the "most lawless and crookedest" in the state.

After the Great Northern brought in homesteaders in the 1910s, Plentywood gained quite a different reputation. Not finding either of the two major political parties to their liking, early homesteaders formed the Farmer-Labor Party. Throughout the 1920s, this socialist-leaning party controlled county politics. In the 1930 general election, 300 Sheridan County residents voted straight-ticket Communist Party.

Today, the county's progressive politics are expressed in the quality of its public institutions, parks, and recreational facilities.

Sights

The **Sheridan County Museum** at the fairgrounds on the east side of Plentywood, tel. 765-2219, contains memorabilia from frontier and homesteading days. On the museum grounds is the **Old Tractor Club**, a huge collection of vintage tractors and farm equipment.

Accommodations
The **Sherwood Inn**, 515 W. First Ave., tel. (406) 765-2810, $37 d, continues the illusion that there are forests here; there is also a lounge (**Robin Hood's**) and restaurant (**Fryer Tuck's**). The truth-in-naming laurel goes to the **Plains Motel**, 626 W. First Ave., tel. 765-1240, a comfortable older lodging. Choose between the new wing ($36 d) or the old ($30 d). There are free campsites at the city park at the north end of Box Elder Street.

Food
For light meals, try the **Alta Vista Café**, 564 W. First Ave., or **Randy's Restaurant**, 323 W. First Ave., tel. 765-1661. **Fergie's Pizza**, 114 S. Main, tel. 765-1744, delivers for free. For steaks, drinks, and dancing, try the **Loft Supper Club**, 105 S. Main, tel. 765-2350, or the **Blue Moon Supper Club** east of Plentywood on Hwy. 5, tel. 765-2491.

Information And Services
Contact the **Plentywood Chamber of Commerce** at P.O. Box 4, Plentywood, MT 59254, tel. (406) 765-1810.

Reach the **sheriff** at 765-1200. **Sheridan Memorial Hospital** is at 440 W. Laurel Ave., tel. 765-1420.

Reach the **U.S. Border Control** at the Port of Raymond, tel. 765-1852.

MEDICINE LAKE NATIONAL WILDLIFE REFUGE

Medicine Lake lies in an old channel of the Missouri River. Before the ice ages, the Missouri flowed north from near Culbertson along this watercourse, eventually to empty into Hudson's Bay. Ice sheets blocked this channel about 15,000 years ago, and the Missouri sought more southerly outlets. Now the broad valley once dominated by the river holds a series of shallow lakes.

Established in 1935, the **Medicine Lake National Wildlife Refuge**, tel. 789-2305, is a superior example of a prairie lake ecosystem. Containing 31,000 acres of lake, wetlands, and prairie, the refuge is home to enormous numbers of ducks (10 different species) and geese, as well as pelicans, herons, grebes, and cranes. Pronghorn and white-tailed deer are common along brushy coulees. In an area called the Sandhills are stands of chokecherry, buffalo berry, and native prairie grasses; hiking trails cross the rolling hills.

In 1976, 11,360 acres of the refuge were designated a wilderness area. No motorized boats are allowed on the lake. On the 18-mile auto tour around the lake, one of the 10 stops is the **Tepee Hills Site.** Here, rings of stone indicate the sites of ancient Indian lodges perhaps 4,000 years old.

THE FORT PECK INDIAN RESERVATION AND VICINITY

East of Fort Peck Dam, the Missouri River flows down a wide fertile valley lined by cottonwood trees. Extending north and south of the river are the relentless and austere plains. Also north of the river is the Fort Peck Indian Reservation, the state's second largest, and home to the Yanktonai Sioux and Assiniboine tribes. Highway 2 follows the course of the Missouri, linking old river-freighting centers and ranch towns like Wolf Point and Poplar.

HISTORY

The Assiniboine Indians moved south out of Canada into Montana in the late 1700s, where they lived along the Missouri River. They became willing partners with the early white traders. In 1837, a boat carrying smallpox reached Fort Union. The disease quickly spread to the Assiniboine natives encamped outside the trading post. Smallpox raged through the Assiniboine Nation, killing an estimated two-thirds of the tribe.

Greatly weakened as a society, the Assiniboine quickly agreed to the constraints and protections of early reservation treaties and settled along the Missouri. When smallpox again broke out amongst the Indians upriver at Fort Belknap, these Assiniboine quickly moved farther down the Missouri to live with the Yanktonai Sioux near Fort Peck, thereby avoiding the epidemic.

The Sioux Nation was one of the greatest of the Indian tribal confederations. The branch that came to inhabit the northern prairies of Montana is called the Yanktonai Sioux. They originally roamed the prairie provinces of Canada until forced into Montana. Here, rolling waves of displaced Indians came to a congested, chaotic halt.

The Yanktonai were part of the alliance that fought Custer in 1876; this triumph didn't forestall their enclosure in the huge Indian territory north of the Missouri the following year. When the Great Northern sought to put a railway across northern Montana in the late 1880s, the U.S.

government renegotiated the reservations to allow the railway right-of-way. The Sioux and Assiniboine were assigned to their present reservation in 1888.

Fort Peck Reservation was one of the worst affected reservations under the Dawes Act. Seeking to turn these nomadic tribesmen into agrarian landowners, this federal program allocated homestead-sized pieces of land to individual Indians. The surplus land then became available to non-Indians. Because of the size of the Fort Peck Reservation (2.1 million acres) and the paucity of Indians (about 2,000 at the time), only 46% of the reservation is now owned by Native Americans.

WOLF POINT

History

Wolf Point (pop. 2,880, elev. 2,004 feet) began as a trading post on the Missouri. The name apparently derives from an event in the fur-trading days. During an especially harsh winter, trappers had good luck trapping and poisoning wolves. However, the wolves froze solid before they could be skinned, so the trappers piled the carcasses along the river's edge, to be skinned in the spring. But when the trappers returned, Indians had taken control of the landing, and the trappers were forced to abandon their booty. The putrefying wolves became a landmark for steamboat crews.

Wolf Point is now a trade town for local farmers and ranchers and a center for the Sioux and Assiniboine. Grain-storage facilities here can warehouse 1.5 million bushels of grain, making Wolf Point one of the state's most important terminals. The Wolf Point Wild Horse Stampede is the state's oldest organized rodeo, and one of the best.

Sights

The **Wolf Point Area Historical Society Museum,** 220 Second Ave. S, tel. 653-1912, contains artifacts from its early frontier and homesteading days, plus a reliquary devoted to native-son trick roper Montie Montana (and his horse Rex).

Seven miles east of Wolf Point, on Hwy. 13, is **Lewis and Clark Memorial Park**. The park straddles the north bank of the Missouri River, and with its wealth of shady cottonwoods is a good picnic area. It was from groves such as these that early wood hawks made a rugged living felling trees to feed the engines of steamboats that trundled the river between St. Louis and Fort Benton. Watch for stumps and fallen trees amongst the younger stands.

Along this stretch of the Missouri, the local Indians too quickly learned that there was money to be made in selling wood. Cedar wood fetched a higher price than cottonwood; the canny natives would paint the ends of cottonwood logs red and then demand cedar prices for it. When the river was too low for the boats to approach the bank where the Indians were trying to sell wood, they would squat in the shallow water with only their heads above water to give the impression that the river was shoulder deep.

Accommodations

In downtown Wolf Point, the **Sherman Motor Inn**, 200 Main St., tel. (406) 653-1100, $28 d, is the town's most comfortable lodging option, with a good restaurant, lounge, and convention facilities on-site. Other motels string along Hwy. 2. The **Big Sky Motel**, 6007 Hwy. 2 E, tel. 653-2300 $28 d, sits on the eastern edge of Wolf Point. The **Homestead Inn**, 101 Hwy. 2 E, tel. 653-1300, $31, is nearer the old center of town.

Rancho Campground is one mile west on Hwy. 2, tel. 653-2500. At the junction of Hwys. 2 and 13 (seven miles east of Wolf Point) is **R.B.W. Campground,** tel. 525-3740.

Food

There are a number of drive-ins and fast-food parlors along Hwy. 2, but it's worth driving downtown to find better atmosphere. The restaurant at the **Sherman Motor Inn**, 200 E. Main, tel. 653-1100, is the nicest in town, with a menu that offers alternatives to the beef pervasive in most eastern Montana eateries; open 6 a.m.-10 p.m.

Join the locals at two venerable downtown cafés for light meals and sandwiches: Both the **Stockman's Café**, 220 Main, tel. 653-2287, and the **Wolf Point Café**, 217 Main, tel. 653-

9910, make one recall when times, and foods, were simpler.

Events

The **Wolf Point Wild Horse Stampede** began in Wolf Point as an Indian celebration of horse racing and horsemanship. Early cowboys found the event to their liking and joined in. The Stampede became a full-blown rodeo in 1915, after it was sanctioned by the Rodeo Cowboy Association. Today, it is the oldest and one of the most prestigious rodeos in Montana, where rodeo events alternate with Indian dancers in a mutual celebration of shared culture. The Wolf Point Stampede is held the second weekend in July, with three separate rodeos and parades. Contact the chamber of commerce for further details.

The Assiniboine celebrate **Red Bottom Day** west of Wolf Point at Frazer the third weekend of June. The powwow involves singing, traditional dancing, a giveaway, and a display of handmade wares.

Information

Contact the **Wolf Point Chamber of Commerce** at 201 Fourth Ave. S, Wolf Point, MT, tel. (406) 653-2012.

Getting There And Around

Amtrak's Western District ends in Wolf Point, and two trains a day pass through. The depot is on Front St., tel. 653-2350. **Big Sky Airlines** flies between Billings and Wolf Point three times a day; call (800) 882-4475.

POPLAR

Poplar (pop. 881, elev. 1,963 feet) is the agency town for the Fort Peck Indian Reservation. Like many a Missouri River town, Poplar had its fitful beginnings as an Indian trading post and freighting center for furs and buffalo robes. Its pulse quickened when the Great Northern went through in 1887, and the Fort Peck Reservation was carved and centered here the following year.

Besides the Indian agency offices, Poplar is home to **NAES College,** a tribal community college, and **A & S Industries.** A & S, a tribally owned business, employs over 400 people to make camouflage netting and medical chests for the U.S. government. A large and heavy-producing oil field lies just north of town.

Sights

The **Poplar Museum** is located east of Poplar on Hwy. 2, in the old tribal jail. In addition to Indian artifacts, the museum also relates the history of the Assiniboine and Sioux reservation. Open daily 11 a.m.-5 p.m. Memorial Day-Labor Day, tel. 768-3916.

Accommodations And Food

Lee Ann's Motel, 150 F St., Hwy. 2, tel. (406) 768-5442, $28 d, offers clean, snug rooms, some with kitchenettes. **Bud's RV Park**, one mile east on Hwy. 2, tel. 768-3392, is open April through November.

Try the **Buckhorn Café**, 217 Second Ave. W (behind the bar) for light meals, with Indian tacos a favorite. Steaks, and good ones, are the specialty at the **American Legion Supper Club**, 127 A St. E, tel. 768-3923.

Events

The **Iron Ring Celebration**, held the third weekend of July in Poplar, commemorates the last Sioux chief with dancing and a powwow. The Assiniboine and Sioux collectively host **Oil Discovery Celebration**, a powwow held the last weekend of August to memorialize the 1950s discovery of oil on the reservation.

Information

Contact the Fort Peck Tribal Council at P.O. Box 1027, Poplar, MT 59255, tel. (406) 768-5311.

FORT UNION AND VICINITY

"A judicious position for the purpose of trade," is what Capt. William Clark recorded at the confluence of Montana's two mighty east-flowing rivers, the Missouri and the Yellowstone. And traders quickly agreed. The American Fur Company built the region's grandest fur-trading post here in 1828, overlooking the juncture of the two rivers. Fort Union prospered in the 1830s and '40s as it became the undisputed focus of the Montana fur trade.

Today, the site is administered by the National Park Service, which is in the process of reconstructing the fort as it stood in 1851.

FORT UNION

History

Lewis and Clark camped at the confluence of the Missouri and Yellowstone rivers on their way into Montana and again as they exited a year later. Upon arriving in late April, 1805, they were glad to have made it to this famous landmark, where the forks of the Missouri divide. The captains allotted each member of the Corps a dram of whiskey in celebration; the fiddle came out, and the evening was spent in song and dance. The expedition continued up the Missouri River.

Though overwhelmed with mosquitoes, on his return trip Clark recognized the strategic na-

ture of this site. These two enormous, easily navigable rivers drained a vast region rich in wildlife. Whoever controlled the Missouri and Yellowstone confluence controlled the wealth of the two river basins.

During the early 1800s, although the Americans controlled the trade on the Yellowstone and had made friends with the Crow Indians, the Missouri River all the way to Three Forks was controlled by the Blackfeet, who, through trade for firearms, were allied to the English in Canada. The Americans attempted again and again to establish trade with the Blackfeet, with uniformly bloody results.

In 1828, John Jacob Astor (of the American Fur Company) ordered Kenneth McKenzie to build a trading fort at the confluence of the Yellowstone and Missouri, and to break the British hegemony over trade in the Missouri. McKenzie dispatched a trapper who spoke the Blackfoot language to induce warriors to accompany him back to Fort Union. Showered with gifts, the Blackfeet shortly entered into trade at Fort Union. With the Blackfeet suddenly compliant, and (starting in 1832) with steamboat service to Fort Union, all of Montana was open for exploitation. Until the 1850s, Fort Union reigned undisputed over Montana trade.

McKenzie, powerful, unscrupulous, and vain, built up Fort Union to be the most elegant habita-

Fort Union

W. C. McRAE

tion west of St. Louis. Liveried servants poured French wines into crystal goblets at his table; bag-pipers piped as he entered his dining room; native chiefs were sometimes greeted by McKenzie in full chain mail. The list of guests at Fort Union reads like a Who's Who of the American West: painters Karl Bodmer, George Catlin, and J.J. Audubon, German Prince Maximilian, Father DeSmet, Jim Bridger, and Governor Isaac Stevens.

The enormous success of Fort Union was not based solely on geography. Although it was illegal to sell alcohol to the Indians, McKenzie established a still at Fort Union and used alcohol to cement native loyalty to his trading post and the U.S. This was not a fine single malt that he traded to the Indians for furs: an early recipe for "Indian whiskey" cut McKenzie's homemade liquor with river water, cayenne pepper, tobacco, sagebrush, and a dash of strychnine.

The damage to the Plains Indians begun by alcohol at Fort Union was hastened by the arrival of the steamboat *Saint Peter* in 1837. The Assiniboine camped at Fort Union contracted smallpox from the crew; from here it spread quickly amongst the Indians in northern Montana. An estimated 15,000 of them died from the disease that year.

As fur-bearing animals in Montana approached extinction, Fort Union waned. By 1867, it had fallen into disrepair; some buildings were dismantled to build Fort Buford two miles downstream, and the remainder was sold by wood hawkers as steamboat fuel.

Sights

Behind 20-foot-high palisades situated on the high banks of the Missouri River, the reconstructed **Fort Union Trading Post National Historic Site** is again the focus of traffic at the Yellowstone and Missouri confluence. The **Bourgeois House** was the home of the fort's factor, or governor. The building was reconstructed as an exact replica of the surprisingly elegant 1851 house seen in paintings of the time; it now houses the visitor center and a good museum detailing the history of trade and early frontier life on the Missouri.

From the palisades, the Missouri and Yellowstone confluence can be seen, and it's easy to imagine steamboats pulling up to the embankment to load up with furs.

The National Park Service is in the process of rebuilding the rest of Fort Union. With the fortifications erected, the **Indian Trade House,** where Natives swapped beaver, mink, and marten skins for rifles, trinkets, and whiskey, is next scheduled for completion.

During the summer the **Fort Union Rendezvous** takes place. At this reenactment of an 1800s trappers gathering, hundreds of buckskin clad, musket-bearing, tepee-dwelling people gather to celebrate frontier-era skills and fortitude. There're also hatchet-throwing contests, food cooked à la frontier, and black-powder rifle shooting. Contact the fort for dates.

It's important to note that Fort Union is not a commercial reconstruction: this isn't a theme park, and it's not just for kids. The fort is one of the most informative and satisfying stops in this part of Montana, definitely worth a detour.

The **Fort Union Trading Post National Historic Site**, Buford Rte., Williston, ND 58801, tel. (701) 572-9083, is located only yards east of the Montana border in North Dakota.

Fort Buford And The Missouri/Yellowstone Confluence

Two miles farther into North Dakota are the remains of Fort Buford. Built in 1866 in the midst of hostile Sioux territory, the fort was conceived less as a military staging site than as a thorn in the side of the Sioux. About half the buildings at old Fort Union were dismantled and brought here to be rebuilt. Little remains but a few frame buildings and the fort's 1860s graveyard; reading the tombstones gives a fascinating glimpse of what life—and death—were like at this frontier outpost.

Just east of the ruins of Fort Buford along the same road is the confluence of the Yellowstone and Missouri rivers. A nice picnic area on a broad embankment overlooks this historic crossroads. A respectful stillness seems to encroach: these two prodigious rivers, meeting beneath yellow bluffs in a tangle of cottonwoods, willows, and a crisp dialogue of waters, have embraced almost all of Montana.

During the heyday of Fort Union, the confluence was farther upstream, near the fort. But in compliance with some fluvial law, their junction has drifted eastward.

CULBERTSON AND VICINITY

As the valleys of the Yellowstone and Missouri prepare to meet, a ridge of high, gray badland buttes rise to the south. To the north, the prairies begin their flat sweep to Canada.

The land here is rich, and grain production has dominated the local economy since the Great Northern Railroad brought homesteaders here to plow. If good soil wasn't enough in itself, nature also found time to bury a wealth of oil here.

Culbertson (pop. 796, elev. 1,921 feet) has come a long way since the day in 1892 when a young woman stepped from the train at Culbertson station and spent some time looking for the town; where she came from, two buildings did not constitute a town. Early ranchers engaged in horse ranching; the many military forts along this length of the Missouri demanded a large number of mounts. Now a pleasant farming town, Culbertson sits at the crossroads between northern Montana and Saskatchewan.

Accommodations And Food

The **King's Inn**, 408 E. Sixth, tel. (406) 787-6277, $30 d, is a modern, attractive motel along Hwy. 2. There's free camping in the city's **Bicentennial Park**.

The **Wild West Diner**, 20 E. Sixth, tel. 787-5374, is a classic roadside café with a pleasingly unassuming menu. **M & M's Place,** 14 E. Sixth, tel. 787-5362, is a family restaurant near the junction of Hwys. 2 and 16.

Information And Services

Contact the **Culbertson Chamber of Commerce** at P.O. Box 633, Culbertson, MT 59218, tel. 787-5821. **Roosevelt Memorial Hospital** is at 818 Second Ave. E, tel. 787-6281.

HIGHWAY 200: FAIRVIEW TO CIRCLE

The highway system in Montana almost exclusively follows river valleys or old rail lines, but there's one marked departure from the general rule. Highway 200 enters eastern Montana near the Yellowstone/Missouri confluence and, like a sensible highway, follows the Yellowstone Valley to Sidney. Then, perversely, it lights off west across the prairie, toward nowhere in particular.

Between Sidney and Lewistown—a distance of almost 300 miles—Hwy. 200 passes through only three towns with gas pumps; their *combined* population approaches 1,500 people. As it connects up these remote enclaves of humanity, Hwy. 200 intersects a part of Montana often called the Big Lonely. Unpopulated, marginally productive, and often starkly beautiful, this is one of the last vast frontiers left in Montana.

Fairview

Squat on the Montana-Dakota state line and 11 miles east of Sidney is Fairview, a small farming town in the heart of sugar beet country. Fairview's principal claim to fame is that half the town is in North Dakota. There's camping in **Fairview City Park**, complete with RV hookups, playground, swimming pool, and picnic facilities.

SIDNEY AND VICINITY

Although stockmen had begun to establish ranches along this stretch of the Yellowstone Valley in the 1880s, it took the Lower Yellowstone Project, a federally funded irrigation project begun in 1904, to put Sidney (pop. 5,726, elev. 1,928 feet) on the map. The wide, fertile valley fell to the plow and hip waders. Sugar beets became the principal crop, inducing Holly Sugar to build a refinery here.

In the 1950s, Sidney found itself on the edge of the Williston Basin, a huge oil reserve. Sidney moved from sugar town to oil town seamlessly, accruing the economic benefits.

Sights

One of the largest community museums in this part of the state, the **Mondak Heritage Center**, 120 Third Ave. SE, tel. 482-3500, open Tues.-Sun., combines the function of a regional art center and local history museum. In addition to displays of area history, the basement houses a re-creation of an old-time Sidney street.

Accommodations

The recent oil boom has had an ameliorative effect on the quality of lodging in Sidney. The **Lone Tree Inn**, 900 S. Central, tel. (406) 482-4520, $36 d, and the **Richland Motor Inn**, 1200 S. Central, tel. 482-6400, $40 d, are both modern, attractive, hotel-like lodging complexes. The **Angus Ranch House Motel**, 2300 S. Central, tel. 482-3826, $22 d, low-slung and rambling, at least preserves the quiddity of a motel. The **Park Plaza Motel**, 601 S. Central, tel. 482-1520, $26 s, near city center, is perfectly adequate but more modest. The **Lalonde Hotel**, 217 S. Central, tel. 482-1043, $23 d, is Sidney's old downtown hotel; though cheap and convenient, it does suffer from a rather dire late-'60s make-over.

Camping

Six miles east of Sidney on Hwy. 200 is **Richland Park**. This fishing-access area and campground is shaded by cottonwood and elm trees, and provides latrines, potable water, picnic facilities, and a playground. If you plan to camp

prickly pear cactus, Opuntia polyacantha

overnight, don't leave Sidney until you get permission and buy a $1 ticket from the Richland County Sheriff's Department, 110 Second Ave. NW, tel. 482-7700.

Food

For breakfast and light meals, try the **M & M**, south of Sidney on Hwy. 200, tel. 482-1714, open daily 5 a.m.-7 p.m., or **Gulliver's**, 120 E. Main, tel. 482-5175, open for breakfast and lunch. There's Chinese cooking at **Eagle Café**, 102 E. Main, tel. 482-1839, open 4:30 p.m.-10:30 p.m., and the **Hunann Restaurant**, 821 S. Central, tel. 482-1118, open 11 a.m.-9:30 p.m.

For steaks or seafood, go to the **South 40**, 207 Second Ave., tel. 482-4999, open Mon.-Thurs. 11 a.m.-10:30 p.m., Fri. and Sat. 11-11, Sun. 9 a.m.-10 p.m.; or the **Triangle**, south of Sidney on Hwy. 23, tel. 482-9948, open nightly from 5 p.m. The dining room at the Lalonde Hotel, called **La Chateau**, tel. 482-1043 serves a good meal, and is open from 6 a.m.-10 p.m.

Transportation

Big Sky Airlines flies into Sidney twice a day from Williston; call (800) 882-4475 for details.

Information And Services

Contact the **Sidney Chamber of Commerce** at 909 S. Central Ave., Sidney, MT 59270, tel. (406) 482-1916. **Community Memorial Hospital** is at 216 14th Ave. SW, tel. 482-7700.

RICHEY

Between Sidney and Circle, Hwy. 200 climbs up over gravel hills and out of the Yellowstone drainage. The countryside opens up into a wide basin garnished here and there with ranch buildings. In good years, deer and pronghorn are abundant, making this area popular with hunters.

The urban instinct is weak here; the little crossroads of Richey (pop. 259) represents one of this region's few experiments in city living. Richey is a pleasant little hamlet dominated by grain elevators; the **Richey Historical Museum**, tel. 773-5656, commemorates the homesteading boom that followed the Great Northern line into town. The **Farmer's Kitchen Café**, tel. 773-5533, serves up tasty food designed to satisfy a ranch-hand's appetite; open 6 a.m.-7 p.m.

CIRCLE

Circle (pop. 805, elev. 2,450 feet) got its start as a cattle town during the open-range years. The biggest outfit hereabouts had a simple circle for its brand, hence the name for the settlement that grew up beside it. Both the Northern Pacific and the Great Northern schemed about extending into Circle; this alone was sufficient to bring in grain-farming homesteaders who had plans for the flat grazing lands of the Redwater River Valley.

South of Circle are the Big Sheep Mountains, obviously named by people who hadn't seen a mountain recently. Actually little more than a series of high sandstone ridges, they mark the watershed between the Yellowstone and Missouri drainages. At one time, Audubon mountain sheep grazed along these chokecherry-laden bluffs. They live on in the name of the mountains only: like the buffalo, early frontiersmen found them an easy, tasty prey, and hunted them to extinction.

Sights

The **McCone County Museum**, west of town on Hwy. 200, tel. 485-2414, contains displays commemorating the Circle's frontier history. On the museum grounds are a restored country schoolhouse, an old church, and a caboose from the Northern Pacific.

Accommodations And Food

The **Gladstone Hotel and Motel**, on the corner of Main and Hwy. 200, tel. (406) 485-3311, $27 d, is Circle's old downtown hotel, listed on the National Register of Historic Places. The **Traveler's Inn**, at the junction of Hwys. 13 and 200, tel. 485-3323, is half open and offers a more modern alternative to the Gladstone; $31 d. There's RV parking at **Scheer's Trailer Court** on First Ave. N, tel. 485-2285.

It's some kind of judgment when the best place to eat is the **Tastee-Freez** on the east end of town, tel. 485-3674, but it's a pretty good Tastee-Freez. Otherwise, try the **Wooden Nickel** on Main St., tel. 485-2575, open 10 a.m.-10 p.m.

Information And Services

Write the **Circle Chamber of Commerce** at Circle, MT 59215, tel. 485-2414. For emergencies, contact the **sheriff**, tel. 485-3405.

There are two service stations, open till 9 p.m. For **road conditions**, call 1-365-2314.

THE BIG OPEN

West of Circle, the farms thin out, the landscape coarsens into badlands, and signs of human habitation grow more scarce. From here to the banks of the Musselshell River 150 miles west, Hwy. 200 traverses a vaguely defined region of ranches, gumbo buttes, sagebrush, coyotes, and cowboys. It's known by many names: Big Dry Country, the North Side, Jordan Country, the Big Empty, the Big Lonesome, and the Big Open.

The last of these gained currency a few years ago when environmental activists proposed turning the area into an enormous wildlife park; it's hard to imagine how much more of a wilderness this forlorn and lonesome land could be. Garfield County, nearly the size of Connecticut, encompasses much of this area; it has the lowest population density in the state, with not quite one person for every three square miles of land.

But if you asked one of the locals, you'd be told there's not much room left. Out here, under a trademark big sky, where single farms and ranches engulf a whole township's worth of land, people get used to taking up space.

For better or worse, this is one of the last outposts of the frontier spirit: cowboy hats are mandatory, the bar doubles as the community hall, and the rodeo club is the biggest extracurricular activity at the high school. Here, more than anywhere else in the state, there is still some Wild left in the West.

JORDAN AND VICINITY

No one comes to Jordan (pop. 494, elev. 2,800 feet) because of its interesting past. There's nothing startling about Jordan's history. Like other late-germinating communities, many of the first settlers were outlaws. Homesteaders drifted through desultorily, recoiling when they discovered what a nasty piece of business the Big Dry Country was. Big ranches and big families have always ruled the rangelands. And now, what makes Jordan exceptional is that it never bothered to change.

Jordan is remote. In 1931, only eight households had running water. Rural homes didn't have electrical service until 1952, and ranches didn't get telephones until 1956. Public transportation? Never had it, probably never will. The most isolated county seat in the lower 48 states, Jordan is 175 miles from the nearest major airport, 85 miles from the nearest bus line, 115 miles from the nearest train line. The local high school serves such a vast area that it maintains the only public coed dormitory in the U.S.

Once discovered, Jordan has always fascinated journalists. A New York radio station in 1930 identified Jordan as "the lonesomest town in the world." A local ranchwoman for years contributed a column called "Timber Creek Riffles" to The Wall Street Journal. Jordan made it to the front page of the nation's papers in the 1970s when, in the aftermath of a break-in at the local drug store, the sheriff deputized the men in the local bar as his posse. The sheriff got his man, but only after the gun-toting mob gave a visiting Associated Press journalist an eyeful of Western color.

A famous TV investigative reporter showed up in town a few years later to film a story about the farm/ranch crisis. Locals in the bar didn't much like his flashy ways; he conducted his on-screen interviews with his nose in plaster.

Despite its reputation as the last holdout of the Old West, Jordan is a friendly town with adequate facilities for the traveler. It is central to great hunting and to recreation and wildlife viewing on the C.M. Russell Wildlife Refuge and Fort Peck Lake.

Sights
The **Garfield County Museum**, just east of town, tel. 557-2517, offers both a historic and prehistoric overview of the locality. A replica of the triceratops found north of town, as well as other fossil remains, are the highlights here. Also on display are homesteader memorabilia, early photos, and a restored one-room school. Open daily June 1-Sept. 1.

West of Jordan about eight miles is a curious landmark known as **Smokey Butte**. This promontory, which rises a thousand feet above surrounding prairie, is the easternmost of the many igneous intrusions that rose into moun-

DINOSAUR COUNTRY

The dun-colored badlands that rise along the Missouri River, fantastically carved by erosion into sharp canyons and buttes, contain one of the world's richest chronicles of early life on earth. Paleontologists discovered some of the first and most important remains of dinosaurs in these desiccated hills; now, the annual arrival of the summer "bone diggers" is almost a traditional event in Jordan.

In 1902, Dr. Barnum Brown of the American Museum of Natural History journeyed to the Jordan area to search for dinosaur remains. Brown cut quite a figure: he reported to the digs in a starched white collar and polished knee boots, popping his gold pince-nez on and off. The existence of large dinosaurs was still a matter of conjecture in scientific circles; the giant reptiles certainly didn't form part of the popular imagination.

What attracted Brown to this area was its Cretaceous-era badlands. Laid down by shallow, marshy seas about 70 million years ago, these layers of mudstone, shale, and sandstone were normally covered by thick, more recent layers of sediment. When the Missouri River cut its present badland canyon, it opened up a gorge through millions of years of geologic history: here, in the arid bluffs of Garfield County, the earth has stored its memories of vanished life. In the stratified layers of sediment revealed by erosion, Brown reasoned, one should be able to find the band corresponding to the "Age of the Dinosaurs."

In a gumbo escarpment on Hell Creek, Brown found much more than he was looking for: two skeletons of *Tyrannosaurus rex*. The fossil-rich Cretaceous sediments, now called the Hell Creek Formation in honor of Garfield County's dinosaur haven, has continued to yield up specimens: in 1988, a Jordan couple found the most complete Tyrannosaurus skeleton to date along the shore of Fort Peck Lake, the seventh found in the area; Triceratops has almost become Jordan's dinosaur mascot; aquatic duck-

billed dinosaurs and the mosasaurus, a sea-serpent-like dinosaur, have also been found in Jordan's Hell Creek Formation. Smaller finds—dinosaur eggs, petrified mollusks and fish—are common.

Later scientists have come to Jordan not to dig bones, but to research theories. It was commonly known that dinosaurs, in fact most early life forms, were found only below a smudgy black band in the gumbo buttes; this thin layer of lignite coal in fact demarcates the Hell Creek and Fort Union sedimentary formations.

Dr. Walter Alvarez from UC Berkeley analyzed this layer from Hell Creek closely, found it contained traces of iridium embedded in similar sediments worldwide, and in 1979 proposed his asteroid-impact theory. According to Alvarez, a massive object from outer space struck the earth, causing a global winter during which the dinosaurs became extinct.

Other scientists dispute the asteroid theory. Eager to prevail, two research groups are currently accumulating evidence in Montana's badlands for competing dinosaur-extinction theories.

JIM MASTERSON

tains in central Montana. More curiously, the rock that makes up Smokey Butte, armolcolite, had only previously been found in rocks collected on the moon.

Accommodations And Food

One of Jordan's old hotels, **The Garfield**, on the corner of Main St. and Hwy. 200, tel. (406) 557-6215, is still in business, and offers rooms in the hotel or in newer motel units; $31 d. **Fellman's Motel**, on Hwy. 200, tel. 557-2209, $35 d, is only a block from the municipal swimming pool. Campers should go to **Kamp Katie**, just west of the bridge, tel. 557-2851, a pleasant-enough campground on the banks of Big Dry Creek.

The **QD's**, tel. 557-2301, west of Jordan on Hwy. 200, is Jordan's only full-service restaurant, open daily 6 a.m.-10 p.m.

Information And Services

Contact the **Jordan Commercial Club** for travel info at P.O. Box 370, Jordan, MT 59337, tel. (406) 557-2480. For emergencies, call the **sheriff** at 557-2882. The **C.M. Russell Wildlife Refuge** maintains a wildlife station in Jordan. The office is along Hwy. 200; tel. 557-6145. Contact the **BLM** at 557-2376; the office is on Main Street.

For local **road conditions**, call 1-365-2314.

THE CHARLES M. RUSSELL NATIONAL WILDLIFE REFUGE

Known to locals, with widely varying degrees of affection, as the "C.M.R.," the 1.2 million-acre C.M. Russell National Wildlife Refuge flanks the entire northern edge of Garfield County along the Missouri River. One of the largest refuges in the nation, the C.M.R. is home to an abundance of wildlife, including elk and bighorn sheep, which were once common on the prairies.

Garfield County contains more of the refuge than any other county; feelings run high here about having such a huge wilderness area (and its champion, The Government) for a neighbor. Many local residents are still bitter about being displaced from their land along the Missouri when Fort Peck was built and about their grazing land in the Breaks being turned into de facto wilderness, and unhappy when what land they have left is overrun by errant herds of deer, pronghorn, elk, and most of all, coyotes.

Unfortunately, heavy-handed interference on the part of the government and sheer old-fashioned cussedness on the part of the locals combine to make the C.M.R. much less accessible to visitors than it should be. Quite apart from the incredible wealth of wildlife—lacking only grizzly bears and wolves to replicate the Missouri River flora and fauna experienced by Lewis and Clark —the Missouri Breaks are dramatic and austere badlands still full of outlaw lore. And at the center of the refuge is Fort Peck Lake, one of the largest manmade lakes in the world, important as a migratory waterfowl stopover, to say nothing about its stellar fishing and recreational possibilities.

There is public access to the refuge and Fort Peck Lake at two sites in Garfield County. The most popular is **Hell Creek State Park**, 26 miles north of Jordan. Developed as a recreation area for local anglers and boaters, Hell Creek offers a campground, marina, store, and cabins. The road in, best attempted in dry weather, passes through rugged badlands. Elk, deer, waterfowl, eagles, foxes, and coyotes are pervasive.

Further afield, and along a dodgier road, is **Devil's Creek Recreation Area**, with undeveloped campsites, about 40 miles west of Jordan. Here, the gumbo buttes, fringed with ponderosa pines, drop away in canyons to the lake's shore. Both sites offer good scouting for fossils.

BOB RACE

THE HI-LINE AND GREAT FALLS

From the dramatic eastern front of the Rocky Mountains to the long views of the Hi-Line, this agricultural heart of Montana has more for the visitor than a look at a topographic map would imply. This is the country where the Nez Percé were finally run down by Army troops and Chief Joseph gave his remarkable surrender speech. It's where dinosaur nests have revised public opinion of the ancient reptiles, transforming them from flesh-ripping brutes into loving parents. It's where Blackfeet have held fast to a small part of the land they used to race across with their horses, and where they now host a big annual powwow. And it's where cowboy artist Charley Russell settled down to work in his log cabin studio.

There's enough quiet history here to keep a buff occupied for days. The Hi-Line was built by the Great Northern Railway—in fact, its name refers to its being the state's northernmost railroad line. Thousands of hard-working homesteaders, many of them European immigrants, took the train to the Hi-Line, stepped off onto

the windswept plain, and dug into the shortgrass prairie.

INTRODUCTION

The Land

Oil and natural gas formed beneath anticlines in far northern Montana. Glaciers mowed down from arctic Canada, leveling the land, forcing the Missouri to shift its channel southward, and plugging outlets to form Glacial Lake Great Falls. The Milk River now flows through what was once the Missouri River's bed.

Mule deer are abundant, and pronghorn, waterfowl, and some elk also live east of the Rocky Mountain Front.

History

The Great Northern Railway defined the development of the Hi-Line. James J. Hill had rails laid across northern Montana after Montanans such as Marcus Daly and Paris Gibson convinced

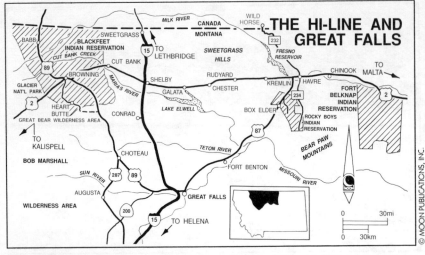

him that it was worth taking the trouble to compete with the Union Pacific, whose line already ran across the southern part of the state. In order to keep the railcars filled, settlers were recruited, both for Gibson's town, Great Falls, and for the northern tier, which would be coaxed into producing grain.

Hill and Professor Thomas Shaw were proponents of dryland farming. Shaw developed a theory that called for deep plowing and unrelenting cultivation of the land, a method that was practiced widely and led to wide-scale erosion. Precious topsoil, catching a windy ride, blew completely out of the state.

Between 1910 and 1918, homesteaders, sometimes derogatorily called "honyockers," swarmed to Montana for free land. Typically a family would get off the train, which had a boxcar full of their possessions, pay a "finder" $20 to lead them to their homestead, and start plowing. During the middle of the decade, the homesteader's life looked good. Wet weather helped crops to flourish, and World War I inflated the price of grain. But when drought set in in 1918 and didn't let up for years, homesteaders scattered almost as fast as the dry topsoil.

Wheat farming has remained a major part of the local economy, and one way of dealing with

MINUTEMEN

Scattered among 23,000 acres of prairie surrounding Great Falls are innocuous-looking chain-link fence and cement enclosures. Tucked away in fields or meadows, these 200 facilities house Minuteman intercontinental ballistic missiles.

Each silo consists of an 80-foot-deep tube, launch equipment, and missile. The silo door *alone* weighs 108 tons. The launch facilities are controlled from a nearby underground chamber. Launch-control chambers have walls 4½ feet thick, and dangle in a 90-foot-deep pit, suspended by cables that allow

the chamber to swing three feet in any direction. The chambers are always staffed, with Air Force officers on 24-hour shifts awaiting launch orders. Malmstrom Air Force Base in Great Falls is the headquarters for the Minuteman missiles.

The missiles are located in Montana for a number of reasons: the launch fuel is very sensitive to humidity, making the arid prairies a natural habitat; and the average elevation of 3,500 feet gives the missiles a head start, realizing a six percent fuel savings. The fact that not many people live hereabouts doesn't hurt, either.

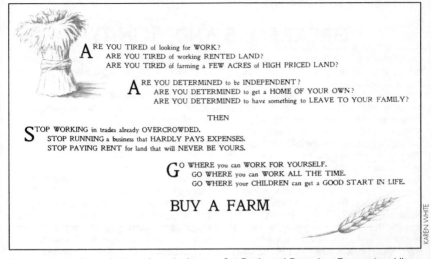

ARE YOU TIRED of looking for WORK?
ARE YOU TIRED of working RENTED LAND?
ARE YOU TIRED of farming a FEW ACRES of HIGH PRICED LAND?

ARE YOU DETERMINED to be INDEPENDENT?
ARE YOU DETERMINED to get a HOME OF YOUR OWN?
ARE YOU DETERMINED to have something to LEAVE TO YOUR FAMILY?

THEN

STOP WORKING in trades already OVERCROWDED.
STOP RUNNING a business that HARDLY PAYS EXPENSES.
STOP PAYING RENT for land that will NEVER BE YOURS.

GO WHERE you can WORK FOR YOURSELF.
GO WHERE you can WORK ALL THE TIME.
GO WHERE your CHILDREN can get a GOOD START IN LIFE.

BUY A FARM

KAREN WHITE

the dry, windy climate is the strip agriculture you'll see wherever wheat's been planted, in which one strip of land is cultivated and the adjoining strip lies fallow.

Transportation
Amtrak's *Empire Builder,* taking its name from James J. Hill's sobriquet, crosses northern Montana once a day traveling between Chicago and the West Coast with stops in Havre, Shelby, Cut Bank, and Browning. Four major airlines serve Great Falls, and **Rimrock Stage** buses, tel. 453-1541, connect Great Falls with Havre, Shelby, and Cut Bank.

Information
Travel Montana provides excellent free travel information. Most of the Hi-Line falls within their Charley Russell Country division. Call (800) 527-5348 for free brochures and maps.

GREAT FALLS AND VICINITY

Great Falls (pop. 56,000, elev. 3,333 feet) suffers the reputation of being Montana's most boring and stodgiest city, and one *can* think of it as a city filled with long, bleak commercial strips and military buildup, but there is reason to stop for more than a fill-up and a Diet Coke. To start with, there's rich Lewis and Clark history here, albeit mostly obliterated by the hydroelectric dams that now rope in the once-awesome Great Falls of the Missouri. There's also the Charles M. Russell Museum, and the unexpected—contemporary art at the Paris Gibson Museum.

The Sun River flows into the Missouri at 10th Street in Great Falls. The Highwood, Little Belt, and Big Belt mountains crop up to the east, southeast, and south of town, while the main spine of the Rockies runs down 50 miles west. But it's the Missouri River that's always defined Great Falls—the falls themselves, remembered in the city's name, the Giant Springs that now nourish hatchery trout, the riverside parks beckoning bicyclists and anglers.

When sheets of glacial ice covered the northern Montana plains 15,000 years ago, present-day Great Falls was under 600 feet of water. Ice dams backed up Glacial Lake Great Falls between Great Falls and Cut Bank, spilling out into the Shonkin Sag.

HISTORY

Blackfeet controlled the area when Lewis and Clark spent June 15-July 15, 1805 negociating the Great Falls of the Missouri, actually portaging 18 miles in 13 days. A grizzly bear chased Lewis into the Missouri at one point; he was also impressed that there were "not less than 10,000 buffalo in a circle of two miles."

Paris Gibson first visited the riverbend site of present-day Great Falls in 1880 and quickly set to building a city there. He conferred with James J. Hill, of the Great Northern Railway, and in 1887 the Montana Central Railroad was built through Great Falls, connecting the Great Northern line to the mining centers farther south.

The Anaconda Company came into town in 1908 and built a copper-reduction plant, powered by a dam on Black Eagle Falls. The cheap electricity generated by the Black Eagle Dam and the others that followed on other falls spurred Great Falls early on to an industrial economy, with attendant labor union and political imbroglios.

SIGHTS

It's worth stopping in Great Falls to visit the **C.M. Russell Museum,** 400 13th St. N, tel. 727-8787. Charley Russell's brilliant colors work in the original paintings as they never quite do in the reproductions found splashed across everything from book jackets to coffee mugs. The museum complex includes Russell's log cabin studio and house. Admission is $3 for adults, $1.50 for students and seniors. Summer hours are Mon.-Sat. 9 a.m.-6 p.m., Sun. 1-5 p.m. Winter hours are Tues.-Sat. 10 a.m.-5 p.m., Sun. 1-5 p.m.

A few blocks from the Russell Museum, at 1400 First Ave. N, tel. 727-8255, the **Paris Gibson Square Center for Contemporary Arts** mounts some surprisingly forward-thinking art exhibits.

The **Cascade County Historical Society**, tel. 452-3462, shares the Paris Gibson building and the museum space there includes historical exhibits. Historical Society members also conduct tours of the Ulm Pishkun, Fort Shaw, and other local historic sites.

Malmstrom Air Force Base has a museum and park open to the public Mon.-Sat. noon-3 p.m., tel. 731-2705. Tours of the base leave from the main gate (Second Ave. S) on Fridays from noon-2:30. Call 731-2427 for tour information.

Twelve miles north of town on Hwy. 87, the 12,300-acre **Benton Lake Wildlife Refuge** harbors nearly 200 bird species, including shorebirds, snow geese, tundra swans, burrowing and short-eared owls, and mammals such as rabbits, deer, and long-tailed weasels. Visitors can stop by April 1-Oct. 31 during the daytime.

Turn off I-15 at the Ulm exit, 15 miles south of Great Falls, and follow the "pishkun" signs six miles along good gravel roads to the **Ulm Pishkun State Monument.** Tepee rings abound near the 30-foot-high buffalo jump, and there are supposed to be some pictographs there, too. Poke around the base of the cliff for decaying buffalo bones, but wear boots to guard against the prickly pear and rattlesnakes, and don't carry off any souvenirs—the area is protected by the State Antiquities Act. A prairie dog town and picnic area share the pishkun site, which is closed October through May.

Springs, Rivers, And Dams
Everywhere you turn in Great Falls, there's a park, and the keynote one—a greenway along River Drive—is worth a special visit. The **Giant Springs Heritage Park** is three miles from downtown, and the BLM Visitor Center there has good brochures describing Lewis and Clark's portage of the falls, as well as information and exhibits on fishing and hunting.

Giant Springs, a gushing natural springs that captured the attention of Lewis and Clark, is part of the Giant Springs Heritage Park. The genesis of this 134,000-gallon-per-minute fountain is in the Little Belt Mountains southeast of Great Falls. Exposed Madison limestone absorbs mountain snowmelt and rain, which then drains and flows through fissures to Great Falls, where it surges up and spews into the Missouri

River. The mineral-rich water has proven to be a good fish-breeding medium, and there's a trout hatchery a stone's throw away from the springs.

Downstream from the springs are overlooks onto the dams that harness Black Eagle and Rainbow Falls. Both of these dams have preserved the essential nature of the waterfalls. From the roadside overlook, look across the Missouri to the town of **Black Eagle,** a company town that was built up around the turn of the century to serve the copper-reduction works.

Head north on Hwy. 87 to visit the **Ryan Dam,** which marks the site of the Great Falls of the Missouri, described by Meriwether Lewis as "the grandest sight I ever beheld," with its roily cascades, foamy spray, and spiky rock projections.

Accommodations
Most of Great Falls's bed and breakfasts are in an older residential neighborhood between downtown and the C.M. Russell Museum. The **Chalet Bed and Breakfast,** 1204 Fourth Ave. N, tel. (406) 452-9001, is a Victorian house almost directly across from the museum. Toward downtown, find the **Old Oak Inn,** 709 Fourth Ave. N, tel. 452-0032; the **Sarah,** perhaps the best appointed of the lot, at 626 Fourth Ave. N,

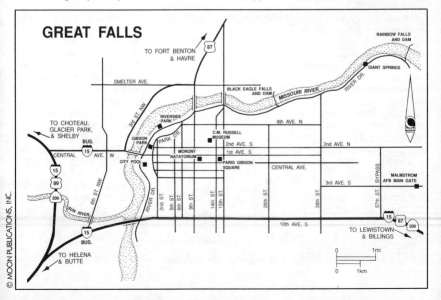

tel. 452-5906; and the **Three Pheasant Inn,** 626 Fifth Ave. N, tel. 453-0519. Bed and breakfast for two runs around $50 at any of these well-maintained homes.

On the downtown side of the Central Avenue strip, the **Royalty Motel,** 1300 Central Ave., tel. 452-9548, is conveniently located and cheap ($20 s), but seedy. Better bets close to downtown would be the **Imperial Inn,** 601 Second Ave. N, tel. 452-9581 or (800) 735-7173 ($34 s), or the **Mid-Town Motel,** 526 Second Ave. N, tel. 453-2411 ($36 s).

For more of a splurge, the **Rainbow Hotel,** 20 Third St. N, tel. 727-8200, or (800) 332-9940 in state, (800) 548-9974 out of state, is a nicely refurbished downtown hotel whose main drawback is probably the convention-hotel aura enveloping it. Singles here start at $52.

Across the Central Ave. Bridge, the **Central West Motel,** 715 Central Ave. W, tel. 453-0161, is well built and has singles from $25. Just down the street at 626 Central Ave. W, the **Edelweiss Inn,** tel. 452-9503, is another reasonably priced alternative ($27 s).

If you're loath to stray off the 10th Ave. strip, try the **Village Motor Inn,** 726 10th Ave. S, tel. 727-7666 ($28 s).

Food And Drink
For a morning jumpstart, **Morning Light Coffee Roasters,** 900 Second Ave. N, tel. 453-8443, has espresso drinks and pastries.

The **Conservatory Restaurant** at the Paris Gibson Square Center for Contemporary Arts is a gem of a lunch spot, open Tues.- Friday. The well-thought-out menu does not allow for picking and choosing, and changes weekly. A three-course lunch is $7. Reservations, tel. 727-8255, are mandatory.

For those who'd rather spend the day at the Giant Springs Park, **Red and Shorty's** is a sandwich joint with an outpost at the park, tel. 452-0308. Downtown, the Great Falls branch of

Bert and Ernie's, a Montana classic at 300 First Ave. S, tel. 453-0601, serves burgers and imported beers.

Mama Cassie's is a casual downtown Italian restaurant and deli with spaghetti dinners starting at $5, deli sandwiches, and good homemade bread. It's at 319 First Ave. N, tel. 454-3354.

At **Murphy's Maverick Bar,** spot the bartender in the family portrait mounted behind the bar. This quintessential Montana bar is at 122 Central Ave., tel. 727-9634.

The **Polar Bear Café,** on Central Ave. W, is worth at least a peek.

Events
The **C.M. Russell Auction of Original Western Art** is an annual March event benefiting the C.M. Russell Museum. Bidders descend from all over the country. Contact the museum at 727-8787 for details.

Montana Roundup Days, at the end of June, features float trips on the Missouri, a rodeo, and assorted "Western" events.

The last few days of July and the first few of August find the **Montana State Fair** at the fairgrounds. **Horse races** are run through the summer.

Recreation
Swim outdoors at the **Mitchell Pool,** just south of the First Ave. Bridge on River Drive. Open swimming hours are 1-8 p.m., adult swim is noon-1 p.m. Admission is $1.75 for adults, 60 cents for children. Serious lap swimmers may prefer the beautifully named, carefully maintained **Morony Natatorium** at 12th St. N and First Ave. North.

Bike or jog along the **River's Edge Trail,** stretching from the 10th Ave. Bridge to Giant Springs Heritage Park.

The Great Falls **Dodgers** are the Pioneer League farm team of the Los Angeles Dodgers. Minorleague baseball fans can catch them throughout the summer at Legion Park. Call 452-5311 for schedule and ticket information.

Charley Russell's studio door

The **R.O. Speck Golf Course** is a busy 18-hole public course on River Rd. next door to Legion Park. Across the river in Black Eagle, the **Anaconda Hills Golf Course** has recently expanded to 18 holes.

Information And Services
The **visitors bureau** of the Great Falls Chamber of Commerce can be reached at 926 Central Ave. or P.O. Box 2127, Great Falls, MT 59403, tel. (406) 761-4434.

The **public library** is at 301 Second Ave. N, tel. 453-0349. Listen to **Montana Public Radio** at 89.9 FM.

Transportation
Great Falls International Airport, southwest of town, is the region's largest, and is serviced by major airlines.

Intermountain Bus and **Rimrock Stage** share a terminal at 326 First Ave. S, tel. 453-1541, and, between the two lines, travel to Shelby, Havre, Lewistown, Billings, Bozeman, Helena, Butte, Missoula, and Kalispell.

Great Falls Transit System runs buses in and around town. Call 727-0382 for schedule information. Hail a **Diamond Cab** by calling 453-3241.

THE HI-LINE

More than any other part of Montana, this is the country the railroad built. James J. Hill, head of the Great Northern Railway, mounted an aggressive campaign to bring European immigrants to the Hi-Line—by train, of course. Towns named Zurich, Malta, Inverness, and Kremlin were supposed to welcome Europeans.

Today, this is the Montana known by Amtrak passengers, wheat farmers, and few others. Almost nobody comes here on vacation, unless it's to help their parents out with the harvest. Glacier Park-bound easterners zip past the grain elevators and filling stations, seldom turning from Hwy. 2 to explore the old downtowns.

For the most part, such lack of curiosity is understandable. There's little here obviously beckoning the tourist to stop and spend much time or money. Barring major car repairs, it's hard to spend much money here, but there are plenty of places to while away a few hours.

HAVRE

You wouldn't know it by the pronunciation, but Havre (HAV-ver, pop. 10,201, elev. 4,167 feet) does take its name from the French city, Le Havre. Originally it was called Bull Hook Siding, but James J. Hill pleaded for a name befitting the dignity of a Great Northern town. The lo-

cals complied, as Hill was ensuring the town's prosperity by making it a railway-division point.

Raucous boom times came to town with the railroad and with cowboys in the 1890s—gambling and prostitution both swelled to legendary proportions. By 1910 homesteaders were piling into the land office at Havre to claim their 160-acre plots. They were, as a whole, a much more serious bunch than railroad workers and cowboys and the bartenders, card sharks, and whores who'd gathered around Hill's esteemed division point, but Havre did its best to resist the new morality imposed by farmers and prohibitionists. Traces of this heritage linger in the drive-up bar and the gambling joints still thriving in downtown Havre. And why Havre's high-school teams are called the "Blue Ponies" is anyone's guess.

Sights
The **H. Earl Clack Museum,** toward the west end of town at the Hill County Fairgrounds, is free and open daily 9 a.m.-9 p.m. from Memorial Day through Labor Day. The **Wahpka Chug'n Buffalo Jump,** behind the Holiday Village Shopping Center, provides the fodder for the museum's most interesting exhibits. Museum personnel lead tours of this *pishkun,* where hordes of bison were driven off a cliff; call 265-9913 for details.

Underground tours visit opium dens and the bootlegging district of Havre's wild past. For information call 265-5547 or stop by 104 Third Avenue.

Northern Montana College has a well-tended campus south of downtown, and is a good place to sit in the shade. The Math-Science Building houses natural history displays, including a stuffed specimen of the extinct Audubon mountain sheep once displayed above the bar of one of Havre's bygone high-class joints.

A rookery, badlands, and a radar base separate Havre from Canada. Fossils and archaeological sights stud the badlands. A glacial ice sheet covered this part of the Hi-Line 10,000 years ago.

The remains of **Fort Assiniboine** are a half mile south of the intersection of Hwys. 2 and 87. The Clack Museum leads tours out to the old fort, built in 1879 to protect U.S. citizens from both the Blackfeet and the feared return of Sitting Bull from his exile in Canada. The fort was converted to an agricultural research station in 1913 and was used to house transients during the Depression.

Rocky Boy Reservation

On the western edge of the Bear's Paw Mountains south of Havre is the reservation named for Chippewa leader Stone Child, called Rocky Boy by the whites. Almost 2,000 Chippewa and Cree share this 108,015-acre reservation, which is owned entirely by Tribal members.

Cree Indians came from the Upper Great Lakes area to the northern plains in the late 1700s and were allies of the Assiniboine and foes of the Sioux and Blackfeet. When bison began to disappear from the plains, the Cree became vagabonds in search of the last herds. They became known for their wandering, and for their alignment with Louis Riel and his band of Metis.

U.S. authorities repeatedly tried to force the Cree to settle in Canada, and for many years, the tribe was homeless. The Cree teamed up with another homeless group, Rocky Boy's band of Chippewa, who had been shorted out of reservation land in North Dakota. When Fort Assiniboine was abandoned in 1911, part of its acreage was set aside as a reservation for the Chippewa-Cree. Reservation life was not easy for these tribes, and employment on the reservation is still difficult to come by.

Accommodations

Havre's old downtown hotel, the **Park,** is at 335 First St., tel. (406) 265-7891. The aptly named **Shanty Motel** has rooms from $20 at 115 Ninth Ave., tel. 265-7076. Singles start at $27 at the **Super 8** on the west end of town, tel. 265-1411. The **El Toro Inn,** 521 First St., tel. 265-5414 or (800) 422-5414 in state, has a Spanish motif and rooms from $30.

Le Havre Town House Inn is a large motel at 629 W. First St., tel. 265-6711, (800) 821-2521 in Montana, or (800) 442-4667 out of state. Single rooms start at $32 and there's an indoor pool and adjoining restaurant. The **Duck Inn,** 1300 First St., tel. 265-9615, is, like the Le Havre, on the fancy side for the Hi-Line. The Duck Inn's restaurant, lounge, and supper club draw a fair crowd, and rooms start at $41.

The **Lions campground** by the museum is okay for RVs but tent campers are better off heading south toward the Bear's Paw Mountains. It's only about 15 miles to the entrance of **Beaver Creek County Park,** tel. 395-4565, a huge park with 250 sites in several discreet campgrounds. Purchase a $5 camping permit at the park office.

Food And Drink

Pizza Hut, McDonald's, and **Kentucky Fried Chicken** all rear their heads on the west end of town, but there are a few alternatives. Chinese restaurants have a long history in Havre—in the early days there was always Chinese food to go with the hell-raising. Today, the **Canton Chinese Restaurant** at 439 First St. W, tel. 265-6666, carries on the tradition.

If you're hungry for a meal that's classy without snobbish overkill, **Navlika's,** just down the way at 415 First St. W, tel. 265-5426, has *good* Italian food and homemade pies. And, while a bit predictable, **4-Bs** rarely disappoints—they have a place at 604 First St. W, tel. 265-9721.

For a less nutritious view of Havre stop by the **Oxford Bar,** 329 First St., where drinks are swallowed unnoticed when the gambling gets hot. **PJ's** also draws on its historic surroundings to buff up its image—there's a bar and restaurant at 15 Third Ave., tel. 265-3211.

The **Duck Inn** has a more refined gaming area, and about the fanciest restaurant in town.

Events

The **Rocky Boy Powwow** is held the first weekend of August near Box Elder on the Rocky Boy Reservation.

The **Hill County Fair** is in mid-August, and mid-September brings **Havre Festival Days**. For more information, call the chamber of commerce at (406) 265-4383.

Recreation

When the sun beats down on the Hi-Line, consider a dunk in the **city pool**, 420 Sixth Ave., tel. 265-8161.

South of town, the **Bear's Paw Mountains** are 50-million-year-old grass-covered volcanic humps. A long county park has several outposts with many campsites and fishing areas, though there aren't many hiking trails. Get a permit before camping or fishing at **Beaver Creek County Park;** they're available for $5 at the park headquarters, about 25 miles south of Havre.

Fish **Fresno Reservoir,** northwest of Havre, for walleye, crappie, and northern pike.

Tribal fishing and camping permits are issued by the Chippewa-Cree at their business office in Box Elder. The tribes also run the **Bear's Paw Ski Bowl,** a small downhill ski area on the **Rocky Boy Reservation.** It's usually open mid-December through April 1.

Information And Services

You'll notice the streets in Havre run parallel to the railroad tracks (Hwy. 2 is First St.); avenues are perpendicular to the tracks.

The **chamber of commerce** is at 518 First St., tel. (406) 265-4383. Find the **post office** at 306 Third Ave; just across from the lively courthouse. The public **library** is just a couple of blocks away at the corner of Third St. and Fourth Avenue. In the same neighborhood, **Big Sky Books,** at the corner of Third and Third, has piles and piles of used books and several tidier shelves of new books, many about Montana.

The **Chippewa-Cree Business Committee** is at Rocky Boy Rt., P.O. Box 544, Box Elder, MT 59521, tel. 395-4282.

Transportation

Amtrak's *Empire Builder* stops at Havre. **Rent-A-Wreck** is right near the train depot, in the Conoco station at 500 First St., tel. 265-1481.

Rimrock Stages provides bus service to the Hi-Line and Great Falls, and stops at the Park Hotel in Havre, 335 First St., tel. 265-6444.

The **Havre Hill County Airport** is serviced by Big Sky Airlines. Budget Rent-A-Car has an office at the airport, tel. 265-1156.

CHINOOK

Chinook, the Hi-Line's remaining cattle town on the Milk River, is named after the warming wind that's saved many a cow from freezing or starving to death.

The **Chief Joseph Battlefield,** 16 miles south of town in view of the Bear's Paw Mountains, has a few plaques and a trail through the grass. Follow the trail and find small markers strewn over the battlefield, marking the sites of deaths and camps.

This is where General Nelson Miles overtook the Nez Percé, who were less than 40 miles from sanctuary in Canada. Here Chief Joseph gave the speech for which he is most remembered:

> . . . *It is cold and we have no blankets. The little children are freezing to death. My people, some of them, have run away to the hills, and have no blankets, no food; no one knows where they are—perhaps freezing to death. I want to have time to look for my children and see how many I can find. Maybe I shall find them among the dead.*
>
> *Hear me my chiefs. I am tired; my heart is sick and sad.*
>
> *From where the sun now stands, I will fight no more forever.*

There's a good local museum, the **Blaine County Museum,** at 501 Indiana, tel. 357-2590. A mural and a slide show on the Nez Percé Battle of the Bear's Paw are featured. From May through Sept., hours are Tues.-Sat. 8 a.m.-5 p.m., Sun. 2-4 p.m. Winter hours are Mon.-Fri. 1-5 p.m.

The **Chinook Hotel,** 62 Third St., tel. 357-2231, is the old downtown hotel. **Bear Paw Court,** 114 Montana Ave., tel. 357-2221, has rooms from $25 s; the **Chinook Motor Inn,** 100 Indiana Ave., tel. 357-2248, is more expensive

($36 s), but has an indoor pool and hot tub, tel. 357-2248.

The **Pastime Lounge and Steakhouse** or the restaurant at the Chinook Motor Inn are the best bets for a meal in this small town.

The **Blaine County Fair and Rodeo** and an accompanying art show and auction are held in mid-July. Contact the **Chinook Chamber of Commerce** at P.O. Box 744, Chinook, MT 59523, tel. 357-2570, for more information.

WEST OF HAVRE

Don't just whiz through **Kremlin.** Stop and look hard for the onion domes rising above the prairie—they're what give the town its name. (Actually, *nobody's* ever seen 'em, except a home-sick Russian homesteader back in 1910 or so.)

The unenlightened may pass south of **Rudyard** on Hwy. 2 and dismiss it as a real hayseed town, but Rudyard natives have ended up doing such diverse things as running pizza chains in Paris and making large conceptual art installations on a farm outside of town. There is even an old downtown hotel in Rudyard—the **Grand Hotel,** tel. 355-4215.

Chester
A dam on the Marias River forms **Tiber Reservoir** (aka Lake Elwell) southwest of Chester. It's the only recreational area for miles around, and is a haven for those seeking **campsites**.

BOB RACE

buffalo berry,
Sheperdia argentea

Boating is popular, fishing is mediocre for rainbows and perch, and there seems to be a largely untapped potential for windsurfing. A float trip along the Marias from below the dam to the Missouri River passes badlands and white cliffs not unlike those of the Wild and Scenic stretch of the Missouri.

If you're not a camper, perhaps you'd like to stay in a motel named after a local point of interest. The **MX Motel** on Hwy. 2, tel. 759-5564, reminds passers-through that some missile silos slumber just off the highway around here.

Galata
Galata is off the highway to the north, but its cemetery is right beside the highway. When this was still cattle country, Galata had the stockyards, while Shelby was in charge of going-to-town provisions and hilarity.

Shelby
A boxcar was thrown from a Great Northern train here in 1891, and the site was named after Montana's general manager of the Great Northern, who swore the place would never amount to much. Shelby developed into a trade center, supplying cowboys and sheepherders with food and wild times. Oil was discovered north of town in 1921, and though the town's population swelled, it didn't quite live up to its own expectations. In 1923, Shelby hosted a prize fight between Jack Dempsey and Tommy Gibbons. A 45,000-seat arena was erected for this occasion; unfortunately, only 7,000 were filled for the fight.

The **Marias Museum of History and Art,** 206 12th Ave., tel. 434-2551, has memorabilia from the big fight, and displays concerning the region's oil wealth.

Sweetgrass border crossing, 24 miles north of Shelby on I-15, is open 24 hours and is the state's busiest port of entry.

Shelby has a few motels. For something nice try the **Crossroads Inn,** Hwy. 2, tel. 434-5134 (it has a pool); for plain old cheap, the **O'Haire Manor Motel,** 204 Second St. S, tel. 434-5555, is just fine. Campers may want to swing seven miles south of town to **Williamson Park** on the Marias River.

Hong Kong Chan's, a Chinese restaurant at 200 Front St., tel. 434-2646, is not as improbable as its name. The **Capital Café** serves regular American food at 248 Main, tel. 434-2991.

Like many hot Hi-Line towns, Shelby has a city **swimming pool,** at 105 12th Ave. N; tel. 434-5311.

Conrad

Conrad, though 24 miles south of the Hi-Line proper on I-15, shares an agricultural heritage and economy with the towns along Hwy. 2. Dryland farming and big irrigation projects took off here and made it a productive wheat-growing area. Conrad is within easy striking distance of Lake Elwell, a minor mecca for recreationists on the prairies.

BLACKFEET INDIAN RESERVATION

Just east of Glacier National Park and the Rocky Mountains, shortgrass prairie rolls across the Blackfeet Reservation, a high plain cut through by creeks and dotted with lakes. Strong west winds, long cold winters, and short hot summers make it difficult to ignore the weather here.

Meriwether Lewis hoped to find the headwaters of the Marias River mingling with those of the Saskatchewan River, up above the 50th parallel. On their return from the Pacific, Lewis and a small party of men traced Cut Bank Creek from its confluence with the Two Medicine River. (These two streams combine to form the Marias.) Unfortunately for Lewis, Cut Bank Creek comes out of the Rockies west of Browning, and, due to cloudy weather, he couldn't see the stars well enough to get an exact reading of how far north he was. All in all, it was enough to cause him to name their terminus "Camp Disappointment." A highway marker and a wind-tossed hilltop picnic area now mark the site.

HISTORY

The Blackfeet, originally from north of the Great Lakes, moved west in the 1600s and established southern Alberta as their territory. What is now known as the Blackfeet Nation is composed of three distinct tribes: the Northern Piegan (Pikuni), the Southern Piegan or Blackfeet (Sisaka), and the Blood (Kainai). By the 1700s, bands of Blackfeet had settled in what is now Montana. The Northern Piegan and the Blood mostly remained in Canada.

The Blackfeet formed tentative alliances with the neighboring Cree and Assiniboine, and considered the more distant Shoshone and Crow their enemies. When they first arrived on the northern plains, the Blackfeet had neither horses nor guns. They drove buffalo over *pishkuns,* steep cliffs, to kill them.

Horses, acquired from either the Shoshone or the Flathead, Nez Percé, and Kootenai tribes, made a tremendous difference in the everyday life of the Blackfeet. Buffalo were much easier to hunt from horseback, and once the tribe began trading for guns, were a snap to shoot down. The Blackfeet became skilled riders, and their fierce reputation was enhanced as they were able to stage wide-ranging raids.

When white explorers and mountain men arrived in the 1800s, the Blackfeet controlled the northern plains. White settlers feared the Blackfeet's raids as much as they vied for their business at trading posts. Early trading posts in

---

BLACK FEET?

Two legends tell of how the Blackfeet got their tribal name. The first, and oldest, story is about a man and his three sons. Following a vision, the man sent his sons west to hunt buffalo. The buffalo were there where they were supposed to be, by the thousands, but they were difficult to approach. The Sun appeared in a second vision and provides the man with black medicine with which to paint his oldest son's feet. It worked—the son was able to run down the buffalo. His descendants are called Blackfeet.

The man's other two sons weren't ignored. One became a warrior—his painted red lips earned his descendants the name "Bloods." The third son returned home with clothes of distant tribes, and his descendants became the Pikuni, or "Far-Off Clothing." Whites translated this into "Piegan."

The less visionary story of the Blackfeet recounts moccasin-blackening travels across scorched praires to reach present-day Montana.

Blackfeet country included Fort Piegan on the Missouri River near present-day Loma.

Contact with white traders and soldiers brought more of the valuable guns and ammunition, but also conflict and disease. The Blackfeet were decimated as much by disease as by battle. Thousands were killed by smallpox and scarlet fever.

The U.S. government was eager to confine the Blackfeet and, in order to start the process along, marked the land north of the Yellowstone and south of Canada's Saskatchewan River, east of the Continental Divide and west of the confluence of the Missouri and Yellowstone rivers, for a Blackfeet reservation. Of course, pressure from whites wanting the land for their own uses resulted in an incredible shrinking reservation. The Blackfeet Reservation now comprises 1.5 million acres, with over a third of that is owned by non-Indians.

Oil drilling on tribal land has provided revenue for the Blackfeet since the early 1900s. Oil and gas now supply the tribe with most of their income and much controversy. Ranching, farming, and a pencil factory also contribute to the reservation economy.

RECREATION

Lakes dot the Blackfeet Reservation, and many of them are worth fishing. The tribe has a fishing information line at 338-7413—they'll provide advice on the necessary permits and current fishing conditions.

Tough Creek Outfitters, Box 216, Browning, MT 59417, tel. 338-7062 or 338-5478, is a fishing-guide business owned and operated by Craig Ollinger, a Blackfeet tribal member. **Morning Star Troutfitters,** tel. 338-2785, also operates out of Browning and specializes in fishing trips on the Blackfeet Reservation.

CUT BANK

This foothills oil and gas town of 3,329 was named by the Blackfeet for "the river that cuts into the white clay bank," or Cut Bank Creek. There was an initial burst of development when the Great Northern Railway came through in the 1890s, and another big spurt in the 1930s when oil and gas were discovered floating at

the top of the giant arch in the bedrock—the Sweetgrass Arch—that stretches across the Hi-Line here. Cut Bank is actually on the eastern edge of the Blackfeet Reservation, but, unlike Browning, it's not a thoroughly Indian town.

Though no tourist town, weary drivers can find a motel room here. The **Northern Motor Inn,** 609 W. Main, tel. (406) 873-5662, is a good deal for $26 s, $35 d. They have an indoor pool and hot tub. Even less expensive, but far more basic, are the old downtown **Pioneer Hotel,** 322 E. Main, tel. 873-4515, and the **Corner Motel,** 201 E. Main, tel. 873-5588. The **Parkway Motel** is a few blocks off the main drag at 7 Third Ave. W, tel. 873-4582. Double rooms are $32.

Café food is served up at two spots on Main Street: **Big Sky Café,** 13 W. Main, tel. 873-2542, and **Burgin's Café,** 109 W. Main, tel. 873-2341. Around the corner, the **Greco,** at 112 N. Central Ave., tel. 873-4353, has tasty baked goods. For a dinner meal, look to the **Village Dining and Lounge,** tel. 873-5005, in the shopping center near the Northern Motor Inn.

The city's heated outdoor **swimming pool** is at 320 Second Ave. W, tel. 873-2452.

The last weekend of July brings Cut Bank's **Lewis and Clark Expedition Festival.** The **chamber of commerce,** P.O. Box 1243, Cut Bank, MT 59427, tel. 873-4041, can supply details.

BROWNING

Browning (pop. 1,170, elev. 4,462 feet) is the headquarters of the Blackfeet Tribe. It's 18 miles east of Glacier National Park and many parkgoers zip through, in a hurry to get to the mountains. Though Browning is not a fancy place—it can be hard to find a pay phone that works, and the café fare is no more compelling than the highway motel rooms—there is a certain spirit to the place, and there are reasons to stop here.

Sights
Browning's main attraction is the **Museum of the Plains Indian,** near the intersection of Hwys. 2 and 89. The exhibits of cultural artifacts are well curated and professionally displayed, the slide show is vivid, and the gift shop is a good place to buy Indian art and jewelry without fear of getting inferior or inauthentic goods and with the assurance that the artist is being fairly compen-

sated. From June through September the museum is open daily 9 a.m.-5 p.m. Winter hours are Mon.-Fri. 10 a.m.-4:30 p.m., tel. 338-2230.

At the same highway intersection, the **Museum of Montana Wildlife** is a jumble of taxidermy, dioramas, and bronze sculptures. It's joined by the **Hall of Bronze,** and artist **Bob Scriver's studio and gallery.** Though a bit of a mishmash, it's worth visiting along with the Museum of the Plains Indian. The museum is open daily, June 1 through Labor Day, 8 a.m.-8 p.m. Adult admission is $2, reduced rates for children and families, tel. 338-5425.

The back roads of the reservation pass homes (with an occasional tepee pitched out back), lakes, oil and gas rigs, and a ceremonial sun lodge (a polygonal log-limbed structure). While common manners dictate that one shouldn't trespass, it is especially important not to enter tribal religious sites, such as a sun lodge.

Among the reservation communities, **Heart Butte** is the most traditional; **East Glacier, St. Mary,** and **Babb** cater to tourists, with many businesses owned by non-Indians. **Cut Bank,** on the reservation's eastern border, has more in common with the Hi-Line towns to the east.

Accommodations And Food

Rooms at **Browning's Glacier Motel,** on Hwy. 2, tel. (406) 338-7004, start at $35 d. The **War Bonnet Lodge,** at the intersection of Hwys. 2 and 89, tel. 338-7610, has double rooms for $47. Browning's no culinary mecca, but there is the 24-hour **Montana Café.**

Events

North American Indian Days are held the second week of July at the powwow grounds behind the Museum of the Plains Indian. Dancing and drumming are the highlights of the weekend activities. Teams of drummers come from all over the West to compete at this powwow, and their drumming is frequently rhapsodic. Stick games, jewelry peddlers, and the bustling encampment of tepees, tents, and pickups round out the scene. Spectators will quickly realize that this is *real,* not something trotted out for tourists, and, while non-Indians are welcome, events aren't geared toward them.

Information

Information is available from the **Blackfeet Planning Department,** P.O. Box D, Browning, MT 59417, tel. (406) 338-7406.

ROCKY MOUNTAIN FRONT

The Rocky Mountains hoist themselves off the plains just west of Choteau and Augusta. It's as dramatic a transition as you'll find in any landscape: flat rangeland to the east, wilderness mountains rising abruptly to the west. Chinook winds blowing down off the mountains warm the plains.

Natural-gas pumps and ABM sites dot the fields stretching out from the Rocky Mountain Front. Controversy has erupted between those who want to develop natural gas (and feel that it can be balanced with wilderness) and those who fear such gas exploration and mining will harm the Front's environment.

CHOTEAU

Choteau is not in Chouteau County; it's the county seat of Teton County. The town (pop. 1,741, elev. 3,800 feet) is built around the county courthouse, smack where Hwy. 287 crosses Hwy. 89.

Dinosaurs used this area as a breeding ground, and paleontologists (led by Jack Horner, now based in Bozeman at the Museum of the Rockies), have pieced together revolutionary dino-life theories based on bones and eggshells excavated here.

The Old North Trail was an important migratory trail for proto-Indians running from the Arctic to Mexico over 8,000 years ago. Traces of it are still visible at the Pine Butte Preserve just west of present-day Choteau.

Catholic missionaries preceded the fur traders who started white settlement here; the town was named after Pierre Chouteau, who was associated with the American Fur Company. The first "u" in the name was dropped to distinguish the town from Chouteau County. When fur trading died out, the economic mantle was picked up by cattle ranchers.

Choteau was home to novelist A.B. Guthrie until his death in 1991. Guthrie, best known for *The Big Sky*, was an environmentalist in this land of ranchers and natural-gas speculators.

Sights

Teton Trail Village, on Choteau's main street, is a cluster of cabins housing curio shops and the **Old Trail Museum.** The museum shows off some of the area's fossils, including dinosaur bones and eggs. Ask the museum proprietor about tours of the dinosaur dig site—they run a van to Egg Mountain every summer afternoon; $7.50 adults, $4 children under 12, tel. 466-5332. The van ends up at the free Egg Mountain tour (see below); the driver, often a local with intimate knowledge of the dinosaur digs, will also discourse on local history and recreation.

The **Pine Butte Swamp Nature Conservancy Preserve** is nestled between the Front Range and a missile silo. The preserve stretches from the mountains to the plains across a rare (for this area) wetland. (More precisely, it's

The Sun River flows from the Bob Marshall Wilderness.

a fen, which means that the water actually flows.) Grizzly bears forage here, and use the brushy swamp as a corridor to the plains, making this the easternmost outpost of the grizzly, which was once a plains animal. Access to the preserve is limited.

Summertime tours are conducted at 3:30 each weekday, starting from the Bellview Schoolhouse, now the preserve's education center. The schoolhouse is five miles west of Egg Mountain on the same road, and the Pine Butte tours are designed to follow the ones conducted on Egg Mountain.

To visit the swamp at other times, drive past the schoolhouse and turn right on a cut-across road. Drive northwest on this road for about two miles to an information kiosk. Park here, read the posted information, and take the trail starting directly across the road from the kiosk. It's a short easy hike up a flower-strewn ridge to a view of the glacier-carved Pine Butte, wetlands, glacial moraines, faint traces of the Old North Trail, and the Rocky Mountain Front.

The Pine Butte Preserve runs summer workshops for both children and adults. Most of these courses run for several consecutive days and focus on the region's natural history, but nature writing and puppet-making have also been offered. Contact the Pine Butte Swamp Preserve, HC 58 Box 34B, Choteau, MT 59422, tel. (406) 466-5526, for schedules and course descriptions.

Freezeout Lake, a waterfowl area and wetlands southeast of Choteau, is a rest stop for migrating birds. Pelicans, blue-winged teal, and marsh hawks reside here, as do snow geese and tundra swans each fall. Nearby Priest Butte was the site of a Catholic mission for the Blackfeet.

Egg Mountain

Staff members at the dinosaur school run free tours of the dig sites. These tours, held at 2 p.m. every day of July and August, are the *only* times the sites are open to the public. It is imperative that unescorted visitors not trespass on Egg Mountain or the bone beds.

To reach the dinosaur fields, turn off Hwy. 287 south of Choteau at the Triangle Meat Packing plant. Follow the little green "Dinosaur School" signs; when the road forks, don't take the road to Pishkun Lake—veer right. There are two big digging sites here—Egg Mountain, where evidence of many dino nests has been unearthed, and the "bone beds," final resting place of many maiasaurs.

Serious amateur paleontologists may find that an afternoon tour is not enough. Students at the "Dinosaur School," supervised by staff from the Museum of the Rockies, are turned loose with jackhammers and screwdrivers, the tools of the paleontological trade here on the east front of the Rockies. Week-long courses ($650-850) are geared toward adults; a two-day parent and child version ($75-115) is also offered. Students board in the camp tepees, eat the camp food, and, presumably, some drink the camp brew— Jack Horner's first grant was $10,000 from Rainier Beer. Contact the Museum of the Rockies at (406) 994-5257 for information on these field courses.

The Old Trail Museum also offers paleontology courses in conjunction with the College of Great Falls. Courses run from two to eight days and cost $100-500.

Accommodations

Country Lane Bed and Breakfast, on Hwy. 89 just north of Choteau, tel. (406) 466-2816, is more of an enterprise than one would expect— there's even an indoor pool. A double room goes for $60.

None of Choteau's motels will bust a traveler's budget—most rooms are less than $30. At the **Western Star Motel,** 426 Main Ave. S, tel. 466-5737, rooms start at $20. The cheery **Belle Vista Motel,** 614 Main Ave. N, tel. 466-5711, has rooms from $26. The **Glenloyd** is a sleepy old downtown hotel, at 415 N. Main, tel. 466-2101.

The free **Choteau city park campground** is right in town; turn off Hwy. 89 at the blinking light and follow the KOA signs. The city park is closer in than the **KOA.** Choose the city park if flush toilets and running water are amenities enough; for hookups, showers, and campground fees, continue on to the KOA.

Mill Falls Campground is small, free, and well situated for hikers. Follow Hwy. 89 north out of Choteau and turn down the road to Teton Canyon.

Ranch Stays
Pine Butte Guest Ranch, on the South Fork of the Teton River, west of Choteau, has been a dude ranch since 1930. The original owners sold it to the Nature Conservancy, an organization whose mission involves buying land for nature preserves. Traditional dude-ranch activities are supplemented here with natural-history studies. Summer rates are $775 a week for adults, $600 for children. During May and September, weekly rates are $100 less, and guests may come for shorter stays (two-night minimum) at $100 a night. Room, board, naturalist tours, and, during the summer season, horseback riding, are included in the fee, as is Sunday transportation to and from Great Falls Airport. Contact the Pine Butte Guest Ranch at HC 58, Box 34C, Choteau, MT 59422, tel. 466-2158.

Another guest ranch between Choteau and the Rockies is the **Seven Lazy P,** P.O. Box 178, Choteau, MT 59422, tel. 466-2044. It's open year-round—both downhill and cross-country skiing are nearby, and during the summer, some naturalist workshops are mixed in amongst the pack trips and fishing. Rates run $85 pp per day (three-day minimum), or $130 a day for pack trips.

Food And Drink
Ice cream is Choteau's most prevalent cuisine. There's an ice-cream parlor in the **Teton Trail Village** and another one right across the street at the **OutPost Deli,** which is also a good spot for a sandwich, tel. 466-5330. The **Circle N,** 925 N. Main Ave., tel. 466-5331, is open for breakfast, lunch, and dinner, and seems to be the only place in town that does not tout its ice cream.

Events
The **Choteau rodeo** happens on the Fourth of July.

Recreation
Take your pick of trails on the South Fork of the Teton River—many of them lead into the Bob Marshall Wilderness. **Our Lake** (called Hidden Lake on the trailhead sign), is three miles up and in. Mountain goats are often visible above the lake. The hike to **Headquarters Pass** starts at the same trailhead (near the Mill Falls Campground) and passes a high waterfall on the Sun River on the way to expansive views. Grizzly bears are sometimes spotted in the area, so take precautions. It's not unusual to run into snowfields on the higher trails even in July.

Rocky Mountain Hi Ski Area has cross-country and downhill trails at Teton Pass. Cross-country skiers headed for the Bob Marshall Wilderness Area often start from Choteau, as roads are plowed all the way to the mountains.

Fish **Pishkun Reservoir,** southwest of town, for kokanee salmon, northern pike, and rainbow trout.

Information
The Forest Service **ranger station** is on Hwy. 89 at the northern edge of town, tel. 466-5341. An information kiosk is set up in Choteau during the summer, and the **Old Trail Museum** is another good source of information, especially for dinosaur details.

The **post office** is at 103 First Ave. Northwest.

AUGUSTA

Twenty-five miles of glacial moraines along Hwy. 287 separate Augusta from Choteau. The Sun River flows east from the Rockies to the Missouri. Blackfeet referred to the Sun as the Medicine River: mineral deposits from a side gulch were used medicinally. Gibson Reservoir, named after Paris Gibson, the founder of Great Falls and initiator of hydroelectric power on the

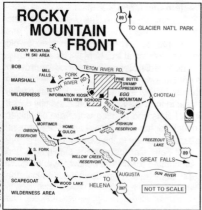

Missouri, is on the Sun River. The dam was built in 1913 primarily to store and divert water for irrigation.

Sights
Gibson Reservoir is 26 miles from Augusta. Reach it via the road toward the south end of town with the sign to Willow Creek Fishing Access Site (Rd. 1081). On the way to the Rocky Mountain Front, the road crosses a moraine strewn with glacial erratics—boulders carried in glacial ice and then dropped where the ice melted. Once the road meets up with the Sun River, you come right up against the rocks, and the whole geologic idea of "overthrust" becomes startlingly clear.

The road ends just past the dam, and trails continue the length of the reservoir, past medicine springs and Native American pictographs, into the Bob Marshall Wilderness. Bighorn sheep, elk, and deer winter north of the reservoir.

The state bought land for **Sun River Wildlife Management Area** in the 1940s to provide wintering ground for the Sun River elk herd. Previous to that, the elk had competed with cattle on the plains and with bighorn sheep in the mountains. Thousands of elk now winter on the moraine between the Gibson Reservoir and Augusta. Hunting is permitted here, though it's prohibited in the Sun River Game Preserve, part of the Bob Marshall Wilderness Area. The range is closed in the winter (though elk are often visible from nearby roads) and open in the summer to birdwatchers, hikers, and mountain bikers.

Accommodations
Billboards along Hwy. 287 herald the roadside **Wagons West** campground, as well as an associated inexpensive motel, tel. 562-3295, and restaurant. The **Bunkhouse Hotel**, 122 Main St., tel. 562-3387, is an old downtown hotel with inexpensive rooms.

Settle in and contemplate geology at **Home Gulch Campground** below Gibson Reservoir on the Sun River, 21 miles from Augusta. Five miles down the road, **Mortimer Campground** perches above the reservoir. A trail leads from Mortimer into the **Bob Marshall Wilderness Area**.

The **JJJ Ranch**, Box 310, Augusta, MT 59410, tel. 562-3653, leads horsepack trips into the Bob Marshall and, for the more sedate, has cabins

on the Gibson Reservoir. Ranch guests are fed whole-grain foods when they're not out on trail rides, fishing expeditions, or photo safaris.

Three campgrounds south of Gibson Reservoir are on Rd. 234 (Benchmark Rd.) west of Augusta. **Wood Lake** is 25 miles from Augusta, **Benchmark** is another five miles down the road, and **South Fork** is yet another mile on, at the end of the road.

Recreation
The trail from Mortimer Campground on Gibson Reservoir goes into the Bob Marshall Wilderness Area.

Trails into the Bob Marshall and Scapegoat wilderness areas start from Benchmark and South Fork campgrounds. A trail starts at the South Fork Campground and passes through the Sun River Game Preserve on its way to the spectacular Chinese Wall, a 13-mile-long, 1,000-foot-tall escarpment on the Continental Divide.

Information
The Forest Service has a **ranger station** just down Willow Creek Rd., tel. 562-3247.

BOB MARSHALL WILDERNESS AREA

The Bob Marshall Wilderness Area was created in 1940, when three national forest primitive areas were combined and named for a New Yorker who was a strong advocate for wilderness and an inveterate hiker.

The Land
The eastern face of the Bob Marshall is characterized by overthrust—old rocks on young. The Sawtooth Range, which forms the Rocky Mountain Front, shows off faults, folds, and overthrusts in the layers of limestone jutting into the prairie. The rocks here are generally younger than those in the more western ranges. Oil and gas speculators have been petitioning the Forest Service since the 1940s for the right to drill in the Bob Marshall and Great Bear wilderness areas.

The eastern side of the Bob Marshall is, as expected, drier, windier, and more sparsely vegetated than the western Swan Range side. Bears, mountain goats (native, not transplants), elk, and bighorn sheep all thrive in this wilderness area.

Getting In

Backpackers should plan to spend a minimum of five days to a week—distances are great. The Forest Service puts out a topographical map of the Bob Marshall, Great Bear, and Scapegoat Wilderness Complex. Use this map or USGS topos to select a route.

Despite its imposing appearance, the Rocky Mountain Front has a number of entrances to the Bob Marshall Wilderness Area. Roads west from Choteau and Augusta end at trailheads, some right near the wilderness boundary. There's a real visual punch gained by entering over the Front Range. The escarpments are pronounced on their eastern faces and trail off more gradually to the west.

The Benchmark trailhead west of Augusta is a particularly popular one, especially with horse packers.

Just to the north, trails from Gibson Reservoir lead right into the wilderness.

From the Headquarters Pass Trail, west of Choteau, continue on to Rocky Mountain Peak, at 9,392 feet the Bob's highest peak. This trail can also be followed to the Chinese Wall.

Destinations

Hikers and packers can start at virtually any trailhead and reach the Chinese Wall. This tall escarpment near the Continental Divide is the hallmark of the Bob and can see a surprising amount of traffic during the summer. For solitude, it's worth studying the maps and consulting with rangers to pick a less traveled area.

West of the Divide, the South Fork of the Flathead River cuts through the Bob and is a favorite with floaters and anglers, who usually come in from Holland Lake, on the western border.

East of the Bob Marshall's divide, anglers go after rainbow, brown, lake, golden, and cutthroat trout. Grayling are here too, but must be released when caught.

The **Sun River Game Preserve** was established in 1912 to protect and develop big-game herds. It now covers much of the eastern half of the Bob Marshall Wilderness Area—the only part of the Bob where hunting is prohibited.

Information

Contact the Forest Service at the Choteau Ranger Station, Rocky Mountain National Forest, Choteau, MT 59422, tel. (406) 466-2951.

BOB RACE

THE JUDITH BASIN AND CENTRAL MONTANA

INTRODUCTION

Central Montana is Montana's hybrid province: hundreds of miles from the Rocky Mountains' front range, isolated mountain peaks rise up like islands from the surrounding prairie. Called outliers, these ranges are literally habitat "islands" to plants and wildlife otherwise found only in the fastness of the Rockies.

The prairies spread around these peaks have been an ample home first to buffalo, and then, in the same pattern as the rest of eastern Montana, to livestock and farmers. But the mountains inevitably intrude, and nowhere on the central Montana prairies are they out of sight.

Central Montana managed to experience, almost headlong and after the fact, every phase of the state's history. Prospectors followed cattle barons, who were hurried out by the railroads and homesteaders. Fossil-fuel exploration followed giddily, and the region's hub city, Lewistown, is now quickly becoming a retirement community.

It seems odd that such a rich, central, and practical region should be one of the last settled in Montana. But the area's potent amalgam presents the traveler with a telescoped menu of the state's best offerings in hiking, hunting, fishing, wildlife viewing, scenery, and flat-out Western culture.

THE LAND

Central Montana is a half-mountain, half-prairie region of high plateaus and mountain valleys, roped in by the rivers that circle, feed, and drain the region. The Missouri River, rising from the south before turning sharply east, borders the area to the west and north; the Musselshell River, flowing east and then abruptly north, delimits central Montana to the south and east. Within this oblong of land has occurred some of Montana's most curious geologic history.

About 50 million years ago vast amounts of magma began to rise randomly along faults and fractures in underlying rock. In some cases, as in the Highwood Mountains, volcanic eruptions occurred. Sometimes the magma pooled under existing sedimentary levels, bulging these strata up to mountain height (the Big Snowy Range). In other cases, magma flowed along fractures until lakes of lava formed at their ends. Erosion has eaten away the softer sedimentary casts, leaving spiny lava outcrops (like Square Butte). Surrounding these mounds and spurs of rock are the rolling prairies.

The molten rock that hardened into mountains in central Montana is quite unusual. Not only has it proved to be rich in gold, silver, and lead, it contains minerals quite rare elsewhere. Shonkinite, a peculiar basalt which makes up the Highwood, Adel, and Bears Paw mountains, is named for Shonkin, Montana. Some of the world's bluest and most valued sapphires are mined on Yogo Creek in the Little Belt Mountains.

During the last ice age, central Montana's mountains stood above and helped block further advance of the continental ice sheet. Huge lakes formed when rivers like the Missouri and Musselshell, which drain northward, could find no escape for their waters. When these lakes burst and formed new river channels, they cut deep valleys. Around Great Falls particularly, minor streams today flow through enormous spillways meant to contain the Missouri.

Climate

The mountains of central Montana are not high by world, or even Montana, standards. However, they are very effective in trapping weather. Winters are harsh, and snowfalls are very heavy. In fact, the state record snowfall was recorded in the Little Belt Mountains (33 feet). Winter can come early, and stay late, especially in mountainous areas.

Central Montana does not suffer the same extremes of summer heat as the rest of eastern Montana. Frequent summer thunderstorms keep the region green, long after the prairie grasses have withered elsewhere.

INFORMATION

Travel Montana's central Montana district is called **Russell Country.** For free travel information contact them at P.O. Box 1366, Great Falls, MT 59403, tel. (800) 527-5348.

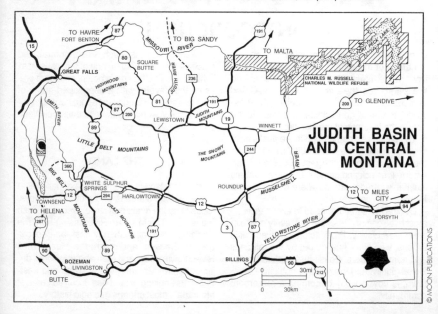

Belt Creek cuts a limestone canyon through the Little Belt Mountains.

The **BLM** office is on Airport Rd., Lewistown, tel. 538-7461. Most of the mountains in the area are part of the **Lewis and Clark National Forest, Jefferson Division**. The Forest Supervisor's Office can be reached at P.O. Box 871, Great Falls, MT 59403.

GETTING THERE AND AROUND

Great Falls and Billings are the closest airports served by major air carriers, although **Big Sky Airlines** has two flights a day into Lewistown from Billings. Call (800) 237-7788 for schedules; one-way fares between Billings and Lewistown can be as low as $25.

Intermountain Buses offers service between Great Falls and Billings, via Stanform, Lewistown, and Roundup. For schedules, contact the Lewistown depot, 102 W. Main, tel. (406) 538-3380.

LEWISTOWN

Lewistown (pop. 6,051, elev. 3,960 feet), nestled along Big Spring Creek at the foot of the Judith, Big Snowy, and Moccasin mountains, is the hub of central Montana (actually, the exact center of the state is located at 1105 W. Main.) Lewistown is a lively trading center for farmers and ranchers in the fertile Judith Basin country, and provides ample facilities and temptations for the traveler. Besides the city's many buildings of historic and architectural interest, within 30 miles are hiking trails, mountain lakes, trout streams, wildlife viewing, and ghost towns.

THE LAND

The Big Snowy Mountains (and their eastern extension, the Little Snowies) form a broad, domed arch rising from the plains. They were formed when magma pushed up from deep within the earth, but rather than erupting as a volcano, it pooled and crystallized. This magma blister elevated its limestone overburden thousands of feet. Today the sharper peaks of the Moccasins and Judiths reveal clusters of magma intrusions; erosion has stripped the softer rock away to expose igneous granite, syenite, and, occasionally, gold.

HISTORY

Big Spring Creek Valley was strategically located as settlement and trade entered central Montana. A trading post founded in 1873, Fort Sherman serviced hunters, trappers, and Crow Indians. The Carroll Trail, a stage route between Missouri River steamboats and the gold camps at Helena, was established a year later and passed near the trading post. Camp Lewis, a temporary military post, was built to protect commerce along the trail in the same year.

The Metis

The first permanent settlement came in 1879, when Metis families settled along Big Spring Creek. The half-French, half-Chippewa Metis had lived in the prairies of the northern U.S. and southern Canada until the Riel Rebellion of 1870. Dislocated by the English, the Metis fragmented and drifted westward in search of a homeland. Louis Riel joined the Big Spring Creek Metis in the early 1880s, but in 1884 he returned to Canada with most of his people to organize and resist English Canadian incursions against the Canadian Metis.

After the second Riel Rebellion failed in 1885, the Metis drifted back into Montana as "landless Indians," most of whom were eventually settled on the Rocky Boy Reservation. Some Metis remained on Big Spring Creek and established homesteads. Francis Janeaux opened a store and platted part of his land for the town that eventually became Lewistown.

Taming The Territory

Meanwhile, the Judith Basin was opening up. Granville Stuart established the DHS, a huge open-range cattle ranch, east of Lewistown in 1880. Other ranchers moved in to graze the rich prairies. Prospectors discovered gold at Maiden in the Judith Mountains the same year. The central Montana gold rush was on, and mining camps like Gilt Edge, Maiden, and Kendall boomed.

Even though the Indian Wars of 1876-77 had effectively crushed the fighting force of the natives of Montana, in 1880 the Army established Fort Maginnis to protect fledgling settlements from Indian attack. None occurred, and the indolent soldiers became more of a problem to local residents than the hostiles they purported to deter. The fort was closed in 1890.

Lewistown remained a rough-and-ready frontier town longer than comparable Montana communities. Rustlers preyed on local ranches, finding ample shelter in the rugged Missouri Breaks north of town. A shoot-out on Main Street ended the career of two suspected ringleaders (known to contemporaries as Rattlesnake Jake and Longhair Owen) in 1884.

Lewistown was incorporated in 1899, and in 1903 the Central Montana Railroad (bought in 1908 by the Milwaukee Railroad) reached this center of mining and ranch trade. What was taken out in cattle or gold was dwarfed by the

GRANVILLE STUART

L.A. HUFFMAN/MONTANA HISTORICAL SOCIETY

Granville Stuart, circa 1883

Granville Stuart, statesman, rancher, vigilante, writer, ambassador, and librarian, was among those early Montana settlers who thrived on challenge. Born of Scottish parents in West Virginia in 1834, Stuart accompanied his family to California during that state's gold rush. While returning to the East, he and his brother James detoured north through Montana. On Gold Creek near Drummond, they discovered gold in 1858. The Stuarts started the Montana gold rush. Granville was canny enough to realize that the *real* way to make money in a gold camp

was to supply goods to miners. He opened a store in Bannock in 1862, and operated a small farm. He saved his money and began to dabble in ranching in the Deer Lodge Valley.

Here he soon ran a lumber company. Stuart was elected to the Territorial Council in 1871, and was twice elected to the lower house, in 1876 and 1879. By 1879, he moved cattle out of western Montana and onto the plains of the east. He helped found the DHS Ranch east of Lewistown, the first large ranch in this part of the state.

Entire towns of rustlers grew up in the inaccessible Missouri Breaks to prey on these early ranches. The Montana Stockgrowers Association at their meeting in Helena in 1884 named Stuart—a founding member—president of their association. Stuart presented cattlemen's concerns to the legislature, and to the administrators of Fort Maginnis, which the Army had built in the hay yard of the DHS Ranch. When the branches of the government failed to adopt appropriate measures, Stuart and vengeance-minded ranchers founded "Stuart's Stranglers," a vigilante gang that broke the back of organized rustling. Estimates of the number of suspected rustlers killed in 1884 vary; at least 25, and as many as 100.

The winter of 1886-87 dealt with Stuart as sternly as others on the Montana prairies. He swore that he never again would winter an animal he couldn't shelter. In 1891, he became the state land agent, and selected 600,000 acres of government land whose proceeds still support the state school system. In 1894, he was named envoy to Paraguay and Uruguay by President Cleveland. Stuart retired to Montana in 1899, and became the Butte public librarian until his death in 1918.

Although not formally educated, Stuart was an avid reader with a taste for Byron, Shakespeare, and the Bible. His memoirs, *Forty Years on the Prairie,* are fascinating reading.

numbers of homesteaders who came in. The Judith Gap and Lewistown area was quickly and heavily settled by hopeful farmers: nearly 6.5 million acres of land were opened for settlement. The hegemony of the open-range ranches was broken, and by 1920 mining had declined in importance. The fertile countryside of central Montana sheltered homesteaders from some of the vicissitudes encountered by other settlers, and the gracious homes and buildings

of Lewistown bear testimony to the community's long-standing stability.

SIGHTS

Historic Lewistown

Lewistown has one of the prettiest physical settings in the state, and almost matches its natural attributes with its graceful turn-of-the-centu-

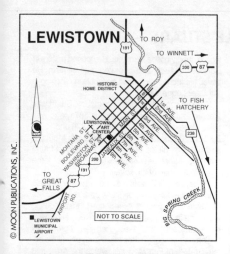

LEWISTOWN

TO ROY

TO WINNETT

HISTORIC
HOME DISTRICT

TO FISH
HATCHERY

LEWISTOWN
ART
CENTER

MONTANA ST.
BOULEVARD ST.
WASHINGTON ST.
BROADWAY

TO
GREAT
FALLS

AIRPORT RD.

NOT TO SCALE

LEWISTOWN
MUNICIPAL
AIRPORT

BIG SPRING CREEK

© MOON PUBLICATIONS, INC.

ry architecture. There are three neighborhoods listed as historic districts in the National Register of Historic Places. The chamber of commerce, 408 N.E. Main, provides brochures with walking tours of Lewistown. Not to miss: the **Fergus County Courthouse**, at 8th Ave. and Main, built in 1907 in mission style; behind it, on Broadway and 7th, is a wooden frame building which originally served as officers' quarters at Fort Maginnis; immediately next door is a wonderful example of a sandstone "four square" home. The **Silk Stocking District**, an area bounded by Boulevard and Washington streets at 2nd and 3rd avenues., contains a mix of arts-and-crafts style and neo-Georgian homes built by early haberdashers (hence the name). Dominant throughout, and especially downtown along Main St., are buildings made of sandstone bricks carved by immigrant Croatian stonecarvers. Less satisfying is the piped music that plays from speakers throughout the town center.

Central Montana Museum
Located in the same complex as the chamber of commerce (403 N.E. Main, tel. 538-5436), this local museum features Indian relics, homesteader memorabilia, and reminders of life on the open range.

Lewistown Art Center
Specializing in Montana art, this small gem of a gallery, 108 8th Ave. N, tel. 538-8278, mixes

traveling shows of regional art with a good selection of art and crafts in its gallery shop. The stone building that houses the art center was built in the 1890s and is a former rooming house and high-school dormitory.

Ghost Towns
Gold was discovered in 1880 in the Judith Mountains; by 1881 **Maiden** claimed a population of 6,000, making it larger than Lewistown, with which it vied for county seat when Fergus County was formed in 1882. To reach Maiden, take Hwy. 191 north from Lewistown for 10 miles, then turn east on a good secondary road for nine miles. This gold camp burned in 1905, making the inevitable ghost town a bit more spectral.

The road up Warm Springs Creek in the Judith Mountains to Maiden is very scenic, and continues five miles over a steep pass to **Gilt Edge**, another gold camp gone bust. Gilt Edge boomed when gold was discovered in the early 1890s. Calamity Jane Canary claimed that Gilt Edge was her favorite town; she also claimed that she was the local law enforcement. A few intact brick buildings and more disintegrating plank buildings remain. Gilt Edge can also be reached by traveling Hwy. 200 east from Lewistown for 14 miles; turn north another mile.

Farther west in the Moccasin Mountains is **Kendall**, a gold camp that reached its zenith in the first years of this century. The foundations of the union hall and a bandstand are amongst the remains. Take Hwy. 191 north to Hilger, then turn west for about six miles.

ACCOMMODATIONS

Hotels And Motels
The **Park Inn International**, 211 E. Main, tel. 538-8721, is Lewistown's most comfortable lodging. The **Park Inn** (known to the locals as the Yogo Inn) caters to the small convention trade and has the kinds of amenities (pool, spa, good restaurant, meeting rooms) that dignify this class of motel ($36 s, $41 d).

Mid-range motels include the **B & B Motel**, 420 E. Main, tel. 538-5496, $25 s, $36 d; the **Mountain View Motel**, 1422 W. Main, tel. 538-3457, $24 s, $32 d; the **Trail's End**, 216 N.E. Main, tel. 538-5468, $24 s, $34 d. The **Super 8**, 102 Wendell, tel. 538-2581, $31 s, $37 d, is located on the hill west of town. The **Historic Calvert Hotel**, 216 7th Ave. S, tel. 538-5411, $12 s, $17 d, is Lewistown's remaining older hotel.

Campgrounds
Mountain Acres is principally an RV park, just north of Lewistown on Hwy. 191, tel. 538-7591. Tent campers will prefer **Crystal Lake** 35 miles south of town (see p. 146), or **Camp Maiden**, located at the summit of the Judith Mountains near the remains of Maiden ghost town. Take Hwy. 191 north 10 miles to Warm Springs Rd., and turn east 12 miles.

FOOD

The **Park Inn,** 221 E. Main, tel. 538-8721, has Lewistown's most varied menu, and features local trout along with beef and seafood. Elsewhere, steaks are the order of the day. The **Hackamore Club,** two miles west of Lewistown

on Hwy. 200, tel. 538-5685; **Bar 19,** a mile north on Hwy. 191, tel. 538-3250; the **Horseshoe Club,** 111 Commercial, tel. 538-9722; and the **4 Aces,** 508 1st Ave. N, tel. 538-9744, are all good supper clubs (with menus heavily weighted to beef) that can't quite decide if they are restaurants, casinos, or bars.

Go to the **Whole Famdamily,** 206 W. Main, tel. 538-5161, or **Sweet Six,** 224 W. Main, tel. 538-3867, for lunch and breakfast. Visit your food roots at a couple of Lewistown diners, the **Snow White Café,** 122 W. Main, tel. 538-3666 ("We use real potatoes"), or the **Empire Café,** 214 W. Main, tel. 538-9912.

RECREATION

Fishing
The Lewistown area offers great trout fishing. Big Spring Creek issues forth from a spring five

CHOKECHERRIES

The chokecherry is one of the few fruits native to the northern prairies. This large deciduous shrub produces sour, aptly-named fruit which played a large part both in traditional Plains Indian culture and in the lives of early settlers.

Chokecherries are a large component of *pemmican,* a staple of the Plains Indian diet. Ground chokecherries were added to powdered dried buffalo meat to form a compound that was both nutrious and mobile. Nomads stored pemmican in buffalo-skin vessels, or in their *parflèche,* for long journeys. When on the move, pemmican was eaten out of hand; it could also be fed into boiling water to make a flavorful soup. Indians also made cakes of dried chokecherries, which were saved and eaten in winter. Chokecherries provided one of the only sources of vitamin C in the Plains diet.

As notable as the chokecherry's gastronomic virtues were its emetic properties. Sufferers of stomach complaints or diarrhea made a tea of chokecherry twigs and barks; relief was quick and lasting. Captain Lewis drank chokecherry tea when he developed intestinal distress along the Missouri; he recovered within hours.

Indians also used chokecherry wood for arrow shafts and bows. Warring and hunting parties used chokecherry wood to build fires; such a fire produced little smoke—a benefit when camping near enemies.

Homesteaders found chokecherries, bitter as they are, to be the prairie's only common native fruit. The *chokecherry,* Prunus virginiana

fruit was carefully gathered and processed into jelly and syrup. To an old-timer, the thought of pancakes and chokecherry syrup brings back happy associations of simpler times.

Mountain ravines and stream sides around Lewistown are still home to stands of chokecherries; recognize them by their pale green-white tufts of flowers, and dark fruit hanging in clusters.

Lewistown is host to the Chokecherry Festival the second weekend of September. There's a street dance, a marathon run, and judges award a prize for the best chokecherry recipe. Use one of these, or consider a batch of chokecherry jelly; simply pick the fruit and prepare according to any recipe for sour cherry jelly. Be careful of the leaves: they contain cyanic acid, and can be poisonous.

miles south of town, and locals consider it one of the best fishing streams in the state. Turn south on First Ave. and follow signs to Heath or the State Fish Hatchery. Warm Springs Creek is also good trout fishing, in a more rural setting. Take Hwy. 191 north 10 miles to the intersection of Warm Springs Creek Road.

Lake anglers are also in luck. **Crystal Lake,** high in the Big Snowy Mountains, affords excellent recreational opportunities, including good fishing for rainbows. No motorized boats are allowed. Good hiking trails, overnight camping, and picnicking make Crystal Lake a popular destination for locals. Crystal Lake is 35 miles south of Lewistown; follow Hwy. 200 west seven miles, then follow well-signed Forest Service roads 28 miles south.

Hiking

The gentle, domed peaks of the Big Snowy Mountains provide surprisingly challenging and rewarding hikes. From the south end of Crystal Lake, **Uhlhorn Trail** leads up an initially steep grade to the Big Snowy Crest. High, moderately flat alpine meadows open out across the saddle of the mountains, with great views across the plains of eastern Montana. At the crest, the trail divides. To the west, a two-mile-long trail leads to Ice Cave, cool and exciting to explore with a flashlight. A longer hike involves following the crest trail to the east. The trail continues through meadows until, about six miles in, the ridge narrows to Knife Blade Ridge. The trail skirts abrupt drops on both sides before reaching Greathouse Peak, about 10 miles from the crest trailhead.

Parks

A nice place for a picnic is the **State Fish Hatchery** on Upper Big Spring Creek. The eponymous Big Spring is the third-largest freshwater spring in the world, discharging 62,700 gallons of water a minute, over three million gallons per hour. Near the hatchery, along the stream and amongst trees, there's a picnic area; tours of the hatchery are available. Follow 1st Ave. south to Country Club Rd., and follow signs for the Hatchery.

Closer to town, **Symmes Park** has a picnic area, tennis courts, a playground, and is located right behind the chamber of commerce and museum at Hwy. 200 and Prospect Avenue. The city swimming pool is in **Frank Day Park,** 6th Ave. and Cook St. (12 blocks south of Main Street).

Along Denton Rd., 10 miles north on Hwy. 191, then west on Hwy. 81 is **Warm Springs,** a natural spring of warm water diverted into a swimming pool. Adjacent is a picnic area. There is a $2 fee for use of the pool and grounds.

Golf

The **Lewistown Elks Country Club,** south of Lewistown on Spring Creek Rd., tel. 538-7075, is a nine-hole course situated above a pastoral mountain stream.

Services

The **Lewistown Area Chamber of Commerce** is at 408 N.E. Main St., Lewistown, MT 59457, tel. 538-5436.

The **Central Montana Medical Center** is at 408 Wendall Ave., tel. 538-7711. **Emergency** is 911.

Winter storms can be intense in the local mountains. To check **local road conditions**, call 538-8731.

If dirty clothes are getting you down, go to the **Wash House,** 511 E. Main, tel. 538-9919.

The **Carnegie Public Library** is at 701 W. Main, tel. 538-5212. The **Post Office** is at 204 3rd Ave. N, tel. 538-3439.

GETTING THERE AND AROUND

Two flights daily on **Big Sky Airlines** link Lewistown with Billings. One-way fare is $25. Contact Big Sky Airlines at (800) 882-4475 for schedules; their number at the airport is 538-2311.

Rimrock Stage Buses run between Billings, Lewistown, and Great Falls. The Lewistown depot is at 102 W. Main, tel. 538-3380.

Cars are available from **Budget Car Rental,** 519 W. Broadway, tel. 538-7701.

FORT BENTON AND BIG SAG COUNTRY

East of Great Falls, the Rockies fade from view, the buttes and peaks of central Montana loom capriciously, and the Missouri leaves its wide valley to plunge into a badland gorge. This transition landscape, between the prairies of eastern Montana and the Rockies' foothills, contains some of the most interesting history, geology, and scenery in the state. Here too are seldom-visited back roads leading to pleasant, isolated towns like Highwood, Stockett, and Eden.

Montana's oldest town is Fort Benton. Steamboats from St. Louis docked here 125 years ago—it was known as the "innermost port"—making it the stepping-off point for thousands of settlers and their chattel.

THE LAND

Geologically speaking, relatively recent events created the distinctive landscapes of the Big Sag area. About 20 million years after the Rockies formed, a vast surge of volcanic activity forced molten rock to the surface in many parts of central Montana.

Not all lava erupted; some molten rock squeezed up through fissures and faults or fed into underground reservoirs, called laccoliths. Erosion has exposed these formations as well, steep vertical ridges of volcanic stone—dikes—running in straight lines across the landscape. Rising spectacularly from the plains near Geraldine is Square Butte, one of the most prominent laccoliths in Montana.

Ice-age glaciers trapped river flow and glacial meltwater, forming Glacial Lake Great Falls. The present site of Great Falls was flooded by 600 feet of melted ice; water stretched from the Highwoods to the Rocky Mountain foothills. As the lake grew and the glaciers receded, this vast body of water cut a new spillway. About 10,000 years ago, the overflow of Glacial Lake Great Falls roared through this channel, until the melting glaciers revealed a lower watercourse. The glacial lake spillway, called the Shonkin Sag by geologists and the Big Sag by locals, remains as a deep U-shaped valley, 500 feet deep and a mile wide, along the base of the Highwood

Mountains and Square Butte. All that remains of the huge river that once flowed here are a few shallow lakes and the spectacular canyon that it cut.

HISTORY

The mix of rich prairie grassland, mountain pastures, and easy access to supplies at nearby Fort Benton gave this area prominence in the early days of open-range ranching. The Milwaukee Road established rail service to the area in 1908, laying track along the Shonkin Sag's old riverbed, thereby opening the region to the homesteader.

Montana's first commercial coal production took place in 1876 at Belt. The high-quality lignite coal was hauled to Fort Benton, whose steamboats demanded a source of fuel. The abundance and quality of the coal drew the attention of Marcus Daly, whose Anaconda Copper Company smelters needed coal. Daly gained control of coal production in Belt in 1893, and established the town as a center for coal refining. One hundred coke ovens and a coal washhouse lined Belt Creek; a branch line of the Great Northern daily carried 1,500 tons of coke to smelters at nearby Great Falls and Anaconda.

The fuel needs of the Great Northern itself led to the development of coal mines at Sand Coulee and Stockett, just west of Belt. All these mining centers fell on hard times when the smelters converted to natural gas and when the railroads converted to diesel fuel. There is no coal production in the area now.

SIGHTS

The Shonkin Sag
Today, the Shonkin Sag is home to the small community of **Highwood**, numerous shallow lakes, and scattered farms and ranches. To reach the Shonkin Sag, follow Hwy. 228 east from Great Falls or Hwy. 331 north from Belt. Highwood sits at the mouth of the Shonkin Sag. From here, gravel roads continue on to Geraldine or to Fort Benton; both are well signed and in good condition.

The Shonkin Sag

W.C. McRAE

The more scenic choice is the Geraldine road. It continues up the Shonkin Sag to the little crossroads of Shonkin, then cuts south into a steep valley in the Highwood Mountains. The road leaves the mountains and again crosses the Shonkin Sag; Square Butte looms to the south across several marshy lakes, and a spiky palisade of igneous rock (a volcanic dike) marches across the valley. The county road ends at Geraldine and Hwy. 80. The landscape is curiously spare and beautiful; this is one of the most compelling side trips in the state.

Shonkin Sag continues southeast, following Hwy. 80 past Square Butte. Here it turns abruptly north, with tiny Arrow Creek borrowing the Missouri's ancient riverbed for that creek's short and uneventful journey northward. Prominent white cliffs cap the ridges east of Square Butte. To the north, the Missouri is flowing through a canyon cut through the same formation; Lewis and Clark were much taken by the White Cliffs along the Missouri, calling them "seens of visionary inchantment."

Travelers unable to make the full sashay around the Big Sag can get a taste of this landscape by taking a shorter side trip to Stockett, south of Great Falls. Before the ice age began, the Missouri flowed in a channel slightly south of its present flow. The little towns of Sand Coulee and Stockett are nestled in the perfect U-shaped valley left when the Missouri abandoned this former channel. To reach Stockett, follow Hwy. 227 south from the outskirts of Great Falls. Off-road enthusiasts can follow gravel roads through gently rolling landscapes, with great views onto the Rocky Mountain Front and the central Montana mountains, by continuing on to Eden, the Smith River Valley, and Ulm.

Highwood Mountains

The Highwood Mountains are the deeply eroded remnants of isolated volcanoes that erupted about 50 million years ago. Although not tall—Highwood Baldy reaches 7,600 feet—these old craters host good trout streams. Like the other ranges of central Montana, the Highwoods don't overwhelm the traveler by size or severity; more meadow than peak, they are islands of green in a sea of grain fields. The Forest Service maintains a popular campground on **Thain Creek**.

Away from the main cluster of peaks, a series of isolated buttes marches to the east. While explosive volcanic events formed the Highwoods, unerupted pools of magma are responsible for these symmetrical but craggy peaks.

The most notable of these lava formations are **Round** and **Square buttes** east of the Highwoods. The unusual magma that formed these extrusions is a dark, crystal-flecked rock called shonkinite, rare enough to be named after the central Montana area where it occurs in abundance. As the pools of shonkinite cooled underground millions of years ago, a lighter igneous rock floated to the top of the laccolith, like cream on milk. Called syenite, it's much lighter colored than shonkinite, and forms the startlingly white cap on Square Butte.

The **Square Butte Natural Area** is a 2,000-acre preserve along the butte's high plateau and peaks, 2,400 feet above the prairies. Maintained by the BLM, this is one of the most unusual destinations in Montana. The steep sides of the butte have protected the native grasses and plants from overgrazing; Lewis and Clark saw such stands of grasses when they crossed the prairies 200 years ago. In a good year the plants reach waist level; some varieties here are no longer found on rangeland. The wildflower display in May and June is astonishing, and deer, pronghorn, and birds are abundant.

The views too are spectacular. The core of the laccolith rises in cliffs and ridges of shonkinite and syenite, hundreds of feet above the plateau. The Shonkin Sag runs along the north side of Square Butte (look for the escarpment of an ancient waterfall in the watercourse). Here, as at few other places, one can truly grasp the expanse of the plains. The mountains of central Montana perforate the otherwise limitless flat horizons stretching outward for hundreds of miles.

While ascending to the Square Butte Plateau is relatively easy, given a high-clearance vehicle and a little chutzpah, getting to the top of the volcanic plug itself requires a rigorous scramble up very rough terrain. Square Butte is much more rugged than it looks from a distance. Don't attempt to climb it alone, and don't feel as if you have to. Heroism isn't required to enjoy the plant and animal life; a good picnic will do the trick.

Square Butte is only accessible through private land. The landowners ask that you check in with them before starting up the butte. The road is a 4WD track, and although adequately maintained, it is quite rocky. Cars with narrower axles than pickup trucks will need to straddle the tracks; low-bellied cars could easily puncture an oil pan on the trademark shonkinite. Although a high-clearance vehicle is preferable for this road, at least one Honda Accord has made it up and back.

To reach Square Butte Natural Area, turn at the community of Square Butte and follow the signs. The road passes through a ranch yard; from here, the top of the plateau is about three miles.

Accommodations

The Big Sag area is within easy driving distance of Great Falls, Lewistown, Stanford, and Fort Benton, each of which offers a full range of lodgings and amenities. To reach **Thain Creek Campground**, follow road signs for Highwood from Hwy. 200, then turn up Highwood Creek for 18 miles on a good gravel road.

Food

In Highwood, the **Willow Tree Café**, tel. 733-2383, serves breakfast and lunch. In Geraldine, the local eatery is **Mike's Bar and Grill**, tel. 737-4541.

FORT BENTON

Once the bustling head of Missouri River navigation, Fort Benton (pop. 1,600, elev. 2,600 feet) is now a quiet, even sleepy town. When the fur trade boomed, steamboats struggled up the narrow, sandbarred waters of the Missouri to discharge fortune-seeking trappers and prospectors and load up with furs. The Great Falls of the Missouri 25 miles upstream prohibited further river travel.

Fort Benton was built in 1846 and served primarily as a fur-trading post. By 1859, the Mullan Road linked Fort Benton with Walla Walla, Washington, the easternmost navigable town on the Columbia River system. The Whoop-Up Trail led from Fort Benton to Alberta, and was used to supply western Canada with illegal "Indian whiskey"; incongruously, the fort was also supply depot for Canadian Mounties charged with bringing order to the wild, whiskey-sotted western provinces.

Of the trading forts built in mid-19th-century Montana, only Fort Benton survives as a town today. History is well displayed in Fort Benton's long, green riverside park. And the Missouri River still flows by, wide and muddy as ever, headed for an area still barely touched by roads.

Sights

Start Fort Benton's walking tour in the city park. The remains of the original fur-trading fort are here, as is the **Museum of the Upper Missouri**, tel. 622-3766, which focuses on the fur trade and steamboat era. Hours are 9 a.m.-7 p.m. daily May 15-Sept. 15. The museum shuts down from Oct. 15 to May 1 and has 1-5 p.m. hours the remaining days of the year.

Fort Benton as it appeared in Harper's Monthly, April, 1867

MONTANA HISTORICAL SOCIETY

Continue walking down the levee to the statue of Lewis, Clark, and Sacajawea sculpted by Browning artist Bob Scriver, the keelboat replica built in the early '50s for the movie *The Big Sky*, and the 15th St. Bridge, which has spanned the Missouri since 1888. Historical signs along the grassy riverside strip discuss riverboats, the fur trade, and wild times in the streets of 19th-century Fort Benton.

Facing the river at 1718 Front St., the **Wild and Scenic Upper Missouri Visitor Center** has wildlife and archaeological exhibits and a Lewis and Clark slide show.

Toward the end of the greenway, read about **Shep**, the faithful sheepherder's dog who, after his master's body was ferried away by rail, met every train into town for over five years. Shep, who was eventually run over by a train, is buried on a hill overlooking the depot where an enormous particle-board likeness of him hovers over the simple concrete grave marker.

Among the town's historic buildings, the **Grand Union Hotel**, 1302 Front St., stands out. It was indeed grand when it was built in 1882, just as the railroad was poised to eclipse steamboat transportation, and is now in a stalled state of renovation.

Three blocks away from the river on 20th and Washington streets, the **Museum of the Northern Great Plains** has an agricultural focus; open 9-7 daily, May 15-Sept. 15.

Accommodations
Of the two motels in town, the **Pioneer Lodge**, 1700 Front St., tel. 622-5441, more closely fits the old downtown motel category, but it's not quite the real thing. The building used to be a general store, and was designed without many windows. In order to bring the rooms up to motel code, windows were put in—but they face onto the hallway, not the Missouri River. Though the rooms ($30 s) are comfortable, they lack telephones, but not TVs. Still, it's more conveniently located, has more character, and is a tad less expensive than the **Fort Motel**, 1809 St. Charles, tel. 622-3312.

RV campers can pull up and spend the night for free in the city park, but there are no amenities. Tent campers aren't encouraged to do the same.

Food And Drink
While the **3-Way Café**, 2300 St. Charles, tel. 622-5681, may have the more titillating name, it's **C-J's Diner**, 1402 Front, tel. 622-5035, that serves up tater tots as a side dish.

Events
A **summer celebration** is held the last weekend of June. Labor Day weekend brings the **Choteau County Fair**.

Missouri Breaks

"SEENS OF VISIONARY INCHANTMENT": THE WILD AND SCENIC MISSOURI RIVER

East of Great Falls, the Missouri River leaves its valley and begins to burrow below the prairie surface. The sluggish river and the deep canyon it cuts were designated a Wild and Scenic River in 1976; 149 miles of river and 131,840 acres of adjacent land are preserved much as Lewis and Clark encountered them. Today, it's one of the great float trips in the nation, with tons of wildlife viewing adding to the historic and scenic value of this last remnant of free-flowing Missouri River.

The Land
The austere gorge cut by the Missouri between Fort Benton and Fort Peck Dam is a relatively recent accomplishment. Until the most recent ice ages, the Missouri flowed north from this point until it debouched into Hudson's Bay. The ice sheets blocked that outlet, and huge ice-age dams, filled with the Missouri's flow and glacial melt, spilled over the plains. Almost surreptitiously, the Missouri began to flow along the southernmost face of the glaciers, slowly cutting a channel all the way to the Mississippi. When the ice sheets began their last retreat 10,000 years ago, the Missouri remained in its new channel.

The precipitous and highly eroded walls of much of the Wild and Scenic Missouri's canyon are known locally as "breaks" or "badlands." These strata are the sedimentary remains of ancient seas washed up in eastern Montana 80 million years ago. The thousand-foot-deep gorge cuts through about 10 million years of this geologic history. Erosion has isolated monoliths of sandstone, craggy outbursts of rock, and sheer cliffs of startlingly white limestone.

The soils are extremely infertile—rich in alkali and salt, they support little plant life except for occasional junipers and ponderosa pines. Along the river, however, there are beautiful groves of shade-giving cottonwoods.

The lower reaches of the Wild and Scenic Missouri merge with the C.M. Russell National Wildlife Refuge. Here, elk, bighorn sheep, deer, beaver, mink, coyotes, and birds in abundance live along the riverbanks.

Recreation
The Missouri River provides the recreational, as well as the historical, focus to Fort Benton. A visit to the BLM's information center at 1718 Front St. will make all but the most hydrophobic start planning a float down the Missouri River.

Just down the park from the remains of old Fort Benton is the **swimming pool**. It's a nice, big pool, and worth the $2 adult, $1 child fee. The **Signal Point Golf Course**, out St. Charles St. past the Shep Memorial, is reportedly the state's most challenging nine-hole course.

Fish the Missouri from Fort Benton's levee for sauger, freshwater drum, and goldeye.

Information And Services
Dial 622-5451 for **emergency** services.

Write the **Fort Benton Visitor's Center**, P.O. Box 988, Fort Benton, MT 59442, tel. 622-5634, for information. Or stop in at **Karen's Insta-Print Studio**, 1402 Front St. (by C-J's Diner) for tourist brochures.

Exploring The Wild And Scenic Missouri By Boat

Only one road crosses the Missouri between Fort Benton and the Fred Robinson Bridge north of Grassrange 150 miles away. Only remote, ranch-access dirt roads even come close to it. Without any doubt, the best way to see the Wild and Scenic Missouri is by boat.

A float trip on the Missouri takes two forms; a guided trip with a guide and outfitter or a well-planned float on your own. Both have advantages. While the traveler's independent streak might initially value a go-it-alone attitude, consider the following:

Remember that there are no towns along the river; no shops, no restaurants, no motels. You have to bring your own water; the muddy water of the Missouri isn't appealing for drinking even when boiled. There are no telephones or ambulances waiting if accidents occur (actually, heat stroke and sunburn are the greatest dangers). The Missouri is not a hasty shoot-the-rapids river; it takes seven days to float all the way between Fort Benton and the Fred Robinson Bridge. And if you do put in on your own, how are you going to get back to your vehicle, several hundred road miles back upstream?

If you decide to float on your own, remember to sign in at the BLM visitor center in Fort Benton before putting in to the river. The stretch of the Missouri between Fort Benton and Loma is an easy one-day float, and is the most heavily used segment of the Wild and Scenic Missouri. For more information, contact the BLM River Manager, Airport Rd., Lewistown, MT 59457, tel. 538-7461. During the summer, the BLM maintains an office at 1718 Front St., Fort Benton, MT 59442, tel. 622-5185.

Outfitters

The following outfitters provide guided trips on the Missouri; each offers different packages involving trips of varying lengths (a minimum number of floaters is also usually demanded), and most also rent canoes or rafts. The BLM provides a complete list of permitted outfitters.

Missouri River Outfitters, Attn. Bob Singer, P.O. Box 1212, Fort Benton, MT 59442, tel. 622-3295. The Grand Old Man of Missouri float trips, Singer is a veteran of nearly 25 years of river outfitting. Guided, fully outfitted trips begin at $75 a day per person. He also rents canoes for $12 a day, and offers a shuttle service.

Missouri River Canoe Rental, Attn. Don Sorenson, R.R. 1, Loma, MT 59460, tel. 378-

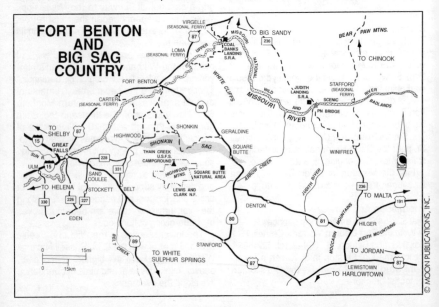

3110, offers bed and breakfast in a historic inn or in homesteaders' cabins. Outfitted float trips range from $55-100 a day per person. Canoes are also for rent, and shuttle service is available.

The **Upper Missouri Keel Boat Company**, Attn. Charles Kincaid, 8385 Buffalo Horn Dr., Helena, MT 59601, tel. 458-5323, recalls the fur-trading days on the Missouri by offering float trips in replica 19th-century keelboats. These fully outfitted trips feature guides in buckskins and camping in tepees, and begin at $200 per day per person. A 40-foot keelboat holds six passengers.

Exploring The Wild And Scenic Missouri By Car

While there's no substitute for a float trip down the Missouri, travelers on a tight schedule or fearful of water retain interesting options. On this section of the Missouri, only one gravel road bridges the river; other less-traveled roads cross the river on ferries.

The **Missouri River ferries** are amongst the last river ferries in the country. Licensed by the U.S. Coast Guard, these cable-drawn ferries connect obscure county roads for ranchers and farmers who live in this lonesome stretch of Montana.

The ferries are free during the day; simply pull up to the landing and drive onto the small plank barge. If the ferry is on the other side, the operator will cross to pick you up. If there is no sign of life, honk your horn. Out of consideration, plan to use the ferries within normal waking hours; there is sometimes a fee for late-night crossings. The ferries normally operate April to Thanksgiving; the rest of the year the river freezes over.

Ferries operate at Carter, Loma, Virgelle, and Stafford. The Carter Ferry links up with a network of country dirt roads in the Fort Benton/Highwood area, making a loop trip easy if dusty.

Loma is where the Marias River flows into the Missouri. In 1805, when Lewis and Clark were traveling up the Missouri to its headwaters, they spent several puzzling days camped at the confluence. Their Mandan informants had not mentioned this particular river coming in from the north, and most of the men in the party believed that this large river was actually the main stream of the Missouri. Lewis, and eventually Clark, thought otherwise, and led the Corps south, along what was, indeed, the Missouri.

The mouth of the Marias became the site of **Fort Piegan**, established in 1831 for trade with the Blackfeet. (If you wonder how the Corps could have been so flummoxed by so small a river as the Marias, remember that it was once much larger and is now impounded for irrigation by Tiber Dam.)

The **Loma Ferry** provides access to forlorn badlands and to dirt roads that become pretty questionable in wet weather. Off-road enthusiasts can make a loop trip through dramatic gumbo breaks and ranchland by starting at the Loma Ferry and coming back out at the **Virgelle Ferry**.

Downstream from Virgelle is the most scenic portion of the Missouri Breaks; **Coal Banks Landing State Park** is a popular departure point for float trips. For cars, the landscapes are dramatic, but there is no road access to the nearby White Cliffs area along the river.

The **Stafford Ferry** is the most remote of the Missouri River ferries, linking dirt roads north of Winifred with a gravel road south of Chinook. It's a long road—about 80 miles—but it passes through breathtaking badlands, along the trail of Chief Joseph's last flight and battle, and through the lonesome and lovely Bear's Paw Mountains. It's countryside not often seen by travelers. Don't attempt this road if rain threatens.

There's a bridge now at the site of the old PN Ferry, at the juncture of the Judith River and the Missouri. The Judith adds its deep valley to the Missouri's gorge, making this a precipitous confluence. It's easily reached north of Winifred, or south of Big Sandy, by good all-weather gravel roads.

Practicalities

The **Loma Motel**, tel. 739-4252, $28 d, also offers an RV campground, and is next door to the **Loma Café**.

The **Virgelle Mercantile** offers B&B accommodations in frontier-era cabins ($40) or in an old storefront inn ($65-85). Evening meals are available by reservation. The Virgelle Mercantile also does business as the **Missouri River Canoe Rental** and offers boat rentals and fully outfitted trips down the Missouri.

There are undeveloped campgrounds at the ranger stations at **Coal Banks Landing** near Virgelle and at Judith Landing north of Winifred.

EAST OF LEWISTOWN

Once the traveler descends from the pass of the Judith Mountains 10 miles east of Lewistown, unadulterated eastern Montana lies ahead. The ponderosa pines quickly thin and give way to shortgrass prairie; mountain valleys flatten into wide coulees surmounted with sandstone bluffs. Ranches displace farms, and gray rain clouds from the west veer upwards, sutured by heat rising off the prairies. Somewhere hereabouts, the Great Plains begin in earnest.

This part of Montana is more often traversed than visited: even by Montana standards, this is pretty forlorn country. Nonetheless it bears the memories of a violent history, sporadic development, and early settlement. Today, in the tradition of the glory days of the West, this outpost of eastern Montana supports large ranches, a vast wildlife refuge, and tiny communities known mostly for their watering holes.

THE LAND

Within the arm formed by the Musselshell River flowing north to meet the Missouri, flat but eroded prairies stretch between Grassrange and Winnett. The plains belie their beginnings as sedimentary seabeds, and, especially to the

north along the present-day Missouri, the effect of Glacial Lake Musselshell.

Geologists discovered one of the first and richest oil fields in this part of Montana in 1920. The Cat Creek Anticline, a buckling of sedimentary layers caused at the same time the mountains rose in central Montana (about 50 million years ago), contains domes of oil-rich sandstone at a depth of about 1,200 feet.

An earlier but less productive oil discovery was made in the impressive Devil's Basin, 27 miles south of Grassrange on Hwy. 87. Here, sandstone layers are so tightly folded by underlying faults that they rise in steep ridges and stalk across a wide, barren valley.

HISTORY

As with the Big Open region just to the east, here the requisite historical phases of boom and development came late and peremptorily. There was little settlement—of a law-abiding sort—until this century, making this one of the last areas of Montana to be settled.

As early as the 1860s, Fort Musselshell, established at the Musselshell and Missouri river juncture, was a busy trade center with the Gros

Homesteading was hard, often discouraging work; rewards were counted in the years survived, the number of acres plowed.

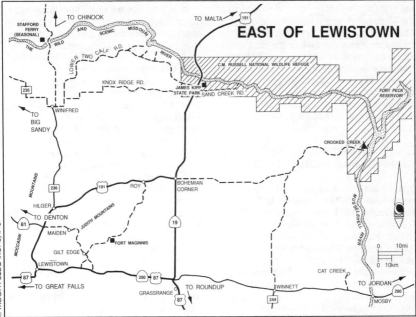

Ventre Indians. By the 1870s, the more hostile Sioux forced abandonment of the trading post. Another trading outpost, Carroll, was established just up the Missouri in 1874. From here, freighters established a stage route west to the gold camps at Helena, in hopes that Carroll's downstream location would displace Fort Benton as the hub of steamboat trade, at least in low-water years. The stages stopped rolling after only one year.

Trappers, wolf hunters, and woodchoppers (for the steamboats) were the only permanent residents of this remote country, and they lived together in rough camps that passed for towns. As steamboat trade dwindled, the settlements increasingly became hideouts for rustlers and outlaws; Kid Curry and his gang had a pied-à-terre in a knocked-together river town called Rocky Point. The Breaks, as this rough country was known, became synonymous with rustlers and ne'er-do-wells. An 1870 census found 170 people living along the Missouri from Fort Benton to North Dakota; the count included only one white woman.

The Open Range

On the prairies that spread out eastward from the Judith Mountains, cattlemen like Granville Stuart soon established huge open-range ranches. By the 1880s, lawlessness was so rife that Fort Maginnis, raised on the flats next to Stuart's DHS Ranch, spent more time pursuing rustlers than intimidating Indians.

The mouth of the Musselshell hosted numerous rustler gangs: in this wild country of brushy badlands, box canyons, and primitive settlements, wayward cowboys could trail stolen cattle and horses into secret ravines, alter their brands, and sell them to traders or trail them to Canada. Once in Canada, they would steal other livestock, and trail them south into the States.

As the situation worsened, Stuart and a posse of like-minded vigilantes met at a bar in Gilt Edge and decided to take matters into their own hands. During the summer of 1884, "Stuart's Stranglers," as the vigilantes called themselves, took the offensive against the organized rustling rings along the Missouri. In a series of shoot-outs and hangings at least 17 men were killed by the vigilantes in Rocky Point, at the mouth of the Musselshell, and other hideouts along the Missouri. Spurred on by their success, Stuart's Stranglers took their show on the road, and in secret raids in other parts of eastern Montana killed an estimated 60 more suspected thieves.

So the ranchers rid themselves of the threat of rustlers; but as these stockmen did not own the land they grazed, soon homesteaders carved the open range into half-section parcels.

CHARLES M. RUSSELL NATIONAL WILDLIFE REFUGE

The Western Unit of the Charles M. Russell National Wildlife Refuge forms the northern border of much of this area. Created in 1936, the 1.2 million-acre C.M.R., as it is known locally, is the second-largest wildlife refuge outside of Alaska. Highway 191 is one of two paved roads into the refuge; the other is 125 miles east. Anyone who wishes to visit the refuge must be willing to drive, sometimes for great distances, on gravel and dirt roads. The rustlers and outlaws who holed up here did so for a reason: it's hard country to navigate. However, isolation conducive to thieving is also conducive to wildlife.

Travelers without high-clearance vehicles are advised to cross the Fred Robinson Bridge on Hwy. 191 and take the **Self-Guided Nature Trail**, a 20-mile loop north of the Missouri. Those with more versatile vehicles can explore the back roads of these rugged, isolated, and uninhabited badlands on the south side.

Sand Creek Trail leaves the pavement four miles south of the Fred Robinson Bridge, at the refuge headquarters, and winds through badlands, with several side roads giving onto the river bottoms. A much longer road (and in bad weather one of more dubious passability) leaves Hwy. 191 near the crossroads at Bohemian Corners (or north from Hwy. 200 at Winnett) and leads into some of the roughest and most historic wildlands in the refuge. **Crooked Creek Recreation Area** is located at the mouth of the Musselshell River, where the waters of Fort Peck Lake meet steep gumbo canyons.

Many travelers will find this rugged but eerily beautiful country reason enough to visit the refuge, but don't forget the wildlife. Deer, prong-horn, and elk range through the refuge in profusion. Bighorn sheep, coyotes, and prairie dogs can be seen by the sharp-eyed, and over 200 bird species have been sighted.

Back Country Byways
The BLM has designated some scenic off-road routes under its protection as "Back Country Byways." The **Missouri Breaks Byway** makes a loop west of Hwy. 191 and travels through rough badlands, with views onto the Missouri River and its canyon. The byway begins within the Charles M. Russell National Refuge and continues along the boundary of the Upper Missouri Wild and Scenic River area. Turn west on Knox Ridge Rd. one mile south of the Fred Robinson Bridge. The most questionable part of the entire route immediately looms as the dirt road climbs up a very steep grade to the top of the breaks. After this point, the road becomes much less stressful; however, do not attempt this route if it's at all wet.

The BLM's designated route splits off Knox Ridge Rd. and turns north toward the river along Lower Two Calf Road. From it, several side roads drop onto the riverbottom. Sweeping views of the Missouri and wildlife sightings make this byway both instructional and awe-inspiring. The route rejoins Knox Ridge Rd. and returns to Hwy. 191 across high prairies.

The entire loop road is 73 miles long; at the western junction of Knox Ridge and Lower Two Calf roads, the traveler can also continue 12 miles to Winifred and paved Hwy. 236.

Campgrounds
Informal camping is allowed in most areas of the C.M.R., with established campgrounds at **James Kipp State Park**, at the Fred Robinson Bridge on Hwy. 191. The campgrounds at **Crooked Creek** have a boat launch, but not fresh water.

Information
Contact the Charles M. Russell National Wildlife Refuge at P.O. Box 110, Lewistown, MT 59547, tel. 538-8706.

WINNETT AND VICINITY

History
Walter Winnett's ranch along McDonald Creek

evolved in 1909 from an open-range camp to a small town as homesteaders who settled the valley needed a center for commerce. The Milwaukee Road extended to Winnett (pop. 188, elev. 2,960 feet) in 1917, just as drought hit. The community began to fray, then in 1919 oil was discovered at Devils Basin, the first oil strike in central Montana. Despite the bad years for farmers, Winnett's population boomed with the hope of more oil strikes. At Cat Creek, on the Musselshell, drillers discovered significant reserves of oil in 1920. A pipeline was laid to Winnett, a refinery established, and the railroad shipped out the first tanker of oil in 1921. By 1923, Winnett had a population of 2,000 people.

But the boom was short-lived; within 10 years, Winnett had lost three-quarters of its population, even though Cat Creek continued to produce oil. Ranching and farming, much of it on arid and marginal land, again took over as the area's primary economy.

Accommodations

In this vast unpopulated area, there are few lodging options. The **Northern Hotel**, tel. 429-7781, is one of Winnett's originals; $15 d. The **Grassrange Motel**, tel. 428-2242, is part of a bar/café complex. Also in Grassrange, the **Little Montana Truckstop**, tel. 428-2270, has an RV park.

Food

In Winnett, the **Kozy Korner**, tel. 429-2621, is open 6 a.m.-9 p.m. At the crossroads of Hwys. 87 and 191, there's the **Bohemian Corner Café**, tel. 464-2321, open 7 a.m.-9 p.m. The **Grassrange Bar**, tel. 428-2242, also serves food.

WHITE SULPHUR SPRINGS AND THE BELT MOUNTAINS

The wide basin of the Shields and Smith rivers extends laterally between the Missouri and Yellowstone drainages. Although hemmed in by five mountain ranges, the valleys are vast and flat: prairie wannabees.

White Sulphur Springs lies at the center of this valley network. The hot springs for which the town is named were first enjoyed by Indians; by the turn of the century, developers advertised them as America's answer to Europe's famous spas in Baden-Baden.

As elsewhere in central Montana, the mountains drew early settlers to mining camps; one of the richest gold strikes in the state was in the Big Belts. The valleys provided ranching, which proved to be a less transitory occupation.

The basin offers unparalleled recreational opportunities. The Shields and Smith rivers, and also Belt Creek, hold pedigrees as great trout streams. The Smith River passes through a deep limestone canyon, making it inaccessible to land vehicles for 61 miles; this section has become a favorite for river floaters.

THE LAND

The basin drained by the Smith and Shields rivers is flanked by mountains that rose in conjunction with volcanic activity in central Montana. The exception is the Big Belt Mountains, which formed as recently as 25 million years ago when bedrock buckled, forcing very old sedimentary layers to the surface. Across the valley, the Little Belt Mountains were formed earlier. The Castle Mountains just to the south erupted about the same time. The molten core of the Crazy Mountains pushed up through still-wet layers of sediment to form serrated peaks. The Bridger Range is a buckle of sedimentary rock that rose as the central Montana volcanoes erupted.

Also forced upwards as the Big and Little Belts buckled were plateaus of Madison limestone. The Smith River cuts a long canyon through this formation; Belt Creek leaves the Little Belt Mountains through an escarpment of limestone.

HISTORY

Diamond City in Confederate Gulch in the Big Belt Mountains was the site of one of the state's earliest and richest gold strikes. Three veterans of the Civil War found the placers in 1864; by 1867 the town's population had swollen to 5,000, with a reputation for wildness and wealth.

The gravels were extraordinarily rich. Legends tell of single pans containing a thousand dollars worth of gold; in one day miners claimed 700 pounds of gold from one strike. But the diggings were shallow; by 1870 the boom was over, and the gold camp deserted. But not before prospectors extracted an estimated $16 million from the gulch.

Miners decamped to the Little Belts and Castle Mountains, and moved onto silver, lead, and copper. Prospectors discovered copper east of White Sulphur Springs in 1866; the mining camp, called Copperopolis, had to send its ore to Wales to be smelted. Production of silver began at Neihart in 1881, and wavered until the Great Northern Railroad built a line up Belt Creek in 1891. Monarch grew up as a commercial and smelting center for local miners. There has been little significant mining activity in the Little Belts since 1900.

The Army built Fort Baker on the Smith River in 1869 to protect the thriving mining camps of Confederate Gulch from Indian reprisal. It was relocated upstream in 1870 and renamed Fort Logan. The fort was never called on militarily, and it was abandoned in 1880. Several original log buildings remain.

Real settlement of the Smith and Shields valleys awaited the railroads and the Homestead Acts. Richard Harlow's much-ballyhooed Montana Railroad bypassed White Sulphur Springs, which angered residents who fancied their town to be a major spa waiting to happen. Harlow instead linked the Missouri River to the silver camp of Castle in 1895. The Milwaukee bought Harlow's "Jawbone" Line in 1908.

White Sulphur Springs finally got its railroad in 1910, when local entrepreneurs built the ambitiously named White Sulphur Springs and Yellowstone Park line. Despite the moniker, the line merely linked White Sulphur Springs to Ringling, 18 miles away.

WHITE SULPHUR SPRINGS AND VICINITY

White Sulphur Springs (pop. 963, elev. 5,200 feet) was named for the white deposits left by the hot water that burbles up in the city's public park just off Hwy. 12. The 115° waters only faintly smell of sulphur, but weary travelers have soaked in them for centuries. Today, the flow is tapped for use in the Hot Springs Motel; it also heats the town bank.

History

White Sulphur Springs had been a popular hot springs for local Indians for many years; Crow chief Plenty Coups recalled pilgrimages by warriors to the medicinal mud baths. James Brewer chanced onto the area in 1866, as stage coaches rumbled through along the Carroll Trail. Brewer developed the hot springs as a stagestop for travelers; references to Baden-Baden, whose famous German springs the waters here are said to resemble, dot his early promotional literature. However, the grand hotel and spa envisioned by early boosters never materialized.

Sights

The gracious homes built in White Sulphur Springs during the 1890s are testimony to the wealth of open-range ranchers who found the wide valleys hospitable for cattle and sheep raising.

The Castle, a mansion built in 1892 out of locally carved granite, now functions as the **Meagher County Historical Museum.** It contains a selection of artifacts from the region's early history, and some beautiful period furniture. The mansion itself is well restored; the carved wood and moldings are to die for. Open Memorial Day-Labor Day, 10-6; $3 admission, tel. 547-3423.

Eighteen miles northwest of White Sulphur Springs along Hwy. 360 are the remains of **Fort Logan,** the military post built in 1870 to defend local mining camps. The log blockhouse still stands on the banks of the Smith River, surveying the valley.

Accommodations

The **Spa Hot Springs Motel,** 202 W. Main, tel. 547-3366, $33 d, has White Sulphur Spring's trademark hot water piped into indoor pools. The Spa also offers guided fishing and float trips. The **Tenderfoot Motel,** W. Main St., tel. 547-3303, $29 d, offers small cabinettes with kitchenettes.

Bed and breakfast accommodations are available in two historic homes: **The Columns,** 19 E. Wright, tel. 547-3666, offers rooms in an 1882 house once owned by writer Walt Coburn. Doubles begin at $40. The **Foxwood Inn** is a 100-year-old, 28-room mansion off Hwy. 360, tel. 547-2224, with double rooms at $42.

Campgrounds: The **Springs Campground,** on Hwy. 89, tel. 547-3921, is convenient for RV campers. Consider camping lakeside at **Newlan Creek Reservoir,** 10 miles north of White Sulphur Springs, or along **Sutherlin Reservoir,** 12 miles east on Hwy. 12.

BOB RACE

Castle Museum

Food

The **Truck Stop Café** on the east end of Main St., tel. 547-3825, is open 5:30 a.m.-10 p.m. As its name suggests, the **Cow Palace**, just south of town, tel. 547-9994, is a supper club offering good steaks. If you don't mind a short drive, the **Newlan Creek Club**, 13 miles north of town on Hwy. 89, features steaks and seafood at the head of a wooded lake.

Recreation

The **Smith River** gets off to an easygoing start in the wide basin around White Sulphur Springs, but soon passes into a narrow canyon cut through extensive limestone formations. Between old Camp Baker and Eden Bridge, a 61-mile stretch, the river can only be reached by boat. The extreme remoteness of this portion of the Smith, along with excellent wildlife viewing and old-fashioned excitement, make this float very popular.

Due to increased traffic on the river, the Dept. of Fish, Wildlife, and Parks asks that floaters make reservations and check local conditions before making the trip, tel. 454-3441. Contact local outfitters for guided floats and fishing trips (see below). The float takes two days, and camping is allowed at designated campsites only, so this trip demands some forethought.

The Smith also offers excellent fishing for brown and rainbow trout. The state maintains two fishing-access sights and campgrounds in otherwise inaccessible portions of the river north of White Sulphur Springs. Take Hwy. 360 west, and follow signs to Smith River (18 miles) or Fort Baker (26 miles).

The following outfitters offer float and fishing trips down the Smith River: **Castle Mountain Fly Fishers**, Box 370, White Sulphur Springs, MT 59645, tel. (406) 547-3366. **Montana River Rats**, Box 604, White Sulphur Springs, MT 59645, tel. 547-3760. **Montana River Outfitters**, 1401 Fifth Ave. S, Great Falls, MT 59405, tel. 761-1677.

Information

The **Meagher County Chamber of Commerce** can be reached at Box 365, White Sulphur Springs, MT 59645, tel. (406) 547-3366. The **Lewis and Clark National Forest** office's address is Box A, White Sulphur Springs, MT 59645, tel. 547-3361.

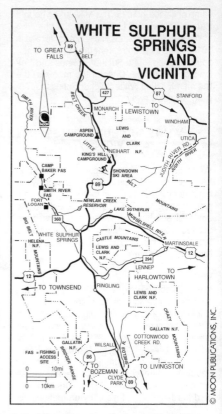

© MOON PUBLICATIONS, INC.

For information about floating the Smith River, contact the **Dept. of Fish, Wildlife, and Parks**, 4600 Giant Springs Rd., Great Falls, MT 59404, tel. 761-5840, or the outfitters listed above.

NORTH OF WHITE SULPHUR SPRINGS ON HWY. 89

Actually anything but little, the Little Belts ramble across 1,500 square miles of central Montana. Formed by underlying folds in the bedrock, these broad arches expose rocks from a hodgepodge of sources, including Precambrian sedimentary rock, limestone, and igneous intrusions. Silver has been mined in the Little Belts since the 1880s, but now more famous are the sapphire mines on Yogo Creek. Originally considered to be detritus from gold placer mining, the blue stones were analyzed and discovered to be sapphires of unusually high quality and a startlingly dark blue color. They occur, like diamonds in South Africa, in a "pipe" only eight feet across and three miles long. Sapphires have been mined commercially since 1896; the mines are not open to the public, but Yogo sapphires are available from local jewelers.

Recreation, however, and not mining, seems to be the future of the Little Belts. Skiing, hiking trails, snowmobile tracks, and great fishing now characterize these pretty but undramatic mountains. **Showdown Ski Area**, high in the Little Belts, holds the state's record snowfall—33 feet of snow in one winter. For your $16 lift ticket, you get 28 runs with a vertical drop of 1,400 feet. Facilities include a cafeteria, bar, ski rentals, and pro shop. Showdown is eight miles south of Neihart, tel. 236-5522.

Neihart

There's not much life left in the old mining town of Neihart. It began in 1881 when silver was discovered; the rail line to Great Falls would have ensured growth if the silver market had remained stable. Neihart was marginalized after the silver crash of 1893. Victorian-era homes and a log school testify to its more affluent days.

One oasis in Neihart is **Bob's Bar and Grill**, tel. 236-9955. Bob's also sells hunting and fishing licences. Forest Service campgrounds abound along Hwy. 89 in the Little Belts. **King's Hill**, nine miles south of Neihart, and **Aspen**, six miles north of Neihart, are convenient to the highway.

The **Belt Creek Information Station** of the Lewis and Clark National Forest is on Hwy. 89 in Neihart, tel. 236-5511.

Monarch

Born a mining camp, Monarch has developed into a tourist center. Its sylvan character, access to fishing in Belt Creek, and bars and restaurants make this a favorite stop for hikers and skiers from Great Falls.

As Hwy. 89 drops out of the Little Belts and onto Belt Creek, 10 miles north of Monarch, a roadside stop overlooks Belt Creek as it issues out of a canyon of white limestone cliffs. At the **Sluice Box State Monument**, trails lead up the creek beneath these cliffs. It's a good spot for a picnic or to try for a trout.

The **Rocking J Motel**, 66 Cascade Ave., tel. 236-5334, provides modest accommodations near Belt Creek; $20 d. As for food, the **Lazy Doe**, tel. 236-9949, serves lunch and dinner, and overlooks Belt Creek. The **Cub's Den Café and Tavern** serves sandwiches and lighter meals, tel. 236-5922.

Recreation

The Little Belts along Hwy. 89 have been mined and logged. Travelers who want to explore the range on foot should hike into the headwaters of the Judith River. The South Fork, Lost Fork, and Middle Fork of the Judith are each served by good trails. The drainages cut through limestone canyons and are de facto wilderness areas.

For access to the hiking trails, follow the Judith River southwest from Utica along a good gravel road toward **Fred Ellis Memorial Recreation Area**. Follow signs to the trailhead.

SOUTH OF WHITE SULPHUR SPRINGS ON HWY. 89

The Shields River

From the western slopes of the Crazy Mountains flows the Shields River. Highway 89 follows the river as it drains southward through lush farm and ranch land. In the 1860s frontiersman Jim Bridger led settlers up the Shields River and over Battle Ridge Pass into the Gallatin Valley to western Montana gold camps. Settlement spread up the valley after the Northern Pacific reached Livingston in 1882; a stage line soon linked Clyde Park to the Yellowstone Valley, and a spur line of the NP extended to Wilsall in the first decade of this century.

In the saddle between the Shields and Smith rivers is Ringling, named for John Ringling, of circus fame, who settled and ranched near here. A division point on the Milwaukee Road, it now contains a grain-alcohol plant that converts local wheat and barley to gasohol. St. John's Catholic Church sits on a bluff above the town, dominating the skyline.

There's good fishing in the Shields River and its Crazy Mountain tributaries. Hiking trails to high mountain lakes in the Crazies depart from trailheads on Cottonwood Creek.

HIGHWAY 12 AND
THE MUSSELSHELL VALLEY

The Musselshell River rises in the peaks of the Crazy, Castle, and Little Belt mountains and flows east through a wide wooded valley, lined with farms and ranches. Here is some of the gentlest beauty in Montana: shaded by majestic cottonwoods, cattle graze along a rushing river flanked by steep sandstone cliffs. And, as everywhere in central Montana, mountains loom in the distance like ramparts.

Rarely in Montana does the integrity of the natural landscape seem so little in conflict with the pursuits of agriculture. The compromise that nature has made with the rancher seems only to have made the landscape more gracious.

Almost nowhere else in Montana have a region and a railroad been so closely linked as the Musselshell River Valley and the Milwaukee Railroad; the solid towns build alongside the railroad reflect the confident dreams of settlers that it brought west. Roundup and Harlowtown have endured as trade centers; however, the scope and solid stylishness of their old town centers contrast oddly with their present, chastened realities. They wear their pasts awkwardly, like ill-fitting clothes—modest communities occupying towns built for larger purposes.

Other settlements—Shawmut, Two Dot, Ryegate—didn't fare as well. Today all but ghost towns, these old communities are stone and brick monuments to the poignant, and mostly unrealized, dreams of an entire generation of Montanans.

Highway 12 parallels the old Milwaukee Road, and serves the farming, ranching, and mining communities that sprawl across this piece of Montana. This is one of the most beautiful drives in the state; and east to west, it's more direct than the freeway.

THE LAND

The Castle and Little Belt mountains formed when magma shot up from deep in the earth, pushing up the earth's surface in broad domes. Eventually, erosion exposed the mountains' granite cores.

The Crazies tell a more unusual creation story. They too were formed by the intrusion of magma, but here the molten rock projected into still-moist sediment. The enormous heat of the magma baked the wet sand and mud into hard metamorphic deposits. Erosion has washed away the softer deposits, leaving the jutting igneous intrusions and their husks of baked sandstone. Glaciers later carved steep valleys into the sharp peaks.

After leaving the mountain valleys, the Musselshell passes into a wide prairie valley with sandstone bluffs flanking the river. Near Roundup, the river cuts into the Fort Union Formation. Its rich veins of coal were mined during the early years of this century.

As Hwy. 12 climbs up out of the Musselshell Valley and into the lower Yellowstone drainage, it crosses a broad saddle of land punctured here and there with oil wells. The bleak prairie surface disguises an anticlinal arch in the bedrock, which trapped significant reserves of oil.

HISTORY

The Musselshell Valley was a rich hunting ground for early Indians, but it didn't historically belong to any single tribe; it was either shared or battled for. In the 1830s, part of the Crow tribe moved north from the Bighorn River Valley and settled along the Musselshell, and became known as the River Crow. Subsequent treaties established the Crow Reservation south of the Yellowstone, and the River Crow were removed from the Musselshell.

By the 1870s, open-range cattle companies grazed the valleys of central Montana. The Army established a trail linking Fort Custer on the Bighorn and Fort Maginnis near Lewistown; it crossed the river near the present town of Musselshell. Texas drovers considered this ford to be the last stop in the long trail from the south; thereafter, cattle fanned out to graze the rich prairies to the north. The Musselshell Valley and Judith Basin remained the province of open-range ranchers for almost 30 years. Two of these ranches—the Two Dot and the Seventy-nine—have passed into Western lore. Uncharacteristically, the big cattle outfits here shared the range with enormous sheep ranches, especially near Martinsdale and Sumatra.

Mining began in the 1880s at Castle, where a rich vein of silver was intermittently exploited. However, central Montana was far from any railroad—ox teams hauled the ore to Helena for smelting—which made further development of minerals unprofitable. Local residents began to call for a central Montana railroad. During the 1890s, Richard Harlow built the Montana Railroad, in fits and starts and as financing allowed, eventually linking Lombard, on the Missouri River, to Harlowtown and Lewistown in 1903.

The Chicago, Milwaukee, St. Paul and Pacific Railroad, on its way to Seattle, laid tracks up the Musselshell in 1908. The firm bought the Montana Railroad from Harlow, thereby extending into the Judith Basin. Coal deposits at Roundup were developed to fuel the Milwaukee's engines.

In 1915 the Milwaukee announced that it would electrify its engines between Harlowtown and Avery, Idaho, which made it at the time the longest stretch of electric railroad in North America. The engines that pushed the trains uphill ran backwards downhill, working both as brakes and as generators to recharge up to 60% of the electricity expended on inclines.

Ad campaigns from the railroad convinced prospective settlers of the richness of central Montana. Towns sprung up along sidings, and farmers claimed the bottomland, half section by half section, signaling the end of the open range. The media trumpeted the bumper crops raised by these first-time farmers, and many immigrants responded, choosing new, seemingly secure lives and opportunities on the Montana prairies.

The decline of central Montana began with the droughts of the late 1910s and continued as later droughts combined with the Great Depression of the 1930s. Nature in Montana proved to be cruel: of the tens of thousands who moved to central Montana during the homestead era, only the frugal, driven, and lucky endured until the 1940s. The rural population decamped; coal mining at Roundup ended in the 1950s, and the Milwaukee Railroad itself, struggling since the 1940s, ended its central Montana service in 1980.

Today, agriculture nevertheless remains the backbone of local economies. Although large farms and ranches have replaced homesteads, for many in central Montana rural life is as unsure nowadays as it was for earlier, perhaps more naive, settlers.

Fishing

The Musselshell River affords good fishing for trout in its upper reaches west of Harlowtown. From Roundup to Fort Peck Lake, catfish, northern pike, and smallmouth bass predominate. Lake fishing at Sutherlin, Martinsdale, and Deadman Basin reservoirs is excellent for rainbow trout.

FORSYTH TO ROUNDUP

Highway 12 crawls out of the Yellowstone Valley and across an arid plain before it drops into the Musselshell River Valley. Forsaken little towns like Vananda follow the old Milwaukee Road. They indicate both the hope and the disillusion of early homesteaders. This is historically sheep and cattle country. The early prosperity of now-flagging communities like Ingomar and Sumatra was linked to vast, nearby stretches of open prairie which needed a railhead for shipping livestock to outside markets.

Within the Musselshell Valley, irrigated farmland replaces the arid plains. Little towns like Melstone (pop. 166, elev. 2,897 feet) and Musselshell, once centers for homesteaders, are today crossroads and gas stations for travelers and local farmers. West of Melstone, the sandstone cliffs and bluffs of the Fort Union Formation shelter the valley; their rich coal veins enriched the local economy when the steam engines of the Milwaukee Railroad crossed the West.

Practicalities

One of the most famous bars in Montana is the **Jersey Lily** in the little community of Ingomar. The bean soup here is the pièce de résistance and enjoys statewide fame. The Jersey Lily is the only business left in town, and only local ranchers and the occasional traveler keep the bar

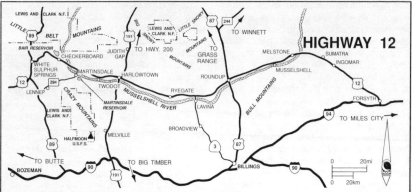

from going the way of the rest of the town. Plank sidewalks, hitching posts, and tumbleweeds in the street aren't added for effect: they're real. Enthusiasts of Western lore can test their mettle at the authentic outdoor privies.

In Melstone, the town café is **Montelone's**, 109 Second Ave. W, tel. 358-2355. It's open 6:30 a.m.-9 p.m.

ROUNDUP

History
Roundup (pop. 1,808, elev. 3,184 feet) was, by dint of etymology, the beginning of the Great Montana Roundup, the centennial cattle drive in 1989. In this it mimicked its frontier role as a center of livestock roundups in the 1880s.

The Milwaukee Railroad put Roundup on the map. In 1908, its steam engines arrived to create a demand for cheap coal in central Montana. The Bull Mountains, an uplift of sedimentary sandstone containing significant amounts of coal, are south of Roundup. Mines here became the Milwaukee's fuel source.

At Roundup, Hwy. 87 intersects north to south. Klein, a largely defunct community just across the Musselshell from Roundup, was once a vibrant mining community. Early immigrants solved the housing problem by building lodgings into the cliffside. Some of these cave-homes are now used for livestock; some still house people. Watch for electric lines and TV antennas.

Sights
The **Musselshell Valley Historical Museum**, 534 First St. W, tel. 323-1403, contains reminders of Roundup's dual heritage as pioneer cowtown and mining camp. Open Memorial Day to Labor Day, 9-6.

Practicalities
The **Sage Motel**, 630 Main, tel. 323-1000, is near the junction of Hwys. 12 and 87; a double room goes for $29. Equally central, and as unassuming, is the **Big Sky Motel**, 740 Main, tel. 323-2303, $30 d. At **Cowbell Park** off Hwy. 12 south of town, there is free overnight camping along the Musselshell River.

The best choice for a quick bite in Roundup is the **Busy Bee** on Hwy. 87, tel. 323-2204. It's principally a diner open 24 hours a day; the large parking lot explains its popularity with truckers. The **Vault**, 201 Main, tel. 323-1229, serves pizza and Mexican food. **Stella's Supper Club**, north of town along Hwy. 87, tel. 323-1166, offers good steaks. Roundup likes good coffee; try a cup at the **Morning Grind**, 119 Main, tel. 323-1579.

Recreation
Pine Ridge Country Club mile west on 13th Ave. W, tel. 323-2880, is a nine-hole course with a log clubhouse dating from 1908. The municipal **swimming pool** is at 700 Third Ave. W, tel. 323-1384.

Information
Contact the **Roundup Chamber of Commerce**, P.O. Box 751, Roundup, MT 59072, tel. 323-1966.

ROUNDUP TO HARLOWTOWN

History

The traveler is rarely out of sight of ponderosa pines on sandstone buttes or of the cottonwood-lined Musselshell on this length of Hwy. 12. As elsewhere on the Milwaukee Road, community hopes ran high; the huge, now defunct hotel at bypassed Lavina testifies to the ambitions of homestead-era settlers. At Barber, among the deserted storefronts is Grace Lutheran Church. Built in 1917 by German homesteaders, it could be the prototype for the Little White Church in the Vail; it is also the smallest active Lutheran congregation in the nation.

Just east of Ryegate, Chief Joseph and the Nez Percé crossed the Musselshell in 1877 as they fled northward to Canada.

Practicalities

In Lavina, **Richard's Café**, south on Hwy. 3, is open 6 a.m.- 8 p.m. If you want a break in Ryegate, try the **Ryegate Café**, 107 First St., tel. 568-9995.

At **Deadman Reservoir**, north of Hwy. 12 between Barber and Shawmut, there are free undeveloped campsights, along with good fishing and views of the Big Snowy Mountains.

HARLOWTOWN

The original settlement at this valley crossroads was called Merino, indicating the importance of sheep and wool production in the area. When Richard Harlow's Montana Railroad reached the village in 1900, the jubilant citizens renamed their town in his honor.

Harlowtown (pop. 1,049, elev. 4,167 feet) was a division station for the old Milwaukee Line; this and a flour mill provided suitable basis for substantial early growth. Harlo (as it is known to locals) has one of the best-preserved town centers in Montana, a perhaps unwelcome benefit of limited recent growth. Immigrant stonesmiths cut sandstone from nearby quarries to build storefronts. Three blocks of the downtown area, now a historic district, are built of this handsome native stone.

At Harlowtown, Hwy. 191 cuts through north to south. Access to the Judith Basin and the Yellowstone Valley make Harlowtown a hub of local travel.

Sights

The **Upper Musselshell Historical Society Museum**, 11 S. Central Ave., tel. 632-4301, contains local memorabilia, the requisite pioneer schoolroom re-creation, old conveyances, and an interesting display of serving vessels carved from 200 different kinds of wood. Open May 1-Nov. 1, Tues.-Sat. 10-5, Sun. 1-5 p.m.

On the corner of Central Ave. and Hwy. 12 is a Milwaukee Road Electric Locomotive built in 1915. Trains pushed by engines like this were the first to climb the Rockies under electric, not steam, power.

Accommodations

One the most spectacular old hotels in Montana is the **Graves Hotel**, 106 S. Central, tel. 632-5855. Built in 1909 as a grand railroad hotel, the Graves is a three-story, block-square sandstone monument to the affluent days of rail travel. Rooms, with every configuration of bed size and bathroom access, range from $14-36. The Graves is listed in the National Register of Historic Places—a must stay for enthusiasts of Western heritage. The dining room serves Harlowtown's best meals (steaks and seafood).

Another, less grand, relic of the railroad era is the **Star Hotel**, 208 S. Central, tel. 632-4786. The lobby café is an authentic throwback to an earlier, happier age, both in menu and appearance. Rooms are available on a bed and breakfast basis, and start at $15.

The **Countryside Inn**, 309 Third Ave. NE, tel. 632-4119, $29 d, is a handsome log motel, once known as the Ranch Autel. The **Corral Motel**, tel. 632-4331, $29 d, is slightly out of town at the western junction of Hwys. 12 and 191.

There's camping at **Chief Joseph Park** near the eastern junction of Hwys. 191 and 12. This three-acre city park also offers a playground, picnic sites, and a fishing pond.

Food

The **Graves Hotel Dining Room**, 106 S. Central, tel. 632-5855, is open for dinner from 5-10 p.m. The coffee shop is open all day. The **Star Hotel Café** 208 S. Central, tel. 632-4786, open 6 a.m.-10 p.m., serves light meals and sandwiches. At the crossroads of Hwys. 191 and 12 is **Wade's Café**, a truck stop open for three meals a day; during the summer, there's a drive-in. Other downtown restaurants include the **Cornerstone**, 11 N. Central, tel. 632-4600, a bakery and café featuring pizza; it's open for breakfast and lunch.

Recreation
The **Jawbone Creek Golf Course**, one-half mile north on Central Ave., tel. 632-9960, is a nine-hole course that incorporates an old cemetery as a hazard.

Information
Contact The **Harlowton Chamber of Commerce**, P.O. Box 694, Harlowton, 59036, tel. 632-4400. The **Musselshell Ranger District Office** is just west of town off Hwy. 12, and can be contacted at Box F, Harlowtown, MT 59306, tel. 632-4391.

HARLOWTOWN TO THE CRAZY MOUNTAINS

West of Harlowtown the horizon is punctuated by the rugged peaks of the Crazy Mountains, the most dramatic of central Montana's ranges. Highway 191 cuts south along the eastern face of the Crazies to Big Timber and the Yellowstone Valley.

The Musselshell River skirts the northern edge of the Crazies; its headwaters are in the more modest peaks of the Castle and Little Belt mountains. Highway 12 follows the Musselshell until it divides; it then follows the North Fork through a canyon and past Checkerboard, a pretty community sadly turned trailer court. Highway 294 follows the South Fork of the Musselshell, and the old Milwaukee tracks, between the Castle and Crazy mountains.

This is rich agricultural land: the wide green valleys provide open winter pasture, while nearby mountain slopes afford rich summer grazing.

History
The upper Musselshell has traditionally been livestock range, especially for sheep; in 1910 one sheep rancher shipped 44 train-car loads of wool out of Martinsdale, the largest single shipment of wool in the state's history. A famous local ranch was the Two Dot, named for its cattle brand. Today, the little settlement of Two Dot, little more than a school and a bar, serves Montana townfolk as a short-hand epithet for any rural eastern Montana community.

At Lennep, one of the Milwaukee's electric powerhouses sits idly beside the road, a remnant of that railroad's early electrified service. Along a gravel road seven miles north of Lennep is the ghost of Castle, a silver-mining town that ran its boom-to-bust cycle in the last decades of the 1800s. Lennep was the site of the first Lutheran church service held in Montana, in 1891; the present church, built in 1910, commands a broad view over the valley.

downtown Harlowtown

Practicalities

The Crazy Mountain Inn, 100 Main, in Martinsdale, tel. 572-3307, offers rooms in a carefully renovated turn-of-the-century hotel. The inn serves the best food—steaks, chicken, and homemade soups—in this part of Montana.

There is free lakeside camping at **Martinsdale Reservoir**, two miles east of town on a local access road, and at **Bair Reservoir**, 11 miles west on Hwy. 12.

Guest Ranches: With the Crazy Mountains as a backdrop, it's no wonder that two of Montana's best guest ranches have developed such devoted audiences. **Lazy K Bar Ranch**, Box 550, Melville Rt., Big Timber, MT 59011, tel. (406) 537-4404, is the state's oldest dude ranch, and perhaps its most exclusive. Writer Spike Van Cleve wrote about his humorous misadventures here with errant guests and horses; the Van Cleve family still owns the ranch.

The **Sweet Grass Ranch**, Box 161, Melville Rt., Big Timber, MT 59011, tel. 537-4477 summer, 537-4497 winter, offers trail rides, fishing, cookouts, and rodeos on a working ranch.

Recreation

The Crazy Mountains' heavily glaciated peaks loom mirage-like above the surrounding plains; isolated and spectacular, they are amongst Montana's undiscovered gems for hiking and high mountain lake fishing. Legends abound as to how they got their name, but they all have to do with women gone crazy with grief.

Hiking trails into the east side of the Crazies depart from the **Halfmoon USFS Campground**, 15 miles west of Hwy. 191 on a good gravel road. There are a number of steep ascents, and the snow lasts well into June at higher elevations, so plan your hikes carefully. A short dayhike of five miles roundtrip from the campground takes the hiker to views of jagged peaks rising impertinently from deep-blue lakes; there's even good trout fishing in the lakes, though not all are easily accessible. Mountain goats were transplanted here in the 1940s and have flourished.

To reach Halfmoon Campground, travel eight miles south of Melville on Hwy. 191; the road passes through bucolic ranchlands before entering the Big Timber Canyon on its way to the trailhead.

Information

For information concerning the Crazy Mountains, contact the **Gallatin National Forest, Big Timber Ranger District**, P.O. Box A, Big Timber, MT 59011, tel. (406) 932-5155.

THE JUDITH BASIN

Bounded by the mountain ranges of central Montana, the broad basin of the Judith River contains some of the richest agricultural land in the state. Streams course through fields and meadows; abundant crops and well-nourished livestock share this fecund domain.

For centuries, this open prairie supported hundreds of thousands of buffalo. After their decimation, the first open-range ranches of Montana prospered here. The Milwaukee Road and the Great Northern vied for supremacy in the Judith Basin, each luring settlers (and hence passengers and freight) by extensive advertising campaigns. The dry-land farms were so successful that the Judith Basin became the poster child of the Montana homestead movement. Unfortunately, even here farmers could not survive on homestead allotments during cycles of bad years.

History

Though not "ghost towns" to the popular mind, many stillborn little rail-side towns are almost completely deserted. Some have become incorporated into nearby farms, or still support a roadhouse. Stop and examine these old towns to understand the lives of the thousands of people who tried to extract a living from the prairies.

Often made of brick, buildings were built to last. Banks were especially solid, much more so than the institutions they housed. Quality schools were also a source of pride to homesteaders, and early automobile garages were sometimes stylish additions to young towns. Unlike comparably sized mining ghost towns, saloons and hotels are much rarer in these agricultural and ranching towns. In comparison to civic architecture, private homes were usually small and unprepossessing; in many cases, farmers stabled livestock in more attractive lodgings than they themselves lived in.

Two-hundred Minuteman missiles are buried in silos across this area of Montana. Currently, their presence is menaced more by superpower friendliness than by enemy attack.

STANFORD AND VICINITY

Stanford (pop. 529, elev. 4,200 feet) was the Judith Basin's most important trade center for grain and livestock in the early 1900s. It has managed to survive the vicissitudes of drought and bad markets better than its neighbors, and the town's wide streets and well-kept homes make it a handsome anomaly in central Montana.

Backroads through the Judith Basin recall a simpler era.

Sights

The **Sod Buster Museum**, five miles west of Windham on Hwy. 200, tel. 566-2281, contains a good collection of Indian relics, old machinery, and homesteader memorabilia.

In Stanford, the **Judith Basin Museum**, 203 First Ave. S, tel. 566-2281, features a collection of over 2,000 salt and pepper shakers, an exhibit on a dastardly white wolf from homesteader days, and frontier-era household items.

Practicalities

Accommodations: The **Sundown Motel**, west along Hwy. 200, tel. 566-2316, is next to Stanford's best steak house. A double room goes for $31. The **By Way Motel**, tel. 566-2943, $30 d, is across from the truck stop of the same name.

Food: The **By Way Café**, south of Stanford on Hwy. 200, tel. 566-2631, is that uniquely Montanan institution, the combination truck stop, restaurant, and liquor store. The **Sundown Inn**, tel. 566-9911, features local beef in its restaurant just west of town. In the center of town is the **Wolves Den**, 81 Central Ave., tel. 566-2451, open for breakfast and lunch.

Hobson And Utica

The **Judith Basin Cattle Pool** was one of the earliest open-range outfits in the state. During the boom years of the 1880s, investors bought cattle and then pooled them together to be run by hired cowboys. Calves were branded with the same brand as their mothers; in the fall, they were sold, trailed to railheads, and shipped to feedlots for fattening.

Utica was the hub for open-range cowboys in the Judith Basin during the 1880s; here, cowboys gathered the immense herds of cattle to divide them according to brand. It was a raucous time: after a summer of sometimes lonely cattle herding, the cowboys had a chance to kick up their heels and celebrate. Painter Charley Russell worked the ranges here, and many of his paintings feature the unique skyline of the Judith Basin.

Not much is left in Utica except a bar and a museum, both appropriate memorials to the ghosts of cowboys past. When the Great Northern line went through, Utica was bypassed for Hobson (pop. 226, elev. 3940 feet), 10 miles down the Judith River.

Sights: The **Utica Museum**, tel. 423-5208, preserves Utica's cowboy heritage with tools, saddles, and wagons from last century.

Food: Light meals are served at Utica's old bar, the **Oxen Yoke Inn**, tel. 423-5530. In Hobson, there's breakfast and lunch at **Cathy's Café**, Main St., tel. 423-5312. The **Hobson Supper Club**, tel. 423-5639, is the local steak house. At the junction of Hwys. 200 and 191 is **Eddie's Corner**, tel. 374-2471, a popular truck stop, open 24 hours a day.

The Judith Gap

Named for the wide and desolate divide between the Big Snowy and the Little Belt mountains, the Judith Gap has been a transportation corridor for centuries. Crow Indians crossed the gap to hunt buffalo in the Judith Basin; Blackfoot warriors later pushed south across the area to menace the Crow along the Musselshell. Traders used this notoriously windy pass to reach erstwhile settlements and gold camps in central Montana. Both the Great Northern and the Milwaukee lines laid track over the Judith Gap to reach homestead towns.

The first settlement in the area was the old crossroads of U-bet, which thrived as a stop on the old Carroll Trail stage line during the 1870s. U-bet was a well-loved watering hole for early cowboys. When Richard Harlow's Montana Railroad pushed through the Judith Gap in 1903, it too named its station U-bet.

During the homestead rush, a telling division of sentiment regarding alcohol led to the establishment of two communities. North Garneill was "dry"; nearby South Garneill (incorporating U-bet) had a guesthouse, saloon, and the accoutrements of an Old West town. In some kind of victory, today only North Garneill survives, if only diffidently and under the abridged name of Garneill.

The **Ubet and Central Montana Pioneers Monument** at Garneill is a huge block of granite on a concrete base. Embedded in the base is an array of local rocks. There are two large, nearly identical pear-shaped stones here, found by early settlers near Winnett. Apparently carved by Indians, their meaning has been lost.

Food: The **Carroll Trail Inn**, in the town of Judith Gap, tel. 473-9992, is open 7 a.m.-7 p.m.

Winifred

The mouth of the Judith River was an important stop for Missouri River steamboats. Camp Cooke was built here in 1866 both to protect travelers from the hostile Blackfoot Indians and to defend the thriving community of Judith Landing that grew up from selling wood to the steamers en route to Fort Benton.

Although not much is left at the old site of Judith Landing, the drive to the confluence of the Judith and Missouri rivers is a spectacular side trip into the Missouri Breaks. Proceed to Winifred along Hwy. 236 north of Lewistown and follow a good gravel road toward the PN Bridge. Soon the farmland falls away in 1,000-foot drops to the rivers below; directly west, an abandoned channel of the Missouri River slumps into the Judith Valley and across the present Missouri. After crossing the PN Bridge, the only span on the Wild and Scenic stretch of the Missouri, Hwy. 236 continues through farmland to Big Sandy, 40 miles distant.

From Winifred a right turn on Knox Ridge Rd. leads to other views of the Missouri Breaks and to the C.M. Russell National Wildlife Refuge (see p. 156)

Food: The **Winifred Tavern and Café**, tel. 462-5426, provides for the needs of local farmers, ranchers, and the occasional traveler, with three meals a day.

A little farther afield, the **Denton Café**, 512 Broadway, tel. 567-2647, makes its own sweet rolls, and is open 6 a.m.-8 p.m.

BOB RACE

SOUTH CENTRAL AND THE MISSOURI HEADWATERS

THE LAND

Rivers roll off south central Montana's mountain ranges and the high Yellowstone Plateau and course north to the Missouri. Mountains and fertile valleys form chains along the riverbeds and the valleys of the big rivers are the sites of settlements and thoroughfares. To the east, prairies spread between the northern Crazy Mountains; the Beartooths loom south. The highest spot in the state is here in the Beartooths, and, not surprisingly, a *lot* of snow falls in the high country near Yellowstone.

Yellowstone's volcanoes covered the Absarokas with lava and ash, and glaciers pushed and carved their way across the region's higher peaks. Faults cut across the mountain ranges, and mountains still tumble.

Flora And Fauna

Lush wide valleys and tight canyons are typical, but plains habitats crop up between the mountain ranges, and there's some tundra on the high peaks. Cottonwood and aspen line the streams; serviceberries provide the locals with the makings of purple serviceberry pie.

Lodgepole pine is the predominant tree species in most of the forests in the headwaters region. They are particularly prone to infestation by pine beetles, which kill the trees. Dead, dry and brittle, the stands become easy fodder for fire, which is the necessary ingredient to break open the pine cones and allow the seeds to germinate.

HISTORY

The hunting ranges surrounding the Missouri headwaters were coveted and often fought over by Native Americans. Bannock, Blackfeet, Crow, Flathead, and Shoshone all considered it sacred hunting ground. As the Blackfeet gained control of the northern plains, they drove other tribes out of the Missouri headwaters area. The

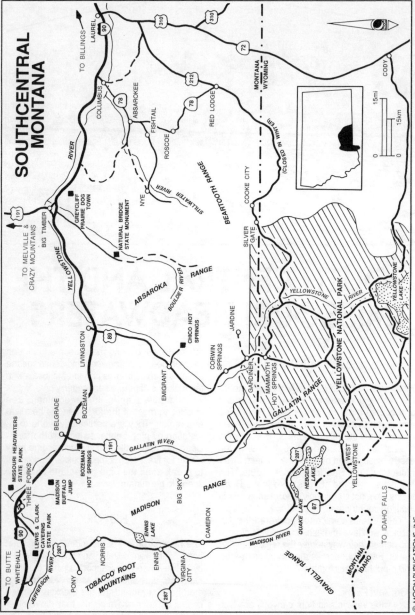

SOUTHCENTRAL MONTANA

© MOON PUBLICATIONS, INC.

Shoshone moved south and west, the Crow tended to stay off to the east, and the Flathead crossed over from the Bitterroot Valley less often.

Lewis and Clark arrived at present-day Three Forks in July 1805, and declared it the headwaters of the Missouri. Clark and his party returned to the forks on their way back east; from the headwaters they traveled up the Gallatin, crossed Bozeman Pass at Sacajawea's suggestion, and reached the Yellowstone River near the site of present-day Livingston. They floated the Yellowstone to its confluence with the Missouri, where they were joined by Lewis and his men.

Fur-bearing animals quickly caught the eyes of white trappers and mountain men. Miners made some forays into the mountains, but homesteaders and ranchers were ultimately more successful. Tourism, spurred on by the dude ranches and maniac fly-fishers, is now evident in most towns.

RECREATION

The Madison, Gallatin, and Yellowstone rivers bait anglers with trout. The hatches of salmon flies and caddis flies are as closely watched as the seasons, and most everyone knows brown from rainbow from cutthroat.

Bitterroot to Beartooth is almost required reading if you want to hike much in the mountains of the headwaters region. Author Ruth Rudner focuses on wilderness areas, and land nominated for wilderness designation in the 1980s. Excellent discussions of the ecology of the specific areas are an important part of this Sierra Club totebook.

THREE FORKS AND
THE MADISON RIVER VALLEY

INTRODUCTION

Even if the notion of the Missouri headwaters doesn't automatically stir your blood, a visit there probably will. There's something *big* about the place where three lively trout streams join up to make their way across the plains that gives the spirit an almost geological uplift.

The Madison, the middle fork of the Missouri, starts in Yellowstone Park and joins with the Jefferson and the Gallatin at Three Forks. Mention of the Madison quickens the pulse of anglers across the U.S.; people come from all over to fish here, and the valley sports a number of guest ranches to accommodate them.

The Land
All three of the Missouri's forks come straight from the mountains. The Madison Range flanks Madison Valley to the east; to the west are the northerly, batholithic and glacier-cut Tobacco Root Mountains and low, southerly Gravelly Range. The northern valley is wide; indeed, between Three Forks and Ennis, Hwy. 287 skirts well west of the Madison, following the Jefferson for awhile, through wide open and rolling plains.

The Gravelly Range is well named. These mountains aren't particularly high, but they do have a fair amount of geology packed into their rubbly composition. For one, the marble that underlies parts of this range has further metamorphosed into talc in some places, making this a major talc-mining area.

The Madison Range has obvious current geologic activity. The eastern front is moving along a fault. A lurching move in August, 1959 precipitated an earthquake that jacked the mountains up and dropped the valley floor. The southern end of Hebgen Lake rose, the northern end dropped, and a rock slide buried campers and blocked the Madison River, forming Quake Lake.

Fishing
Fish the Madison for brown or rainbow trout, and be prepared to catch a generous number

of whitefish as well. Along with the beautiful riffles and incredible trout fishing come crowds. To avoid them, look for spots far from Hwy. 287 and fish early or late in the season. Although the high waters make most stretches of the Madison too turbulent for fly-fishing until about July, some stretches (especially inside Yellowstone Park) are okay for flies by early June, and turbulent waters don't seem to deter anglers when the salmon flies hatch around the end of June.

July and August are when the caddis hatch, and anglers flock to the upper Madison. Below (north of) Ennis Lake, the river warms up too much for good summer fishing; try this area in the spring or fall. Fly-fishing is usually good through mid-October on most of the Madison.

Some areas of the Madison River are closed to fishing from a boat, bait fishing is prohibited along some stretches, and in some spots, catch-and-release fishing is mandated. Special regulations will usually be posted at fishing-access areas, but check ahead with the Department of Fish, Wildlife, and Parks or your fishing guide.

THREE FORKS

Three Forks (pop. 1,200) gets its name from the headwaters of the Missouri. The confluence of the Gallatin, Madison, and Jefferson rivers occurs on a wetland plain surrounded by mountains just north of town.

Just west of Three Forks, Hwy. 287 follows the Jefferson River through sedimentary, fossil-ridden limestone that's been jostled into a tilted position. For a few miles the land is open and dry; past Lewis and Clark Caverns, the Madison River flows through a gorge of high, buff-colored hills. This road, which eventually leads to Cardwell, is a pleasant alternative to the interstate.

History
White westerners may experience a certain resonance in reliving Lewis and Clark's visit to the headwaters of the Missouri, but there's also a

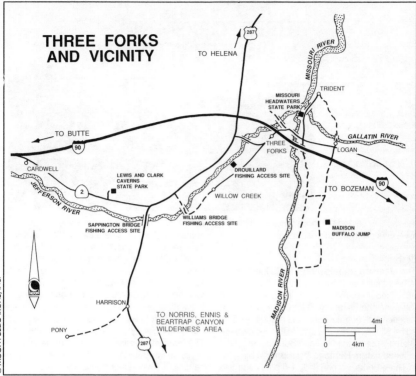

THREE FORKS
AND VICINITY

TO HELENA

MISSOURI RIVER

TRIDENT

MISSOURI
HEADWATERS
STATE PARK

GALLATIN RIVER

TO BUTTE

90

CARDWELL

THREE
FORKS

LOGAN

LEWIS AND CLARK
CAVERNS
STATE PARK

DROUILLARD
FISHING ACCESS SITE

JEFFERSON RIVER

2

WILLOW CREEK

TO BOZEMAN

90

SAPPINGTON BRIDGE
FISHING ACCESS SITE

WILLIAMS BRIDGE
FISHING ACCESS SITE

MADISON
BUFFALO JUMP

MOON

MADISON RIVER

HARRISON

TO NORRIS, ENNIS &
BEARTRAP CANYON
WILDERNESS AREA

PONY

287

0   4mi

0   4km

© MOON PUBLICATIONS, INC.

rich Native American heritage to the area. Before Lewis and Clark floated through, the Three Forks area was well traveled. It was a disputed hunting area and the site of frequent battles between the Crow and the Blackfeet. The mountain and river bands of the Crow had regular rendezvous at the headwaters, where they'd hunt, fish, and, later, trade with whites.

When the Corps of Discovery reached the Missouri headwaters on July 27, 1805, Lewis and Clark concluded that none of the three rivers was sufficiently larger than any other to warrant calling it the Missouri, and the other two feeder streams. They solved this dilemma by declaring them "three noble streams," and took the opportunity to name them after the President (Jefferson), the Secretary of State (Madison), and the Secretary of the Treasury (Gallatin). Actually, river-naming was not foremost in Lewis and Clark's minds—they were far more preoccupied with meeting the Shoshones, from whom they hoped to obtain horses.

The Blackfeet thwarted the business of a small trading post established in 1810 on the spit of land between the Jefferson and Madison rivers. Gallatin City was built at the headwaters in 1864, and prospered for a few years. The settlement was established here under the premise that steamboats could navigate the Missouri to this point. Of course, the Great Falls of the Missouri were not properly taken into account, and when Fort Benton became the head of navigation on the Missouri, Gallatin City foundered. Some of the buildings were moved from the original site near the mouth of the Gallatin across the Madison-Jefferson, and this second Gallatin City, with its ferry service to the mining towns to the west, became an important food supplier. Bozeman ultimately outstripped Gallatin City as a commercial center and when

*Missouri Headwaters
State Park*

JUDY JEWELL

the railroad skirted the three forks in 1883, the town was pretty much abandoned.

Sights
The **Madison Buffalo Jump State Monument** is less than seven miles south of Logan on I-90. Wander around the steep cliff, contemplate the bone shards, and wait for the landscape to turn rich with buffalo, deer, and pronghorn. The same $3 fee admits you to both the Headwaters State Park and the Madison Buffalo Jump.

Headwaters Heritage Museum, on Main St. in Three Forks, is open daily 1-5 p.m. June 1 to Labor Day, tel. 285-3495. A railroad dispatch office and a hat shop are among the exhibits.

Pony, just below the Tobacco Root Mountains about 30 miles southwest of Three Forks, is just shy of being a ghost town. There are a few fancy new houses on the hills above the abandoned Victorians and brick bank building. Pony took its name from Tecumseh "Pony" Smith, who mined gold here in 1868. Gold, silver, and some tungsten were mined in Pony through the early part of this century. The Pony Bar, which is still doing business, used to be a boardinghouse for men. When the second floor residents got tired of running downstairs and out back to the outhouse, they constructed a "pee trough" running down the hallways and into a drainpipe.

Southwest of Pony, through Potosi Canyon, is Potosi Hot Springs, a site undeveloped save for a small Forest Service campground.

Missouri Headwaters State Park
Try to visit this site, where the Madison, Jefferson, and Gallatin rivers join up to form the Missouri, early or late in the day, when the light comes in low and opens you up to some special magic held by the rivers and bluffs. The park is four miles north of I-90 at Three Forks, near the town of Trident. Good information stations discuss local flora and fauna as well as Corps of Discovery history. There's a $3 entrance fee. The headwaters site includes an old hotel and log cabin from Gallatin City. There's also a small cave with several faded and damaged Native American **pictographs**—follow the trail south from the main interpretive center to see it.

If birdwatching appeals to you more than steeping yourself in Lewis and Clark lore, the Missouri headwaters has herons, osprey, Canada geese, and songbirds along the headwaters trail. Climb Lewis Rock or Fort Rock to scan the cliffs for golden eagles. Vegetation here is characteristic of the plains: prickly pear and pincushion cacti, bluebunch wheatgrass, big sagebrush, saltbush, and buckwheat brush. The headwaters area is also a popular fishing spot.

Accommodations
Sacajawea Inn, 5 N. Main, tel. 285-6934, is the best place to stay for miles around. The huge old hotel was built in 1910 and recently completely refurbished. Rooms run $45-80.

Alternatives are the **Broken Spur Inn,** 124 W. Elm, tel. 285-3237, $29 s, or the **Park Hotel,** a classic but dilapidated two-story wood frame downtown hotel at 114 Main St., tel. 285-3457. Just past "downtown," find the **Lewis and Clark Motel** at 510 Main, tel. 285-3454.

Camping

The **Headwaters State Park campground** has brushy riverside sites perfect for those on a Lewis and Clark pilgrimage. Read the journals first and you'll know to bring mosquito repellent. The $7 fee includes day use.

There's also a large state park campground at **Lewis and Clark Caverns,** open May through September.

The campground at **Beartrap Hot Springs** is convenient, if occasionally boisterous. If you find it tough to leave the hot springs, or if the hot bath-cold beer combination proves a little too seductive, plunk down $13 for a tent or trailer site. Head east on Hwy. 84 for nine miles to find **Red Mountain,** a free BLM campground near the bridge over the Madison River. For a secluded spot, try **Potosi,** a free primitive Forest Service campground about eight miles south of Pony.

Food And Drink

Of the two good dining bets around Three Forks, the particularly surprising one is the **Blue Willow Inn,** six miles down the road from Three Forks in Willow Creek, tel. 285-6660. Breakfast, lunch, and dinner are all a cut above what you'd expect to find out here, and both the restaurant and the bar are easy spots in which to while away a couple of hours. The menu is a combo between "international" dishes such as seafood fettucine, and "country cookin'," like chicken-fried steak; a large breakfast runs $4-5; dinners are about $10.

The **Sacajawea Inn's** restaurant goes a step farther in the gourmet direction—appetizers of Provencal-style pizza and $10-15 dinners of rosemary-garlic lamb chops or chicken with sauterne sauce can make one inquire about long-term rentals at the inn. The dining room is closed on Tuesdays; during the winter, call 285-6934 to make sure they're open at all.

In downtown Three Forks, the **Headwaters Café** is at 105 S. Main, tel. 285-9892. **Charlie's,** 24 W. Main, tel. 285-3536, is open for dinner Wed.-Sun. and has enchiladas and pizza as well as $10 sirloin, chicken, or shrimp dinners.

Jonathan's, 117 N. Main, tel. 285-2314, has a supper-club atmosphere, with dinners starting at less than $10. The **Prairie Schooner,** not far from Main St. at 10770 Hwy. 287, tel. 285-6948, has inexpensive café breakfast, lunch, and dinner food, including buffalo burgers and huckleberry shakes.

Events

The Three Forks **rodeo** is held the third weekend of July. A **Lewis and Clark Pageant** is staged also in July, right around the time of year the Corps of Discovery first passed through.

Each September, Headwaters Park is the site of the **John Colter Run,** a seven-mile dash through the prickly pears (clothing and shoes are permitted).

Fishing

Fish the Missouri headwaters; there's fishing access at the **Headwaters Park.** Near Three Forks, **Drouillard Fishing Access Site** offers entry to the Jefferson River on Hwy. 10 two miles west of Three Forks. The **Sappington Bridge** crosses the Jefferson on Hwy. 287 at Hwy. 10, and the **Williams Bridge** is just to the east. The Jefferson is deeper and slower than the riffly Madison, but fishing very early or late in the day will often yield brown trout as well as a host of less prestigious whitefish, carp, chubs, and suckers.

Cobblestone, Grey Cliff, and **Black's Ford** fishing-access sites are on the lower Madison River between Hwy. 84 and the Missouri headwaters. To reach this stretch of the Madison, head south on Hwy. 286 (off I-90 east of Three Forks) or east from Norris on Hwy. 84, then north on Hwy. 286. Camping is permitted at these undeveloped riverside spots, but care should be taken not to stray onto the surrounding private land without permission. The relatively warm lower Madison, while popular, does not share the incredible reputation of the river's cooler upper reaches.

There are several pulloffs on Hwy. 84 near the bridge nine miles east of Norris, and the more ambitious angler can head up the trail into Beartrap Canyon.

*Woolly scholars find new use
for one-room schools,
Willow Creek*

JUDY JEWELL

Beartrap Canyon, a BLM wilderness area east of Norris, is a steep gorge cut by the Madison River. A hiking trail starts three miles down a dirt road from the Red Mountain campground (about nine miles east of Norris on Hwy. 84) and runs seven miles up the canyon. A dam at the southern end holds back Ennis Lake; hiking is prohibited around the dam, forcing hikers to retrace their steps to leave the canyon. The trail is popular with both hikers and anglers and can get crowded on summer weekends.

Bear Trap Hot Springs is just east of Norris on Hwy. 84; it's $3.25 for a soak. At this relaxed operation, the pool is small and lined with wooden boards. Hot water shoots into the air and showers down onto a corner of the pool.

Information

Reach the **Three Forks Chamber of Commerce** at P.O. Box 1003, Three Forks, MT 59752, tel. 285-6857. Visit the **library** at 121 Second Ave. E, tel. 285-3747.

ENNIS AND VICINITY

Ennis (pop. 773, elev. 4,927 feet) became a supply station for the gold towns of Virginia City and Nevada City shortly after gold was discov-

ered in Alder Gulch. Since then, ranching has become the economic mainstay. Many of the area's ranches are now owned by wealthy (and sometimes famous) investors who hire real ranchers to manage and run the cattle. Anglers flock to Ennis in the summer, when it's hard to believe that the population is only 773.

Sights

For Virginia City, see p. 250 and for Nevada City, just west of Ennis, see p. 252.

The **Ennis National Fish Hatchery** breeds rainbow trout 12 miles south of Ennis. It's open to visitors, tel. 682-4847.

It takes all day to drive from Ennis to Sheridan if you go via the Gravelly Range, but you'll likely see elk, moose, pronghorns, many deer, grouse, and a sheep or two. Stop at the Ennis ranger station and pick up their brochure on the Gravelly drive. Don't figure on taking your two-wheel-drive Dodge Dart on this 60-mile rangeland tour if the road is wet or snowy; it gets pretty steep.

Accommodations

Dude ranches surround Ennis, and there are some more conventional motels here too. **Riverside Motel,** 346 E. Main, tel. 682-4240, is a good budget choice—it's right by a little riverside park.

El Western Motel and Resort, on Hwy. 287 S near the river, tel. 682-4217, is a little fancier, with motel rooms and cabins starting at $40.

If a pool is important, try the **Sportsman's Lodge,** north of town on Hwy. 287, tel. 682-4242 ($28 s), **Hickey's Four Seasons Motel,** on the downtown strip at 222 Main, tel. 682-4378 (both a pool and a hot tub here), or **Rainbow Valley Motel,** on Hwy. 287 south of town, tel. 682-4264, $40 and up, with lower winter rates.

Lake Shore Lodge, P.O. Box 134, McAllister, MT 59740, tel. 682-4424, rents cabins on Ennis Lake. Camping space for RVs and tents, outfitter services, and boat rentals are all available here.

Ranch Stays Diamond J Ranch, P.O. Box 577, Ennis, MT 59729, tel. 682-4867, 14 miles east of Ennis, has 10 cabins available June through Sept. for three-day or week-long stays. In addition to fishing and horseback riding, the Diamond J has indoor tennis courts and a swimming pool.

The Old Kirby Place, south of Cameron, is noted for its log lodge and bunkhouse dating from the 1880s and its celebrity guests. Fishing, rather than horseback riding, is the focus here. A week's stay is $850 (includes all meals). Contact Walter Kannon, West Fork Bridge, Madison River, Cameron, MT 59720, tel. 682-4194. During the winter, Mr. Kannon is at Box 104, Sugar Loaf, NY 10981, tel. (914) 469-4380.

Also near Cameron is the **CB Ranch,** P.O. Box 604, Cameron, MT 59720, tel. 682-4954. Rates are $600 a week for a single person, or $500 pp for a double room. It's not a big outfit; only about a dozen guests are here at a time. The CB is a working family-owned cattle ranch and, though most guests come to fish, horses are available.

Camping

Ennis Fishing Access Site, just out of town on the south side of the bridge, is a more developed campground than most of the state's fishing access sites. The camping fee is $3, and the amenities include pit toilets and running water.

Once you get south of Cameron there are plenty of public campgrounds. **West Madison** BLM campground is three miles west of the McAttee bridge; **South Madison** is another BLM campground, about six miles south of the McAttee Bridge and a mile off Hwy. 287.

About 34 miles south of Ennis, near the West Fork rest area, find both **West Fork** and **Madison River** forest service campgrounds ($6 fee). In the same area, find **West Fork Cabin Camp,** a private outfit with housekeeping cabins and an RV campground. Since it's on the Madison River, fishing is taken seriously. Call 682-4802 for reservations.

Food And Drink

The **Continental Divide** is Ennis's high-toned restaurant. Like others of its ilk in Montana, it's not too intimidating to be a real treat. Dinners run $15-20, with a logical emphasis on steak and seafood. Call 682-7600 for reservations, but don't expect to find it open during winter months. For a quick bite, **Bettie's Café** is off the main drag by a couple of blocks, tel. 682-9905. Local ranchers hang out at the **Silver Dollar Saloon,** tel. 682-9901. Pizza and sandwiches are on the bar menu, and in the adjoining steak restaurant a prime rib dinner goes for $7.95; tel. 682-4808. Down the road in Cameron, find the **Cameron Café,** tel. 682-4950, and, for a spirited Saturday night, the **Blue Moon Saloon.**

Events

Mid-June brings **Pioneer Days** to Ennis. The Fourth of July weekend **rodeo** is taken seriously here. Mid-October, shortly after the start of hunting season, Ennis holds a wild game cookoff. Call the chamber of commerce at 682-4388 for details.

Recreation Madison Meadows is a public, nine-hole golf course just west of town, tel. 682-7468. Public **tennis courts** are adjacent to the golf course.

Many old logging roads in the hills south of Ennis are closed to motorized traffic and make good mountain bike routes. Get the current road closure information at the Ennis ranger station. The Gravellys are popular with elk hunters, but the recent road building and logging has threatened elk habitat, partly because all the logging roads have brought more hunters to previously remote areas.

September brings upland game bird hunters to the area for Hungarian partridge and sharptail, blue, and ruffled grouse.

Fishing And Floating

The state maintains several fishing-access sites on the Madison River near Ennis. **Ennis FAS** is on Hwy. 287 just south of Ennis; **Burnt Tree Hole** is a mile west of Ennis on Hwy. 287, then two miles south on the county road; **Eight Mile Fork** is four miles down the same county road; **Varney Bridge** is another six miles down the road. All these spots have informal camping sites; there's a $3 fee to camp at Ennis. To reach **Valley Garden FAS,** turn north onto the county road from Hwy. 287 a quarter mile south of town and travel two miles. **McAtee Bridge,** 18 miles south of Ennis, also provides access to the Madison.

Ennis Lake (aka Ennis Reservoir or Meadow Lake), is a silty, shallow reservoir backed up by a rather small Montana Power dam on the Madison just below the lake. Because it's so shallow, Ennis Lake gets very warm during the summer. The warm water makes for pleasant swimming, but causes rampant algae growth and is generally rough on fish downstream. Resorts and ranches surround Ennis Lake.

Float the Madison, but take care where you go. Beartrap Canyon is for whitewater experts, and the segment between Cameron and Ennis is tough for a novice to navigate. A popular and easy trip runs 30 miles from Quake Lake (put in at the Hwy. 87 bridge four miles from the lake) to the Varney Bridge, in Cameron. This stretch of the river passes several campgrounds. Fishing from a boat is restricted on certain stretches of the Madison. Check the current regulations before casting a line.

Shopping

Like much else in Ennis, shopping revolves around fishing. There are several fly-fishing shops in town: **Bob's Tackle Box,** tel. 682-7234, **Madison River Fishing Co.,** 109 Main St., tel. 682-4293, **Headwaters Angling,** tel. 682-7451, and **The Tackle Shop,** tel. 682-4263. These shops can recommend guides.

There are a couple of galleries in town, too, and it should come as no surprise that the **Fly** **Fisherman's Art Gallery** is one of them. The other is the **Hole-in-the-Wall Gallery.**

Information

The **Madison Valley Public Library** is at 210 E. Main, tel. 682-7244. Ennis's **Chamber of Commerce** can be reached at P.O. Box 291, Ennis, MT 59729, tel. 682-4388. The **ranger station** is just west of town on Forest Service Rd., tel. 682-4253.

Contact the **sheriff** at 843-5351, the **fire department** at 682-4800, and the **ambulance** service at 682-4222. Call the **Madison Valley Hospital** at 682-4274.

HEADING TOWARD IDAHO

If you aren't able to make the drive in to Red Rocks Wildlife Refuge (see p. 242), but would like to see some wildlife, try **Cliff Lake** and **Wade Lake.** These turquoise lakes are about six miles west of Hwy. 287 via Forest Service Rd. 8381 (find this road just north of where Hwy. 87 joins Hwy. 287).

The road into the lakes passes the ghost town of Cliff Lake, crosses the "Missouri Flats," a high sagebrush prairie with abundant bird life, and climbs to the forested lakeshores. Trumpeter swans sometimes appear here in the winter; raptors live and nest on the lakes. Moose are also common.

There are three Forest Service campgrounds in the area: **Wade Lake, Hilltop,** and **Cliff Point,** as well as the utterly charming **Wade Lake Resort,** tel. 682-7560, which has simple cabins for rent year-round, 55 km (35 miles) of groomed cross-country ski trails in the winter, and boats for rent during the summer. Cabins run $35-65 a night, with a two-night minimum stay.

The southern road to Cliff and Wade lakes snakes in through humpy sagebrush and pine-covered hills from Hwy. 87, north of where Raynolds Pass crosses the Continental Divide at a remarkably level 6,834-foot pass into Idaho. It takes its name from Captain Raynolds, who headed a scientific expedition in 1860. Jim Bridger was the scientists' guide. There's now a fishing-access site just south of Hwy. 287 near Raynold's Pass.

QUAKE LAKE AND HEBGEN LAKE

Driving south on Hwy. 287 towards Hebgen Lake, the mountains rise off the plain of the Madison Valley. Hebgen Lake is the reservoir formed by the damming of the Madison River in 1915. The lake's north side has a smattering of resorts and private campgrounds; several public campgrounds are on the less-trafficked south side of the lake.

Late on the night of Aug. 17, 1959, the Madison River Canyon shuddered as an earthquake measuring 7.1 on the Richter Scale started a giant landslide. A 7,600-foot-high mountain collapsed into the river, burying campsites at the Rock Creek Campground and damming the Madison to form Quake Lake. A couple of large fault blocks dropped and tilted north. A huge tidal wave swept across Hebgen Lake, over the 1914 Hebgen Dam and into the Madison River canyon. Amazingly, Hebgen Dam held.

Dead trees now stand in Quake Lake, the Madison River is still choked with rubble, and a "ghost village" near the east end of Quake Lake is a jumble of buildings swept up and dropped by floodwaters. Reach the ghost village via the road across from Cabin Creek campground. A visitor center now overlooks the site of the landslide. It's open Memorial Day-Labor Day, tel. 646-7369.

Accommodations
Parade Rest Guest Ranch, near Hebgen Lake at 7979 Grayling Creek Rd., West Yellowstone, MT 59758, tel. 646-7217, caters to anglers, though horseback riding is included in the $93 pp per day tariff. Rates are 20% less in the off-season and include all meals. Parade Rest has close ties to many local fishing guides, and while the ranch can set you up with a guide, it's best to arrange this well in advance. **Firehole Ranch,** 11500 Hebgen Lake Rd., tel. 646-7294, is luxurious.

Moderately priced lodgings dot the north shore of Hebgen Lake. (Hebgen Lake Rd. here is the same as Hwy. 287.) None of these are fancy, but they're good resting places, and just enough removed from the hubbub of Yellowstone National Park to afford real relaxation.

Campfire Lodge Resort, 8500 Hebgen Lake Rd., between Hebgen and Quake lakes by Cabin Creek, tel. 646-7258, has cabins, sites for tents and RVs, a café, and boat rentals. **Kirkwood Ranch Motel,** 11505 Hebgen Lake Rd., tel. 646-7200, is on Hebgen Lake and also rents boats. **Hebgen Lake Lodge,** 14320 Hebgen Lake Rd., tel. 646-9250, has both motel and lodge rooms, a marina, and camping out back; **Lakeview Cabins,** 15570 Hebgen Lake Rd., tel. 646-7257, are next to the lake and the U.S.S. Happy Hour Bar. On Hwy. 191, just south of where Hwy. 287 comes in, the **Madison Arm Resort,** tel. 646-9328, has an RV campground and a marina.

Cabin Creek and **Beaver Creek** Forest Service campgrounds are on the Hwy. 287 side of Hebgen Lake. To the east, **Rainbow Point** (on the Grayling Arm of Hebgen Lake) and **Bakers Hole** (on the Madison River above Hebgen Lake) are public campgrounds close to West Yellowstone and often full of RVs. **Spring Creek, Rumbaugh Ridge,** and **Lonesomehurst** are seldom-mentioned Forest Service campgrounds on the south shore of Hebgen Lake.

A lot of snow falls here in the winter, and virtually all of these places shut down between late September and early May. Winter travelers can reserve a Forest Service cabin on the Hebgen Lake Road by calling 646-7369. It's available from Nov. 20 to April 1.

Food And Drink
The resorts along the north shore of Hebgen Lake offer what there is to be found in the way of food and drink. The **U.S.S. Happy Hour,** 15400 Hebgen Lake Rd., tel. 646-7281, is a particularly appealing bar with a view of Hebgen Lake. If it's choice you want, head down the road to West Yellowstone, where restaurants proliferate.

Recreation
The **Lee Metcalf Wilderness Area,** just north of Hebgen Lake, and the adjacent **Cabin Creek Wildlife Management Area** are crisscrossed with trails. Several trails start at the end of Beaver Creek Rd., and a trail heads out from Cabin Creek Campground to the wilderness area and other trails. Consult a Gallatin Nation-

al Forest map, available from the ranger station in West Yellowstone or Ennis before setting out. Fish Hebgen Lake for brown and rainbow trout. Cutthroat, whitefish, and some arctic grayling also live here.

People do windsurf on Hebgen Lake, but it's probably not worth planning an entire vacation around it.

There's backcountry cross-country skiing on Hebgen Mountain and less challenging trail ski-ing at Refuge Point on Hebgen Lake. Stop by the ranger station in West Yellowstone for more information.

Information
A deluxe **visitor information center** sits above Quake Lake. The **Hebgen Lake Ranger Station** is actually on the northern edge of West Yellowstone, tel. 646-7369.

(top) the Kootenai River west of Libby (Judy Jewell); (bottom left) heading into the Bob Marshall Wilderness Area west of Choteau (Judy Jewell); (bottom right) in the high country (Judy Jewell)

(top) Sportsmen bar, Butte (Brian Foulkes); (bottom) Butte by night (W.C. McRae)

THE GALLATIN VALLEY

Highway 191 follows the west Gallatin River north from Yellowstone Park through a valley speckled with dude ranches and resorts. The Madison Range, including Spanish Peaks, is west of the Gallatin Valley; the Gallatin Range to the east.

In the rugged northern part of the Madison Range, Precambrian basement rock juts up as high as 11,000 feet. Legend has it that these "Spanish Peaks" were named for Spanish trappers from Mexico who showed up in the area in 1836 and, in 1863, had a run-in with some Crow Indians.

Just below the Madison and Gallatin ranges, the West Yellowstone Basin is a high plain layered with obsidian sand from volcanic eruptions and silt deposits from melting glaciers. It was the site of the Bannock Trail, which led Indians to eastern buffalo-hunting grounds. Hwy. 191 follows the route of a road cut in 1911 from Bozeman to West Yellowstone.

Tourism is not new to the Gallatin Valley. The Milwaukee Pacific Railroad built the Gallatin Gateway Inn in 1927 at the terminus of their tourist spur line down from Three Forks. Tourists generally dined at the hotel but slept in their train cars before boarding buses to Yellowstone Park. Once tourists began traveling more by car than by train, the elegant hotel foundered.

Sights

Big Sky, Montana's largest ski resort, is on Lone Mountain about an hour north of West Yellowstone. The slopes of Lone Mountain have been grazed since the 1890s, and dude ranches began to spring up a few years later. When native son Chet Huntley retired from the newscasting business, he started up Big Sky Resort in what he figured was the ideal spot to blend development with the natural environment. Who'd have figured? The unprepossessing Huntley Lodge and its swarming parking lot now teeter on the edge of overwhelming nature.

Development here has not led to street addresses—businesses are located by the "village" they occupy: the Huntley Lodge and ski lifts are in the development known as Mountain Village; Meadow Village is toward the base of the mountain.

To experience Huntley's ideal, stay in one of the many well-appointed hotel rooms, but try to escape the network of shops and pizza parlors for at least a little while.

Soldier's Chapel commemorates Montana's native sons who died in the infantry in World War II. The log chapel is on Hwy. 191 near Big Sky. Sunday services are held here.

In the **Gallatin Petrified Forest,** at the southern end of the Gallatin Range, trees are still standing beneath layers of volcanic tuff. Purchase permits to collect the petrified wood for $5 at ranger stations in West Yellowstone, Gardiner, Livingston, or Bozeman.

Accommodations

There are several lodging options at Big Sky. Motel rooms, cabins, and condominiums are all available at different elevations on Lone Mountain. A shuttle bus runs between all the lodging spots and the ski lifts.

At the bottom of the hill, **Best Western Buck's T-4 Lodge,** on Hwy. 191, tel. (800) 822-4484 or 995-4111, has rooms starting at $39 s, $49 d. The **Golden Eagle Lodge** is at the Meadow level of the mountain, and has single rooms from $40, doubles from $45, tel. (800) 548-4488. They also have reasonably priced suites housing up to eight people.

Rooms at the **Huntley Lodge** in the Mountain Village, tel. (800) 548-4486 or 824-7767, start at $99 s, $111 d. Huntley also has condominium units for rent, starting at $220 a night. Also in Mountain Village, the less luxurious **Mountain Lodge,** tel. (800) 831-3509 or 995-4560, has rooms from $38 s or d. Summer rates run at least $10 less at all these places.

North of Big Sky, in the town of Gallatin Gateway, the **Gallatin Gateway Inn** has been beautifully restored as a historic landmark. Rooms with a bath down the hall start at $45, rooms with a bath start at $65. Reserve by calling 763-4672.

Ranch Stays

Lone Mountain Ranch, halfway between the highway and the ski lifts, tel. 995-4644, is a little different from the other Big Sky lodgings. Originally a working cattle ranch, it has become a great cross-country ski resort and, during the summer, a dude ranch with special fishing and cooking programs. Any number of different packages are offered, but a standard seven-day stay costs $1100 s, $750 for each additional person.

320 Ranch, a guest ranch since the turn of the century, is 12 miles south of Big Sky and six miles north of Yellowstone Park, tel. 995-4283. Cabins are for rent by the night (from $30), week (from $200), or month. Guest ranch activities such as horseback riding and fishing can also be arranged. This is also a good place to stop for a meal.

Campgrounds
At the southern end of the valley, **Bakers Hole** is the closest public campground to West Yellowstone. It's just three miles north of town on Hwy. 191. Blue herons nest on the Madison River just across from the campground.

For the frugal traveler, **Spire Peak** is a small, free Forest Service campground about 15 miles southeast of Gallatin Gateway.

young dude rancher saddles up

Food And Drink
Well, there's plenty of it. Down in Meadow Village, **Edelweiss Restaurant,** tel. 995-4665, serves bratwurst and schnitzel dinners for around $15. Also in Meadow Village, and in the same price range, **First Place,** tel. 995-4244, offers more mainstream fancy fare. Moderately priced Italian and Mexican dinners share the bill at **Rocco's,** yet another Meadow Village eatery, tel. 995-4200.

Halfway up the hill, the **Lone Mountain Ranch** serves up Big Sky's best meals each night at 6:30 p.m. (reserve by calling 995-4644). The views from the comfortable Lone Mountain bar are seductive after a few times around the cross-country ski trails.

At the top of the hill, **Huntley Lodge** has a fancy dining room. For Italian food, try **Andiamo** in the Arrowhead Mall. Sandwich shops, pizza joints, and cafeterias are all well represented and easy to find in Mountain Village.

Reasonably priced meals with little culinary pretention abound at the **Corral Café,** five miles south of Big Sky on Hwy. 191, tel. 995-4249. The **Half Moon Saloon,** three miles south of Big Sky on Hwy. 191, is a comfortable place to stop for a beer. Almost to Yellowstone, the **320 Ranch** serves good Montana-style steak, trout, and fish dinners, tel. 995-4283.

In the northern part of the valley, almost to Bozeman, the **Gallatin Gateway Inn,** tel. 763-4672, has elegant and thoughtfully prepared dinners running $10-20.

Events
During January, Big Sky holds a free "Learn to Ski" day and a winter carnival. In July, the **Big Sky Arts Festival** sponsors a concert series, bringing classical, jazz, and country music to the slopes every weekend. Call 995-4211 for exact dates and details.

Skiing
Big Sky does have good downhill skiing. An average of 400 inches of snow falls each year, and the resort has plenty of lifts to manage the crowds. The vertical drop is 3,030 feet, and the longest runs go on for three miles. Lift tickets are $30 a day for adults, $15 for children 12 and under. Half-day and multi-day rates are also offered, as is night skiing Dec. 26 to March 31.

Cross-country skiers can buy daily passes ($8 full day; $6 half day) for the trail network at **Lone Mountain Ranch,** tel. 995-4644. The 45 miles of groomed trails cross a variety of terrains with some good views of the Gallatin Valley. Lessons and guided tours are also offered.

Cross-country skiers can also head to the Spanish Creek Cabin on the edge of the Lee Metcalf Wilderness Area, about 10 miles north of Big Sky. It's rented out Dec. 15-March 31 for $20 a night. Call the Bozeman Ranger Station at 587-6920 for reservations.

The Gallatin is popular with whitewater enthusiasts; it's a challenging river to float. Don't put into the West Gallatin (the main stem of the river that starts in Yellowstone and merges with the East Gallatin near Bozeman) without plenty of whitewater experience under your belt. The section of the river above Big Sky is particularly wild. Two rafting outfitters have their headquarters on Hwy. 191 at the Big Sky turnoff. **Adventures Big Sky,** tel. 995-4211 or 995-2324, and **Yellowstone Raft Co.,** tel. 995-4613, both run daily whitewater trips. Adventures Big Sky also rents **mountain bikes.**

Fishing access to the main stem West Gallatin River is easy; the road runs alongside it much of the way from Yellowstone to Bozeman, and there are many pulloffs—de facto fishing-access sites. There's an official site at the Axtell Bridge, between Gallatin Gateway and Bozeman Hot Springs. Fish don't grow large in the cold waters of the upper Gallatin, but most anglers pull something from the riffly waters of this stretch. The West Fork comes in near Big Sky, and the combined waters flow through a canyon with exceptionally good fishing. Fishing from a boat is prohibited on the Gallatin.

The salmon flies hatch from late June through early July on the Gallatin, but there's good fishing for brown and rainbow trout April through October. **Gallatin Riverguides,** Box 212, Big Sky, MT 59716, tel. 995-2290, leads fishing trips year-round, $160 per day, with substantial reductions for groups of two or three. Lone Mountain Ranch and 320 Ranch also provide fishing guides.

Hikers flock to the Spanish Peaks during the summer. Trails, most more suitable to overnight backpacking than to day-hiking, cross the peaks. Trailheads sprout on Hwy. 191 between Big Sky and Bozeman; the Cascade Creek hike is especially popular, and the trail can be crowded on the weekends. Pore over the Gallatin National Forest map to construct a long backpacking trip in this spectacularly scenic area.

The **Arnold Palmer Golf Course,** a challenging riverside course at the Meadow Village, was indeed designed by Palmer. It's open to the public, call 995-4706 for a tee time.

Information And Services

Big Sky Resort Association is at Box 1, Big Sky, MT 59716, tel. (800) 548-4486 or, in Montana, (800) 824-7767.

Contact the **sheriff** at 585-1475, the **fire department** at 585-1390, and the **ambulance service** at 585-1480.

Transportation

Continental, Alaska, and Delta airlines all fly into the Bozeman airport. **Karst Stage,** tel. 586-8567, runs a shuttle from the airport to Big Sky, and shuttle buses run frequently between Big Sky's Meadow and Mountain villages. See p. 189 for car rentals in Bozeman.

BOZEMAN AND VICINITY

Bozeman (pop. 22,660), home of Montana State University, is at the foot of the Gallatin Valley, with the Gallatin Range (and its Spanish Peaks) and Madison Range to the south, the Bridger Range to the northeast, the Tobacco Roots farther west, and the Big Belts way off north and west. It's safe to wear your Birkenstocks in Bozeman—its elevation of 4,754 feet puts it just high enough to be inhospitable to rattlesnakes.

HISTORY

Native Crow, Blackfeet, Bannock, Shoshone, and Flathead referred to this area as the "Valley of the Flowers." It was a sacred hunting ground and neutral territory.

White settlers named the city for John Bozeman, mountain man and immigrant guide of the 1860s. Bozeman's trail, essentially a spur of the Oregon Trail leading to Montana's gold country, ran along what is now a section of I-90. Frequent attacks by Sioux and Cheyenne bands plagued sojourners on the Bozeman Trail. Bozeman himself was killed, perhaps by Blackfeet (or perhaps by a business colleague, perhaps by a jealous husband), near Livingston in 1867. Largely as a reaction to Bozeman's murder, Fort Ellis was established in 1867 at the site where William Clark and his party camped in 1806. It was the supply post for the Cavalry during the Battle of the Little Bighorn in 1876 and provided military escort for railroad surveyors in the 1880s.

Even before the Northern Pacific Railroad came through in 1883, Bozeman had the bearing of a civilized town set down in the wilds. One fortune-seeker who passed through Bozeman in 1882 claimed it was the nicest place he'd been since St. Paul. In a letter to his sister, he told of "2 Churches, Court house, fine large brick school and the nicest lot of small dwelling houses all painted white with green lawns and level as a floor. There are lots of brick store buildings here. That is something you don't see the whole length of the Yellowstone River."

Bozeman is still just a touch on the prissy side, at least for Montana. The students look wholesome, and some of the stores aim for large pocketbooks. It's an easy place to visit and is well situated for recreationists, but for those who savor quirky dashes of humanity, Bozeman may be just a little too *normal*.

SIGHTS

Historical Bozeman
To embark on a historic downtown walking tour, with a foray into residential areas, start at the large brick building at Main and Rouse; it once housed City Hall, but was first the opera house, with the original sign remaining over the front door for years afterward. Historic business buildings along Main St. include the Baxter Hotel (eat in one of the restaurants it now houses, or simply step in and admire the lobby), the Hotel Bozeman, the Ellen Theatre, and Holy Rosary Church. Historic homes cluster in the neighborhood between Main St. and the university, especially along Willson Avenue. The Sigma Alpha Epsilon fraternity house at Willson and College is known locally as the Storey Mansion. It was the home of the son of Nelson Storey, the first cattleman to drive cattle up from Texas to the Gallatin Valley.

Sunset Hills Cemetery, immediately south of Lindley Park, is now home to John Bozeman, Chet Huntley, and most of the people that Bozeman's buildings and streets are named for. The old part of the cemetery is off to the west; if you're really interested in exploring the graves, stop in a bookstore and pick up a copy of the cemetery guide produced by MSU art students.

Montana State University
Montana State University, founded in 1893, is the state's oldest and largest university. Originally the "Ag School" in the state system, it is now a haven for some 10,000 outdoorsy students with a technical bent.

Museums
At the southeast corner of the MSU campus, S. 7th Ave. and Kagy Blvd., find the **Museum of the Rockies.** If you like dinosaurs, modern art, pioneer history, or astronomy, this may be the

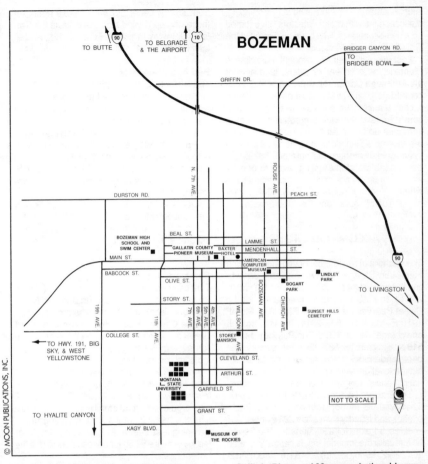

BOZEMAN

TO BUTTE
TO BELGRADE & THE AIRPORT
BRIDGER CANYON RD.
TO BRIDGER BOWL →
GRIFFIN DR.
N. 7th AVE.
ROUSE AVE.
PEACH ST.
DURSTON RD.
BEAL ST.
BOZEMAN HIGH SCHOOL AND SWIM CENTER
LAMME ST.
GALLATIN COUNTY PIONEER MUSEUM
BAXTER HOTEL
MENDENHALL ST.
MAIN ST.
AMERICAN COMPUTER MUSEUM
BABCOCK ST.
BOGART PARK
LINDLEY PARK
TO LIVINGSTON
OLIVE ST.
STORY ST.
BOZEMAN AVE.
CHURCH AVE.
SUNSET HILLS CEMETERY
19th AVE.
11th AVE.
7th AVE.
6th AVE.
5th AVE.
4th AVE.
WILLSON AVE.
COLLEGE ST.
TO HWY. 191, BIG SKY, & WEST YELLOWSTONE
STOREY MANSION
CLEVELAND ST.
ARTHUR ST.
MONTANA STATE UNIVERSITY
GARFIELD ST.
TO HYALITE CANYON
GRANT ST.
KAGY BLVD.
MUSEUM OF THE ROCKIES
NOT TO SCALE
MOON
© MOON PUBLICATIONS, INC.

spot for you. Though synergy is not always at work in the eclectic collection, you're likely to find something that interests you. It's a good place to take the kids, and adults will enjoy it more if they read Jack Horner's book, *Digging Dinosaurs,* before their visit. Horner is a renowned paleontologist in charge of the museum's impressive paleontology department.

Admission is $3 for adults, $2 for children, $10 for a family; the planetarium is another $2.50 apiece. The museum is open daily 9 a.m.-8:30 p.m. from Memorial Day through Labor Day; during the winter, hours are Mon.-Sat. 9 a.m.-4:30 p.m., Sun. 1-4:30 p.m.; tel. 994-2251.

Gallatin Pioneers' Museum, in the old county jail at 317 W. Main, tel. 585-1311, is open weekdays June to Sept. 2-5 p.m., Tues. and Thurs. 2-4 p.m. in the winter. The museum only took over from the jail in 1982, and there are still jail cells and a gallows amongst the Indian artifacts, old household items, and barbed wire collections. Look for the display of tiny carved Montana agates, the products of a Gallatin County couple's lifelong hobby. A dollhouse-size bar, complete with back bar and bottles, is particularly charming.

Fort Ellis, the site on Hwy. 187 where Clark and his party camped July 14, 1806, and which later became an Army fort, is no longer standing, but local guys with metal detectors have turned up a number of relics, which are on display at the Gallatin Pioneers' Museum.

Lest you think that all historical museums in Montana focus on early settlers, take note of the **American Computer Museum,** 234 E. Babcock St., tel. 587-7545. You'll not see one old kitchen utensil in this surprisingly absorbing museum. Instead, ponder computers that seem immense and confusing and realize that they are little more than a dozen years old. It is worth being guided around; the curator's talk is understandable and interesting, even to one for whom computers are little more than smart typewriters. Summer hours are daily 10-4; winter hours: Tues., Thurs., and Sat. noon-4 p.m.

ACCOMMODATIONS

The plethora of reasonably priced motels along both Main St. and 7th Ave. makes it easy to find lodging in Bozeman unless it's a big weekend for the MSU Bobcats, graduation, or the Sweet Pea Festival. Try the **Blue Sky Motel,** 1010 E. Main, tel. 587-2311. It has a hot tub and charges $28 s, $32 d. The **Rainbow Motel,** 510 N. Seventh, tel. 587-4201, has singles for a pool, cinderblock walls, and a hospital smell, but the location is convenient and there's a little hot pot and instant coffee packets in the rooms.

The **Bobcat Lodge,** 2307 W. Main, tel. 587-5241, with its indoor pool and sauna, kitchenettes and laundry room, has $28 singles, $31 doubles, $4 extra for a kitchenette. The **Econo Lodge,** aka the Imperial Inn, is centrally located at 122 W. Main, tel. 587-4481 or (800) 332-7666 outside Montana, $28 s, $34 d. And there's a **Super 8** in Bozeman, at 800 Wheat Dr. (near the freeway interchange), tel. 586-1521 or (800) 843-1991, $31 s.

Also near the I-90 interchange, and a step up in ambience and price, find the **Bozeman Inn,** 1235 N. Seventh, tel. 587-3176 or (800) 648-7515, $39 s. The **Best Western Gran Tree Inn** is nearby at 1325 N. Seventh, tel. 587-5261 or (800) 624-5865 outside Montana, $58 s. Both of these motels have swimming pools.

The **Holiday Inn,** 5 Baxter Lane, 587-4561 or (800) HOLIDAY, also has a pool and rooms

from $61. A better bet for a deluxe hotel, for those who don't mind a bit of a drive, is the **Gallatin Gateway Inn,** 76405 Gallatin Rd., at Gallatin Gateway, tel. 763-4672, rooms from $45.

Bed And Breakfasts

The **Voss Inn,** 319 S. Willson, tel. 587-0982, is Bozeman's premier bed and breakfast. The six guestrooms range in price from $40-65 and are furnished with antiques.

Each of the three rooms at **Torch and Toes,** 309 S. Third Ave., tel. 586-7285, has a personal touch from the proprietors' family. Rooms run around $40; the inn, like the Voss, is in a historic neighborhood between the university and downtown Bozeman.

Skiers will find the hewn-log **Silver Forest Inn** conveniently located. It's at 15325 Bridger Canyon Rd., near downhill and cross-country ski areas, tel. 586-1882. The five rooms run $55-70.

Camping

Tent campers will almost certainly want to head for one of the three campgrounds in the Hyalite Canyon: **Langhor** is 11 miles south of town on Hyalite Canyon Road. **Blackmore** and **Hood Creek** are another five and six miles down the same road. Reach Hyalite Canyon Rd. by heading south on 19th Street.

Another reasonable camping bet is the **Bozeman Hot Springs KOA,** eight miles south of town on Hwy. 191, tel. 587-3030. The springs fill one large and several small indoor pools—outside the bathhouse, it's a KOA campground. Camping fees start at $12, with an extra dollar fee to swim (it's $2.50 for noncampers to use the hot springs).

FOOD AND DRINK

Downtown

The 1939 WPA Guide Book characterized Bozeman as:

> an old and decorous town. Local ordinances prohibit dancing anywhere after midnight and in beer halls at any time. It is illegal to drink beer while standing, so all Bozeman bars are equipped with stools.

So sit down and have a drink at the **Robin Lounge** in the old Baxter Hotel. Also in the Baxter, 105 W. Main St., tel. 586-1314, the **Rocky Mountain Pasta Company** and the **Bacchus Pub** share the elegant old hotel lobby. The Bacchus is a popular lunch spot, where the cook may be heading east for a Ph.D., and the Pasta Company is a good dinner spot.

At the **Western Café,** 443 E. Main St., tel. 587-0436, cinnamon rolls come out of the oven at 8 a.m., tabs must be paid before the first of the month, the grill cook's quick, and there's a jackalope head mounted above the milk dispenser. They open at 5 a.m. The Western's main competition, the **Cowboy Café,** 215 E. Main, tel. 586-1420, opens at 6 a.m. and stays open for dinner. They have American and Mexican diner fare.

For those who would rather drink coffee than eat, the **Leaf and Bean,** 35 W. Main, tel. 587-1580, is a good place to hunker down with the morning paper. They serve some pastries and a full range of espresso drinks. **Wild Flour Bakery,** 19 S. Willson, tel. 587-8110, is the best place in town to load carbohydrates.

John Bozeman's Bistro, 242 E. Main, tel. 587-4100, serves lunch and dinner daily, and weekend breakfast. The food is good American-bistro-ex-hippie style, there's plenty of it, it's easy to eat for less than $10, and the atmosphere is comfortable if not stimulating.

Pay just a touch more for a really good lunch or dinner at **Ira's on Main,** 233 E. Main, tel. 587-9999 (dinner reservations recommended). The food is fresh and well prepared; dessert-lovers will be particularly impressed. And, for tasty, if trendy, nouvelle-Southwest fare, try **Sundog's,** a recent start-up at 39 E. Main, tel. 586-0038. Fajitas and grilled tuna are specialties; dinners run $10-15.

University District

Near the university, there are some casual places catering to students and locals. The **Pickle Barrel** is not much bigger than the genuine item. All they've got are sandwiches, but they're giant, satisfying things, with any of the steak and cheese sandwiches getting a special recommendation. There are picnic benches out front if you want to hang around and eat, then finish the gorge with an ice-cream cone from the equally tiny place next door (it's actually part of the Pickle Barrel, but the buildings are too small to fit main course and dessert in the same place). They're across from the university at 809 W. College (During the winter, they also operate a place at the Bridger Bowl). Open for lunch and dinner, with free delivery, tel. 587-2411.

For a full sit-down-inside meal, **Casa Sanchez** is right around the corner at 719 S. Ninth, tel. 586-4516. It's a pleasant place in an often-crowded small house serving moderately priced Mexican lunches and dinners.

Columbo's Pizza and Pasta, 1003 W. College, tel. 587-5544, features cheap dinners (some less than $5) from "all natural ingredients"—not surprising, as they share a mini shopping center with the local food co-op.

Seventh Avenue

If you're staying on the N. Seventh Ave. motel strip and lack the energy to leave your street, there are alternatives to McDonald's and Taco Bell. **Tom's Green Grill,** 319 N. Seventh, is open 24 hours for diner food, including good ice-cream concoctions and homemade pie. At the Bozeman Inn, 1235 N. Seventh, the **Avellino,** tel. 586-1535, advertises "a touch of Italy, a taste of Montana," featuring Italian cuisine with Montana beef and veal. Dinners run $10-15.

EVENTS

The Gallatin County Fairgrounds is the site of the **Montana Winter Fair** late each January. Unlikely as it may seem, it's a wintertime version of a state fair.

One of Bozeman's pleasant surprises is the **Intermountain Opera,** tel. 586-8729, which stages one production a year (with two performances). Pablo Elvira, a Gallatin Valley resident who sings with New York's Metropolitan Opera, is frequently featured in these mid-May productions.

Mid-June, the **College National Finals Rodeo** comes to the MSU fieldhouse. It's a popular show, and tickets for the final rounds can be hard to come by at the last minute. Reserve the $6-8 tickets in advance from the College National Finals Rodeo, 502 S. 19th St. #303, Bozeman, MT 59715, tel. 994-4813.

The **Sweet Pea Festival** dominates Bozeman's social scene during the first weekend of

August. Booths from local restaurants line up along Main St. for the **Taste of Bozeman,** a big picnic-cum-dinner party that kicks off the festival weekend. As the arts festival bustles in Lindley Park, people gear up for the Sweet Pea Ball, held at the Gallatin Gateway Inn. A parade and plenty of musical and arts events are scheduled for the festival weekend. For specifics on any events, call the chamber of commerce at 586-5421 or (800) 228-4224.

September marks the start of the season for the **Bozeman Symphony Orchestra and Symphonic Choir.** Performances occur approximately once a month through April. Call 585-9774 for the season's schedule.

RECREATION

Pools And Parks

The **city pool** is adjacent to the high school at 1211 W. Main, tel. 587-4727. Adults pay $2, swimmers under 18 or over 54 are charged $1. Regular morning, noon, and evening lap swims are scheduled. For a relaxed paddle around a hot-springs pool, **Bozeman Hot Springs KOA,** 133 Lower Rainbow Rd., tel. 586-6492, charges $2.50. During the summer, the outdoor pool in **Bogart Park** is open afternoons and evenings. Lake swimmers may prefer Glen Lake at **East Gallatin State Recreation Area** on Manley Rd. in the northeast corner of town.

Of the many parks in Bozeman, the visitor is most likely to spend time in **Lindley Park** on the south side of E. Main St., just out of downtown. The Sweet Pea Festival overruns the park early each August, and it's a good spot for a picnic at other times. **Bogart Park,** on S. Church, has an outdoor swimming pool, an ice rink, and a summertime Saturday-morning farmers' market. Just south of Bogart Park, pick up the **Gallagator Linear,** a walking, running, skiing, and biking trail that runs from S. Church Ave. and Storey St. to Third Ave. and Kagy Blvd.

Hiking

Hyalite Canyon is about half an hour south of town via S. 19th and Hyalite Canyon Road. Drive to the end of the road to launch a five-mile hike past nearly a dozen waterfalls to Hyalite Lake, then go another two miles to reach Hyalite Peak. One drainage over from the Hyalite Lake hike, Emerald Lake is another five-mile hike to a pretty lake in a high cirque. Turn left off the road shortly after the youth camp at Hyalite Reservoir to reach this trailhead.

The trails in this area are well maintained and well signed, indeed, many of the trails, campgrounds, and fishing-access points in the Hyalite Canyon are designed to allow people of differing physical abilities to use them. The trails are rated from easiest to most difficult; one of the easy trails is a half-mile paved loop from Langhor Campground with nature trail signs in both type and braille.

Bozeman's student population finds ample time for outdoor recreation.

W.C. McRAE

Of the three official **campgrounds** in Hyalite Canyon, **Langhor** is closest to town, in a brushy meadow next to the creek. **Blackmore** and **Hood Creek** are both alongside the reservoir. Blackmore is wooded; Hood Creek is more open, right by the water, and next door to the Hyalite Youth Camp.

North of town, the **Bridger Foothills National Recreation Trail** starts at the **M Picnic Area** on Bridger Dr. and continues for 21 miles to the Fairy Lake Campground. From there, it's a two-mile hike to **Sacajawea Peak**. To drive to the **Fairy Lake Campground**, take Bridger Dr. for 24 miles to Forest Rd. and go another seven miles to the campground.

Skiing
Big Sky, one hour to the south (see p. 181), is the state's biggest downhill ski resort, and the site of good cross-country skiing at **Lone Mountain Ranch,** tel. 995-4644.

Bridger Bowl, 16 miles northeast of town up Bridger Canyon Rd., tel. (800) 223-9609 or 587-2111, is Bozeman's local ski mountain. It's just as snowy as Big Sky and a lot less glitzy.

Cross-country skiers can head up Bridger Canyon to **Bohart Ranch Cross Country Ski Center,** 16621 Bridger Canyon Rd., tel. 586-9070. During the summer the trails are used for mountain biking, hiking, and horseback riding.

Bangtail, 508 W. Main, tel. 587-4905, rents cross-country skis in the winter and mountain bikes once the snow's gone. Ask for their map of the area's mountain-bike trails. **Chalet Sports,** at Main St. and Willson Ave., tel. 587-4595, also rents both skis and bikes.

Other Activities
Cottonwood Hills on River Rd., tel. 587-1118, is Bozeman's nine-hole public golf course.

For those who aren't fans of the fairways, perhaps the **Skate Palace** at 2015 Wheat Dr., tel. 586-7770, holds more appeal.

SHOPPING

There's plenty of shopping to be done on and around Main Street. Two Western-clothing stores share a downtown block—both **McCracken's,** 131 E. Main, tel. 586-9570, and

Country West, 137 E. Main, tel. 587-4548, offer real ranch wear and a polite tolerance of shoppers who don't really need it.

T. Charbonneau Trading Company, with its allusion to Sacajawea's husband, is an upscale "Western lifestyle" place with bent-willow furniture and French designer cowboy clothes. It's a block off Main at 37 S. Willson, tel. 587-9198. For stylish women's wear with a Western twist, **Jones and Co.,** 27 E. Main, tel. 587-0883, has outfits that won't look out of place in Indianapolis or Baltimore. Likewise **Rising Sun Leather** at 307 E. Main, tel. 586-0222—wander to the back of the store and try on the great woolen coats by a local designer. Even budget travelers can get outfitted at **Rethreads,** a great used-clothing shop at 24 W. Main, tel. 586-1219.

Northern Lights, 1716 W. Babcock, tel. 586-2225, has equipment and clothing for hikers, climbers, campers, and cross-country skiers. They're located near the Patagonia mail-order headquarters, and often have good deals on Patagonia clothing.

Montanaphiles and baseball lovers alike will thrill to the collection at **Vargo's Books,** 1 E. Main St., tel. 587-5383. The shelves are packed with new and used books on topics both mainstream and obscure. **Country Bookshelf** is an exceptionally good general bookstore at 28 W. Main, tel. 587-0166.

TRANSPORTATION

Gallatin Field is eight miles west of town, near Belgrade. Serviced by Delta, Alaska, and Continental airlines, flights come in daily from Salt Lake City and Denver. Roundtrip fares from the West Coast run $250-300.

Automobile rentals are available at the airport through **Budget Rent-A-Car,** tel. 388-4091 or (800) 527-0700; **Avis,** tel. 388-6414 or (800) 311-1212; **Hertz,** tel. 388-6939 or (800) 654-3131, and **National,** tel. 388-6694 or (800) 227-7368. Near the airport, at 21000 Frontage Rd., find **Thrifty Car Rental,** tel. 388-3484 or (800) 367-2277, and **Payless Car Rental,** tel. 388-3348 or (800) PAYLESS. There's also bus service between Gallatin Field and downtown Bozeman.

For budget car rentals in downtown Bozeman, try **Rent-A-Wreck,** 5 E. Mendenhall, tel.

587-4551 or (800) 421-7253. They offer a free airport pick-up service, as does **U-Save,** 506 N. Seventh, tel. 587-9716 or (800) 444-9716.

Greyhound stops in Bozeman on its way down I-90; catch it at 625 N. Seventh Ave., tel. 587-3110. **Rimrock Stages** provides bus service to Helena and Missoula from the same bus terminal (same phone number, too).

City Taxi, tel. 586-2341, offers another way of shuttling around town or to Big Sky or Yellowstone.

SERVICES AND INFORMATION

The **Bozeman Area Chamber of Commerce** is at 1205 E. Main, tel. 586-5421 or (800) 228-4224, but the **Visitor Information Center** at 1001 N. Seventh is a better place to stop for brochures and conversation.

Dial 911 for the **police** or **fire** departments; 587-0911 reachs the **ambulance** service. **Bozeman Deaconess Hospital** is at 915 Highland Blvd., tel. 585-5000.

Find the **public library** at 220 E. Lamme, tel. 586-4787; it's open Tues.-Saturday. Pick up **National Public Radio** at 89.3 FM in and around Bozeman.

The **Montana Department of Fish, Wildlife, and Parks** has an office at 1400 S. 19th, tel. 994-4042.

The **post office** is in the Federal Building at 32 E. Babcock.

LIVINGSTON AND THE PARADISE VALLEY

Back when passenger trains still crossed southern Montana, Livingston was the gateway to Yellowstone National Park. Park-goers would change trains at the Livingston depot, and take the rail spur to Yellowstone.

Nowadays, travelers with a little time to pass can stock up on some of the world's most coveted flies in Livingston, cast them into the Yellowstone River, soak in the hot springs at Chico, or wander out of the broad, sun-filled Paradise Valley into the Absaroka-Beartooth Wilderness Area. There's really no sense in a pell-mell dash to often-hectic Yellowstone Park when there are so many places to linger just to the north.

LIVINGSTON

Livingston's a really weird place. Stand by the jukebox at a downtown bar and a lovely woman in evening dress may invite you to party with Tom McGuane and Peter Fonda. Or maybe you'll be the lucky person to meet the guy dressed in full buckskins, up visiting from L.A. At the very least you'll hear a good fishing story.

While Bozeman quickly gained a reputation as a straight-laced town, Livingston, 26 miles east, never had any such reputation to live down. It's a town with a history of such Wild West legends as Calamity Jane and Kitty O'Leary, aka Madame Bulldog. (Calamity Jane's reputation must have softened over the past century, for there's now a beauty salon named for her in Kalispell, featuring brow arching and facial waxing as well as haircuts.)

Livingston, the Park County seat (pop. 6,700, elev. 4,490 feet), is situated at the wind-tossed northern end of the Paradise Valley. The Absaroka and Gallatin ranges flank the valley. After its northerly run up from Yellowstone Park, the Yellowstone River turns east at Livingston, where I-90/94 meets the river and ushers it from the state.

History
Mt. Baldy (aka Mt. Livingston), southeast of Livingston in the Absaroka Range, was the site of winter vision quests by Crow braves. William Clark camped on the Yellowstone River south of Livingston on July 15, 1806. Several days later, Crows stole his party's horses, forcing the explorers to build dugouts and bullboats.

Livingston's mild climate led Nelson Story to select it for the terminus of his cattle drive from Texas in 1866 à la Larry McMurtry's *Lonesome Dove*—a trip prescient of Montana's development as cattle country.

Tourist development began in the 1860s when a physician established a hot-springs resort east of Livingston near Springdale. In 1867, trail guide John Bozeman was killed in a narrow part of the Yellowstone Valley 13 miles east of Livingston. A highway marker on I-90 commemorates him.

The Railroad
The Northern Pacific laid rail tracks across the Yellowstone in the early 1880s. Two merchants bent on supplying the railroad promptly founded Clark City, on the southeast side of present-day Livingston. They didn't realize that the NP had already planned to build the town of Livingston in the same area. Within months, Livingston (named for a railroad official) sprouted right next to the railroad tracks, and the Clark City entrepreneurs moved to the new townsite.

The railroad established Livingston as a major division point and locomotive repair site, and a boom set in. Ever since then, Livingston's history has been a cycle of booms and busts. When tourists flocked to Yellowstone Park via train, rail passengers debarked the main N.P. line to catch the Park Branch Line to Gardiner and Livingston flourished.

With the good times came legendary rambunctiousness:

*The old **Bucket of Blood**, 113 Park St., one of the many old-time Montana saloons so named, was probably a little rougher than most. It . . . was the center of a group of resorts of the same kind including a gambling dive run by Tex Rickard, Kid Brown, and Soapy Smith until the Klondike rush took them off to the Yukon. Madame Bulldog, once Kitty O'Leary, ran what was* *euphemistically known as a dance hall. Her joint, she said, was a decent one. Announcing that she would stand for no damfoolishness, she saved the wages of a bouncer by polishing off roughnecks herself. Her dimensions, like her sensibilities, were pachydermal; she tipped the scales at 190, stripped. And stripped she was most of the time. Calamity Jane was one of her associates for a time, but legend has it that they fell out, whereupon Madame Bulldog tossed Calamity into the street, "as easy as licking three men." When asked whether Calamity Jane really tried to fight back, one who knew both women replied succinctly, "Calamity was tougher'n hell, but she wasn't crazy!"*

-WPA Guide to Montana

When the Burlington Northern closed down its southern Montana lines in 1986, things looked grim. Since Montana Rail Link bought the southern Montana line and its shops in 1988, there's been a bit of an upturn.

Sights

The Northern Pacific Railroad Depot, built in 1901-1902, resembles an Italian villa. It's now called the **DepotCenter** and houses the Livingston Chamber of Commerce and a well-curated historical, cultural, and art museum. The DepotCenter, 200 W. Park, tel. 222-2300, is open from June through mid-October, Mon.-Sat. 9-5, Sun. 1-5; winters, Thurs.-Sun 1-5. Admission is $2 for adults and $1 for children and seniors.

The other historical museum in town, the **Park County Museum,** is crammed into an old

CALAMITY JANE

It's a little hard to pin down the facts on Martha Jane Cannary, largely because, under the name of Calamity Jane, she was one of the West's most notorious liars.

Martha Cannary's father moved his wife and children west from Missouri in the early 1860s. He may have been a Mormon lay preacher bound for Salt Lake City, but the Cannarys seem to have landed in Virginia City, Montana, during the 1865 gold rush. As a teenager, Martha Jane set to wandering around the West, picking up what work she could.

Though Jane expressed both an aptitude for and interest in such male-dominated adventures as Army scouting and prospecting, prostitution became her calling, like many other women of the West. "She was given to shooting up saloons, and to raising hell with tongue and quirt," says the WPA Guide to Montana. Perhaps she was a lover of Wild Bill Hickok's, but more likely not. Stories of Calamity's secret marriage to Wild Bill, and of their daughter, Janey, are unsubstantiated, but her theatrical bent did lead to a stint with Buffalo Bill's Wild West Show. Her theatrical career, however, as well as many other projects, was cut short by her alcoholism.

Castle, Harlowtown, Big Timber, and Livingston were all her haunts. Calamity Jane lived in Livingston off and on—she had a cabin at 213 Main Street for several impoverished and unhappy years. Calamity Jane was 51 when she died outside Deadwood, South Dakota, in 1903. According to her wishes,

she was buried next to Wild Bill Hickok in the Deadwood cemetery.

For a fact-based, eloquent novel, try Larry McMurtry's *Buffalo Girls*, which chronicles the lives of Calamity Jane and her comrades.

Calamity Jane

schoolhouse and a hundred-year-old Northern Pacific car at 118 W. Chinook St., tel. 222-3506. Among the displays are a room devoted to railroading and a bicycle collection. The Park County Museum is open June 1 to Labor Day, noon-5 p.m. daily.

Livingstonians ran amok in the late 1970s, listing every eligible site on the National Register of Historic Places. There's great pride taken in the restoration of downtown buildings to their original Western look, and it does look splendid. Much of the restoration has been accomplished by public grants with matching funds from local businesses. Look for elaborate brickwork and faded signs painted on the sides of the downtown buildings. Wander down some of the residential streets. Yellowstone St., three blocks west of Main, was a very toney address around the turn of the century. The east side of town, near G and Callender, was the figurative "other side of the tracks," where the blue-collar railroad workers lived. To round out the tour, visit the 300 block of South B St. The four matching houses on the east side of the street were once Livingston's brothels.

Accommodations

The **Talcott House Bed and Breakfast Lodge,** 405 W. Lewis, tel. 222-7699, has elegant rooms with large breakfasts and a workout room for $55-65 d. Both kids and dogs are welcome.

Rooms at the **Murray Hotel,** across from the DepotCenter at 201 W. Park, tel. 222-1350, start at $21 s. Like much of the rest of downtown, the Murray is listed in the National Register of Historic Places. Though they've hosted "writers, artists, and film people," nowadays it's largely a residential hotel with a lively bar and a café that draws in railroad workers. Still, it's not *too* creepy, and its interior architecture recalls the grander side of the Old West.

There are lots of motels in Livingston and, by Montana standards, they're a little more expensive than their appearances would suggest. They're here to house the fly-fishers and Yellowstone-goers, and the rates at most places plunge during the off-season.

A block down from the Murray, the **Guest House Motor Inn,** 105 W. Park, tel. 222-1460, has doubles from $35. On the east end of town on Hwy. 85, the **Rainbow Motel,** tel. 222-3780, has a campground and $30 double rooms. **Parkway Motel,** on the edge of town at 1124 W. Park, tel. 222-3840, has a pool and rooms from $40 d. There's also a pool at the **Del-Mar Motel,** I-90 Business Loop W, tel. 222-3120, $36 s, $44 d. At the **VIP Motel,** on the West Park strip near I-90, tel. 222-3600, morning donuts and coffee are included with the $45 rooms. The **Super 8,** 108 Centennial Dr., tel. 222-7711, comes in a little cheaper at $32 s, $36 d.

Doubles are $50 at the **Best Western Yellowstone Motor Inn,** 1515 W. Park, tel. 222-6110 or (800) 528-1234. The comparably priced **Paradise Inn** is near the freeway exit on the west end of town, tel. 222-6320. Both the Paradise and the Best Western have indoor pools.

The **Forest Service** rents several cabins in the Livingston district for about $20 a night. Call the ranger station at 222-1892 for details and reservations.

Unless you're looking for RV camping, it's better to drive a ways up the Paradise Valley to find a site. But, in a pinch, there are private campgrounds in Livingston: try the one associated with the **Rainbow Motel,** tel. 222-3720, or the **Rock Canyon Campground,** which has tepees for rent three miles south of town on Hwy. 89, tel. 222-1096.

Food And Drink

Martin's Restaurant, next to the depot, tel. 222-2311, remains a traditional 24-hour railroad café. Across from the depot, the **Murray Cafe** is another unpretentious spot for breakfast, lunch, or dinner.

The back bar at the **Livingston Bar and Grill,** 130 N. Main, tel. 222-7909, dates to the early 1900s, and it was supposedly Calamity Jane's favorite spot in Livingston. Montana trout and beef are featured in the restaurant, as are buffalo burgers.

Don't be surprised to find yourself propped up against a bar in Livingston. The town's wild reputation is supported by a wealth of bars. The **Mint Bar** on Main and Callender has a card room and the ubiquitous electronic gambling machines. The **Murray Hotel Bar** may host tea-drinking hotel residents early in the evening, but eases into rowdiness later at night. The **Sport,** a bar with good burgers, has been gussied up a bit, apparently with tourists in mind.

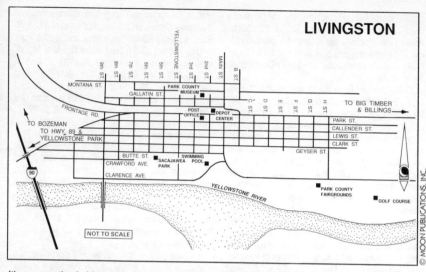

It's easy on the timid traveler without succumbing to blandness.

Wilcoxson's, Livingston's ice cream, is available in most grocery stores throughout the state.

Events
The **Livingston Roundup Rodeo** is on the Fourth of July weekend. It kicks off with a parade and segues into a lively Professional Rodeo Cowboys Assn. (PRCA) rodeo. Reserved seats at the rodeo cost $8, general admission is $5, children $3.

The **Yellowstone Boat Float,** a three-day mid-July event, runs 110 miles from Livingston to Columbus, following the route of Captain Clark and his party on their return from the Pacific. The float is open to all, any sort of boat is permitted, and, like the river, it's "wet, wild, and dam free." Contact Yellowstone Boat Float, Inc., P.O. Box 1000, Laurel, MT 59044 for more information and exact dates.

During the second week of August, Livingston hosts the **Park County Fair.**

Recreation
The nine-hole **Livingston Golf and Country Club** is a public course on River Dr. at the foot of Main St., tel. 222-1031.

Because the Yellowstone is such a popular and accessible floating river, shuttle services have sprung up to transport floaters' cars from the put-in point to the take-out point. Check with fishing and tackle shops for the details and phone numbers.

The city **swimming pool** is near the foot of Main St. just east of Sacajawea Park and just north of Miles Park.

Livingston Cycle, 117 W. Callender, tel. 222-2628, sells, rents, and repairs bicycles.

Arts
It may be a little surprising that a scrappy railroad town like Livingston has become something of an artists' colony. But the beautiful light and stunning scenery (not to mention the trout fishing) of the Paradise Valley work in counterpoint to Livingston's raucous edge to make this one of the state's most prestigious addresses.

Russell Chatham is Livingston's most renowned artist. His oils and lithographs evoke the places where the plains come up against the mountains. Chatham's work is represented in town by the **Wishing Tree Galleries,** 120 N. Main, tel. 222-7528. Other galleries along the same stretch of Main St. are the **Danforth Gallery,** 106 N. Main, which focuses on innovative, quality crafts, and the **Wade Gallery,** 116 N. Main, tel. 222-0404.

Shopping

Don't look for $60 French jeans in Livingston, but there's Western wear, books and a little of most everything else at **Sax and Fryer,** 109 W. Callender Street. **Gil's** carries every variety of Western souvenir at 207 W. Park. Next door, fly-tiers start early at **Dan Bailey's Fly Shop,** an angler's supply mecca. Bailey's flies are so renowned they're practically pedigreed . . . and, they're available by mail order from 209 W. Park, Livingston, MT 59047, tel. 222-1673. Just south of Livingston on Hwy. 89, **Anderson's Yellowstone Angler,** tel. 222-7130, is another source of tackle and guidance.

Information And Services

The Livingston **Chamber of Commerce** is housed in the old baggage room of the Livingston Depot Center, 200 W. Park, tel. 222-0850.

For information on hiking, camping, Forest Service cabin rentals, and fishing, stop by the ranger station on Hwy. 89 about a mile south of Livingston, tel. 222-1892.

Livingston Memorial Hospital is at 504 S. 13th St., tel. 222-3541. The **post office** is at the corner of Main and Callender. **Olson's Laundry,** at D and Park, tel. 222-7428, is open daily 8 a.m.-10 p.m.

Getting There

The **Greyhound** depot is at the Stop Over Café, 332 S. Main St. Three eastbound and three westbound buses pass through daily. For schedule information call 222-2231. **TW Services** buses use the same depot and run to Yellowstone Park during the summer months. There's a bus leaving Livingston each morning at 8:15 a.m. It arrives in Mammoth at 9:35 a.m. and continues on a tour through the park. Bozeman and Billings have more car rental agencies, but **Rent-A-Wreck** has an office at Park and 6th, tel. 222-0071 or (800) 255-0071. Reach **VIP Taxi** at 222-0200.

PARADISE VALLEY

The Land

The never-dammed Yellowstone River flows past the Absaroka Range to the east and the Gallatin Range to the west. The broad valley narrows upriver, squeezing down to form Yankee Jim Canyon near Yellowstone Park.

Yellowstone's volcanoes spat out the Absaroka Range—a high lava field with relief etched by erosion from water and glacial ice. The Absarokas are lush, wet mountains, more characteristic of western Montana than the dry peaks east of the Divide. The same lava flows covered folded sedimentary rocks of the Gallatin Range.

History

The Crows lived along the upper Yellowstone for two hundred years before white explorers and mountain men arrived. Jim Bridger cut up and down the valley in the 1840s.

Gold, but not much of it, was mined in the 1860s. Emigrant Gulch was the site of the first strike in 1864, and a short-lived mining town called Yellowstone City sprouted on the hillside of the gulch. Old Chico was another mining camp, where one of the world's largest gold dredges scraped a trickling stream.

By the 1880s, coal had replaced gold as the valley's main lode. Coke ovens were built west of Livingston to produce fuel for the smelters in Anaconda.

Both cattle and sheep ranching have long been important in the Paradise Valley, but subdivisions have carved big outfits into a panoply of ranchettes near Livingston.

The **Church Universal and Triumphant** (known locally as CUT) has bought up an enormous tract of land north and west of Gardiner. Underground bunkers and storage tanks have been carved into the ground west of Corwin Springs. These survivalist measures are mandated by the group's spiritual leader, Elizabeth Claire Prophet, who has predicted pending nuclear holocaust.

The church has not engendered good feelings amongst most Montanans. Some people think of the problems that came about when the Bhagwan Shree Rajneesh bought a huge ranch in Oregon. Many cite the church's lax environmental precautions. During the spring of 1990, an oil storage tank ruptured and spilled thousands of gallons of oil, imperiling a nearby trout stream. The church's plans to tap the area's geothermal resources have provoked concerns about the impact this would have on Yellowstone Park.

Sights

Come to the Paradise Valley for the Yellowstone River, its valley, and the surrounding mountains. A few miles south of Livingston, the paved but potholed East River Rd. leaves Hwy. 89. Both roads along the Yellowstone are lovely, but the East River Rd. gives a better view of the way people live in the valley.

The upper Yellowstone River cuts through the gneiss of narrow **Yankee Jim Canyon** 15 miles north of Gardiner. Jim George, aka Yankee Jim, built the first road into Yellowstone National Park. He charged a toll to travel the road, and when the Northern Pacific claimed its right to the roadbed, the railroad was forced to build Yankee Jim another road further up the hill.

The **Gallatin Petrified Forest** is west of Hwy. 89 up Tom Miner Creek. Permits, available for $5 at ranger stations in Gardiner, Livingston and Bozeman, are required for collecting petrified wood.

Just southwest of Corwin Springs, near the Church Universal and Triumphant's holdings, Mt. Cinnabar has a red streak, called the Devil's Slide, and originally reckoned to be cinnabar. Actually, it's not mercury, but a clinker coal seam making it red.

Jardine, an old mining ghost town five miles up Bear Gulch from Gardiner, has seen several spurts of mining activity. Both gold and arsenic were mined here, with arsenic production continuing until the end of World War II. The late 1980s saw another attempt to mine gold from Jardine, but the town is notable chiefly as home to some well-preserved mining relics. Hiking trails starting in Jardine lead into the Absaroka-Beartooth Wilderness.

Chico Hot Springs Lodge, halfway between Livingston and Gardiner in Pray, is the sort of spot you want all your friends to know about, and everybody else to ignore. The lodge here is built around a large hot springs-fed swimming pool. The rooms in the circa-1900 lodge are cramped and spartan, but the rooms aren't where most guests spend their time. There's plenty of recreation in the Paradise Valley, soaking and swimming in the pool, surprisingly elegant dinners in the hotel dining room, and rowdy good times in the lively bar. There's an outfitter on the premises with fishing gear and bicycles for rent. Rooms in the lodge start at $34 d; there

are motel rooms ($49 d), cabins ($50-110), and condos ($115-275) available, too. Call 333-4933 to reserve rooms or meals.

Other Accommodations

Pine Creek Cabins, 12 miles south of Livingston on East River Rd., tel. 222-3628, are quintessential Montana resort cabins—rustic, cheap, and with easy fishing access to the Yellowstone. There's also a Forest Service campground two miles up Pine Creek from the hamlet of Pine Creek. Pine Creek Falls is a short hike from the campground, and Jewell and Pine Creek lakes are three miles up the trail.

The Forest Service has a cabin for rent up Trail Creek, 20 miles southwest of Livingston. The cabin is rented year-round for $20 a night; winter visitors may need skis or a snowmobile to navigate the final three miles of the road.

Mountain Sky Guest Ranch is an upscale outfit south of Emigrant, P.O. Box 1128, Bozeman, MT 59715, tel. 587-1244 or (800) 548-3392. Riding, fishing, tennis courts, a pool, hot tub,and sauna are all available here. Rates start at about $1000 a week per person for a shared room, with reduced rates for children.

Snow Bank Forest Service campground is 20 miles south of Livingston on Hwy. 89, then another 15 miles east on Mill Creek Road. Closer to Gardiner and Yellowstone Park, **Tom Miner/ Petrified Forest** Forest Service campground is eight miles west of Hwy. 89 on Tom Miner Rd. (36 miles south of Livingston). The Gallatin Petrified Forest is a two-mile hike from the campground. The many fishing-access sites on the Yellowstone are de facto campgrounds.

Recreation

Bicycling: The East River Road is for cyclists who don't mind a few potholes. Mountain bikers will want to turn off the main road and head up into the hills. Rent bikes from the outfitter's shop at Chico Hot Springs—after a day or two on the bicycle saddle, the pool at Chico is hard to pass up.

Floating the Yellowstone: The upper stretches of theYellowstone River, particularly through Yankee Jim Canyon, have some challenging whitewater. After the river leaves Yankee Jim Canyon and enters the Paradise Valley, it calms down enough for novice floaters to navigate it without much difficulty. Gardiner's **Yel-**

spring mountain biking north of Chico Hot Springs

JUDY JEWELL

lowstone Raft Company, tel. 848-7777, runs raft trips on the Yellowstone.

Fishing: The Yellowstone River is a blue ribbon trout stream. Most everybody that fishes here uses flies, and the local fishing shops are quick to advise you on what'll work best. Summer and fall are the most popular seasons to fish the Yellowstone. Early in the summer, the salmon flies and caddis flies hatch. Later on, around August, trout feed on grasshoppers near the river's edge. Numerous fishing-access sites dot both Hwy. 89 and the East River Road.

Besides the Yellowstone, there are a couple of "spring creeks" that challenge the skillful angler. The two most notable of these, Nelson's and Armstrong's, are on private land and a fee is charged for fishing them. For details, ask at Dan Bailey's Fly Shop in Livingston or at any other local angler's shop.

Hiking: Mill Creek reaches into the Absaroka-Beartooth Wilderness Area. The lower stretches of the Mill Creek Rd., from the town of Pray to the wilderness boundary, are good for mountain biking, and the foot trail continues into the wilderness area. Thompson Lake, Elbow Lake, Mount Cowan, and Passage Creek Falls are some of the destinations for hikers. The Snowbank campground is a handy jumping-off point.

In the Gallatin Range, hike or cross-country ski just about any drainage: Trail Creek (there's cross-country skiing in the vicinity of the Forest Service cabin there), **Big Creek** (28 miles south of Livingston, then west up Big Creek Road), **Rock Creek** (with access to a trail network), or **Tom Miner Basin** (and the nearby Gallatin Petrified Forest).

GARDINER

Used to be, Gardiner was just another way in to Yellowstone National Park. Now, mention the town and you'll quickly draw comments on Elizabeth Claire Prophet and her Church Universal and Triumphant (CUT). These espousers of eminent apocalypse have laid their own history down beside a heritage of gold mining, tourist trains, and wildfire.

As if politico-religious controversy wasn't enough, local ranchers want to shoot buffalo. Buffalo frequently carry brucellosis, a bacteria that causes abortions in newly-infected cattle. For several years, bison straying from Yellowstone Park have been hunted by Montana and National Park wildlife officals and by private hunters, who can enter a lottery for a buffalo tag. This practice enrages animal rights activists and some environmentalists.

But, for the average traveler, Gardiner (pop. 600, elev. 5,314 feet), isn't far removed from what is expected at the gateway to America's oldest national park. The motels and souvenir shops are somewhat less daunting than those in

West Yellowstone, and elk and deer wander from the park to graze on ornamental shrubbery and linger on lawns. Gardiner's small enough not to need real street addresses—just squint hard and you'll find what you're looking for.

The Gardiner entrance to Yellowstone is marked by the Roosevelt Arch, dedicated in 1903 by Theodore Roosevelt. It's the only park entrance open to cars year-round. The road between Gardiner and Cooke City is plowed during the winter.

Accommodations

During the summer, many of the accommodations in Gardiner are expensive—even the **Super 8,** Hwy. 89, tel. 848-7401, charges $60 a night. Park-goers may prefer to reserve in advance and stay in the lodge or cabins at Mammoth Hot Springs, which has more moderate prices.

From mid-September through May, lodging prices drop significantly.

On Hwy. 89, the **Flamingo Motor Lodge,** tel. 848-7536, and **Hillcrest Cottages,** tel. 848-7353, have lodgings for around $40. In the same price range are the **Town Motel,** Park St., tel. 848-7322, and **Wilson's Yellowstone River Motel,** just east of Hwy. 89 near the park entrance, tel. 848-7303.

The **Best Western by Mammoth Hot Springs** is set back off the highway just north of Gardiner on Hwy. 89, tel. 848-7311.The comfortable rooms run $65 d.

Paradise, tel. 848-7684, and Rocky Mountain, tel. 848-7251, are RV-style campgrounds right in Gardiner. **Eagle Creek** is a Forest Service campground four miles northeast of town.

Food And Drink

The gamut of tourist restaurants is represented in Gardiner. **Bear Country Restaurant,** tel. 848-7188, is open for breakfast, lunch, and dinner until 9 p.m., a stone's throw from the Roosevelt Arch. For sandwiches, try the **Sawtooth Deli,** tel. 848-7600, or the **Town Café,** tel. 848-7322, or grab a burger at the **Corral Drive Inn,** tel. 848-7627. Gardiner's fancy restaurant is the **Yellowstone Mine** in the Best Western, tel. 848-7336. It's open daily for breakfast and dinner. If you're hungry, but don't feel compelled to stop in Gardiner, the **Ranch Kitchen,** seven miles north of town in Corwin Springs, tel. 848-7891, is operated by Church Universal and Triumphant members, who cook with lots of fresh vegetables and whole grains.

Sundries

The rodeo comes to Gardiner in mid-June. Call the **chamber of commerce,** tel. 848-7971, for the exact date.

Boats aren't allowed on Yellowstone Park's rivers, but **Yellowstone Raft Company,** headquartered in Gardiner, runs trips on the Yellowstone, Gallatin, and Madison rivers. The Gallatin National Forest has a **ranger station** in Gardiner near the park entrance, tel. 848-7375.

BIG TIMBER TO LAUREL

The Boulder River falls between the Absarokas and the Beartooths to Big Timber, passing ghost towns, church camps, and dude ranches on the way. Around Big Timber, the Yellowstone River changes from a cold-water trout stream to the broad, warm home of paddlefish.

History

This whole area was Crow territory before white settlers moved in. It's reckoned that the Verendrye party passed by the Boulder River and Big Timber Creek in 1741 as they traveled down the Yellowstone from the Musselshell River. The next white explorers were Captain Clark and his brigade, who camped near Hunter's Hot Springs in July of 1806.

It wasn't until 1873 that a rancher settled in the area. When the railroad came through, a small settlement sprang up near the mouth of the Boulder River. This town, called Dornix (meaning "Rock Pile"), never made it as a railway station. In 1883, the town of Big Timber was founded just to the west. Ranching, especially sheep ranching, has always figured more than railroading, and now, along with tourism and recreation, supports the local economy.

BIG TIMBER

Big Timber (pop. 1,557), a usually quiet ranch town, is not a forested spot. William Clark named Big Timber Creek for the stand of cottonwoods shading its confluence with the Yellowstone. Today, it might be called "Big Wind" or "Crazyview," for the frequent gusts and the nearby mountain range are far more noticeable than the trees.

Sights

Like nearby Livingston, Big Timber has tried to make something of local artists. For a look at Sweet Grass County art, stop by **Zemsky/Hines Gallery** at 100 E. Third St., tel. 932-5307. The late

Spike van Cleve, a rancher from Melville, was a raconteur of ranch life, and his granddaughter Barbara, a photographer now based in New Mexico, has stunning black-and-white photos hanging in the Grand Hotel and in the Kirby real estate office-cum-art gallery, 100 McLeod Street. **Cabin Creek Studio** houses sculptor Lyle Johnson, who is known for his Western bronzes.

Big Timber is also home to a couple of quirky museums. The **Sweet Grass County Museum,** 120 McLeod St., is open Tues.-Sat. 10 a.m.-4 p.m. It features displays of the area's geology and natural history. **Victorian Village** is a large and well-tended historical museum and antique store begun as a Washington man's private collection; it is now continued by his family. Summer hours are daily 9 a.m.-5 p.m.; spring and fall, Sat, and Sun. 10 a.m.-4 p.m.; closed Oct. through February.

Yellowstone cutthroat trout of all ages live in the pools of the **Fish Hatchery** north of town on McLeod St., tel. 932-4434. Trout are taken from the hatchery to stock lakes across the state.

Exit the corpse-strewn freeway at Greycliff to visit the communal burrows of **Greycliff Prairie Dog Village.** From May 1 to Sept. 30, there is a $3 per vehicle entrance fee.

The **Crazy Mountains,** north of Big Timber, are a spectacular, isolated range (see p. 164). To reach them from Big Timber, drive north on Hwy. 191 (the road to Harlowtown) and follow signs for Big Timber Canyon. Halfmoon USFS campground and a trailhead into the mountains are about 15 miles from the pavement.

Accommodations

The **Grand Hotel,** a hundred-year-old hotel on McLeod St. in Big Timber, maintains the original restaurant and bar, and the hotel has been restored as a bed and breakfast. This is a great place to stay— the rooms are cozy, the full breakfasts are staggeringly good, and there's a sauna in the upstairs hallway. Rooms with breakfast run from

BOB RACE

prairie dog

downtown Big Timber

JUDY JEWELL

$55 (shared bath) to $85 (private bath), about $20 less in the off-season, tel. 932-4459.

The **C.M. Russell Lodge and Motel,** tel. 932-5245, and the **Lazy J Motel,** tel. 932-5533, are both on Hwy. 10 in Big Timber and have rooms starting around $30.

Spring Creek Camp and Trout Ranch has cabins and some tent sites, but is essentially an RV park two miles south of Big Timber on Boulder River Road.

The **Big Timber KOA** is near the Greycliff exit, nine miles east of Big Timber, tel. 932-6569. Besides tent and RV sites, there are cabins for rent, a swimming pool, and hot tubs.

Nineteen miles north of Big Timber, up Big Timber Canyon, **Half Moon campground** features hiking trails into the Crazy Mountains.

Food And Drink

You can breakfast at the **Grand Hotel** only if you're a guest there, but lunches and dinners are served up to the public, and there's a friendly bar off to the side of the lobby. Northern Italian entrees are interspersed among the steaks on the dinner menu (dinners run $15). Next door to the Grand, **Prospector Pizza** is a popular and inexpensive place to eat.

Events

The **rodeo** is held the last weekend in June. Equally popular is the **cutting horse show,** held at the fairgrounds during the last weekend in July. Cutting horses are trained to separate specific cattle from a herd without causing a fracas. For more information call the chamber of commerce at 932-5131.

Recreation

Sun-baked I-90 travelers may enjoy a stop at the **Big Timber Waterslide,** nine miles east of Big Timber at exit 377, tel. 932-6570. The water park is open June 1 through Labor Day, 10 a.m.-7 p.m., admission $10.95 for ages seven and above, $8.50 for ages two-six.

The nine-hole public **Overland Golf Course** is a mile east of Big Timber on Hwy. 10., tel. 932-4297.

Boulder River **fishing-access sites** include **Big Rock,** four miles south of Big Timber and **Boulder Forks,** in McLeod. Fish the Yellowstone from **Grey Bear,** seven miles west of Big Timber, or **Greycliff.**

In the Crazy Mountains, hiking trails start from the **Halfmoon campground.**

Information

Write to the **chamber of commerce** at Box 1012, Big Timber, MT 59011, or call 932-5131. Reach the **Forest Service** at 932-5155.

BOULDER VALLEY

It's hard to pick Montana's most beautiful river valley, but this one's a strong contender—small wonder, then, that celebrities and novelists have become the modern-day homesteaders here.

Sights

Drive up the Boulder River Valley 25 miles south of Big Timber to the **Natural Bridge State Monument.** The limestone cliffs have been warped, lifted, dropped, and eaten away by weak riverwater acids, leaving a spectacular gorge with a 100-foot waterfall. The eponymous natural bridge across the falls collapsed in 1988. Trails course the park, but there are no campsites.

Just down the road from the natural bridge, the **Main Boulder Ranger Station** dates from 1905. There are pictographs in the caves west of the ranger station.

Forty miles up the Boulder River from Big Timber, the ghost town of **Independence** recalls a past of gold mining and stock-promotion schemes. The final four miles of the drive to Independence are best driven in four-wheel-drive.

Accommodations

The Boulder Valley didn't support miners or farmers for long, but dude ranchers have done well by it. The **Hawley Mountain Guest Ranch,** 45 miles south of Big Timber, has reasonably priced week-long packages including cabin, meals, horseback riding, and river floating. Information is available by writing to Box 4, McLeod, MT 59052 or calling 932-5791. Also near McLeod is the **Burnt Leather Ranch,** West Boulder Rd., McLeod, MT 59052, tel. 932-6155 or 222-6795.

For less expensive lodgings, the tidy **McLeod Resort,** Box 27, McLeod, MT 59052, tel. 932-6167 or 932-6169, has a campground ($8), cabins ($10 and up), and apartments ($27.50 and up). Both the cabins and the apartments have cooking facilities, but cooking utensils are not provided.

The Gallatin National Forest is studded with campsites south of Big Timber, but you've got to drive a ways to get to them. **Falls Creek Campground** is 30 miles south of town on Boulder River Road, with **Aspen Grove, Chippy Park,** and **Hell's Canyon** campgrounds all within the next 10 miles. **Hicks Park Campground** is 50 miles south of Big Timber on the same road. Turn right at McLeod to reach the **West Boulder Campground,** 30 miles southwest of Big Timber, with a trail into the Absaroka-Beartooth Wilderness.

Food And Drink

If the name of the **Road Kill Bar and Café** makes you grin, you'll love the place itself. This McLeod landmark is a convivial place to stop for a drink or a meal. Note the arched plank ceiling in the bar.

COLUMBUS AND BEYOND

Columbus, 37 miles east of Big Timber at the mouth of the Stillwater River, is renowned for the **New Atlas Bar,** which has a great backbar and more animal heads than most people have seen in a lifetime. Before the New Atlas, Columbus was known for its frequent name changes. Before landing on the present name, it was called Eagle's Nest, Sheep Dip, and Stillwater.

The jagged peaks of the Beartooth Range form the jawline of the horizon to the south. On the road down from Columbus, through Absarokee to Red Lodge, the fine views of former Crow country recall lost freedom and buffalo hunts.

Spend the night at **Oliver's Bed and Breakfast**, on Main St. in Absarokee, tel. 328-4813, stop for a coke at the Fishtail Mercantile (Fishtail also supports a restaurant and bar), fish the Stillwater River and wonder how it ever got that name, camp at Pine Grove or Emerald Lake campgrounds out of Fishtail, or at Jimmy Joe or East Rosebud Lake out of Roscoe. For a traveler with no pressing schedule, this is dinking-around country.

LAUREL

Located at a transportation crossroads, Laurel is a town often passed through by history. What with railroading and refining, it maintains an industrial ambience at odds with the fruitful valley it sprawls in. Boosters of Billings repeat a mantra about the day when Billings stretches clear to Laurel. It's not clear that there's much to gain or lose for either city; it's hard times for the farms in between, however.

History

As the Nez Percé Indians fled from the Battle of the Big Hole in 1877, they struck eastward toward Yellowstone National Park. Here they hoped to encounter their allies the Crow, and seek asylum in southeastern Montana. Repudiated by the Crow, who were by this time working closely with the Army, the Nez Percé leadership realized they had but one choice remaining: escape to Canada.

They pressed up the valley of the Clark Fork of the Yellowstone, and crossed the Yellowstone at Laurel. Colonel S.D. Sturgis and the new Seventh Cavalry caught up with the Nez Percé on Sept. 13 about nine miles north of Laurel, in Canyon Creek. Indian sharpshooters took positions in the sandstone bluffs above the valley, and held off the infantry until the Indian caravan was safe in the Musselshell Valley. At the Battle of Canyon Creek, the Army lost three men, the Nez Percé claimed three wounded.

Laurel grew up as the railhead for the Red Lodge-area coal mines that fuel the Northern Pacific's Montana steam engines. Laurel became the railroad hub of the entire Yellowstone Valley after the Great Northern and the Chicago, Burlington, and Quincy railroads made Laurel a division point. Access to rail lines made Laurel a candidate for other industry. Currently, a Cenex oil refinery dominates the skyline.

Sights

Follow Hwy. 532 north of Laurel nine miles to visit the scene of the Canyon Creek battle. The Chief Joseph-Sturgis Battlefield Monument commemorates the event.

Closer to town, in Fireman's Park, a newly unveiled statue of Chief Joseph serves as a memorial to the combatants at the battle.

Accommodations And Food

Best Western Locomotive Inn, 310 S. First Ave., tel. (800) 528-1234 or 628-8281, has a pool, nice restaurant, and sauna; $30 s, $42 d. The **Welcome Travelers Motel,** 620 W. Main, tel. 628-6821, has doubles starting at $36. **The Laurel Ridge Motel,** 1403 E. Main, tel. 628-2000, has comfortable rooms beginning at $32 d.

The **Locomotive Inn Restaurant,** 310 S. First Ave., tel. 628-7969, is Laurel's nicest place to eat, with the fairly requisite menu of steaks, chicken, and seafood. For family dining, try the **Owl Diner,** 203 E. Main, tel. 628-4522, open Tues.-Sat. 24 hours, Sun. and Mon. 5 a.m.-10 p.m.

Information

Contact the **Laurel Chamber of Commerce** at P.O. Box 395, Laurel, MT 59044, tel. 628-8105.

ABSAROKA-BEARTOOTH

THE LAND

This is Montana's high country: Granite Peak, towering 12,990 feet in the Beartooth Range, is the state's highest point and a formidable climb. Geologically and ecologically different, the Absaroka and the Beartooth ranges share a plateau and a wilderness area. The accommodating Beartooth Plateau tilts from a low northwestern Absaroka corner to the soaring Beartooths in the southeast.

The Beartooths were uplifted, eroded, partially blanketed with lava from Yellowstone's volcanoes, and covered with glaciers. The limestone cliffs of the Beartooth Range rise from high tundra cut through by steep canyons.

The weather in the Beartooths can change quickly and with arctic severity. Come prepared for a snowstorm, even in midsummer.

The Beartooths are largely above the timberline, and alpine meadows are the characteristic vegetation. The growing season here is about 45 days, and the plants and the soil are sensitive to trampling. During the late summer, snowbanks sometimes turn pink as microorganisms on the snow's surface die and turn red.

RED LODGE

Red Lodge (pop. 1,958, elev. 5,555 feet) is perhaps best known as the start of the Beartooth Highway.

Purportedly, a band of Crow Indians settled in the Beartooths and decorated their lodges with red clay. Once part of the Crow Reservation, this area was taken from the Indians in 1882 and coal mining commenced a few years later. The mines became the basis for the town, and many immigrants came to work in Red Lodge; Finns were particularly well represented. Mining dropped off in the 1930s and an explosion at the nearby Smith Creek Mine in 1943 halted large-scale coal mining in the area. Red Lodge is now a resort for travelers on the Beartooth Highway. The town has made an effort to round out its tourist offerings with a petting zoo, a ski resort, lots of restaurants, and the annual Festival of Nations.

Sights

Downtown Red Lodge is riddled with historic preservation. Pick up a walking-tour map from the chamber of commerce and ramble through the sandstone and brick edifices of the late 1800s.

The **Carbon County Historical Museum,** open during the summer, has all the expected pioneer paraphernalia, and an additional tidbit—Liver Eatin' Johnson's cabin. It's probably apocryphal, but Mr. Johnson was said to have avenged his Flathead wife's death by eating the livers he'd ripped from Crow Indians.

Coal Miner's Park, at the north edge of town, is home to the **Red Lodge Zoo** and hiking, biking, and cross-country skiing trails. Admission to

marker at the site of the original Crow Agency near Roscoe

the petting zoo is $2 adults, $1.50 children (free under age two). Hours are daily 10 a.m.-7 p.m. during the summer, tel. 446-1133. A precursor of the Red Lodge Zoo was the See 'Em Alive Zoo, operated by a fox farmer in the 1930s.

Accommodations

The old downtown hotel choice in Red Lodge is, without question, the **Pollard Hotel** at 2 N. Broadway, tel. 446-2860. Back when it was known as the Spofford, it hosted Calamity Jane and Buffalo Bill. Now there's even a sauna; rooms start at $33 s, $44 d.

Willows Inn bed and breakfast at 224 S. Platt, tel. 446-3913, is an old Victorian home with a supplemental two-bedroom cottage.

For budget accommodations, the **Valli Hi Motor Lodge,** 320 S. Broadway, tel. 446-1414, has single rooms starting at $25. If you yearn for predictability amidst the chaos of nature, there's a **Super 8** at 1223 S. Broadway, tel. 446-2288. Summertime rates here start at $33 s, $36 d, including a breakfast bar and use of a hot tub.

For a full-scale resort, the **Rock Creek Resort** is 4 miles south of town on Hwy. 212, tel. 446-1111. Single rooms start at $40, and accommodations include three-bedroom townhouses for $140 a night. There's no pool here, but there are tennis courts.

Camping

The Red Lodge **KOA,** four miles north of town on Hwy. 212, tel. 446-2364, has a swimming pool and sites for both RVs and tents at $9 a night. **Perry's Camper Park** is 1 1/2 miles south of town, tel. 446-2722. To find Forest Service campgrounds, head south on Hwy. 212. Reach **Cascade** and **Basin** campgrounds via Red Lodge Mountain Rd., which starts right near the ranger station. These are good spots for hikers wanting to head into the Absaroka-Beartooth Wilderness.

Farther south on Hwy. 212, find turnoffs for **Sheridan** and **Ratine. Parkside, Limber Pine, Greenough Lake,** and **M-K** are all part of the Rock Creek Recreation Area 11 miles south of Red Lodge and virtually at the foot of the Beartooth Highway. All these spots but Cascade, Ratine, Sheridan, and M-K have running water and charge $6 to camp.

Food And Drink

It's not hard to find a meal in Red Lodge—the town supposedly has more restaurants per capita than any other place in Montana. **Natali's** has reasonably priced breakfasts, lunches, and dinners with good burgers and some European touches at 115 S. Broadway, tel. 446-3333. **Pius's International Room** is the fancier dinner restaurant end of the same establishment.

In keeping with the melting-pot ethic of Red Lodge, try one of Montana's few Japanese restaurants: **Kiyoko's,** 718 S. Broadway, tel. 446-2606, open for lunch and dinner.

17 Broadway, (aka The Restaurant), tel. 446-1717, is another good dinner spot, with some pasta entrees in among the steaks.

For a casual lunch or dinner, **Bogart's** has good pizza and Mexican food in a comfortable, relaxed setting at 11 S. Broadway, tel. 446-1784. Breakfasts, particularly the sourdough pancakes, are the highlight at **P.D. McKinney's,** open for breakfast and lunch at 407 S. Broadway, tel. 446-1250.

A bright spot for coffee snobs afoot in Montana, **The Coffee Factory Roasters,** 6 S. Broadway, tel. 446-3200, roasts beans and serves up espresso and desserts.

Events

The **Red Lodge Music Festival** brings top high-school musicians to train with professionals. Both students and faculty perform over a nine-day span in mid-June.

The **Red Lodge Rodeo** is on Fourth of July weekend.

Mountain men descend on Red Lodge in late July and early August. Spend a week at the rendezvous for $15 ($25 family rate) or come in on a day pass for $3 (children $1). The encampment on the south end of town features trade goods, including buckskin garments, black-powder rifles, Indian beadwork, and pewter ware. More information is available from **Jeremiah Johnson's Trading Post,** tel. 446-3535, or the chamber of commerce, tel. 446-1718.

Ethnic diversity is celebrated each August during the nine-day **Festival of Nations.** Since the focus is on cultures that make up Red Lodge, expect to celebrate Scandinavian Day, Scottish Day, German Day, Finnish Day, Yugoslavian Day, English-Irish Day, Italian Day,

Montana Day, and All Nations Day. The town fills up for this celebration, so be sure to book rooms in advance if you want to stay in Red Lodge during the second week in August.

Personalized events can be had at the **Canyon Wedding Chapel,** four miles south of Red Lodge, P.O. Box 605, Red Lodge, MT 59068, tel. 446-2681. Both religious and civil wedding ceremonies are held here.

Recreation

Red Lodge Mountain is a ski resort six miles west of town. Snowmakers are used early in the season, which runs from early December through mid-April. Spring skiing is especially popular at Red Lodge. The vertical drop is 2,016 feet, and five chairlifts ferry skiers up the 30 slopes. Nearby **Red Lodge Nordic Ski Area,** tel. 446-3158, has nine miles of groomed trails, with lessons and rentals available.

Head up the West Fork of Rock Creek for hiking and fishing. The often-crowded **Wild Bill Lake,** six miles from Red Lodge on West Fork Rd., is wheelchair-accessible for fishing. Toward the end of the road, trailheads sprout up. Just out of Basin Campground, the **Basin Lakes National Recreation Trail** is an easy day-hike leading to two lakes (with some brook trout) and a few tumbledown prospectors' cabins. At the road's end, the **West Fork Trail** puts you at the Absaroka-Beartooth Wilderness boundary, and a one-mile hike from a waterfall, five miles from a mountain lake, and 10 miles from Sundance Pass.

Golf at **Red Lodge Elks Golf and Country Club,** southwest of town on Red Lodge Mountain Rd., tel. 446-1812.

Shopping

Red Lodge supports a surprising number of gift shops with a Native American bent—there are more bear claws and porcupine quills for sale along Broadway than, probably, any place else in the U.S. **Broadway Bookstore,** 13 S. Broadway, tel. 446-2742, continues this theme with a good selection of books on Native American topics.

Transportation

Fly into Billings on Northwest, United, Delta, or Continental. Car rentals are available at the Billings airport (see p. 53).

Cody Bus Lines has service between Billings and Cody, Wyoming via Red Lodge. Call them at 446-2304 or (800) 733-2304 for schedule information.

Information And Services

The **Chamber of Commerce Visitor's Center** is on the north edge of town, tel. 446-1718. The **ranger station** is on Hwy. 212.

Carbon County Memorial Hospital is at 600 W. 21st St., tel. 446-2345. Call the **police** at 446-1313; the **ambulance** and **fire department** are at 446-1212.

The **Carnegie Library** is at 3 W. 8th St., tel. 446-1905.

BEARTOOTH HIGHWAY

Make sure there's gas in the tank and that you have a few hours to spare before setting out on the 68-mile-long Beartooth Highway. Built in 1936 and recently designated a National Scenic Byway, the road climbs to 10,942 feet and crosses alpine meadows and snowfields. The road's summit is called the "Top of the World," and, once each July, on an unannounced date, the Red Lodge Chamber of Commerce serves free drinks by the side of the road. The alcoholic beverages of yore have been replaced by soda pop.

The road climbs Rock Creek Canyon out of Red Lodge and switches back four times, crossing as many vegetation zones. Douglas fir and lodgepole pine grow in the valley; the first switchback brings Engelman spruce into view; up toward the timberline subalpine firs grow in bunches on dry, scrabbly cliffs; where they let off, alpine meadows sprout boulders and wildflowers.

Near the Beartooth Pass, pink snow betrays the presence of high-altitude algae.

This drive is a veritable geology lesson; watch for the Bear's Tooth, a tall spire left after a glacier devoured the rest of the peak. The Beartooth Range itself takes its name from the eerily ursine appearance of its grinning limestone cliffs. North of the summit of Beartooth Plateau, Granite Peak juts above the landscape.

The high country around the Beartooth Highway is crossed by hiking trails and speckled with lakes. For a short hike through an alpine meadow, drive up to the fire lookout on **Clay**

Butte, and hike a little over a mile along the ridge.

For a longer trek, take trail #614 at the switchback in the road up to the lookout, and hike about four miles (generally downhill) around Beartooth Butte to Beartooth Lake. There's a lovely campground at Beartooth Lake, and a loop hike around the butte passes several other lakes in its seven-mile course.

Remember that the road dips down into Wyoming here—buy a Wyoming fishing license in Cooke City or at the Top of the World store before going after the rainbow, cutthroat, and brook trout in Beartooth Lake.

Many of the alpine lakes on the Beartooth Plateau have been stocked with trout. The hikes in are lovely, the fishing's generally good, and Pat Marcuson details every fish-bearing Beartooth lake and stream in *The Beartooth Fishing Guide*, published by Falcon Press.

Campgrounds

You won't find any motels along the road from Red Lodge to Cooke City, but there are plenty of places to pitch a tent along the Wyoming stretch of the Beartooth Highway. High on the Beartooth Plateau, **Island Lake**, about 40 miles west of Red Lodge, and **Beartooth Lake**, three miles farther west, have trails leading to the many alpine lakes to the north. **Fox Creek**, seven miles east of Cooke City, and **Crazy Creek**, two to three miles farther east, don't have the alpine quality of the higher campgrounds, but they are convenient and attractive wooded riverside spots.

COOKE CITY

John Colter was the first white in the area, leading the 19th-century parade of mountain men, traders, prospectors, and speculators. Until 1882 this was still recognized as Crow land, and relatively few whites intruded. By 1883, Cooke City, named after the son of a Northern Pacific financier, was a booming mine town. Gold, silver, and lead were extracted from the mountains. Because of the remoteness, the boom didn't last. Unmined lodes remain around Cooke City, but it's still hard to get to them, and the mining costs are reckoned to be too high to maintain much of an operation.

Recently, however, mining speculation has started anew. Plans are afoot to mine gold, copper, and silver from a site called the New World Mine, just north of town. Local businesses are starting to rename themselves to attract the prospective 300 New World Project construction workers, and local environmentalists have formed the Beartooth Alliance, a branch of the Northern Plains Resource Council, to address concerns about wildlife habitats, water quality, and conflicts with recreation and community values.

Otherwise, Cooke City (elev. 7,651 feet) is a tourist town. There's just one street to reckon with here, and it's easy to walk from one end of it to the other. Even in the summer, when drivers spill off the Beartooth Highway, there's an easygoing, rustic flavor. During the winter, when the Beartooth Highway shuts down, Cooke City is open via the road through Yellowstone Park to Gardiner. Silver Gate, three miles west of Cooke City, was established as a resort town shortly after the Beartooth Highway was built. Together, the two towns have about 75 year-round residents, though this, and much else may change with the advent of large-scale mining.

Accommodations

Most accommodations in Cooke City are serviceable, but neither fancy nor expensive; most double rooms are $30-35. **Bearclaw Cabins**, tel. 838-2336, **Alpine Motel**, tel. 838-2262, **High Country Motel**, tel. 838-2272, and **Elkhorn Lodge**, tel. 838-2332, are all basic lodgings right along the main drag of Hwy. 212. **Hoosier's Motel**, tel. 838-2241, has rooms from $32 s, and the added attraction of the **Hoosier Bar**, a 7.651-foot-high paean to Indiana.

With double rooms going for $47, the **All Seasons Inn**, tel. 838-2251, is a bit more expensive and a bit less spartan than the other lodgings in town.

Chief Joseph, Soda Butte, and **Colter** are Forest Service campgrounds just east of Cooke City on the Beartooth Hwy.

Food And Drink

Sit, dizzy from the elevation, on the front porch of the **Beartooth Café,** gobble carrot cake, and stroke Buster, the yellow lab. Wander down the street to the **Hoosier Bar,** or stop in for pie at **Joan and Bill's,** tel. 838-2280. As evening falls, Cooke City takes on the aroma of fried chick-

Cooke City

JUDY JEWELL

en—either **Ma Perkins** or Joan and Bill must be offering it as a $6 dinner special. Dinners at the Beartooth Café are trendier and more expensive, with a good selection of imported beers.

Pick up basic groceries and a truckload of ambience at the **Cooke City Store,** tel. 838-2234, a historic general store and de facto community center.

Recreation

There is some gold in the hills around Cooke City, and fortune-seekers may enjoy panning in the local streams.

Beartooth Plateau Outfitters, P.O. Box 1127, Cooke City, MT 59020, tel. 838-2328, runs hunting, fishing, and horse-packing trips. Down the road in Silver Gate, **Castle Creek Outfitters,** tel. 838-2301, has similar services.

Northeast of Cooke City, on the edge of the Absaroka-Beartooth Wilderness, there's a "grasshopper glacier," a glacier with dark bands of grasshoppers frozen into it. Apparently, the grasshoppers were migrating to the plains when overcome by fierce mountain weather. The frozen grasshoppers are cloaked by snowfall during most of the year, but in August the previous year's snow has usually melted away, exposing the would-be migrants. To reach the glacier, drive a high-clearance 4WD up the LuLu Pass-Goose Lake Rd. (near the Colter campground). The road stops at the Absaroka-Beartooth Wilderness border. Continue on foot (or horseback) along the old road to Goose Lake, then take the trail northeast to the saddle between Sawtooth Mountain and Iceberg Peak. Turn right at the saddle, and climb the first rock ridge, from which the glacier is visible on the north side of Iceberg Peak. The hike from the road's end to this point is four miles. Topographical maps of the area are available at the Cooke City Store. Hikers should prepare for harsh weather any time of year.

YELLOWSTONE NATIONAL PARK

INTRODUCTION

Most of Yellowstone National Park is in Wyoming, but three of its entrances are in Montana. See Don Pitcher's *Wyoming Handbook* for information on the rest of the park. Entrance to the park costs $10 per car, or $4 per person on bicycle, motorcycle, bus, or snowmobile, good for a week. A Golden Age Passport gives those over age 62 free admission to national parks.

The park is set up for motorists—spin through a couple of loops, watch Old Faithful spew, cruise by Yellowstone Lake, peer down into Yellowstone Canyon. If you're lucky, maybe you'll see some wildlife. This is all reasonably satisfying, but perhaps not worth the veritable pilgrimages people make to Yellowstone.

There are plenty of ways to make a park visit more enriching. Read up on natural history and geology. If you're anything of an angler, bring fishing gear and pick up a free fishing permit at a visitor's center or ranger station. Find out from a ranger where wildlife is likely to be spotted and spend some time there with binoculars and perhaps a camera or sketchpad. Follow the trail of the Nez Percé through the park, or become obsessed with the exploits of mountain men such as John Colter.

Classes at the **Yellowstone Institute** can provide focus. For course listings, write P.O. Box 117, Yellowstone National Park, WY 82190, or call (307) 344-7381, ext. 2384.

Yellowstone Park closes for a couple of weeks early in Dec. and from mid-March until May, but for those willing to make the effort to get in there during the winter months, there's a wilder park to explore than most summertime visitors glimpse. Winter snows drive the animals down to lower elevations where they find easier winter grazing.

The Land

This land has as violent a geology as can be imagined. Six hundred thousand years ago, a volcano erupted from the deep magma pocket underlying Yellowstone and left an immense hole, or caldera, gaping in the central part of what is now the park. Subsequent lava flows filled the caldera, and glaciers refined the landscape, carving out Yellowstone Lake.

The Madison and Gallatin ranges are to the west and north of Yellowstone Park's high plateau; the Absaroka Range is off to the east. South of Yellowstone, in Wyoming, the Tetons shoot to 12,000 feet.

Flora And Fauna

The wide range of habitats in Yellowstone can be broken down into ecological zones: The aquatic zone is home to trout, beavers, moose, eagles, osprey and otter. Low grasslands include grasses and shrubs, rabbits, badgers, pronghorn, and, in the winter, elk and bison. Mixed forest contains aspen in recently burned areas, Douglas fir, shrubs and berries, elk, mule deer, mountain lions, and coyotes. A dense lodgepole forest blocking enough light to an understory and the animal life dependent on it; a climax forest of Engelmann spruce and subalpine fir; and areas of alpine tundra. Elk, deer, and bears are attracted to the edges between high meadows and forests.

Yellowstone National Park cannot be thought of as a distinct entity. Surrounding areas are also part of the ecosystem, and the tendency of animals to naturally walk across unnatural park boundaries can be a source of conflict. Witness the buffalo, host to brucellosis, a microorganism benign to infected buffalo, but which causes abortions in cattle. Neighboring ranchers are in favor of shooting buffalo found straying from the park, and whether this should be permitted, and by whom, has caused no end of brouhaha in the area around Gardiner.

History

The history of the Sheepeaters, thought to be descendants of outcast Bannock and Shoshone Indians, tells of being in the area around the Yellowstone geysers "from the beginning."

John Colter was the first white to describe the fantastic land of fire pots and blow holes, which was soon called "Colter's Hell." After years

the Beartooth
Mountains

TOM VANDEL

of a reputation charged by mountain men's tall tales, the U.S. Geological Survey explored Yellowstone in 1870, which led to its establishment as the first national park in 1872. For 14 years, park superintendents and their small crews worked as virtual volunteers marking park boundaries and routing poachers and other troublemakers. In 1886, the Army took over, and spent the next 30 years bringing law and order to Yellowstone. Since 1916 the rangers of the National Park Service have patrolled the park.

Over the past century, notions as to how a national park should be managed have changed considerably. Bears were once tourist attractions as they begged for food at campsites and foraged in the open garbage dumps; they are now managed to maximize their "wildness." Fire control procedures have also changed, with no little controversy resulting from the massive wildfires of 1988.

Information
The **Yellowstone Association** sells books in park visitor centers, and it runs educational programs and the **Yellowstone Institute,** with classes ranging from Yellowstone history to wildlife photography to astronomy. The institute is based in the old "Buffalo Ranch" in the Lamar Valley. For information on the association or the institute, write to P.O. Box 117, Yellowstone National Park, WY 82190, tel. (307) 344-7381, ext. 2384.

WEST YELLOWSTONE AND VICINITY

West Yellowstone (elev. 6,666 feet) is the west entrance to the park, and the site of a stiff competition between nature and motel space. The 1939 WPA guide characterized West Yellowstone as a town "full of eager competition and alert service . . . [where] every variation of western costume appears." There's all the tourist schlock you'd expect, and the out-of-doors is purveyed as recreation, a commodity that'll bring people here and make them spend money. But never mind. If tourism gets you down, come in the off-season (spring) and share the place with buffalo grazing on south-facing hills, huge crows, relaxed locals, and false-fronted buildings shut down 'til the crowds return.

History
Sheepeater Indians made fine arrowheads from the local obsidian and left pictographs on canyon walls near West Yellowstone. White homesteaders started to dribble into the West Yellowstone basin in the mid-1870s once a road was built into the newly formed national park. When the Nez Percé crossed the park in 1877, they nabbed several of the early park tourists, killing a couple, but treating the survivors well.

In 1907 West Yellowstone became an official park entrance, and a town was platted. A tourist train from the main Union Pacific line in Ashton,

Idaho, began operating in 1909 and the train depot became a hub of West Yellowstone. By 1915, cars were being driven into the park, and the railroad was eventually supplanted by the highway down the Gallatin Valley from Bozeman.

Sights

Yellowstone National Park itself is the main reason to come to "West," and the **Museum of the Yellowstone** offers a good preview of the park. Wildlife, historical, and art exhibits are housed in the old Union Pacific Railroad Depot at 124 Yellowstone Ave., tel. 646-7814. The bookstore here is worth a browse; it has a strong regional section and a good selection of field guides

The **Federation of Fly Fishers' International Fly Fishing Center,** 200 Yellowstone Ave., tel. 646-9541, has fly-fishing displays, a library, and a casting pond. It's open June 15 to Sept. 30, and admission is free.

Gray Line offers bus tours of Yellowstone Park originating from 211 Yellowstone Ave. (across the street from the Fly Fishing Center) in West Yellowstone, tel. 646-9374. Buses run around either the "lower loop" (includes Old Faithful, Yellowstone Lake, and the Grand Canyon of the Yellowstone; $27.50 for adults, $25.50 for 62+ seniors, $11 for children 3-11, $22 for teens 12-17) or the "upper loop" (Norris Geyser Basin and Mammoth Hot Springs; $26.50 for adults, reduced rates for children and seniors). There's also a tour of Quake Lake and the mining towns of Virginia City and Nevada City ($26.50 and down).

Accommodations

The motels belonging to the West Yellowstone Chamber of Commerce offer one number to call from out of state to book a room in any of the member motels: (800) 521-5241; the local number is 646-7832. The budget hotel choice is the

WEST YELLOWSTONE ACCOMMODATIONS

Name	Address	Phone	Rates	Features
Madison Hotel	139 Yellowstone Ave.	646-7745	$12-14 dorm $25 d private room	historic building, hostel atmosphere
Alpine Motel	120 Madison Ave.	646-7544	$28	closed Nov. 1-April 30
Al's Westward Ho	16 Boundary St.	646-7331	$27 and up	closed Nov. 1-April 30
Lazy G Motel	123 Hayden St.	646-7586	$28 and up	lower winter rates
Lionshead Super 8	1545 Targhee Pass	646-9584		sauna and hot tub
Dude Motor Inn and Roundup Motel	3 Madison Ave.	646-7301	$44 and up	lower winter and shoulder-season rates; closed mid-March-April and late Oct. to mid-Dec.
Stage Coach Inn	209 Madison Ave.	646-7381	$45 and up	snowcoach headquarters, sauna
Best Western Desert Inn	133 Canyon Ave.	646-7376	$53 and up	much lower winter, spring, and fall rates; pool
Best Western Executive Inn	Dunraven & Gibbon Ave.	646-7681	$55 and up	lower winter, spring, and fall rates; pool
Best Western Crosswinds Inn	201 Firehole Ave.	646-9557	$57 and up	lower winter, spring, and fall rates; pool

Madison Hotel, sort of a cross between an old downtown hotel and a youth hostel at 139 Yellowstone, tel. 646-7745. It was built in 1912 and remains open Memorial Day-Oct. 1. There's also the Madison Motel at the same address and phone number. The **Gallatin National Forest** rents cabins at Beaver Creek, off Hwy. 287, and at Cabin Creek, off Hwy. 191 north of West Yellowstone. Contact the Hebgen Lake Ranger District, P.O. Box 520, West Yellowstone, MT 59759, tel. 646-7369, to make reservations.

The eight campgrounds in the town of West Yellowstone are mostly for RVs, though a few do have spaces for tents. **Rustic RV Park, Wagon Wheel RV Park,** and **Hideaway RV Park** reserve some space for tent campers. Forest Service campgrounds down the Madison Valley offer more options for tenters.

Food And Drink

Bears are the first thing that come to mind when contemplating West Yellowstone's dining venues. For a hearty breakfast or cheap dinner, try the **Running Bear Pancake House,** 538 Madison, tel. 646-7703. The **Three Bears Restaurant** cooks more steaks than pancakes at 217 Yellowstone Ave., tel. 646-7811. The Three Bears is open for breakfast and dinner, but not lunch.

Departing from the bear theme, the **Silver Spur Café,** 111 Canyon St., tel. 646-9400, is a good place to breakfast with the locals—it's open for breakfast, lunch, and dinner. The nearby **Sunflour Bakery,** 29 Canyon St., tel. 646-9737, is *the* place for cinnamon rolls.

Across from the bakery, **Thiem's Café,** 38 Canyon St., tel. 646-9462, is a good cubbyhole to tuck into for a soup and sandwich lunch. Head toward the back of the **Book Peddler,** 106 Canyon St., tel. 646-9358, where soup and sandwiches, pastries, and espresso are served.

Many of West's restaurants are associated with motels, of these, the **Rustler's Roost** in the Best Western Pine Motel, 234 Firehole Ave., tel. 646-7622, stands out. Their menu includes elk and buffalo dinners for about $15.

Head about eight miles west to **Alice's Restaurant,** 1545 Targhee Pass Hwy. (Hwy. 20), tel. 646-7296, for schnitzel or trout dinners for about $10.

Events

The **Rendezvous Cross Country Ski Race** is held early in March. A winter festival has sprung up around this event. The spring months are relatively quiet in West Yellowstone. Plowing the roads into the park provides jobs for weeks, and they're usually clear by May. There's a steady pitch of activity all summer long, punctuated by such events as the August **Federation of Fly Fishers Conclave.** Call the chamber of commerce at 646-7701 for more information.

Recreation

Wagons and Trails West, on Yellowstone Ave. next to the Information Center, offers summertime trail rides and stagecoach tours.

Rent bikes from **Yellowstone Bicycles and Video,** 132 Madison Ave., tel. 646-7815. **Gallatin Fats Cyclery,** tel. 646-9318, rents bikes and runs mountain-bike tours to guest ranches and to Red Rocks Wildlife Refuge. The Rendezvous cross-country ski trails (see below) are well suited to summer mountain biking. A bicycling and walking route runs along the old Union Pacific rail bed from West Yellowstone to Island Park, Idaho.

During the winter, the only ways into the park from this direction are via cross-country skis, snowmobile, or snowcoach. Heated, 10-passenger coaches equipped with ski racks ferry passengers to Old Faithful and other thermal basins. For those who don't want to just ride around in the coach, drivers are accustomed to serving as skiing advisors and shuttlers.

Rendezvous Cross Country Ski Trails comprise 15 miles of trails groomed for both traditional cross-country and freestyle (skating) skiing. The trailhead is just off Yellowstone Ave., about three blocks west of Canyon Street. Loops can be selected according to skill and stamina, and, for that special Montana touch, there's a biathlon loop for gun-slinging skiers.

The **Riverside** trails start where Madison Ave. ends (at Boundary). These trails aren't as meticulously groomed as those at Rendezvous, but they offer a little more scenic punch. The trail network goes right into the park, where it runs along the Madison River. It's easy skiing, with a basic trip of about 2$^1/_2$ miles. There's a good chance of seeing wildlife from these trails.

West Yellowstone has promoted itself as the "Snowmobile Capital of the World." There are hundreds of miles of snowmobile trails, and it's a good way to explore large areas of Yellowstone Park in the winter. Snowmobiles can be rented at **Rendezvous Snowmobile Rental,** 429 Yellowstone Ave., tel. 646-9564, or from **Westgate Station,** 11 Yellowstone Ave., tel. 646-7781 or (800) 735-6339 for reservations. Rentals at both places start at about $65 a day.

Fishing

West Yellowstone is a good hub for fishing the area's trout streams. The Madison, both in and out of the park, is the most celebrated river, but there are smaller streams worth fishing: Grayling, Duck, and Cougar creeks, and the South Fork of the Madison. Venture into nearby Idaho and try Henry's Fork of the Snake River. Fishing season gets going on Memorial Day weekend (except on Yellowstone Lake and its tributary streams, where the season opens June 15) and runs through the first Sunday of November. State fishing licenses aren't needed inside the park, but a Yellowstone fishing permit, available free from any park visitor center or ranger station, is required.

If you need someone to initiate you into the mysteries of fly-fishing, find a guru in a guide. Even experienced anglers can benefit from a guide's knowledge of local conditions. They don't come cheap, however. **Bud Lilly's Trout Shop** (39 Madison Ave., tel. 646-7801) offers instruction for $100 a day. They also run a five-day fly-fishing school with room and board at a local guest ranch for $1140. **Madison River Outfitters,** 117 Canyon St. (Box 1106), tel. 646-9644, is another good source of fishing expertise in West Yellowstone.

Shopping

Shops line Canyon Street. (aka Hwy. 191, the road to Bozeman). Pick up western or outdoor clothing, fly-fishing paraphenalia, or that souvenir T-shirt. Two good bookstores are the **Bookworm,** 14 Canyon St., tel. 646-9736, and the **Book Peddler,** 106 Canyon, tel. 646-9358. Add to these the bookshop in the **Museum of the Yellowstone** and the traveler who's content to curl up and just *read* about Vacationland is headed for pure bliss.

Fishing shops include **Madison River Outfitters,** 117 Canyon St., tel. 646-9644, **Bud Lilly's Trout Shop,** 39 Madison Ave., tel. 646-7801, **Blue Ribbon Flies,** 309 Canyon St., 646-7642, **Jacklin's Fly Shop,** 105 Yellowstone Ave., 646-7336, and **Eagle's Tackle Shop,** 3 Canyon St., tel. 646-7521. Most of these places

also sell outdoor clothing and most can arrange guided trips.

Entertainment

Playmill Theater limits its season to the summer months, when it presents family entertainment each evening at 29 Madison Ave., tel. 646-7757.

Information And Services

The **chamber of commerce** at 100 Yellowstone Ave., 646-7701, has the expected array of brochures and a friendly staff. **Yellowstone National Park** has an information line at (307) 344-7381, and the **Hegben Lake Ranger Station,** just north of West Yellowstone on Hwy. 191, tel. 646-7369, can provide information on the nearby Gallatin National Forest. **Southwest Montana Avalanche Advisory,** tel. 587-9784, posts daily avalanche reports outside the post office during the winter. The **library** is at 100 Yellowstone Ave., tel. 646-9017.

911 is the emergency phone number. The **police** and **ambulance** are housed at 124 Yellowstone Ave. A **medical clinic,** tel. 646-7668, and a **social service center** share the address of 236 Yellowstone Ave.

The **post office** is on Madison Ave. Both a laundromat and showers are open every day at the **Canyon St. Laundry,** 312 Canyon St., tel. 646-9649.

Transportation

West Yellowstone Airport is open during the summer, but it's often easier to fly in to Bozeman and catch a bus to West Yellowstone. **Karst Stages** runs morning and evening buses from the Bozeman airport and the Greyhound terminal to West Yellowstone. If you don't mind spending around $100 for a taxi, Bozeman's **City Taxi** will ferry you down to West Yellowstone.

Amtrak stops at Pocatello, Idaho, some 160 miles from West Yellowstone. Buses run between the two towns in the summer, and it's easy enough to rent a car in Pocatello any time of year.

MAMMOTH HOT SPRINGS AND VICINITY

The grand arch leading into Yellowstone from Gardiner, dedicated by Theodore Roosevelt in 1903, was the original entrance to the park, and is still the only entrance open to cars year-round.

(top) fossil-rich badlands in eastern Montana (W.C. McRae); (bottom left) beargrass and Indian paintbrush light an alpine meadow (Judy Jewell); (bottom right) Centennial Mountains (Judy Jewell)

(top) alpine meadow on the Beartooth Highway (Judy Jewell); (bottom) Glacier National Park in winter (Tom Vandel)

Elk winter around Mammoth, spending much of their time, it seems, in the hotel parking lot.

Sights

Stop by the **visitor center** for an overview, a movie, and, if necessary, fishing or backcountry permits. Schedules for ranger-led hikes and discussions are also available.

A boardwalk climbs the terraced hot pools. The pools are not static; as the flow of hot groundwater through limestone changes, so do the formations. Groundwater combines with burps of carbon dioxide from underground magma to form carbonic acid, which dissolves limestone. Limey carbonated water emerges from the ground as Mammoth Hot Springs and the lime is deposited as travertine. Thermophilic bacteria and algae live in the hot water, tinting the white travertine with their brilliant colors. Pick up a brochure at the foot of the trail to take the self-guided tour of the springs. Take care to stay on the boardwalk; the hot pools are frequently boiling hot, and they may have very thin crusts around them. People and animals have died in thermal pools.

The Army was the original overseer of the park, and their headquarters, Fort Yellowstone, is behind the visitor center. It has been used as the **National Park Service Headquarters** since 1918.

During the summer, the Mammoth campground amphitheatre is the site of nightly talks by park rangers.

For a roadside glimpse of the park, try the TW Services **bus tour of the Grand Loop.** Re- serve a $22 seat (half-price for kids) by calling (307) 344-7311, or sign up at the activities desk in the Mammoth hotel. **Gray Line Tours,** tel. 646-9374, also runs tour buses into the park.

Midway between Mammoth and Tower Junction, the **Blacktail Plateau** offers both a scenic drive and hiking trails. Follow the dirt road through grasslands and along a stretch of the old Bannock Trail, used by the Bannock Indians to cross from present-day Idaho to the eastern plains.

Accommodations

Mammoth Hot Springs Hotel, open May 25-Sept. 15, has both hotel rooms (starting at $32) and cabins (sans bath, $23; with a bath, $47). Like the other Yellowstone hotels, it's operated by TW Services; call (307) 344-7311 for reservations.

The campground at Mammoth is small by local standards—only 85 sites. It's open year-round and costs $8 a night.

Food And Drink

Mammoth Hot Springs Hotel Dining Room is a *relatively* fancy, relatively pricey restaurant open during the hotel's season. The **Terrace Grill** (aka Mammoth Fast Foods) is in the same complex and has a slightly longer season, from mid-May through late September, and a decidedly casual atmosphere. The **Mammoth General Store** offers basic foodstuffs year-round. And remember, you didn't come to Yellowstone for a culinary experience.

Terraced pools at Mammoth Hot Springs

JUDY JEWELL

Recreation

Hot springs empty into the Gardner River at the 45th parallel, and this is one place where hot springs bathing is sanctioned. The parking lot is just over the state line into Montana. It's about a five minute walk down the path to the springs, which are officially open 8 a.m.-6 p.m. Remember to bring a bathing suit.

Register for **trail rides** at the Mammoth Hotel activities desk.

Information And Services

General park information is dispensed at the **visitor center** in Mammoth, and by telephone, tel. (307) 344-7381.

Dial **911** for emergencies. The **Mammoth Hot Springs Clinic** is near the visitor center and is open on weekdays all year, tel. 344-7965.

The main Yellowstone **post office** is to the side of the park service administration building in Mammoth. Foreign currency can be exchanged at the front desk of any Yellowstone hotel, and there is a bank machine in the lobby of the Old Faithful Inn.

TOWER JUNCTION AND VICINITY

Tower Junction is where the Mammoth-Cooke City road is joined by the road to Yellowstone Canyon. There's a small settlement here—a ranger station, a lodge with cabins, and a campground three miles south at **Tower Falls.** The falls, nestled into a rocky gorge, are a popular sight. A more meditative viewing is often afforded by taking the short but steep hike to the bottom. Bannock Indians found a safe place to cross the Yellowstone River just above the falls; it's now referred to as Bannock Ford.

Elk and bison winter in the **Lamar Valley,** east of the Tower Junction. Coyotes are also commonly spotted jogging across the valley floor.

Accommodations

Cabins at **Roosevelt Lodge** start at $17 for a rustic cabin without a bath; a cabin with a bath is $47. There's an emphasis on things Western here—stagecoach rides leave several times a day for a half-hour tour, and cookouts at nearby

Yancey's Hole involve a horseback or church-wagon journey.

Nearby campgrounds include **Tower Falls,** open late May to mid-Sept., **Slough Creek,** open late May through Oct., and **Pebble Creek,** open mid-June to early September.

Food And Drink

If you want a meal that's longer on the experience than on the cuisine, try the TW-sponsored **Old West Dinner Cookout.** Jump on a horse or climb into a church wagon at Roosevelt Lodge and ride to Yancey's Hole for a slab of steak and other picnic fare. Reserve a space by calling TW at (307) 344-7311. The **Roosevelt Lodge** prides itself on the ribs served at its family-style restaurant.

Recreation

The **Buffalo Plateau Trail** swings north of the park into Montana on its 21-mile run from the trailhead three miles west of Tower Junction to Slough Creek Campground. It's best to wait until late July for this hike—the varied terrain includes Slough Creek, which can be difficult to cross when it's carrying lots of water. **Slough Creek Campground** is also the trailhead for an 11-mile hike (or wintertime cross-country ski trip) up Slough Creek to the northern edge of the park. Full descriptions of these and other hikes are included in the Sierra Club totebook, *Hiking the Yellowstone Backcountry,* by Orville Bach. Hikers should also check with park rangers to learn about current trail conditions.

In the winter, the road to **Tower Falls** becomes a cross-country ski trail. A private viewing of the falls is worth the three-mile, generally uphill, slog.

Specimen Ridge, southeast of Tower Junction, sports a petrified forest; indeed petrified forests are stacked deep in this area. The mud and ash coughed up by volcanoes provided soil on which new trees could grow, only to be covered when the next volcano erupted. Erosion has uncovered some of the top layers; it's conjectured that 44 layers of forest exist. Naturalists lead day-long hikes on Specimen Ridge during July and August; details are available at any park visitor center.

BOB RACE

SOUTHWESTERN MONTANA

Southwestern Montana is rich in almost every meaning of the word. Early prospectors found some of the richest gold deposits ever discovered here along the flanks of the Rocky Mountains. Hardrock mining earned Butte the sobriquet, "the richest hill on earth." At one time Helena boasted more millionaires per capita than anywhere else in the nation.

The boom that fed this early growth has largely gone bust. Nowadays, residents measure their wealth in the majestic beauty of the mountains, the free-flowing rivers filled with trout, and the potent culture of old cities and towns whose rich culinary heritage is still keenly observed.

Native Montanans know that some of the best recreation in the state is here. The Jefferson and its tributaries provide blue-ribbon trout fishing, whitewater rafting, and streamside campsites. Enormous national forests provide unparalleled camping, hiking, and wildlife-viewing opportunities: the Beaverhead National Forest alone is larger than many Atlantic states.

INTRODUCTION

THE LAND

The area's rich mines extract mineral riches from intrusions of molten granite that punched up through existing mountain formations about 70 million years ago. Although some of the magma erupted as volcanoes, much simply hardened at shallow underground depths. Called batholiths, these bodies of rock are sometimes vast and richly infused with valuable minerals. The mines at Helena, Boulder, Butte, and Silver Star all tapped into the same enormous formation, the Boulder Batholith.

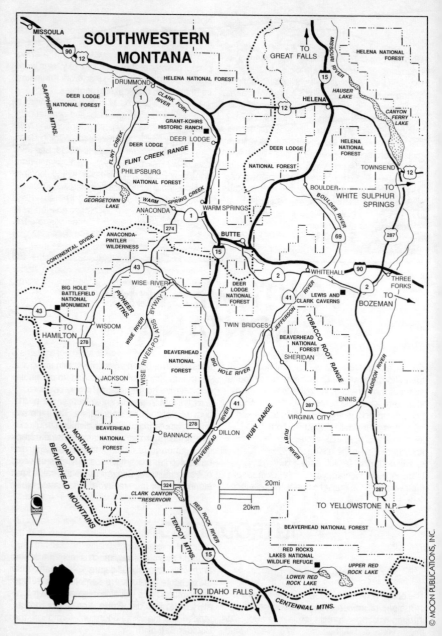

SOUTHWESTERN MONTANA

HISTORY

Gold first brought settlers to this part of the state. Beginning at Bannack in 1862, then Virginia City, and then in almost every ravine throughout the area, prospectors found mineral wealth. Gold camps sprang up, the easily panned gold played out, and the settlement moved on.

This early, colorful era of Montana's mining history ended when silver replaced gold as the mineral of choice. Silver demanded mills and smelters for extraction, which required costly investment. Soon the ripsnorting life of the prospector was replaced by a corporate payroll, panning for gold in a lonely stream was traded for a shift underground with a crew of workers.

Whereas the early transitory life of the placer miner left few monuments, corporate mining from the 1880s to the 1930s built cities of worldwide influence. Butte was perhaps the richest mining center the world has known. Were Butte a nation, it would rank fourth in world copper production. During the 1880s Butte was the largest silver producer in the world; W.A. Clark, the man who led the development of silver mining, became the eighth-richest man of his day. Helena's Montana Club became the Pacific Northwest's first private club: membership was only open to millionaires (50 Helena citizens in the 1880s qualified).

This wealth built imposing cities; the swaggering, cosmopolitan savoir faire of foreign workers, who came streaming in to work the mines, contributed to their cultural richness.

Life in Butte and other mining communities in southwestern Montana changed dramatically in the early 1900s when, after Copper King Marcus Daly's death, his Anaconda Mining Company acquired Clark's Butte holdings, and then bought out Heinze. Suddenly, fractious and rambunctious Butte, and the many mining, logging, and industrial businesses it controlled in the region, were owned by a single, corporate entity. Fierce labor-management battles ensued, with lethal disputes and martial law being more the rule than the exception in 1910s Butte.

Mining went into decline during the Great Depression. Butte, Anaconda, and many other old mining centers are still searching for a stable economic base to replace the copper, silver, zinc, and lead of yesterday.

FLORA AND FAUNA

The southwestern corner of Montana contains a unique mix of plant and animal life. In an hour, a hiker could easily pass from an arid prairie environment of sagebrush and pronghorn, through verdant forests of lodgepole pine, spruce, and fir, and explore alpine tundra life along the many crenellations of the Continental Divide.

Especially notable in this area are the large populations of mountain goats and Bighorn sheep along the peaks of the Flint Creek and Anaconda-Pintler wilderness areas. Prairie fowl, such as sage grouse, seem out of place when sighted with 10,000-foot peaks in the background.

Two otherwise rare species occur in southwestern Montana. Biologists feared that the trumpeter swan was extinct in the U.S. until they found several nesting pairs in the 1930s at Red Rock Lakes in the extreme southwest corner of the state. The lakes are now a wildlife refuge; trumpeters have since reestablished their territory over other parts of the Pacific Northwest.

KAREN WHITE

pronghorn, Antilocapra americana

Another species rarely found outside of Alaska and northern Canada is the arctic grayling, a long-finned cousin to the trout. While not abundant, the grayling occurs in streams along the Big Hole drainage.

PRACTICALITIES

Information
Travel Montana, the state tourism bureau, provides good free information on events, sights, and lodgings. Southwestern Montana is contained in their **Gold West** region. Call (406) 846-1943 for details.

Getting There
Helena and Butte are both served by major airlines. **Greyhound** travels along I-90, linking Butte, Deer Lodge, and Anaconda to Seattle and Chicago. **Intermountain buses** link Helena and Dillon to Greyhound at Butte.

Driving can be hazardous in winter; call 494-3666 for local **road conditions**.

BUTTE

Butte (pop. 33,336, elev. 5,755 feet) is at once unique and Montana's most representative city. Touted as "the richest hill on earth," Butte was the nation's largest single source of silver in the 1880s and the largest source of copper for the following 30 years.

This early and extreme wealth gave Butte a singular history and destiny. The town's politicians utterly dominated Montana government for the first 50 years of statehood. It became the first industrialized city in the state, and it was also the largest until the 1960s.

Montanans from other parts of the state have always been deeply ambivalent about Butte: its political infighting, religious rivalries, hot temper, and its wealth and self-importance created a statewide atmosphere of distrust. However, many of the things that now seem typically Montanan—the can-do swagger, spirited politics, the jocular and embracing sociality, its unspoken sense of neighborliness, even its food and drink (and the gusto and quantity in which they're consumed) reached a zenith in the early days of Butte.

The city's greatest resource was always its people, the swirling mix of Irish, Poles, Italians, Slavs, Chinese, and others who forged the cosmopolitan set of neighborhoods known as Butte. Billings now makes much of being Montana's largest city, and enjoys likening itself to a youth-ful Denver. Early in the 1900s Butte had nearly as large a population tucked into a steep swale on Silverbow Creek; with its bluster and ethnic diversity, Butte was more like Chicago than any other city in the West.

Butte is now the exoskeleton of a much larger city. Some of the charm and much of the history of the old city still remain: people still self-assuredly bustle, good food and drink are unquestionably an elemental part of daily life, and the old mansions and civic buildings that great wealth built still stand beside the ugly smokestacks, head frames, and piles of tailings.

HISTORY

The Copper Kings

When the first placer miners arrived near Butte in 1864, they discovered pits dug with elk antlers: apparently Indians also knew of the area's gold deposits. But prospecting for gold requires water, and here, in this basin just under the crest of the Continental Divide, scarcely a stream runs. The gold camp drifted along until 1874, when the first silver claims were made. Abundant quartz in the Butte area contained an unparalleled richness in silver. The rush was on.

News of the silver strikes spread quickly, attracting miners and entrepreneurs from through-

Early mining in Butte wreaked environmental havoc.

MONTANA HISTORICAL SOCIETY

out the West. Two stand out. William Clark, a canny businessman, banker, and former miner from the Bannack gold-rush days, gained control of one of the richest mines. In 1876, Marcus Daly arrived in Butte from Colorado, sent by mining investors to scout out the mines of Butte. Both men controlled enough capital to develop the rich mineral deposits of Butte.

Silver isn't free-occurring, like gold. It must be milled out of the rock, usually quartz, in which it is suspended. This shift in method produced far-reaching changes in the Montana mining West. The gold camps inhabited by free-spirited prospectors quickly evolved into industrial towns dominated by the political and corporate interests of mine and smelter owners.

Clark became the first of the mining kings of Butte by owning not only mines, but also the supply stores, transportation systems, real estate, banks, and processing plants necessary for the development of Butte.

Daly was the first industrialist to recognize the potential of the Butte copper deposits. He bought up the now-legendary Anaconda Mine, and discovered veins of nearly pure copper 100 feet across; this mine alone produced more than 50 million pounds in 1887. Before anyone else realized the value of copper—copper for electric wire was only just becoming a worthwhile commodity—Daly had bought up the mines adjacent to the Anaconda. He built the city of the same name 26 miles west of Butte where he sent copper ore to be smelted.

Besides investment capital, the third component needed to make Butte boom was the railroad. The Utah and Northern reached Butte in 1881, suddenly linking Butte minerals with a world in the midst of industrialization and modernization.

A City Of Immigrants

Mining on this scale demanded thousands of miners. Beginning in the 1880s, a vast influx of foreign miners flooded into Butte from eastern and northern Europe, from Italy and Ireland, and from Wales and Cornwall. By 1885, 22,000 people lived in Butte. These men and their families brought to Butte the dreams and enthusiasm of immigrants. Butte was opportunity, financial stability, and excitement.

The social and civic life of Butte was a wild tapestry fashioned from bits and pieces of each incorporated culture. Bars and restaurants were open 24 hours a day, as mines were worked day and night. Each ethnic group had its own neighborhood and customs. Greyhound coursing, Irish football, cockfights, opium dens and secret Chinese societies, fancy-dress balls, a noted opera house, gambling and prostitution, St. Patrick's Day and Balkan feasts combined with a dozen other celebrations and cultural traditions—all these mutated into a uniquely energetic way of life called Butte.

But there was also a dark side. Mining is dangerous work. Quite apart from the obvious risk of cave-ins, the dust and fumes in the mines contributed to everything from respiratory diseases to cancer. Above ground, air pollution was absolutely treacherous. In the 1890s, smoke and fumes so darkened the air that streetlights burned night and day. Vegetation ceased to grow; dogs and cats were found dead in the streets from ambient poisons.

The Birth Of The Anaconda Company

The most noteworthy battles among the Copper Kings, especially Clark and Daly, were not fought over mining claims or wealth, but rather for prestige and politics. Daly connived to deny Clark a seat on the U.S. Senate; Clark won his battle to keep the state capital out of Daly's "company town" of Anaconda. Both men wielded enormous power in the state; each shamelessly manipulated the newborn state government to benefit mining in general, and, when possible, used the government to spite his arch rival's ambitions.

Augustus Heinze, the last of the Copper Kings, arrived in the late days of Butte's zenith. Basically a spoiler, in 1900 he manipulated mining laws and bought judges to press his claim to holdings already developed by Daly. The ploy ultimately made Heinze a wealthy man, but his antagonism forced investors in Daly's Amalgamated Copper Company to rethink and streamline their operations. Amalgamated Copper turned mean. It had already purchased Clark's mining empire; with Heinze out of the way, it had total control over Butte. With more benevolent figures like Daly dead and Clark removed from the scene, corporate mining triumphed, and the swashbuckling days of Butte were over. Amalgamated Copper, also known as the Anaconda Company or simply "The Company," by

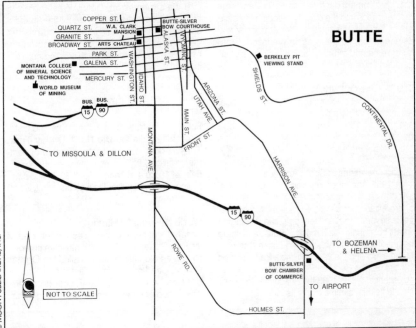

1903 practically ran the state from boardrooms in New York City.

Labor Vs. Management

Butte labor was highly organized; the Butte Miners' Union was formed in 1878, and was Local No. 1 of the Western Federation of Miners. Daly and Clark were both tolerant of the unions, and Butte had never seen significant labor-management action.

But when the ownership of the mines moved out of state and became depersonalized, the stage was set for confrontation. Increased rancor characterized the relations of management and labor, but the real battles were fought within the rank and file. Divided between conservative, accommodationist members and more radical workers, some of whom organized for the "Wobblies," or the Industrial Workers of the World (IWW), the labor movement in Butte shattered completely. As conditions in the mines worsened and management demanded lower pay, the two union factions adamantly disagreed about what action to take. Violence broke out: in

June, 1914, the old Union Hall was bombed in Butte, two men were shot, and miner set upon miner.

Finally, in September, the governor was forced to declare martial law. Left-wing leaders of the union tried and imprisoned, and the elected mayor and sheriff of Butte, both Socialists, were removed from office.

Of course, this was music to the corporate ears of the Anaconda Company, which chose this moment to break the back of the union: Anaconda disavowed both union elements, and declared the Butte mines an open shop. Events flared up once more in 1917, when 164 miners died in an underground fire. Workers again organized, again with the help of the IWW. Anaconda refused to bargain with the miners, and Butte went out on strike. The Company sent in 200 detectives to infiltrate the movement. One night, masked men forced an IWW leader from his bed, dragged him behind a car to the outskirts of Butte, and hanged him.

The lynching threw Butte into pandemonium. Fearing a renewed shutdown of the mines, the

U.S. government declared martial law and sent federal troops into the city. By branding the strikers as antiwar and seditious, the Company and its governmental allies again prevailed. Butte labor remained strongly, but not effectively, organized thereafter.

The Decline Of Butte
During the Great Depression, the price of copper fell from 18 cents a pound in 1928 to five cents a pound in 1933. The decline of Butte had begun. The old veins were playing out and the ore was getting more costly to extract. Besides, the Anaconda Company had more cost-effective mining operations in South America.

In 1955 Anaconda opened the Berkeley Pit, an open-pit mine meant to revitalize Butte mineral production. However, surface-mining copper veins several thousand feet deep meant digging a vast hole underneath much of Butte, and some neighborhoods, notably the old Italian district of Meaderville and the vast Columbia Park, toppled into the pit. The Berkeley Pit in its turn reached obsolescence, and in 1983 the Anaconda Company closed its mines in the city of its birth.

Butte struggles on. Denny Washington, a Montana-born industrialist, bought the Anaconda Company properties in 1985, and has developed low-overhead, low-labor methods of extracting profits from the rich ore and rich heritage of Butte.

SIGHTS

For a quick introduction to the sights and history of Butte, take the **Old No. 1 Trolley Tour.** The half-hour tour leaves the chamber of commerce office, 2950 Harrison Ave., tel. 494-5595, daily at 10:30 a.m., and 1:30, 3:30, and 7 p.m., Memorial Day to Labor Day; $4 per adult, $2.50 for children.

World Museum Of Mining
Located west of Montana Tech at the end of W. Park St., tel. 723-7211, the museum complex sits on an old mining claim, called the Orphan Girl. Included on the grounds is a head frame, ore carts, a locomotive, and other hardware. The indoor museum contains mining tools,

BUTTE ACCOMMODATIONS

Name	Address	Phone	Rates	Features
Best Western Copper King Inn	4655 Harrison Ave.	(800) 332-8600, 494-6666	$50 s, $55 d	conference center; pool
Best Western War Bonnet Inn	2100 Cornell Ave.	(800) 443-1806, 494-7800	$55 s, $60 d	pool, exercise room
Butte Plaza Inn	2900 Harrison Ave.	494-3500	$53 s, $53 d	near shopping
Capri Motel	220 N. Wyoming	(800) 342-2774, 723-4391	$30 s, $35 d	downtown
Finlen Motor Inn	100 E. Broadway	723-5461	$24 s, $27 d	downtown
Mile Hi Motel	3499 Harrison Ave.	494-2250	$23 s, $26 d	pool
Super 8	2929 Harrison Ave	(800) 848-8888, 494-6000	$34 s, $42 d	convenient to freeway
Town House Inn	2777 Harrison Ave.	(800) 442-4667, 494-8850	$41 s, $46 d	Butte's largest
Copper King Mansion B&B	219 W. Granite	782-7508	$55-95	historic mansion with period furnishings

Park Street, Butte, circa 1920

steam engines, ore samples, and a large number of old photos and memorabilia from the boom years of Butte.

In the same complex is **Hell Roarin' Gulch,** a replica of a mining camp from 1900. A millinery shop, Chinese herb store, bank, print shop, school, post office, and other period buildings have been faithfully reconstructed. Open daily 9-9, June 1 to Labor Day; 10-5 April to June and Labor Day to Thanksgiving, and closed during the winter; free admission.

Adjacent to Hell Roarin' Gulch is the **Neversweat and Washoe Railroad,** tel. 723-4349, which gives a guided rail tour of Butte's mining sights. The track is a segment of the rails that once linked the Butte mines with the Washoe smelter at Anaconda. A 1925 railcar follows six miles of track from the World Museum of Mining to the Kelly Mine on the hill behind downtown Butte. Tours are offered on the hour, 10 a.m.-noon and 2-5 p.m.; $4 adult, $2.50 children.

Montana Tech

Montana College of Mineral Science and Technology, better known as Montana Tech, sits on a bench of Big Butte, the promontory just west of downtown. Established in 1900, the college teaches mineral science and other professional and technical curricula. The four-year institution currently has an enrollment of 1,800 students.

From the ramparts of the campus there are great views over the city to the Continental Divide; a statue of Marcus Daly shares the view from the university's entrance on Park Avenue.

Visit the **Mineral Museum,** in Tech's Main Hall, where 1,300 mineral specimens are displayed. In a separate, darkened room is an interesting exhibit of fluorescent minerals.

Downtown

Butte's magnificent homes and commercial and civic buildings attest to its early wealth and importance. Much of downtown Butte is protected as a national landmark and many individual buildings are on the National Register of Historic Places; the chamber of commerce provides a brochure with a walking tour of historic buildings.

The following are open to the public: the **Copper King Mansion,** 219 W. Granite, tel. 782-7580, was built in 1888 by William Clark at a time when he was one of the world's richest men. This three-story brick High Victorian mansion contains 30 rooms, many with frescoed ceilings, carved staircases, inlaid floors, and Tiffany windows. Clark spent $300,000 on the building, and imported many craftsmen from Europe. The third floor boasts a 60-foot-long ballroom and a chapel. The mansion is open for tours daily 9:30-4:30; $4.50 adults, $4 seniors, and $3 students, under six free.

Clark's son Charles was so taken by a chateau he visited in France that he procured the plans and had it reconstructed in Butte. Now known as the **Arts Chateau,** at 321 Broadway, tel. 723-7600, it serves as Butte's community arts center. Open Tues.-Sat. 10-4 and Sun. 12-5, Memorial Day-Labor Day, and Tues.-Sat. 12-5 the rest of the year.

The showpiece of Butte civic architecture is the **Butte-Silver Bow Courthouse,** 155 W. Granite, built in 1910. A lovely stained-glass dome tops the four-story rotunda, murals decorate the ceilings, and oak fixtures predominate throughout. Butte leaders spent almost twice as much on this courthouse as the state spent on the Montana Capitol.

Overlooking Butte from the fastness of the Continental Divide is *Our Lady of the Rockies,* a 90-foot statue of the Virgin Mary. Completed in 1985, the monument was the result of six years of volunteer community work, including building the access road to the site, 8,510 feet above sea level. There is a viewing point at Continental Drive and Pine. Tours to the statue are arranged as interest allows; $10 adult, $9 seniors, $5 children. To schedule, call the Our Lady of the Rockies Foundation office, 432 N. Main, tel. 782-1221.

Berkeley Pit

Veering from the high to the low, there's the Berkeley Pit, the enormous open-pit copper mine just next to downtown Butte. Due to the high costs of hardrock underground mining, in 1955 Anaconda began stripping low-grade copper ore from the surface. Eventually, the Berkeley Pit reached a depth of 1,800 feet; the gulf from side to side is more than a mile across. Mining continues here at a greatly reduced pace and today, the pit is filling with water—Montana's deepest body of water. It is also probably its most toxic water, percolating up as it does through abandoned mine shafts.

FOOD

Only in Butte could one even begin to make the argument that there is a Montana cuisine. Its large ethnic population and its intense urban character gave restaurants a prominence and an enthusiastic clientele—very atypical in frontier Montana. Butte specialties include the pasty, brought over from Cornwall, and the pork-chop sandwich. Meals in Butte were traditionally served in courses; the price of dinner included a relish tray, bread sticks, soup and salads, a pasta course, the entree, and dessert. This evening's worth of food and service is called

eating "Old Meaderville" style, for the Meaderville Italian neighborhood that collapsed into the Berkeley Pit, fine restaurants and all.

Fine Dining

Possibly the best restaurant in Montana is the **Uptown Café,** 47 E. Broadway, tel. 723-4735, where the best of Butte tradition meets lively up-to-the-minute sauces and ingredients. The wine list is intriguing, the ambience light and friendly, and the food—with fresh seafood, veal, and desserts as specialties—is superb. Open for lunch weekdays 11 a.m.-2 p.m., Tues.-Sat. 5-10 p.m. for dinner.

Montana's most famous restaurant is **Lydia's,** 5 Mile, Harrison Ave, tel. 494-2000. Italian food, old-fashioned but highly creditable, is served in an atmosphere of slightly dated chic. Open nightly 5:30-11:30.

In terms of atmosphere, the **Copper King Mansion Restaurant,** 219 W. Granite, tel 782-7580, is in a class of its own. Diners feast amongst the antiques in W.A. Clark's fabulous home. The food—chicken, veal, and steaks—is as refined as the setting. Open Mon.-Sat. 6-10 p.m.

Chinese Food

Growing up in Montana, there were two pieces of received wisdom about Butte restaurants: there was Lydia's, the fanciest restaurant in the state, and there was Chinese food. Long before Pacific Rim cuisines caught the American imagination, there were little neighborhood Chinese shops that divvied out tasty, inexpensive Chinese food from *very* unassuming storefronts. Visit these landmark Oriental restaurants as much for the sense of a lost era as for the perfectly commendable Chinese food.

Peking Noodle Parlor, 117 S. Main, tel. 782-2217, open 5 p.m.-3 a.m., lies at the top of a stairway, above two deserted storefronts. Screw up your courage and climb the stairs to enjoy cheap, simple chow meins and noodle dishes. **Ming's,** 116 W. Park St., tel. 782-7058, open 11:30 a.m.-10 p.m., is another misleadingly stark venue that was serving Szechuan food long before it was mandatory.

Other Options

Butte also has good Mexican food. **La Toucan Cantina,** 8 W. Park, tel. 723-6160, specializes in

THE BUTTE PASTY

One of Butte's enduring gastronomic standbys is the pasty (pronounced PAST-ee), a meat pie native to Wales and Cornwall. Early miners brought the pasty with them from their Celtic homelands; here, as there, the savory and resilient pasty made a convenient lunch down in the mine. Pasties are still common in Butte, where they remain an alternative to their cousin the hamburger. And, believe it or not, natives really do argue about who makes the best pasty in Butte.

Gamer's, 15 W. Park, tel. 723-5453, certainly makes one of the best, and you can buy the recipe for a dollar; Joe's Pasty Shop, 1641 Grand Ave., tel. 723-9071, also bakes highly touted examples of pasty art. On Saturday, the Butte Hill Bakery, 7 S. Montana, tel. 723-4828, makes pasties from additive-free ingredients.

However, you needn't call Montana for takeout to enjoy pasties at home. The following recipe is as old as the proverbial richest hill on earth, compliments of Butte.

Dough
1½ c. white flour
½ t. baking powder
¼ t. salt
¼ c. butter or shortening
¼ c. cold water

Mix dry ingredients, and cut in butter or shortening with a pastry knife. Add water gradually and stir until a ball of dough is formed. Knead lightly for a 10-20 .seconds.

Filling
½ lb. steak, diced into small cubes
1 medium onion, chopped finely
1 small turnip, chopped finely
1 medium potato, diced
2 T. butter

Mix the steak and vegetables. Divide the dough in two, and roll into a circle about the size of a pie pan. Place one half of the meat mixture on half of the dough circle to within one inch of the edge. Sprinkle the meat with salt and pepper, and put 1 tablespoon of butter on the meat. Enclose the meat by folding over the other half of the dough circle. Seal edges with fork tines. Repeat with remaining ingredients.

Place the pasties on a baking sheet. and slit a small hole in the top. Bake at 400 for 45 minutes. occasionally pouring a teaspoon of water in the slit to keep the meat moist. Reduce heat to 350 and bake for another 15 minutes. Serve warm with lots of gravy.

Makes two pasties.

Tex-Mex dishes in an attractively renovated bank building; open Mon.-Thurs 11 a.m.-9:30 p.m., Fri.-Sun. 11 a.m.-11 p.m. **Café La Cosina,** 625 E. Front, tel. 723-9008, is a step down in decor, but the food is spicy and well prepared; open 11 a.m.-8:30 p.m., Sun. 4-8:30 p.m.

Don't count Butte out for steaks. At the **Lamplighter,** 1800 Meadowlark Ave., tel. 494-9910, open nightly 5-10 p.m., you can have Yorkshire pudding with your prime rib. With pasta, steaks, ribs, and seafood, **Jacalyn's,** 3502 Harrison, tel. 494-3851, open for three meals a day, is a convenient, highly palatable compromise between other Butte venues.

For breakfast or lunch, **Gamer's,** 15 W. Park, tel. 723-5453, is an absolute must. This dark little diner is filled with the gregarious charm of its owner, who teases and entertains the customers with an unending flow of chatter. Gamer's is the ultimate in self-service: not only are guests encouraged to keep their own coffee cups filled, they also make their own change out of the till. The food, especially the pasties and baked goods, is tasty and satisfying.

For something uniquely Butte, try **Pork Chop John's,** at 8 Mercury, tel. 782-0812 (downtown), or 2400 Harrison, tel. 782-1783 (on the strip), open 10:30 a.m.-10:45 p.m. The boneless porkchop sandwich is a Butte original; as you savor it, think of all the hungry miners who also gained satisfaction here.

ENTERTAINMENT

Nightlife
Within a state that already has a rowdy reputation, Butte bears the sybaritic crown; in the Butte

equation, bars are elemental. Remember that, in Montana, you don't have to drink alcohol to go out to bars; bars are What You Do. The **M & M** is probably the most famous bar in the state; the mix of gambling, a 24-hour café, and a clientele of hardened bar-goers makes this institution one of Butte's most authentic assets. A night out on the town in Butte should also include the **New Deal Bar**, 333 S. Arizona, the **Sportsman**, 18 N. Main, the **Silver Dollar**, 133 S. Main, and **Maloney's**, 112 N. Main.

Recreation
Stodden Park, at Sampson and Utah streets, tel. 494-3686, has a swimming pool, picnic grounds, tennis courts, and a nine-hole golf course.

Fourteen miles north of Butte on I-15 (at the Elk Park exit) is **Sheepshead Mountain Recreation Area**. This fishing and wildlife-viewing facility is completely accessible to wheelchairs. It's a stopover for migrating waterfowl, and moose and elk are frequently sighted.

The **Butte KOA** is off I-90's exit 126, two blocks north, tel. 782-0063.

INFORMATION AND SERVICES

The **Butte-Silver Bow Chamber of Commerce** is at 2950 Harrison, Butte, MT 59701, tel. (406) 494-5595.

St. James Hospital is at 400 S. Clark St., tel 782-8361. **Emergency** is 911.

The main **post office** is at 701 Dewey, tel. 494-2107. The **library** is at 106 W. Broadway, tel. 723-8262. The *Butte Standard* is the local daily paper. National Public Radio is at 99.3 FM.

The **Suds and Fun Laundromat** is open 24 hours a day at Dewey and Harrison, tel. 494-7004.

TRANSPORTATION

Butte is served by **Horizon** and **Delta airlines**. Also at the airport, south off Harrison Ave., are **Avis**, tel. 494-3131, and **Budget**, tel. 494-7573, car rental agencies. **Greyhound** and **Intermountain bus lines** link Butte to other Montana cities. The bus station is at 105 W. Broadway, tel. 723-3287. For a cab, call **City Taxi**, tel. 723-6511.

THE UPPER CLARK FORK RIVER VALLEY

Silver Bow Creek drains the Butte Basin before charging almost 1,000 feet down a narrow channel to the wide valley below. Here the creek is renamed the Clark Fork River, and it begins to pick up the many tributaries that will eventually make it one of the most important arms of the mighty Columbia.

Early settlers knew this as the Deer Lodge Valley. The state's first ranches grew up when some miners recognized that a quicker and more dependable profit could be made selling agricultural products to the booming mining towns.

Today, this open stretch of the Clark Fork River Valley is the stepping-off point for hikes in the rugged Flint Creek Range, and fishing in the newly vivified Clark Fork River is both popular and possible; in the recent past it was neither. Deer Lodge boasts of being the second-oldest town in the state. Certainly its old prison and ranch museum deserve a visit.

FAIRMONT HOT SPRINGS

This old hot-springs spa, halfway between Butte and Anaconda, went through a major face-lift to become one of the premier resorts in Montana. The hot springs here fill four pools, two of them Olympic-sized, with one of them indoors; the others are meant for soaking weary muscles. Other facilities tempt the visitor with more active enterprises. Tennis courts, an 18-hole golf course, horseback riding, a petting zoo, and hay- or sleighrides (depending on the season) round out the activities.

Fairmont makes the most of its proximity to fishing and watersports at Georgetown Lake and skiing at Discovery Basin, and offers special ski packages in conjunction with the latter. Cross-country skiers love Fairmont; after a day in the Pintlers or the Flint Creek Range, a good hot soak takes the creak out of tired muscles.

A full range of rooming options includes suites and kitchenettes; double rooms start at $75. The food's fine, considering the variety of clientele they have to please. There's dancing and drinks in the lounge.

Some resorts with Fairmont's amenities and potential would discourage kids. Not here. This is a great place to take a family. There are enough supervised activities here that harried parents might even be able to have some time to themselves.

Contact Fairmont Hot Springs at 1500 Fairmont Rd., Anaconda, MT 59711, tel. (406) 797-3241. Rooms begin at $59, double occupancy.

DEER LODGE

Named for a salt lick popular with deer during frontier days, Deer Lodge is the center of a vast valley full of history and recreation.

History

The Mullan Road, a northern version of the Oregon Trail that ran between Fort Benton and Walla Walla in the 1860s-80s, dropped into the Clark Fork Valley near Deer Lodge. The valley, with its abundant water and forage, was popular with pioneers who had just traversed the prairies and Continental Divide.

With as much prescience as savvy, Canadian trader Richard Grant and his sons Johnny and James began trading cattle in the 1850s along the Oregon Trail in Idaho. With cattle fattened on western Montana grasses, the Grants would trade westbound pioneers one fat, healthy cow for two emaciated specimens that had just crossed the prairies. It didn't take long for the Grants to amass a *huge* holding of cattle. In 1862 Johnny Grant established a base ranch in the Deer Lodge Valley, Montana's first. When the gold rush began in the 1860s, cattlemen like the Grants were already in place to sell beef to hungry miners.

When the first influx of prospectors swooped into Bannack in 1862, some disenchanted souls decided to explore the new territory for other options. Amongst them was a German named Conrad Kohrs. After a stint as Bannack's butcher, he put together his own cattle herd and went off to Deer Lodge Valley. He bought Johnny Grant's ranch and never looked back. Building on Grant's base, Kohrs was the foremost rancher in Montana for almost 40 years.

The valley was as kind to other farmers and ranchers. Deer Lodge's ornate Victorian homes are witness to the prosperity and aspirations of these early settlers. The fact that early legislatures established the State Home for the Insane in Warm Springs, the State Tuberculosis Sanitarium in Galen, and the State Penitentiary in Deer Lodge is indicative of their political clout.

While the valley prospered due to the proximity to Butte and Anaconda markets, the pollution of these two industrial centers was at odds with the farms and ranches. The WPA *Guide to Montana* in 1939 describes the waters of Silver Bow Creek just above present-day Fairmont Hot Springs as "muddied with the refuse of Butte mines, though in places it is intensely blue from dissolved copper salts." The Clark Fork was unable to support aquatic life until the 1960s, after 10 years of cleanup. In 1903, after cattle began dying in fields from poisoned air, the smelter at Anaconda extended its smokestack 300 feet in order to disseminate its smoke higher in the atmosphere.

Between stricter mining regulations and the demise of mining in general, the valley has returned to a degree of its former integrity. A portion of the Clark Fork by Warm Springs is such hot fishing that it is now regulated by the Dept. of Fish, Wildlife, and Parks.

Old Montana Prison Complex

The Old Montana Prison, 1106 Main St., is the core of a series of neighboring historical exhibits. Montana Territory first established a penitentiary in Deer Lodge in 1871, but the disturbingly attractive buildings now open to the public were begun in the 1890s. The castellated, three-story cell block of red brick was built in 1912. It contains 200 cells, each six feet by seven feet. W.A. Clark financed the construction of the prison theater in 1919. The oldest structure is the quarried sandstone guard wall, 24 feet high, and buried four feet below ground, built in 1893.

All these structures, and others, were built by enforced convict labor, a practice later outlawed. After a violent prison riot and investigation into the deteriorating conditions at the old prison, a new facility was built in 1979.

Most of the facility is open for self-guided tours. Check out the gun ports in the shower room, the "galloping gallows" for off-premises executions, and maximum security's Black Box.

The **Montana Law Enforcement Museum** is located in the prison. Here is a memorial to officers slain in the line of duty, as well as curiosities such as Lee Harvey Oswald's handcuffs.

Resist the reaction to find all this really creepy, and do visit the old prison. On the one hand, the perfectly preserved quarters and facilities tell a grim story of prison life in the recent past. But, almost eerily, the handsome architecture and pleasing symmetry of the row upon row of empty cells give the prison a forlorn but intense beauty.

Also in the prison complex is the **Towe Ford Collection,** the world's second-largest antique Ford automobile collection. Edward Towe began his hobby in 1953 with the acquisition of a 1923 Ford Model-T Runabout; the collection now comprises over 100 automobiles. Some of the standout cars: the 1931 A-400 convertible sedan, a 1955 Thunderbird, and Henry Ford's personal "camper," a modified 1922 Lincoln that served as a picnic basket on wheels when Henry Ford went for weekend getaways.

From Labor Day to Memorial Day, the prison complex is open daily 8 a.m.-9 p.m. During April, May, Sept., and Oct., it's open daily 8:30-5:30; during the winter it's open Mon.-Fri. 9-4, Sat. and Sun. 10-5. Tickets are $3; call 846-3111 for details.

Museums

Across the street is the **Powell County Museum**, 1193 Main St., tel. 846-3294. It contains dinosaur bones, Indian tools, mining equipment, cowboy gear, and other relics of Powell County's rich history. Nearby is **Yesterday's Playthings**, 1017 Main St., tel. 846-1480, a doll and toy museum. The collection features 1,000 antique dolls from the private collection of Genevieve Hostetter.

Grant-Kohrs Ranch National Historic Site

The old Grant-Kohrs Ranch just north of Deer Lodge on Main St. contains the home and outbuildings of Montana's earliest ranch. The ranch is open 9-5:30 daily June 1-Labor Day, 9-4:30 the rest of the year. Admission is $1, or $3 for families. Contact the Grant-Kohrs Ranch Office for more information, 316 Main St., Deer Lodge, MT 59722, tel. 846-3388.

THE GRANT-KOHRS RANCH NATIONAL HISTORIC SITE

The Grant-Kohrs Ranch is a fascinating glimpse into the real life of cowboys and ranchers of early Montana.

Johnny Grant's 1862 log home was considered the finest house in the territory. Conrad Kohrs bought the operation in 1866 and began a series of improvements. To the back of the old house Kohrs attached a brick addition for a formal dining room, a large kitchen, and second-story bedrooms. The barns and stables were extensive; by the 1880s, Kohrs grazed cattle on over a million acres of open-range prairie and meadow across four states and southern Canada. Even after the disastrous winter of 1886, Kohrs was able to ship 8,000-10,000 cattle a year to eastern markets.

Kohrs reduced the size of the ranch in the 1910s, and the Deer Lodge holdings stayed in the family until 1972 when the National Park Service bought the ranch to preserve it as a historic monument. The old 23-room ranch house is wonderfully intact, a delightful mix of Victoriana and frontier living. Kohr's wife Augusta acquired an impressive array of valuable furniture—especially impressive since much of it came to Montana by steamboat and then overland to the Deer Lodge Valley.

The house is open for guided tours only; no more than 12 may tour at once, and admission is on a first-come basis. Apply at the ticket office. The outbuildings contain old tools, horse-drawn conveyances, and period equipment. The old bunkhouse was in many ways the center of the ranch; here, the hired men ate, played cards, and slept while in camp. Their spare rooms and modest environs contrasts vividly with life in the Big House.

Historic Downtown

Deer Lodge was home to a number of early ranchers and settlers whose fine period houses attest to their wealth and ambition; the city's commercial and civic buildings reflect a shared economic self-assuredness. The state's first college buildings, built in 1878, are now used by the local school district.

At the Courthouse Square stand the Powell County Courthouse, a statue and fountain commemorating John Mullan and pioneers who came west along the Mullan Road, and a Milwaukee Road engine originally built to sell to the Soviet Union. There are an abundance of lovely old homes, including the girlhood home of Jeanette Kelly, the original "Betty Crocker."

Accommodations

The **Big Sky Best Western Motel**, 210 Main, tel. (406) 846-2590, $34 d, has a pool and is convenient to the Grant-Kohrs Ranch. **Scharf's Motor Inn**, 819 Main, tel. 846-2810, $29 d, is on the other end of town, near the old prison. The **Downtowner Motel**, 506 Fourth St., tel. 846-1021, $32 d, is a quiet block off Main Street. The **Super 8**, 1150 Main, tel. 846-2370, $30 s, $34 d, offers a pool and is right off I-90. The Deer Lodge **KOA Campground**, tel. 846-1629, is at 413 Park.

Food

For the best steaks in this old ranching town, go to the **Broken Arrow Steak House**, 317 Main, tel. 846-3400. For family dining try **Scharf's**, 819 Main, tel. 846-3300; open for three meals a day, it's next door to their motel. The **Old West Bakery**, 321 Main, tel. 846-2142, offers its version of Butte's pasty in beef or chicken. The **Nickelodeon Café**, 502 Main, tel. 846-3026, combines light meals with ice-cream fountain favorites. As ever, the redoubtable **4-Bs**, 130 Sam Beck Rd., tel. 846-2620, serves good family meals 24 hours.

Recreation

The Flint Creek Mountains rise directly west of Deer Lodge. These jagged peaks harbor many high mountain lakes linked with good hiking trails. From the **Racetrack** Forest Service Campground, a rough road continues eight miles to Indian Meadows trailhead. Here, a series of alpine lakes repose beneath the 9,000-foot Twin Peaks. The lakes are high enough to be undependable as fisheries. To reach Racetrack, turn west at Warm Springs and continue 10 miles on a good road.

Hikes to other high mountain lakes begin at Tin Cup Lake, eight miles west of Deer Lodge, off Montana State Prison Road; and west of Rock Creek Lake, about 15 miles northwest of Deer Lodge on Forest Service Rd. 168. Consult the

Deer Lodge National Forest Map and the Ranger Station, 91 N. Frontage Rd., tel. 846-1170.

The city **swimming pool** is at 703 Fifth Street. **Deer Lodge Golf Club**, tel. 846-1625, welcomes visitors to its nine-hole course just west of town.

Information And Services

The Deer Lodge **Chamber of Commerce** is at 1171 Main, Deer Lodge, MT 59722, tel. (406) 846-2094. The **post office** is at 510 Main, tel. 846-1882.

The **Powell County Memorial Hospital** is at 1101 Texas St., tel. 846-2212. **Emergency** is 911.

Contact the Deer Lodge **Ranger Station** at 91 N. Frontage Rd., tel. 846-1170.

DRUMMOND

Between Deer Lodge and Drummond, the Clark Fork Valley is squeezed by the Flint Creek Mountains and the Garnet Range into an increasingly narrow valley. Mining makes a reprise here; at Garrison, phosphate is mined for fertilizer, and near Gold Creek, Granville Stuart made the first gold strike in the state.

History

Settlers during the 1860s rode steamboats to Fort Benton and then continued west to the Columbia on the Mullan Road, a rough trail scouted out by the Army. When gold was dis-covered in this part of Montana, some travelers were beguiled by the specter of quick wealth and stayed to stake a claim. The Mullan Road wound down the Clark Fork along this valley.

Montana's gold rush began here. In 1860, James and Granville Stuart were panning in Gold Creek when their pans showed color. Word of the gold strike brought in a flood of prospectors from the spent gold rushes in other parts of the West. Gold Creek was never a rich producer compared with some of the astonishingly fecund findings elsewhere in Montana, and only a few temporary shacks ever occupied this gold camp. Years later, better technology allowed developers to extract the remaining gold with dredges—as the mounds of tailings attest.

Gold Creek had its second day of fame when the Northern Pacific Railroad, built west from Chicago and east from Portland, met here in 1883. Northern Pacific president Henry Villard was present to drive the last spike linking the nation's second transcontinental railroad.

Accommodations And Food

The **Wagon Wheel Motel and Café**, at Front and C streets, tel. (406) 288-3201, $30 d, features comfortable rooms and good home cooking. The **Sky Motel**, east on Main St., tel. 228-3206, $32 d, offers rooms in individual cabins. The **Star Motel,** 170 W. Front, tel. 228-3272, $33 d, offers kitchenettes.

The **D-M Café**, 112 W. Front, tel. 288-9909, serves three meals a day of hearty food designed to satisfy hard-working ranch hands.

PINTLER SCENIC ROUTE

Montana Hwy. 1 leaves the Clark Fork Valley at Anaconda to wind through high mountain valleys, past ghost towns and old mining centers. The highway plunges down to join the Clark Fork and I-90 at Drummond. This alternative to the freeway doesn't involve any extra mileage, and leads to plentiful scenic and historic sites.

Anaconda is the town that Marcus Daly built. As the smelter of Butte's enormous reserves of copper and zinc, Anaconda became a powerful city, very nearly edging out Helena as capital of Montana.

Philipsburg is a convivial old silver town with a wealth of century-old storefronts, private homes, and civic structures. Located in a steep draw beneath craggy peaks, "P-Burg," as Montanans call it, is one of the most picturesque towns in the state.

Recreation ranges from skiing at one of Montana's best ski areas to lake fishing at 5,500 feet to sapphire hunting and exploring the ghosts of the mining towns that didn't quite make it.

THE LAND

For most of its distance, Hwy. 1 travels along Flint Creek. Its high north-issuing valley is flanked by two very different but related types of mountain ranges. The low, undramatic ridges of the Sapphire Mountains to the west once were sedimentary deposits in present-day Idaho. Great domes of magma bulged up beneath them, forcing these old layers up to great, but unstable, heights. As the underground swellings of magma grew even higher, huge blocks of the rock detached and skidded eastward on seams of molten rock.

The Sapphires came to rest in Montana, leaving the deep Bitterroot Valley in their wake. The land lying in front of the bulldozing Sapphire block became intensely folded and warped, eventually rising up to become the rugged Flint Creek Range.

The magma that lubricated the east-thrusting Sapphire Range apparently oozed out onto the newly formed Flint Creek Range, coating the crumpled landscape with lakes of mineral-rich granite. The silver deposits that sponsored such mining camps as Philipsburg and Granite were mined out of this formation, called the Philipsburg Batholith.

ANACONDA

To the industrialists who built Butte, its incredible mineral wealth was only half the equation. A *lot* of water was needed to refine the ore. Butte, in an arid basin near the Continental Divide, had scarcely enough water for prospectors to successfully pan for gold.

Copper King Marcus Daly decided rather than bring the water to the ore, that he'd take the ore to a better water source. He went to the Warm Springs Creek Valley, 26 miles west of Butte, to establish a smelter. Daly platted the town in 1883, and named it "Copperopolis." As unlikely as it now seems, Montana already had a settlement with that consonant-rich appellation, and the new town was renamed Anaconda (pop. 10,278, elev. 5,331 feet) for Daly's mine in Butte.

The **Washoe Smelter**, towering on a hill above Anaconda, became the largest copper smelter in the world. Daly established the Butte, Anaconda, and Pacific Railroad solely to transport the ore from his Butte mines to the Washoe. The smelter could process 1,000 tons of ore an hour; it employed about 3,500 workers. The immense smokestack that rose above Anaconda became a landmark; 585 feet high, nearly seven million bricks were used in its construction.

Anaconda was a classic "company town." Daly was inordinately proud of the town that he founded, and he graced it with fine city buildings. When Montana became a state in 1889, Daly mounted a huge campaign to name Anaconda the new capital. He immediately clashed with W.A. Clark, who favored retaining Helena, the territorial capital. A classic Copper King feud ensued. Daly spent $2.5 million promoting Anaconda and disdaining Helena and Clark. Clark painted a picture of Anaconda as a grimly obedient company town, and minted copper dollars as exemplars. In 1894, Helena won out, but by fewer than 2,000 votes.

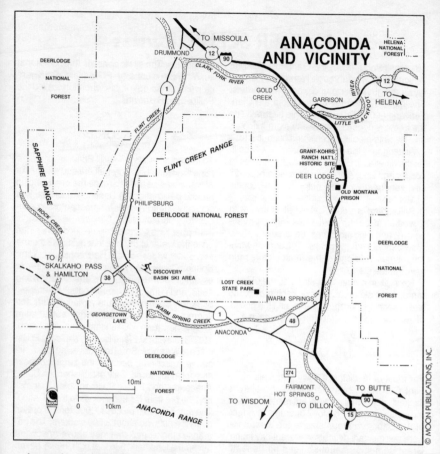

ANACONDA AND VICINITY

© MOON PUBLICATIONS, INC.

Anaconda was inexorably tied to the fate of Butte. When Butte stumbled, Anaconda also faltered. After years of failing business, the Anaconda Company closed the Washoe Smelter in 1983.

Sights

Anaconda has preserved its historic town center. One of the most imposing buildings is the old **City Hall,** 110 E. Eighth St., tel. 563-8421. Built in 1894 with typical Daly zest and aplomb, it now houses the city's museum, a gallery, and a craft store. The **Deer Lodge County Courthouse,** at the south end of Main St., dominates the town. Built in 1898, it features a rotunda, a copper-clad cupola, curving staircases, and a dumbwaiter to convey books from floor to floor.

An art-deco extravaganza, the **Washoe Theatre** at 305 Main is one of Anaconda's most stellar showcases. As befits the town, the hammered metal-leaf decorations are almost overwhelming. The imposing **Hearst Free Library,** 401 Main St., was an 1898 gift to Anaconda from William Randolph Hearst's mother, Phoebe.

Accommodations

Right downtown is the **Marcus Daly Motel,** 119 W. Park, tel. (406) 563-3411, $34 d; it's both comfortable and convenient. The **Trade Wind Motel,** 1600 E. Commercial, tel. 563-3428, $29 d, offers nonsmoking rooms and kitchenettes. The **Vagabond Lodge Motel**, 1421 E. Park, tel. 563-5251, $25 s, $30 d, is an attractive brick inn on the road out of town. Probably the most unusual lodging in Anaconda is the **Copper Town Inn**, 23 Main St., tel. 563-2372, whose 10 rooms are decorated with period furniture and named for famous Anacondans; all rooms have double beds and are $20. **Big Sky RV Park**, 200 N. Locust, tel. 563-2967, has fishing access on Warm Springs Creek and is near public parks.

Food

Like a lesser Butte, Anaconda has a reputation for good food and entertainment. **Barclay II Supper Club**, 1300 E. Commercial, tel. 563-5541, is Anaconda's most stylish restaurant, serving large Italian-influenced meals in many courses; open 5-10 p.m. The landmark hotel in Anaconda was the **Montana Hotel** built by Marcus Daly as the city's showcase. Unfortunately, it was gutted by fire in the 1970s. Its handsome and substantial skeleton was revivified as the **Montana Supper Club**, 200 N. Main, tel. 563-5602. Enjoy steaks and seafood in the shadow of the old hotel's arches. The **Haufbrau**, 111 Hwy. 1 W, tel. 563-9982, is a good family restaurant with pizza as a specialty.

Recreation

Georgetown Lake, 15 miles west of Anaconda on Hwy. 1, provides fabled fishing and watersports access, with plenty of campgrounds (see below). Closer to Anaconda and less overrun with locals are a couple of wildlife viewing areas. **Lost Creek State Park**, six miles off Hwy. 48, two miles east of Anaconda, is a campground in a narrow limestone canyon. A waterfall, interesting geology, and mountain goat and Bighorn sheep make this a nice alternative to urban RV sites.

Mount Haggin Wildlife Management Area offers stunning views onto local mountains and also the chance to see bashful moose and elk. Mount Haggin is popular with cross-country skiers in winter and mountain bikers in summer. To reach Mount Haggin, follow Hwy. 274 14 miles south from Anaconda; watch for the sign for **Mule Ranch Vista**. With 54,137 acres under protection, Mount Haggin is the state's largest wildlife-management area.

Information And Services

The **Anaconda Chamber of Commerce** is at 306 E. Park, Anaconda, MT 59711, tel. (406) 563-2400.

The **Community Hospital of Anaconda** is at 401 W. Pennsylvania, tel. 563-5261. Emergency is 911.

The **post office** is 218 Main St., tel. 563-2241.

GEORGETOWN LAKE

Georgetown Lake, at the upper reaches of Flint Creek, is one of the state's oldest hydroelectric projects. The lake is incredibly popular with the locals, and good restaurants and recreation areas ring the shoreline. By winter, the lake is renowned for ice fishing.

Flint Creek was first dammed in 1885 and was further developed in 1891 when the silver mines in Philipsburg demanded a source for electric power. In the 1890s, Marcus Daly's Butte, Anaconda, and Pacific Railroad ran weekend trains to the lake for the workers in Butte and Anaconda. A steamboat plied the lake, offering excursion trips.

Today, boating, windsurfing, and fishing are the preferred pastimes at Georgetown Lake, although many people simply go there to "weekend" at their cabins.

Discovery Basin Ski Area

Located 20 miles west of Anaconda in the Flint Creek Range, Discovery Basin offers a vertical drop of 2,700 feet along 13 runs. Full rental facilities are available, as well as food and beverage services at the ski lodge. A lift ticket costs $14.50 for adults. For more information contact Discovery Basin, P.O. Box 221, Anaconda, MT 59711, tel. (800) 332-3272 in state, or (800) 443-2381 out of state.

Accommodations And Food

The following hotel/restaurant combinations offer good food, plus access to the lake and nearby Discovery Basin skiing. **Georgetown Lake Lodge**, Denton's Point Rd., tel. (406) 563-7020, $32 d, is the area's most evolved accommodation; there's also an RV park. The **Brown Derby Inn**, 13902 Hwy. 1, tel. 563-5072, $26 d, is convenient for passers-through; the restaurant is dependable. The **Seven Gables Resort**, 18 S. Hauser, tel. 563-5052, $31 d, is just off the road to Discovery Basin, and offers rooms, a restaurant, and a bar.

Camping is easy at Georgetown Lake, with an abundant mix of private and public campgrounds in the area. At **Denton's Point KOA**, west two miles on S. Shore Rd., tel. 563-6030, there's a marina with a bar and restaurant. Just up the road is **Georgetown Lake KOA**, tel. 563-3402, open all year.

PHILIPSBURG

Between Georgetown Lake and Philipsburg, Hwy. 1 follows Flint Creek down precipitous Flint Creek Canyon to the Philipsburg Valley. The terrain becomes much more hospitable to ranching, and between Philipsburg and Drummond the landscape becomes increasingly agrarian.

Whether it is the community's isolation or the integrity of its Victorian-era architecture, Philipsburg has recently gained the reputation as a refuge for artists.

History

A lone miner discovered silver ore at Philipsburg (pop. 925, elev. 5,195 feet) in 1864, but he didn't pursue his claim. His barroom oratory about the rich deposits, however, attracted more ambitious miners. In 1866, the rich Hope Mine, Montana's first silver mine, was established, and by the next year the camp boasted 700 inhabitants. The silver deposits were rich enough to attract the Northern Pacific's spur line to Philipsburg in 1887.

The Bimetallic Mining Company entered the town in 1885. At the time it was the largest silver mill in the state and its smoke stacks still tower over Philipsburg. Its demand for power led to the creation of Georgetown Lake.

Four miles farther up the mountain from Philipsburg was Granite, whose rich mines earned it the nickname "Silver Queen." Granite boomed along with Philipsburg; $30 million of silver was mined there during the 1880s. Granite suffered more grievously when the bottom fell out of the gold market in 1893. Within hours of the mines closing, 3,000 miners and their families reportedly descended on Philipsburg to with-

DEGREES OF GREY IN PHILIPSBURG

You might come here Sunday on a whim.
Say your life broke down. The last good kiss
you had was years ago. You walk these streets
laid out by the insane, past hotels
that didn't last, bars that did, the tortured try
of local drivers to accelerate their lives.
Only churches are kept up. The jail
turned 70 this year. The only prisoner
is always in, not knowing what he's done.

The principal supporting business now
is rage. Hatred of the various grays
the mountain sends, hatred of the mill,
The Silver Bell repeal, the best liked girls
who leave each year for Butte. One good
restaurant and bars can't wipe the boredom out.
The 1907 boom, eight going silver mines,
a dance floor built on springs—
all memory resolves itself in gaze,
in panoramic green you know the cattle eat
or two stacks high above the town,
two dead kilns, the huge mill in collapse
for fifty years that won't finally fall down.

Isn't this your life? That ancient kiss
still burning out your eyes? Isn't this defeat
so accurate, the church bell simply seems
a pure announcement: ring and no one comes?
Don't empty houses ring? Are magnesium
and scorn sufficient to support a town,
not just Philipsburg, but towns
of towering blondes, good jazz and booze
the world will never let you have
until the town you came from dies inside?

Say no to yourself. The old man, twenty
when the jail was built, still laughs
although his lips collapse. Someday soon,
he says, I'll go to sleep and not wake up.
You tell him no. You're talking to yourself.
The car that brought you here still runs.
The money you buy lunch with,
no matter where it's mined, is silver
and the girl who serves your food
is slender and her red hair lights the wall.

—Richard Hugo

draw their bank accounts and purchase one-way tickets out.

Sights

Philipsburg never really grew much after the century turned, and the old town has remained intact. The chamber of commerce passes out a brochure for a walking tour to 32 historic buildings. Note especially the well-preserved Victorian storefronts downtown, many with original signage. The grade school, built in 1894, is the oldest school building in Montana still in use.

The ghost town of Granite is four miles southeast of Philipsburg on a gravel road. The handsome Miner's Union Hall, a three-story brick structure, is one of the few buildings still standing.

Accommodations And Food

The **Burg Motel**, 1005 Broadway, tel. (406) 859-3959, is open year-round and also has an RV park. **Kaiser House Bakery and Restaurant**, 217 E. Broadway, tel. 859-3953, open for three meals a day, is a good place for a light meal. Behind the dour storefront at **The Gallery Café**, 127 E. Broadway, tel. 859-3534, is good food and the atmosphere of a Richard Hugo poem; open 6 a.m.-8 p.m.

Information

Contact the Philipsburg **Chamber of Commerce** at P.O. Box 661, Philipsburg, MT 59858, tel. (406) 859-3256. The **Philipsburg Ranger Station** can be reached by calling 859-3211.

THE SKALKAHO PASS ROAD

Six miles south of Philipsburg, Hwy. 38 leaves Hwy. 1 and winds west through the Sapphire Mountains, eventually dropping into the Bitterroot Valley at Hamilton. Travelers should consider this 50-mile drive, mostly on gravel roads, for several reasons. For anglers, the road passes the upper reaches of Rock Creek, one of Montana's premier fishing streams. Amateur prospectors can try their hand at sapphire mining along its banks. At the crest of Skalkaho Pass, 32 miles from Hwy. 1, Skalkaho Falls roars down under the highway and makes a great place to picnic. Although hiking isn't necessary to enjoy the falls, the ambitious can hike up a trail about a quarter mile from the falls, toward the pass. Finally, Skalkaho Pass Rd. connects two otherwise distant valleys along a route with great scenic value.

Skalkaho Pass Rd. is closed from mid-October to June. Early or late in the season, call the Highway Department, tel. 859-3932, to be certain the road is open.

At Rock Creek, the **Gem Mountain Sapphire Mine**, 13 miles west of the junction with Hwy. 1, tel. 859-3530, offers buckets of sapphire-rich gravel to process. The sapphires come in a number of shades (classic blue being one of the rarest) and are relatively easy to find. You can choose to wash the gravel yourself, for the real prospector experience, or buy prewashed concentrated gravel by the bucket. The gravel is placed on sorting tables, and then it's up to you to spot the gems. The staff are happy to help—they even offer a faceting and mounting service—and the experience makes a good family outing. There's informal picnicking and camping along Rock Creek near the mine.

Anglers will want to leave Hwy. 38 for Rock Creek Rd., and follow it to its confluence with the Clark Fork River. The upper reaches of Rock Creek receive a lot less attention than the more developed areas closer to Missoula, but the fishing is as good.

THE BIG HOLE RIVER COUNTRY

The Big Hole is known as the "Valley of 10,000 Haystacks" for the stacks of loose, unbaled hay that the local ranchers persist in using for hay storage; ranches don't have much truck with labor-saving technology. Time has not forgotten this isolated valley, but neither has it been thinking of the Big Hole very recently.

The Big Hole River flows north, draining a huge, very high valley lying between the Bitterroot Mountains on the west and the Pioneer Mountains on the east. After bumping into the Anaconda Range, the river does a U-turn and flows south, picking up the west-slope drainage of the Pioneers.

For anglers and floaters, the river's the thing. Fishing in the Big Hole is superlative, and the rafting challenging. And for hunters, this is the best hunting ground for pronghorn in the state, outside of the prairies of eastern Montana. Amateurs of history can hike the trails and war fields of the Battle of the Big Hole, where in 1877 the Nez Percé fought the U.S. Army as the Indians tried to flee incarceration on reservations.

To comprehend the Big Hole's allure, understand that this is still the West. Resorts haven't yet replaced ranches. You can catch trout elsewhere in Montana, but here you can share a drink and tell your fish stories to a hired hand or cowboy—not a conventioneer.

THE LAND

The Big Hole Valley, and the Pioneer and Bitterroot mountains that ring it, are the result of ancient mountain-moving on an enormous scale. As the North American continent split away from its neighbors on the Ur-continent of Panagaea, the collision of the continent and the Pacific Ocean floor produced huge amounts of molten rock. As the landmass continued to flow over the ocean floor, the magma forced up the sedimentary layers that had formed the edge of the old continent.

The enormous pool of magma that formed is known as the Idaho Batholith. It grew so large and forced the older layers of rock so high that

eventually, about 70 million years ago, these sedimentary levels skidded off to the east on molten subterranean lubricant, and deep valleys formed in their wake. The Pioneer Range is one of the most easterly of the fragments set adrift by the rising of the new Rocky Mountains; it made its 50-mile journey east in about a million years. The Big Hole Valley is the void left as the old mountains bulldozed eastward.

The Big Hole Valley is some of the highest, flattest land in Montana. Almost all of the farm and ranch land hovers well above 6,000 feet, in wide valley swatches 15 miles across. However, the original gorge cut when the rock mass careened eastward was much deeper. Wells dug in the Big Hole penetrate through 14,000 feet of sediment before striking bedrock.

HISTORY

Feeling conceptual, Lewis and Clark in 1805 named the three forks of the Jefferson River Wisdom, Philanthropy, and Philosophy. In time, Wisdom River became the less abstract Big Hole River, so named by later ranchers impressed with the vast real estate hemmed in by towering peaks.

Ranches spread into the valley in the 1880s and the area quickly became synonymous with big cattle outfits. No one has come forward with an explanation for the Big Hole's penchant for unbaled hay. Perhaps it is local pride. The contraption used to stack loose hay, a "Beaver Slide Stacker," which conveys hay up a sloping wooden structure and dumps it onto the stack, was invented by a local rancher in 1910.

BIG HOLE NATIONAL BATTLEFIELD

The Nez Percé

One of the most famous Indian battles in Montana history involved an Indian tribe not indigenous to the state. The Nez Percé homeland was the region where Oregon, Washington, and Idaho meet; there they were semi-nomadic fishers, hunters, and gatherers. The Nez Percé Nation was a largely peaceable confederation of loosely knit tribal units, each under a powerful chief.

By the 1850s, white settlement began to displace the Nez Percé. An 1855 treaty confined them to a reservation; as the boundaries included their traditional homeland, and since the treaty also restricted white settlement on their land, they complied.

By 1863, however, more stockmen, miners, and settlers were encroaching on Nez Percé land. A new treaty was drawn up, reducing the reservation to one-quarter of its former size. The Nez Percé chiefs whose land was still within the reservation signed the new treaty; those chiefs whose land was being taken away refused. The U.S. government, on the pretext that the signature of any Nez Percé chief represented the commitment of the whole tribe, ordered the "non-treaty" Nez Percé onto the new reservation.

While both the Indians and the U.S. Indian Bureau dallied for several years without strict enforcement of the order, increasing pressure from settlers—especially after Custer's rout in 1876—made compliance a priority. In 1877, the U.S. Army was sent in to compel the delinquent Nez Percé to the reservation.

At this time, a band of young warriors attacked and killed four white settlers, whom the Indians believed guilty of earlier murders of Nez Percé elders. Fearing harsh retaliation and foreseeing a dismal future for the tribe, five bands of the non-treaty Nez Percé—about 800 people—fled eastward from the Wallowa Lake area of northeastern Oregon. After two skirmishes in Idaho, where the Indians eluded the Army, the Nez Percé realized they had to leave the area completely. They crossed over to Montana, intent on journeying to Crow country on the Yellowstone, where they hoped to reestablish the tribe.

The Battle Of The Big Hole

Once in Montana, the pace of the exodus slowed, and after pushing up the Bitterroot Valley, the Nez Percé camped on the western side of the Big Hole Valley. Here, they considered themselves out of reach of the Army for a few days. They stopped to cut new travois poles and to ready themselves for more traveling.

The Nez Percé knew that the Washington-based Army detachment was two weeks behind them. However, they didn't realize that the Seventh Infantry, under Col. John Gibbon of Fort Shaw, had moved south to ambush them. In the early morning of Aug. 9, 1877, a Nez Percé sentry rode into the advance guard of Col. Gibbon's forces. He was shot and killed, and the gunfire awoke the rest of the Indian warriors. The infantry mounted a full attack on the Nez Percé as they awoke from their tepees, killing women, children, braves, and elders indiscriminately.

Indian warriors quickly took up defensive positions, and with sniper fire forced the Army back onto the side hill. Both sides sustained heavy losses.

The Nez Percé successfully besieged the Army troops the rest of that day and night, until the Nez Percé had struck their bivouac, and fled eastward to an uncertain future.

The Battlefield

Hike the trails here not just for their history, but for the quiet beauty of this lush meadow flanked by mountains and a hastening stream.

The **visitor center,** tel. 689-3155, open daily 8 a.m.-8 p.m. Memorial Day to Labor day, 8 a.m.-5 p.m. the rest of the year, provides audiovisual displays that explain the background of the Nez Percé flight and the Big Hole battle. Exhibits include artifacts of the battle and items from the daily life of the early settlers and the Indian tribes who contested here in 1877.

An extensive network of self-guided hiking trails links the sites of the battle. From the parking lot, a half-mile trail leads to the site of the Nez Percé camp; a shorter trail leads to the siege area. Here, for devotees of military strategy, interpretive signs chart the development of the battle in great detail. A somewhat steeper hike leads to the site of the howitzer captured by the Nez Percé with great views over the battlefield and the Big Hole Valley.

For hiking of a different magnitude, the **Nee-Me-Poo Historic Trail** passes through the Big Hole Battlefield. This 1,500-mile hiking and backpacking trail follows the route of the Nez Percé from Oregon to the Bear's Paw Mountains, where the Army finally apprehended the fleeing Nez Percé.

Accommodations

There are picnic facilities at the lower parking lot, along the river, but camping is not allowed. The closest services are in Wisdom, 10 miles east. The **Trail's Rest Campground**, tel. 689-3149, is open June-Sept. only, one mile west of the battleground on Hwy. 43.

THE BIG HOLE

Although the Big Hole River itself is over 100 miles long, the term "Big Hole," frontier-ese for a deep wide valley, refers to the river's upper basin. Here, between Jackson and Fishtrap, is fabled ranch country, rivaling only eastern Montana for its eternal flatness and traditional Western ways. Here too is great fishing for the discriminating angler, with rushing streams full of scrappy brook trout and rare arctic grayling. Almost all river access is through private land; be sure to ask permission from the landowner.

Jackson

Lewis and Clark passed through here in 1805 and stopped at the local hot springs. Not content with just a soak, the Corps also cooked their dinner in the 138° water. Now, as then, this little community is known mostly for the springs.

The **Jackson Hot Springs Lodge**, off Hwy. 278, tel. (406) 834-3151, operates a small resort at the spot where Lewis and Clark dined. Open year-round, the lodge caters to summer anglers and tourists, but really gears up for winter guests. Nearby are excellent cross-country trails, some groomed and others informal; snowmobilers also use the lodge as a center. Lodging at the resort is in freestanding cabins; rates begin at $24 a night. Food, drink, and entertainment are provided at the lodge.

Rose's Cantina, tel. 834-3100, is open for three meals a day and offers an unlikely special: Rose will cook your fresh-caught trout and, for a couple dollars, provide hash browns and a salad. If you are passing through Jackson in August,

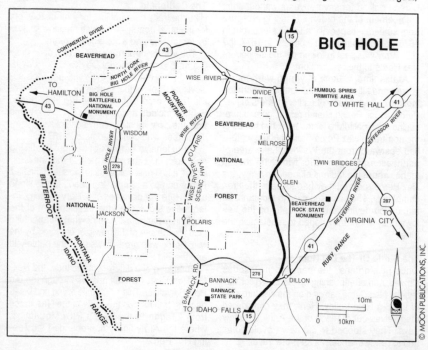

ask about their **Girls Only Rodeo**, usually held the second weekend.

Wisdom

This little crossroads—more an outpost than a town—is a trading center for the cattle ranches and hay farms that stretch across the wide valley. Higher civilization is making inroads, however. As a sign of changing times, Wisdom supports both watering holes for local ranch hands and a tony fine-art gallery.

Practicalities: Lodging in Wisdom is fairly perfunctory. Made of logs, the **Nez Percé Motel**, tel. (406) 689-3254, $28 d, is the most attractive option. The **Sandman Motel**, tel. 689-2689, $22 d, offers a laundromat.

The centers of life in Wisdom are its bars and restaurants. **Fetty's Bar and Café**, tel. 689-3260, is a local institution serving three meals a day. The **Antler Bar** is a popular place for a drink; it's not unlike having a beer in a taxidermy shop.

The really incongruous business in town is the **Wisdom River Gallery**, tel. 689-3400, open daily 9-5. Here, the art of the West rubs cheeks with the life of the West. This fine selection of blue-chip Western art, from the likes of Gary Carter and Beverly Doolittle—and some local talents—somehow finds a market in Wisdom. There's a café in the back of the gallery.

The **Wisdom USFS Ranger Station** can be contacted at 689-3243. **Emergency** is 911.

Wise River

Between Wisdom and Wise River, the Big Hole Valley narrows. The river enters a canyon and picks up speed. Rainbow and brown trout begin to dominate the waters, in numbers and sizes that excite a national audience of fly-fishers. There are a number of fishing-access sites as the river enters its canyon, good for anglers, also handy for floaters. At the town of Wise River, the river of the same name enters the Big Hole. A designated scenic byway along Hwy. 484 begins here.

A couple of lakes in the Anaconda Mountains to the west are of interest to the traveling angler. **Mussigbrod Lake**, 23 miles northwest of Wisdom, has some of the best arctic grayling fishing in the Lower 48. There's also a Forest Service campground. There's a campground too at **Pintler Lake**, 10 miles off Hwy. 43 up Pintler Creek Road. The lake offers good fishing for rainbow and cutthroat, and a very scenic base camp for explorations of the surrounding pine forests.

Practicalities: What passes on the map for a town at Wise River is in fact a couple of bars at the junction of the Big Hole and Wise rivers. Not to sound dismissive: a couple of bars do a town make, at least out here in fly-fisher's heaven.

The **Wise River Club**, tel. 832-3258, is a taciturn old bar full of antiques and stuffed animals. It's still enough of a local's bar to be at once suspicious and friendly. The restaurant is open for three meals a day. The Club's motel has rooms at $28 d; there is also limited camping for RVs.

Outfitters and guest ranch resorts provide accommodation options for hunters and anglers. The **Sundance Lodge**, Box F, Wise River, MT 59762, tel. 689-3611, is a year-round resort that offers hiking, horseback riding, hunting, and, of course, fishing and float trips. Lodging is in cabins or in the lodge; meals are provided. Rates begin at $40 a day.

The **Complete Fly Fisher**, P.O. Box 127, Wise River, MT 59762, tel. 832-3175, promises great fishing and great cooking for their guests. **Stockton Outfitters**, P.O. Box 9, Wise River, MT 59762, tel. 832-3138, offers fishing and float trips in addition to guest ranch activities.

Big Hole River Outfitters, P.O. Box 156, Wise River, MT 59762, tel. 832-3252, offer accommodations to their angler guests. **Pioneer Outfitter**, Charles Page, Alder Creek Ranch, Wise River, MT 59762, tel. 832-3128, offers big-game hunting as well as fishing expeditions.

The **Wise River Ranger Station** can be reached at 832-3178.

THE LOWER BIG HOLE RIVER

Downstream from the community of Divide, the Big Hole, heretofore great fishing, becomes a blue-ribbon trout fishery. Brown trout are both huge and abundant. Mid-June, when the salmon flies hatch, marks a frantic season for fish and fishers alike. To the misfortune of trout, there are several good fishing-access sites between Divide and Glen.

Divide

Floaters need beware of a diversion dam just upstream from Divide. Here, water from the Big Hole River is pumped over the Continental Divide to Butte at a rate of five million gallons a day. In its day, the pump station was quite an engineering feat; it's on the National Register of Historic Places.

For hikers, often overlooked is the **Humbug Spires Primitive Area**, a day-hike into an area of geologic interest. Intense faulting has fractured granite extrusions into steep, sharp needles that resemble menhirs. About three miles in, the trail reaches a watershed, and there's a good view over the spiny valley. Exit I-15 at Moose Creek Rd., three miles south of Divide, and turn east.

Melrose

Somewhere near Melrose, the Big Hole leaves its steep-sided canyon and resolutely flows to its appointment with the Beaverhead River. This is a good place to leave the freeway and follow old Hwy. 10. From Glen, off-road enthusiasts can follow a gravel road along the Big Hole River as it trends east to the Beaverhead. It's a pretty drive, becoming dramatic as it approaches historic Beaverhead Rock from its backside.

Melrose lolligags along the old rail sidings that spawned its early growth, a town caught in the midst of a stretching exercise. This pleasant hamlet is known for its fishing; with several fishing-access sites, an attractive motel, a café and bars, it's no wonder that anglers flock here.

Practicalities: The Sportsman Motel, N. Main, tel. (406) 835-2141, $36 d, is a handsome log motel complex. Down the street is the **Quack-Quack Café**, tel. 835-9421, open 7 a.m.-9 p.m.

As elsewhere on the Big Hole, outfitters await in abundance. **Ray's Guide Service**, Box 70, Melrose, MT 59743, tel. 835-3091, offers float fishing on local rivers. **Bacon Outfitters**, P.O. Box 163, Melrose, MT 59743, tel. 835-2691, and **Sundown Outfitters**, P.O. Box 95, Melrose, MT 59743, tel. 835-2751, both offer big-game hunting in addition to fishing trips.

THE PIONEER MOUNTAINS

Surrounded on three sides by the meanderings of the Big Hole River, the Pioneer Mountains are in fact two different ranges divided down a north-south axis, linked yet separated, sort of like the underside of a coffee bean. These out-of-the-way mountains come to life in the winter, as a hot springs resort and a good downhill-ski area combine to bring in the locals. The Wise River drainage is popular with anglers; there are several large Forest Service campgrounds with fishing access along the river.

Highway 484 transects the Pioneer Mountains, from Wise River in the north through Polaris to Hwy. 278 in the south. The Forest Service has designated this part-gravel, part-paved route as the Wise River-Polaris Scenic Byway.

Maverick Mountain Ski Area

The legendary heavy snows of southwestern Montana are put to good use at Maverick, which boasts 215 inches of base snow at the summit of the runs. The vertical drop is 2,120 feet. Maverick Lodge offers full pro shop, rental, and food facilities; cross-country skiers are welcome. A lift ticket is $14 a day. Call 834-3454 for details.

The closest lodging is at the **Grasshopper Inn**, tel. (406) 834-3456, $40 d, at the base of the slopes beside the near-ghost town of Polaris. Open 9 a.m.-9 p.m., the restaurant is good, the bar lively, and the motel-style rooms are comfortable.

Elkhorn Hot Springs

This venerable resort is the other popular lodging for skiers. Cross-country skiers converge here; with 40 kilometers (25 miles) of cross-country trails managed by the resort, an entire mountain range of informal trails to explore, and a good hot soak to come home to, this is near-heaven (at 7,385 feet, literally so). In summer, the hot springs are popular for hikers. There are two outdoor mineral pools, plus a sauna.

Rooms are either in the lodge (bathroom down the hall) or in rustic cabins scattered amongst the trees. The restaurant in the lodge is open for three meals a day. Rooms start at $16 d. Elkhorn Hot Springs is 13 miles north of Hwy. 278 on Hwy. 484. Contact Elkhorn Hot Springs at P.O. Box 514, Polaris, MT 59746, tel. 834-3434.

Crystal Park

At this Forest Service-maintained site, on Hwy. 484 16 miles north of Hwy. 278, rockhounds can dig for quartz crystals. It's also a nice spot for a picnic; fire grates and water are provided.

THE SOUTHWEST CORNER

Montana school children are taught to recognize the state's western boundary as Abraham Lincoln's long-faced profile. The scruff of Lincoln's beard is Beaverhead County, the state's largest and one of its most varied. The Continental Divide careens along towering snow-capped peaks, which ring in valleys so broad, flat, and covered with sagebrush that ranchers from eastern Montana could feel at home: this is western Montana's prairie province. Some of the oldest and largest ranches in Montana stretched across these high flatlands.

History was quick to find this corner of Montana. High on a forgotten pass between Montana and Idaho is Sacajawea Historic Area, where the Corps of Discovery crossed the Continental Divide. Bannack State Park, Montana's best preserved ghost town, commemorates the state's first city and first territorial capital. Red Rock Lakes National Wildlife Refuge is one of the nation's most important bird sanctuaries. It is a primary breeding ground for trumpeter swans, once feared extinct.

With two million acres of national forest in Beaverhead County alone, and a vast network of streams forming the Missouri's most distant headwaters, southwest Montana has plenty of room for outdoor recreation. Yet the great fishing, hunting, and hiking opportunities in this lovely corner of Montana are blessedly free of crowds.

History

The Shoshone Indians were the first Montana-area Natives to acquire horses. They stormed north through the upper Jefferson River drainages to threaten and finally dominate the high plains east of the Rocky Mountain front in the 1750s. The Blackfeet Federation, moving south from Canada with guns obtained from the British, halted the Shoshone's expansion. The Shoshone were forced back into Idaho by the 1800s, where Lewis and Clark first encountered them.

Monida Pass, now part of I-15, is one of the lowest and gentlest of passes over the Continental Divide. It provided access to some of the

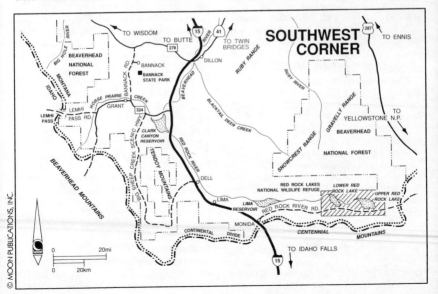

earliest migrations of non-Indian settlers. Prospectors found rich gold pannings along Grasshopper Creek in 1862. Bannack sprung up in response, becoming the first real town in Montana. By the time it became the territorial capital in 1864, Bannack boasted hotels, a governor's mansion, churches, and a Masonic temple.

Montana's vigilante movement was born in Bannack. The first elected sheriff, Henry Plummer, was a smooth operator who ran a gang of road agents—deceptively called the Innocents—on the side. Miners and travelers were preyed upon until the vigilantes prevailed and hanged over 20 suspected outlaws.

The stage line that extended from the Union Pacific in Utah to the Montana gold fields was replaced in 1880 by the first railroad to reach the state, the Utah and Northern. Access to transport made silver camp Butte into a boom town, and although gold had already played out in southwest Montana, the railroad boosted the fortunes of nascent stock ranches. The enormous basins from the Centennial Range in the south to the Big Hole Valley to the west provided rich grazing.

THE RED ROCK VALLEY

The Red Rock River, the most distant headwater of the Missouri, drains a broad valley overlooked by the Continental Divide, but not by much. This is high country: the valley stretches out prairie-like at elevations above 6,000 feet.

History

Shoshone Indians used the Red Rock Valley as a trail eastward to buffalo country on the Yellowstone. After gold was discovered in the region, its wide valleys, with access to markets in early mining camps, made this one of Montana's first livestock ranges. When the railroads came north to take out ore in the 1880s, sheep raising became an important component of the local economy.

This remote and beautiful valley, ringed with high but rounded peaks, would probably be ignored by the traveler if it weren't for Red Rock Lakes. At these marshy lakes, biologists discovered trumpeter swans in 1933, once feared extinct in the U.S.

Trumpeter swans formerly ranged over much of the continent. However, during the 19th century, hunters found a vigorous market for quill pens, powder puffs, and swan meat. As the homestead movement changed the environment of eastern Montana, with land falling to the plow and marshes being drained, populations plummeted. Biologists found only 66 trumpeters in 1933 at Red Rock Lakes, the last individuals of the species in the U.S.

The U.S. Department of the Interior established the 40,300-acre **Red Rock Lakes National Wildlife Refuge** in 1935. Currently, 600 trumpeters summer here, and, as geothermal activity maintains ice-free water temperatures year-round, the winter population swells to 2,000.

BOB RACE

trumpeter swans, Cygnus columbianus

The Defenders of Wildlife, a group concerned with wildlife preservation, have called the refuge one of the most beautiful in America. Upper and Lower Red Rock Lakes are nestled beneath the 9,800-foot Centennial Mountains. A total of 258 bird species have been sighted at the lakes. This isolated corner of Montana is home to a variety of wildlife, including moose, deer, elk, pronghorn, and fox.

To reach the refuge, turn at Monida, just below the Continental Divide on I-15. The reserve begins a rattly 28 miles up a gravel road. Wildlife viewing is best between May and November, which is about the only season the road is dependably passable. The reserve can also be reached in good weather from Idaho, on the Red Rock Pass Rd., from Hwy. 87, 17 miles from West Yellowstone. For more information, contact the Refuge Manager, Red Rock Lakes NWR, Monida Star Rt., Box 15, Lima, MT 59739, tel. 276-3347.

Recreation

Fishing is allowed in most areas of the refuge, and provides good sport for trout anglers. Non-motorized boats are allowed on some areas of the lakes; check with refuge managers. Arctic grayling are caught in streams that feed the lakes. Hunting is permitted in designated areas of the refuge for specific species.

Practicalities

The closest motel is the **Kalbas Korners Holiday Motel,** 111 Bailey St., tel. 276-3535, $28 d, in Lima. Otherwise, this is camping country. There are two campgrounds at the wildlife refuge, one at each lake, and each at lake-side, meaning great views but also potential mosquito assault.

Guest ranches and outfitters provide an alternative to camping. **Rush's Lakeview Guest Ranch,** Monida Star Rt., Lima, 59739, tel. 276-3300, offers a full range of recreation and wildlife viewing opportunities year-round. Lakeview is the headquarters of the refuge, but offers no amenities. Make sure your gas tank is full before heading up.

Kalbas Korners Café, tel. 276-9998, in Lima serves really good food way off the beaten path; open 6 a.m.-10 p.m. Likewise, **Yesterday's Café,** tel. 276-3319, in Dell, serves superior home-style cooking in a refurbished country schoolhouse; open Sun.-Fri. 7 a.m.-9 p.m.

HORSE PRAIRIE VALLEY

The Red Rock River meets Horse Prairie Creek at Clark Canyon Reservoir, and the Beaverhead River issues forth. While the reservoir is popular with local boaters and anglers, and old ranches fill the wide valley traditionally known as the Horse Prairie, travelers will want to explore the area to relive some of the most stirring moments of the Lewis and Clark Expedition.

History

As the Corps of Discovery pushed up the Jefferson River, searching for the headwaters of the Missouri, Sacajawea began to recognize landmarks of her childhood.

Recognizing the need for horses to proceed over the difficult Continental Divide that faced them, Lewis and three men went ahead to scout for the Shoshone, into whose homeland Sacajawea insisted they had entered. Lewis sighted the expedition's first Indian in Montana in the Horse Prairie Valley, and continued over Lemhi Pass to encounter a Shoshone lodge near Tendoy, Idaho. After tenuous negotiations for horses, the Shoshone agreed to backtrack with Lewis and his party to meet the rest of the Corps.

As the party approached, Sacajawea began to suck her fingers, a sign that she recognized her kin. A Shoshone woman broke rank and ran forward to embrace Sacajawea, recognizing her from her childhood. When Sacajawea was summoned to interpret the dialogue between the Europeans and the Natives, she entered the tent where the men were conversing, and immediately recognized her brother Cameahwait, who was now chief of the Shoshone.

Consider for a moment what the negotiations for horses and supplies entailed. Sacajawea translated her brother's Shoshone terms into Minataree, which her husband Charbonneau understood. He in turn spoke French to a French-speaking member of the Corps, who then translated the terms into English for Lewis and Clark. However circumlocutious, the translations worked. The Corps traded for 24 horses, and on August 29, 1805, the entire party climbed over Lemhi Pass and the Continental Divide, into Spanish territory.

Lemhi Pass

A drive up the steep, graveled road to Lemhi Pass (elev. 7,373 feet) is a must for any Lewis and Clark buff with a high-clearance vehicle. Turn off Hwy. 324 onto the Lemhi Pass Rd., and follow the road, sometimes more rock than gravel, for about 20 miles. From the top, the Montana/Idaho border, mountains stretch to the west as far as the eye can see. A sign commemorates the Corps' historic ascent and subsequent descent into Idaho.

Just below the crest of the pass, on the Montana side, the state has established **Sacajawea Historical Area,** with picnic facilities and a small campground. Here, where a tiny spring gushes out of the rock only yards from the Continental Divide, Lewis thought he had found the "most distant fountain of the waters of the Mighty Missouri." (It's not; that distinction goes to Hellroaring Creek south of the Red Rock Lakes.) The party of four drank from the spring, and stood astride it "exultingly," thankful to have lived to put a foot on each side of the "heretofore deemed endless Missouri."

Today's visitor will be unable to resist doing the same. Bring a picnic; this is an enchanting spot and you'll want to stretch your legs before bumping back down to the valley. A Forest Service road continues into Idaho; it's quite steep and not advised for cars. Check with the Salmon Ranger Station, tel. (208) 756-2215; sometimes the road is closed due to logging.

Recreation

There's good fishing for trout in Clark Canyon Reservoir, although the barren, treeless setting and the seemingly always under-filled lake are charm-free. The 5,000-acre lake is popular with boaters from Dillon. The Red Rock River just above the lake is good fishing for cutthroat and rainbows.

Practicalities

Dillon is the closest center for amenities, although at the little crossroads of Grant, the Horse Prairie Hilton advertises both beer and welding. There are six free campgrounds on the shores of the Clark Canyon Reservoir.

BANNACK

Bannack is a well-preserved ghost town whose remains commemorate the rich 1862 gold strike on Grasshopper Creek, the scene of some of Montana's most violent early history. Bannack State Park is self-guided and undeveloped; visitors are free to explore this fascinating old territorial capital at will and without threat of gift shops.

History

Prospectors gone bust in the Colorado gold boom came north to southwest Montana, and in 1862 discovered gold at Grasshopper Diggings, about 20 miles west of Dillon. The first of the great Montana booms was on. A sign, written in axle grease, stood at the confluence of the Beaverhead River and Grasshopper Creek:

Tu grass Hop Per digins
30 myle
Keep the trale nex the bluffe.

By winter, a thousand rag-tag adventurers, many refugees from the Civil War, assembled on the banks of Grasshopper Creek. They named their camp Bannack (symptomatically misspelled) for the native Bannock Indians.

When it came to law and order, which the advent of sudden great wealth demanded, early Montanans just faked it. Henry Plummer was a veteran of California and Nevada gold rushes, and his urbane good looks and considerable charm won the trust of Bannack (and later Virginia City) voters who elected him sheriff.

At the same time, Plummer also secretly led a band of road agents of considerable ruthlessness. These ruffians and killers preyed on travelers, authorities, Indians, and anyone else who got in their way. Bannack in 1863 was the West of Hollywood: gunfights in the street, men gunning each other down over cards, strangers killing strangers for the way they looked. Especially at risk were travelers between Bannack and Virginia City; stage robberies were customary; cold-blooded murder frequent.

Even for the Wild West, violence in Bannack was excessive: during the first year of Plum-

W.C McRAE

Bannack, Montana's first capitol, is one of the state's best-preserved ghost towns.

mer's stint as sheriff, the Innocents, as he called his gang, killed over 100 men. As many deaths probably went unreported; in a gold camp of several thousand miners, the summer's orgy of lawless killings claimed a significant percentage of the population.

Once Grasshopper Creek froze up, and panning ceased for the winter, outraged citizens decided to take the law into their own hands. A secret alliance of men formed a Vigilance Committee, and codified their own set of laws and punishment (invariably death), a secret oath, and their cabalistic secret number 3-7-77, with which they marked their victims.

The vigilantes moved quickly. In a period of two weeks, 24 of Plummer's gang were summarily hanged. Plummer's last words were "Give me a good drop."

The experience of lawlessness enforced the need for a stronger civil authority. In 1864, the miners in Bannack and Alder Gulch sent Judge Sidney Edgerton to petition the U.S. Government for territorial status, which the Senate granted and President Lincoln signed on May 26. Bannack became the first territorial capital when Edgerton convened the first legislature here; his house became the first Governor's Mansion.

Bannack's prominence had already begun to fade as the far richer colors of Alder Gulch attracted upwards of 10,000 miners by 1864. The territorial capital followed the miners to Virginia City. Little remained of Bannack by 1890.

Bannack State Park

Over 60 structures remain standing at Bannack. The streets, homes, hotels, and civic buildings extend along Grasshopper Creek in various stages of disrepair. The entire park is self-guided: explore at will, being careful of dubious stairways and decrepit second stories. The old hotel is rumored to be the most photographed site in Montana. Other buildings of note are the Governor's Mansion, the Masonic Hall, jail, and Methodist Church. The third weekend of July is Bannack Days at the state park. Events include a black-powder shoot, horse and wagon rides, and a buffalo steak barbecue. Call 834-3413 for details.

Entry is $2 per vehicle, and is open all year in good weather, daylight to dark. Call 834-3413 for more information. To reach Bannack, turn off Hwy. 278 and follow a good gravel road for three miles. From the south, Bannack can be reached from Hwy. 324 at Grant, 11 miles along a gravel road.

Practicalities

The closest lodgings and food are in Dillon, 25 miles east. There are two campgrounds at Bannack State Park.

DILLON

Even if Dillon (pop. 8,424, elev. 5,057 feet) weren't the center of a vast region of broad fertile valleys filled with old ranches and rushing streams brimming with trout; even if Dillon weren't surrounded by national forests and wildlife refuges; and even if Dillon wasn't close to the crossroads of Lewis and Clark, Chief Joseph, Henry Plummer, and a territory's worth of early miners and ranchers, Dillon would deserve the traveler's attention.

Dillon is an authentic old trade town that has managed to endure the recent economic malaise of the agricultural West without facing extinction or resorting to survival as a self-parody for tourists. Filled with historic architecture but kept young by the presence of students at Western Montana College, blessed with fine restaurants, and faithful to the old bars that—then, as now—have consoled cowboys, sheepherders, and miners, Dillon is one of Montana's most bewitching small cities. There may be more urbane entertainment in Helena or Missoula, but in its unassuming way, Dillon keeps itself—and the complicit traveler—happily bemused.

HISTORY

Dillon began in 1880 as the northern terminus for the narrow-gauge Utah and Northern Railroad as it pushed into Montana to service the mines of Butte. Within a year, prosperous Dillon petitioned to take seat of enormous Beaverhead County from Bannack. The railroad brought a boom to the nascent cattle and sheep industries in the broad valleys that ringed the new city. Rich ranchers soon built mansions in Dillon, and invested in commercial ventures. Gold, lead, and silver miners, in their on-again, off-again fashion, found a better market for the metals along the new rail corridor, and frequented businesses in the new town.

By 1893, Dillon was prominent enough to attract the State Normal School, provided for by the third legislative assembly. The first building, a magnificent Queen Anne extravaganza, was completed in 1897.

Dillon was for many years the railhead for the state's largest wool-producing area, as sheep were especially well suited to the high mountain valleys of southwestern Montana. Irrigated farming, and cattle and sheep ranching, remain the economic backbone of Dillon.

SIGHTS

Historic Dillon
For a city of its size, Dillon has an array of architectural styles. The Beaverhead County Museum provides a free brochure, "Historical Tour of Dillon," covering many of the local curiosities.

Some highlights: the **Beaverhead County Courthouse,** Pacific and Bannack streets, was built in 1889 and contains a four-faced Seth Thomas clock in its tower. The **Dillon Tribune Building,** Bannack and Idaho streets, housed Dillon's first newspaper; the 1888 facade is made entirely of pressed metal. One of the grandest of all the old hotels in Montana is **Metlen Hotel** built in 1897 as "one of the best, if not the best, constructed edifices in the state." A little down on its luck today, the Metlen is still an imposing monument to the era of grandiose railroad hotels.

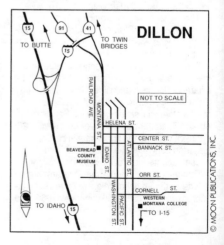

"Old Main," Western Montana College

Orr Mansion, at the south end of Idaho St., is flanked by estates of other early entrepreneurs. William Orr was a California cattleman who brought his herd north to the Beaverhead country in 1862. Success was more or less immediate, and by 1864, Orr began to build his Italianate villa.

At the **Beaverhead County Museum,** 15 S. Montana St., tel. 683-5027, a towering Alaskan brown bear (mounted, of course) oversees the exhibits of Indian artifacts, early ranching curios, and mining memorabilia.

Western Montana College
Of The University Of Montana
The 34-acre State Normal School, established to train teachers for Montana's classrooms, was established in Dillon in 1893. The original structure, added to in 1907, forms Old Main, an imposing and distinctive brick edifice incorporating eclectic design elements, ranging from Gothic tracery windows to Queen Anne towers.

Recent economic circumscriptions by the state Board of Regents have forced the college to affiliate with the University of Montana in Missoula. Western Montana College specializes in training prospective teachers for Montana's rural schools. It also organizes the state's Elderhostel program. The campus switchboard can be reached at 683-7011; the mailing address is 710 S. Atlantic, Dillon, MT 59725.

PRACTICALITIES

Lodging
The Creston Motel, 335 N. Atlantic, tel. (406) 683-2341, $22 s, $26 d, is clean and comfortable, and within walking distance to downtown. Up the street near the college is the **Crossroads Motel,** 1004 S. Atlantic, tel. 683-2378, $29 d; there's a restaurant next door.

Undoubtedly the most famous hostelry in Dillon is the **Metlen Hotel,** 5 S. Railroad Ave., tel. 683-2335. Built in 1897, the Metlen has somehow endured, mostly as a residential hotel. It's a grand old white three-story, block-square building, with neon tracery in the windows and a general—and delicious—sense of over-ripe datedness. If for no other reason, travelers should support this anachronism of a hotel (the downstairs bar notwithstanding) simply because it still exists. Bathroom-down-the-hall doubles begin at $16.

Other accommodation options involve less history but more comfort. The **Best Western Paradise Inn,** 650 N. Montana, tel. 683-4214, $36 s, $42 d, is Dillon's plushest lodging, with a pool and restaurant. The **Town House Inn,** 450 N. Interchange, tel. 683-6831, $33 s, $37 d, also has a pool. The **Super 8,** 550 N. Montana, tel. 683-4288, $33 s, $39 d, and the **Sundowner Motel,** 500 N. Montana, tel. 683-2940, $27 s,

$31 d, contiguously offer several hundred rooms. If you're heading to Twin Bridges, the **Sacajawea Motel**, 775 N. Montana, tel. 683-2381, $25 d, is on your way.

If you want to go native, stay at a guest ranch. The **Beaverhead Ranch,** run by Gary and Sonia Williams at 4325 Old Stage Rd., Dillon, MT 59725, tel. 683-2126, and **Hildreth Livestock Ranch,** with Henry and Trudi Hildreth, P.O. Box 149, Dillon, MT 59725, tel. 681-3111, are both working ranches that welcome travelers.

Camping

The **Dillon KOA,** 735 W. Park, tel. 683-2749, has a pool. The **Southside RV Park,** exit 62, right on Poindexter, tel. 683-2244, has a lovely location on Blacktail Deer Creek. The **Bureau of Reclamation campground** at Barretts, five miles south on the frontage road, sits right on the Beaverhead River as it leaves its canyon. North of Dillon, on old Hwy. 91, **Skyline Trailer Court and Campground,** tel. 683-4692, offers fishing and miniature golf.

Food

Dillon's best meal is served at **Bannack House**, 33 E. Bannack St., tel. 638-5088, whose Italian specialties are welcome and delicious, and whose wine list is lengthy; lunch 11-2, dinner 4-11, closed Mondays. **The Lion's Den**, 725 N. Montana, tel. 683-2051, is a supper club serving steaks and seafood; there's dancing later in the evening. The best pizza in town is at **Pappa T's,** 10 N. Montana, tel. 683-6432.

The **Paradise Inn Restaurant**, 660 N. Montana, tel. 683-6422, has an eclectic menu well based in beef.

For a memorable breakfast or lunch, crowd into the **Metlen Café,** tel. 683-2335, in the back of the Metlen Hotel, 5 S. Railroad. The food is good and abundant, and you get to watch expert fry cooks at work. If breakfast pastries or light meals are more your style, try **Anna's Oven**, 120 S. Montana, tel. 683-5766, a bakery with coffee, rolls, and sandwiches to go.

RECREATION

You can't swing a cat in Dillon without bumping up against great recreation opportunities. Dillon is the natural hub for the entire southwestern corner of Montana, where fishing, hiking, hunting, camping, and exploring the outdoors in general are incarnated in rich abundance.

Fishing

The races and runnels that form the fabric of the Jefferson River are all legendary, highly productive fisheries. The Beaverhead River forms below Clark Canyon Dam; between here and Dillon is some of the most challenging and satisfying trout fly-fishing in Montana. Much of this fast-flowing river is fished best by floating; during high flows, travelers should consider enlisting the aid of outfitters. Of course, one river does not an anglers' paradise make: the Ruby, Big Hole, and Red Rock rivers, not to mention the mountain streams that feed them, are all within easy casting distance from Dillon. Don't miss Blacktail Deer Creek, just southeast of Dillon, for more leisurely, streamside fishing for brookies and cutthroat.

Hiking

With the Continental Divide arrayed around the perimeter of southwestern Montana, it's no wonder there's great hiking and camping just about everywhere that's uphill. A Beaverhead National Forest map reveals hikes in every direction, but there are a few isolated ranges that avid hikers should try to visit.

The Snowcrest Range contains rugged and seldom-visited 10,000-foot peaks, with large populations of elk and mountain goats. The mountains divide the Ruby, Red Rock, and Blacktail Deer drainages, in a remote area. The Snowcrests are about 20 miles southeast of Dillon along Blacktail Deer Creek Road. Even more remote and rugged are the mountains at the head of Big Sheep Creek (turn west at the Dell exit, 45 miles south of Dillon, and follow signs for Big Sheep Canyon).

Between the Beaverhead Mountains (guardians of the Continental Divide) and the Tendoy Mountains fan out the tributaries of Big Sheep Creek. Trails lead up to glaciated valleys and knife-edge ridges along the Montana-Idaho border. Check with the Forest Service office in Dillon for details.

Outfitters

All of the following provide guided fishing excursions on local rivers, and most offer lodging and hunting trips: **Beavertail Outfitters,** Dennis and Jerry Jo Rehse, 2590 Carrigan Ln., Dillon, MT 59725, tel. 683-6232. **Dave Wellborn, Outfitter,** 775 Medicine Lodge Rd., Dillon 59725, tel. 681-3117; he also offers excursions on mountain bikes. **Diamond Hitch Outfitters,** Robert McNeill, 3405 Ten Mile Rd., Dillon, MT 59725, tel. 683-5494; the McNeills offer backcountry pack trips. **Frontier Anglers,** Tim Tollett, Box 11, Dillon, MT 59725, tel. 683-5276. **Last Best Place Tours,** Graeme McDougal, 11805 Hwy. 324,

Dillon, MT 59725, tel. 681-3131; offers a number of adventure trips throughout Montana.

INFORMATION AND SERVICES

The **chamber of commerce** is at 15 S. Montana, Dillon, MT 59725, tel. (406) 683-5511. The **Dillon City Library** is at 121 S. Idaho, tel. 683-4544. The **Clean Critter Laundromat** is at 230 N. Montana, tel. 683-4010.

Emergency is 911. **Barrett Memorial Hospital,** tel. 683-2323, is at 1260 S. Atlantic.

The **Dillon Ranger District,** Beaverhead National Forest, is at 610 N. Montana, Dillon, MT 59725, tel. 683-3900. The **BLM** office is at 1005 Selway Dr., Dillon, MT 59725, tel. 683-2337.

Transportation

Greyhound buses connect Dillon with Butte and Idaho Falls. The depot is at 17 E. Bannack, tel. 683-2344.

ALDER GULCH AND THE RUBY RIVER VALLEY

At Virginia City in Alder Gulch prospectors stumbled onto one of the richest gold strikes in history. The settlement that sprang up, once called "Fourteen-mile City" for its attenuated slouch down the steep gulch, became the second capital of Montana Territory. Virginia City has survived as other gold camps have not; it is still the governmental seat of Madison County, and amongst the deserted buildings are shops, hotels, and restaurants that belie its guise of a ghost town.

HISTORY

In 1863, one year after the first big gold strike in Montana, a group of prospectors led by Bill Fairweather left Bannack for the Yellowstone Valley. En route, they were harried by Crow Indians and turned back. After pitching camp in the Gravelly Range, the prospectors decided to pan for tobacco money. Their panning turned up rich color, and the miners realized they had discovered a major gold deposit at Alder Gulch.

They vowed to keep silent about their claims, but after they returned to Bannack, their free-spending ways drew the attention of other prospectors. When they started back to Alder Gulch, hundreds of miners followed them, each hoping to cash in on the presumed new strike. Within a year, 10,000 hopefuls lived in settlements along Alder Gulch.

Gold Camp

The tremendously rich gold-bearing gravels of Alder Gulch lay beneath a considerable weight of overburden. Shafts and tunnels had to be dug and the gravel hoisted out to the surface. The gravel was then shoveled into a "rocker," where water sloshed away lighter materials while the gold nuggets tumbled into baffles on the bottom of the device. If the claim was near streams, water could be diverted into sluice boxes. Dozens of miners could work along a sluice, sometimes hundreds of feet long. During the first five years of mining operations in Alder Gulch, an estimated $40 million was extracted, and by 1928 the total exceeded $100 million, with gold at $16 an ounce.

Although Bannack came first as a gold camp, Virginia City is Montana's first incorporated town; as the gold at Bannack played out quickly, mining continued at Virginia City. When the second territorial congress convened in 1865, it met at the state's population center, Virginia City, thereby elevating it to territorial capital. It remained so until 1875.

When Montana became a territory in 1864, an official court system was put in place, though vigilantes retaliated against presumed wrong-doers for several more years. Other institutions soon followed: the state's first school district was established in Virginia City in 1866.

After miners removed the richest deposits of gold in Alder Gulch, more advanced technology allowed the processing of low-grade ore and tailing from early mining to extract trace deposits. The large berms of gravel at the little town of Alder reveal the debris of gold-dredging operations from the early 1900s. Although gold-seekers still pan for gold, and mines south of Virginia City produce gold and silver, the talc mines in the Ruby Range are now the area's largest operations.

VIRGINIA CITY AND NEVADA CITY

Montana's second territorial capital (pop. 142, elev. 5,760 feet) is that oxymoronic anomaly, a working ghost town. Five streets of original and restored buildings from the 1860s and '70s define the town, which led to Virginia City's designation as a national historic landmark in 1962. But the town never died. Virginia City is still the county seat, and behind its false fronts and log-frame structures, cafés and shops serve locals year-round.

Sights

Virginia City is best thought of as an open-air museum of the early mining West. While strolling along the board sidewalks, poke into the old buildings. Those that aren't currently in business have been restored and contain artifacts of the boom years of Alder Gulch. Most of the following structures lie along Wallace Street, now Hwy. 287.

The **Madison County Courthouse** built in 1876 still serves as the seat of local government. The territorial offices were housed on the second floor of **Content Corner** building. The **Montana Post Building,**with its display of printing equipment, was home to Montana's first newspaper. Within **Vigilante Barn** the Montana vigilante movement was supposedly born.

The **Pioneer Bar** is an authentic restoration of a mining-era watering hole. The **Bale of Hay Saloon** contains period mechanical peep shows. The **Masonic Temple,** built of cut stone, still houses lodge meetings. The **Madison County Museum** contains artifacts from the Alder Gulch mining days, including furniture, clothing, and photos, and a collection of barbed wire. The **Thompson-Hickman Memorial Museum and Library,** tel. 843-5346, contains the preserved club foot of a desperado and other vigilante mementos, as well as ore samples and mining equipment.

Other buildings have been restored to serve their original purposes, as barbershops, grocery stores, and other small business of an early mining camp-cum-state capital.

A short walk south on Jackson Street leads to **Alder Gulch Discovery Monument,** which commemorated the original gold strike of 1863. North on Fairweather Street about half a mile to a bluff above town is the **Boothill Cemetery.** Here are buried three road agents who were hanged by vigilantes during their brief tour of duty. Bill Fairweather was buried here until re-interred in a new cemetery with more law-abiding

neighbors. Fairweather maintained the respect of the citizens of Alder Gulch by riding along Wallace Street, scattering gold dust for children and the less fortunate. From Boothill there is also a good view of Alder Gulch.

Montana's oldest summer stock theater group, the **Virginia City Players,** perform at two of Alder Gulch's historic buildings. As the **Opera House,** they perform period melodramas and comedies. Tickets are $10 adults, $5 children; the theater is open June 8-Sept. 7; shows start at 8 p.m. At the **Gilbert Brewery** the Players host a vaudeville variety show. Now restored as a bar, Montana's first brewery provides musical cabaret June 21-Sept. 14. Admission to the show is $8 adult, $5 children. For more information on the Virginia City Players, call 843-5377.

Credit for the restoration of Virginia City belongs to Charles and Sue Bovey, who worked hard in the 1940s to preserve the old frontier town. They bought many of the dilapidated buildings and restored them to their original condition. Heirs of the Boveys are threatening to sell the properties due to the high cost of insurance and upkeep. Owners of a California theme park are reportedly interested in acquiring the buildings and moving them there to enhance the park's verisimilitude. The National Park Service is negotiating to buy the property.

Accommodations And Food

The **Fairweather Inn,** 305 W. Wallace St., tel. (406) 843-5377, $28 s, $42 d, is a lovingly restored Victorian hotel. Rooms go fast, so call ahead for reservations. It is open from June to mid-September only. Virginia City's two bed and breakfast inns are open year-round in National Historic Register Homes: The **Virginia City Country Inn,** 115 E. Idaho, tel. 843-5515, and the **Stonehouse Inn,** 306 E. Idaho, tel. 843-5504, both offer lodging in restored and period-furnished rooms; doubles begin at $40.

The **Virginia City Campground,** tel. 843-5493, just east of Virginia City, offers mini-putt golf and gold panning for the kids.

The **Virginia City Café,** 210 W. Wallace, tel. 843-9997, is open for lunch only. The **Morning Sun Restaurant,** 118 W. Wallace, tel. 843-9998, is open 8 a.m.-5 p.m. Other establishments close during the winter.

Nevada City

Virginia City's sister city one mile downstream grew up in the boom days of placer mining in Alder Gulch. Abandoned by the 1880s, the ghost town was restored in the 1950s by Charles and Sue Bovey, the driving force behind Virginia City's renovation. The Boveys brought in period buildings from other ares of Montana, creating an outdoor museum of early mining in Montana.

In addition to restored shops and businesses, the **Alder Gulch Short Line Steam Railroad Museum** contains a collection of rolling stock and engines from the early days of railroading. The $5 admission includes fare on the narrow-gauge rail line running between Nevada and Virginia cities. Also of interest is the **Nevada City Music Hall,** which houses an astonishing collection of old mechanical music machines. Check behind the Nevada City Hotel to glimpse the renowned two-story outhouse.

Practicalities: The **Nevada City Hotel and Cabins,** tel. 843-5377, $38 s, $50 d, is an authentic hostelry restored with an eye to modern comforts. The front part of the log hotel was a stage stop during the gold boom. The cabins are original miners' lodgings.

The **Star Bakery Restaurant** is a charming little café for light meals. Amenities in Nevada City are open from June to mid-Sept. only.

RUBY RIVER VALLEY

During the 1860s and '70s, the stage route called the Vigilante Trail ran from Alder Gulch down the Ruby River to Twin Bridges, and thence to Bannack or Helena. Thievery along this route led to the establishment of the Vigilantes. Here, too, traders and farmers began communities that would outlast the mining boom.

The Ruby River rises in the gentle peaks north of Red Rock Lakes. Native Americans called the Ruby Passamari, or "Stinking Water," for the sulfur springs along its banks. The Ruby River, later named for the deceptive red garnets that early settlers mistook for rubies, is interred at Ruby Reservoir, where much of its flow is diverted into irrigation canals.

Alder

After low-tech placer mining extracted the richest gold deposits along Alder Gulch, gold dredges were brought in to rework the displaced, lower-grade gravel. The banks of pebbles at Alder are the remains of this process.

Dredging in the Ruby Valley reached its height during WW I, when Harvard University sponsored the operations. Sixty years later, the banks of dredged gravel remain unreclaimed and unproductive.

The Northern Pacific built a branch line from Whitehall to Alder in the early 1900s to take out the dredged gold and other precious metals from the nearby hills. Today, talc mines in the Ruby Range are the area's most important mining operations. Watch for the white mounds near railroad sidings.

At Alder, a gravel road leads south seven miles to Ruby Reservoir. There is a free campground, and when the lake's not drawn down by irrigation, boating and fishing. Keep an eye out for garnets. A fair gravel road (eventually becoming Forest Service Rd. 100) continues up the Ruby River, where better fishing and great vistas reward the off-road enthusiast. About 20 miles from Ruby Reservoir is a Forest Service campground, called Cottonwood Camp. Forest Service Rd. 100 enters the Red Rock Valley just above the Red Rock Lake game refuge.

Accommodations And Food

The **Virginia City KOA**, tel. (406) 842-5677, is in fact just east of Alder, and is open to campers all year. A number of guest ranches service anglers, hunters, and outdoor recreationists. The **Buckboard Guest Ranch**, Box 136, Alder, MT 59710, tel. 842-5384, is a working cattle ranch that provides lodging and guide services to anglers, photographers, and hunters on the upper Ruby River. **Tate's Upper Canyon Guest Ranch**, Box 109, Alder, MT 59710, tel. (800) 735-6514, operates a lodge for anglers, hikers, and horseback riders.

The **Alder Steakhouse and Bar**, tel. 842-5159, open 4-10 p.m. daily, is the local supper club.

Laurin

Laurin preserves a hint of this tiny community's Gallic genesis in its pronunciation: with little apparent respect for the original French, you say Law-RAY. Jean Baptiste Laurin established a trading post and stage stop along the banks of the Ruby River in the late 1860s, and eventually amassed large agricultural holdings in the area.

Virginia City and Alder Gulch

W.C. McRAE

Laurin built St. Mary's Church, a handsome and substantial Catholic church constructed of local stone, as a gift to the town he founded.

The **Vigilante Inn**, tel. 842-5982, is Laurin's sole restaurant, serving breakfast and lunch.

Robber's Roost

Three miles downriver from Laurin, along the old stage route between Alder Gulch and Bannack, is the roadhouse and bar once known as Pete Daly's Place. This log two-story bar and dance hall was built in 1863 and became associated with Henry Plummer and his band of ne'er-do-wells. After two outlaws were lynched by vigilantes nearby, Pete's Place became known as Robber's Roost. Bullet holes in the walls attest to the character of the Alder Gulch bar scene.

A full-length porch with hitching rail gives onto the first-floor bar and gambling hall; upstairs was the dance floor. On the veranda, dancers could catch a breath of air or desperados could plot mayhem, as the situation demanded.

Robber's Roost now sits in the yard of a private farm. It's open to the public as an antique store-cum-museum. Call 842-5304 for details.

Sheridan

Sheridan (pop. 652, elev. 5,079 feet) was established in 1866 as mining spread from Alder Gulch northeast to the Tobacco Root Mountains. Sheridan grew into a prosperous trade center for miners and ranchers, reflected in the handsome period storefronts.

Accommodations And Food

Established in 1878, the **Ruby Hotel**, 110 N. Main, tel. (406) 842-5710, is a charming old brick hotel with second-story balconies; rooms begin at $14. A more modern alternative is the **Mariah Motel**, 220 S. Main, tel. 842-5491, $32 d. **Zak's Inn Guest Ranch**, 2905 Hwy. 287, Sheridan, MT 59749, tel. 842-5540, offers access to fishing and other outdoor activities in the lower Ruby Valley.

In the basement of the Ruby Hotel, the **Sump Saloon** serves sandwiches and light meals. The **Sheridan Bakery and Café**, 201 S. Main, tel. 842-5716, open 7 a.m.-4 p.m., closed Sun., is a friendly diner with home-baked goods. The **Log Cabin Café**, tel. 684-5252, open for three meals a day, lies between Twin Bridges and Sheridan.

INFORMATION

Contact the **Virginia City Chamber of Commerce** at P.O. Box 67, Virginia City, MT 59759, tel. (406) 843-5377.

Contact the **Sheridan Chamber of Commerce** at P.O. Box 613, Sheridan, MT 59749. The **Sheridan Ranger District Office** of the Beaverhead National Forest is at P.O. Box 428, Sheridan, MT 59749, tel. 842-5432.

The **Madison County Sheriff** can be reached at 843-5351. The **Ruby Valley Hospital** is at 220 E. Crofoot, Sheridan, tel. 842-5453. Dial 494-3666 for **road conditions**.

THE JEFFERSON RIVER VALLEY

At Twin Bridges, the Jefferson River collects its mighty tributaries—the Big Hole, Beaverhead, and Ruby rivers—and flows north to its appointment with the Missouri at Three Forks. For much of this 80-mile journey, the Jefferson and its valley are open, wide, and relaxed, as if they too enjoy the spectacular mountain scenery rising above them. The ragged peaks of the Tobacco Root and Highland mountains contain granite intrusions that are cousins to the mineral-rich formations near Butte.

The Jefferson's deep holes and brushy banks which hampered Lewis and Clark's journey upriver now excite sportsmen. Brown trout of storied size lurk in the shade of the overgrowth, and river floaters, more captivated by the rugged mountain scenery than challenged by the current, enjoy the river's leisurely pace.

East of LaHood, the river drops into the Jefferson Canyon. Stop and watch for bighorn sheep along the high sheer cliffs. In a limestone formation high on the side of the canyon are the Lewis and Clark Caverns, one of the largest developed cavern systems in the nation.

HISTORY

After Lewis and Clark ascended to Three Forks in 1805, their journey then became a series of conjectures about which river fork, and fork of forks, to follow to the Continental Divide. At Three Forks, the Corps chose the Jefferson. They could have saved themselves hundreds of miles of rambling in the upper Jefferson drainages if they had heeded Charbonneau's advice and traveled up Pipestone Creek, near Whitehall. They would have surmounted the Continental Divide in 20 miles, and found themselves in the Columbia River drainage.

Near Twin Bridges, the captains chose to follow the Beaverhead River. A few miles upstream, Sacajawea recognized Beaverhead Rock, an immense limestone outcropping rising above the river, as a landmark for her people, the Shoshone.

One of the most stirring stories of the Montana frontier involves John Colter, a member of the Corps, who could have little imagined the conditions under which he would next see the Jefferson. Colter didn't return to St. Louis with the rest of the Corps in 1806, preferring to stay in Montana and lead the life of a mountain man.

In 1808, while trapping on the lower Jefferson with a companion, Blackfeet Indians ordered them ashore, immediately killing the other trapper. Colter was stripped of his clothing and given a 200-yard headstart in a footrace for his life. After killing his closest pursuer with a stolen spear, Colter dived into the Jefferson and hid beneath a shelter of driftwood and overgrowth. The Blackfeet searched the area, prodding the brushy riverbank with spears. Colter remained in the river until nightfall, when the Blackfeet abandoned their search.

Barefoot and in the buff, Colter started up the Gallatin River, crossed the Bozeman Pass, and followed the Yellowstone River to its confluence with the Bighorn. Colter covered 300 miles in seven days, living on berries and seeds. When he arrived at Fort Remon, his fellow trappers especially noted his sunburned hide—and his appetite.

The gold rush of the 1860s produced the inevitable smattering of gold camps in the Jefferson Valley, with towns like Silver Star booming when the gold market allowed. Marble quarries and open-pit talc mines have proved to be more resilient, and more profitable. The real economic vitality of the region derives from the ranches that spread across this wide valley.

The little crossroads of LaHood is named for Shadan LaHood, a Lebanese immigrant who moved to Montana in 1902. After a few years of selling dry goods to settlers from his horse-drawn wagon, he established a general store along the Jefferson River. LaHood Park, at the site of the original store, became the first Civilian Conservation Corps camp in the nation.

LEWIS AND CLARK CAVERNS

Leave I-90 at Three Forks or Whitehall and follow back roads through the Jefferson River Canyon for a scenic loop-road alternative to the freeway. The quickening pace of the river as it cuts through walls of steeply tilted sedimentary rock makes this a popular expedition for floaters.

High on the north side of the canyon, in a vein of exposed limestone, is Lewis and Clark Caverns State Park, on Hwy. 10, 19 miles west of Three Forks, or 13 miles east of Whitehall. When a ramrod of granite magma thrust up the Tobacco Root Mountains about 70 million years ago, sedimentary layers laid down hundreds of millions of years earlier rose to flank the new mountains in steeply pitched strata. In an exposed face of Madison Limestone, rainwater began to erode into the porous rock. Many millions of years later, water has cut 3,000-foot-long chambers and passageways, 300 feet below the surface, making this the third-largest cavern in the U.S.

Water carrying minute traces of minerals has stained the many stalagmites and stalactites into wonderful colors. Fanciful minds have assigned the caverns' rich abundance of exotic formations theme chambers, with such names as Hell's Highway, the Lion's Den, and the Organ Room.

Guided tours are offered 9 a.m.-7 p.m., June 15-Labor Day. From May 1 to June 14 and from Labor Day to Sept. 30, tours are offered 9 a.m.-5 p.m. Tickets are $3. Tours last about two hours; visitors should be sure on their feet and ready to negotiate stairs; take a jacket, as the caverns remain at 50° fahrenheit.

The caverns are three miles from the highway. Along the route is a campground, several picnic areas, and a vista point overlooking the Jefferson. Light snacks are available at the visitor center. There is also a self-guided nature trail near the upper picnic area; watch for snakes.

For more information contact Lewis and Clark Caverns, P.O. Box 648, Whitehall, MT 59759, tel. (406) 287-3541.

WHITEHALL AND VICINITY

The town of Whitehall sits along the Jefferson River in the shadow of the main spine of the Rocky Mountains. Originally a stage stop between Helena and Virginia City, Whitehall was named for the large white ranch house of an early settler. The town evolved once the Northern Pacific pushed through in 1889.

Located on the edge of the Boulder Batholith, which provided Butte's legendary mineral wealth, Whitehall saw its share of early prospectors. Not all the riches are historic: two large gold and silver mines still operate in the area.

Accommodations And Food
The **Chief Motel**, 303 E. Legion, tel. (406) 287-3921, $35 d, is a solid older motel along Hwy. 10. The **Rice Motel**, 7 N. A St., tel. 287-3895, $25 d, also offers fishing trips under the name **Cutthroat Outfitters**.

For good food, the best choice is **Land of Magic Too Supper Club**, 27 W. Legion, tel. 287-5252. Open for three meals a day, it specializes in steaks and seafood.

the ever-present
Montana rodeo

TOM VANDEL

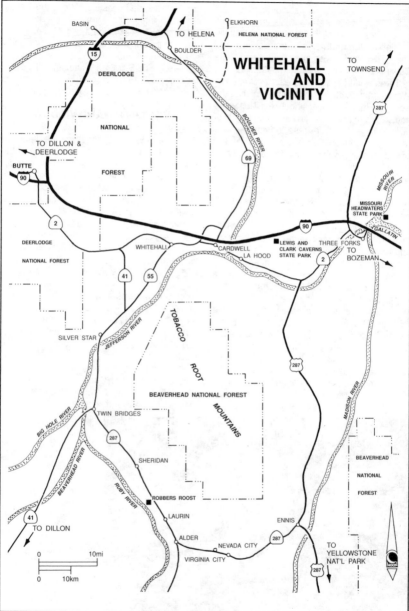

WHITEHALL AND VICINITY

Silver Star

Silver Star has settled into a gentle doze after an eventful early history. One of the oldest settlements in the state, the town's founder, Green Campbell, was issued Montana land patent #1 in 1866. The town sits on the southernmost extreme of the rich Boulder Batholith, and miners extracted hefty amounts of gold, silver, and lead from the Highland Mountains. Silver Star was the only town between Virginia City and Helena during the high-flying 1870s, booming as it serviced the needs of local miners and settlers.

Legend contends that Edward, prince of Wales, spent three days in Silver Star in 1878. It's been pretty much downhill ever since.

Accommodations And Food: The old and highly creditable **Star Bar**, tel. 287-3648, serves a filling lunch and dinner. **Jefferson River Park**, one mile south of Silver Star, tel. 684-5262, is a lovely campground right on the Jefferson River.

TWIN BRIDGES AND VICINITY

Twin Bridges slumbers near the confluence of the Ruby, Beaverhead, and Big Hole rivers. Lewis and Clark rested here before continuing up the Beaverhead. At Three Forks, the captains named the mightiest of the Missouri forks for President Jefferson. At the forks of the Jefferson, they decided to name each for the cardinal virtues of the president: Philanthropy, Philosophy, and Wisdom. Later settlers waxed less poetic, renaming the rivers the Ruby, the Beaverhead, and the Big Hole. History is silent as to whether the later generation considered these attributes of President Jefferson.

With all these rivers about, the mystery is not which two bridges spawned the town's name, but why there were *only* two. Twin Bridges found itself at the center of commerce and transportation for southwestern Montana. By 1884, three daily stagecoaches passed through the town. Reflecting its then centrality, Montana Territory in 1889 built the first normal school in Twin Bridges. After political maneuvering, the state moved the normal college to upstart Dillon in 1893. The school buildings became the State Orphans' Home shortly thereafter. The facility had been home to over 5,000 children before it was closed in 1975. The buildings can be seen just west of town along the road to Dillon.

Accommodations And Food: The somewhat faded **Kings Inn**, 307 S. Main., tel. (406) 684-5639, offers kitchenettes; double rooms begin at $35. The **Blue Anchor Bar and Café**, 102 N. Main, tel. 684-5655, is open for three meals a day. Just outside of Twin Bridges, on the way to Sheridan, is the **Log Cabin Bakery and Café**, 25 Middle Rd., tel. 684-5252.

Beaverhead Rock

Between Dillon and Twin Bridges is Beaverhead Rock, a landmark to settler and Indian alike. The excited Sacajawea recognized the huge outcropping, and told the rest of the Corps that they were in her homeland. Three hundred feet high, it is apparently the leading edge of land thrust eastward by mountain-building to the west.

I-15 CORRIDOR, BUTTE TO HELENA

Between Helena and Butte, I-15 crosses over the Boulder Batholith, an intrusion of magma that shot up from the bowels of the earth like a piston about 70 million years ago. The formation is made largely of granite, but in places it also contains an almost incomprehensible wealth of minerals. Near towns like Clancy and Jefferson City, gold was panned, mined, and dredged. The orderly dikes of processed gravel tailings from streambeds lie like welts across the landscape.

The old town of Boulder lies at the center of this rich mining area. Its spent mines have recently been put to new use. Radon gas, in low concentrations, occurs naturally in the mine-shafts. People who suffer from a variety of ailments—from cancer to asthma to lupus—have found relief descending the mines and breathing the radon-rich air. Called "health mines," these strictly non-AMA approved facilities have become so popular that peak seasons are reserved for weeks in advance.

HISTORY

About 120 years ago, this forlorn piece of non-descript mountain landscape was one of the busiest and most populated in Montana. Rich but diffident deposits of gold first attracted placer miners in the 1860s. Gold camps sprang up in every gulch. After the surface deposits were exhausted, many camps developed into industrial mining towns, as capitalists brought in more highly mechanized techniques to mine and smelt underground silver, lead, and gold. A final reprise of Montana's mining boom years came in the early decades of this century, when gold dredges reworked the tailings from old mines for the trace amounts of gold missed by earlier mining methods. By redigesting mining refuse and stream bottoms in a rich muddy soup, dredges were able to isolate what mineral wealth remained, leaving acres of mine tailings.

Between Helena and Boulder, place names recall important early settlements and boomtowns: Jefferson City, Prickly Pear Gulch, Montana City, Wickes, Corbin—towns that once vied

with Helena and Butte in importance during territorial days. Now, little remains, save a citation in a history book and mounds of worked gravel, these towns long ago having slumped from catalepsy into dilapidation.

Boulder and Basin survived the decline of Montana's mining industry by establishing a somewhat more diversified economy. As early as the 1880s Boulder Hot Springs attracted tourists and weekenders to its spa resort. Boulder was also the trade center for ranchers in the Boulder River Valley. Basin struggled on as a rail center for local gold and silver mines until the 1940s, when the presence of uranium met the demands of a changing world. After a brief flurry of activity, these radium-rich mines became the radon health mines that currently energize the local economy.

BOULDER AND VICINITY

Named for the large stones littered around its valley, Boulder (pop. 1,316, elev. 5,158 feet) began as a stage stop between Fort Benton and Virginia City in the 1860s. Its prominence as a trading center was enhanced when the state built the **Montana Home for the Feeble-minded** here in 1892. Now known as the Montana Development Center, the facility houses and trains developmentally impaired citizens.

Old Boulder
The town center of Boulder, with its sprawl of red-brick storefronts, retains much of the flavor of a frontier commercial center. Its most prominent landmark is the **Jefferson County Courthouse**, built in 1889. Its grand scale and gargoyles betray the German education of John Paulsen, who also designed the administration building for the Home for the Feeble-minded. Both are listed on the National Register of Historic Places.

Boulder Hot Springs
One of the earliest tourist facilities in the state, this resort began in 1883 as a spa for the rich and

influential in Helena and Butte. Over the years, the lodge has been redesigned and reinterpreted in fashionable, ever more grandiose, architectural vernaculars. The earliest wooden-frame hotel was replaced by a Queen Anne clapboard lodge, only to be renovated in Spanish mission style. The imposing lodge at Boulder Hot Springs is undergoing another rejuvenation. No lodging or food is currently available, but the hot pools remain open. Boulder Hot Springs is three miles south of Boulder on Hwy. 69. Direct inquiries to P.O. Box 1020, Boulder, MT 59632, tel. 225-4273.

Elkhorn

The silver-mining town of Elkhorn began in the 1870s, and flourished until the early 1890s, when the international silver market bottomed out. Although only the ghosts of the town remain, Elkhorn is reckoned to be one of the best-preserved mining camps in the state. Buildings of note: **Gillian Hall**, a two-story bar and dance hall; and **Fraternity Hall**, a meetinghouse in neoclassical style. Elkhorn is six miles south of Boulder on Hwy. 69, then 12 miles north on graveled Elkhorn Road. During winter months, the trip is best made on cross-country skis.

Accommodations And Food

Castoria Inn, 211 S. Monroe, tel. (406) 225-3549, dates from 1889 and is listed on the National Register of Historic Places. It currently offers bed and breakfast starting at $29; rooms in the motel are $26 d. The **Linn Motel**, 410 N. Main, tel. 225-3365, $25 d, and the **O-Z Motel**, 114 N. Main, tel. 225-3364, $21 d, are both older motels in the center of historic Boulder.

For campers, there are pleasant RV parks with easy access to fishing in the Boulder River.

RADON GAS HEALTH MINES

In 1950, a California woman who suffered from arthritis accompanied her husband into a uranium mine near Boulder. She noted a marked relief from the constant pain to which she had long grown accustomed. She related her experiences to a fellow arthritis sufferer; her friend's stay in the Boulder mine produced the same rapid recovery.

Word of the "miracle cure" soon spread, reaching an early peak when *Life* magazine sent a news team to cover the "stampede" of people coming to seek this underground cure.

Just why the cure seems to work hasn't been adequately explained. Radon gas is a naturally occurring gas formed when radium, in the process of aging, oxidizes. This radioactive gas occurs in Basin-Boulder mines in levels deemed safe for miners, but in concentrations considered therapeutic by the mines' many promoters. Sympathetic researchers contend that radon gas stimulates the pituitary gland to produce health-giving hormones and natural steroids, which can ease or eradicate the pain of conditions caused by hormonal dysfunction.

The recommended "cure" involves a careful regimen of contact with radon gas. Patrons are asked to spend no more than one hour at a time in the mines, no more than three times per day. About 30 hours of contact with radon gas is considered to be the optimum treatment. Within the mines, there are sofas, tables, and chairs for the visitors' comfort; card games and reading are the usual pastimes.

Radon-gas therapy is *not* medically accepted in the United States; mine owners stress that the mines are open for people seeking *non-medical* treatment. There is no guarantee of cure.

There are, however, many moving testimonials from people who have found relief from aggravated and long-standing afflictions by undergoing a "health mine cure." Indeed, the European medical establishment is less hostile to radon-gas therapy than its North American compatriots. The list of physical conditions for which radon gas may be efficacious grows as the number of afflicted visitors grows. Sufferers of arthritis, migraines, eczema, asthma, diabetes, and allergies have testified to the mines' healing virtues.

If you have questions about the "health mines," contact the **Boulder-Basin Chamber of Commerce,** Box 68, Boulder, MT 59632, or contact the following mines directly: **Free Enterprise Health Mine,** Box 67, Boulder, MT 59632, tel. 255-3383; **Merry Widow Health Mine,** P.O. Box 129, Basin, MT 59631, tel. 255-3220.

Radon therapy is very popular; if you are considering a visit call ahead for reservations, and don't be surprised if the facilities are all booked up.

Try the **Sunset Trailer Court**, Fourth and Adams, tel. 225-3387, or **Phil and Tim's RV Park**, one-quarter mile south of I-15 on Hwy. 69, tel. 225-3370.

Phil and Tim let Vicki run **Vicki's Café,** open 6 a.m.-2 p.m., in **Phil and Tim's Bowling Alley**, tel. 225-3201. Otherwise, try **Mountain Good Restaurant**, tel. 225-3382, open daily 6:30 a.m.-8 p.m.

BASIN

Located in narrow Boulder River Canyon, Basin is an old mining town that has avoided the narcoleptic destiny of many other mining camps. By luck or connivance, Basin always successfully managed to market what it has.

Gold prospectors such as Granville Stuart helped found the community, but it was silver mines that put Basin on the map during the 1880s.

Basin fell into a long doze after a spurt of gold mining during the 1920s, then reactivated

when the uranium market developed during World War II. The radon gas present in many of the old mines is now marketed for its reputed health-giving benefits.

Basin's main street exhibits structures from more prosperous times. The **Masonic Hall** dates from the turn of the century, as does the old boardinghouse in the Sockerson Block. Watch the hillsides near Basin for old flumes and mine adits.

Accommodations And Food

Most of the health mines provide accommodations and campgrounds for their guests. Be sure to reserve ahead. The campground at the **Merry Widow Health Mine**, two blocks off Basin Creek Rd., tel. 225-3220, is open to the public but spaces go quickly.

The Silver Saddle Bar and Café, tel. 225-9995, open 7 a.m.-8 p.m., serves good basic food in an authentic Western atmosphere.

HELENA

Montana's capital city straddles one of history's richest gold strikes—Last Chance Gulch. Unlike its contemporary boomtowns, Helena (pop. 24,569, elev. 4,124 feet) managed not only to survive but to prevail through good times and bad. Like a snake swallowing its tail, Helena transformed itself from seething gold camp to trade center, then to capital city, and finally into a cultural and tourist center.

In Montana, only Butte can approach Helena in sheer historicity, but history has left Helena a richer legacy of monuments and architecture. From the elegance of the state Capitol and the Cathedral of St. Helena to the stone shacks on Reeder's Alley, the highs, lows, and middlings of the state's history each have here their testimony. Excellent museums and galleries present and preserve the best of Montana's past and present.

People in Helena are both insiders and outsiders. The state is by far the city's largest employer, and Helena's bright, friendly character derives in part from internalizing the lessons of political life. Citizens greet you as if they want to be popularly elected. The real politicians are pretty obvious: spot the ill-fitting Western dress jackets, the clumsy handbags and unsensible shoes, and the telltale chummy complicity.

But come the weekend, the insiders go outside. Helena is unbelievably well situated for recreation. With fishing and boating on nearby lakes on the Missouri, hiking and skiing in Helena National Forest, and exploring old ghost towns and other reminders of the past always just nearby, the Helena area tempts the traveler with a rich brew of history and outdoor activity.

HISTORY

Helena began, as did so many other gold camps, as the cry went up, "Just one last chance before we leave." In this case, four Confederate ex-soldiers were panning in 1864 for gold in a narrow gulch called Prickly Pear, just below the crest of the Continental Divide. The "Four Georgians," as they were later known, found color in their pans in the draw they called Last Chance Gulch. Word spread and the rush was on. By 1876, the town had grown to 4,000 inhabitants.

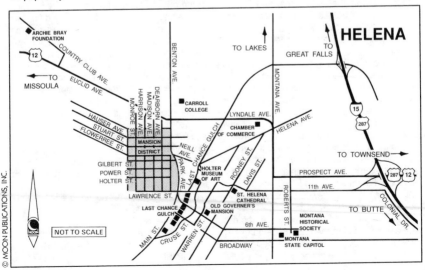

© MOON PUBLICATIONS, INC.

At the time, Montana was a territory lacking a cohesive center. Due to the boom-and-bust nature of its initial settlements, the focal point of Montana moved from strike to strike. The earliest territorial capital of Bannack was almost deserted by the time the center of government moved to Virginia City. In turn, Helena attracted the capital in 1875.

Helena had advantages that the other mining centers lacked. The gold, then the silver and lead, were richer in Helena than in other early settlements. Helena was midway on the stage routes between Fort Benton, the uppermost steamboat reach on the Missouri, and Virginia City and other mining areas in southwestern Montana. Newcomers quickly realized that wealth was in trade, not mining, and gravitated to Helena, the largest center of population in the territory. Trade quickly underpinned mining to support Helena's economy. Sometime miners, now important captains of industry, built huge mansions on the city's west side.

Battle For The Capital

Helena first overtook Virginia City in 1875, when voters chose it to be the territorial capital. The real battle began when Montana was recognized as a state in 1889. The feud between Copper Kings Marcus Daly and William Clark ricocheted across the state. What had been a grudge match of political influence became war as each backed a different city to be capital of the new state of Montana in a statewide election in 1894.

While each of the industrialists had solid power bases in Butte, the wrangle involved Anaconda, the city that Daly built, and the established capital of Helena, where Clark had major mining investments. The attack politics of our time could take lessons from the acrimonious battles of the Copper Kings. Each controlled newspapers; each shamelessly bought and influenced votes. ("It came through the transom" is an expression still used in Montana to explain a windfall gift from a patron.) In the end, Helena only just won the statewide vote, retaining its hold on the capital.

Helena continued to hold sway over the rich and powerful during the late 1890s and early years of the 1900s, as is witnessed by its elaborate architecture of the period. Be they ranchers,

miners, or tradesmen, the rich from across the state hadn't "arrived" until they had engaged in the mansion-building competition that thrived on the west side of Last Chance Gulch. The concentration of wealth in Helena is legendary. In the late 1880s there were more millionaires in Helena per capita that anywhere else in the nation.

The old economic and historical center of Helena is Last Chance Gulch, the main street that winds along Prickly Pear Creek, where original mining claims became building sites as the city evolved from mining to commerce. An urban-renewal project during the 1970s sought to preserve Last Chance Gulch by declaring it a pedestrian zone.

SIGHTS

The Montana State Capitol

The State Capitol, 1301 Sixth Ave., was begun in 1899. This imposing structure, domed with a cupola of Butte copper, was enlarged in 1912 by the extensions containing the present legislative wings. The statue on the dome commemorates an odd episode in Montana history. After the bruising fight for state capital between Helena and Anaconda, the Capitol Commission ran off with the books. When this statue arrived at the railroad station from a foundry in Ohio, no one knew who ordered it, who paid for it, or what it was meant for. The foundry's records were shortly destroyed in a fire, leaving the mysterious statue no history, and no future. The builders of the Capitol needed statuary for the top of its dome, and the *Goddess of Liberty* found its way to the top of the Montana State Capitol.

Significant paintings and murals decorate the Capitol. In the House Chambers hangs *Lewis and Clark Meeting the Flathead Indians at Ross' Hole* by Charley Russell, one of his largest and most acclaimed works. In the lobby of the House of Representatives are six paintings detailing the state's history by E.S. Paxson. Tours of the Capitol are given on the hour, Mon.-Sat. 9 a.m.-5 p.m., Sun. 11-4.

The Capitol Area

Known in local parlance as the East Side, the area around the capitol is directly south of the

Montana state capitol

downtown area and contains many buildings of historic interest.

Probably the first thing a summer visitor should do while in Helena is take the quick city tour offered by **Last Chance Tours,** tel. 442-6880. This open-air tour train does a quick drive-by of most of Helena's historic and scenic properties; the traveler can decide what to explore in further depth. On the route are buildings in the Capitol area, Last Chance Gulch, Reeder's Alley, the mansion district, and Carroll College. Catch the "Last Chancer," as the tour train is nicknamed, just outside the Montana Historical Society at Sixth Ave. and N. Roberts, across the street from the capitol. Tours begin at 9:30 a.m. and continue on the half-hour until 4:30 p.m.; fare is $3.

The **Montana Historical Society,** 225 N. Roberts, tel. 444-2694, is Montana's premier museum, mixing fine art, an exhibit charting the state's history, and changing exhibits. Of special interest is the **MacKay Gallery of Charles M. Russell Art,** one of the nation's largest public collections. If Western art seems like an oxymoron to you, come marvel at the brilliant use of color and composition by this unschooled cowboy artist.

The **Montana Homeland Exhibit** tells the story of Montana, beginning with Indian prehistory and moving on through the era of settlement. Three rooms contain over 2,000 artifacts. Other galleries change exhibits, but often contain fascinating displays of frontier photographs. Of interest to historians and researchers are the **Library and Photo Archives.** Open Mon.-Fri. 8 a.m.-6 p.m., weekends 9 a.m.-5 p.m., Memorial Day-Labor Day; Mon.-Fri. 8 a.m.-5 p.m. and Sat. 9-5 the rest of the year; admission is free.

From 1913-1959, Montana's governor lived at the **Old Governor's Mansion,** 304 N. Ewing, tel. 444-2694. Built in 1883 by a local entrepreneur, the 20-room residence is now owned by the Montana Historical Society, which has restored the ornate building to its historic splendor. Free tours operate on the hour, 9 a.m.-5 p.m.

The **Cathedral of St. Helena,** 509 N. Warren, tel. 442-5825, was begun in 1908 but wasn't finished until 1924. Modeled after the Cologne Cathedral, Helena's bishopric dominates the skyline with its 230-foot twin spires. Its stained glass was fashioned in Germany, although the images of the Seven Sacraments seem out of a Burne-Jones Pre-Raphaelite painting. The cathedral is open to visitors 9-5, unless services are taking place. Free tours are available, call 442-5825.

Last Chance Gulch

In the 1860s, Prickly Pear Creek snaked down from the mountains through a thicket of mining claims called Last Chance Gulch. As mining gave way to commerce, the gulch remained the main street; its winding path, and especially the one-claim-sized business buildings, still reflect its mining past. The old business district of Helena

HELENA AREA ACCOMMODATIONS

Name	Address	Phone	Rates	Features
Best Western Colonial Inn	2301 Colonial Dr.	443-2100	$50 s, $56 d	Helena's most lavish
Days Inn	2001 Prospect Dr.	(800) 325-2525, 442-3280	$35 s, $40 d	
Econo Lodge	524 Last Chance Gulch	442-0600	$26 s, $34 d	right downtown
Jorgenson's Holiday Motel	1714 11th Ave.	442-1770	$29 s, $34 d	restaurant
Lamplighter Motel	1006 Madison	442-9200	$23 s, $26 d	
King's Rest Motel	1831 Euclid	442-6384	$28 s, $33 d	off Hwy. 12 W
Park Plaza Hotel	22 N. Last Chance Gulch	(800) 332-2290, 443-2200	$48 s, $53 d	downtown's best
Motel 6	800 N. Oregon	442-9990	$24 s, $31 d	pool
Shilo Inn	2020 Prospect	(800) 222-2244, 442-0320	$47 s, $53 d	pool
Kozy Motel	836 W. Jackson	442-4570	$23 s, $25 d	
Helena Super 8	2201 11th Ave.	(800) 848-8888, 443-2450	$35 s, $41 d	
Alladin's Coach House East	2101 11th Ave.	443-2300	$36 s, $39 d	indoor pool
The Sanders Bed and Breakfast	328 N. Ewing	442-3309	$46-70	historic 1875 B&B, nonsmoking
Upcountry Inn	2245 Head Ln.	442-1909	$40-50	rural location; restaurant

is still impressive, even after a 1933 earthquake destroyed some of its buildings.

Much of Last Chance Gulch is now a pedestrian mall, designed to make this historic main street more attractive to tourists and business. Have a look at the handsome, empty storefronts and decide if it has worked.

The extensive infrastructure of historic business buildings in Helena prove that the capital's most significant occupation was commerce, not mining. Several walking-tour maps to the Last Chance Gulch area are available from the chamber of commerce and from Downtown Helena, 121 N. Last Chance Gulch, tel. 442-9869. Notable buildings not to miss:

The Power Block, 58-62 N. Last Chance Gulch, was built in 1889; note that on the southeast corner, each of the five floors has a corresponding number of windows. The Securities Building, 101 N. Last Chance Gulch, built in 1886, is a Romanesque former bank with curious carved thumbprints between the first-floor arches. The Montana Club, 24 W. Sixth, was Montana's most prestigious private club: membership was open only to millionaires. The club's present building was designed by Cass Gilbert, who designed the U.S. Supreme Court Building.

The Atlas Building, 7-9 N. Last Chance Gulch, is one of Helena's most fanciful; on a cornice upheld by Atlas, a salamander and lizards do symbolic battle. **Reeder's Alley,** 308 S. Park, is a winding series of one-room brick shanties built in the 1870s to house the mining camp's many bachelors. Today, it's a theme alley dedicated to shops and places to eat.

Visit the Norwest Bank, 350 N. Last Chance Gulch, tel. 447-2000, to see the **Gold Collection,** displaying gold in many forms, from nuggets to leaves.

West Side Mansions

Montana's grandest historic homes grace the hillside above Helena. In an area roughly bounded by Stuart, Monroe, Dearborn, and Power streets stand dozens of imposing monuments to the economic clout of their merchant, mining, or ranching owners. The mansions display a bewildering assortment of styles; Mark Twain described these Helena homes as "Queen Anne in front and Mary Ann behind." In all their opulence, these are what money could buy in Helena during the boom years from 1880-1900.

None of the old homes are regularly open for viewing, but a walk through these beautiful old neighborhoods is a must for anyone with an interest in historic homes.

Downtown Environs

Given all the beautiful architecture in Helena, it is ironic that the city's most distinctive building is the **Civic Center** on the corner of Neill and Fuller, built in 1921 as the Masonic Algeria Shrine Temple. This exercise in high camp is a Moorish revival edifice with a 175-foot minaret, onion dome, and intricately modeled exterior brickwork. It now houses Helena's municipal offices.

Overlooking Helena from the northeast is **Carroll College,** a private Catholic college with a student body of 1,400 students. Carroll stands on 63 acres atop a bluff still known as Capitol Hill. The site was offered for the state capitol in 1895, but the landowner wanted $7000 for the real estate, and the frugal Capitol Commission went elsewhere.

Fort Harrison

Established in 1895, Fort Harrison, just north of Helena on Hwy. 12, was one of the Army's last defensive garrisons against ructions in the West. Although the troops were never called out, the fort remained active through World War I. By 1922, the fort was given over to the Veterans Administration, and turned into a large veterans' health facility. Fort Harrison still operates as a veterans' hospital, but its most interesting buildings are its 1905 officers' quarters. Built of brick, these imposing three-story duplexes boast wide verandas and gabled roofs. Turn-of-the-century Army life in Montana was extremely genteel, judging by these lodgings. Buildings at Fort Harrison are closed to the public.

Frontier Town

Goofy but beguiling at the same time is Frontier Town, 15 miles east of Helena on Hwy. 12, at McDonald Pass, tel. 442-4560, an Old West theme fort built by eccentric second-generation cowboy John Quigley in the 1940s and '50s.

Last Chance Gulch's old mining distirct has been reclaimed as a pedestrian mall.

W.C. McRAE

Quigley was seemingly driven to build this faux frontier village along the Continental Divide: often working alone, he felled trees, raised log buildings, built furniture, and accumulated period furnishings.

The result is Frontier Town, with a main street of shops filled with goods, a chapel that's popular for nuptials, an Indian village, a vast restaurant and bar complex, and a gift shop. It's just as odd as its description. Sit (in stools made of saddles) at the bar (made of one huge Douglas fir log), and toast the obsession of John Quigley. The restaurant serves quite good food, by the way. Open daily 9 a.m.-10 p.m., April to October; admission is $2.

THE ARTS

Theater
Helena is proud of its newest addition to its arts, the **Myrna Loy Center for the Performing Arts,** 15 N. Ewing, tel. 442-0287. Named for the film actress who hailed from the Helena area, the center is housed in the revamped old 1880s jail. A performance space, gallery, and art-film theater (the Second Story Cinema) combine to make this a jewel in Helena's cultural crown.

The **Grandstreet Theatre**, 325 N. Park, tel. 442-4270, is Helena's community theater. Grandstreet works closely with drama students from Carroll College, and conducts a theater school for young people.

Galleries
The **Holter Museum of the Arts**, 12 E. Lawrence, tel. 442-6400, displays changing exhibits of contemporary art, and offers workshops and readings. Summer visitors should check out the Western Rendezvous of Art, a large hanging of noted Western artists' works; in the middle of August, the works go on sale. Open Tues.-Sat. 12-5, Sun. 12-4; free admission.

Several private Western-art galleries range along Last Chance Gulch, including **Ghost Art Gallery,** 21 S. Last Chance Gulch, tel. 443-4536, and **Cason Gallery,** 7 N. Last Chance Gulch, tel. 443-5919.

The **Archie Bray Foundation**, 2915 Country Club Dr., tel. 443-3502, is a studio workshop, classroom, and gallery for ceramic artists. The brickyard and kilns of **Western Clay Manufacturing Company** have stood just outside Helena for over 100 years. Archie Bray, whose father began the business, was approached by local artists to use the brickyard's huge beehive kilns to fire ceramics. Bray, already active in the Helena arts scene, decided to dedicate a portion of the factory to the ceramic arts. In 1951, he founded the Archie Bray Foundation, now a world-famous facility for training talented young potters and a space in which resident artists can experiment and exhibit.

Visitors can watch potters in workshops and view works for sale in the gallery. The old kilns and outbuildings still stand, while avante-garde ceramics, colorful and abstract, are strewn about with guileless abandon.

FOOD

It makes a certain sense, in a town fueled by the business of politics, that there are as many or more good choices for lunch in Helena as for dinner. Clustered in the Last Chance Gulch area are several good restaurants that serve a busy and boisterous lunch clientele. **Bert and Ernie's,** 361 N. Last Chance Gulch, tel. 443-5680, open 11 a.m.-10 p.m., serves a sandwich-dominated menu with a wide selection of beers.

For lunch in a Helena institution, go to the **Rialto,** 52 N. Last Chance Gulch, tel. 442-1890. Try the burger in this venerable old bar with a café up front; the grill is open 11-9. For a deli sandwich, go to **Stove Top Deli,** 42 S. Park, tel. 442-3354.

The **Windbag Saloon**, 19 S. Last Chance Gulch, tel. 443-9669, open 11 a.m.-10 p.m., was a brothel named Big Dorothy's until 1973. With this colorful history, and filled with namesake politicians, the Windbag is one of Helena's unique restaurants. The burgers are the thing for lunch, with steaks on the dinner menu; open 11-2:30 and 5-9:30. With less atmosphere but, as ever, good food at a good price, there's **4-Bs,** 900 N. Last Chance Gulch, tel. 442-2083; open 24 hours.

For a snack or pick-me-up, Helena has good coffee and sweet treats. The **General Mercantile,** 413 N. Last Chance Gulch, open 9-6, serves Italian sodas and espresso coffee drinks. Likewise, if a sojourn in Montana has you longing for decent coffee, address your needs at

Morning Light Coffee Roasters, 503 Fuller, tel. 442-5180, open 7:30 a.m.-10 p.m.

Helena's most famous sweets sanctuary is **Parrot Confectionery,** 42 N. Main, tel. 442-1470, a soda fountain and candy factory that isn't just old-fashioned, but actually *old.* Try the handmade chocolates or a malted milk; the Parrot's sole feint to solid food is its renowned chili; open 9-6. For ice cream, go to the **Ice Cream Parlor,** 718 Logan, tel. 442-0117, open 8 a.m.-11 p.m. It's also a good place to take the kids for a light supper.

Fine Dining

There's also good dining in the downtown area. Northern Italian appears **On Broadway,** 106 Broadway, tel. 443-1929, open 5:30-10 p.m., in a light, airy red-brick atmosphere. The **Stonehouse,** 120 Reeder's Alley, tel. 449-2552, while it remains firmly grounded in good beef, is probably Helena's most innovative restaurant. The Stonehouse is located in an 1890s structure listed on the National Register of Historic Places. Open Mon.-Sat. 11:30 a.m.-2 p.m., Sun.-Thurs. 5-9 p.m. and Fri. and Sat. 5-10 p.m. **Victor's,** in the Park Plaza Hotel, 22 N. Last Chance Gulch, tel. 443-2200, open 6 a.m.-10 p.m., serves an eclectic menu; seating is available on the patio.

If you're up to the drive, the restaurant at **Frontier Town,** 15 miles east of Helena on Hwy. 12, tel. 442-4560, serves tasty re-creations of frontier dishes and of course great steaks. The dining room is open Mon.-Sat. 5-10 p.m., Sun. 1-8 p.m.

RECREATION

Hiking is as close as **Mount Helena,** the city's 620-acre park on the west side of Last Chance Gulch. Seven trails wind up and across the mountainside, some ascend to Mount Helena's 5,468-foot peak, and others dawdle in meadows. To reach the park, follow the ravine behind Reeder's Alley on foot or drive to the top of Adams Street behind the mansion district.

The municipal **swimming pool** is at Memorial Park, 1200 Last Chance Gulch, tel. 449-3483. There're **tennis courts** at the park behind the Civic Center (Neill and Park streets.) and at Barney Park, Cleveland and Hudson streets. Both parks also have picnic facilities and playgrounds.

Holter, Hauser, and Canyon Ferry lakes just to the east of Helena provide excellent fishing, boating, and even windsurfing.

The **Helena KOA Campground,** three miles north on Montana Ave., tel. 458-5110, has a pool and playground.

INFORMATION AND SERVICES

The **Helena Chamber of Commerce** is at 201 E. Lyndale, Helena, MT 59601, tel. (406) 442-4120.

The central **post office** is at 2300 N. Hastings, tel. 443-3304. The **Lewis and Clark County Library** is at 120 S. Last Chance Gulch, tel 442-2380.

St. Peter's Hospital is at 2475 Broadway, tel. 442-2480. Emergency is 911.

The **Helena National Forest Ranger Station** is at 2001 Poplar St., tel. 449-5490. The **State Fish, Wildlife, and Parks office** is at 1420 E. Sixth Ave., tel. 444-2535.

The *Independent Record* is Helena's daily paper. **National Public Radio** is at 91.7 FM and 107.1 FM.

The **Eleventh Ave. Clean and Coin Laundromat** is at 1411 11th Ave., tel. 442-9395.

TRANSPORTATION

Helena is served by Delta and Horizon airlines. The **airport** is east on Washington St., or take the Airport exit from I-15. **Intermountain** and **Rimrock buses** link Helena with Missoula, Butte, and Great Falls. The **bus station** is at 5 W. 15th St., tel. 442-5860.

Hertz rents cars at the airport, tel. 442-8169. **Rent-A-Wreck** car rental is at 3710 N. Montana, tel. 443-3635. **Budget Car Rental** is at 1930 N. Main, tel. 442-7011. Call a **cab** at 449-5525.

TOWNSEND AND THE UPPER MISSOURI VALLEY

At Three Forks, the Jefferson, Madison, and Gallatin unite into the Missouri River. Throwing off any trace of its mountain-bred fussiness, the Missouri flows north with stridency.

Think of the country between Three Forks and Holter Dam (the last of the three back-to-back dams that over-anxiously corral the newly minted river) as practice for the Missouri's long journey across the plains. To accustom the river to flat-land agriculture, it flows through a wide, prairie-like valley consecrated to ranches. As if to teach the headlong Missouri to slow down, three reservoirs within 60 miles impound it. Having learned prudence, the river is released to warm up, bear silt, and shoulder its responsibilities as a prairie river.

It's no wonder, with such an abundance of water around, that Townsend and aptly named Broadwater County boast of their recreational facilities. Perhaps not surprising in an area so close to the state capital, there is an embarrassment of riches in state parks along the Missouri, providing fishing, hunting, boating, and windsurfing opportunities. Visitors can even engage in a more traditional pastime. Several old mines provide pay dirt and teach prospecting skills.

TOWNSEND

Townsend (pop. 1,635, elev. 3,833 feet) has always made the most of its location. Platted in advance of the arrival of the first Northern Pacific train in 1883, Townsend was laid out with a deliberate sensibility, as if it were intended for bigger things. Prosperous farmers and ranchers along the Missouri nourished the strapping town; with the completion of Hwy. 12, linking central Montana to the west, Townsend became a transportation crossroads. When the Canyon Ferry Dam was built in the 1940s, Townsend planted its flag over the lakes' recreational opportunities.

Today, Townsend is a pleasant town, filled with trees and parks, seemingly dedicated to recreation on the nearby lakes and along the Missouri River.

Sights
At the **Broadwater County Museum,** 133 N. Walnut, tel. 266-5252, there are relics of the region's history, including early mining tools from Confederate Gulch.

Where the Missouri River enters the Canyon Ferry Reservoir just north of Townsend is **Canyon Ferry Wildlife Management Area.** Here, in a 5,000-acre delta wetland, is an exceptional viewing point for migrating waterfowl and nesting birds, including ospreys and loons. Beavers and white-tailed deer are also present. From Townsend, follow Hwy. 12 east to Harrison Rd., and turn north one mile.

Accommodations And Food
Lodgings in Townsend are comfortable and convenient for both travelers and watersport enthusiasts. The **Mustang Motel,** 412 N. Front, tel. (406) 266-3491, $28 d, and the **Lake Townsend Motel,** 413 N. Pine, tel. 266-3461, $26 d, are both along Hwy. 12. To find campgrounds, follow hwys. 12 or 284 north along Canyon Ferry Lake; the state maintains 25 of them, mostly toward the north end of the lake.

Good, no-nonsense beef and seafood menus characterize the food choices in Townsend. The **Fireside Supper Club,** one mile east on Hwy. 12, tel. 266-3516, is a dependable choice for an evening meal. As much landmark as restaurant/bar is **The Mint,** 305 Broadway, open 6 a.m.-midnight; it also has lighter meals and sandwiches. **The Horseshoe,** 500 N. Front, tel. 266-3800, is open for three meals a day for good, quick food.

People drive from Helena just for the pizza at **Rosario's,** 316 N. Front, tel. 226-3603. If you're up for a drive, then try the **Deep Creek Restaurant,** 11 miles east of Townsend on Hwy. 12, tel 266-3718; open daily 5-9 p.m. Steaks and fresh fish are served in a remote and beautiful canyon.

Recreation
The upper Missouri Valley is lined by the Elkhorn Mountains to the west and the Big Belt Moun-

tains to the east, each a part of the immense Helena National Forest. While these ranges are not particularly developed for the hiker and camper, the combination of mountain shelter and verdant river meadows makes the area famous for its hunting.

The following outfitters offer both guided fishing trips and big-game hunting expeditions: **Monte's Guiding and Mountain Outfitting,** 16 N. Fork Rd., Townsend, MT 59644, tel. 266-3515; **Greyson Creek Meadows Recreation,** 699 Flynn Ln., Townsend, MT 59644, tel. 266-3612; **Elkhorn Outfitters,** P.O. Box 1339, Townsend, MT 59644, tel. 266-5625.

Information

Contact the **Townsend Area Chamber of Commerce** at P.O. Box 947, Townsend, MT 59644, tel. (406) 266-3911.

The **Helena National Forest Office** is at 415 S. Front, tel. 226-3425.

THE UPPER MISSOURI LAKES

North of Townsend, three dams in rapid succession impound the Missouri. As they are near major population centers and are served by good roads, these lakes are among the most popular and developed in Montana. Canyon Ferry, Hauser, and Holter lakes are well trod by local anglers, boaters, and campers, but they bear up pretty well, considering their heavy use.

The range of recreational options is boggling—there are 25 state parks on Canyon Ferry Lake alone—which makes a brief overview difficult. Contact the Department of Fish, Wildlife, and Parks, 1420 Sixth Ave., Helena, tel. 444-2535, for more complete information.

Canyon Ferry Lake

The largest of the three lakes on the upper Missouri, Canyon Ferry Dam was built in the 1950s by the Bureau of Reclamation. Canyon Ferry backs up 25 miles of reservoir, with almost 80 miles of shoreline. At the south end, nearest Townsend, the lake is widest and the surrounding countryside rolling, gentle, and treeless. To the north, the reservoir narrows and begins to flow into a steep canyon.

On the east side of the lake, about 18 miles north of Townsend, is a sharp ravine in the Big Belt Mountains called Confederate Gulch. In 1864, a couple of Confederate soldiers discovered incredibly rich gravel beds here. While it lasted, individual pannings yielded up to $1000 in gold. A boomtown surged up immediately; called Diamond City, it grew to 10,000 people and was as rowdy and tough as the situation and era allowed. By the 1870s the gold played out, but one last blast with a huge water cannonlike hydraulic sluice dislodged another million dollars. Today, almost nothing remains of the fabulously rich workings of Confederate Gulch.

There are, however, rich fishing and boating today at Canyon Ferry. The lake is heavily and regularly stocked with rainbow trout, and they are usually hungry and scrappy enough to make a lucky angler feel skilled. Most of the facilities, both public and private, cluster at the northern end of the lake.

Follow Canyon Ferry Rd. (or Montana Ave.) east nine miles out of Helena to reach the lake. If coming north on Hwy. 12, turn on Hwy. 284 eight miles out of Winston. Windsurfers can rent equipment at **Big Sky Windsurfing** at Yacht Basin Marina, 7035 Canyon Ferry Rd., tel. 475-3557. The marina also rents all manner of boats, and has a bar and restaurant to boot; tel. 475-3125.

On the southern end of the lake the state parks thin out. The most convenient **campsites** are at Silo, seven miles north of Townsend on Hwy. 12, where there are both public and private campgrounds. At the privately owned **Silo's RV Park** there's **Silo's Inn** bar and restaurant, open 5-9 p.m., tel. 266-5622.

Hauser Lake

Built in 1908 by Montana Power, Hauser Dam is named for Samuel Hauser, an early Montanan who advocated damming the Missouri to harness electricity for regional mining enterprises. At this 3,720-acre lake, heavily used for boating and water-skiing, the fishing is okay, including a population of smallmouth bass and kokanee salmon.

There are two scenic, practically adjacent public campgrounds on Hauser Lake. If the beach at **White Sandy,** seven miles northeast off I-15 on Hwy. 453, is full, then continue a few yards farther to **Black Sandy.**

While at Hauser Lake, try your hand at sapphire mining. The **Spokane Bar Sapphire Mine,** 4397 Hart Dr., tel. 227-8989, 10 1/2 miles east of Helena on York Rd., and the **Eldorado Sapphire**

Mine, 6240 Nelson Rd., tel. 442-7960, both offer buckets of sapphire-laden gravel. Here the novice can wash gravel to discover highly colored sapphires as well as garnets, rubies, and gold.

Holter Lake

Holter lake is the most awe-inspiring of the three upper Missouri lakes. Behind the dam lies the Gates of the Mountains, so named by Meriwether Lewis:

> *this evening we entered the most remarkable clifts that we have yet seen. these clifts rise from the waters edge on either side perpendicularly to the hight of 1200 feet. solid rock for the distance of 5³/4 miles. I entered this place and was obliged to continue my rout until sometime after dark before I found a place sufficiently large to encamp my small party; from the singular appearance of this place I called it the gates of the mountains. July 19th, 1805*

The Missouri cut a deep gorge through thick deposits of limestone; although the flooding of Holter Dam (built in 1913) has lessened the rush of the river through these gates, this is still a startlingly dramatic landscape of geologic and human history.

Do not resist the temptation to take a float trip through the Gates of the Mountains. Wildlife viewing, historical vignettes, geologic curiosities, and drop-dead beautiful riverscapes make this one of Montana's most compelling side trips.

Gates of the Mountains, Inc., two miles east from the Gates of the Mountain exit off I-15, tel. 458-5241, offers guided open-air riverboat tours of the entire canyon. During the two-hour trip travelers usually see bighorn sheep, mountain goats, eagles, ospreys, and deer. Guides point out Indian pictographs along the limestone cliffs.

The river cruises begin on Memorial Day and end in September. Call for times. Tickets are $5.50 adult, $4.50 senior, and $2.50 children.

Plan your day carefully, and disembark the boat at Meriwether Picnic Area. The boat captains allow passengers to break the trip at this point. Here, at the site of Lewis and Clark's 1805 camp, are trails that lead up into the **Gates of the Mountains Wilderness Area,** a 28,560-acre wildlife reserve within the deep limestone canyons along the east side of the Missouri River. Be certain to know when to expect a returning riverboat; save your ticket stub.

There are three public campgrounds along Holter Lake, all on the east side. Turn south on Recreation Rd., just east of Wolf Creek, and cross the bridge. Continue three miles to **Holter Lake State Park.** Four miles up the same road are **Log Gulch** and **Departure Point state parks.**

BOB RACE

NORTHWESTERN MONTANA
INTRODUCTION

THE LAND

Northwestern Montana is characterized by a series of forested mountain ranges (the Cabinets, Missions, Bitterroots, Flatheads, Salish, Whitefish, Purcell, Swans), running generally northwest to southeast, and the valleys that separate them. Although this is a mountainous area, it's not particularly high by Montana standards; in fact, Montana's lowest spot (1,892 feet) is where Clark Fork River enters Idaho near Troy in the state's northwest corner.

Rivers

The Clark Fork of the Columbia is the main river in these parts, flowing from its headwaters in the Rockies near Butte, through Missoula, into Idaho's Lake Pend Oreille. The Kootenai River and its reservoir, Lake Koocanusa, drain the

northwestern corner of the state and spill into the Columbia River in British Columbia. Flathead Lake and the branches of the Flathead River that feed and drain it are other important features of northwestern Montana.

Formation Of The Landscape

Most of the exposed limestones, mudstones, and sandstones in northwestern Montana dates from the Precambrian era. Many contain fossils of blue-green algae, which were the only life form capable of existing in the steamy, carbon-dioxide-saturated air.

The Rocky Mountains began to form some 175 million years ago. The westward-drifting North American continent collided with the plate of the Pacific Ocean floor. The resulting crushing pressures, combined with faults, buckled large chunks of the earth's crust into mountain ranges. In other areas, tension across the crust stretched and broke it into a jumble of rocks. Old rocks sometimes landed on top of younger ones, reversing the intuitive order of geology. Once the Rockies had been formed, Montana was left with a topography that we'd recognize, though it's been modified by erosion and glacial action.

During alternating wet and dry geologic periods, layers of soil were laid down, then eroded off the hillsides when the climate dried. This eroded soil filled the valleys and was cut through by rivers that flowed during wetter times.

The glaciers that intermittently crept over northwestern Montana roughly 10,000 to 100,000 years ago refined and honed the landscape into something like its present form. When glaciers plowed through, they scoured out U-shaped valleys; they came from either side of mountain peaks and carved razor-sharp pinnacles; they pushed rocks and soil into gargantuan piles known as glacial moraines.

Glacial Lake Missoula

Glacial ice dammed the Clark Fork River in northern Idaho approximately 15,000 years ago, forming Glacial Lake Missoula, which filled the valleys of western Montana. River water ultimately floated the ice dam like an ice cube in a glass of water, and the lake drained with spectacular force, coursing over the scablands of western Washington and leaving its mark as far away as the Columbia River Gorge. The ice dam on the Clark Fork settled back down into the riverbed and once again plugged the outlet. The lake filled again, drained again, and was reformed at least 41 times in a little over 1,000 years. Each cycle was shorter, and the lake didn't fill as deep. The record of these successive fillings and drainings can still be seen as a series of faint, perfectly horizontal lines on the sides of Mt. Jumbo and Mt. Sentinel above Missoula.

Climate

This is a moderate area, with considerable Pacific influence. The Rockies shelter the land west of them from frigid continental winds, but snow does pile up in northwestern Montana. The stretch of I-90 just east of Lookout Pass gets particularly snowy. January tends to be the coldest month. Daily minimum temperatures average around 10-12° F, shooting up to average daily highs of around 28°.

July is ordinarily the hottest month throughout the region, with temperatures normally getting above 80°. Thunderstorms are not uncommon on summer afternoons. May and June are typically the rainiest months. Missoula usually receives about 13 inches of rain a year, Kalispell about 16, and Libby about 18.

FLORA AND FAUNA

Flora

Thanks to the warm wet weather that blows over the mountains of Washington and Oregon from the Pacific Ocean, northwestern Montana's forests resemble those of the Pacific coast with their abundance of conifers, including Douglas fir, western red cedar, and western hemlock. Ponderosa pine, lodgepole pine, and western white

TIMBER

The timber industry has not stepped lightly in northwestern Montana in the past decade. In the 1980s, the region's two timber giants, Plum Creek and Champion International, abandoned sustained-yield forestry and cut heavily for maximum immediate profit. Timber-industry officials and some congresspeople argue that such intensive logging is necessary to keep the regional economy afloat.

These huge clearcuts have affected water quality, wildlife habitats, and aesthetics. The Blackfoot River, site of Norman MacLean's *A River Runs Through It*, now disappoints anglers as silt dribbling down from clearcuts (and pollution from abandoned mines) has destroyed spawning grounds.

Northwestern Montana has been so seriously overcut that the Forest Service has scaled down logging operations on some of its land in an effort to mitigate the damage done nearby by private companies. These attempts to slow excessive logging were dealt a blow in 1991, when Regional Forester John Mumma, who was behind the Forest Service cutbacks, was transferred from the territory. Richard Manning, formerly a reporter for the *Missoulian* who was pulled from the environmental beat after too much investigative reporting, has written *Last Stand*, a riveting book chronicling overcutting in the Swan Valley.

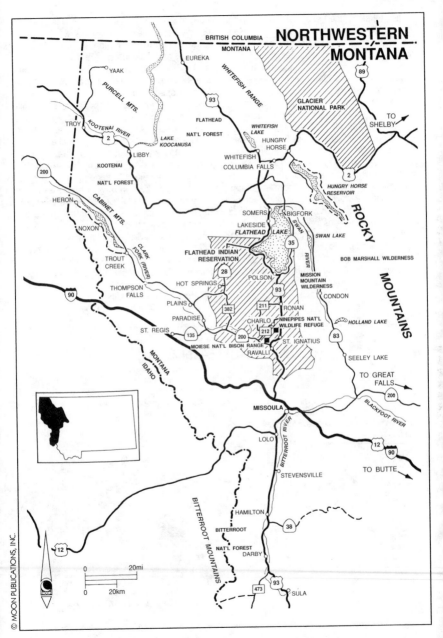

NORTHWESTERN MONTANA

BRITISH COLUMBIA
MONTANA

EUREKA

WHITEFISH RANGE

89

GLACIER NATIONAL PARK

TO SHELBY

YAAK

PURCELL MTS.

93

FLATHEAD

NAT'L FOREST

WHITEFISH LAKE

TROY

KOOTENAI RIVER

2

LAKE KOOCANUSA

LIBBY

HUNGRY HORSE

WHITEFISH

COLUMBIA FALLS

HUNGRY HORSE RESERVOIR

KOOTENAI

NAT'L FOREST

ROCKY

200

HERON

CABINET MTS.

SOMERS BIGFORK

LAKESIDE FLATHEAD LAKE

SWAN LAKE

35

NOXON

CLARK FORK (RIVER)

FLATHEAD INDIAN RESERVATION

SWAN RIVER

BOB MARSHALL WILDERNESS

TROUT CREEK

28

POLSON

MISSION MOUNTAIN WILDERNESS

MOUNTAINS

THOMPSON FALLS

HOT SPRINGS

93

90

PLAINS

382

211

RONAN

CONDON

PARADISE

CHARLO

HOLLAND LAKE

ST. REGIS

135

200

212 NINEPIPES NAT'L WILDLIFE REFUGE

83

MOIESE NAT'L BISON RANGE

ST. IGNATIUS

RAVALLI

SEELEY LAKE

MONTANA
IDAHO

TO GREAT FALLS

200

MISSOULA

BLACKFOOT RIVER

LOLO

BITTERROOT RIVER

12

90

TO BUTTE

STEVENSVILLE

HAMILTON

BITTERROOT MOUNTAINS

38

BITTERROOT

NAT'L FOREST

DARBY

12

0   20mi
0   20km

473

93

SULA

© MOON PUBLICATIONS, INC.

pine are other Pacific trees that are important to the landscape and economy of western Montana. There's also a good sprinkling of trees more characteristic of the Rockies, such as Engelmann spruce, western larch, and subalpine fir.

The bitterroot, the state flower, was an important food for the Flathead Indians. It is most abundant in the valley that bears its name, where it flowers early in the summer. Subalpine wildflowers bloom wildly on the mountainsides once the snow has melted. Look for glacier lilies, beargrass, Indian paintbrush, and lupine.

Shrubs tend to grow at lower elevations than the wildflower meadows. Huckleberry bushes run amok in the open areas of northwest Montana. Look to meadows, old burns, and clearcuts for the most intense growth. Berries begin to ripen at lower elevations toward the end of July, moving upward as the summer progresses. When in huckleberry country keep an eye out for bears, which love to feast on the tasty fruit.

Oregon grape and kinnikinnick (whose bark was smoked as tobacco by the Indians) are other common shrubby plants in northwestern Montana forests.

Fauna

Grizzly bears live in some of the more isolated areas of northwestern Montana, including the Cabinet and Mission mountains wilderness areas. Black bears are more widespread. Don't mess with either. (See general "Introduction" for bear specifics.)

Bighorn sheep can be spotted on steep hillsides throughout the state's northwestern corner. There's a special bighorn viewing area on Hwy. 200 just east of Thompson Falls, and a de facto one along Hwy. 2 west of Libby. They also live on the National Bison Range in Moiese, which is also just about the only place you'll see buffalo, except those kept in private herds as ranch stock or a tourist attraction. Elk, white-tailed and mule deer, moose, and mountain goats are among the other ungulates, or hoofed animals, that inhabit northwestern Montana.

Mountain lions have a reputation for being rather elusive, but they've been reported to roam the streets of Columbia Falls and send joggers up trees in Missoula's Greenough Park.

There's an astounding variety of birdlife in northwestern Montana—bald eagles, ospreys,

ROCKY MOUNTAIN CAMELS

Camels in the Rockies? Well, *yeah*—why not? Strong, don't drink too much . . . So thought the U.S. Army in the 1860s, when some innovative military man began importing camels to use as pack animals. While perhaps more efficient than the customary mules, camels weren't so easy to boss around. Apparently they were harder to recognize, too—several of the camels on the Mullan Road were shot after being mistaken for moose.

woodpeckers, dippers, Clark's nutcrackers, western tanagers, great blue herons, hawks, owls, vultures, blue grouse, ruffed grouse, magpies, and hummingbirds. There are a host of waterfowl and shorebirds around Ninepipe and Pablo wildlife refuges in the Mission Valley. Loons nest in several lakes near Eureka and in the Swan Valley.

Dams and development have altered the riparian ecology in northwestern Montana. Native fish, including bull trout, westslope cutthroat, and whitefish have, to greater or lesser extents, survived environmental changes, including the addition of nonnative species such as kokanee salmon.

There are three major trout species in northwestern Montana: cutthroat, bull, and rainbow. The westslope cutthroat is Montana's state fish and, while not officially endangered, it is the object of some concern. Catch-and-release fishing is generally recommended, and in some places mandatory, for cutthroat. Bull trout, also referred to as Dolly Varden trout, live primarily in the Flathead River system. Rainbow trout are widespread, and are especially prolific in the Kootenai River, where they're native.

Kokanee (pronounced COKE-knee) salmon were introduced to the Flathead system in the 1930s and flourished there for about 50 years. In recent years, Flathead populations of this landlocked salmon have declined precipitously, most likely because of competition with mysis shrimp. Kokanee are still plentiful in other lakes, including Lake Mary Ronan, west of Flathead Lake, and Lake Koocanusa.

HISTORY

Because of the mountainous terrain and dense forests, northwestern Montana wasn't settled or developed by whites as early as other areas of the state. There wasn't a whole lot of activity in this country until the railroad, especially the Great Northern, came through in the early 1880s. Then other development was spurred on, particularly the timber industry and northwestern Montana became a stronghold of the region's economy.

Native Americans

The original inhabitants of western Montana are known largely through the mythology they've engendered. The Flathead people have stories of those who preceded them in Montana—dwarves, giants, and "the foolish folk," a crass and bumbling bunch who, as the legend goes, died out when the last few fools went over Spokane Falls in a canoe. Anthropologists posit that these early inhabitants were from the Pacific coast. A few traces of jewelry made from saltwater shells have been found, and the people seemed to have a physical stature similar to that of modern coastal tribes. Beyond that, these people and their lives remain a mystery. The Kootenai, Pend d'Oreille, and Flathead tribes took up residence in Montana around the 1500s, a couple of hundred years before Plains Indian culture was really established.

Northwestern Montana is now home to Salish and Kootenai tribes. The term "Salish" refers to a language family common to several Pacific Northwest tribes. Salish speakers in northwestern Montana include the Flathead and Pend d'Oreille. The Kootenai have their own distinct language, which seems to be unrelated to any other (though some anthropologists link it to the Algonquian language group common to many tribes in the northeastern U.S. and Canada).

The Flathead Indians came to the Bitterroot Valley from the west. Although they made regular trips to the plains to hunt buffalo, the Flathead also ate many wild roots and berries. During the spring and early summer months, women dug the roots of camas, bitterroot, and wild carrots. The roots were eaten raw, boiled and roasted in stone-lined pits, or sun-dried for later use. Later in the summer, serviceberries, chokecherries, and huckleberries were picked. Some of the berries were dried, pulverized, and mixed with dried meats. Flathead men fished for trout, char, whitefish, and suckers with basket traps, weirs, spears, or poles with animal-hair lines and hooks carved from bone or hawthorn.

Confusion abounds as to why the Flathead are called that. Several barely plausible theories exist, but one confusing fact is that they did *not* flatten their heads.

The Pend d'Oreille lived in the Mission Valley and westward into eastern Washington. They were on friendly terms with the Flathead tribe; indeed, when the Flathead arrived in the Bitterroot Valley, the Pend d'Oreille who were living there moved north to the Jocko and Mission valleys so that the Flathead could settle in the more southern Bitterroot region.

The Kootenai came from the north and settled in and around the Tobacco Plains region (near present-day Eureka), with nomadic bands ranging from southeastern British Columbia, through northern Idaho, and into northern Montana. There were two main branches: The Upper Kootenai, who lived closer to the Rockies, were frequent buffalo hunters on the plains. The Lower Kootenai were river people who fished more than they hunted, but traded with the Upper Kootenai for horses and buffalo meat. Today, the Kootenai live on the Flathead Reservation, mostly around Elmo on the west side of Flathead Lake, and are part of the Confederated Salish and Kootenai Tribes.

Early White Explorers

Lewis and Clark just skirted the lower corner of northwestern Montana on both legs of their expedition. They met a band of Flathead Indians in the Bitterroot Valley and traded with them for horses. Although they found the Salishan language spoken by these people as bizarre as Welsh, Clark proclaimed the Flathead "the likelyest and honnestst Savages we have ever yet Seen." Lewis and Clark don't seem to be the ones who coined the term "Flathead." In fact, Clark referred to them as the Tushepau, and comments more on the "gurgling" language than on the shape of anyone's head.

On their return trip, the entire Corps of Discovery camped at Traveler's Rest (on Lolo Creek near the Bitterroot River), and Meriwether Lewis cut through the Hell Gate Canyon with several other men on the way north to explore the Marias River.

Other areas of the state saw quick American fur-trading action soon after Lewis and Clark reported their finds to the nation. But northwestern Montana was dominated by the Canadian fur companies. Many of the trappers and traders were French Canadian; a substantial number of them married Native American women, and today there are still a number of northwest Montanans with French surnames, especially on the Flathead Reservation.

David Thompson, an English-born explorer, astronomer, and geographer for both the Hudson's Bay and North-West companies, was the first white person to travel into the northwest

corner of Montana. In 1807, he traveled down the Kootenai River from Canada and into Montana. Over the next few years, he set up trading posts along the Kootenai and Clark Fork rivers and became the first white man to travel the entire length of the Columbia River, which he mapped from mouth to source. Thompson spoke several Indian languages, and won the trust and respect of local Indians.

In 1841 St. Mary's Mission was founded in the Bitterroot Valley after repeated requests for Catholicism from the Flathead and Nez Percé of the area. Father Pierre deSmet, the missionary dispatched to found St. Mary's, was also Montana's first agriculturalist. He planted oats, wheat, and potatoes at the mission. This was probably also an initial attempt to make Indians into farmers. Troubles arose between the missionaries and the Flathead and, in 1850, St. Mary's was sold to John Owen, who made it into a trading post.

The St. Ignatius Mission was originally established near the present-day Washington-Idaho border. It did not prosper there, and when Montana Indians requested another mission, Father DeSmet and Father Adrian Hoecken moved St. Ignatius to what is now known as the Mission Valley.

White Settlement

Much of western Montana was opened to white settlement following a reservation treaty enacted in 1855 between Isaac I. Stevens, governor of the Washington Territory (which at the time included Montana), and the Flathead, Pend d'Oreille, and Kootenai tribes. The Hellgate Treaty established the Jocko Reservation (now known as the Flathead Reservation) in the Jocko and Mission valleys. The Pend d'Oreille and the Kootenai agreed to live on the reservation and the Flathead chose to remain in the Bitterroot Valley south of Missoula. In 1872, the Bitterroot Valley was opened for homesteading, but some Flathead Indians remained in the area until 1891, when they were forced to move to the reservation.

It took John Mullan and his crew from 1858 until 1862 to build a military wagon road from Fort Benton to Walla Walla, Washington. This was a particularly vital stretch of road, as Fort

Benton marked the farthest point that steamboats could travel up the Missouri River, and Walla Walla provided access to the Columbia River. His route has held up well; I-90 follows its course from Deer Lodge to the Idaho line.

John Mullan also has the distinction of having written the first travel guide to Montana. In 1865 he authored the *Miners' and Travelers' Guide to Oregon, Washington, Idaho, Montana, Wyoming and Colorado.* As may be expected, the Montana portion follows the Mullan Road.

Development

The late 1800s brought railroads through northwestern Montana. The Northern Pacific followed the Clark Fork and the Great Northern cut across the northern edge of the state. Timber was needed to construct the railroad lines, and, once the trains were running, they were able to transport the abundant local timber to other areas of the state and nation. The smelter in Anaconda burned endless cords of wood, and large timbers were required to prop up mine shafts.

As the number of homesteaders increased, so did the pressure on the Indians. In 1877, Chief Joseph's retreat led nervous homesteaders in the Bitterroot Valley to petition the government for military forts. Fort Missoula and Fort Fizzle were built to protect the white settlers.

The 1887 Dawes Act allotted parcels of reservation land to individual Indians in an effort to make them understand the concept of *owning* the land. Unalloted land was often dealt to the U.S. government and then thrown open to white homesteaders. The Dawes Act was repealed in 1934, when tribal, rather than individual, identity was emphasized in the Tribal Reorganization Act. Under these provisions, the Confederated Salish and Kootenai Tribes were incorporated. By that time, much of the land within the confines of the Flathead Reservation was owned by non-Indians, as it remains today.

Northwestern Montana is still one of the wilder areas of the country. Logging roads may crisscross the forests, but it's still easy to find an isolated spot to set up camp or to fish. The economy is still dependent on the vagaries of the timber industry.

PRACTICALITIES

Hunting

Hunters benefit from the vast tracts of public land in northwestern Montana. Most appreciate that it's laced with logging roads, making it easier to get into fairly wild areas. In order to curb the number of hunters in some areas, roads may be closed to motor vehicles during the hunting season. Local ranger stations or state Department of Fish, Wildlife, and Parks offices will have information on road closures.

While the thick growth of trees and brush can make hunting difficult throughout much of northwestern Montana, this habitat harbors many animals. Elk, deer (mostly white-tailed, but also some mule deer), and black bear are commonly hunted. It's easy for Montana residents to pick up the necessary licenses for these animals. Nonresidents should apply for a combination sportsman's license well in advance of hunting season. A limited number of tags to hunt mountain goats, bighorn sheep, and moose are awarded by a computer lottery during the summer.

Driving

There's a lot of logging activity in northwestern Montana, and the savvy driver will keep a sharp eye and ear out for log trucks, especially on Forest Service roads. Be ready to head toward the ditch, and always give way to the log truck, because the driver and can not make fast stops.

MISSOULA

Missoula, tucked in a fertile valley and filled with students, loggers, and artists, is the hub of western Montana. The Missoula Valley has always been a crossroads, first for Indians, then for white settlers, nowadays for Montana's major highways. It remains a great focus and jumping-off point for the traveler.

The city (pop. 43,000) takes its sense of confluence seriously. Practically within city limits the Clark Fork is joined by the Blackfoot and Bitterroot rivers and several smaller streams. As home to the University of Montana, Missoula is a center of learning and is by and large the cultural center of the state. The city's wood-products industries provide a fairly stable economic base. Missoula has preserved much of its historic architectural character, and offers good restaurants and a full-bodied nightlife. Missoula's nickname, the Garden City, is apt. As a locale, it's about as temperate, fertile, and hospitable as these things get in Montana.

But Missoula is more than a picturesque university town. The university population is notoriously Bohemian and political, while the working core of the city is unmitigatedly blue collar. Depending on the perspective, Missoula is either a working-class town with a radical university imposed on it, or a liberal arts college town infiltrated by the proletariat. But the juxtaposition works: scratch a logger and find a poet.

For many visitors, Missoula, or something like it, is the very image of what they expect of all Montana. However, Montanans from the rest of the state mistrust Missoula. To them the town is Montana with an attitude. Much of the East vs. West dichotomy of Montana is really shorthand for ambivalence about Missoula and the progressive politics and life-styles that emerge from it. Throughout the rest of Montana, the university is disdainfully referred to as "the dance school."

For a traveler, Missoula is an agreeable home base for excursions into the wonders of western Montana. However, for a visitor with a little time and a taste for artistic and political ferment, Missoula can become addictive. The city's saloons and salons are filled with testimonials of those who planned to pass through, but have yet to leave.

THE LAND

Missoula (elev. 3,205 feet) is at the mouth of Hell Gate Canyon, the Clark Fork River's path between Mt. Jumbo (north) and Mt. Sentinel (south) on the eastern edge of town. But the valleys are what define Missoula's geography. Five valleys nearly converge here—the Flathead-Jocko from the north, the Hell Gate and the Blackfoot from the east, the Bitterroot from the south, and the Missoula Valley from the west.

This bowl-like setting makes for both pleasingly temperate weather and the dreaded phenomenon of winter temperature inversion, in which warm, moist air is trapped and held in the valley by high pressure aloft. This stagnant air is apt to contain particulate pollution, largely from wood stoves.

HISTORY

With the five valleys nearly converging here, it's no surprise that the area has long been used as a thoroughfare. Salish Indians lived to the west and traveled through Hell Gate Canyon to reach buffalo-hunting grounds east of the mountains. They were regularly attacked by the Blackfeet as they entered the canyon, thus giving the passage a formidable reputation. In fact, "Missoula" is from a Salish word which has been variously translated as "by the cold chilling waters," "river of awe," or simply an exclamation of surprise and horror.

The first white settlers seemed to agree. As the story goes, French trappers were horrified when they came across the remains of all the Salish who never made it through the canyon and called it Porte de l'Enfer, which, anglicized, became Hell Gate. It's markedly different from the pleasant, seemingly benign city that Missoula has become.

The first whites on record to explore the Missoula area were Meriwether Lewis and a brigade of his men on their return trip from the Pacific. Lewis and his group camped at the confluence of the Rattlesnake and Clark Fork rivers in July

1806, and headed through Hell Gate Canyon without incident.

White Settlement

The Hell Gate Treaty of 1855 opened Missoula and much of western Montana to white settlement (see Northwestern Montana's "History"). The treaty council took place about seven miles west of Missoula (on present-day Hwy. 263) where a state monument can now be found.

In 1860, C.P. Higgins and Frank Worden, the area's first white settlers, established a trading post, Hell Gate Ronde, four miles west of what is now downtown Missoula. Within the year, a log cabin was standing at the mouth of the Rattlesnake, and by 1863 the Mullan Road was running through Hell Gate Canyon and is now Front Street in downtown Missoula. Once the road was open, Worden and Higgins built a sawmill, flour mill, and store at the intersection of the Mullan Road and Higgins Avenue, along the banks of the Clark Fork. Their enterprise, named Missoula Mills, quickly replaced Hell Gate Ronde as the hub of settlement action.

When Chief Joseph and the Nez Percé retreated across Montana in 1877, Missoula citizens asked the federal government for protection from the Indians, and Fort Missoula was hastily established just southwest of town.

Development

Missoula's growth was really spurred on by the arrival in 1883 of the Northern Pacific Railway. The town was a division point and repair center for the line. In 1885 Missoula was incorporated as a city, and by 1925 the population had climbed from 300 to 12,000.

Timber was also important to Missoula's development. In 1886, A.B. Hammond built what was reputedly the world's largest lumber mill at Bonner (seven miles east of Missoula). It produced timbers for railroads and mines as well as construction lumber.

When other Montana cities vied for the state capital and

prison, Missoula alone attempted to land the university. It was established (as Montana State University) in Missoula in 1895. Since then it has become a major cultural force, as well as one of the city's leading employers.

Another major employer in contemporary Missoula is the U.S. Forest Service. The regional office was established here in 1908. The wood-products industry, dominated by Champion International and Stone Container, is the main source of jobs in Missoula today. As befits its history as a transportation corridor, Missoula is now home to a large number of truck drivers—trucking employs roughly as many Missoulians as the university.

The railroad, however, is no longer the force it once was in Missoula's development: both of the city's depots are now restaurants, and the Burlington Northern pulled out of town in the late 1980s. But the purchase of rail lines by freeway builder and mining entrepreneur Denny Washington does seem to be breathing some life into the region's rail business, and his Montana Interlink cars are now riding the rails through Missoula.

Logs choke the Blackfoot River east of Missoula, circa 1900.

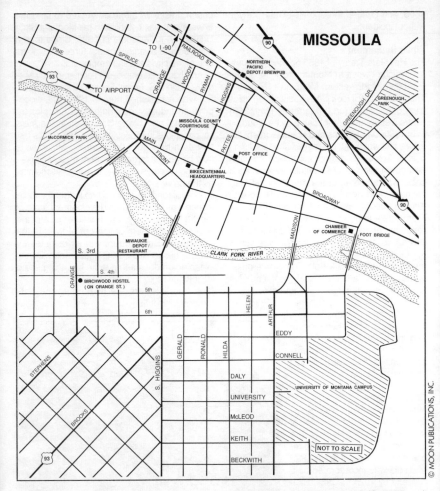

SIGHTS

Most of Missoula's historic downtown is located on the north side of the Clark Fork. The historic residential areas are across the river, near the university.

Downtown

The old business district was located near the river, along the Mullan Road (now Front St.), on which early settlers traveled west. However,

most of the early buildings burned in 1884, and when the city rebuilt, the influence of the incoming Northern Pacific Railroad attracted the downtown northward from the Clark Fork along Higgins Avenue.

Many of these early buildings remain. The **Missoula Mercantile building** (now the Bon) at the corner of Front and Higgins, was built between 1882 and 1891. The Merc (as it was known) was established in 1866 and was the primary mercantile establishment in the city for over a century. Note the cast-iron front facing Higgins Avenue.

FORT MISSOULA

Fort Missoula was built in 1877 in response to the movement of the Nez Percé and white settlers' fear of the increasingly recalcitrant Flathead Indians. However, the threat of Indian attack never really materialized and troops at the fort saw real action only once, at the Battle of the Big Hole in 1877. There, troops from Fort Missoula attempted an ambush of Chief Joseph's retreating Nez Percé and were disastrously defeated.

Thereafter, the story of Fort Missoula ceases to resemble that of the embattled frontier fort and begins to take on more curious dimensions. In 1888, the Twenty-fifth Infantry Corps, an all-black regiment under the authority of white officers, was garrisoned at the fort. In 1896, bicycle enthusiast Lieutenant James Moss established the Twenty-fifth Infantry Bicycle Corps, which sought to test the potential of the bicycle as a military conveyance. The lieutenant, in comparing the bicycle to the horse, reasoned that the bike "doesn't require as much care. It needs no forage; it moves much faster over fair roads, it is not as conspicuous . . . it is noiseless and raises but little dust."

In order to prove to General Nelson Miles that the bicycle was a viable means of troop transport, the following year Moss and 20 men left Missoula on bicycles, bound for St. Louis—1,900 miles overland. The trip, made on mud trails and sandy paths, took only 41 days. The Army higher-ups were not impressed, and the Bicycle Corps returned to Missoula by train.

During World War I the fort served as an Army training center, and during the Depression it was the regional headquarters for the Civilian Conservation Corps (the CCC). During World War II, 1,200 Italian seamen and 650 men of Japanese descent were detained at the fort, and following the war, it was a prison for court-martialed military personnel.

Fort Missoula was closed as a military post in 1947. The fort presently houses government offices and a historical museum, and its grounds are used for such benign displays as dog shows.

North on Higgins is the **Higgins Block** (1889), containing well-preserved late 19th-century commercial architecture. On the corner, beneath a prominent cupola, is a gingerbread bank in the Queen Anne style. Farther along the same block are other old stores, now housing trendy businesses. One vintage interior worth visiting, **Butterfly Herbs,** has an espresso bar in the back.

The **County Courthouse,** 200 W. Broadway, was constructed in 1910. This large, three-story edifice is noteworthy for its murals. These scenes from Montana history were painted by Edgar Paxson, who was called Cot-lo-see, "He Who Sees Everything," by admiring Indians.

Missoula's two **train stations** are imposing and handsome. The Northern Pacific depot was built in 1889 at the north end of Higgins Ave., and the Spanish-style Milwaukee depot was built in 1910 under the Higgins Avenue Bridge on the south side of the Clark Fork. Neither is in operation as a rail depot, but both are noted, in renovated form, for their bars and restaurants.

The **Missoula Museum of the Arts,** 335 N. Pattee, tel. 728-4447, is in the city's old Carnegie library. It houses a small permanent collection and displays traveling art exhibits.

During the summer, **walking tours** of the town are offered ($5 for adults, $4 for students and seniors). Or, if you prefer, see the sights from a horse-drawn cart. Reservations are required; call Discover Missoula Montana at (406) 721-8389 for details.

The University Area

The **University of Montana** is located on the south side of the Clark Fork, at the mouth of the river's Hell Gate Canyon. A green and leafy campus built around a central oval, it's a pleasant place to explore, as is the university district, an area of grand and historic old homes.

For the youthful traveler, the campus is a good center for information about what's going on in Missoula. Flyers and posters abound and the campus paper, the *Kaimin,* is printed four times a week and has good listings. The university also offers the traveler easy access to cultural amenities in short supply elsewhere in Montana, and provides cheap eats and entertainment. The general information number for the campus is 243-0211.

The university, established by the Montana Legislature in 1895, has developed into an academically broad-based institution with a strong liberal arts emphasis. Its schools of journalism and forestry are nationally recognized. The university is proud of its ability to produce Rhodes scholars: only five public institutions in the U.S. have produced more.

But the university has had its share of problems in recent years. During the 1960s, the campus was convulsed with political activity and social unrest. However vital these movements were in their day, they served to alienate much of the state's population, who saw the unrest as a result of the university's teachers and curriculum. The university has fallen on rough economic times of late, partially because legislators find it easy to cut spending for the university due to its reputation as a breeding ground of discontent. Faculty and administration have worked hard to repair the university's image in the rest of the state and have met with some success. Current student enrollment is over 10,000 students, the highest in the university's history, and a decade of faculty cuts seems to be at an end.

The earliest remaining building on campus is the **University Hall,** built in 1899. Besides containing the university president's office, the building's central tower houses a carillon. At noon each day, students are serenaded by a quarter-hour recital of bell music.

Behind University Hall is **Mansfield Library,** named for Montana's former senator Mike Mansfield and his wife, Maureen. After a week or two in rural Montana, the traveler may enjoy catching up on events in its periodicals section.

Across a grassy mall from the library is the **University Center,** a modern three-story building constructed around a central atrium. It's a good place to hang out and watch student behavior. On the second floor, in the Copper Commons and the Gold Oak Room, quick and inexpensive food is available. Also on the second floor is the UC Lounge, a quiet study area with easy chairs. On the ground floor is the UC Bookstore, a good all-purpose bookstore and art-supply source, tel. 243-4921. The university post office is also located in the bookstore.

One of the university's newest additions is the **Montana Theatre,** which houses two stages for live theater. Call 243-4581 for current listings.

For a bird's-eye, or rather a mountain goat's-eye, view of the university and the city, climb up Mt. Sentinel to the university's "M." It's a 40-minute hike from the trailhead at the north end of the UC parking lot.

The university district is one of Missoula's most pleasant neighborhoods and contains some interesting architectural specimens. Some of the old homes have been turned into fraternity or sorority houses, but others remain private homes. None are open to the public, but a stroll or drive through the area is a pleasant way to learn that Missoula took its turn-of-the-century affluence seriously. The grandest homes face onto Gerald Avenue (parallel one block east of South Higgins). See especially the neoclassical mansion at 1005 Gerald (built in 1902-03), once the home of John R. Toole, a prominent early Montana politician and industrialist; and the university president's house at 1325 Gerald, built around 1930. A good brochure, "Historic Missoula," is available from the chamber of commerce.

Another landmark of sorts in the university district is **Freddy's Feed and Read,** a small cooperative grocery and alternative bookstore at 1221 Helen, tel. 549-2127. It remains a very good bookstore, and has fine whole foods, but its niche in history will be its reputation, from the 1960s and '70s, as a focus of social and political change. Freddy's, as a "radical bookstore," became a catalyst for the sorts of liberation of thought that flourished during the period of the store's founding. Of course, that era seems as remote now as the era of the city's mansions, but Freddy's is a useful monument to what access to the written word once meant.

Greenough Mansion

A little farther afield is the old Greenough Mansion (now the Mansion Restaurant and the Highland Golf Course Clubhouse), a magnificent old mansion from whose deck bar one can take in a nice panorama of Missoula. The mansion was built in 1897 in what is now Greenough Park. When Interstate 90 cut through the lower end of the park in the 1960s, the mansion was destined to be demolished. Instead, a group of citizens prevailed and it was cut in pieces and hauled up the mountainside and reassembled were it now stands, at 102 Ben Hogan Dr., tel. 728-5132.

To get there, take South Higgins to Pattee Canyon Rd., turn left, and take the immediate right on Whitaker Drive. Follow it till the road ends at the golf course.

Fort Missoula

Of the 1877 fort site, two original buildings remain (a stone powder magazine and an officers' quarters) and are now part of the **Fort Missoula Historical Museum,** which contains exhibits of local history. Other buildings of interest have been relocated to the fort, including an old church, a schoolhouse, and a Forest Service lookout tower. The rest of the fort now houses National Guard and Forest Service offices. The wide boulevards, green lawns, and white military buildings evoke a real sense of history, if not nostalgia.

During the summer, Fort Missoula is open Tues.-Sat. 10-5, and Sun. noon-5. Winter hours are Tues.-Sat. noon-5, tel. 728-3476. To get there, take Hwy. 93 south to Reserve St., turn right, and follow signs at the junction with South Avenue.

Smokejumping Training Center

Undeniably unique to Missoula and a curious source of pride to natives is the Forest Service Smokejumping Training Center, tel. 329-4900. Here, firefighters are trained in the science of fighting forest fires, as well as the art of parachuting into forest wildfires. The center is open to visitors and features exhibits, films, a diorama, and a tour of the parachuting base. The center is just past Johnson Bell Airport, on Hwy. 93.

ACCOMMODATIONS

Because Missoula is a real crossroads, a great number and variety of lodgings are available. Unless there's a big football game, graduation, or some other major event going on at the university, you'll have little trouble finding something.

Hostels And B&Bs

The **Birchwood Hostel** is at 600 S. Orange, tel. (406) 728-9799. Take the Orange St. exit from I-90 across the bridge. The hostel offers 22 beds in a common bunkroom, one private room, showers, a kitchen, and a laundry room. The proprietor maintains a good "what's happening in Missoula" bulletin board and library. Check-in time is from 5-10 p.m., and a bed costs $6 a night for youth hostel members, $8 a night for nonmembers.

Once the home of the university's second president, **Goldsmith's,** 809 E. Front, tel. 721-6732, is Missoula's top-flight bed and breakfast. Relocated to the north bank of the Clark Fork and renovated to its original 1911 splendor, Goldsmith's boasts six rooms at a range of $45-65, including continental breakfast.

Hotels And Motels

None of the original old hotels downtown is still operating, but in the downtown area there are plenty of perfectly adequate motels along East and West Broadway. The **Sweet Rest,** at 1135 W. Broadway, tel. 549-2358, has a lobby full of taxidermy and unspectacular rooms for less than $20. The **Bel Aire,** 300 E. Broadway, tel. (800) 543-3183 in Montana, (800) 543-3184 out of state, has an indoor pool and hot tub and rooms for $25 d.

A step or two up in price and amenities is the **Red Lion,** located directly across from the university on the Clark Fork, at 100 Madison, tel. 728-3100 or (800) 547-8010. Right downtown is the new **Holiday Inn Missoula Parkside,** 2005 Pattee, tel. 721-8550.

If you are coming in from the south, the 93 Strip (as it's called) also offers many and adequate lodgings. The **4-B's Inn,** on the outskirts of the strip at 3803 Brooks, tel. 251-2665, is near a dependable 4-B's restaurant.

Campgrounds

There are three private campgrounds in Missoula. The **El-Mar KOA** (complete with swimming pool, hot tub, and cabins) is open all year at 3695 Tina Ave. (exit 101 off I-90), tel. 549-0881. **Out Post Campground** is on Hwy. 93, two miles north of I-90, also open year-round. **Jim and Mary's RV Park,** Hwy. 93, one mile north of I-90, tel. 549-4416, is an adults-only campground with no tent sites. They're open April 1-Oct. 30. The Department of Fish, Wildlife, and Parks operates a couple of campgrounds a little farther from town. To reach **Chief Looking Glass,** travel 14 miles south of Missoula on Hwy. 93 (to milepost 77), then go one mile east on the county road; open May 27-Sept. 15. **Beavertail Hill,** open May 20-Sept. 15, is a quarter mile south of the Beavertail Hill exit off I-90 (milepost 130, 26 miles southeast of Missoula).

MISSOULA ACCOMMODATIONS

Name	Address	Phone	Price	Features
Sweet Rest Motel	1135 W. Broadway	549-2358	$17 d	decidedly budget ambience
Brownie's Plus Motel	1540 W. Broadway	543-6614	$31 d	clean and friendly spot
City Center Motel	338 E. Broadway	543-3193	$28 d	burger restaurant adjoining
Downtown Motel	502 E. Broadway	549-5191	$30 d	
Campus Inn	744 E. Broadway	549-5134	$30-$40 d	small pool
Uptown Motel	329 Woody	549-5141	$31 d	
Bel Aire Motel	300 E. Broadway	543-3183 or (800) 543-3184	$35 d	indoor pool and hot tub
Red Lion Motel	700 W. Broadway	728-3300 or (800) 547-8010	$59 d	pool
Village Red Lion Inn	100 Madison	728-3100 or (800) 547-8010	$69 d	on the Clark Fork River, pool and hot tub
Holiday Inn Missoula Parkside	200 S. Pattee	721-8550, (800) 824-4536 in Montana, (800) 523-1408 out of state	$62 d	indoor pool, hot tub, and sauna
4 B's Inn	3803 Brooks	251-2665	$38 d	hot tub
Super 8	3901 Brooks	251-2255	$3 d	free continental breakfast
Orange Street Budget Motor Inn	801 N. Orange St.	721-3610 or (800) 328-0801	$44 d	free continental breakfast, exercise room

FOOD AND DRINK

Food

There are reasons to linger over Missoula's relative abundance of more than passable restaurants. For the traveler coming to Missoula from the east, this may be the first ethnic food seen in days. For the traveler heading into eastern Montana, Missoula may be the last place to enjoy a choice beyond fast food and steaks. Expect restaurants to be busy—Montanans like to eat out. Every franchise imaginable is to be found along the Hwy. 93 strip. However, for those with a hankering for something local, Missoula shouldn't disappoint.

On campus, eating cheap is easy at the University Center, where the **Copper Commons** cafeteria is open 7 a.m.-10 p.m. during the week, and 9-9 on weekends. Down the mezzanine, the **Gold Oak Room** is open for lunch. Both these dining areas offer good values in uncomplicated food. Other university dining rooms are open only to residential students.

A funkier mix of Missoulians is on view at the **Old Town Café,** where huge breakfasts are the order of the day. The rough-hewn decor melds with the new granola/old hippie ambience, 127 W. Alder, tel. 728-9742.

Especially convenient for those staying at the youth hostel, but worth the easy walk or drive from the Broadway motel strip, is **Zorba's Greek**

Cuisine, 420 S. Orange, tel. 728-9259. Watch earnest Greek music videos, chat with the waitresses, brush elbows with the local literati, and fill up for $6-7.

A healthy lunch can be had at **Mammyth Bakery,** 131 W. Main, tel. 549-5542. They also sell good whole-grain baked goods. Another bright spot downtown is **Greenleaf Deli,** on Front St. at Higgins, tel. 728-5969. Lunchtime sandwiches and soup give way to good, reasonably priced continental cuisine in the evenings.

One local burger joint is the **93-Stop-and-Go,** at 2205 Brooks. There are those who swear by their Duper Sauce. Here, as elsewhere in the state, **4-B's** restaurants are dependable purveyors of inexpensive standard American fare in pleasant enough surroundings. The chain began in Missoula (before spreading across the state and region) and the city is blessed with four different locations. Most 4-B's are open 24 hours, making them popular with a late-night student crowd: 301 E. Broadway, tel. 543-7366; 700 W. Broadway, tel. 728-2663; I-90 and Hwy. 93, tel. 721-2771; Reserve and Hwy. 93 S, tel. 251-5882.

Other all-night hangouts are associated with downtown bars. Open for food and gambling is the **Oxford Club,** at North Higgins and Pine. Although not for the faint of heart or the easily appalled, the Ox is a Missoula fixture. Late at night, this is local color at its most opaque. The Oxford's brains and eggs is considered a rite of passage of sorts. The server calls the order by shouting, "He needs 'em."

Higher up on the food and spending chain are some ethnic and tony restaurants. The **Mustard Seed** offers good if not complex Chinese-inspired food in a pleasant environment at 419 W. Front, tel. 728-7825. Good Mexican food is available at **Casa Pablo's,** 227 W. Main, tel. 721-3854. It's a good place to go if you're really hungry since portions are huge, and there's plenty of atmosphere in the well-preserved turn-of-the-century dining room (formerly a bar). The waiting area is a gem of an art deco cocktail lounge.

Missoula's favorite pizza is found at **Zimarino Brothers** (aka **Red Pies Over Montana**) at 424 N. Higgins, tel. 549-7434. It's not recognizably Chicago- or New York-style: it's authentic Missoula pizza, judging from its popularity. Zimari-

no's also offers a selection of pasta dishes. For *cuisine,* try the **Alleycat Grill.** It's tucked in the alley behind the Top Hat at 125 W. Main, tel. 728-3535. Reservations are often necessary at this hip café.

For a splurge, the **Northern Pacific Restaurant** offers an international menu in a white linen atmosphere, at the end of N. Higgins, tel. 549-7434. In the same neighborhood, The **Depot** at 201 W. Railroad, tel. 728-7007, offers steaks and seafood in conjunction with a much-vaunted salad bar.

Higher up on the hill above Missoula is the **Mansion Restaurant,** in the old Greenough Mansion. The view and ambience are outstanding, and the food—steak and seafood—isn't bad either; 102 Ben Hogan Dr., tel. 728-5132.

Drink
Nowhere does Missoula's unique mix of population become more apparent than in its many and bustling watering holes. Some bars are of interest because of their historic character, others because of the characters they attract. Remember that bar life in Montana is primarily social in nature. Bars are where people meet up. There is no stigma attached to not drinking alcohol. Even if you don't care for a drink, go along for the friendly welcome. Be prepared, however, for lots of unrepentant gambling and a certain loss of ambience to the chattering of electronic gaming devices.

The downtown area is chockablock with curious old bars. The **Missoula Club,** 139 W. Main, is a peanut-shells-on-the-floor, grill-in-the-back sports bar, with fixtures unchanged since the 1940s. The Mo Club can get pretty busy at night, but it's a great place to hole up late in the afternoon. Don't attempt to resist their grilled hamburgers. They are, in their simplicity, the stuff of legend.

Also legendary, but for different reasons, is the **Oxford Club** at Pine and North Higgins. Although not always edifying, it has character by the bottleful and a certain attraction for writers. Watch the creative writing students who eye the bar's sullen denizens, waiting for epiphanies. Another bar with an edge to it is the **Stockman's,** 125 W. Front, popular with poker players. Its motto, "Liquor up front, Poker in the rear," has had habitués chortling for decades.

The Oxford Club has gained reknown for its gambling and 24-hour café.

JUDY JEWELL

More standard youthful hangouts are the **Rhino,** 158 Ryman, and the **Top Hat** at 134 W. Front. The latter offers live music (blues and swing, mostly) in an atmosphere heavy with Missoula's peculiar, indolent funkiness.

If you're searching for the gay bar in town, descend the steps at 225 Ryman Ave. to the **AmVets** (yes, the AmVets) **Bar.**

Red's White Sox Bar, at 217 Ryman, is a safe haven for Chisox fans and others willing to stand up for a favorite team. (Missoula has a rookie-league baseball team—the Mustangs.)

Missoula's own locally brewed ale is available at the **Northern Pacific Brew Pub,** at the end of N. Higgins. During the summer bands play on the veranda and hamburgers are bbq'd to order. Not to be outdone, Missoula's other train depot-cum-bar, the **Milwaukee Station,** under the south side of the Higgins Bridge, offers drinks on its lawn beside the Clark Fork.

EVENTS

Early each April, the university plays host to an international **wildlife film festival.** Call the university's information line at 243-4636 for schedules.

A Native American **powwow** is held annually, usually in May, in the university field house. The chamber of commerce, tel. 543-6623, can provide exact dates and times.

The 221-mile bicycle **Tour of Swan River Valley** is an annual springtime event. Register well in advance for the TOSRV ride; it's sponsored by the Missoula Bike Club, tel. 728-7984.

Missoula's Mendelssohn Club sponsors a midsummer choral festival, drawing choirs from all over the world for a series of free concerts. Contact the **International Choral Festival,** 210 E. Pine St., Missoula, MT 59802, for specifics.

The **Western Montana Fair** is held in Missoula during the third week of August. It's time to take in a rodeo, a delectable Montalado (a Montana-style enchilada), the llama pavilion, and coin-operated animal tricks that will send chills up the spine of any animal-rights activist.

RECREATION

Swimming

Missoula is a good place to get some exercise after a long car trip. The university's indoor **Grizzly Pool** has regularly scheduled public hours; adults pay $1.50 for a swim and sauna, children $1.25. Call 243-2763 for the schedule. Outdoor pools are in McCormick Park, at the west end of the Orange St. Bridge, tel. 721-PARK, and at Playfair, behind Sentinel High School (facing onto Bancroft St., tel. 721-PARK).

Bicycling

Missoula has a reputation as a great bike town, and these days everybody seems to be on a mountain bike. The **Rattlesnake National Recreation Area,** a corridor through the Rattlesnake Wilderness, is a mountain biker's dream, but be sure to avoid cycling in the adjacent wilderness area; maps are available at local outdoor stores.

Mount Sentinel's summit can be reached by riding out Pattee Canyon Rd. to the unmarked, gated Crazy Canyon Rd. and climbing to the top of the 5,158-foot peak. A less strenuous fat-tire ride is on the path along the Clark Fork, perhaps venturing east of downtown into the **Kim Williams Nature Area,** named for the late National Public Radio commentator, whose voice represented all things Missoulian to many across the country. Pick up a copy of Bikecentennial's mountain bike map of the Missoula area at their office, or see *Mountain Bike Adventures in the Northern Rockies* by Michael McCoy for details on these and other rides.

Mountain bikes can be rented at the **Braxton Bike Shop,** 2100 South Ave., tel. 549-2513. **Open Road,** 525 S. Higgins, and **New Era,** 101 Brooks, are bike shops in the downtown area.

Bicycle enthusiasts will do well to stop by the **Bikecentennial** headquarters, 113 W. Main, tel. 721-1776. They publish a small bicycle-touring map of Missoula as well as a host of other maps for routes stretching across the nation. Bikecentennial operates bicycle tours and is a clearinghouse for information on cycle touring. There's always chance for casual or obsessive bike talk at their offices.

Golf

Nine-hole public golf courses include the **Highlands Golf Club** at 102 Ben Hogan Dr., featuring the historic Greenough Mansion as its clubhouse/restaurant, tel. 728-7360; and the course on the **University of Montana** campus, tel. 728-8629. **Larchmont Golf Course,** 3200 Old Fort Rd., tel. 721-4416, has 18 holes.

Skiing

There are two downhill ski areas just outside Missoula. **Montana Snowbowl** is the big one—it has 25 runs, reaching up to three miles long, and a 2,600-foot vertical drop. It's about 12 miles out of town, reached by taking the Reserve St. exit from I-90 and driving north on Grant Creek Rd. to Snowbowl Rd., tel. (406) 549-9777. Lift tickets at Snowbowl are $18 for adults, $9 for children, with lessons and student, senior, and half-day rates available. Both skis ($12 per day) and snowboards ($15 per day) can be rented.

Marshall Ski Area, with its seven runs and 1,500-foot vertical drop, is seven miles east of Missoula just off Hwy. 200, tel. 258-6619. Rates are $14 for a full day of skiing and $10 for a half day, with reduced rates for students and children. Marshall has night skiing on selected evenings.

Nightingale Nordic is a privately owned cross-country ski area 16 miles west of Lolo on Hwy. 12, tel. 273-2415 or 273-0655. Over 10 miles (17 km) of tracks are groomed for both traditional cross-country skiing and skate skiing. Trail passes cost $5 for adults and $3 for children. There's also a rental shop and snack bar in the cabin that serves as a lodge.

There are a couple of popular cross-country ski areas in the Garnet Range east of Missoula. **Garnet Resource Area,** a BLM-operated ghost mining town, has 55 miles of ski and snowmobile trails. Follow Hwy. 200 east five miles to Garnet Range Rd., then turn south and follow signs along the Forest Service road. Or follow I-90 26 miles to Bearmouth and turn north five miles on Hwy. 10 to Bear Gulch Road. Follow signs for Garnet.

Skiers can rent cabins in and around the town of Garnet, but there's no driving in to them—food and gear must be packed in. Maps and rental information are available from the BLM office at 3255 Fort Missoula Rd., tel. 329-3914.

The University of Montana School of Forestry, tel. 243-0211, maintains the **Lubrecht Experimental Forest** and its half- dozen cross-country ski trails. From Missoula, take Hwy. 200 to Greenough. Turn right (east) one-half mile beyond the post office and go another quarter mile to Lubrecht Camp. A map of the trails can be picked up at the forest headquarters at Lubrecht Camp.

Closer to town, the **Rattlesnake National Recreational Area and Wilderness** has miles of trails; many are suited for skiing. Consult the RNRAW map, available at outdoor stores, for possibilities.

Fishing

Fishing in Missoula can be as unpremeditated as throwing a line into the Clark Fork from a bridge in the middle of town. The Clark Fork, which was horribly polluted until cleanup measures were taken in the 1970s, is now home to some trout.

Excellent fishing spots abound within an hour's drive of town. The **Clark Fork, Blackfoot, and Bitterroot rivers** harbor rainbow, brown, cutthroat, and Dolly Varden trout. **Rock Creek** is reached by traveling 26 miles east of Missoula on I-90 to exit 126. Rock Creek has been designated a blue-ribbon trout stream, though it is not necessarily an *easy* stream to fish. Catch-and-release fishing is enforced along the middle stretch of the creek and fishing with bait is prohibited, except by children.

Campsites along Rock Creek range from **Ekstrom's Stage Station,** a full-service tent and RV campground (complete with flush toilets, hot showers, a store and swimming pool) one-half mile from the freeway on Rock Creek Rd., tel. 825-3183, to **Siria,** a small, bare-bones Forest Service campground with no drinking water, 29 bumpy miles up Rock Creek Road.

The **Montana Department of Fish, Wildlife, and Parks** has an office in Missoula at 210 39th St., tel. 721-5808.

SHOPPING

For many travelers, Missoula will either be one of the first or one of the last places visited in Montana. Missoula's shops offer the visitor either a last chance to stock up on vital comestibles and to drink that final espresso, or the first opportunity in days to assuage deprivations incurred further inland.

Butterfly Herbs, 232 N. Higgins, tel. 728-8780, offers tea, coffee, herbs, spices, soaps, and in fact a little of everything. The store itself is a well-preserved specimen from the turn of the century. The back of the store is a good espresso bar and café.

The **Good Food Store,** 920 Kensington, tel. 728-5823, is Missoula's best source for natural and health foods.

Freddy's Feed and Read, near the university at 1221 Helen, tel. 549-2127, is the place for good literature and alternative books (it's also a natural foods grocery). The **Bird's Nest,** 219 N. Higgins, tel. 721-1125, is a center for new and secondhand regional books, and **Fact and Fiction,** at 216 W. Main, tel. 721-2881, is a good general bookstore. Most periodicals are available at **Garden City News,** 329 N. Higgins, tel. 543-3470. Out-of-state newspapers are a specialty.

Because of Missoula's access to the outdoors, recreation stores are important to the visitor. A good source of equipment, either for sale or rent, is the **Trailhead** at N. Higgins and Pine, tel. 543-6966. The staff are usually able to offer good advice on local trails and conditions. **Rent-a-Sport,** 2300 Brooks, tel. 549-8225, rents almost everything associated with sports and recreation.

TRANSPORTATION

Air

Johnson Bell Airport is on Hwy. 93 just north of town, tel. 728-4381. Continental, Delta, Horizon, Northwest, and United Express airlines fly into Missoula, but don't expect to find bargain airfares. Shuttle service is available from the airport, tel. 542-7433.

Automobile

All roads lead to Missoula. I-90 will get you there. So will Hwys. 93 and 200. Highway 12 jogs north to join with I-90 in Missoula. Bicycle touring notwithstanding, a car provides you with the most opportunities to get to the really great places. Auto rentals are available at the airport—Hertz, Budget, National, and Avis all have headquarters there. In town, some of the cheaper places include **Rent-A-Wreck,** 2401 W. Broadway, tel. 721-3833 or (800) 421-7253; **Payless,** 200 S. Pattee, tel. 728-5475 or (800) 237-2804; and **U-Save,** 3605 Reserve St., tel. 251-5745 or (800) 426-5299.

Bus

The **Greyhound** station is at 1660 W. Broadway, tel. 549-2339. Greyhound buses run three times daily along the interstate. Several smaller bus lines operate out of the same terminal (same telephone number, too). **Intermountain Trans-**

portation goes between Hamilton and Kalispell, and to Great Falls via Lincoln. **Rimrock Stage** goes to Helena and Bozeman, and **Missouri Valley Trails** goes to Helena.

Mountain Line Transit operates the city buses, and 40 cents will get you wherever they go. Buses run Mon.-Saturday. Most buses leave the downtown from Main between Pattee and Higgins; others run along Main and can be boarded at the corner of Broadway. Mountain Line's main office is at 1221 Shakespeare, tel. 721-3333. Call them or stop by for schedules, which are also available at several locations around town, including the University Center, the library, and the Birchwood Hostel.

Taxi

Taxi service is provided by **Yellow Cab,** tel. 543-6644. A shuttle service, tel. 542-7433, is available from Johnson Bell Airport.

SERVICES

For emergency, police, fire, and ambulance, dial 911. The **police station** is at 201 W. Spruce, tel. 523-4777.

The main Missoula **post office** is at 1100 W. Kent, tel. 329-2200, but the downtown Hellgate Station, 200 E. Broadway, tel. 363-1445, may prove to be more convenient.

The city's two major hospitals are **Community Hospital,** 2827 Fort Missoula Rd., tel. 728-4100, and **St. Patrick's,** located right downtown at 500 W. Broadway, tel. 543-7271. The **Blue Mountain Women's Clinic,** 715 Kensington Ave., tel. 721-1646, offers health services for both women and men.

The **First Interstate Bank** at 101 E. Front, tel. 721-4200, is the main bank in town, and the place to go to exchange foreign currency.

If you become truly enchanted with Missoula, you may find yourself at 539 S. Third Ave. W, tel 720-7060. This is where the **Job Service** is located.

Are dirty clothes taking over your suitcase? Well, positively snappy laundromats abound in Missoula. The following are particularly conveniently located: **Dud's-n-Sud's,** Toole Ave. and W. Broadway, tel. 549-1223, is near a strip of inexpensive motels. Toward the university, a couple of places cater to students: the **Dry Cleaning and Laundry Shoppe,** at 700 S.W. Higgins, tel. 728-7245, has a pleasant enough "study area" complete with an aquarium and a TV. **Sparkle Laundry,** 812 S. Higgins, is outfitted with a TV, video games, and a frozen-yogurt concession. **Grime Busters,** 1202 W. Kent (near Brooks), tel. 721-3429, has the ultimately practical sideline— a used-clothing store. They also do dry cleaning.

INFORMATION

The Missoula **Chamber of Commerce,** at the corner of Van Buren and Front, tel. (406) 543-6623, has racks brimming with brochures on Missoula and the surrounding area. They range from the strictly commercial to a well-done brochure on Missoula's historic buildings. The chamber of commerce will also keep you abreast of "What's Up in Missoula," with their weekly updated telephone recording, tel. 728-INFO (4636).

The regional **U.S. Forest Service** office, at 340 N. Pattee, tel. 329-3511, sells national forest maps for $2 apiece, a little cheaper than you'll find in most retail outlets. This also is a good place for general information on hiking and camping in national forests.

The **Department of Fish, Wildlife, and Parks** has a regional office at 3201 Spurgin Rd., tel. 542-5500. They'll offer advice on fishing and hunting, and can provide a list of public campgrounds.

The **public library,** always a good source of information, is at 301 E. Main. What you don't find on their shelves may well be in the stacks of the **university library.** Of particular interest here is the Mansfield collection, located on the third level down. United States Senator Mike Mansfield left his papers to the University of Montana, and they're housed down here along with a great collection of regional history.

THE BITTERROOT VALLEY

Probably nowhere else in Montana provides such a diverse and satisfying unity of attractions as the Bitterroot Valley. First of all, let's make it clear that the Bitterroot is stunningly beautiful. The Bitterroot River, flanked by groves of cottonwood, winds through a wide fertile valley of farm and pasture land. The heavily wooded humped arch of the Bitterroot Mountains rear back to reveal precipitous canyons and jagged peaks. Historic, quiet old towns slumber in a purposeful way: there are comings and goings, but no commotion.

Opportunities for recreation are almost limitless. The Bitterroot River provides great fishing; the Bitterroot National Forest offers thousands of acres of wilderness, with over 1,600 miles of maintained trails to dramatic peaks, pristine lakes, and wildlife viewing. Across the valley to the east, the Sapphire Range offers gem hunting and more wildlife habitat. Proximity to Missoula lends sophistication to the services in the Bitterroot, but also engulfs the lower valley with residential subdivisions.

Although hardly a crossroads, the Bitterroot Valley has played a role in most of the major economic and historical developments of Montana. Saint Mary's Mission, the first permanent structure erected in Montana, was established in 1841, and Stevensville became the first white-established town. While little mining went on in the Bitterroot, much of the food for the booming mining towns to the east was raised here. And while relations between early settlers and the local Flathead Indians were strikingly amicable, Chief Joseph and his Nez Percé fled up the Bitterroot on the way to the bloody Battle of the Big Hole. The Bitterroot has been sheltered from some of the excesses of the rest of the state's history, while benefiting from its rich past.

When you hear talk about the people "up the Bitterroot," the speaker usually has one of two stereotypes in mind. One would be a cartoon out-of-state artist or retiree whose earnest allegiance to fly fishing or other supposed Montana ways makes real Montanans roll their eyes. The second is of an extremely conservative, almost cultist, backwoods survivalist. The Bitter-root has attracted a new kind of pioneer who finds in the isolation a chance to home-school the kids and a haven from the threat of creeping communism and the loss of the gold standard.

Just south of Hamilton is the small community of Grantsdale, settled exclusively by a sect of the Church of Jesus Christ of Latter-day Saints. Although members of the community follow the directives of original 1880s Mormon dogma, many have been excommunicated for practicing polygamy.

THE LAND

The Bitterroot River flows north in a wide valley between two mountain ranges. The Sapphire Range to the east is characterized by relatively low, forested peaks. To the west rise the deep canyons and jagged peaks of the Bitterroot Mountains, whose rugged watershed forms the Montana/Idaho border.

The Bitterroot Range was formed as the granite of the Idaho Batholith rose to the surface. The immense rock slabs, on whose molten slopes the Sapphire Range skidded eastward, survived to coat the eastern slopes of the batholith. It is this sheet of diagonally pitched rock, called Bitterroot mylonite, which stretches up the valley, lending the range its distinctive, evenly hunched edge. Behind this thousand-foot-thick veneer of rock rear the heavily glaciated granite peaks of the Idaho Batholith, here called the Bitterroots.

The Bitterroot River flows north in the gulf created as the Sapphires continue to slouch eastward away from their original home. While the streams that flow out of the Sapphires have better fishing, the Bitterroot drainages are more distinctive and better explored. Curiously evenly spaced down the length of the valley, these streams debouch from alpine lakes in rounded valleys scooped out by glaciers, then fall quickly through narrow canyons gashed through the resistant mylonite.

When talking of the Bitterroot River it is prudent to note a point of confusion. The human mind is curiously unable to deal with a north-flowing river. Some instinctive sense recognizes north as uphill. "Upriver" could be any direction but south. So be warned: the lower reaches of the Bitterroot are north, near Missoula; farther south, beyond Darby, is the upper Bitterroot. When the locals talk about going "up the Bitterroot" they are talking about going south.

Flora And Fauna

The wildlands of the Selway-Bitterroot Wilderness and the Bitterroot National Forest protect many species of wildlife, though none are unique to the Bitterroots. Elk, bighorn sheep, and mountain goats are frequently encountered, as are smaller mammals like the pika and badger. Os-

preys nest along the Bitterroot River, and bald eagles are frequent visitors to the valley.

Because the Bitterroot Range rises 5,000 feet—from the valley floor to its highest peaks—in three miles, a variety of ecosystems sustain a wide cross section of plant life. These range from the sage and juniper of the valley floor to the fir and larch forests of the upper reaches, with ponderosa pine mediating the transition. The subalpine larch, a deciduous conifer, clings to rock faces high above the point where other trees cease to grow.

HISTORY

In 1805, Lewis and Clark passed down the Bitterroot Valley from the south, over Lost Trail Pass. The Corps of Discovery had already crossed the Continental Divide at Lemhi only to discover that, although the Salmon River in Idaho flowed into the Columbia drainage, it did so as the aptly named "River of No Return." The Salmon was hopelessly impassable. The Corps climbed up into Montana again, this time to follow the Bitterroot down to Lolo Creek, where they established a favorite camping spot, called Traveler's Rest. From here, the Corps followed Lolo Creek up and over Lolo Pass, and down more hospitable drainages to the Columbia. The following year, they retraced their trail to Traveler's Rest. Clark and half the Corps returned up the Bitterroot to cross over Gibbon Pass into the Big Hole.

Lewis is responsible for the name of the plant that gives this valley its name. While local Indians found the roots of the bitterroot both tasty and fortifying, Lewis pronounced it bitter and nauseating. His name now identifies the plant in Latin *(Lewisia rediviva)*.

The Bitterroot Valley, with its fertile bottomland and protected climate, from the first attracted farmers. The discovery of gold in nearby valleys and the establishment of mining boomtowns created a demand for foodstuffs. As farmers moved into the area, they began to pressure the government to remove the Flathead from the valley, and in 1872 James Garfield, who later became the 20th U.S. president, was sent to transfer the Indians north to the Mission Valley.

THE BITTERROOT

While the Bitterroot lily, Montana's state flower, is found in most of the western part of the state, eponymous urgings make the Bitterroot Valley a good place to plan a sighting. The roots of these beautiful light pink flowers were a staple of the Indian diet. Legend contends that the plant sprung from the tears of a Flathead mother whose family was starving. The sun, hearing the mother's lament, sent a bird as a messenger to turn the bitter tears into a plant whose roots were nutritious (and equally bitter) but whose beauty reflected the devotion of the grieving Flathead matron.

Bitterroot was eaten fresh in season, and also dried for use in the winter or when traveling. The Flathead boiled or steamed the roots, then mixed them with berries, marrow, or meat. Although the snow-white meat of the root is bitter to the point of nausea to the unsuspecting, the Flathead found that if gathered before flowering or dried sufficiently, the bitterness was much reduced.

The bitterroot formed an essential part of the Indian diet, and elaborate rituals accompanied its harvest. Amongst the Flatheads, a venerable woman led out the other female gatherers. When they reached the first bitterroot, the leader would stick her elkhorn digger at the base of the plant. After the others planted their diggers, a prayer was offered and the first plant was uprooted. Only after the prayer was offered was the season open; to dig before the ceremony was to invite a small harvest. The following day the first root was given to the chief and a day-long feast ensued.

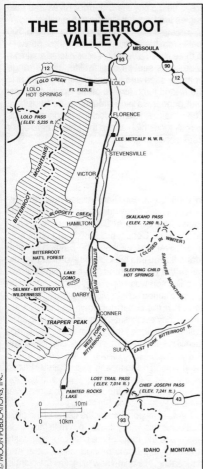

THE BITTERROOT VALLEY

MISSOULA

LOLO CREEK
LOLO HOT SPRINGS
FT. FIZZLE
LOLO
LOLO PASS (ELEV. 5,235 ft.)
FLORENCE
LEE METCALF N.W.R.
STEVENSVILLE
VICTOR
BLODGETT CREEK
HAMILTON
SKALKAHO PASS (ELEV. 7,260 ft.)
(CLOSED IN WINTER)
BITTERROOT NAT'L FOREST
BITTERROOT RIVER
SLEEPING CHILD HOT SPRINGS
SAPPHIRE MOUNTAINS
LAKE COMO
SELWAY - BITTERROOT WILDERNESS
DARBY
CONNER
TRAPPER PEAK
WEST FORK BITTERROOT R.
EAST FORK BITTERROOT R.
SULA
LOST TRAIL PASS (ELEV. 7,014 ft.)
CHIEF JOSEPH PASS (ELEV. 7,241 ft.)
PAINTED ROCKS LAKE
43
0   10mi
0   10km
IDAHO / MONTANA
BITTERROOT MOUNTAINS

© MOON PUBLICATIONS, INC.

barricade at Fort Fizzle and proceeded up the Bitterroot. No shots were fired as they passed through the valley. Once over the Continental Divide in the Big Hole, however, Colonel John Gibbon and 183 men ambushed the Nez Percé at the Battle of the Big Hole, August 9, 1877.

Agriculture

Farming really took hold in the Bitterroot after the Northern Pacific extended a spur line to Hamilton. One of the largest enterprises in the valley was Marcus Daly's Bitterroot Stock Farm. The copper magnate from Butte preferred the Bitterroot as a summer home, and he built a magnificent mansion on his 26,000-acre holding. Considering the fact that Daly modeled his farm on an Irish manor, it's no surprise that race horses were the most noted of the farm's products.

In the early years of this century, the Bitterroot was home to an elaborate irrigation scheme that turned the valley into a huge apple orchard. The Big Ditch, as it was functionally named, provided water to the eastside bench land, which was divided into subdivisions of 10 acres each. At the height of apple euphoria, 22,000 acres of the Bitterroot were in fruit production. The soil and climate didn't quite live up to the exaggerated promises of the developers, and by the 1950s apple production ceased to be a significant element of the area's economy.

While agriculture remains important in the Bitterroot, much of the farmland in the lower valley has now been subdivided into small "ranchettes." This part of the valley has largely been converted into a bedroom community of Missoula.

RECREATION

The Bitterroot National Forest contains 1.6 million acres, with nearly 750,000 of these protected as wilderness. Forest Service roads provide entrance for mountain bikers or off-road-vehicle enthusiasts, while 950 miles of maintained trails give hikers access to some of the most tortured geology and pristine landscapes in the Rockies.

All the larger streams that feed into the Bitterroot River harbor rainbow, cutthroat, and brook trout, and some of the higher lakes in the Bitterroots, such as the Big Creek Lakes, are known for good fishing.

Five years later, the Nez Percé passed through the Bitterroot on their tragic flight across the Northwest. Under the leadership of Chief Joseph, the band of about 700 Indians and nearly 2,000 horses traveled from Idaho down Lolo Creek and up the Bitterroot toward Crow country, fleeing the Army infantry. Chief Joseph vowed to the Army and the Bitterroot settlers to march peaceably through the settled areas of the Bitterroot, in return for unmolested passage. The offer was not accepted officially, and the Nez Percé simply skirted a hastily constructed

For the angler, though, the real news is the Bitterroot itself. The river seems largely untainted by the effect of a century's worth of foresting, farming, suburban sprawl, and irrigating. In fact, even in the busy heart of the valley, the cottonwoods and willows that line the shore shield the angler from the realities of Bitterroot development. The trout here are both numerous and large. Rainbows and browns fill up the majority of creels, but cutthroat and the elusive Dolly Varden are also apprehended. The lower part of the river near Missoula is where the lunkers are most likely lurking (along with rumors of largemouth bass), while farther south, up Connor way, is where the trout are thickest.

The state has established six fishing-access sites on the river, and there's also easy access from bridges. At no place is the Bitterroot far from the road, though remember to ask for permission before crossing private land. Boat rentals are available in Hamilton, and organized float and fishing trips are offered by the region's many outfitters.

THE LOWER BITTERROOT

From Hamilton (pop. 2,700, elev. 3,600 feet) north to Missoula, the Bitterroot is at its most genteel. Excluding lodges of typically nomadic Indians, this part of the valley is the oldest continuously inhabited area in Montana, and it

shows. Interesting old Victorian farm houses are scattered amongst the fields, and isolated apple trees from once substantial orchards can still be seen in meadows. Main streets have changed little since they were built. Despite the crags of the Bitterroot Range rising to the west, here the Bitterroot feels lived-in and comfortable.

The visitor should leave Hwy. 93 as soon as possible (at Florence at the Missoula end, and at Hamilton from the south) and instead take the East Side Highway, MT 269. While 93 is undeniably a faster road, it's also very busy (commuters' cars sport the bumper sticker declaring "Pray for me. I drive Highway 93"). The East Side Highway affords the best views onto the Bitterroots and goes through the pretty towns of Corvallis and Stevensville. It also avoids the more obvious effects of the subdivisions in the lower valley, the part of the Bitterroot that is not so much Missoula's bedroom as its stable.

Try to pick up a copy of a handy brochure called "East Side Highway: Bitterroot Valley Scenic and Historic Drive" from a tourist bureau in Hamilton or Stevensville. As you drive through these old communities, you'll want to know more about the architecture and history.

History

Father Pierre-Jean deSmet established St. Mary's Mission near Stevensville in 1841. It was abandoned in 1850, and the land was purchased by John Owen to build Fort Owen, a

John Owen built Fort Owen from the remains of Montana's first Catholic mission.

JUDY JEWELL

trading post and Indian agency. After gold was discovered in nearby valleys, Owen and the other frontiersmen living in the valley found a market for the agricultural riches of the Bitterroot in the mining boomtowns.

Fort Fizzle, up Lolo Creek, was the rampart thrown up in 1877 to prevent Chief Joseph from passing through the Bitterroot Valley (see "History" above).

Marcus Daly, one of the Copper Kings of Butte, established Hamilton in 1890, at the southern end of a Northern Pacific spur line and near his vast estate and mansion, the Bitterroot Stock Farm. Hamilton became Ravalli's county seat in 1898, and several civic structures from this era still grace the town.

Hamilton is also known for the Rocky Mountain Research Laboratory, where research on Rocky Mountain spotted fever was conducted. The fever, which is spread by ticks and is debilitating if not fatal to humans and livestock, is endemic to parts of the Bitterroot. The discovery of a treatment opened infested and otherwise uninhabitable areas of the valley.

Sights

Hamilton is rather unique in the fact that it didn't just spring up as opportunity (or the railroad) allowed. Rather, like Athena, it sprang fully formed from the brow of copper magnate Daly, who, after designing his model Irish manor, decided to establish a model town nearby. In 1890, Daly brought in planners who laid down a city complete with free plots for churches, ready-designed banks, shops, schools, and rather glorious homes—in essence, a ready-made town. As a result, Hamilton wears its age very gracefully. Stop to picnic or let the kids loose in one of its parks. An easy stop for either one is a small playground only one block west of Hwy. 93 on Bedford, two blocks south of Main. There's a more substantial park where Madison St. bumps up against the Bitterroot River.

Saint Mary's Mission at Stevensville was rebuilt in 1866 by Father Anthony Ravalli out of the original hewn logs of the 1841 structure. The one-room chapel with front belfry is open to the public Wed.-Sat. 10 a.m.-4 p.m., Sun. 10 a.m.-2 p.m.; $2 admission, tel. 777-5734. The interior, with its wood-burning stove and wainscoting, is pretty much as Father Ravalli left it.

Also on the grounds are the mission pharmacy and a graveyard. While Father Ravalli's grave is meant to be the draw here, more curious is the sign indicating "Indian Graves," before an open field. Saint Mary's Mission is on Fourth St. two blocks west of Main.

What's left of **Fort Owen** is just east of Hwy. 93 on the Stevensville cutoff (follow signs for the Fort Owen Monument after the Forest Service office). The original 1850 structure evolved from the log palisade of a frontier trader into an adobe-brick fortress with turrets and walkways after Owen became the federal Indian agent to the Flathead. Of the original buildings, one barracks remains and serves as a museum with interpretive exhibits. The fort is on private land and is open during daylight hours.

Marcus Daly bought his Bitterroot Stock Farm in 1889, and built the **Marcus Daly Mansion** in 1897. After his death, the house was enlarged in 1910 to its present Georgian revival splendor. Built primarily as a summer home for the Daly family, "Riverside," as the mansion was known, looks over the Bitterroot Valley to the rugged peaks in Blodgett Canyon, and vies with the Bitterroots themselves for splendor. The house remained in private hands until 1987, when it was acquired by the state.

Riverside is probably the most beautiful estate in Montana. A tree-lined boulevard leads to 50 acres of grounds, which contain an arboretum of specimen trees, a swimming pool, a playhouse, and a tennis court. The 24,213-square-foot mansion contains 42 rooms, 24 of which are bedrooms and 15 are baths. Some of the original furniture and most of the old fixtures remain. The grounds alone are worth a strolling tour.

The mansion is located four miles south of Corvallis and two miles north of Hamilton on MT 269. After leaving the highway, follow a boulevard about a mile until you reach the grounds. Riverside is open from April-Oct., Tues.-Sun., 11 a.m.-4 p.m.; $3 admission, tel. 363-6004.

Daly's most famous race horse was Tammany Hall. In keeping with the Daly tradition, Tammany did not simply have a stable, but a brick edifice called Tammany Castle. To see what upscale horses lived in at the turn of the century go one mile east of Hamilton on MT 269. Look to the south about 100 yards. The stable is not open to the public.

Hamilton contains a number of handsome old homes and public buildings. The **Ravalli County Museum** is housed in the Old Ravalli County Court House, built in 1900. This stone and brick landmark bears a resemblance to the University of Montana's Main Hall. The museum has a good collection of Flathead Indian artifacts, pioneer-era memorabilia, and an exhibit on wood ticks. The museum is at the corner of Bedford and Third streets. Summer hours: Mon.-Fri. 10 a.m.-4 p.m., Sun. 2:30-5 p.m.; winter hours: Mon., Wed., and Fri. 1-4 p.m., Sun. 2:30-5 p.m. No admission fee. Like the court house, the **City Hall,** at 175 S. Third, is on the National Register of Historic Places.

Accommodations

There's one motel in Stevensville, **St. Mary's Motel and RV Park,** along Hwy. 93. Singles are $25, doubles $30, tel. (406) 777-2838. There are more to choose from in Hamilton. Economical lodging can be found at the **Ravalli Motel,** $25 s, $32 d, at 515 N. First St., tel. 636-3255; at **Deffy's Motel,** $23 s, $25 d, 321 S. First St., tel. 363-1244; at the **Sportsman,** $22 s, $28 d, 410 N. First St., tel. 363-2411; and at the **Bitterroot Motel,** $22 s, $28 d, 408 S. First St., tel. 363-1142. The "First St." that these motels share as an address is actually busy Hwy. 93. The only motel not on First St. is the **City Center Motel** at the quiet end of Main Street, $22 s, $26 d, 415 W. Main, tel. 363-1651. You can pay more money for lodgings along First at **Best Western Hamilton Inn,** $32 s, $38 d, 409 First St., tel. 363-2142 or (800) 426-4586.

For a slightly different twist in lodging, consider staying at one of the local hot springs resorts. Some of the best in the state are in the Bitterroot Valley. **Lolo Hot Springs Resort** is 30 miles up Hwy. 12 along Lolo Creek (38500 Hwy. 12, Lolo, MT 59847, tel. 273-2290). The mineral water is channeled into a large swimming pool, and there's a motel (rooms start at $52), camping, and a bar. Lewis and Clark camped and bathed here. Nowadays, these hot springs are popular with skiers returning from a long day in cross-country heaven at Lolo Pass.

There's a little less funk involved at **Sleeping Child Hot Springs,** just south of Hamilton. In addition to the 98° pool, there are two hotter tubs, a restaurant, and a lodge. Rooms start at $60. After turning onto Hwy. 38 toward Skalkaho Pass, follow signs for the hot springs, which are about 10 miles up a well-maintained road. Sleeping Child is open Thurs.-Sun. noon-11 p.m. (around the clock for weekend hotel guests). For information, write Box 768, Hamilton, MT 59840, or call 363-6250.

For the resort-minded, the Bitterroot offers a wide variety of guest ranches and upscale lodges. One of the more unusual of these is the **Selway Lodge.** It has no vehicular access; guests must ride or hike the 15 miles into the lodge. Nature studies are a specialty. Your bill will be $1200 for a two-week stay. Write Box 1100, Hamilton, MT 59840, tel. 636-2555, for details.

Camping

The U.S. Forest Service maintains a number of campsites in the Bitterroots. Most require a fair amount of determination to make use of: some are essentially trailheads into Bitterroot canyons, and others demand long dusty drives on county roads, but some are handy enough for the more casual traveler to consider.

Lewis and Clark Campground is 12 miles west of Lolo on Hwy. 12, and for the angler, right on Lolo Creek. An even more enticing fishing/camping site is the state's **Chief Looking Glass Fishing Access Site,** which is a developed campsite as well. Look for the fishing-access sign on Hwy. 93 about midway between Lolo and Stevensville, at milepost 77. Then turn east one mile to the river.

Charles Waters is a developed site at the trailhead up Bass Creek, with access to hiking up the canyon and fishing in the stream. Watch for the Forest Service sign for Bass Creek Trail four miles south of Florence or four miles north of Stevensville on Hwy. 93. It's about three miles in to the campsite.

There's more luxury at some of the area's private campgrounds. If you're driving south from Missoula, the first you'll find north of Hamilton is **Rockford's Campgrounds,** one mile south of Victor. As with motels, Hamilton is where the action is in campgrounds. **Bitterroot KOA** has a pool and showers and is eight miles south of Hamilton on Hwy. 93, tel. 363-2430. **Angler's Roost,** three miles south of Hamilton, offers most facilities, tel. 363-1268.

Food And Drink

The hungry traveler will not want for opportunities to fill up in the Bitterroot. There are so many cafés and restaurants along the road that one imagines that Bitterroot residents do little but journey from coffee klatch to lunch and back again. The traveler can't go far wrong with most Bitterroot eateries, and there are a few worth planning ahead for.

Glen's Mountain View Café in Florence is an ordinary enough little roadside café with extraordinary pastries. Not that the rest of the menu is lacking (Glen's raises its own beef), but the pies are reckoned to be the best in the state. Glen's is right on Hwy. 93 at Florence, tel. 273-2534.

The Fort Owen Inn is near the site of old Fort Owen. It's a Western kind of place well used by locals as a hangout and dance hall. The steaks are the news here. The supper club offers a selection of 10 cuts of well-marbled beef. The Fort Owen Inn is right off Hwy. 93 at Stevensville, tel. 777-3483.

The Banque in Hamilton offers well-prepared food in a historic bank building, lending the dining enterprise a kind of ersatz Montana elegance. The savvy traveler will not be surprised to learn that steaks headline the menu. The Banque is at 225 W. Main, tel. 363-1955.

If you want serious steak eating, then find your way to the **Wagon Wheel Steak House** just south of Hamilton on Hwy. 93. Since the steaks are hand-carved, you can order them to fit enormous appetites. Standard menu cuts stop at 24 ounces. The Wagon Wheel has a homey, local air, perfect for the kind of engorgement that's inevitable here, tel. 363-1434.

No serious traveler wants to pass a good bakery by, and **Wildflour Bakery,** 923 First St. N, tel. 363-5420, certainly rates a stop for herb bread or raisin bars.

Recreation

Any creek worth mentioning in the Bitterroots has a trail up it, and all are worth considering for a hike. The Forest Service map of the Bitterroot National Forest will apprise the hiker of dozens of likely destinations. The traveler with some time to spend in the Bitterroots can ask locals for recommendations (every undergrad at the University of Montana has a favorite valley) or ask rangers for the inside scoop. But if you have only a day to spend in the lower Bitterroots, consider one of the following.

A largely overlooked long day-hike (or unstressful overnight trip) that's close to Missoula leads to **Peterson Lake** up the Sweeney Creek drainage. You'll need a vehicle, because the allure of the hike is how high the trailhead is. Forest Service roads (turn west on Forest Service Rd. 1315, two miles south of Florence) will take the hiker most of the way up the canyon wall to a trailhead. After a couple miles of easy traversing, the hiker drops onto alpine lakes, with the car having done most of the climbing.

Another popular ascent of intermediate challenge involves climbing **St. Mary's Peak.** Again, this hike boasts a trailhead midway up the mountain, and one of the great views that the peak affords is onto the local lookout tower. From Hwy. 93, go two miles south of the Stevensville turnoff. A brown sign promising St. Mary's Peak points up the switchbacks of Forest Service Rd. 739.

The **Blodgett Creek Canyon** just west of Hamilton is probably the most beautifully precipitous of the many valleys gashed in the side of the Bitterroots. Although the landscape is very rugged, the trail is relatively level and well maintained. There's no hidden reward at the trail's end, so hike in until lunch seems propitious, and come back out. Back roads out of Hamilton itself lead to Blodgett Creek trailhead, or turn west two miles north of Hamilton on Hwy. 93, just north of the Bitterroot River Bridge.

The **Lee Metcalf National Wildlife Refuge** is a good place for short hikes along the Bitterroot River. It's a good place too for adding the word "riparian" to your vocabulary. This riverside refuge is full of ospreys, eagles, and whatever migrating birds need a place to spend the night. White-tailed deer and coyotes also live here. In the summer, after nesting season, a two-mile loop trail is open through the refuge. Two shorter trails are open year-round, and picnics are encouraged. From the East Side Highway (Hwy. 269), watch for the binocular signs indicating a sanctioned wildlife-viewing area, either just south of Florence or just north of Stevensville.

Another place for nature viewing is the **Bitterroot Wildflower Area.** During late spring, the area is blanketed with a colorful display of local bloomers. In June, watch for the eponymous Bitterroot lily. At other times of the year, the traveler with a hankering for a stroll gets great views onto the Bitterroot Valley. When the signs on Hwy. 93 point east to Corvallis, turn west instead and follow signs to an old logging road up the side of the Bitterroot Range.

Cross-country skiing is pretty much the order of the season after snowfall, and is as casual as just parking the car and putting on your skis. Any of the Bitterroot canyons are good bets, and are even more pleasant covered with snow, as they tend to be pretty rocky and rugged in summer. The real treasure for cross-country skiers, though, is Lolo Pass. Snow simply dumps along the pass all winter, but the Highway Department keeps the road open. Lolo Pass is 37 miles east of Lolo on Hwy. 12. It's very popular, but it's still possible to strike out and get away from the crowds.

There are **public golf courses** in Stevensville and Hamilton. The Stevensville course, just north of town on Wildfowl Lane, tel. 777-3636, has nine holes; the Hamilton Golf Club, on Golf Course Rd. southeast of town, tel. 363-4251, has an 18-hole course.

Outfitters

If the thought of all that nature in the Bitterroot makes you a little jumpy or just lonely, consider hiring an outfitter to ease that transition into the wilderness. After seeing the piles of flyers at the chamber of commerce, you'll wonder if there's anyone in the Bitterroot who is *not* an outfitter or who at least doesn't run a "guest ranch." The following are just highlights of what's available, but an inquiring letter to the chamber will be sure to result in cascades of mail.

Catch Montana offers fishing and floating vacations in the Bitterroot, Box 428, Hamilton, MT 59840, tel. (800) 882-7844. **Rocky Mountain Adventures,** Box 1574, Hamilton, MT 59840, tel. 363-3344, offers hunting and fishing trips and horse or rafting excursions. **Continental Divide Outfitters** at Box 462, Corvallis, MT 59828, tel. 961-4867, will take you hunting and fishing and offers "bunkhouse" accommodations. **Lone Tree Outfitting,** 1531 Iron Cap Rd., Stevensville, MT 59870, tel. 777-3906, offers big-game hunting to both the able and the handicapped.

Shopping

The most obvious craft in the Bitterroot Valley is log-house construction, but even if you're not in the market for a new house, the Bitterroot offers clever windsocks in the shape of enormous flowers at **Wind Related.** There's a shop at the factory along Hwy. 93 north of Hamilton, tel. 363-1050.

Mountain Outfitters Supply repairs bikes at 248 W. Main, tel. 363-3131.

Hamilton supports a good general bookstore, **Chapter One,** 219 Main, tel. 363-5220 and one focussing on used and paperback books, **Rocky Mountain House,** 140 Second St. N, tel. 363-2662.

Transportation

The Bitterroot Stage goes back and forth between Missoula and Darby once a day, and stops just about everywhere along Hwy. 93, tel. 363-2282. **Rent-A-Wreck** operates along Hwy. 93 north of Hamilton, tel. 363-1430.

Services

The **Marcus Daly Memorial Hospital** is at 1200 Westwood Dr. in Hamilton, tel. 363-2211. The Hamilton **sheriff** can be reached at tel. 363-3033.

Hamilton's **post office** is at 340 W. Main. There are also post offices on the main streets of Stevensville, Corvallis, and Victor.

The **Main Street Wash O Mat** is at 711 W. Main in Hamilton, tel. 363-9969.

Information

The **Bitterroot Valley Chamber of Commerce** is just east of the stop light in Hamilton, 105 E. Main, tel. 363-2400.

The **Bitterroot National Forest Headquarters** is in Hamilton at 316 N. Third, tel. 363-3131. The **Stevensville Ranger District Office** is at 88 Main St., tel. 777-5461.

The **Hamilton Public Library** is at 306 State St., tel. 363-1670.

Read the *Ravalli Republic* to keep up on who's been arrested for what, and how big a fish they've caught lately.

THE UPPER BITTERROOT

The Bitterroot Valley narrows upstream from Hamilton, and the character of the land changes.

The river flows faster and the mountains encroach. With rocky ramparts closing in, the Bitterroot ceases to be a broad valley with farms and subdivisions and becomes a wooded canyon. Here, loggers and (for want of a better term) woodsmen predominate. For the traveler, recreation is the draw in the upper Bitterroot.

The Land

Darby marks the southern edge of old Lake Missoula, when in the bad old days the entire Missoula Valley system was alternately underwater and drained as the ice age saw necessary. At Connor, just south of Darby, the Bitterroot divides into the West Fork and the East Fork. The highway also divides. Highway 93 follows the East Fork up Lost Trail Pass over the Continental Divide into Idaho or into the Big Hole Valley. The West Fork proceeds up Hwy. 473 first along a paved road, then along an improved road to Painted Rocks Lake.

The West Fork remains mostly canyon country, but at Sula on Hwy. 93 the East Fork opens onto pastureland. All of a sudden it's cattle country, a last reprise of the Bitterroot Valley before it disappears into the heights of the Continental Divide.

History

Lewis and Clark straggled off Lost Trail Pass in September of 1805 after being foiled on their way to the Columbia by the chasms of the Salmon River. They crept back into Montana via the Bitterroot, and almost immediately met a lodge of Flathead Indians. At present-day Sula, the Corps of Discovery found 400 Flathead and 500 horses encamped, and quickly made friends. Remember the landscape. The enormous painting in the Montana House of Representatives in Helena depicts this meeting.

The valley at the junction of the East Fork and Camp Creek later became known as Ross's Hole. Alexander Ross was a Canadian trapper who nearly died of cold here with his family in 1824.

The Nez Percé passed through Ross's Hole in 1877 on their way to the Battle of the Big Hole, only minutes over the Continental Divide. While the tribal leaders felt they had escaped the pursuing Army, others, with "medicine powers," began to foresee the coming ambush. By this time, the Army, under the command of General Gibbon, had caught up with the fleeing Indians, who unwisely took a break from their flight from Idaho once they had reached Montana.

Accommodations

Darby is a rough-hewn little town that seems to have changed little from its early logging days. Its lodging facilities haven't changed much, either. Bearing in mind that rustic is the operative word, try **Honey's Motel,** Old Darby Rd., tel. 821-3111. To stay in mini log cabins, go to the **Log Cabin Motel,** Hwy. 93 S, tel. 821-3282.

If you have something more luxurious in mind (remember, again, that you are in remote Montana), try the **Lost Trail Hot Springs.** While hot springs resorts can veer from the near-bizarre

*Mission Mountains
from Ninepipes
Wildlife Refuge*

JUDY JEWELL

and seedy to the over-sanitized and commercial, Lost Trail strikes a happy balance. It provides convention facilities (for very small conventions) and the hot mineral water that you expect, but also offers recreational opportunities like mountain biking, hiking, cross-country skiing, horseback riding, fishing, plus the usual bar and restaurant facilities. Lost Trail Hot Springs is seven miles south of Sula on Hwy. 93, and six miles north of Lost Trail Pass (motel rooms are $45, cabins with two beds are $55). The address is simply Sula, MT 59871, tel. 821-3574.

Another lodging option is the **West Fork Lodge,** five miles south of Connor on MT 473, West Fork Rd., Darby, MT 59829, tel. 821-3069. It offers cabins and a motel (each $35 a night), and a one-stop-shop store, bar, and café.

Camping

The Forest Service maintains a number of campgrounds in the upper Bitterroot, mostly off the beaten path. A couple are handy for casual campers who don't want to get too far off the highway. **Indian Trees** is six miles south of Sula, at a location where Flathead women once spiked ponderosa pines to extract sap, which was used as a sweetener. Lewis and Clark camped at **Spring Gulch,** and so can you. The campground is right on the East Fork River, five miles north of Sula on Hwy. 93. The **Sula Store** offers campsites at the beginning of the canyon leading from Ross's Hole.

Recreation

The upper Bitterroot has reserved some of the best recreation for those willing to drive the extra miles to get there. You can grow hoarse talking about the hiking possibilities in the Bitterroot, whether the upper valley or the lower, but probably the most astonishing ascent of the entire range is the climb up **Trapper Peak.** At 10,157 feet, it's the highest mountain in the Bitterroots, and—wait for it—not even a particularly difficult day hike. The trailhead is reached by following West Fork Rd., MT 473, at Connor. Once you pass the Trapper Peak Civilian Jobs Corps Center, go almost seven miles to the signs pointing to the Trapper Peak trailhead. Switchbacks take you most of the way up the back of the mountain, though there's enough slogging left to

satisfy more energetic hikers. If you do only one ascent in the Bitterroots, this should be it.

If a day on the mountain isn't possible for you, then enjoy the other end of Trapper Peak at **Lake Como.** This lake just west of Darby is nestled in a valley rimmed by the most unrestrained peaks in the Bitterroots. It should be no surprise that other people know of Lake Como (the Italian Lake Como is its namesake and chief rival in beauty), and don't expect to be the only campers at the lake. There's good trout fishing but too many speedboats to make it a bucolic getaway. There's an easy eight-mile loop trail around the lake. Watch for Lake Como signs five miles north of Darby.

Another good but slightly longer day-hike will take the curious to **Overwhich Falls,** which drops 200 feet along the wall of the Continental Divide near Lost Trail Pass. It's about six miles in, but after following the switchbacks up to the trailhead, it's fairly easy going. From the Indian Trees Forest Service Campground follow the signs for Road 729 to Porcupine Saddle. From the trailhead, the trail follows Shields Creek to the falls.

Painted Rocks Lake is a reservoir on the West Fork of the Bitterroot that receives a lot less activity than Lake Como and offers better fishing. There are Indian pictographs on the rocks to the west of the lake. Painted Rocks Lake is 23 miles southwest of the junction of Hwys. 473 and 93.

The Bitterroot south of Darby (upstream—we told you this would get confusing) becomes a stream with fast action. The river's never far out of sight, and access is easy if you maintain the courtesy of asking permission to cross private property. There's one fishing-access site that warrants mention. The **Hannon Memorial Fishing Access Site** at Connor allows the angler to fish both the East and the West forks of the Bitterroot as they converge. Camping is allowed.

Information

The **Sula Ranger Station** is just south of Sula on Hwy. 93. The address is simply Sula, MT 59871, tel. 821-3201. The **Darby Ranger Station** can be contacted at Box 266, Darby, MT 59829, tel. 821-3913. The **sheriff** can be reached at 363-3033.

FLATHEAD RESERVATION

INTRODUCTION

The Flathead Reservation measures about 65 by 35 miles east to west. Of about 6,500 tribal members, some 3,800 live on the reservation. The Flathead population is centered at Arlee; most of the Kootenai tribal members live near Elmo. The reservation is managed by the Confederated Salish and Kootenai Tribes, with headquarters near Pablo. A council of 10 elected members, each representing a district of the reservation, governs the tribes.

The Culture Committee of the Confederated Salish and Kootenai Tribes works to keep traditions alive on the reservation. A longhouse in St. Ignatius is used for spiritual ceremonies and storage of herbs and medicinal plants, and a summer camp immerses tribal youngsters in native language and traditions. Along with the preservation of traditional ways comes preservation of natural resources, and the Confederated Salish and Kootenai Tribes have earned a reputation as environmental stewards. Several businesses are run by the tribes, including S and K Electronics, a high-tech firm north of Pablo.

The Mission Mountain Tribal Wilderness is the first place in the United States where "an Indian nation has designated Tribal lands as a wilderness preserve" (from highway marker). It covers the west side of the range's peaks; to the east, it's the Flathead National Forest, with access from Hwy. 83 in the Swan Valley. Any hiking or camping in the Mission Mountain Tribal Wilderness requires a tribal conservation permit, available at many local stores. A three-day conservation permit costs $3; in order to fish on tribal land, an $8 conservation and fishing permit is required.

HISTORY

Salish-speaking Indians originally lived near the Pacific coast. Legend has it that an argument developed as to whether flying ducks quacked with their wings or with their bills. The ones who voted for the wings ended up moving to the Bitterroot Valley. Most Salish-speaking tribes still live near the coast. When the wing-quacker group, which became known as the Flathead Salish, arrived in the Bitterroot Valley, the Pend d'Oreilles who were living there moved north, apparently as a gesture of friendliness.

The Pend d'Oreille also speak a Salish language. Their base was the area around present-day Paradise and Plains and, though they hunted in western Montana, they didn't make regular buffalo-hunting expeditions to the plains.

Until the Blackfeet moved onto the Montana plains in the mid-1700s, the Flathead Salish spent a great deal of time on the eastern plains hunting buffalo. Travel to the west was more limited, generally just far enough to fish for salmon west of Lolo Pass. Camas, bitterroot, and serviceberries were other dietary staples. The Flathead still gather these plants.

MONTANA HISTORICAL SOCIETY

Chief Charlo resisted relocation from the Bitterroots to the Flathead Reservation.

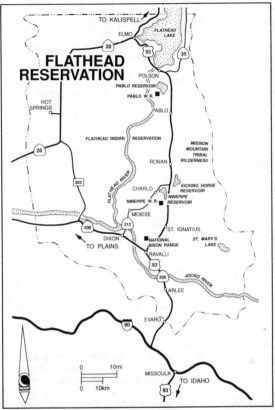

FLATHEAD RESERVATION

© MOON PUBLICATIONS, INC.

date the white homesteaders. Maintaining a good relationship with whites was important enough to Chief Charlo that he refused to help his friend Chief Joseph of the Nez Percé on his flight east. He told Joseph that if the Nez Percé caused any harm to the settlers in the Bitterroot Valley, the Nez Percé could expect the Flathead to defend the whites.

Charlo never signed the reservation treaty. However, in 1872 Arlee, a Flathead war chief, did sign it, and he thus won recognition from the U.S. government as head chief of the Flathead tribe. Charlo stayed behind in the Bitterroots until 1891, when he told the government agents who were pressuring him to move, "I will go—I and my children. My young men are becoming bad; they have no place to hunt. I do not want the land you promise. I do not believe your promises. All I want is enough ground for my grave."

During the early years of the Flathead Reservation, Indians lived in both log cabins and, weather permitting, in tepees. Many took up farming, with a number of successful farms eventually dotting the valley. In 1910, under the Dawes Act, the government allotted each Indian family a parcel of reservation land. The remaining land was made available to white homesteaders. Non-Indians flooded in, and they now comprise about 80% of the population on the Flathead Reservation.

Lewis and Clark and early white settlers found the Flathead to be friendly and helpful. The Flathead continued good relations with white settlers, with many intermarriages. They also got along well with Iroquois and other East Coast Native Americans who moved out west with fur trappers and traders in the early 1800s.

The 1855 Hellgate Treaty formed the Flathead Reservation, but Victor, head chief of the Salish, refused to move his people from their home in the Bitterroot Valley. By the 1870s, the influx of white settlers into the valley made the government attempt to foist a new treaty onto the Flathead. Charlo, Victor's son and the new head chief of the tribe, held firm against moving to the reservation in the Jocko/Mission Valley, but he and his people did what they could to accommo-

RONAN AND VICINITY

Ronan was named for Peter Ronan, an Indian agent. The area around Ronan was part of the Flathead Reservation until 1910.

The **"Garden of the Rockies"** pioneer museum is on Round Butte Rd., five blocks west of Hwy. 93. There are mock-ups of a doctor's office, barber shop, schoolroom, kitchen, bedroom, and living room. Expect a friendly volunteer to give you a personalized tour; perhaps you'll get a demonstration of a favorite object, such as a hand-pumped vacuum cleaner.

Pablo, five miles north of Ronan, is the headquarters of the Confederated Salish and Kootenai Tribes and home of **Salish-Kootenai College,** which offers programs in general studies, Native American studies, nursing, and a range of human services and vocational fields. The college library is a good place to read up on the Salish and Kootenai Tribes. Both traditional and modern Native American art are represented in the college's collection.

Pablo National Wildlife Refuge, off Hwy. 93 about five miles north of the Ninepipes Refuge, is a similar waterfowl sanctuary and is governed by similar regulations.

Accommodations
There's only one motel in town, the **Starlite,** at 18 Main St. SW, tel. (406) 676-4800. A room here won't run more than $25.

Mission Meadows Campground, two miles north of Ronan, then half a mile west of Hwy. 93, has 15 tent and 85 RV spaces. It is open year-round and offers, along with all the usual campground amenities, an indoor heated pool, hot tubs, and a laundromat, for $11 per night, tel. 676-5182.

Food And Drink
The **Rabbit Tree Inn** at 405 Main St. in downtown Ronan is a reasonably priced breakfast, lunch, and dinner spot with a complete bar. **Santorno's,** a moderately priced Italian restaurant on Hwy. 93 just north of Pablo, tel. 676-4859, is one of the area's most popular dinner spots.

Allentown Restaurant is five miles south of Ronan on Hwy. 93, just across from one of the pullouts for Ninepipes Wildlife Refuge. The menu departs a bit from the fancy steak and seafood fare, though that's still a major focus, and there's been some attention given to the wine list. Dinners run around $15. Breakfast and lunch are also served. The Allentown attracts locals who, at night, may happen upon its bar midway along journeys elsewhere.

Events
Ronan celebrates **Pioneer Days** during the second week of August, complete with the obligatory rodeo. Call the chamber of commerce at 676-8300 for more information.

Recreation
Ronan's nine-hole **golf course** is three miles west of Hwy. 93 on Round Butte Rd., tel. 676-4653. Greens fee is $9 for nine holes, $14 for 18.

Information
Write to the **chamber of commerce** at P.O. Box 254, Ronan, MT 59864, or call them at 676-8300.

Ronan has a small **library** on the corner of Main and Second streets, tel. 676-3682. There's also a library on the campus of the Salish-Kootenai College, tel. 675-4800.

ST. IGNATIUS AND VICINITY

Saint Ignatius is a reservation town at the feet of some stunningly jagged peaks. It's home to the Salish Cultural Committee, tel. 745-4572, and a longhouse, located near the St. Ignatius Mission, used for spiritual and ceremonial events.

National Bison Range
It may sound a little boring, driving around in your car for two hours on a one-way road, staring out the window for a glimpse of shaggy critters. But it's not. The National Bison Range has two driving tours, and it's worth taking a couple of hours to go on the long one. Stop in at the visitor center and find out where the herds have been spotted recently. Bison are the main attraction, but expect to see bighorn sheep, pronghorn, elk, mule deer, white-tailed deer, and mountain goats as well. Even if all the animals are in hiding, the land, the sky, and the light are beautiful here. As with most wildlife viewing, it's best to visit early in the morning or around dusk.

The National Bison Range was established in 1908, in response to concern that the buffalo had been slaughtered to the point of extinction. Part of the original herd was purchased from the Conrad family of Kalispell, who were early buffalo ranchers. A bison roundup is held in early October at the Bison Range.

The Bison Range is on a parcel of land carved from the Flathead Reservation by Hwy. 212 near Moiese. If you're approaching from Hwy. 93, catch Hwy. 212 between St. Ignatius and Ronan. If you're on Hwy. 200, there's a turnoff to Hwy. 212 near Dixon. The visitor center at the entrance of the range collects a $2 fee and dispenses brochures.

If there's no time for a tour, at least be sure to keep your eyes peeled as you drive Hwy. 93 north of Ravalli. Sometimes the bison come down off their mountain to water just a hundred yards or so from the highway.

Fort Connah

In 1846-47, Angus McDonald (a Canadian fur trader who, like David Thompson, had a good reputation with the local Indians) built Fort Connah as a Hudson's Bay Company trading post six miles north of St. Ignatius on Post Creek. It was the last of the Company's trading posts in the United States, and was situated near an Indian trail in hopes that such a location would give the Canadian traders an edge on the increasingly competitive American fur traders. Fort Connah operated until 1871. The one building that remains is on private land.

St. Ignatius Mission

Saint Ignatius became, in 1854, the site of the second Catholic mission in Montana. Father Adrian Hoecken, a Jesuit priest, originally established the mission in Idaho, but it was moved to the Mission Valley at the behest of the Pend d'Oreille Indians. A boys' school, a mill, and a press (which printed a dictionary of the Pend d'Oreille language) eventually grew up around the mission.

One of the Jesuits' original log buildings (a chapel that doubled as living quarters for the priests) still stands beside the brick church, which was built in 1891. The church deserves as much of a look as the wooden chapel; there are striking murals inside, painted by Brother Joseph Carignano, the mission cook. While these murals may not initially impress those who hold them up against St. Paul's Cathedral or Chartres, they clearly succeed in illustrating the life of Jesus and in imparting biblical stories to the Indians. Sunday mass is still held weekly at 9:30 a.m. (Good Friday and Easter services at

the mission church have developed into a uniquely Flathead Catholic ceremony.)

Ninepipes Wildlife Refuge

This wetland waterfowl refuge is north of the bison range, between Hwy. 93 and Hwy. 212. The large reservoir and many smaller lakes are rimmed with marshlands, making it difficult to hike from many of the roadside viewing points. The best views are generally from the road that goes along the northern edge of the reservoir off of Hwy. 212. The many "pothole" lakes around the refuge were dug out as glaciers moved across the land some 12,000 years ago.

Ninepipes is in the path of a major migratory flyway in the Rocky Mountain Trench. Prime birdwatching occurs in September. Canada geese, mergansers, mallards, redheads, great blue herons, grebes, double-crested cormorants, American wigeons, pintails, whistling swans, California gulls, ring-billed gulls, pheasants, bald eagles, and American avocets are some of the birds you might spot here.

Check at the headquarters of the National Bison Range for information on the birds and regulations. (There are information sites at the various roadside viewing areas, but they seem to be perpetually out of brochures.) Since the refuge is on tribal land, a tribal fishing permit is

F.J. HAYNES/MONTANA HISTORICAL SOCIETY

St. Ignatius Mission, 1884

required before throwing a line into the reservoir. Permits are available at local sporting-goods stores and at the tribal headquarters in Pablo. No hunting is permitted on the refuge, and it is closed during both waterfowl-hunting season (in the fall) and nesting season (March through mid-July).

Accommodations
Doug Allard's Lodgepole Motel ($21 s) on Hwy. 93 in St. Ignatius, tel. 745-9192 or 745-2951, is part of a complex that includes a museum, a small grocery store, and a trading post with a good selection of beadwork done by tribal members. There's also a chance for a close view of some buffalo here; Allard has a small herd fenced in to the side of the trading post.

Mandorla Ranch Bed and Breakfast, 6873 Allard Rd., tel. 745-4500 or (800) TLC-MONT, is east of St. Ignatius beneath the peaks of the Mission Mountains. Rates range from $35 for a single room with a shared bath to $80 for a double suite with a fireplace and private bath. Breakfast is included with all the rooms, and dinner can be arranged for an extra fee. **Cheff's Ranch** is just down the road from Mandorla's. They have dude-ranch packages and offer horseback rides twice daily for ranch guests and others.

Camping
Free camping behind the senior center in Charlo is provided by the Lions Club. It's a convenient place to stay if you want to get an early jump on bird and animal watching. For a post-bison beer, stop in to the **Branding Iron Bar** in Charlo.

Bison Park Campground, tel. 745-4268, is near the junction of Hwy. 200 and Hwy. 93 in Ravalli. It's open year-round, charges $4, and has showers and a laundromat. **Bison View Campground** is on Hwy. 200 two miles west of its junction with Hwy. 93. It's $7 per night and also has showers and a laundromat.

Food And Drink
A number of cafés in the Southern Flathead Valley, especially those near the National Bison Range, feature buffalo burgers. This low-cholesterol meat is reported to taste something like venison. It comes from bison raised on ranches, not from the tourist attractions roaming the bison range. **Bison View Café,** next to the Bison View

Campground on Hwy. 200, is one of these places. They also feature huckleberry milkshakes. The **Bison Inn,** on Hwy. 93 in Ravalli, serves buffalo burgers as well as more standard diner breakfasts, lunches, and dinners.

Recreation
To explore the **Mission Mountain Tribal Wilderness,** first pick up a tribal recreation permit ($3 for a three-day permit available at Allard's Trading Post). And, unless you know the area, a map of the Flathead National Forest or the Flathead Reservation is another essential.

Kicking Horse Reservoir is just east of Hwy. 93 across from the turnoff to Hwy. 212. It's the site of a Job Corps program run by the Confederated Salish and Kootenai Tribes.

Saint Mary's Lake is less than 10 miles from St. Ignatius on St. Mary's Lake Road. (Find the road just southeast of the mission and follow it as it turns to a fairly bumpy, dusty gravel road, turns left, and heads into the hills.) There are several places to pitch a tent around the lake, and it's worth taking along fishing gear and a tribal fishing permit—there are some lunker trout around here. Just over a mile up the road is the first of the **Twin Lakes,** which are a little more isolated and quieter than St. Mary's. (No motorboats are allowed on the Twin Lakes; St. Mary's does permit them.)

Shopping
Doug Allard's Trading Post (in the same complex as the motel, museum, and bison herd) has a wide selection of beadwork done on the Flathead Reservation. Expect to find some great beaded earrings and hair ornaments, as well as less apparently traditional beaded cigarette-lighter covers. A couple of miles north of Allard's, the **Four Winds Trading Post** specializes in moccasins, Indian artifacts, and toy trains. Preston Miller, proprietor of Four Winds, also collects historic buildings from around the Mission Valley and has moved several to the trading post.

Events
Arlee, 15 miles south of St. Ignatius on Hwy. 93, is the site of the **Fourth of July Powwow** held annually by the Confederated Salish and Kootenai Tribes. It's a major event, not to be missed if you're anywhere in the area. Expect to

see both traditional and fancy dancing to the accompaniment of amazing drumming. Groups of drummers, as well as individual dancers, compete for prize money. In another area of the powwow, the sounds of hand drums signal stick games, which are ritualistic and high-stake gambling competitions. For those not up to the complications and $100 ante of a stick game, poker and blackjack games are set up in small shacks.

Jewelry, crafts, and cassette tapes of popular drum groups are for sale at a number of booths. There's also plenty of food, including fry bread and "Indian tacos." The powwow grounds are the site of an encampment during this long weekend. Tepees, tents, and campers crowd into the dusty field and the celebration goes on late into the night. The powwow grounds are right in Arlee, just east of Hwy. 93. There is no admission fee, non-Indians are welcome, and drugs and alcohol are strictly prohibited.

HOT SPRINGS

The western part of the Flathead Reservation has a couple of commercial hot springs in and around the town of Hot Springs. **Camp Aqua Bathhouse,** five miles off Hwy. 28 at Hot Springs, is a place to relax in a private room with a "plunge," a steam room, a shower, and a toilet. The plunge is like a cement baby pool, with hot water. It's not a posh place; it *looks* like a few aqua-colored double-wides thrown together—the floors are cement, the Formica's cracked, and the steam room barely warms up. But no matter, this place somehow has the feeling of a refuge, a place where chills and bone weariness melt away and you're left with your pores open to the rolling hills and golden light of the surrounding reservation. The bathhouse is open year-round from noon to 10 p.m. An hour-long soak costs $4. There are a couple of apartments available for rent by the night here ($15-35), but most people just come for a soak.

If you do want to spend the night within an easy sniff of the waters, **Symes Hotel and Medicinal Waters** in the town of Hot Springs, tel. 741-2361, has rooms with bathtubs plumbed with the local sulfurous brew. The room rates will make even a devoted camper consider taking a real bed for the night—a double room goes for $15. The hotel has the air of faded therapeutic benefits; the rooms are clean and comfortable, but you may feel it's improper to speak above a whisper.

If you're ready to pull out all the stops in Hot Springs, the **Hot Springs Spa,** tel. 741-2283, has hot tubs, massages ($20), and rooms starting at $15 (or $150 a month).

Locals mix with day-trippers up from Missoula at the free, informal, outdoor hot pool back behind the old bathhouse in Hot Springs. When you hit the T-intersection in town, take a right, follow on up the hill, and bear right. There is some talk of plans to renovate the old bathhouse and return it to its previous status as a tourist destination.

Free camping is provided by the Lions Club on Hwy. 28 between Plains and Hot Springs. It's an informal, indeed bare-bones, place up on a bluff.

Perma

Perma is on the bank of the Flathead River, which flows into the Clark Fork near the junction of Hwys. 135 and 200. Salish and Kootenai Indians made annual trips to this area to dig camas root.

This was Pend d'Oreille country, and traces of their vision quests remain near Perma. Just across the bridge to Hot Springs, a dirt road turns off abruptly to the left, then follows the river a mile and a half down to a clearing near the bend. It takes a little looking, but several red ocher animal figures and a number of hatch marks (which may count the days a young Pend d'Oreille spent on a vision quest) are visible on a cliff by the clearing. This is reservation land, so get a tribal permit before poking around or fishing.

FLATHEAD LAKE

Flathead Lake fills a trench carved by glaciers during the Pleistocene epoch. A terminal moraine at the foot of the lake divides the Flathead Valley from the Mission Valley to the south. Until glacial ice receded, Flathead Lake drained to the west in the area of Big Arm. The outlet is now via the lower Flathead River, which exits the lake at Polson and flows into the Clark Fork around Paradise. Kerr Dam, just southwest of Polson, controls the water level of the lake and the Lower Flathead River.

Three upper forks of the Flathead River join above Kalispell to pour into Flathead Lake. The North Fork originates in southeastern British Columbia, the Middle Fork rises in the northern part of the Bob Marshall Wilderness (near the southern edge of Glacier National Park), and the South Fork flows from the southeastern region of the Bob Marshall Wilderness, via Hungry Horse Reservoir.

HISTORY

David Thompson was the first white in the area (1808). While he was residing at his Saleesh House, a trading enterprise near present-day Thompson Falls, his Indian neighbors told him of Flathead (Salish) Lake. Thompson was guided there in 1809. Jocko Finley, a Scot-Indian, assisted Thompson and became a major fur trader in the southern Flathead Valley. Fur trappers worked the Flathead Lake area from about 1810 through the middle part of the century. Fort Connah, south of Flathead Lake in the Mission Valley, was the main trading post for the region.

Steamboats ran on Flathead Lake in the late 1800s and early 1900s. Their route was from Demersville (a now-defunct town on the Flathead River, halfway between Kalispell and Flathead Lake) down to Polson.

The first white settlers on the eastern banks of the lake arrived in 1891 and quickly lit upon the idea of growing cherries there. Homesteading started in earnest around 1910, when reservation land became available to non-Indians under the Dawes Act. Fruit orchards grew up all along the eastern shore of the lake. They've been subject to periodic killing frosts, most recently in 1989.

RECREATION

Fishing the upper forks of the Flathead depends to a large extent on what's spawning at the moment. These are cold rivers with few nutrients. Many of the fish in them are from the lake, heading upstream to spawn. Fall is the season for kokanee (but since kokanee are now in short supply in Flathead Lake, this isn't much of a season). Cutthroat and Dolly Varden (bull) trout spawn in the spring.

The southern half of Flathead Lake falls within the confines of the Flathead Reservation; anglers should make certain to have the necessary tribal permit, available from sporting goods stores or from the tribal office in Pablo.

Water levels are highest in May and early June, making this the best time of year for river running.

POLSON

Polson (pop. 2,800, elev. 2,949 feet) is tucked into a glacial moraine at the foot of Flathead Lake where the Lower Flathead River drains from the lake. Highway 93 takes a turn here and becomes an east-west road for its run through Polson. It's the county seat of Lake County and the business center of Flathead Lake and the upper Mission Valley. Montanans also tend to think of cherries when Polson is mentioned, though many of the trees around Flathead Lake were killed by the severe 1989 frost.

History
Ferry service across the Lower Flathead River began in the mid-1800s, and in 1880 a store was built at the foot of the lake. By 1898, there was enough of a town to warrant a post office, and it took its name from David Polson, who'd been ranching about five miles northwest of town since 1870.

THE KOKANEE'S DEMISE

Native fish in the Flathead River system include westslope cutthroat trout, Dolly Varden (or bull) trout, and mountain whitefish. Introduced species include kokanee salmon (the freshwater version of sockeye), lake, rainbow, and brook trout, and northern pike.

The prized kokanee salmon once made up 90% of the fish in Flathead Lake, but in recent years they've virtually disappeared, and whitefish are the dominant species.

Mysis shrimp, another introduced species, may be to blame for the kokanee's demise in Flathead Lake. Apparently, the tiny shrimp, originally introduced as fish food, beats the salmon to food sources deep in the lake and wins the competition for habitat.

BOB RACE

Kokanee salmon

Sights

Flathead Lake is the big attraction here. There's plenty of public shoreline and several parks that make appealing sitting, swimming, fishing, or boat-launching spots. **Boettcher Park** is toward the eastern edge of town, **Sacajawea Park** is right downtown off Kootenai Ave., and **Riverside Park** is on the east end of the bridge over the river.

Lake cruises on the *Port of Polson Princess* run daily during the summer, leaving from a dock just east of downtown on Hwy. 93. A three-hour tour departs daily at 1:30 and makes a loop around Wildhorse Island. The fare is $12 for adults, $6 for children. Two-hour sunset cruises depart at 6:30 p.m.; $10 for adults, $5 for children. Family rates and senior citizen discounts are offered.

Polson is a treasure trove for small-museum aficionados. The **Polson-Flathead Historical Museum** at 704 Main St.; is a dark, jumbled place that houses a stuffed steer named Rudolf, the State Fiddlers' Hall of Fame, and a seven-foot sturgeon caught in Flathead Lake in 1955 and reputed to have been the Flathead Mon-

ster. Summer hours are Mon.-Fri. 9 a.m.-6 p.m., Sun. noon-6 p.m., $1 donation requested.

A recent addition is the **Miracle of America Story Museum** on Hwy. 93, just below Hwy. 35 junction ($1 admission, open Mon.-Fri. 9 a.m.-5 p.m., Sun. 2-6 p.m.). The large boat outside the museum is the *Paul Bunyan,* a log towboat. Inside, the intrepid museum-goer will find a unique homage to cleanliness: a collection of antique vacuum cleaners. Music lovers will thrill to the sound of the violano, a coin-operated violin-piano combination.

If it's not too much of a letdown to visit a dam after steeping oneself in our nation's heritage, the **Kerr Dam,** a 204-foot-tall concrete arch dam, is eight miles from Polson on the Lower Flathead River. It was built during the Depression and opened in 1939. It is operated by the Montana Power Company, which leases the land from the Confederated Salish and Kootenai Tribes. Reach it by heading west on Seventh Ave. to Hwy. 354 and following the signs. (This makes a nice bike ride if you don't mind rolling hills with one steep climb.) A long flight of steps leads to a vista over the dam before the road goes down to the power station.

Accommodations

There are several inexpensive motels along Hwy. 93 just east of Polson's city center: **Marina Motel,** with rates from $26 s, $29 d, backs onto Flathead Lake, tel. (406) 883-4397. **Cherry Hill Motel** has duplex units on a bluff overlooking the lake, tel. 883-2737, and the **Sleepy Tiger Inn** is a friendly motel with free donuts and coffee just across the road from the lake, tel. 883-3120; rates start at $26 s. There's also a **Super 8** along this same stretch, tel. 883-6266 or 883-6251. For more expensive digs (and use of an outdoor hot tub), the **Best Western Queens Court** is just up from the Sleepy Tiger on Hwy. 93, tel. 883-5385. During the summer, rooms are $51 s and $59 d; winter rates run about $20 less.

Riverside Park, just west of the city center and east of the bridge, has camping for both tents ($5) and RVs ($10). It's not the most lovely campground on Flathead Lake, but it's convenient to breakfast or dinner in town.

Food And Drink

Try the **Port of Polson Galley** at 318 Main, tel. 883-6200, for breakfast, lunch, or dinner. It's the only place in town to find food that strikes a gourmet note, and it manages to do it without being the least bit stuffy or snooty. **La Porta Vista,** on Main St. at Hwy. 93, has Mexican food and a view of the lake, tel. 883-2585. The **4-B's** at the intersection of Hwys. 93 and 35, tel. 883-6100, has the basic but satisfying fare that Montana travelers have come to expect.

Entertainment And Events
The former golf course clubhouse is now the **Polson Performing Arts Center,** home to the Port Polson Players, a summer theater. The season starts in July, with plays Wed.-Sun. evenings at 8 p.m. Recent productions have been *The Nerd* and *Dames at Sea.* For information about what's on and reservations, call 883-9212.

Fiddle players flock to Polson the fourth weekend of July for the **Montana State Fiddlers' Contest.** Call 883-5969 for details.

Recreation
All manner of watercraft, from sailboards to houseboats, can be rented in Polson. Try **Big Sky Houseboat Adventures** for a sailboat (starting at $10 per hour, with half-day, daily, and weekly rates available), sailboat ($30 per hour), ski boat ($40 per hour including ski gear), or houseboat ($300 per day, $1500 per week). Call 883-3700 or (800) 443-6644.

"SWIMMER'S ITCH"

There are swimming beaches at almost every park on Flathead Lake, and by mid-summer the water is warm enough for enjoyable swimming. There is one special caveat here, though. Once the water warms up, it is home to a parasite known as "swimmer's itch." It's easy enough to figure that this is something to avoid, and there are a number of theories about how to do just this. First, adults and strong swimmers are less prone to swimmer's itch. Apparently the parasite lives in the warmer shallow water, where children are more likely to play. Repeated ins and outs of the water also seem to encourage the parasite to cling to one's skin. Local wisdom has it that coating your body with suntan lotion or any other oily substance will protect you from swimmer's itch. Calamine lotion and cortisone creams are the usual remedy, should precautions fail.

The Lower Flathead River has spectacular badlands scenery and some thrilling rapids just below Kerr Dam. The Buffalo Rapids are a challenging stretch of whitewater for experienced rafters. Those with less than expert whitewater skills should put in the river at the Buffalo Bridge, about 10 miles below Kerr Dam, or sign on with the **Glacier Raft Company,** which has a branch at Riverside Park in Polson that operates tours of the Lower Flathead River, including Buffalo Rapids.

Polson's 18-hole **golf course** is east of downtown on the lake side of Hwy. 93. Nine holes cost $9; 18 holes cost $16. Call 883-2440 for a tee time or more information.

There's a good swimming beach right near the golf course in Boettcher Park.

Since the southern half of Flathead Lake is on the reservation, fishermen need a tribal permit, which can be purchased at many stores in Polson. Although there's been a sharp decrease in the number of kokanee salmon in the lake in recent years, there are still lake trout, whitefish, and some cutthroat trout throughout the lake, as well as largemouth bass and perch in warm, shallow spots, such as Polson Bay. Fishing Flathead Lake requires some thought about water depth and temperature. The *Angler's Guide to Montana* has tips about which fish live where and when.

Although the Lower Flathead River doesn't have much in the way of trout, there are plenty of big pike.

Services
St. Joseph Hospital, Skyline Drive, tel. 883-5377, has 24-hour emergency service. The local **laundromat** is on the corner of First St. and Hwy. 93, by the stoplight. The **post office** is at 219 First St. East.

Information
Contact the **Polson Chamber of Commerce** at P.O. Box 677, Polson, MT 59860, tel. (406) 883-5969.

The public **library,** near the lake at First St. E and First Ave. W, tel. 883-4003, has several cases of books on Montana, a good variety of magazines, and lovely views onto Flathead Lake. Across the hall in the same building, find **Sandpiper Gallery,** with its displays of regional arts and crafts.

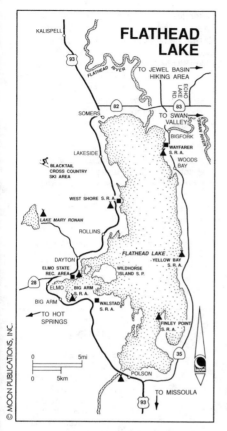

WEST SIDE OF FLATHEAD LAKE

Driving along the west side of Flathead Lake, you get a good view across the water to the Mission Mountains. There's more of an open feeling to this side of the lake than to the east side—off to the west the rolling Salish Mountains gentle the light and lend a glow to the surrounding land and sky.

Wildhorse Island
There are indeed wild horses on this island near the Big Arm of Flathead Lake. There's also a thriving herd of bighorn sheep and a wealth of birdlife, including ospreys, bald eagles, red-

tailed hawks, and Canada geese. The island exists because its rock base resisted the plowing action of the glacier that scooped out Flathead Lake. It was used as a sort of safe house for the local Flathead and Pend d'Oreille horses when Blackfeet came on raids.

Private concerns took over the island for many years, but it became a state park in 1977 and in 1983 the BLM began turning horses loose there. In 1940, two bighorn sheep were transplanted there as a tourist attraction. The herd grew to beyond what the island could support, and many sheep died of starvation before the Montana Department of Fish, Wildlife, and Parks began moving Wildhorse Island bighorns to other areas of the state.

Wildhorse Island is a day-use park; camping and fires (including campstoves) are prohibited, and there are still some private land holdings to avoid. You'll need a boat to get here. Boats can be rented in Big Arm for the trip to the island. Motorboats are recommended; they go for $30 a day at the Big Arm Resort and Marina. The *Port of Polson Princess* cruises from Polson around Wildhorse Island every day of the summer at 1:30, but it doesn't dock.

Angel Point, north of Wildhorse Island near Rollins, is the site of several pictographs. The red drawings, which have suffered from vandalism, are only visible from a boat on the lake.

Camping
Big Arm State Recreation Area, just north of milepost 74 on Hwy. 93, has camping for $7 per night (includes the $2 day-use fee). It's a good spot if you want to swim or boat, but the campsites are packed close together, making it a little uncomfortable for just plain camping. Don't expect to find peace and solitude here, but it's a lovely lakeside spot, and it's understandable why families flock here. **Elmo State Recreation Area,** on Hwy. 93 right near the turnoff for Hwy. 28 (to Hot Springs and Plains), is an open lakeside site, with a tenters' area right down by the water. This campground has showers, a rarity in the public campgrounds of Montana.

Between Dayton and Lakeside on Hwy. 93, **West Shore State Park** is yet another state campground on Flathead Lake. The $7 fee includes both day use ($2) and camping.

Elmo

Elmo is the site of the **Standing Arrow Pow-wow** during the third weekend of July. Though not as large as the powwow held in Arlee, it's a good opportunity to see dancing, drumming, and stick games. The **Kootenai Cultural Committee,** tel. 849-5541, the Powwow's sponsor, has its headquarters in Elmo.

Dayton

The **Mission Mountain Winery** has some vineyards, a winery, and a tasting room in Dayton. They produce mostly Johannesberg riesling and a "blush" wine called "Sundowner," but they also have a dry chardonnay and a cabernet sauvignon for those who are willing to pay more than $6 per bottle.

Lake Mary Ronan

Lake Mary Ronan is six miles off Hwy. 93 near Dayton. It's a popular place to fish, especially for kokanee salmon, which flourish here as they used to in Flathead Lake. Since the lake is not on reservation land, only a state fishing permit is needed. There are several resorts on the lake, all with cabins, tent and RV camping, and restaurants.

Lake Mary Ronan Resort, tel. 849-5454, has cabins with bedding (but no cooking gear) ranging from $35-70 per night, and campsites from $8. They also have a restaurant and a lounge with country music on the weekends. Boat rentals start at $10 per day, and showers are $2.50 if you're not staying at the resort. A friendly attitude is both preached and practiced here.

Mountain Meadows Resort, tel. 849-5459, is, if anything, an even friendlier place than Lake Mary Ronan. Cabins here run $30 per night, camping from $10, and boat rentals for $30 per day.

Camp Tuffit, tel. 849-5220 has the feel of your aunt's back yard—very pretty, well manicured, with green grass and Adirondack chairs, but perhaps a little cloistered. Cabins start at $17.50 a night and go to $54 for a multiroom cabin with a pool table. Boats go from $10-22 per day. There isn't really any tent camping here, but RV spaces are $8 per night.

Lambeth State Park has a $2 day-use admission fee, with an additional $4 for camping.

Lakeside

There are several motels in Lakeside. The **Northernaire Motel,** tel. 844-3864, has double rooms looking out onto the lake $39-48. The **Lake-Shore Motel,** tel. 844-3304, has small cottages from $40 s to $50 d. Both of these motels have swimming beaches and docks; the Lake-Shore also rents boats and canoes.

The **Blacktail Inn,** 105 Blacktail Rd., tel. 844-3055, is a good bet for food and drink in Lakeside. They are open for breakfast, lunch, and dinner, and serve a dinner buffet in addition to some fairly standard menu selections.

Blacktail Cross Country Ski Area is about eight miles from Lakeside. Pick up a trail map and brochure at the ranger station in Bigfork, the Forest Service office in Kalispell, or at the Lakeside Grocery and Deli. The trails, which range from easy to difficult, are at about a 5,500-foot elevation, which means a fairly long skiing season and a chance to get above the clouds. If you have two vehicles, park one at the lower parking lot and use it to shuttle back to the upper lot at the end of your ski tour. Only upper lot

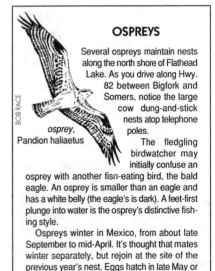

OSPREYS

Several ospreys maintain nests along the north shore of Flathead Lake. As you drive along Hwy. 82 between Bigfork and Somers, notice the large cow dung-and-stick nests atop telephone poles.

osprey,
Pandion haliaetus

BOB RACE

The fledgling birdwatcher may initially confuse an osprey with another fish-eating bird, the bald eagle. An osprey is smaller than an eagle and has a white belly (the eagle's is dark). A feet-first plunge into water is the osprey's distinctive fishing style.

Ospreys winter in Mexico, from about late September to mid-April. It's thought that mates winter separately, but rejoin at the site of the previous year's nest. Eggs hatch in late May or early June. Canada geese may compete for osprey nests.

parking is necessary if you plan to ski the easiest (and the only groomed) trail of the network. Do not ski on the road. There is log-truck traffic on it, even in winter.

Somers

The **Osprey Inn Bed and Breakfast** at 5557 Hwy. 93 S, tel. 857-2042, has a cabin by the lake as well as B&B rooms in the main house ($80 for a double with a private bath).

EAST SIDE OF FLATHEAD LAKE

Sights

Cherry orchards are both a business and an attraction around Flathead Lake. Cherries are usually harvested beginning around the third week of July.

The University of Montana runs a biological station at Yellow Bay. Limnology, the study of the life of lakes, ponds, and streams, is a major research focus here. The biological station has conducted most of its research on water quality and plankton, but the recent acquisition of a research boat will enable them to study the lake's fish. Summer classes in freshwater biology and ecology are offered for credit and for audit. The summer term runs for eight weeks, with housing available in cabins or dorm rooms.

For more information, call 982-3301. If your interest is more casual, drop by the station. Students are often pleased to discuss their research, and there are newsletters and bulletin boards to browse.

Accommodations

Schiefelbein Haus, tel. (406) 887-2431, is a small motel near the Finley Point cherry orchards. Rooms are $35, or $45-55 with kitchens. They also have a German-theme restaurant. **Jorgensen's Cabins,** tel. 887-2724, and **Pineglen Resort,** tel. 887-2455, are in the same Finley Point neighborhood.

The campgrounds off Hwy. 35 can be quite pleasant during off-peak times, and crowded and noisy during summer weekends. **Finley Point State Recreation Area** is four miles off Hwy. 35 on cherry-tree-studded Finley Point. It has a boat launch ($2 for day-use, plus an additional $4 to camp). Just above the Finley Point

turnoff on Hwy. 35 is the **Rocky G Campground,** a Good Sam Park trailer campground. It has a restaurant with Mexican food. The **Yellow Bay State Recreation Area** and campground is right next to the University of Montana's Biological Study and Research Station.

BIGFORK

Bigfork is a Montana anomaly. It's a resort community, one of the few in the state, and it seems to lack the sort of brawn that is pervasive elsewhere. The town is situated on a bay where the Swan River empties into Flathead Lake. The year-round population of about 1,100 can rise exponentially during the summer. It's a fairly charming place with an interesting group of residents in the off-season, but things get a little claustrophobic when the summer crowds gather. The high summer season does bring the attraction of the theater, but if you're looking to get away from cute shops and condominiums, you may want to steer clear of Bigfork. (On the other hand, if you crave homemade whole-wheat herb bread, be sure to at least swing through town.)

Tourism is obviously the mainstay of Bigfork's economy, but agriculture, especially fruit-growing, is also of some importance. A number of artists have taken up residence in Bigfork, adding a cultural depth that represents Bigfork at its best.

History

Bigfork was founded in 1902, about the time the hydroelectric plant at the mouth of the Swan River was built to supply electricity for Kalispell. The electric company is still here, and the bridge is the best place to stand and ponder how it works. (Water from the Swan River is diverted to a higher level, then dropped through turbines to generate power.)

Accommodations

Timbers Motel is on Hwy. 35, tel. (406) 837-6200. Rooms here start at $40 s, $47 d, with winter rates running about $10 less. There's a pool, a sauna, and an outdoor hot tub, and the setting, back off the highway in some trees, is rather snug. **Marina Cay** is a resort motel, the sort of place that draws a lot of conventions. It's right on the bay, and has a pool and a couple of hot tubs. Rooms start at $47 s ($37 winter), $49 d ($38 winter), tel. 837-5861.

At $20 s and $30 d, **Schwartz's Bed and Breakfast** is the least expensive of the B&Bs in town. It's at 890 McCaffery Rd., tel. 837-5463. **O'Duachain Country Inn Bed and Breakfast,** 675 Ferndale Dr., tel. 837-6851, has rooms for $50 s, $60 d, and $85 for a suite. Reduced winter rates are available, and they have a hot tub.

Flathead Lake Lodge is a well-established dude ranch that runs close to $1000 per week, per person (includes all meals and activities). Contact them at P.O. Box 248, Bigfork, MT 59911, tel. 837-4391, if you're up for a family ranch vacation with swimming, fishing, tennis, and windsurfing mixed in with the horseback riding and campfire sing-alongs.

Wayfarer State Recreation Area is a campground just across Hwy. 35 from the main road into Bigfork. It's open mid-May to mid-September and charges $7 per night. There are several RV campgrounds near Bigfork; **CJ's RV Resort** is west of Bigfork on Sylvan Drive, **Bigwoods Campground** is a half mile south of Bigfork on Hwy. 35.

Food And Drink

The **Bread Board Bakery** is not to be missed if you're even close to passing through Bigfork. Their breads are wonderful, and the cinnamon rolls and other pastries are worth more than a casual nibble. It's right downtown, at 439 Bridge St. (right by Electric Ave.), tel. 837-6644. Hang out and listen to the locals reminisce about Grateful Dead concerts or discuss where to find essential car parts.

The **Bigfork Inn,** tel. 837-6680, is a more elegant and expensive proposition, worth a visit if you're not pinching too many pennies. **La Montana Cantina,** 425 Grand Ave., tel. 837-5550, has Mexican food for lunch and dinner and American breakfasts. The **Garden Bar** is a casual place to drop in for a beer. The bar itself is chatty and friendly, and the tables out back provide a quiet place to sit and read in the afternoon.

Korner Kitchen, at Hwys. 35 and 83, is a family restaurant featuring buffalo burgers and broasted chicken. **Bronsten's Cheese** is locally made, and distributed to grocery stores throughout the state. It's worth a try.

Entertainment

Bigfork is known throughout the state for its summer theater productions; the **Bigfork Summer Playhouse** mounts Broadway musicals Mon.-Sat. evenings all summer. A brochure and schedule of upcoming plays is available from P.O. Box 456, Bigfork, MT 59911, tel. 837-4886.

This town makes a big deal of holidays. Christmas brings lots of lights and conifer boughs, then there's Easter, cherry blossoms (early May), the playhouse's opening night, Fourth of July, a whitewater festival (mid-May), a Festival of the Arts (early August) . . . it's hard to arrive in Bigfork when there's *not* something going on.

Recreation

In keeping with its role as a resort village, Bigfork has an 18-hole public golf course. The **Eagle Bend Golf Club** is on Holt Dr. west of Hwy. 35, tel. 837-5400. It's gotten high ratings from *Golf Digest* magazine and from Montana golfers. During the summer, the greens fee runs $15 for nine holes, $28 for 18.

Sailboat tours of Flathead Lake start at the Flathead Lake Lodge.

Jewel Basin Hiking Area was set aside as an easily reached wilderness-like area. There are 35 miles of trails that make day-hike loops or longer backpack trips. To get there from Bigfork, take Echo Lake Road off Hwy. 83. (It can also be reached from the west side of the Hungry Horse Reservoir.) An extremely helpful map will cost $1 at the Forest Service offices in Bigfork, Hungry Horse, or Kalispell.

Hikes take you through wildflower meadows and thickets of subalpine fir. Climbing in from the west, you'll first have expansive views of the Flathead Valley and Lake, then pass over a ridge and realize that Jewel Basin is indeed a basin. It's hard to say which are the jewels—the lakes that stud the basin or the Indian paintbrush, bear grass, fireweed, and showy daisies strewn through the meadows. Some of the lakes are stocked with trout.

Shopping

Several arts and crafts galleries are in downtown Bigfork. The **Bigfork Art and Cultural Center,** 525 Electric Ave., shares a building with the public library. The **Bridge Street Gallery and Wine Café,** 408 Bridge St. (open only during the summer) sells wine by the glass, bottle, or case alongside the art exhibits. **Gary Riecke's studio** (across from the Bigfork Inn) features Western and wildlife art.

Electric Avenue Books, 490 Electric Ave., tel. 837-6072, is a good general bookstore (open in summer daily 9 a.m. to 10 p.m.) with a congenial atmosphere. It's a pleasant place for a bookstore lover to pass an hour or so on an inclement day. **Bay Books and Prints,** on Grand Ave., tel. 837-4646, specializes in books on Montana. Charley Russell and Lewis and Clark buffs will find it especially hard to leave without a book or two. Most of the books are used, with a good selection of rare and out-of-print titles.

The place closes up during the winter, when the owner heads to Arizona.

Information
The **chamber of commerce** is at 645 Electric Ave., tel. 837- 5888. The **library** is at 525 Electric Ave., with the Art and Cultural Center.

You're not too likely to run into a **metaphysical center** in too many other small towns in Montana. But there's a place here at 440 Osborn, tel. 837-4683, where you can purchase metaphysical books and tapes or have palm, psychic, or tarot readings, or even drop in for the weekly open session of group channeling.

THE SWAN AND BLACKFOOT VALLEYS

INTRODUCTION

The Swan Valley is not as large and broad as the valleys to the west of it, but it is beautiful with its two rivers and many lakes, the Swan Range shooting out to the east, and the Mission Mountains stacking up high in the southwest. This valley between the Bob Marshall and Mission Mountains wilderness areas is a popular vacation spot for Montanans, but it doesn't draw the crowds that you'll find around Flathead Lake, Bigfork, or Glacier National Park.

Even the amateur geologist can pick out the signs of the glaciers that formed the Swan Valley. Drive down Hwy. 83 and look up at the jagged peaks and high cirques of the Mission and Swan ranges. Visit the Mt. Morrell Lookout and see some of the glaciers that remain on the Mission Range. Notice the distinctive pothole lakes southeast of Salmon Lake. And the big lakes—Seeley, Salmon, Alva, Placid, and Inez—all were formed when glaciers melted 10,000 years ago.

Wildlife viewing is a special attraction of the Swan Valley and its many lakes. While a canoe is probably the best vehicle for nature watching around the lakes and rivers here, keep your eyes open while you're driving or biking Hwy. 83; there are several designated wildlife-viewing areas, mostly featuring water birds.

Toward the southern end of the valley, Salmon Lake, Seeley Lake, and Lake Alva are

nesting sites for loons. These large, white-neck-laced, solid-boned birds are known for their eerie wails and their diving abilities. (Loons have been reported to dive up to 200 feet, though usual dives are much more shallow.) During the loons' nesting period (May through mid-June), it is important to stay well away from the nests, especially while fishing on the lakes. The presence of humans can cause the loons to abandon their nests.

The Timber Industry In The Swan Valley
Highway 83 is Swan Valley Highway. It's a lovely road to drive, but to venture far off it often means an eyeful of clearcuts.

The railroad received land grants here, the checkerboarded square miles that, in many places, were sold or leased to homesteaders. Timber companies bought some of this land in northwestern Montana, but the railroad held onto a lot of it. In 1968, Burlington Northern bought a

loon, Gavia immer

small Montana timber company called Plum Creek and proceeded to have it harvest the old-growth timber on its land-grant land. The clearcuts here were a mile square—larger than most. Increasing environmental awareness over the past decade has led to smaller clearcuts, but Plum Creek's business and logging practices still raise the hackles of environmentalists, sportsmen, and some Forest Service personnel.

With land in Washington, Idaho, and Montana, Plum Creek has become one of the largest timber companies in the Northwest. In Washington, much of their timber harvest is sold as "raw" unmilled logs to foreign countries, especially Japan. The profits from these raw log exports have been sunk into Plum Creek's operations in Idaho and Montana, where they are able to outbid smaller local outfits. Needless to say, this has put a fatal pressure on many smaller mills.

The large clearcuts in the Swan Valley have threatened watersheds and grizzly habitats. Because of the scope of the logging on private lands, the Flathead National Forest has taken the uncommon precaution of withholding timber sales on national forest tracts adjacent to private lands that have been grossly overcut by Forest Service standards.

Recreation

The lakes and the easy access to mountains and wilderness are the main recreational attractions of the Swan Valley, but there's more here than boating, fishing, hiking, hunting, and horseback riding.

Highway 83 through the Swan River Valley is the stage for a popular bicycle tour held every spring. The **Tour of the Swan River Valley** (TOSRV West) starts in Missoula, heads up the Swan Valley, and back down through the Mission Valley. Even with summer traffic, Hwy. 83 is a good cycling road with plenty of rest stops and campsites.

The Swan Valley has surprisingly good cross-country skiing in the winter. It's high enough to have snow when it's raining in nearby Missoula.

SWAN LAKE

The **Swan River National Wildlife Refuge** is a nesting area for bald eagles, blue herons, and other birds. Canada geese, whistling swans,

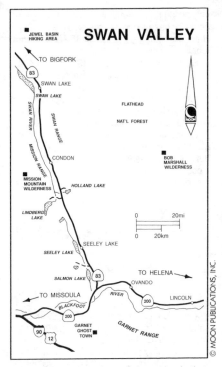

and mallards winter here. Other animals that can be spotted in this marsh, grassland, and river habitat include elk, moose, deer, beaver, river otter, muskrat, and both grizzly and black bear. The refuge is on the Swan River in the northern part of the Swan Valley, near the town of Swan Lake.

If the Swan Valley's rivers and lakes put you in the market for a canoe, stop for a look at laminated woodstrip canoes at **Morley Cedar Canoes** in Swan Lake, tel. 886-3342.

Accommodations

At the north end of Swan Lake, the **Swan Lake Recreation Area** includes a Forest Service campground ($7 per night) on the east side of the highway and a day-use area with a swimming beach and a boat launch on the west side. **Point Pleasant State Forest Campground** is a small, free campground seven miles south of Swan Lake.

Burggraf's Countrylane Bed and Breakfast, Rainbow Dr., tel. (406) 837-4608, is a small

B&B with rooms for $60-70. It's right on Swan lake, and has canoes for guests to use.

HOLLAND LAKE AND CONDON

Accommodations
Holland Lake Lodge is at the end of Holland Lake Rd., tel. (800) 648-8859. It's a downhome kind of place, with tasty, substantial meals, minimalist rooms with bathrooms down the hall, and a friendly bar and lounging area. One needn't be a guest in the lodge to dine or drink there. Rooms are a bargain at $32.50 a night; there are also some cabins for $42-52, and canoes for rent ($4 an hour). During the winter, cross-country ski trails are maintained, and, if you visit in the middle of February, you may have the opportunity to rub up against the unique subculture of dogsled racing. This is the turnaround point in a 500-mile dogsled race that starts and finishes in Helena.

Also near Condon, the **Double Diamond Guest Ranch,** tel. (406) 754-2351, has nightly bed and breakfast accommodations ($65 d) as well as weekly guest ranch packages ($590) which include meals, a horse, and use of all the ranch facilities (including a hot tub and sauna). The ranch also rents a remote cabin year-round.

Holland Lake is the site of one of the prettiest, and sometimes one of the most crowded, Forest Service campgrounds in the area ($7 per night). It's south of Condon, and east of Hwy. 83 on Holland Lake Road. The lake contains cutthroat, bull, and rainbow trout and kokanee salmon.

Holland Lake is a popular departure point for horse trips into the Bob Marshall Wilderness Area and, in addition to the traditional Forest Service campground, there's a horse-packers' campground a little farther down the road from the Holland Lake campground. **Owl Creek Packers' Camp** charges a $4 corral fee. At the road's end there are short hiking trails for the casual dayhiker as well as trails leading into the Bob Marshall Wilderness Area. The hike in to Holland Falls is not difficult (three miles for the roundtrip).

Food And Drink
The dining room at **Holland Lake Lodge** is open to the public, and it's worth a visit. During the summer, when a professional chef is in residence, the dinners ($10-15) are particularly in-spired. But even the simpler lunch menu and winter fare has some treats; the "Gut Bomb" is a locally renowned burger.

The **Hungry Bear Restaurant** south of Condon, tel. 754-2240, is basically a steak house, though they do serve pizza and huckleberry daiquiris.

Recreation
Holland Lake is the trailhead for a popular trail into the Bob Marshall Wilderness Area. It's about 10 miles from road's end to the wilderness boundary, and most people entering this way go around Upper Holland Lake and up over Gordon Pass toward the South Fork of the Flathead River.

Across Hwy. 83 from Holland Lake, several roads lead west from Condon toward the Mission Mountains Wilderness Area. The Lindbergh Lake road leads to a campground (free, no water) and several trailheads. Lindbergh Lake is, indeed, named for Charles Lindbergh, who camped here not long after his trans-Atlantic flight. Hikers should pick up either a Flathead National Forest map (south half) or a more detailed Mission Mountains Wilderness map. Both are available at the ranger station in Bigfork. Be aware that the Mission Mountains are home to some grizzly bears.

Horse-pack trips and other services are provided by **Holland Lake Outfitters,** P.O. Box 1017, Condon, MT 59826, tel. 754-2533 or (800) 648-8859.

BOB MARSHALL WILDERNESS AREA

The Bob Marshall Wilderness Area was formed in 1964, when 950,000 acres were set aside to remain forever wild. In 1978, the Scapegoat Wilderness was added to the south, and the Great Bear Wilderness to the north of the Bob Marshall. The three contiguous areas include a million and a half acres, falling roughly east of the Swan Valley. The designated wilderness areas receive heavy use during the summer and fall. Backpacking and horse packing are the main summer activities, while hunting predominates in the fall, starting mid-September.

Great Northern Mountain (8,705 feet) is the highest spot in the Great Bear Wilderness. The Middle Fork of the Flathead runs through the

Great Bear. The South Fork of the Flathead River starts as Danaher Creek deep in the Bob and flows toward the southern tip of the Hungry Horse Reservoir.

The Chinese Wall is an impressive and popular destination. It's where, to the west, the earth's crust thrust upward, and forced the eastern part to slide underneath it for a distance of about 20 miles. Haystack Mountain provides a good view of the Chinese Wall from the west.

Access To The Wilderness

Napa Point Road starts near the headquarters of the Swan River State Forest and provides access to the **Inspiration Pass** trailhead. It's a challenging but fairly lightly used trail. Sup Creek Campground near the trailhead is a good place to spend the night before embarking on the full-day's hike to Sunburst Lake.

Smith Creek Pass also receives less traffic than many of the other trails that lead into the wilderness. To reach the trailhead, take Falls Creek Rd. (across from the Condon Work Center on Hwy. 83) four miles to Smith Creek Road. Make a sharp right and drive another mile to the trailhead. The climb up the west side of the pass is not easy, and coming down the east side can be even tougher.

Gordon Pass, starting from Holland Lake, is well maintained and heavily used by horse packers and hikers. Big Salmon Lake is a popular destination. Trails come at it from every direction, but the shortest route is from Holland Lake.

Pyramid Pass, with a trailhead near Seeley Lake, leads to the headwaters of the South Fork of the Flathead River. Reach the trailhead by taking Cottonwood Lakes Road (just north of the town of Seeley Lake) to Morrell Road (#467). Turn left on Morrell Rd. and travel for six miles to Pyramid Pass Rd. (#4381, aka Upper Trail Creek Road). Turn right and drive six miles to the trailhead. Pyramid Pass is a steep climb and receives medium to heavy use by both backpackers and horse packers.

From the south, reach the **North Fork of the Blackfoot** trailhead by taking Hwy. 200 to five miles east of Ovando and turning up the North Fork of Blackfoot Road. Drive four miles to North Fork Trailhead Road, and take it seven miles to the trailhead. It's a fairly heavily used trail, with both foot and horse traffic.

For jump-off points on the eastern edge of the Bob, see "Rocky Mountain Front"; for northern entry points, see "Hungry Horse" below.

SEELEY LAKE AND VICINITY

It's a town with all services, the only place in the Swan Valley that can really boast that. J.B. Seeley was the first white resident and the lake and the town that now bear his name support a community of summer homes and dude ranches. The timber industry is a major employer of the year-round residents.

At the junction of highways 200 and 83, this is one landmark you can't miss.

Accommodations

A few notches fancier than Holland Lake Lodge to the north, the **Double Arrow Lodge** is a gem of a Swan Valley hideout. Rooms in the 1930s-era lodge start at $45 a night, homey cabin rooms are $35 a night and up, and larger log lodges rent for $125 or $250 a night. Breakfast (with the best coffee for miles around) and use of a large indoor pool are included. Horseback riding costs extra. The Double Arrow, P.O. Box 747, Seeley Lake, MT 59868, tel. (406) 677-2777, is open year-round.

At the **Duck Inn Motel,** on Hwy. 83, tel. 677-2335, rates start at $23 for pretty basic accommodations. **Elk Horn Motel and Café,** tel. 677-2278, has rooms for $30 d at the north end of Seeley Lake. **Wilderness Gateway Inn,** tel. 677-2095, at the south end of town, is a spiffier place than the typical Swan Valley motel. Rooms are $35 s, $41 d, with a variety of discounts offered.

Tamaracks Resort, on the north shore of Seeley Lake, tel. 677-2433, rents cabins with kitchens for $45-$100 a night. There's also an area for RV and tent campers.

There are three **national forest campgrounds** around Seeley Lake: Big Larch is closest to the highway on the east side of the lake; River Point and Seeley Lake are farther around the southern and western sides of the lake. Just south of Seeley Lake, the campground at **Placid Lake** is usually less crowded than its northern counterparts.

Food And Drink

Double Arrow Lodge, two miles south of Seeley Lake, tel. 677-2777, serves Sunday brunch and elegant dinners, with meals such as mango chicken and grilled Kentucky bourbon steak running just less than $15.

Recreation

The **Clearwater Canoe Trail** is really a floating and hiking loop trail. There's a three-mile canoe segment from an access point off Hwy. 83 four miles north of the town of Seeley Lake, then a one-mile hike back to the put-in spot. The meandering Clearwater River is a good place to watch birds. Keep a special eye out for loons.

Morrell Lake and **Morrell Falls** are on a national recreation trail north of Seeley Lake via Cottonwood Lakes Rd. to the east of Hwy. 83. It's

an easy two-mile hike in to the falls (actually a 100-foot-long lower fall topped by a series of smaller falls and cascades). **Morrell Mountain Lookout** is about 18 miles from the highway via Cottonwood Lakes Rd. (follow it for nine miles) and Road 4365 (follow it for another nine miles). It's a rough drive in a passenger car, and it's wise to check with the ranger station (tel. 677-2233) for current road conditions. The lookout has views of the Mission Mountains, the Swan Range, and the Blackfoot and Clearwater valleys.

Mission Mountains Wilderness Area falls on the eastern part of the mountains' divide; the western part is the Mission Mountains Tribal Wilderness and is managed by the Confederated Kootenai and Salish Tribes (see "St. Ignatius"). The wilderness managed by the Forest Service has about 45 miles of trails. While some people do take horses into the Missions, the steep terrain makes hiking more practical and popular. There are a number of trailheads into the Mission Mountains Wilderness Area. They include Glacier Creek, Cold Lakes, Piper Creek, Fatty Creek, Beaver Creek, Lindbergh Lake, Jim Lakes, Hemlock Creek, Meadow Lake, and Elk Point. Maps of the Mission Mountains Wilderness or the southern half of the Flathead National Forest are available at the ranger station in Bigfork.

Seeley Lake is a good place to fish for bass, and it's also stocked with rainbow trout. To the south, Salmon Lake has rainbow and cutthroat trout and kokanee salmon.

The **Double Arrow Lodge** runs an outfitting service, tel. 677-2411 or 677-2317.

Information

The **Seeley Lake Ranger Station** is about three miles north of town, at the northern end of Seeley Lake. Besides the expected Forest Service brochures and maps, a good selection of field guides is sold here.

Services

Seeley Lake has a **clinic** at the north end of town with a nurse on call 24 hours at 627-2277. For **emergency** services, call 911.

With showers as well as a laundromat, **Cher's Wash House,** back behind the mercantile, is a godsend to backpackers just coming out of the Bob Marshall or Mission Mountains wilderness areas.

BLACKFOOT VALLEY

The Blackfoot River is well known to local anglers and floaters. It's a lovely, undammed river noted for its variety of fish habitats and its 30 miles of "recreation corridor," which allows easy public access to the river.

Meriwether Lewis traveled along the Blackfoot River after he and William Clark split up on their return trip across Montana. Lewis noted two swans near the mouth of the Clearwater River. You're unlikely to find swans here nowadays, but there is some attractive countryside near the ranching towns of Greenough and Ovando. Read Norman Maclean's classic, *A River Runs Through It,* to get a feel for the place.

There was a gold strike here, at roughly the same time in 1865 that President Lincoln was assassinated—hence the name of the gold-laced Lincoln Gulch and of the valley's major town.

Sights

The **Blackfoot-Clearwater Wildlife Management Area,** east of Hwy. 83 and north of Hwy. 200, includes the southern part of Salmon Lake as well as the lower Clearwater River. Near the junction of the two highways the land is prairie, but the northeastern corner of the area rises into forested mountains. The entire area is closed Dec. 1-May 15, but open to hunters and anglers at other times of the year (within the restrictions of hunting season, of course). There are plenty of deer and elk here, and black bear, grouse, and waterfowl.

Garnet Ghost Town is run by the BLM. To reach it, take Hwy. 200 about 24 miles east of Missoula and turn south at Greenough Hill. The rough Garnet access road is 11 miles from the turnoff.

Accommodations

The town of Lincoln has several motels. None of them are fancy or expensive, but most are serviceable and have charming names and friendly proprietors. **Lincoln Lodge** is off the highway on Sleepy Hollow Lane, tel. (406) 362-4396. Rooms start at $25 d. **Leeper's Motel,** tel. 362-4333, has separate units in a grove of trees just back from Hwy. 200. The **Three Bears,** tel. 362-4355, has log cabins. Both Leeper's and Three Bears charge about $32 d. Every room in the similarly priced brick **Blue Sky Motel,** tel. 362-4450, boasts a fireplace.

Food And Drink

There's not a lot to choose from, but Lincoln has a sprinkling of cafés plus the old and venerable **Lambkin's,** tel. 362-4271, a good place for such standard fare as chicken-fried steak. The **Seven Up Supper Club,** east of town on Hwy. 200, tel. 362-4255, is a good log-lodge Western steak house, open Tues.-Sat. 5-10 p.m., Sun. 2-10 p.m. Down in Ovando, **Trixie's Antler Bar** has a far-reaching reputation as a *real* Montana bar, the kind that posts a sign bidding customers to leave their guns outside.

Recreation

Fishing, especially for brown trout, has long been a major preoccupation in the Blackfoot Valley, but past mining and ongoing heavy logging have deteriorated the fishing. Be sure to check the current fishing regulations for the Blackfoot and its tributaries. Catch-and-release is required for cutthroat and bull trout. For the more prevalent brown and rainbow trout, check current regulations.

The **Clearwater Bridge** is a fishing-access site on Sunset Hill Rd. (which intersects Hwy. 200 just east of Greenough Hill). Farther down Sunset Hill Rd. is another fishing-access site. To reach the **Scotty Brown Bridge,** turn down the gravel road seven miles east of Clearwater Junction on Hwy. 200. It's marked with a fishing-access-site sign, and the road leads to several fishing and camping sites.

Blackfoot River Road has two junctions with Hwy. 200, one just north of the McNamara Bridge (14 miles east of Missoula) and the other at the Roundup Bridge (28 miles east of Missoula). There are a number of fishing-access sites along this road, most with undeveloped campsites nearby.

During the winter, the recreational focus shifts to snowmobiling. There are over 200 miles of groomed trails, many of them springing from a hub in Lincoln.

NORTH OF FLATHEAD LAKE

KALISPELL

There's something that makes Kalispell more likeable than the sum of its parts. Perhaps the synergy starts with the name. It rolls off the tongue in just the right way, and it *means* something . . . it's the Kalispel Indian word for "Prairie above the Lake."

Drive around northwestern Montana for a while and, by the time you pull into Kalispell, you'll feel that you're in a real city. Indeed, Kalispell, the county seat of Flathead County with a population of roughly 12,000, is the metropolitan center of northwestern Montana. On a summer afternoon, the intersection of Highways 2 and 93 has the closest thing to a traffic jam you'll ever find in the whole state.

While it's in no way a university town (Flathead Community College does have its base here though), Kalispell has a just touch of artistic college-town hipness, which is kept from becoming cloying by the prevailing rugged, full-bodied atmosphere.

The Land

Kalispell is on the Flathead River near the point where the Stillwater and Whitefish rivers converge with it (elev. 2,930 feet), about seven miles above Flathead Lake. It's at the upper end of the Flathead Valley, and the mountains visible to the north are part of the Whitefish Range, to the east, the Swan Range. The Flathead River between Kalispell and Flathead Lake is as convoluted as the folds of a brain.

History

In the days before the railroad, Flathead Lake steamers made it up as far as Demersville, a now nonexistent town four miles southeast of Kalispell. Charles Conrad, a Fort Benton freight kingpin, got a hot tip from the head of the Great Northern Railway, Jim Hill, to move west to the Flathead area. Conrad did, and in 1891 the Great Northern arrived. Demersville and Ashley (half a mile west of present-day Kalispell) picked up and moved to form Kalispell. Conrad prospered and became a uniquely Montanan model citizen, keeping his own buffalo herd (on what is now known as Buffalo Hills, just north of downtown).

Sights

The **Conrad Mansion** is at 330 Woodland Ave., tel. 755-2166. It's open to the public with guided tours from May 15 to Oct. 15 ($4 for adults, $1

FRANK JEWELL

Conrad Mansion

KALISPELL ACCOMMODATIONS

Name	Address	Phone	Rates	Features
Rose Briar Inn	24 1st Ave. W	752-8887	$23 d	largely residential, weekly rate available
Kalispell Hotel	8 1st St. W	752-3616	$54	casino and restaurant downstairs
Aero Inn	1830 Hwy. 93 S	755-3798 or (800) 843-6114	$40 s, $45 d	indoor pool, hot tub, sauna
Super 8	1341 1st Ave. E	755-1888	$36 s, $41 d	lower winter rates
Motel 6	1540 Hwy. 93 S	752-6355	$33	
Glacier Gateway Motel	264 N. Main	755-3330	$39 d	kitchenettes available
Blue and White Motel	640 E. Idaho (Hwy. 2)	755-4311	$32 s $37 d	indoor pool, sauna, and hot tub
Kalispell Motel	801 Hwy. 2 E	257-3094	$24 d	
Alpine Motel	1009 Hwy. 2 E	257-7155	$34 d and up	
Vacationer Motel	285 7th Ave. N E	755-7144	$24	
White Birch Motel	17 Shady Lane	752-4008	$25	kitchenettes available
Cavanaugh's at Kalispell Center	20 N. Main	752-6660	$62 s, $72 d	winter rates available, indoor pool, sauna, and hot tub

for children under 11). The mansion was built in 1895 and was, for most of the next 80 years, home to members of the Conrad family. None of the original architecture was changed during this time. When the home was donated to the city of Kalispell in 1975, the interior and exterior were renovated, and the mansion is now considered one of the best examples of Pacific Northwest turn-of-the-century architecture.

Woodland Park, on 2nd St. north of Woodland Ave., is a lovely city park, with rose gardens, a duck pond and lagoon, a large swimming pool, and a track. It was originally part of Charles Conrad's estate.

The **Hockaday Center for the Arts,** 2nd Ave. E and 3rd St., tel. 755-5268, hangs some striking and innovative contemporary art. Anyone who thinks that conceptual art is solely an urban phenomenon should stop in and see what's going on in the studios of Two Dot and Bozeman. Gallery hours are Tues.-Sat. 10 a.m.-5 p.m.; admission is free. There's a small crafts shop in the gallery, which is housed in the old brick Carnegie library building. The center also sponsors Arts in the Park weekend in July.

Horse-drawn carriage rides in Kalispell run on summer evenings from the Outlaw Inn and Cavanaugh's. Call **Cahoon Clydesdales** at 756-8544 to reserve. Rides for a party of four run $20 for a half-hour, $40 for an hour. The Cahoons also run trail rides just outside downtown Kalispell ($10 for an hour-long ride).

On Hwy. 2 13 miles west of Kalispell, be sure to stop near milepost 108 to see the Indian pictographs on the cliffs on the north side of the road.

Accommodations

During the summer, Kalispell's motels can fill up quickly with people on their way to and from Glacier National Park. It's wise to reserve in advance.

Budget travelers will be cheered to find the **Kalispell/Whitefish AYH Hostel** at 2155 Whitefish Stage Rd., three miles north of Kalispell. Hostel members, bicyclists, and motorcyclists pay $10 a night; nonmember rates are $12. The hostel has two mountain bikes for loan, and the accommodating proprietor will pick guests up from the airport or train station for a donation. Call (406) 756-1908 for reservations, and try to check in by 8 p.m. (The hostel closes down from 9 p.m.-5 p.m. daily.)

Camping

There's not much in the way of peaceful tent camping in Kalispell, but there are a handful of RV-style campgrounds right in town. **Greenwood Trailer Village,** on Hwy. 2 just east of its intersection with Hwy. 2, tel. 257-7719, has some tent sites. The fee is $7 per night and the campground is open April through October. **Glacier Pine RV Campground** (with 75 tent sites) is one mile east of Kalispell on Hwy. 35, tel. 752-2760. Their season parallels Greenwood's, with a fee of $8 per night. **Rocky Mountain Hi** costs $7 per night and is open year-round. It's four miles east of Kalispell on Hwy. 2, then follow the signs, tel. 755-9573. **Lake Blaine Resort** is nearby, at the junction of Hwys. 2 and 35.

There are some less developed campgrounds a little farther from town. **Ashley Lake State Recreation Area** is 16 miles west of Kalispell on Hwy 2, then 13 miles north on the county road that starts around milepost 105. It's $3 a night for a relatively peaceful campground with running water, pit toilets, and fishing for cutthroat and kokanee. The campground is officially open from mid-May to mid-September. Still farther west of Kalispell (32 miles) is the **McGregor Lake** Forest Service Campground. Even though it's on the edge of a burn, it's not a bad spot, and has a few relatively isolated tent sites. Lake trout are the big fish here, but kokanee salmon, cutthroat and brook trout, and yellow perch are also caught. Also on McGregor Lake, the **Saddle Tramp Inn,** tel. 858-2253, rents cabins for about $15 a night.

Food And Drink

El Oso Chico, at 2316 Hwy. 2 E (one mile past the turn at K mart), is the place to eat piles of cheap Mexican food. (Dinners run less than $6.) The green chili is fiery, but don't expect to quench your thirst with a beer—no alcohol is served. Closed Mondays; tel. 752-4772. **Dos Amigos** is a little fancier, a bit more expensive, and generally easier on the stomach lining. It's open for lunch and dinner right downtown at 25 2nd Ave. W, tel. 752-2711.

Also downtown, at 221 S. Main, the **Lighterside** is a casual and friendly place for inexpensive diner-style food. They're open Mon.-Sat. 7 a.m.-9 p.m. The **Legacy,** 325 1st Ave. E, tel. 257-7121, is not open for dinner, but they serve up very good breakfasts and lunches Mon.-Saturday.

Moose's Saloon, 173 N. Main, tel. 755-2338, is usually a fun place to spend an evening throwing peanut shells on the floor while drinking beer and listening to local musicians.

Recreation

The 27-hole **Buffalo Hill Municipal Golf Course** is at the north end of Main St., tel. 756-4545. Greens fee is $9 for nine holes, $23 for 18 holes at this well-maintained course, which is, in the winter, a handy spot for cross-country skiing. Continue an in-city ski tour into the nearby **Lawrence Park,** a relatively wild city park.

Lone Pine State Park is five miles southwest of town off Foys Lake Rd. (get there from Hwy. 2 via Meridian Road). It's set up on a hill, and hiking trails lead to overlooks with a good view of Kalispell and Glacier National Park.

The **city pool** is in the middle of Woodland Park, tel. 753-4628. Adults pay $2, reduced rates for children and seniors. **Second Wind Sport and Fitness Center,** at 205 Sunnyview Lane (on Buffalo Hill just north of the city center), tel. 752-4100, has a large indoor pool. Nonmembers can swim for $3.75 ($2 for children, $8 for a family).

Bikology, 155 N. Main, tel. 755-6748, has a few bicycles for rent at $10 per day.

For those who scorn the aerobic tension of swimming or hiking, **Big Sky Archery,** 2333 Hwy. 2 E, tel. 752-4526, has indoor archery lanes; the **Strike Zone** has both miniature golf and batting practice cages (24 swings for a dollar), 1335 Hwy. 2 W, tel. 257-7272.

Shopping

Kalispell's a big enough city to do some serious stocking up in; indeed it's the commercial center for this part of the state. There's also some fairly interesting recreational shopping to be done here.

For high-quality local crafts, **Hockaday Center for the Arts** has a small crafts shop tucked into its gallery space.

Sportsman and Ski Haus is a large store at 40 E. Idaho (right by the intersection of Hwys. 2 and 93). It's open every day and has a good selection of sporting, skiing and camping goods. They also rent just about any kind of sporting equipment imaginable, from wet suits to mountain bikes to tennis racquets. **Rocky Mountain**

Outfitters, 135 Main St., has high-quality camping and rock-climbing equipment. Both Sportsman and Rocky Mountain stock well-made clothing by such companies as Patagonia and Woolrich.

Events

The **Northwest Montana Fair** is held at the fairgrounds in Kalispell in mid-August every year. Call 752-6166 for exact dates.

Information

The **chamber of commerce** is downtown at 15 Depot Loop, tel. 752-6166. During the summer, a **visitors information center** is head-

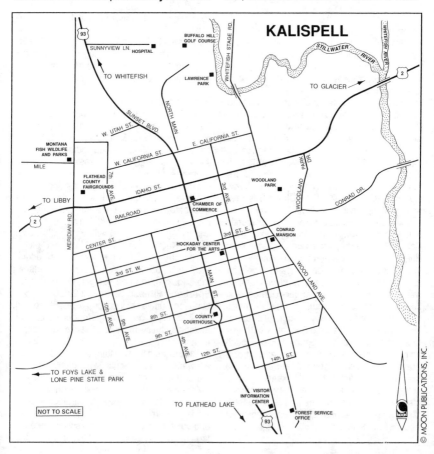

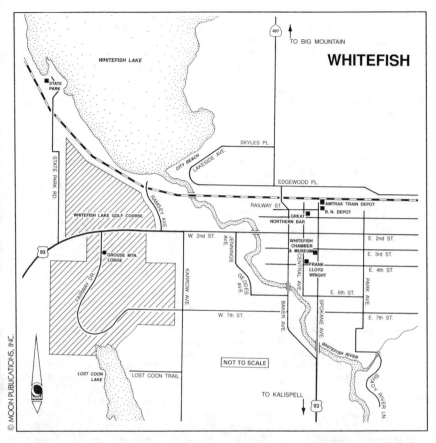

quartered on Hwy. 93 at the south end of town. They have more of a spectrum of information than the chamber of commerce does, plus they're located right next door to the **Flathead National Forest Headquarters,** tel. 755-5401. The Forest Service office has a variety of pamphlets and fliers, plus some books for sale from the Glacier Natural History Association.

The regional office of the **Montana Department of Fish, Wildlife, and Parks** is at 490 N. Meridian Rd., tel. 752-5501 or, for a 24-hour recording, 257-4630.

The Flathead Chapter of the **Montana Wilderness Association** can be reached at Box 543, Kalispell, MT 59903. The **Swan View Coalition** is another environmental "watchdog"

group, focusing on timber issues, at P.O. Box 1901, Kalispell, MT 59903.

The **public library** is at 247 1st Ave. East.

Services

Dial 911 for fire, police, or medical emergency help. **Kalispell Regional Hospital,** tel. 752-5111, is the biggest and most complete hospital until you get to Missoula. It's on Sunnyview Lane, off Hwy. 93 just north of downtown.

The **post office** is on the corner of 1st Ave. W. and 3rd Street.

The **Washing Well Laundry,** 720 W. Idaho (Hwy. 2 W.) is one conveniently located laundromat. There's also a laundromat in the Fred Meyer store on Hwy. 2 E., tel. 755-2002.

Transportation

Glacier International Airport eight miles northeast of Kalispell on Hwy 2 is served by Delta, Horizon, Northwest Airlink, and United Express.

Rental Cars: At the airport, find **Avis,** tel. 257-2727; **Budget,** tel. 755-7500; **Hertz,** tel. 257-1266 or (800) 654-3131; **Sears,** tel. 755-6181; and **National,** tel. 257-7144 or (800) 227-7368. **Rent-A- Wreck,** tel. 755-4555 or (800) 654-4642, is located at 1194 E. Idaho and has service to the airport. So does **U-Save,** 1010 E. Idaho (at Balding's Cars and Trucks), tel. 257-1958 or (800) 272-USAV. **Ugly Duckling** is at 191 Seventh Ave. NE, tel. 752-6800.

Intermountain Transport is at 15 E. 18th St. in Kalispell. A bus leaves for Missoula (where it connects with the I-90 Greyhound) each morning at 10:30; the bus comes in at 1:30. A trip from Kalispell to Missoula is $24 one way, $38 roundtrip.

WHITEFISH

Whitefish, pop. 4,300, calls itself the "recreation capital of Montana." It's a likely enough claim, what with the town's 3,033-foot setting at the base of a major ski mountain some 40 miles from Glacier National Park. To orient yourself in Whitefish, it may help to realize that Hwy. 93, that great north-south road, turns to the west as it heads north from Whitefish.

History

Fur trading and logging brought the first white settlers to this area, but it took the railroad to bring about permanent and stable settlements. In 1893 Whitefish became a division point for the Great Northern Railroad. Railroad workers flooded into town, and the bars followed. In 1904 Whitefish supported 14 saloons. Central Avenue was a muddy rut then; the Cadillac Hotel, at the corner of Central and Railway, had a wooden boardwalk built on stilts to avoid the mud.

Whitefish was originally densely forested. It took six years to clear land for the city, and for many years tree stumps poked up in the middle of streets, giving the town the nickname of Stumptown.

The railroad activity helped loggers to prosper but thwarted the trapping trade, although trapping for beaver, mink, and muskrat continued around Whitefish until the 1960s.

Sights

Most people come here for the proximity to Big Mountain and Glacier National Park. In fact, that's why most of the local people ended up here. It's the sort of place a skier or avid outdoorsperson moves to.

Surprisingly enough, Whitefish has a **Frank Lloyd Wright building,** but only the most fervid architectural buff would find it particularly interesting. It's on Central Avenue between Third and Fourth streets, and looks like any old one-story modern office building, currently housing insurance offices and opticians.

The old **Great Northern depot** is currently used by Burlington Northern, and there is a push on to save it as a historic site. The Whitefish Chamber of Commerce would like to use it as its headquarters. The depot is styled along the same lines as the Glacier Park chalet hotels.

Accommodations

Most of the motels, especially the less expensive ones, are on the southern edge of town on the Hwy. 93 strip. There you'll find a **Super 8,** 828 Spokane Ave., tel. 862-8255 or (800) 843-1991, with single rooms from $40 ($33 spring and fall). The **Chalet Motel,** 6430 Hwy. 93 S, tel. 862-5581, boasts an indoor pool, sauna, and hot tub. Summer and winter rates are $36 s, $42 d; spring and fall rates drop to $32 s, $36 d. **Mountain Holiday Motel,** at 6595 Hwy. 93 S, tel. 862-2548 or (800)5 43-8064, has both indoor and outdoor pools, a sauna, and a hot tub. Summer and winter rates are $36 s, $44 d; spring and fall rates start at $32 s, $36 d.

The **Duck Inn,** 1305 Columbia Ave. (just off Hwy. 93, behind the Mountain Holiday Motel and overlooking the tiny Whitefish River), tel. 862-3825 or (800) 344-2377, is heavily imbued with personal identity, largely focusing on the image of a duck. Rooms run from $46-66, whether you're alone or with another person.

The **Downtowner Motel,** 224 Spokane Ave., tel. 862-2535, has a health club on the premises with weight-lifting apparatus, exercycles, and stairstep machines. Also downtown, the **Garden Wall Bed and Breakfast,** 504 Spokane Ave. (Hwy. 93), has a cozy feel to it. Rooms with shared bath are $75, $85 with a private bath; tel. 862-3440. At the **Castle Bed and Breakfast,** 900 S. Baker, tel. 862-1257, home-made breakfast breads are a highlight, and rooms run $40-75.

If you're traveling top end, **Grouse Mountain Lodge,** across from the golf course at 1205 Hwy. 93 W is the deluxe place to stay in White-fish. Summer and winter rates are $77 s, $87 d; spring and fall, $50 s, $60 d. For this, you get access to a pool, a sauna, three hot tubs, tennis courts, and pleasant rooms that look out onto a golf course rather than onto a highway strip; tel. 862-3000, or in Montana, (800) 621-1802, and outside Montana, (800) 321-8822.

Camping

Whitefish Lake State Recreation Area is about two miles west of town off Hwy. 93. Pick this as your place to stay if you're after convenience, if you want to spend some time near civiliza-tion, if you want to eat out or shop in Whitefish, or if you want a handy launching-off spot for a trip to Glacier National Park. It's a crowded place, even for a state park campground. There's a boat launch and a swimming beach popular with local kids (there's a $2 day-use fee, $7 for camping). The campground has run-ning water and flush toilets and it's open mid-May through mid-September.

Out of town, **Tally Lake** (USFS) is open Memorial Day through Labor Day, $4 per night. It's six miles west of Whitefish on Hwy. 93, then 15 miles west on FS Road 113. Several trails originate from various points around Tally Lake. From the campground, the Tally Lake Overlook is a 1.2-mile hike. The Boney Gulch trail is a steep three-mile trail. Its trailhead is on Road 913 about three miles from the campground.

If you have a backpacking trip in mind, the Reed Divide Tally Mountain Bill Creek Trail be-gins at the junction of Road 913, some two miles from the campground, and runs nearly the length of its name, some 20 miles. For the less driven hiker, the Stove Pipe Canyon Trail is just one mile long and goes into a canyon that is true to its name. This trail starts off Road 2924 on the west side of the lake.

Big Mountain Accommodations

Big Mountain sports a variety of accommoda-tions—you'll generally pay more for the conve-nience of skiing to your door, but there are fre-quent "deals," especially for groups.

The **Alpinglow Inn,** tel. 862-3511, is just across from the lifts and adjacent to the cross-country trails. There are two outdoor hot tubs and two saunas. Summer rates start at $52 s, and go to $72 for a six-person room. During the winter, package deals are available starting at $305 for five nights (double occupancy). **Kan-**

The Whitefish train depot was modeled after the Glacier Park Lodge.

dahar Lodge, tel. 862-6098, is a fancy mountain lodge near the slopes; rooms run $62-104, depending on the season. Suites with kitchens are available.

Edelweiss Condominiums, tel. 862-5252 or (800) 662-2270, are also right in "downtown" Big Mountain. Kitchens and fireplaces are standard in the condos. High season (mid-Dec.-early Jan.) range from $120 per night for a studio, to $280 for a large condo for four to eight people. Summer rates are substantially lower. Lift tickets are included in the rental price. At nearby Anapurna, tel. 862-3687 or (800) 243-7547, the year is divided into six seasons and rates vary accordingly. Condominiums, duplexes, and houses rent from $60 to $400 a night.

Hibernation House, tel. 862-3511 or (800) 858-5439, is an "economy bed and breakfast hotel" for those who want to stay on Big Mountain but are on something of a budget. It's just a short distance from the slopes, and winter packages start at $255 for five nights, double occupancy.

Ptarmigan Village, tel. 862-3594, is three miles from the ski lifts and has singles ($70-120, depending on season), doubles ($115-185), and triples ($145-240). They offer a discount for a stay of five nights or more.

Food And Drink

Buffalo Café, 516 E. 3rd, tel. 862-2833, is populated with an easy mix of locals and tourists. The breakfast menu features about half a dozen variations on huevos rancheros and at least as many omelettes. They're open for breakfast and lunch. There's a good variety of hefty sandwiches for $3-4 at Whitefish Sandwich Shoppe, 235 Central Ave., tel. 862-3354.

The Great Northern Bar and Grill, 27 Central Ave., tel. 862-2816, is a friendly, low-key bar with sports on the TV in the front and sandwiches and spaghetti served up at the tables in the back. It's open for lunch and dinner, and usually has live music in the bar on weekend nights.

For a fancier dinner, walk down a block to Stumptown Station, 115 Central Ave., tel. 862-4979. Expect to spend at least $10 for a full dinner, but light meals and the bar menu offer a less expensive way to enjoy the atmosphere. There's a pleasant outdoor patio where, during the summer, lunches and drinks are served.

Casey's, a casino bar at 101 Central Ave., tel. 862-8150, is housed in Whitefish's oldest building. It was built in 1903, when Whitefish was a rollicking railroad town.

The Bulldog, 144 Central Ave., tel. 862-5601, is known as a good bar to hang out in and maybe munch a burger. Kitchen Connection, 242 Central Ave., bills itself as a gourmet food shop. It's open Mon.-Sat. 9 a.m.-5 p.m., and offers sandwiches, salads, and pastries.

Stageline Pizza, one of four in the northwest Montana chain, at 901 Wisconsin, tel. 862-4441, has free delivery and reasonably priced pizzas with all the standard add-ons, including sauerkraut. O'Piccolo's is the fancier pizza joint, at 550 Edgewood Pl. (at the corner of Edgewood and Wisconsin, just over the viaduct of the road to Big Mountain), tel. 862-5495. O'Piccolo's specializes in deep-dish pizza and also serves pasta dishes and calzone.

Jimmy Lee's, 6550 Hwy. 93 S, is a popular local spot for typical Chinese fare. It opens at 5 p.m. for dinner; meals run $5-8. "Jimmy's lunch" is a particularly tasty noodle dish.

Dos Amigos, Wisconsin Ave. (on the road to Big Mountain), tel. 862-9994, has good Mexican food. This is the original Dos Amigos; the one in Kalispell followed after this place proved such a hit.

Skiing

Of course there's plenty of downhill skiing on Big Mountain, tel. 862-3511 or (800) 858-5439, or in Canada, (800) 637-7547. It's the largest ski resort in the state, with 45 runs, the longest of which is two miles. The elevation at the summit of Big Mountain is 7,000 feet, the base is at 4,600 feet, and the vertical drop is 2,170 feet. The season runs from Thanksgiving through Easter, and there are lights for night skiing. Lift tickets cost $25 for adults, $21 for 13- to 18-year-olds and for seniors, $14 for children 12 and under. Night skiing is cheaper: $9 adults, $7 teens and seniors, and $6 children. There's a whole resort area built up around the ski area, with several hotels, a handful of restaurants, a grocery store, a day-care center, and ski rentals.

The Big Mountain Nordic Center is just below the main parking lot. Its 15-km (10-mile)trail network is rather challenging for both winter skiing (including skating) and summer mountain biking.

The Forest Service (irregularly) maintains cross-country ski trails at **Round Meadows,** about 10 miles northwest of town. Take Hwy. 93 north to Star Meadows Road. A trail map is available from the ranger station in Whitefish or the Forest Service office in Kalispell. The elevation here is relatively low (approx. 3,300 feet), and good skiing is generally limited to late December through early March. Once the snow melts, mountain bikers take to the trails here.

Other Recreation

Even during the summer, there's plenty of reason to make the steep tortuous drive (or bike ride, for the ambitious and low-geared) to Big Mountain. The **Danny On Trail** leads from the main parking lot 3.8 miles up to the summit. There are plenty of huckleberries on the trail late in the summer, and spur trails offer wildflower meadows and vistas of the Flathead Valley. For $9 ($7 for children and seniors), you can buy a ride up on the chairlift and either hike or ride back down. The thrifty will appreciate the free ride down on the chairlift that's available to those who make the hike up. The entire trail is usually clear of snow from July through mid-September.

The Forest Service has an information center in the basement of the Summit House and, on Tuesday afternoons in the summer, hosts an environmental lecture series.

Glacier Cyclery, 336 2nd St., tel. 862-6446, has a good-looking fleet of mountain bikes for rent at $15 per day. Hours are Mon.-Fri. 10 a.m.-6 p.m., Sat. 10 a.m.-3 p.m. The staff will provide you with a hand-drawn bike map of the area and suggest rides; they also sell Flathead National Forest maps with good mountain-bike roads highlighted. During the summer, Glacier Cyclery stables a fleet of mountain bikes on Big Mountain.

Whitefish Stage Road, about a mile east of Hwy. 93 (via Hwy. 40), is a good bicycle route to Kalispell. Even though there's not much of a shoulder, it doesn't have a lot of traffic if you avoid the rush hours.

There are a couple of fitness clubs in town. One is part of the **Downtown Motel,** and the other, **Unique Physique,** is at 131 Central Avenue. A day's pass is $5 at either place. Neither has a swimming pool; the best bets for summer swimming are **City Beach** or the beach at

Whitefish Lake State Recreation Area ($2 for day use). Boat tours of the lake start at City Beach.

As befits the recreational capital of Montana, Whitefish has two golf courses. If you're a duffer, you'll probably be most comfortable at **Par 3 on 93,** tel. 862-7273. If you've got a good swing and the right clothes, the **Whitefish Lake Golf Course** is one of the best courses in the state. This country club-like course is on Hwy. 93 W., across from the Grouse Mountain Lodge, tel. 862-4000.

Drive north to fish in **Upper Stillwater Lake,** off Hwy. 93 just north of Olney. The lake reportedly has Dolly Varden, cutthroat, rainbow, and brook trout, perch, and northern pike in it. There's a small undeveloped lakeside campground.

Shopping

The streets of downtown Whitefish are lined with shops and galleries. **Artistic Touch,** 209 Central Ave., tel. 862-4813, has an excellent selection of high-quality crafts. Just across the street at 238 Central Ave., tel. 862-9043, **O'Keef's** has attractive, though pricey, jewelry and crafts. **Tomahawk Trading Company,** 419 2nd St., tel. 862-9199, features Indian jewelry.

If you're traveling Montana with your campstove and espresso pot, a stop at **Montana Coffee Traders,** tel. 862-7633, is almost imperative. It's south of town at 5810 Hwy. 93 S, about a quarter mile south of the Hwy. 40 intersection. Besides a variety of home-roasted coffee beans, there's a selection of coffee-drinking paraphernalia, locally made and imported gifts, and a little garden center that springs up in the front yard during the spring and summer.

Third St. Market, at the corner of 3rd and Spokane, tel. 862-5054, is the local health-food store. Many of the towns in this part of Montana have small health-food stores, but this one is more of a complete food store and community rendezvous than most.

Sportsman and Ski Haus has a branch at 105 Baker Ave. tel. 862-3111. It's open every day and stocks all sorts of sporting and skiing equipment.

Transportation

Amtrak stops at the N. Central Ave. depot, tel. 862-2268, on its way across the top of the country. The *Empire Builder* runs between Chicago and Seattle or Portland, and stops in Whitefish each day. The eastbound train comes through around 6:30 a.m.; westbound at approximately 11:30 p.m. A roundtrip ticket from Chicago costs $205; from Portland, it's $118.

Intermountain Transport uses Stumps Pumps, a gas station at 403 2nd St. E, tel. 862-6700, as its Whitefish terminal.

The **Duck Inn,** tel. 862-3825 or (800) 344-2377 is the rental car agent in town.

Information
The **Whitefish Chamber of Commerce** at 525 E. 3rd St., tel. 862-3501, publishes a very helpful tabloid brochure that includes a walking tour of the downtown area. There's also a small historical museum, replete with an old saxophone, lovely quilts, and an extensive collection of high school yearbooks, housed with the chamber of commerce.

The **Whitefish Ranger Station** is on Hwy. 93 near the turnoff for the Whitefish Lake State Recreation Area (and next door to Grouse Mountain Lodge).

Services
The **post office** is at 424 Baker Avenue.

Martin's Laundromat, at the corner of 3rd and Baker, is as convenient as any in western Montana. It's no chore to toss a load into the washer and wander through the shops and galleries while it's spinning.

COLUMBIA FALLS

There are no falls in Columbia Falls (pop. 3,000, elev. 2,960 feet). When it was time to name the town, Columbia was the initial choice. Since that name had already been taken, "Falls" was tacked on for the euphony it lent.

When Columbia Falls was established in the 1890s, it was supposed to have become a division point for the Great Northern Railway. Kalispell, then Whitefish, became the actual division points, leaving Columbia Falls built to a rather grander scale than its activity would warrant.

Today, Columbia Falls (pop. 3,000) is the industrial center of the Flathead Valley. Aluminum smelting is big business (Anaconda Aluminum is based here). Timber is also important—Plum Creek, the timber giant, has a big new mill with plenty of logs in the yard.

For the traveler, Columbia Falls is a handy jumping-off point for both Hungry Horse Reservoir and Glacier National Park. There are several motels and enough stores to do some last-minute stocking up before heading into the mountains.

Accommodations
Mountain Shadows Motel, at the junction of Hwys. 2 and 206, tel. (406) 892-7686, has rooms for $29 s, $33 d, and operates a campground with spaces for both tents and RVs. At the same intersection, the **Old River Bridge Inn** has singles starting at $37 ($34 winter), doubles from $40 ($37 winter), and an indoor pool, tel. 892-2181.

Big Creek is a Forest Service campground 21 miles north of Columbia Falls on Road 210 where Big Creek runs into the North Fork of the Flathead River. During the summer it's one of the quieter spots around, and, at $4 a night, one of the least expensive.

Food And Drink
The **Pines Café** is a handy stop along Hwy. 2, tel. 892-3712, featuring inexpensive breakfasts, mounted fish, and a museum. For a downtown café, try the **Columbia Café,** 509 Nucleus Ave., tel. 892-3166. Also downtown, **Chan's Restaurant,** 612 Nucleus Ave., tel. 892-3938, has Chinese and American lunches and dinners. The **Nite Owl** is a bar and restaurant with pizza, chicken, and ribs at 522 Ninth St. W, (tel. 892-3131.

Both the **Old River Bridge Inn** and the **Mountain Shadows Motel** have restaurants.

Recreation
The **Meadow Lake Country Club** at 1415 Tamarack Lane, tel. 892-3242, has a nine-hole golf course open to the public.

Services
For **emergency** services, call 911. The **post office** is at 530 First Ave. West. Lovers of cleanliness will want to stop by **Falls Coin Laundry and Car Wash** on Hwy. 2 W, tel. 892-4200.

Information

The Columbia Falls **Chamber of Commerce** is at 233 13th St. E, tel. 892-2072. The **Flathead County Library** has a branch at 130 Sixth St. W in Columbia Falls.

HUNGRY HORSE

Hungry Horse is the next town down the road from Columbia Falls. There's obviously a story surrounding the name of the town. During the severe winter of 1900, two draft horses used for logging the area wandered off. Tex and Jerry were found about a month later, all scraggly and hungry.

Though there'd been settlements in the area since the turn of the century, the Hungry Horse post office wasn't established until 1948, when the federal government began planning to dam the South Fork of the Flathead River. The dam was completed in 1952.

Sights

Fans of dam technology will want to tour the visitors' information center at the **Hungry Horse Dam**, four miles south of town. The 564-foot-high concrete dam holds back the 34-mile-long Hungry Horse Reservoir. Guided tours of the dam are offered during the summer months.

A road circles the reservoir and provides access to a number of trails into the surrounding national forest and wilderness areas. Jewel Basin Hiking Area lies to the west of the reservoir, the Great Bear Wilderness is to the east, and the Bob Marshall Wilderness is to the south. Great Northern Mountain, east of the reservoir, rises to an elevation of 8,720 feet. The Middle Fork of the Flathead River flows into the southern end of the reservoir. You'll see a myriad of Bible camps around the reservoir, and there's no dearth of public campgrounds.

Hungry Horse Reservoir is a good place to fish for cutthroat and bull trout; most people fish from boats, and the best fishing is during the late summer and fall.

Camping

There are eight Forest Service campgrounds around the Hungry Horse Reservoir. It's necessary to bring your own drinking water to all of them; even those that once had piped water have had their services cut back. Because of these cutbacks, all the public campgrounds around Hungry Horse Reservoir are now free.

Doris Point Campground is eight miles down Road 895 from Hungry Horse; **Lost Johnny Point** is a mile farther, **Lid Creek** is 15 miles from Hungry Horse; **Lakeview** is 24 miles; **Handkerchief Lake** is 35 miles from Hungry Horse on Road 895, then another two miles on Road 897. There's a trail from Handkerchief Lake up to the Jewel Basin Hiking Area. **Spotted Bear** is at the south end of the reservoir, 55 miles from Martin City on Road 38 (and about equal distance form Hungry Horse). **Elk Island** (accessible only by boat), **Murray Bay,** and **Emery Bay** are along the east side of the reservoir. Emery Bay is the closest spot to Martin City; it's seven miles down Road 38.

Food

The huckleberry is the culinary specialty of Hungry Horse. The **Huckleberry Patch** at 8858 Hwy. 2 E, tel. 387-5000, is a convenient place to load up on gifts of huckleberry preserves and to toss down a slice of huckleberry pie or a huckleberry milkshake in the café. (They also offer all-you-can-eat spaghetti for $3.95.) It's easy enough to pick your own berries. They start ripening around mid-July, and almost any trip off Hwy. 2 into the hills will lead to good picking—but watch out for bears, they feast on berries to prepare for hibernation.

Great Bear Wilderness Area

The Great Bear Wilderness Area comprises 285,771 acres just south of Glacier National Park, north of the Bob Marshall, on the west side of the Continental Divide. A small airstrip at Schafer Meadows is an unusual feature of this wilderness area. It's possible to fly in: **Strand Aviation,** tel. 247-7678, and **Eagle Aviation,** tel. 755-2376, will fly three to five people in for between $115 and $135, with extra fees for heavy or bulky equipment.

Trailheads from the Spotted Bear Ranger Station lead to Lodgepole Creek and the Spotted Bear River. Just about every trail in the wilderness complex will go into the valley of the South Fork of the Flathead River. The headwaters of the Middle Fork of the Flathead River are in the Great Bear Wilderness.

Information

The *Hungry Horse News* is the newspaper of record in these parts, definitely worth picking up if you want to read a weekly paper loaded with stories of mountain lions in the streets, bear maulings and bee stings in Glacier Park, and numerous DUI violations.

The Forest Service has two ranger stations in the area. One is in Hungry Horse, tel. 387-5243, and the other, which is staffed during the summer months only, is at Spotted Bear, at the southern end of the Hungry Horse Reservoir.

NORTHWEST CORNER

This is big timber country. You'll see lots of acid-green signs, like "This family supported by timber dollars" or "We support the timber industry." Roughly a third of the work force is directly employed by the wood-products industry, and logging pervades just about everyone's life in one way or another. There's a swagger in the calk boots and a pride in hauling logs.

But the forests are disappearing, and it's on everybody's mind. The old growth has been depleted to the point where mills have found it necessary to retool their equipment to accept smaller logs. Compromises that once seemed impossible have been hammered out by environmentalists and timber officials concerning additional wilderness areas. There are proposed additions to the Cabinet Mountains Wilderness, as well as proposals to mine under the existing wilderness area.

THE LAND

The Kootenai (pronounced KOOT-nee) National Forest is the defining physical feature of this corner of the state. It has a Pacific quality, and its lush hillsides are drained by the Kootenai and Clark Fork rivers and a host of smaller rivers and streams. Trees are everywhere, and where they aren't, their absence is more than conspicuous—it's almost an affront to those who don't depend on logging for a living.

Western red cedar, western hemlock, western white pine, whitebark pine, lodgepole pine, ponderosa pine, alpine larch, western larch, mountain hemlock, grand fir, subalpine fir, Douglas fir, Engelmann spruce, juniper, cottonwood, quaking aspen, alder, and paper birch are all native to northwestern Montana. Years of forest management have changed the composition of the new growth forest to increase their timber yields. Timber managers often replant only a single, fast-growing tree species, changing the forest from a diverse system with literally dozens of different species to a "mono-crop" similar in composition to a potato patch.

Although erosion increases and water quality decreases, logged areas do support both plant and animal life. Wildflowers bloom in clearcuts, huckleberries and elderberries invade, and deer and elk populations flourish in open areas created by timber cutting. There are also moose in the forested areas here, and some bighorn sheep and mountain goats on the hillsides.

Experienced mushroom hunters might try collecting morels in old burn areas and beneath Douglas fir and ponderosa pine trees. Moist spring weather can bring about a veritable fungal bloom in open areas.

HISTORY

The Kootenai

The Kootenai Indians moved from the north to the Tobacco Plains area around present-day Eureka and along the Kootenai River around the 1500s. The Upper and Lower Kootenai had different cultural traditions and lived in different areas, but they thought of themselves as one people. The Upper Kootenai lived closer to the Rocky Mountains and had more of a plains tradition than did the Lower Kootenai, who used canoes more than horses and caught more salmon than buffalo. After the Blackfeet arrived on the plains in the 1700s, the Kootenai largely restricted their travel to the west side of the Rockies.

Though many of the Kootenai people in Montana now live on the Flathead Reservation (mostly around Elmo), the name, "Kootenai," whose origin is uncertain, still brings to mind the mountains, tall trees, and rushing waters of the northwest corner of the state. (Some sources say their name means "Deer Robes" and alludes to their skill as deer hunters and tanners, but this is not certain because "Kootenai" is not even a word in the Kootenai language.)

Whites Arrive

David Thompson was the first white man in the area. He explored the Kootenai River in 1808 and portaged around Kootenai Falls. He sent Finan McDonald to the area near Libby to establish a trading post for the North-West Company. Trappers and fur traders followed in the wake of Thompson and McDonald, but it took gold and silver to bring a significant number of white settlers to the region. Placer mining started in 1869 and continued for about 20 years.

Even with trapping and mining activity, this corner of Montana was an isolated place until the Great Northern Railway came through in 1893. The railroad truly opened the north to development. Not only was there an easy way to get into the area, there was a way to haul abundant natural resources, particularly the trees, away. The growth of the timber industry was thus linked to the railroad.

Though much of the focus today is on the forests, mines still operate around Libby and Troy. Improved methods of extracting minerals and rising prices fuel interest in both small and large operations. In fact, there are prospectors who want to build tunnels under the Cabinet Mountains Wilderness area to extract the silver and copper deposits there.

This area, which for years was so remote and hard to penetrate because of its densely forested mountains, now has an abundance of roads. More than 7,000 miles of roads have been built in the Kootenai National Forest, with another 50-75 miles added each year.

BULL RIVER ROAD AND CABINET MOUNTAINS WILDERNESS

Bull River Road (Hwy. 56) runs from Hwy. 200 (just west of Noxon) to Troy. The Bull River and several lakes are along the road, and the Cabinet Mountain Wilderness is just to the east. Fishing is good in the river (but not spectacular in Bull Lake, which does not feed the river). There's a good chance that wildlife will be somewhere along this road almost anytime you drive it. You'll probably see deer, and there are also plenty of elk and moose in the area.

Highway 56 was an Indian trail; it was also used by smugglers bringing Chinese laborers down from Canada to work on the construction of the Northern Pacific Railroad.

Ross Creek Cedar Grove

Ross Creek Cedar Grove is about four miles off Hwy. 56 just south of Bull Lake (17 miles north of Hwy. 200). The gravel road has a steep section and isn't suitable for large RVs. The western red cedar forest here is a Pacific rainforest, a little unusual for Montana. It gets 50 inches of rain a year, so don't be surprised if you take the mile-long nature hike in a shower. The raised boardwalk trail on the interpretive hike protects the forest floor and makes it easy to hike in the rain. There are trails up the Middle Fork and the South Fork of Ross Creek starting from the parking lot of the cedar grove.

Indian history records that Bull Lake was formed when a landslide blocked a stream and destroyed a camp. There is still some evidence of such a slide at the foot of the lake.

Cabinet Mountains Wilderness

The Cabinet Mountains Wilderness comprises nearly 95,000 acres in the Kootenai National Forest. It can be reached from Hwy. 56 or Hwy. 200. Snowshoe Peak is the high point in the wilderness, at 8,738 feet. There is good hiking here, and some rock-climbing on the peaks.

To reach the trail to **St. Paul Lake,** a 4,715-foot-high lake in a cirque beneath St. Paul Peak, go up East Fork Rd. off Bull River Road. About a mile up East Fork Rd. is a Forest Service sign noting directions and distances to several trailheads. The St. Paul Lake trailhead is four miles from this point, up a gravel road that's easy to drive in a passenger car until the final short descent to the trailhead, which requires some caution. The hike in to the lake is four miles each way; the roundtrip is a good day's walk for the average hiker. The trail, which is shown on the Kootenai National Forest map, passes through some old-growth western red cedar and western hemlock before it reaches the lake. Even if you don't want to take the hike up to the lake, consider fishing the East Fork of the Bull River for trout.

Accommodations

The **Bull River** Forest Service Campground is by the Cabinet Mountains where Bull River runs into the Clark Fork. Dirty campers can wander just west of the campground to a private RV campground with showers for rent.

Big Horn Lodge is about seven miles from Hwy. 200 on Bull River Road. The lodge is attractive, the proprietor friendly, and the food good. Bed and breakfast rates start at $52 s, $70 d; for $80 s or $135 d, all meals are included. Guided trail rides and fishing trips are also

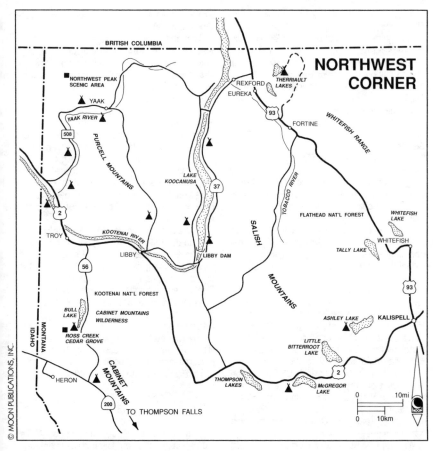

available, and the proprietor's son, Rus Willis, is one of the area's most successful hunting guides.

There's camping on the road to the Ross Creek Cedar Grove. **Bad Medicine** Forest Service Campground is two miles off Hwy. 56 overlooking Bull Lake. There is a boat launch at this cedar-scented site.

TROY AND VICINITY

At 1,892 feet, Troy is the lowest point in Montana. It's a town of about 1,100 on the west bank of the Kootenai River, which flows north-

west from Troy into Idaho. The Purcell Mountains are to the north of Troy, the Cabinet Mountains to the south. Ice-age glaciers covered the Purcells and ground them down to softer peaks. To the south, glaciers carved valleys and cirques in the Cabinet Mountains, but did not cover them so completely as to smooth them out.

The Yaak River drains the Purcell Mountains in the far northwest corner of the state and flow into the Kootenai river just west of Troy. The Yaak has gained a certain literary fame since writer Rick Bass moved to the area and wrote *Winter Notes* about snow, woodcutting, and isolation. The road between Yaak and Rexford has both densely forested areas and massive clearcuts. It's illustrative of the northwest timber industry.

Though the timber industry provides the basis for Troy's economy, both the railroad and mining have been important to the town's development. Mining still plays a major role. The ASARCO mine began processing copper and silver in 1981.

The high school team is, of course, the Trojans.

Sights

Troy's **historical museum** is housed in an old railroad building on Hwy. 2. Old railroad and logging equipment figure prominently in the collection, but one special prize is a cigar lighter. There's a short nature trail behind the museum.

Troy's as good a place as any to stock up on groceries, and the IGA (across the street from the museum) has the special attraction of mounted animal heads all over the walls.

Accommodations

There are a couple of inexpensive motels along Hwy. 2 in Troy. At the **Holiday Motel,** 213 E. Missoula (Hwy. 2), tel. (406) 295-4117, you won't spend over $24 for a double. The **Ranch Motel,** 914 E. Missoula, tel. 295-4332, charges $22 for a single, $26 for a double.

Yaak River Campground (USFS), seven miles west of Troy on Hwy. 2, is a good entrance or exit campground to the state. There are plenty of paths down to the river. Head up the Yaak to **Yaak Falls Campground,** set by a cascade eight miles up from Hwy. 2.

Whitetail Campground is on a quiet stretch of the Yaak River; it's not a bad place for a swim. **Pete Creek** is an exceptionally pretty campground set on a bluff above Pete Creek, just west of the town of Yaak.

McAffie's, tel. 295-4880, operates a lodge, a restaurant, a fly-fishing shop, and an outfitting service on Yaak River Road between Pete's Creek and Yaak.

Food And Drink

The **Silver Spur Restaurant,** on Hwy. 2 W, tel. 295-9937, is a popular family place, but the sort of popular family place that's got a log cabin motif and a bar. It's the best bet for a dinner in Troy, though the adventurous may prefer the

Trojan Lanes, a bowling alley-cum-casino-cum-dinner spot on Hwy. 2.

Though the Trojan Lanes does serve pizza, a less scary bet is the **Gold Nugget,** a cubbyhole of a pizza place on the east edge of town. **R Place** is a tiny, inexpensive burger joint across from the museum. They also serve sandwiches, fish, and Mexican food.

Recreation

Pulpit Mountain Trail, a national recreation trail, is a five-mile (one-way) hike just north of Troy. It passes an old fire lookout on Pulpit Mountain and has good views of the Cabinet Mountains. The easiest way to walk the trail is to start from the trailhead on Lynx Creek Rd. and hike to where the trail comes out on Rabbit Creek Road.

To reach the **Northwest Peak Scenic Area,** turn up the Pete Creek Rd. just west of Yaak. This is an isolated area of the state, and it's rare to see many other hikers on the trails. One of the more popular trails leads to Northwest Peak. It's a two-mile hike to the peak, which has grand views and a deserted lookout.

Information

The **ranger station** is on the west edge of town; visitor's information is dispensed at the historical museum, and the **public library** is at the corner of Third and Spokane, tel. 295-4040.

LIBBY

Libby's a timber town, through and through. It's 2,066 feet and the population is approximately 2,600. It's in the Kootenai River valley, with the Cabinet Mountains to the south, the Purcell Mountains to the northwest, and the Salish Mountains to the northeast. Though it's not an obvious tourist town, it's easy to spend a day or two in the area.

History

David Thompson's reconnoitering in 1808 resulted in a small influx of fur traders during the first half of the 1800s, but little development occurred until gold was found in 1865. A mining town was thrown up by Libby Creek in the 1880s, and it moved to wherever the gold seemed to be. Sometimes the development was called New Town; other times Old Town seemed the more appropriate name. The name of a prospector's daughter ultimately won out. Libby ended up in its present location when the railroad came through in 1892.

Trees were initially harvested for mine timbers, then for railroad bridges and ties. Ultimately, the timber industry eclipsed both mining and the railroad, and has become the mainstay of Libby; the Champion Mill is a major employer.

Mining, however, still figures in the local economy. Perhaps it's not the sort of mining that one thinks of immediately, but W.R. Grace and Co. has a vermiculite mining and processing operation in Libby. Vermiculite, used as an insulation material and as a potting-soil additive, is a type of mica that becomes light and puffy when it's heated.

Sights
The **Heritage Museum** on Hwy. 2 is a large polygonal log building. The dark interior is full of display cases brimming with Libby's old musical instruments (including two ukelins, one pianoette, two mandolin harps, and the sheet music for "Let Me Call You Sweetheart"), household implements, and logging equipment. There are special displays on the region's wildlife, logging, and mining. Open daily and admission is free.

Of the several historical buildings in downtown Libby, the oldest is what is now the dentist's office at 209 W. Second Street. It was built in 1899 and was originally the Libby hospital. The ballpark across the street was once the site of an Indian camp. One place that's changed a bit over the years is the white and red apartment building on E. First St. across from the train depot. It was once known as Helen Hunter's Place, and, in 1906, was Libby's first brothel.

Montana City Old Town is south of Hwy. 2 on Main St., then right at the radio station, tel. 293-8426. In addition to false-fronted stores, there's a theater company that puts on vaudeville acts and dramas in the Opera House.

If you're out to relive Libby's history, it may be more profitable to pan for gold on Libby Creek than to watch vaudeville or go glassy-eyed over displays of old kitchenware. Gold was discovered in Libby Creek in 1865, and was mined fairly intensively around the turn of the century. There's still some gold there, though. The original dredging equipment got only 85-90% of what gold was in the creek. What's left is most likely to be found near the bottom of gravel piles left by early miners. The Forest Service has an area set aside for gold panning on Libby Creek; it's important not to search outside the designated area, as there are a number of mining claims staked close by.

To reach the **Libby Creek Gold Panning Area,** turn from Hwy. 2 onto Bear Creek Rd. (seven miles south of Libby) and drive 18 miles to the small parking area beside Libby Creek. (Or take Libby Creek Rd., 12 miles down Hwy. 2 from Libby, and follow it just over 10 miles to the panning zone.) Howard Lake Campground is a mile south of the gold-panning area. If you tire of prospecting, follow Libby Creek Road (the road that goes west at the Howard Lake junction) to its end and take an easy two- mile roundtrip hike along Libby Creek past an old miner's cabin.

The **Champion plywood** and sawmill plants run free tours on weekdays in the summer. Stop by Champion's main office at 1 p.m. or call 293-4141. Be sure to wear long pants and sturdy shoes on this one-hour, mile-long tour.

For a look at the cascading, 200-foot-high **Kootenai Falls** from the highway, there's a turnout on Hwy. 2 about five miles west of Libby. This is one of the few waterfalls on a major Northwest river that hasn't had its power harnessed to electrical generators. A trail leads from the casual campground by the highway pullout, across a bridge over the railroad tracks, and down to viewpoints of the cascades. Continue west on the trail to a swinging footbridge downstream from the falls. Bighorn sheep are often seen just east of here grazing on the cliffs across the river.

Kootenai River Road runs west along the north side of the river, starting at Hwy. 37 just over the bridge from downtown Libby. The road is closed to motor vehicles about seven miles from there, and it makes an enjoyable walk. Before white men came to the area, this was an Indian trail. The WPA Guide to Montana speaks of ceremonial sweat baths used by the Kootenai Indians along this trail where Pipe Creek flows into the Kootenai about five miles west of Libby.

This stretch is now pretty developed, and you can't see the broken rocks anymore, but, if you walk down the closed part of the road, you'll get a feeling for why this spot was used for ceremonial sweat baths.

Walk far enough along this trail, and you'll reach Kootenai Falls. Actually, this is a good mountain bike ride-hike combination. The first couple of miles are along an old road dotted with abandoned cabins. When the road runs out, leave your bike and take to foot. The trail isn't always apparent, but if you keep to the ridge just above the river you'll be okay. Near the head of the falls the trail traverses rock slides. This is a good place to turn back. Even if you can see the swinging bridge below the falls, don't try to hike there. It gets dangerous quickly, and you'll understand why the Kootenai Indians built rock cairns to ensure safe passage around the gorges and cataracts.

Accommodations

Perhaps the most interesting accommodation in the Libby area is the **Big Creek Baldy Mountain Fire Lookout,** available for $25 per night. It's about 26 miles from Libby via Pipe Creek Road. The cabin is equipped with everything but sleeping bags and food. Reservations and the key to the lookout are available from the Libby Ranger Station, one mile northeast of Libby on Hwy. 37, tel. 293-7741.

There are a host of inexpensive motels along and around Hwy. 2 in Libby. **Sandman Motel** is set back off Hwy. 2 just a bit. It rents doubles for $28 and has an outdoor hot tub. Some rooms have microwaves and refrigerators. **Rainbow Motel,** 505 10th St., tel. 293-8661, has rooms for $18 s, $22 d.

Venture Motor Inn, Hwy. 2 W., tel. 293-7711, is the deluxe place to stay in Libby. It has a fitness center, heated pool, and hot tub starting at $36 a night.

There's a **free campground** behind the Libby Chamber of Commerce building. It's a bit too much in the thick of things for tent camping, but the convenience and the price are enticing. **Scholl's Conoco** on Hwy. 2 has RV camping and, important for tent campers, showers. Between Libby and Troy, the **Lions Club** maintains a free primitive campground at the Kootenai Falls viewpoint. A trail leads down to the falls. **Carrigan,** yet another free campground 12 miles up Pipe Creek Rd., is isolated, with no running water, and is run by Champion.

Native American travelers and railroad builders both found it tough to skirt Kootenai Falls' narrow gorge.

Food And Drink

The **Red Dog Saloon** is seven miles up Pipe Creek Rd. in Libby, on the way to Turner Mountain. It's a little way off the main drag, but haven't you been craving a pizza with whole-wheat crust? It's a friendly local hangout for both food and drinks.

La Casa de Amigos serves up Mexican and American lunches and dinners downtown on California Avenue. There's a **4-Bs** at 442 Hwy. 2, tel. 293-8751. And, if it's steak you're after, **M-K Steak House** on Hwy. 2, tel. 293-5686, is the place to eat in Libby. For a bar with live music on the weekends, try the **Pastime,** 216 Mineral Ave., tel. 293-9925. The Pastime has been around since 1916, when it was known as the Pastime Pool Hall. Note the original carvings behind the bar.

Events

Logger Days are held in mid-July every year. Libby's **Nordicfest** is held the third weekend of

September. It features Scandinavian food, crafts, music, and dancing.

Recreation

The 23-mile **Skyline National Recreation Trail** starts at the west fork of Quartz Creek, northwest of Libby, and ends in the Yaak Valley.

The Kootenai River is popular with rafters and canoeists. The Canoe Gulch Ranger Station on Hwy. 37 is a good put-in spot, and boats can be taken out in town just below the California Ave. Bridge. The trip is a little too challenging for inexperienced river runners, and it's important to remember that Kootenai Falls, five miles downstream from Libby, are not passable.

There are large rainbow trout living below Libby Dam, but those who fish this part of the Kootenai River should pay close attention to the water level; release of water from the dam can cause quick rises. Fishing is best when the

---

WESTERN LARCH

A northwest Montana hillside strewn with yellowing "evergreen" trees does not necessarily mean blight. It may be a stand of larch, or tamarack trees.

Western and alpine larch, both found in northwest Montana, are the only conifers starting each spring with a fresh growth of needles. Around mid-September, the trees respond to the shortening days with yellowed needles, which drop before winter hits.

The larger, more common, western larch trees grow at lower altitudes than their alpine relatives. North-facing slopes provide good habitat for the hardy western larch, which can withstand fires and temperature extremes that thwart other species.

Larch wood is dense and durable—good for hot fires and for structural support. Because of a funny incompatibility with concrete (the wood secretes a concrete-weakening sugar), it's not used as much for construction as expected, but some larch extracts are used pharmaceutically and in baking powder.

Larch needles usually collect in piles beneath their trees, but enough end up in streams to form a regional collectible—larch balls. These wads of larch needles, sometimes the size of a grapefruit, have been packed together by river currents and eddies.

---

water level drops. For water-release schedules, call Libby Dam's River Discharge Information at 293-3421.

The downhill ski area at 5,952-foot **Turner Mountain,** 22 miles up Pipe Creek Rd. from Libby, has a 2,400-foot vertical drop.

There are groomed **cross-country ski trails** at Bear Creek and Flatiron Mountain near Libby. Few of the logging roads around Libby are plowed in the winter. Stop by the ranger station to find out which roads have been set aside for skiers. Snowmobilers should check with the Forest Service to see which roads are designated for snowmobile use.

Cabinet View Golf Course, tel. 293-7332, is a nine-hole course (with plans to expand to a full 18 holes). Fees for public use are $8 for nine holes, $14 for 18.

There's bowling at **Lincoln Lanes,** 138 Commerce Way, tel. 293-3123.

Shopping

Little Bear Tipi Pole Company, 22983 Hwy. 2 S, about 20 miles from Libby, tel. 293-9880, is a genuine old hippie enterprise, replete with tepees for sale and for rent.

Cabinet Books and Music, in the Libby Shopping Center, has a selection of regional books along with mainstream paperbacks.

Information

Visitors information is proffered on Hwy. 2 at Fireman's Park, tel. 293-5110. The **Libby Ranger Station** is across the river, a half mile north on Hwy. 37, tel. 293-7741. Another ranger station is at **Canoe Gulch,** 13 miles north of Libby on Hwy. 37, near Libby Dam.

Services

For **police or ambulance service** in Libby, call 293-4112. The **fire department** answers at 911. **Saint John's Lutheran Hopital** is at 350 Louisiana Ave., tel. 293-7761.

Two of the laundromats in Libby are **Janet's,** 221 W. Ninth, and **A & J Suds and Scrub,** 1770 Hwy. 2 West.

Transportation

Amtrak stops in Libby; the eastbound train comes through at 4:30 a.m., the westbound at 11:30 p.m. **Libby Cab** operates 24 hours a day in Libby and Troy, tel. 293-7349.

LAKE KOOCANUSA

Ninety-mile-long Lake Koocanusa, framed by the Purcell and Salish mountains, was formed in 1972 when the Libby Dam backed up the Kootenai River from just above Libby all the way north into Canada.

Libby Dam now provides hydroelectric power, via the Bonneville Power Administration, to much of the Northwest and stores water in Lake Koocanusa to prevent flooding downstream. Water is released from the dam to supply the 17 dams downstream on the Columbia River. The dam itself is a straight axis, concrete gravity dam: it holds back Lake Koocanusa by its own weight.

The Libby Dam has an attractive **visitor center,** tel. 293-5577, 17 miles north of Libby. The center is open late May through early September, 9:30-6, for guided tours of the dam and powerhouse. There's a boat launch and picnic area.

Paved roads circle a good portion of Lake Koocanusa. Highway 37 runs along the east side; Forest Service Road 228 follows the western shore. There are only a couple of places to cross the lake. Libby Dam has a bridge, and Montana's highest and longest bridge spans the lake just south of Rexford.

The name "Koocanusa," derived from "Kootenai," "Canada," and "U.S.A.," was coined by residents of Rexford, a town largely flooded by the lake. Part of the town simply picked up and moved to higher ground, a grand tradition among dam-flooded sites. Actually, Rexford had already moved once before that; it was originally built right along the banks of the Kootenai River and was moved alongside the railroad tracks in the early 1890s.

Accommodations

Either rooms in a large log house or a big tepee can be rented at **Trail's End Bed and Breakfast,** tel. (406) 889-3486, on Trail's End Rd. near Lake Kookanusa and Sophie, Moran, and Tetrault lakes. Singles cost $25, doubles $35. **Yoder's Bed and Breakfast,** 5611 W. Kootenai Rd., tel. 889-3466, is on the west side of Lake Koocanusa 11 miles from the Canadian border in the Amish community of West Kootenai. It's a secluded spot with both cabins and bedrooms in

the main house available. Rates are $24 for one person, $38 for two, up to $60 for four. Yoder's closes down from January through March.

Two cabins are rented out by the town of Rexford: a one-bedroom cabin is $35 per night and $150 per week; the two-bedroom cabin is $50 per night and $225 per week. To reserve, call 296-2867 or 296-2439.

Campsites are abundant around Lake Koocanusa. On the west side, six miles above Libby Dam, is **McGillivray,** a large Forest Service campground and recreation area ($6 per night). There's a boat launch and a swimming area on the lake at McGillivray, but they can only be used when the lake is filled with water, generally any time after early July. If McGillivray is too crowded, check the sign at the entrance for smaller and less developed campgrounds in the area.

Rexford Beach Campground is one of the few national forest campgrounds where reservations can be made with a toll-free phone call. It will cost $6, in addition to the usual $7 camping fee, but to gain that peace of mind that reservations lend, call (800) 283-CAMP (2267). **Tetrault Lake** and **Sophie Lake** north of Rexford, near Lake Koocanusa, both have Forest Service campgrounds by them.

Rocky Gorge and **Peak Gulch** are Forest Service campgrounds on Lake Koocanusa on Hwy. 37 south of the Lake Koocanusa Bridge. **Mariners' Haven,** tel. 296-3252, is a private campground near Rexford with tepee rentals, a grocery store, and marina.

Recreation

There is good fishing around Libby Dam, most notably for kokanee salmon. Bald eagles are onto this one, too, and can be spotted here in the fall, swooping down for spawning kokanee. Late October through mid-November is the peak season for eagle viewing. Arrive early in the morning and you may see 40 or 50 eagles just downstream from the dam.

Just up the road from the visitor center is a trail (approx. two miles) to Alexander Mountain, continuing on another mile and a half to Fleetwood Point.

The short trail to Little North Falls (off Road 228) is handicapped-accessible.

Information

The **Canoe Gulch Ranger Station,** tel. 293-7773, or 293-5758 for a recording, on Hwy. 37 just south of its junction with Road 228, has information on recreation around Lake Koocanusa.

EUREKA

Eureka (pop. 1,200, elev. 2,577 feet) is located on the Tobacco River in the Tobacco Valley (so named because that was a crop grown by the area's Kootenai Indians, though some sources contend that missionaries attempted to grow tobacco here, and the name comes from their failed efforts). The Tobacco Valley was formed by glacial action, and it joins Plains and the Paradise Valley in the hotly contested battle over who gets the title of "banana belt of Montana." The mountains off to the east are part of the Whitefish Range.

History

The Tobacco Plains were home base to the Kootenai Indians, who hunted, fished, and gathered in the Kootenai River basin. The northern part of Hwy. 93 was originally an Indian trail and was used later by fur traders and pack trains traveling between Missoula and Vancouver, B.C. David Thompson was in the area in 1808; he was the first white to see it. Trappers, traders, prospectors, and homesteaders began to settle the valley in the early 1880s. The first homesteaders were stockmen who established ranches in the town of Eureka.

Eureka, like the rest of northwestern Montana, has a timber-based economy. There's a little twist on it here, though; Eureka calls itself the "Christmas tree capital of the world." Farming supplements timber around Eureka; in fact, coming in to Eureka from the big timber country to the west, it looks strikingly agricultural.

Sights

Eureka doesn't just have the standard small-town historical museum; rather, it has a full-blown **historical village** near the south end of downtown. Most of the buildings there are salvaged from the town of Rexford. The old Rexford general store now houses a museum, which boasts, among the old books and papers, an ancient permanent-wave machine. Be sure to take your camera and flash attachment in with you, as you'll want to get the caretaker's permission to drag a chair over by the machine and have your picture taken with the wicked-looking clamps and wires dangling around your head. Another oddity here are larch balls, which can be had for a quarter each. Larch balls form when larch trees drop their needles into a stream and the currents and eddies form the needles into a ball.

There's an Amish community centered in West Kootenai and Rexford, on the west side of Lake Koocanusa about 14 miles north of the Koocanusa Bridge. The **Kootenai General Store** is a good place to stop to get the feel for the community, which formed in the 1970s when about 20 families moved here from the Midwest. They hold an annual auction of quilts, furniture, and prefabricated log homes in mid-June. For the exact date, contact Kootenai Log Homes, 5388 West Kootenai, Rexford, MT 59930, tel. 889-3258.

When Libby Dam flooded the Kootenai River to form the lake, fish habitats were destroyed. **Murray Springs Fish Hatchery,** seven miles northwest of Eureka, near the north end of Lake Koocanusa, was built in 1978 in an attempt to restore cutthroat trout to the area.

Murphy Lake, 14 miles southeast of Eureka on Hwy. 93, is home to a loon population as well as a host of other animals, including horned grebes, bald eagles, herons, ospreys, white-tailed and mule deer, and beavers. Be sure to respect the privacy of nesting loons.

Accommodations

It's not expensive to stay the night in Eureka. The **Creek Side Motel,** 1333 Hwy. 93 N, tel. (406) 296-2361, has rooms for $24.50 per night. They also have a campground with sites for both RVs and tents, plus shower and laundry facilities. **Ksanka Inn,** Hwy. 93 and Hwy. 37, tel. 296-3127, is a store and bakery in addition to a motel. Rates here run $24.50 s, $29.50 d. South of Eureka, **Grave Creek Bed and Breakfast,** five miles east of Hwy. 93 on Graves Creek Rd., tel. 882-4658, has rooms with private baths; $29 s and $40 d.

Crystal Lakes Condominiums, northeast of Fortine on Hwy. 93, tel. 882-4586, face onto the Whitefish Range. This resort area includes a pool, hot tub, tennis courts, and cross-country ski trails. Rates here start at $42 for a single studio with a kitchen and run to $139 for a group of eight in a two-bedroom unit. There's a public nine-hole, par-three golf course across the highway from Crystal Lakes. **Meadow Creek Golf Course,** tel. 882-4474, has its headquarters and clubhouse at Jerry's Saloon, Steakhouse, and Golf. Greens fee is $6.

North of Eureka, the Ten Lakes Scenic Area has two campgrounds, **Big Therriault Lake** and **Little Therriault Lake.** To the south, **Murphy Lake, North Dickey Lake,** and **South Dickey Lake** all have campgrounds. Murphy Lake has a small loon population, which is protected during nesting season by boating restrictions on the southern end of the lake.

Food And Drink
Time Out Café on Dewey Ave. (Hwy. 93) tel. 296-2197, draws a big local crowd. It has a salad bar. The sporting will undoubtedly venture into **TJ's Restaurant and Lounge,** which houses a card room and a pawn broker on Hwy. 93 next to the Big Sky Lanes, tel. 296-3174. **Espinoza's,** at 113 Dewey Ave., tel. 296-3360, has Mexican food and a full line of burgers and café fare, including great milkshakes. Even for dinner, it's hard to spend more than $6-7. **Albinia's** is the restaurant, lounge, and casino side of the operation. The obligatory **Stock-man's Bar** is a good bet if you want a beer with your burger.

Recreation
Ten Lakes Scenic Area is adjacent to the Canadian border near Eureka, and has been nominated for wilderness-area designation. To reach the Ten Lakes area, turn off Hwy. 93 at Grave Creek (about 10 miles south of Eureka) and follow the road for 30 miles, almost to its end. Several hiking trails start at the end of the road (just beyond Little Therriault Lake) and lead to many of the lakes in the area.

Paradise and Bluebird lakes are the closest, about two miles in, with about a 1,000-foot elevation gain. A pamphlet with a rough trail map is available at the Murphy Lake Ranger Station south of Eureka. Pick up a map of the Kootenai National Forest for clearer detail.

Information And Services
The **Eureka Ranger Station** is on the north edge of town, at 1299 Hwy. 93, tel. 296-2536 or 296-2769 for recorded information. There's also a ranger station at Murphy Lake, south of Eureka, tel. 882-4451.

Police, fire, and ambulance emergency in Eureka is 911. **Eureka Laundry and Lockers** is at 308 Dewey Ave., tel. 296-2204.

THE LOWER CLARK FORK

ALONG I-90

Mile Zero! No Services! Hearts soar with the ebulliant welcome to Montana. Is it really different here already? Well, it *is* an hour later than in Idaho.

Think of John Mullan as you drive along I-90. The military road he built from Fort Benton to Walla Walla, Washington, followed this same route from the Idaho line to Frenchtown, then along what is now Hwy. 263 into Missoula.

For a first chance-last chance Montana campground, you can't get much more convenient than **Cabin City** Forest Service campground. It's a little over two miles off I-90 at exit 22, just east of DeBorgia and 22 miles from the state line. Unless you hit a busy weekend, it's not as crowded as one would expect. The campsites are set in a lodgepole pine forest, and there's a three-quarter-mile nature hike down to Twelvemile Creek. The campground is open from late May through early September, $4 per night.

St. Regis is where the St. Regis River flows into the Clark Fork. The St. Regis parallels the freeway to the west of town, the Clark Fork to the east. At the town of St. Regis, the Clark Fork makes a sharp turn to the east. Hwy. 135 follows it along the lovely stretch to Hwy. 200.

Superior was a mining boomtown. Gold was discovered on a stream called Cayuse Creek in 1869 and, over the next year, 10,000 people swarmed to the mining camp. Other strikes in the area shifted the activity from place to place. In some areas, such as Louisville, Chinese miners moved in to the abandoned shacks and gleaned the remaining gold. Mining booms came intermittently over the next few decades, but pretty much ended in 1910, when a huge forest fire destroyed the Keystone mine and most everything else for miles around.

Alberton (pop. 384) was originally a railroad town. It was a division point for the Milwaukie Road, whose depot has been restored and is visible from the freeway. Alberton has a packed-to-the-gills used bookstore, **Montana Valley Books,** and it has a notorious gorge. **Alberton Gorge** (aka Cyr Canyon) is a 20 mile stretch of whitewater on the Clark Fork River. There are plenty of fishing-access sites along the Clark Fork that can be used to put in and take out boats. It's an especially challenging run when the river is high—only experienced paddlers should attempt it before August. Even when the water level drops, it's not a trip for beginners, though both the **University of Montana Outdoor Recreation Program,** tel. 243-5072, and Missoula's **Western Waters River Trips,** tel. 728-6161 run raft trips through Alberton Gorge. Those who aren't tempted by whitewater may choose to fish this section of the Clark Fork for brown, cutthroat, rainbow, and bull trout.

Frenchtown was settled by French Canadians as the Mullan Road was being built. It's now a mill town and a bedroom community of Missoula.

THE ROAD TO PARADISE

Highway 135 follows the Clark Fork River from I-90 at St. Regis to Hwy. 200 just east of Paradise. **Cascade Campground** is a small, basic, roadside Forest Service campground ($4, with smelly pit toilets and hand-pumped water). It's on Hwy. 135 six miles south of Hwy. 200. There's a surprising amount of roadside noise generated by Hwy. 135, but the setting is nice; there is a hike up to a waterfall, the Clark Fork River is just across the road, and if it's chilly, there's a hot springs resort less than four miles up the highway.

Quinn's Hot Spring Resort, three miles south of Hwy. 200 on Hwy. 135, tel. 826-3150, charges from $9.36 for tent camping, up to $13.56 for a full hookup. For a dip in the 96° outdoor swimming pool, adults pay $2.50 (included in camping fee), $2 for children, $2.25 for seniors. There's a small grocery store with washing machines, a bar, and a supper club (with Sunday brunch at 10). Non-campers can get a motel room or a small cabin for $20-44.

PARADISE AND PLAINS

Paradise may have originally been "Pair-o-Dice," after a roadhouse on the road along the Clark Fork. But Paradise isn't such a bad name in itself. There's the river, the mountains, and the banana belt. Not much else, but hey, who needs it?

Plains was originally called "Horse Plains." Its moderate climate made it a favorite spot for Indians and their horses to spend the winters.

Sights
In Plains, the old Horse Plains Jail is at the corner of Blake and McGowan a block north of Hwy. 200. The Wild Horse Plains School House is a log building dating from 1878. It's on the west end of town next to the highway.

Accommodations
While there's no particular reason to spend the night here, Plains does have several inexpensive motels: the **Owl Motel,** 304 W. Meany, tel. 826-3691, the **Tops Motel,** 340 E. Railroad, tel. 826-3412, and the **Harwood Motel and Trailer Court,** east of Plains on Hwy. 200, tel. 826-3623. There are several cafés, restaurants, and bars in Plains, including the **Wildhorse Bakery Restaurant** and Lounge at 102 E. Railroad.

THOMPSON FALLS

Thompson Falls (elev. 2,463 feet, pop. 1,300) was named for David Thompson, the geographer and trader who established his Saleesh House here in 1809. The trading post was used, though perhaps not continuously, by Thompson and other North-West Company employees until the early 1820s. There's no trace of the Saleesh House left at its original site about two miles east of Thompson Falls on the north shore of the Clark Fork River, but there is a memorial to David Thompson across the highway from the timber staging area just east of town.

Like many in Montana's history, Thompson Falls residents of the 1880s decided that a little direct action would enhance their town. They felt that Thompson Falls had been unfairly over-

looked by the Northern Pacific Railway, so they piled logs onto the railroad tracks. When the train was forced to stop, the locals boarded it and persuaded the passengers, emigrants from the east, to settle in Thompson Falls.

The falls were dammed in 1916, backing up a two-mile-long reservoir behind the dam. There are two more dams downstream from this one, making the Clark Fork more like a lake than a river for much of its course from Thompson Falls to the Idaho state line.

Sights
Thompson Falls Island, at the foot of Gallatin St., is a day-use park that's closed to automobiles. It's full of bluffs and rocky rises, a good place to hike around and watch the birds, including the osprey nesting on the bridge. Keep an eye peeled for Canada geese. Like the Canadian employees of the North-West Company in the early 1800s, they seem to like this area.

The local **historical museum** is housed in the old jail, behind the police station on Madison St. It's open during the summer Mon.-Fri. 9 a.m.-5 p.m.

East of Thompson Falls, the **KooKooSint Mountain Sheep Viewing Area** is a roadside pullout with several informative signs. (Koo-KooSint is the name given David Thompson by the local Indians. It means "Man who looks at stars.") Bighorn sheep were eaten by the Flathead Indians and by Thompson, who found them a welcome addition to his sparse winter diet. You're most likely to see sheep here in the spring, when they're at lower elevations eating the new grass, or during late November or December, when they descend to feed in the valleys and mate. Open, south-facing slopes provide a winter habitat. The lambs are born in early May on the high ridges, and the sheep summer in the mountains. Mountain sheep have spongy hooves with hard edges to lend traction and support, allowing them to traverse slopes easily and quickly.

Accommodations
Hotel Black Bear (with bar and café), 919 W. Main, tel. 827-3951, has rooms for the daring from $12 s. It's an old downtown hotel gone somewhat to seed.

For more comfortable accommodations, **Falls Motel,** 112 Gallatin, tel. 827-3559, has a hot tub in a pleasant little solarium, rooms from $24 s, $38 d. Just west of town, **Rimrock Lodge** tel. 827-3536, has a good restaurant and rooms for $27 s, $30 d.

Thompson Falls State Recreation Area is a mile west of Thompson Falls just off Hwy. 200 on the Clark Fork. It costs $6 a night to camp in a riverside spot with running water but no other amenities. **Copper King** and **Clark Memorial** are free Forest Service campgrounds with no running water up the Thompson River Road (catch this road five miles east of town). Copper King is four miles off Hwy. 200; Clark Memorial another mile and a half up the road.,

Recreation
The **Thompson Falls Golf Club** is a nine hole public course just northwest of town near the state recreation area.

Several looped hiking trails lead to small lakes in the Lolo National Forest north of Thompson Falls. Reach the **Four Lakes Creek** trailhead by driving north of the Thompson River Rd. (which intersects Hwy. 200 five miles east of town)

bighorn sheep, *Ovis canadensis*

BOB RACE

about six miles, turn left onto the West Fork Thompson River Rd., and follow it, bearing left as it becomes Four Lakes Creek Rd. (Forest Rd. 7669), some eight miles to the trailhead. A Lolo National Forest map will detail the trails.

Fishing access to the Thompson River is easy; a road runs along it almost the entire way from Hwy. 200 north to Hwy. 2. Expect to pull mostly rainbow trout, and perhaps some brown or Dolly Varden trout from the stretch near Hwy. 200.

Food and Drink
Ferk's, 809 Main St. (tel. 827-9994) has good burgers and is, in general, a pleasant place to dine in Thompson Falls. The **Rimrock Lodge** has serves breakfast, lunch, and dinner.

NORTH OF THOMPSON FALLS ON HWY. 200

Trout Creek
Trout Creek is west of Thompson Falls and 15 miles east of Noxon. It has a few motels, a recreation area with a small swimming beach, and a ranger station. Several outfitters operate out of Trout Creek, including one that specializes in hunting and fishing trips for people with disabilities (Jerry Malson Outfitting and Guiding, 22 Swamp Creek Rd., Trout Creek, MT 59874, tel. 846-5582). **North Shore Campground** is a National Forest campground on Noxon Reservoir about two miles west of Trout Creek.

If you're in the mood to drive back roads, **Vermillion Falls** is 12 miles from Trout Creek on the Vermillion River Rd. A couple of miles farther along the road, find **Willow Creek Campground,** a small, free, and primitive (no water) Forest Service campground.

Noxon
There's a dam on the Clark Fork at Noxon, a small town on the west bank of the river. The 190-foot-high dam, which harnesses the Noxon rapids, was built in 1959 and has two viewpoints less than a mile from Hwy. 200. The **Noxon Motel,** tel. 847-2600, just across the bridge from Hwy. 200, has a hot tub.

Heron

The Cabinet Gorge was named by David Thompson, who thought of the French word for a small room when he saw the high rock walls that formed the gorge. Of course, there's a dam here now, just over the state line into Idaho.

The **Wilderness Lodge,** Rt. 2, Box 41, Heron, MT 59844, tel. 847-2277, is tucked away on Elk Creek in the northern Bitterroot Mountains. Motel rooms and cabins are rented by the day and the week.

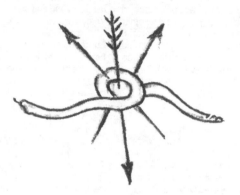

BOB RACE

GLACIER NATIONAL PARK

Glacier National Park contains over 1,500 square miles of extraordinarily scenic wilderness. Towering, glacier-pocked summits bend over mirror-like lakes. Wildlife, from wolves to bald eagles, from moose to ptarmigans, inhabit the park's thick forests, streamsides, and rocky promontories; over 60 species of mammals and 200 species of birds make their homes in Glacier. Easily one of the most spectacular drives in the country is Going-To-The-Sun Road, which climbs from lakes and forest, up the sheer face of the Rockies to a fragile, alpine meadow almost 7,000 feet above sea level.

Glacier is a park for the outdoor-minded: you'll want to leave the car behind. Over 700 miles of hiking trails link backcountry peaks and lakes. In winter the park's roads double as cross-country ski trails.

Sometimes called the "Crown of the Continent" for its staggeringly rugged skyline, Glacier, and its Canadian cousin Waterton Park, forms one of the crown jewels of the National Park system.

INTRODUCTION

THE LAND

Peak for peak, and valley for valley, Glacier National Park contains some of the most astonishing geology in the country. Three geologic stages have successively acted on the land; each leaving distinctive and unique features.

Belt Sedimentary Rock

The rocks that form the mountains of Glacier National Park were laid down when the area was resting under primordial seas. The profusion of primitive algae and limestone indicate that the oldest formation in the park, the **Altyn Formation,** developed under a shallow sea perhaps 1.5 billion years ago. Altyn Formation,

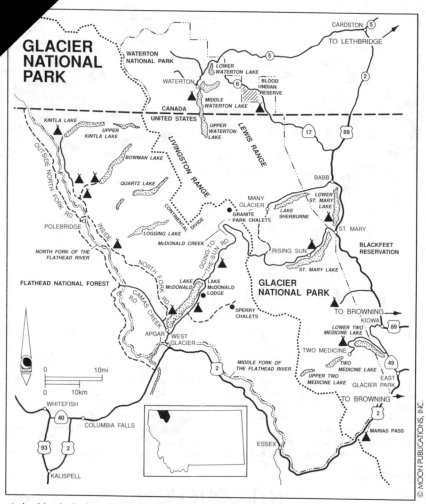

GLACIER NATIONAL PARK

stark white, is the bottom tier of the immense layer cake that is Glacier National Park.

In response to ancient geologic forces, the seafloor fell; plant life here ended, but fine grey silt began to accumulate. Almost 2,700 feet of this barren clay, called the **Appekunny Formation,** sits on top of the fossil-rich Altyn. About 900 million years ago, the **Grinnell Formation** began layering on top of the Appekunny Formation in the increasingly shallow seas. These two formations, together over 5,500 feet thick, comprise the most

evident and colorful of the geologic layers in the park. Iron traces in the Grinnell Formation, which formed in oxygen-rich shallow seas, were transformed by pressure and heat into hematite, a barn-red mineral. Similar sediments from the Appekunny Formation, which formed deep in the sea where there was little oxygen for the iron to bond with, instead reacted with silicate minerals to form a dull green chlorite. At their juncture, red and green layers overlap, indicating an interregnum of shifting sea levels.

BEAR GRASS

Bear grass covers the slopes of Glacier in July and August. But not every summer brings a bumper crop, and it has less to do with the year's weather than it does the plant's life cycle. An individual bear grass plant blooms only once every seven years. Some years, the torch-like stalks are abundant; other years they're a mere scattering.

Native Americans used the long, tough leaves of the plant (a member of the lily family) for trading, especially with Pacific Coast tribes, who wove the leaves into clothing and watertight baskets. Some tribes also ate the roasted root.

Though bears don't eat bear grass, elk and mountain goats do.

In time, the shallow seas again supported life. The resulting sedimentary limestone, called the **Helena** or **Siyeh Formation,** contains rich deposits of primitive algae. This 3,500-foot thick deposit is shot through with a volcanic sill, a thin band of once-molten rock that squirted through the Helena Formation along a horizontal fault about 750 million years ago. It's easily recognized as the resistant layer of black rock sandwiched between thick bands of white limestone.

On the very highest peaks of Glacier Park, at elevations above 7,000 feet, the two youngest of the Precambrian formations, the **Snowslip** and **Shepard,** rise as horns above deeply glaciered valleys. To capture the full mystery of the park, remember that the peaks of these 10,000 mountains are capped with rock that was once sediment in a shallow sea, before vertebrate life began on earth.

The Lewis Overthrust
When the North American and Pacific plates collided some 150 million years ago, much of the rock near the old seacoast buckled and warped into mountains. However, the 18,000 feet of proto-Glacier Park sediments that had accumulated under the Precambrian seawater were durable enough that, instead of fracturing into a bull-dozed rubble, they split along a deep horizontal fault roughly parallel to the soil surface.

The ancient Precambrian sediments of Glacier Park became a wedge of rock cut loose from its moorings.

As mountain-building to the west continued, this free-floating bit of geologic history was gouged up out of the bowl it was formed in, and pushed eastward onto the top of younger rock. Under continued pressure from the elevating bulwark of the new Rocky Mountains, the rocks of Glacier Park slid east almost 35 miles over the top of much younger Cretaceous-era deposits. View the leading edge of the overthrust from Two Medicine Lake or other sharp cliffs along the eastern front, where the mountains of Glacier National Park seem to rise up like a wall of rock out of the prairie. Almost three miles high, with ancient sedimentary layers still intact, the rock block of Glacier Park is literally sitting on top of the plains.

Glaciation
During the last ice age, glaciers filled the park. Like a scoop pulled through a block of ice cream, these glaciers deepened, rounded, and straightened the park's valleys. The largest glaciers scoured out St. Mary's and McDonald valleys. Dammed by moraines, these now hold lakes with expansive views up to narrow peaks, also carved by glaciers.

bear grass, Xerophyllum tenax

Hanging valleys were cut when two glaciers intercepted one another—the smaller glacier left a scooped valley high above the larger valley floor. Sometimes two or more glaciers formed on different sides of a peak; when they finished carving out **cirques** on each side, little was left of the original peak but a craggy **horn.** Other glaciers formed along a mountain ridge, and edged downstream in a parallel movement. The peaks that divide these U-shaped valleys are fin-like: when marshalled into regiments, as along Lake McDonald or St. Mary's Lake, they look like upside-down boats, keels pointed skyward.

The glaciers that carved the peaks and valleys in Glacier National Park disappeared about 10-12,000 years ago; the small glaciers currently found in the park are much younger. Since the 19th century, the remaining glaciers have lost almost three-quarters of their mass due to warmer temperatures and decreased snowfall.

FLORA AND FAUNA

Glacier National Park rises from a high-plains ecosystem on the east, to alpine tundra along the Continental Divide, and back down to Pacific forests, all within 25 miles. It's an amazingly concentrated venue for viewing many of Montana's wide-ranging animals and plants.

Flora

Plants, more than animals, reflect the quick-changing and numerous ecosystems in the park. Skirting Lake McDonald and other westside lakes are forests of red cedar, Douglas fir, and hemlock. Watch for skunk cabbages and bracken ferns in marshy lowlands. Farther up mountain slopes are extensive stands of lodgepole and deciduous, cone-bearing larch, indicating an on-going history of forest fires.

Along the Continental Divide are expanses of alpine tundra. The midsummer wildflower display, including lemon-yellow glacier lilies, dark blue gentians, pink heathers, and the greenish-white spires of bear grass, is spectacular. Examine rocky outcrops for colorful lichens.

The east side of the park is much drier, with aspen commingling with the dominating conifers. Wildflowers include red and white geraniums, Indian paintbrush, gaillardia, and pasque flowers.

Fauna

Although grizzly bears are the most talked about animal in the park, they are much less numerous than the smaller black bears. Both species deserve respect. Recognize grizzly bears by the hypertrophied shoulder muscles which form a substantial hump just behind the neck. Generally a mottled brown color, grizzlies also have a dish-shaped face. Black bears aren't always black; often brown or cinnamon colored, at 200 pounds they are a third the size of their grizzly brethren.

Mountain goats haunt the peaks and escarpments of Glacier Park. Near Logan Pass, they gather at natural salt licks in the cliffs above the road. Bighorn sheep, a few wolves, white-tailed deer, and moose comprise other large mammals. Near streams, watch for beavers and river otters; hoary marmots abound along hiking trails; ground squirrels nose into pant legs and lunch bags at every picnic area.

Ospreys and bald eagles are the park's principal birds of prey. Watch for water ouzels (aka "dippers") near streams; they're not drowning themselves, they're diving and bouncing around underwater looking for food. A hatch of ptarmigans sauntering across the road often brings traffic to a halt.

HISTORY

Salish tribes west of the Continental Divide traditionally traveled over Marias Pass on yearly trips to hunt buffalo. After the Blackfeet Indians moved to prairies east of the park in the late 1700s, they consolidated their hold over the entire area; Marias Pass became the scene of bloody battles when Salish hunting parties encountered Blackfoot warriors.

Early frontiersmen who explored the Glacier Park area also had to be wary of the Blackfeet. Peter Fidler, an agent of the Hudson's Bay Company and in 1792 the first white to tour the Glacier Park area, did so in the company of Blackfoot warriors. Twenty years later, trapper Finian MacDonald crossed Marias Pass with a group of Flathead Indians and was immediately ambushed by the Blackfoot landlords.

Under pressure from the railroads, miners, and settlers, the Blackfeet sold the eastern slope of the park in 1895 for $1.5 million, thus opening the area up for business. Copper mining was a bust, as was oil exploration. Tourism, amply advertised by the Great Northern Railroad, which in 1891 completed its service through Marias Pass just south of the park, was left as the area's economic mainstay. Conservationists, leagued with powerful railroad interests, sought to establish the area as a national park. In 1910, President W.H. Taft signed the bill creating Glacier National Park.

Between 1910 and 1917, the Great Northern spent $1.5 million developing tourist facilities. It built a series of huge lodges, chalets, and tent camps, each a day's horseback ride away. The Great Northern's recommended itinerary of hikes, fishing, and trail rides required a full week to "do" the park.

This leisurely, genteel, and recreation-oriented era was challenged in 1933 when the CCC finished the Going-To-The-Sun Road, thus introducing the automobile to Glacier Park's backcountry. The volume and pace of traffic in the park quickened; in 1925, only 40,000 people visited Glacier; in 1936, 210,000 visitors traveled through, many simply to experience the Going-To-The-Sun Road. The old Great Northern facilities fell into disuse, and strip towns grew up on the outskirts of the park to service the needs of motorists. Fragile ecosystems in the park began to deteriorate under the weight of increased traffic. Tourism in Glacier reached a nadir during the late 1960s, when a survey found that the average tourist spent only 25 hours in the park.

Glacier Park's backcountry is still not on the typical tourist's itinerary, and many people still zoom over Going-To-The-Sun Road on a cross-country road-trip blitz. But increased environmental awareness since the 1970s has multiplied the number of people who linger amongst Glacier's unique topology and wildlife haunts.

ACCOMMODATIONS

The enormous lodges built by the Great Northern Railroad still stand at East Glacier, Waterton, and Many Glacier, and have become near trademarks for the park itself. These old lodges are tremendously evocative and charming, but rooms aren't cheap, and for the money, the amenities aren't great. That having been said, you simply must stay in at least one of these old landmarks.

For hikers, backcountry chalets are another option. Sperry Glacier and Granite Park Chalets are remnants of the Great Northern's heyday in the park. Each a day's hike from Logan Pass, these chalets offer an evening meal, dormitory-style lodging, breakfast, and a pack lunch. Reservations are required, often months in advance. Call **Belton Chalets,** tel. 888-5511, for information or reservations.

Campers are in luck. There are good campsites at each entry to the park, and at lakeside recreation areas. Motels abound just outside of the park boundaries, particularly near the west entrance.

GETTING THERE AND AROUND

Kalispell (p. 286) and Great Falls (p. 125) offer the closest airline service to the park. **Amtrak** stops at East Glacier and Belton (aka West Glacier) when the park is open, May 15-Sept. 15. Amtrak stops at Essex year-round.

Red roll-back-top buses operate out of the lodges at East Glacier, Many Glacier, Waterton, and Lake McDonald and offer guided tours of the park and a shuttle service from one lodge to another.

INFORMATION

Contact the **Superintendent, Glacier National Park,** West Glacier, MT 59936, tel. (406) 888-5441, for more information.

MANY GLACIER

Aside from the Going-to-the-Sun Road, this is the most popular and the most spectacular area of Glacier National Park. The mountains are *right there,* with the Garden Wall as a backdrop to the southwest, and a glacier but a day-hike away. Many Glacier is spectacular enough to warrant a quick detour just for a snooze on the hotel veranda, but it also makes a good base for several days' worth of hiking, canoeing, and bicycle or horseback riding.

The Land

Head up any of the numerous valleys converging on the hotel and, on the way to high cirques and glaciers, observe all four of Glacier's geologic formations. Tan Altyn limestone is exposed in the hotel parking lot. Climb through the green layers of Apekunny mudstone, look for mud cracks and ripple marks in the red Grinnell muds, then scale the buff-colored Helena (or Siyeh) Formation, where large stromatolites abound. High on the Garden Wall, the Purcell diabase layer is a dark, 100-foot-tall layer of igneous rock that shot up through the muds and limes until it spread into a yielding gap in the sedimentary layers. The molten intrusion seared the adjacent limestone layers, turning them to marble.

Just east of Many Glacier is the edge of the Lewis Overthrust. Chief Mountain, visible from the road between Babb and Waterton National Park, is the far eastern outpost of the overthrust of Precambrian rock, and the leading edge of the Rocky Mountains. Younger Cretaceous shales, buried by older rocks in most of Glacier Park, take over the valley floor just east of the mountains.

Glaciers filled Swiftcurrent Valley and left their trademark U-shaped valleys running down from the peaks and converging in Many Glacier Valley. Valley floors here are striped with moraines and dotted with glacial lakes, which get colder and more milky-blue as they near their glacial sources. Cirques tucked into the face of the Garden Wall were the starting point for many glaciers, and the Grinnell and Gem glaciers still creep across the shady flank of the arête.

History

Copper was discovered in the Altyn Formation in 1892. Within a few years, the Blackfeet were forced to sell much of their reservation land, allowing prospectors free reign over the east face of the mountains. A mining town was erected near Lake Sherburne, but it proved hardly worth digging for the small amounts of copper embedded in the limestone. Even though the first oil ever found in Montana came from a local copper mine, the town of Altyn didn't live long enough to see the national park established in 1910.

STROMATOLITES

The limestones of the Helena Formation are shot through with stromatolites, the vestiges of blue-green algae. You'll see them on the hike to Grinnell Glacier—the three-foot cabbage flower designs make rock ledges look like they're covered with giant chintz bedspreads.

Blue-green algae, still around today, are so primitive they don't even have cells. These photosynthesizers have been tossed into their own non-plant, non-animal kingdom called Protista.

In Precambrian time, blue-green algae lived in shallow seawater and, as they photosynthesized, developed a crusty outer layer of calcium carbonate.

This crust would block incoming sunlight and inhibit photosynthesis, so the algae would ooze out and spread over the top of its own crust, like it was just another sunny rock to lay on. In this way, thick reefs of algae grew.

It's reckoned that, as other forms of life developed, blue-green algae became a popular food, and big algal reefs became a thing of the past. That's why giant cabbage-like stromatolites, the remnants of the algal crusts, are hallmarks of Precambrian rocks. Since the stromatolites are not the dead algae themselves, but a metabolic by-product, they are not true fossils.

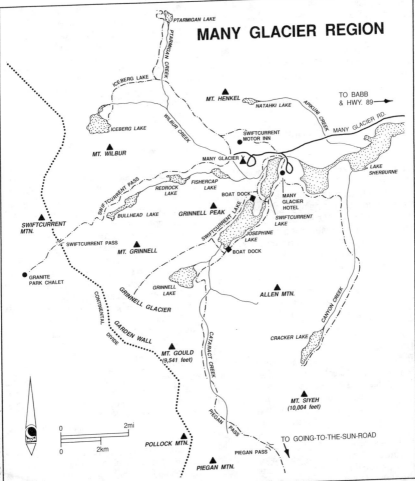

MANY GLACIER REGION

In 1919, a dam, approved and set in motion before the establishment of the park, impounded Swiftcurrent Creek and enlarged the existing Lake Sherburne.

SIGHTS AND ACTIVITIES

Park Tours
Cruise the park in an open-top red tour bus. A $25 half-day tour travels the east half of Going-To-The-Sun Road to Logan Pass. For the full Going-To-The-Sun Road circuit, take the $40 full-day ride to Lake McDonald. A day-trip to Canada's Waterton National Park will cost $31.

Boat Tours
Scenic cruises of Swiftcurrent and Josephine lakes leave the hotel boat dock several times daily. Grinnell Glacier, only partially visible from the hotel, comes into view as the boat crosses Josephine Lake. The one-hour tour is $6.50 for

adults, $3.25 children. It's easy to hop off the boat for a hike or a picnic at Josephine Lake, and then catch another boat back to the hotel.

Evening Presentations

Each evening at 8, a talk or slide show is held in the hotel basement. Try to catch a Blackfoot tribal member's cultural presentation—there's usually a seamless blend of legend and history.

RECREATION

Short Hikes

Of the many hikes in the Many Glacier area, the one around Swiftcurrent Lake is the simplest, if the least spectacular. It's a good evening stroll from the lodge or campgound, two miles of flat lakeside terrain. The trail occasionally breaks out of the trees for views of the Garden Wall and nearby mountains. Pick up a nature guide at the official trailhead, the picnic area halfway between the lodge and the campground.

Another easy walk combines a $6.50 boat trip to the far end of Josephine Lake with a two-mile RT hike to **Grinnell Lake,** a milky aqua lake full of icy water and glacial flour from Grinnell Glacier.

Day Hikes

Park naturalists lead several different hikes each day in Many Glacier Valley. Hikers with a modicum of stamina and a passing interest in geology should try to catch the naturalist-led hike to **Grinnell Glacier.** In combination with a boat shuttle across Swiftcurrent and Josephine lakes ($6.50), the hike is eight miles RT with a 1,600-foot elevation gain. (Forgo the boat rides and it becomes 11 miles.) Grinnell Glacier reached its peak size during a sort of minature ice age in the 1800s. Melting since then has left two smaller glaciers: **The Salamander** clings high on the Garden Wall; **Grinnell Glacier** proper is below and to the left. A warming trend starting in the 1980s has enlarged the iceberg-laden lake below the glacier, making it particularly hazardous to walk onto the glacial ice.

Watch out for bears on the trail to **Iceberg Lake,** an aptly named glacial lake 4.7 miles from the trailhead in the Swiftcurrent parking lot. The trail crosses alpine meadows before dropping into a cirque holding the milky blue lake. Moun-

tain goats, marmots, and an occasional bear share this path with a myriad of hikers.

Take the same intial stretch of trail to reach **Ptarmigan Falls** (two miles) and **Ptarmigan Lake** (4.3 miles). The waterfalls and flower-strewn meadows make up for the steepness of the trail. Hikers reaching the lake with unbounded energy should go another mile to the 183-foot-long **Ptarmigan Tunnel,** which emerges onto the north face of the Ptarmigan Wall, looking out to the Belly River country.

Longer Hikes

For an extended jaunt, start at the camp store parking lot and head up Swiftcurrent Creek past **Red Rock Falls,** cross the Divide at **Swiftcurrent Pass** and join up with the **Highline Trail** on the other side. It's eight miles from the trailhead in the campstore parking lot to the **Granite Park** chalets (and campground), and another eight miles from the chalets to Logan Pass.

Start at the hotel, pass Josephine and Grinnell lakes, and skirt Mt. Siyeh and Going-To-The-Sun Mountain on the 12-mile route across **Piegan Pass** to **Going-To-The-Sun Road.** Geology, wildflower meadows, waterfalls, mountain goats, and big views are highlights of this hike. There are no backcountry campgrounds along this trail.

Boating

Rent a canoe or rowboat for $5 an hour at the boat dock behind the hotel. Determined canoeists will heft their boats a quarter mile over the moraine separating Swiftcurrent and Josephine lakes. The isolation and views from Josephine Lake are worth the portage.

Motorboats, except for the "scenic cruise boats," are prohibited on Swiftcurrent and Josephine lakes, but are allowed on the larger Lake Sherburne.

Horseback Riding

The corral behind the Many Glacier Hotel parking lot is the starting point for a number of regularly scheduled guided horseback rides. An all-day ride over Swiftcurrent Pass to Granite Park Chalet leaves each morning at 8:45 ($47), with the option of an overnight stay at the chalet (book a chalet visit well in advance). Other day-long rides go to Poia Lake ($43) and Cracker Lake ($38).

JUDY JEWELL

*Explore the
Many Glacier region
on horseback.*

Shorter rides are $20-25 and leave several times a day for Grinnell Lake, Josephine Lake, or Cracker Flats. If horses and guides are available, private trail rides cost $12 an hour. Call 732-5597 to register for all rides in advance.

Fishing

There are trout in Swiftcurrent Lake, but they're not always eager to swallow a hook. Both Josephine and Grinnell lakes are home to brook trout—it's worth the extra hike to Grinnell Lake for both the beautiful turquoise lake and the fish. For a change from the trout, head down to Sherburne Lake for northern pike.

ACCOMMODATIONS

The **Many Glacier Hotel,** a 200-room Swiss-style chalet in an isolated valley on Swiftcurrent Lake, is currently managed by the huge Greyhound-Dial Soap corporation, which seems to be letting it run down a bit. The tacky early-'70s dorm decor is only ameliorated by the perfect setting and the stunning views from the lobby windows. Geology comes right down to meet you here, and wildlife is often spotted on the slopes across the lake. The hotel is open from the second week of June through the first week in September; rooms run $67-79 s, $74-86 d.

The **Swiftcurrent Cabins** are especially popular with families; at $20 and up, they're not expensive, and, though they lack toilets and kitchens, they evoke pleasant hazy memories of some idealized summer camp or the perfect 1962 family vacation.

Less appealing than the lodge or cabins, but sometimes available on short notice, are motel rooms in the **Swiftcurrent Motor Inn.** At $51-57 s, $55-61 d, they cost considerably more than similar accommodations elsewhere, but hey, do you really have a choice? Both the motel and the cabins have short seasons—late June through Labor Day.

Make reservations for any of these places by calling 226-5551 mid-May through September or (602) 248-6000 October through mid-May. From Canada, call (403) 236-3400 year-round.

No reservations are accepted for the **Many Glacier Campground,** so campers need to grab a spot early in the day—it's often full shortly after noon. The campground's season runs from mid-June through the third week in September.

FOOD AND DRINK

The dining room at the **Many Glacier Hotel** has a continental, Swiss-inspired theme. It's the same meat and fish supplied to other Glacier Park hotels, but here it's sauced and stuffed, rather than grilled or breaded and fried. In the hotel basement, **Heidi's** serves ice cream and hot dogs. The two hotel bars have a tightly meshed, if seemingly senseless, schedule.

There's a coffee shop and a camp store down by the **Swiftcurrent Motor Inn** and cabins. They're standard national park issue.

INFORMATION AND SERVICES

Rangers dispense trail information and back-country permits from their station near the campground. Glean general trail information and specifics on bus tours and hotel activities from the information desk in the **Many Glacier Hotel lobby.**

The most coveted of all camper services—**showers and a laundromat**—are in the Swiftcurrent cabin complex. Purchase shower tokens at the camp store.

Transportation

Many Glacier is 12 miles west of Babb, a crossroads town on the Blackfeet Reservation nine miles north of St. Mary. Travelers relying on public transportation can catch a **red bus** from any Glacier Park lodge to the Many Glacier Hotel.

LOGAN PASS TO ST. MARY

From the Highline Trail at Logan Pass to Two Dog Flats around St. Mary Lake, the scenery on the east face of Glacier National Park is just as spectacular as, and more exposed than, that on the west side of the Divide. Geology is suddenly lucid as red Grinnell rocks and the green rocks of the Appekuny Formation glow in the morning light bouncing off St. Mary Lake. Westbound travelers will do well to stop in the St. Mary information center and purchase a copy of *Geology Along Going-To-The-Sun Road,* a book explaining roadside geology markers.

East of the pass, drying winds blow across stands of aspen and cottonwoods to the plains, which suddenly replace the mountains a few miles east of St. Mary.

SIGHTS

Logan Pass

Logan Pass, at 6,680 feet, is an alpine-arctic tundra environment. Even though the landscape here is shaped by a harsh climate, it's not able to withstand flower-picking or trampling by hordes of hikers. To learn more about alpine ecology, stop in for a naturalist's talk at the visitor center. Talks are usually scheduled for 11 a.m., noon, and 1 p.m. daily from early June through Labor Day. The visitor center stays open as long as the road is passable—usually from June through October.

Glaciers started on either side of the divide at Logan Pass and eventually ran backwards into each other—rather than leaving a spiky arête like the Garden Wall, chiseled away on both sides, the wall was entirely eroded.

St. Mary Lake

Even non-hikers will want to stop at the **Sun Point** trailhead and walk a few yards to the "peak-finder." Of the nine peaks visible from Sun Point, **Going-To-The-Sun Mountain** stands out at 9,942 feet. The mountain, whose name was taken for the road, recalls Napi, the Blackfoot Old Man, who left his home in the sun to help the Blackfeet. Once he had finished his work on earth, he returned home via this mountain.

Boat tours of St. Mary Lake set out several times a day from the dock across from the Rising Sun complex. The 7 p.m. sunset cruise is popular but, unlike the daytime rides, it's not accompanied by a park naturalist. The one-hour ride costs $7 for adults, $3.50 for children.

For those who stick to the road, there's an official photography turnout overlooking **Wild Goose Island.** A real snob will pass this up, but it *is* a great cliché of a place to stop and put the instamatic to work.

RECREATION

Hikes Around Logan Pass

Glacier Park's most popular trail is the boardwalk from Logan Pass to **Hidden Lake Overlook,** a three-mile RT hike through delicate alpine meadows, home to marmots, ptarmigan, and mountain goats. The weather can be blustery up here, even in mid-summer, and the 500-foot climb to over 7,000 feet above sea level can be surprisingly fatiguing.

For a fairly level trail that goes on for miles, the **Highline Trail** can't be beat. It's the main route to Granite Park chalet, and can be frustratingly crowded, but the above-timberline views, bear grass meadows, and chattering marmots are absorbing enough to eclipse the other hikers.

Hikes Around St. Mary Lake

Walk out to **Sun Point** for a view of St. Mary Lake and the surrounding mountains. This was the site of the most elaborate of the Glacier Park chalets, which fell into disuse once the Going-To-The-Sun Road became the focus of a trip to the park, and was dismantled in the late 1940s. From Sun Point, the trail skirts the lakeshore for less than a mile to **Baring Falls.**

Sunrift Gorge is on Baring Creek just above the falls—cap off the Sun Point walk by taking the spur trail and climbing to the gorge. Or, follow the lead of most gorge-viewers, and park in the Sunrift Gorge pullout and walk 50 yards up the path to the narrow chasm, formed not by erosion, but by a vertical slip of the rock.

Those in search of a *real* hike will want to continue past Sunrift Gorge to **Siyeh Pass** and

Preston Park. This is no easy amble—the trail shoots up once it leaves Baring Creek and Siyeh is Glacier's highest pass. As one would expect, persevering hikers are rewarded with great views and a delicate alpine environment. After passing alpine larch trees at Preston Park, the Siyeh Bend cutoff trail heads back to Going-To-The-Sun Road, making this a 12-mile hike. (Actually, most people do this hike in the opposite direction—it's an easier uphill but with less spectacular views.) Park naturalists set out daily at 9 a.m. from Siyeh Bend on Going-To-The-Sun Road, marshalling hikers along on one of the park's best naturalist-led hikes.

An eight-mile hike to **Gunsight Lake** starts at either Sun Point or, more commonly, at the Jackson Glacier Overlook west of St. Mary Lake on Going-To-The-Sun Road. There's a campground at Gunsight Lake; Gunsight Pass is another *steep* two miles up the trail. From the pass, the trail drops down to Lake Ellen Wilson, Sperry Chalet, and ultimately reaches the road again at Lake McDonald Lodge. The whole Gunsight Pass route takes two or three days to hike. Besides the inevitable switchbacks and vistas, expect to see mountain goats along this trail.

Boating And Fishing
Though boats are permitted on St. Mary Lake, there's no place to rent them. Anglers generally prefer boat fishing to bank fishing on St. Mary Lake, which is not really known for good fishing, but does have some whitefish, rainbow, and brook trout. Hikers are rewarded by better fishing at Red Eagle Lake, south of the park entrance, or Gunsight Lake.

Cross-country Skiing
Loop trails around **Red Eagle Valley,** near the park entrance, offer several miles of skiing for beginning and intermediate skiers. For those who want more of a challenge, Red Eagle Lake is a 14-mile RT along Red Eagle Creek.

ACCOMMODATIONS

Granite Park Chalet is perched on an igneous outcropping at the north end of the Garden Wall. Four trails lead to the chalet; the most popular is the seven-mile-long, stunningly beautiful, nearly level Highline Trail, which follows the base of the Garden Wall from Logan Pass. Other trails come in from the loop on Going-To-The-Sun Road (four miles), over Swiftcurrent Pass from Many Glacier (eight miles), and from Goat Haunt at the head of Waterton Lake (an approximately 23-mile backpacking trip via the northern extension of the Highline Trail).

There's a certain appeal to hiking into the backcountry with nothing but a toothbrush and a change of underwear on your back—in truth, it's best to bring water, a few handfuls of trail mix, and some warm clothing. Once you arrive at the chalet, meals are provided.

Reserve a simple, electricity-free, $60 pp room at Granite Park early—a year in advance is not unreasonable—by contacting Belton Chalets, P.O. Box 188, West Glacier, MT 59936, tel. 888-5511.

Rising Sun Motor Inn is operated by the Glacier Park concessionaire, Greyhound-Dial, near St. Mary Lake. Uninspiring motel rooms and cabins have the familiar steep tariffs of the other park lodgings—$61 for a double motel room, $50 for a cabin. For reservations, call 226-5551 mid-May through Sept.; (602) 248-6000 in the winter.

At the St. Mary crossroads, the **St. Mary Lodge,** tel. 732-4431, is (some would say, thankfully) *not* a Glacier Park, Inc. enterprise. The views don't suffer for being just outside the park boundaries, and the accommodations are every bit as comfortable as, and a touch cheaper than, those inside the park. Double rooms in the main lodge are $55; renovated rooms in the annex are $61. None of the rooms either here or in the park lodges have TVs or radios, but who needs 'em when there's Singleshot Mountain out there?

Campgrounds
The **Rising Sun Campground** isn't particularly appealing in itself—83 shrubby, often hot, sites, but it's just across the road from St. Mary Lake; there's a hiking trail heading up Rose Creek to Otokomi Lake, and there are pay showers in the nearby cabins complex.

Just inside the park boundary, the rather drab **St. Mary campground** is about twice as large as Rising Sun, but not so well-positioned for boaters and hikers. It is, however, open for free, primitive camping in the off-season (Sept.-May).

Chewing Blackbones KOA, north of St. Mary on Hwy. 89, tel. 732-4452, is a large Black-

JUDY JEWELL

*Glacier Park's
mandatory photo stop
at Wild Goose Island
rarely disappoints.*

feet-owned campground on Lower St. Mary Lake. It's a good bet when the park campgrounds are full. There's another KOA in St. Mary, tel. 732-4422.

FOOD AND DRINK

Hungry travelers should note that between Lake McDonald and St. Mary, Rising Sun is the only place to buy food. The **Rising Sun** coffee shop serves Indian tacos as well as all the most predictable café breakfasts, lunches, and dinners. Like the motel, the coffee shop is open mid-June through late September. A camp store with a small grocery section is the alternative to the coffee shop.

There's a better meal waiting in St. Mary. The **Snowgoose Grille** at St. Mary Lodge features whitefish from St. Mary Lake and other entrees which occasionally transcend the expected steak, trout, and chicken dishes. Try the

homemade sourdough scones or one of the huckleberry concoctions. The Snowgoose is open for breakfast, lunch, and dinner mid-May through Sept., tel. 732-4431.

Also in St. Mary, dare yourself to try "semi-fast food," including Indian tacos, at the **Hog and Jog Café. Johnson's,** on the north end of town, tel. 732-5565, takes pride in home cooking and large portions—refuel after a long hike with their pie and cinnamon rolls.

INFORMATION

Rangers at the **Logan Pass Visitor Center** keep the fireplace stoked on chilly days, and dispense maps, backcountry permits, and advice. More detailed maps and books on the park's trails, geology, and history are available from the **Glacier Natural History Association** here. The setup is much the same at the St. Mary Visitor Center, just inside the eastern park entrance.

EAST GLACIER AND VICINITY

While East Glacier is not the best base for a several-day tour of the park, it is a handy entrance point for travelers from the east. Camp or hike at nearby Two Medicine lakes, with all the scenery and far less company than you'll find at Many Glacier or Lake McDonald.

There's more of a Native American presence here than in many other areas of the park. Even though most of East Glacier is controlled by non-Indians, it is within the Blackfeet Reservation boundaries, and is part of an area historically and culturally important to the Blackfeet.

The Land

The Lewis Overthrust came to a halt just west of present-day East Glacier, and its leading edge is visible at Running Eagle Falls near Lower Two Medicine Lake. The hard Precambrian rock of the Lewis formations rolled on top of a younger, softer shale, which has worn away to form the gentler, hilly landscapes east of the overthrust.

Glaciers dug out the bottoms of the three Two Medicine lakes (upper, middle, and lower). Moraines formed dams, allowing water to fill the troughs. Two Medicine Valley is surrounded by peaks, many adorned with waterfalls and hanging valleys.

Floodwaters coursed the Two Medicine area in 1964 and 1975, uprooting trees and boulders. There's still flotsam and jetsam along the stream banks, and boulders prematurely rounded by torrents of sandy floodwater.

History

Blackfeet camped in the Two Medicine Valley, and gathered by the middle lake to make medicine. The name "Two Medicine" may harken to a time when, because of a dispute, one group camped on the upper lake, another group on the lower, or it may refer to the two different waterfalls manifested at Running Eagle Falls. When white prospectors exhibited interest in the northern Rockies, the Blackfeet were forced onto a reservation and ceded their mountain territories—the land which now comprises the eastern half of Glacier National Park.

Rising Wolf Mountain, just north of Lower Two Medicine Lake, was named for the first white man in the area—Hugh Monroe, a Hudson's Bay trapper who came to the area in 1815 and married a Blackfoot woman.

When James J. Hill was planning the route of the Great Northern Railway, he heard rumors of a "lost" pass over the Continental Divide. In the winter of 1889, railroad surveyor John J. Stevens found Marias Pass and deemed it navigable by rail.

Early national park visitors typically pulled in on the train from the east, disembarking at East Glacier and spending a night at the lodge before saddling up to ride the circuit of backcountry chalets and tent camps in the company of a guide. For a hearty evocation of such a trip, read Mary Roberts Rinehart's *Through Glacier Park in 1915*. Once Going-To-The-Sun Road was built, auto travel supplanted both the train and the horse, and the spotlight was off the massive Glacier Park Lodge.

SIGHTS

East Glacier

Stop by the Glacier Park Lodge to sit in the lobby and write postcards or wander through the gardens. Blackfeet culture is the focus of twice-weekly evening talks in the hotel lobby; one need not be a hotel guest to listen in. Check the lecture schedule at the information desk in the lobby.

The **John L. Clarke Western Art Gallery** displays the work of western artists, including the eponymous Clarke, a part-Blackfeet, part-Scottish wildlife sculptor who lived in East Glacier from the early 1900s until his death in 1970.

Park Tours

Red roll-back-top buses depart from Glacier Park Lodge for loop tours of the park every day at 10 a.m. The day-long trip costs $43.50 ($21.75 for children under 12). Half-day excursions to Two Medicine Lake leave at 9:30 a.m. and 1:30 p.m., $7.25 roundtrip.

Two Medicine

Two Medicine has some of the park's most spectacular scenery, but it's a ways from the

JUDY JEWELL

Eagle Falls in June

Going-To-The-Sun Road drag strip, and is often overlooked.

A glacier gouged Lower Two Medicine Lake at the foot of purplish-red Rising Wolf Mountain (elev. 9,505 feet). Backcountry chalets were built by the Great Northern—the Two Medicine chalets were the first stop on a horseback circuit popular in the pre-automobile days. One wood chalet remains as the Two Medicine camp store.

Boat tours of Two Medicine Lake leave the dock at 10:30 a.m. and 1, 2:30, and 3:30 p.m. daily. The 45-minute tour costs $5 for adults, $2.50 children.

RECREATION

Hikes Near Two Medicine Lakes

It's a short walk from the well-marked bridge over Two Medicine Creek through some conifers and across a rocky creekside to **Running Eagle Falls** (aka Trick Falls). When there's plenty of water, it appears to be like any other waterfall. The "trick" comes when water volume decreases late in the summer, and water spouts from a hole beneath the main shelf of the falls. Look at the rim of the falls for the fault line marking the eastern edge of the Lewis Overthrust. Running Eagle, or Pitamakan, was a Blackfoot woman who reportedly led warriors over Cut Bank Pass on raids against Flathead and Kootenai tribes to the west.

Combine a hike to the fork-topped **Twin Falls** with a boat ride across Two Medicine Lake. Naturalist-led trips leave the Two Medicine boat dock at 1 and 2:30 p.m. daily for the cruise and two-mile hike.

For a full day's hike, **Upper Two Medicine Lake** is five miles from the Two Medicine Campground. The trail runs along the south shore of Lower Two Medicine Lake—to shorten the hike, catch the tour boat to the head of the lake.

Triple Divide Peak

Hike eight miles up the valley of Cut Bank Creek to **Triple Divide Pass.** The trail starts at the campground and, after a hike and a final scramble from cairn to cairn, reaches the spot where Atlantic, Pacific, and Hudson Bay creeks issue from the divide.

Boating

Canoes, rowboats, and motorboats are rented for $5-10 an hour at the boat dock on Lower Two Medicine Lake. Though motorboats are permitted, speed is limited to 10 mph.

Fishing

Pick up a tribal permit at the lodge or Two Medicine camp store to fish the Two Medicine River or Lower Two Medicine Lake. Once inside the park boundaries, stop by any visitor center or ranger station and get park fishing regulations (no license is necessary). Brook and rainbow trout lurk in Lower Two Medicine Lake and Cut Bank Creek.

Horseback Riding

Horseback rides are offered by East Glacier's **Great Bear Outfitters,** tel. 226-9220. A one-hour ride is $10; it's $18 for two hours, and $2 for a short pony ride. Great Bear also has guides for big game hunting in the fall.

Bicycling

Scenic View Bike Rentals, in the lot next to John L. Clarke Western Art, tel. 226-9238, charges $3 an hour.

Golf

The nine holes of the **Glacier Golf Course** span Hwy. 49 just north of the lodge. Since the course is run by Glacier Park, Inc., it keeps the same season as the lodge. Call 226-4411 for tee times.

Cross-country Skiing

Once the snow starts piling up (late December), it's easy to strap on skis at East Glacier and glide to Two Medicine Lake. On nice days, it's an easy day-trip.

ACCOMMODATIONS

Step upstairs from **Brownie's Market** to find a charming youth hostel with sloping linoleum floors and lots of old photos and books in the sleeping rooms. Dorm-room beds go for $10 a night for AYH members; $13 for nonmembers. A private room is $15 s ($18 nonmember), or $20 d ($23 nonmember).

Glacier Park Lodge charges $68-81 s, $75-89 d, tel. 226-5551 (mid-May through Sept.) or (602) 248-6000 (Oct. to mid-May). It's a spectacular building, with huge Douglas fir timbers forming the Ionic columns in the Grecian Revival lobby, meticulously groomed gardens out front, and a heated pool out the back door. The lodge is open Memorial Day through early September, and is big enough to house conventions.

Between the youth hostel and the lodge fall several small motels, most of which house guests in detached, cabin-like units. All these places are adequate; none are fancy. **East Glacier Motel,** tel. 226-5593 (summer) or 226-4465 (winter), has cheery motel rooms and cottages (some with kitchens) for $27 and up. At **Jacobson's Cottages,** tel. 226-4422, conventionally shaped units ($34 d) are tucked behind the A-frame office. Cabins at **Sears Motel** are $32 s, $36 d, tel. 226-4432. Rooms at the **Mountain Pine Motel** are comfortable, $40 d, tel. 226-4403.

There's a more secluded feeling to the cabins at **Bison Creek Ranch** two miles west of town on Hwy. 2, tel 226-4482. Two-person cabins run $25-40.

Off-season travelers should look to **Porter's Alpine Motel,** off Hwy. 2, tel. 226-4402. Double rooms are $39 from mid-June through mid-Sept., $32 the rest of the year.

For RV campers, the **Y Lazy R** RV park is behind Porter's Motel near the intersection of Hwys. 2 and 49.

Camp on **Two Medicine Lake,** 12 miles from East Glacier via Hwy. 49. The national park campground here is open from the second weekend in June through Labor Day. Campfire presentations by park naturalists and Blackfoot tribal members are held every evening at 8 p.m. at the amphitheatre in Loop B. The **Cut Bank Campground,** reached via a gravel road north of Kiowa, is more primitive and secluded. It's open from the beginning of June through mid-September.

Head west of East Glacier on Hwy. 2 to reach Forest Service campgrounds. **Summit Campground,** near the rest area at Marias Pass, is 10 miles from East Glacier. Historical cachet and convenience are the most this campground has to offer, but it's got plenty of both, and there are often empty spaces when the national park campgrounds are full. **Devil's Creek Campground** is another six miles southwest on Hwy. 2.

FOOD AND DRINK

For a good meal, head to the junction of Hwys. 49 and 2. The **Villager Dining Room,** tel. 226-4464, puts a tasty, innovative twist on their dinners ($6-15)—even the chicken salad makes you notice that it's *good* food, and special care is lavished on desserts. The adjoining **Villager Café** slings breakfast eggs and hash browns for $3. On the same block, **PJ's Diner** is a cubbyhole café with similar $3 breakfasts and huckleberry shakes.

Right in the cabin-motel heart of East Glacier, the **Thimbleberry** serves good, though not outstanding, American food breakfast, lunch, and dinner, tel. 226-5523.

Not to forget the **Goat Lick Steak and Rib House,** the western-theme Glacier Park Lodge dining room, with fried bread and steak specialties. Dinners here run $10-15.

A **campstore** at the Two Medicine Campground sells groceries and camping provisions during the campground's season. The store is housed in the one remaining Two Medicine chalet.

West of East Glacier, at Marias Pass, is **Summit Station,** a bar and restaurant (with a prime rib special on the weekends) tel. 226-4428.

INFORMATION AND SERVICES

There's no Glacier National Park visitor center in East Glacier, but the **information desk** at the lodge is staffed by generally helpful people. The **ranger station** at Two Medicine Lake has more specific information on nearby hiking trails.

The **post office** is east of Hwy. 2, behind the Glacier Park Trading Company. A **laundromat** and **showers** are two blocks south at the Y Lazy R RV park behind the Exxon station.

Transportation

Amtrak stops at the East Glacier Park station during the summer. The westbound train comes through around 7:30 p.m., eastbound service is around 9 a.m. daily. From September through May, the train stops in Browning rather than East Glacier; check exact dates with Amtrak, tel. (800) 872-7245.

Car rentals are $45 a day from **Rent-A-Wreck** at the Sears Motel, tel. 226-9293. The first 100 miles are free, then 25 cents per mile is charged.

WEST GLACIER PARK AND THE MIDDLE FORK OF THE FLATHEAD RIVER

The Middle Fork of the Flathead River runs out of the Bob Marshall and Great Bear wilderness areas and along the southwest border of the park to West Glacier. West Glacier, while more restrained than its Yellowstone counterpart, certainly exudes the last-chance-to-buy aura of a town on the brink of a national park.

SIGHTS

Of all the sights one can afford, save your money for a **helicopter ride** over the park. Call the Vista Motel, tel. 888-5311, for reservations; two passengers are $330 an hour, or $170 for a half-hour, or $100 for a 15-minute ride. Tours are also run by **Minuteman Aviation** at Great Northern Whitewater, tel. 387-5340.

For those who wish to remain more firmly planted, amble over to the Belton Chalets and dream of spending a night there, preparing to take the train back east, after a week of horseback chalet-hopping through the park. Until the Going-To-The-Sun Road was built in the 1930s, this is how most people toured the park. Romantic as it seems, it was obviously a vacation for the wealthy. For better or worse, the paved road opened the park to middle-class tourists.

It's amazing how gravity has gone awry just outside the park entrance. The **House of Mystery** bends all the rules on Hwy. 2 west of West Glacier, tel. 892-4550. Another local roadside attraction, the **Glacier Park Maze,** tel. 387-5902, is a two-story, mile-long science fair experiment. Both these places are open May-September.

Head about 35 miles south on Hwy. 2 to visit the **goat lick,** a mineral-laden cliff that provides goats with salt. A parking area near milepost 182 vents onto a short trail to the overlook. Spring is the big mineral-licking season; evenings in early June are certain to keep visitors entranced with billy, nanny, and kid goats. Binoculars help.

RECREATION

Hiking

Most of the hikes in this part of Glacier are long backpacking trips on little-used trails into wild country. Animals, including bears, abound in these woods and stream bottoms. Glacier Park maps show trails along every creek. Those planning to hike in the area should seek up-to-date trail information from the Walton Ranger Station on Hwy. 2 near Essex, tel. 888-5628. They can also provide backcountry permits, which are required for overnight hikes; in this section of the park, there is no constraint but good sense concerning where to camp.

A couple of shorter hikes do originate at the Walton Station. Hike to **Ole Creek** and follow the trail as far as you'd like. The same trailhead provides access to the **Scalplock Lookout,** four unrelentingly steep miles to great views.

Leave the highway about two miles east of the goat lick to find a trail into the Great Bear Wilderness Area.

For a guided expedition into the park, contact **Glacier Wilderness Guides,** P.O. Box 535, West Glacier, MT 59936, tel. 888-5333, or in Montana (800) 521-RAFT.

Boating

Several whitewater companies are based in West Glacier. Float trips on the Middle Fork of the Flathead comprise most of their scheduled outings, though arrangements can be made to float the South Fork (in the Bob Marshall Wilderness Area) or the North Fork (in the northwest corner of Glacier Park). **Glacier Wilderness Guides,** tel. 888-5333, **Glacier Raft Co.,** tel. 888-5454 or (800) 332-9995, **Great Northern Whitewater,** tel. 387-5340 or (800) 535-0303, and **Wild River Adventures,** tel. 888-5539 or (800) 826-2724, offer similar trips and prices. Day-long floats run about $50, half-days are about $25, and dinner trips are $35. Each of these companies will provide longer trips, with the option of adding hikes and horseback rides to the river-running.

The Middle Fork is a Wild and Scenic River, and this official designation is particularly apt in its upper reaches in the Bob Marshall and Great Bear Wilderness areas. It's possible to fly in to float this wilderness river; the Schaeffer Meadows airstrip is near the river in the Bob Marshall.

The wilderness stretches of the river are not easy; indeed they can be dangerous for novice rafters. Even the lower reaches are better floated in a raft or kayak than a canoe, and anyone with questionable skills should sign on with an outfitter. Early summer is the best time to float the Middle Fork; water levels are high, but not at flood stage, and some of the chill has gone out of the air.

Fishing

The stretch of the Middle Fork of the Flathead paralleling Hwy. 2 isn't a particularly noteworthy fishing stream, but its upper reaches in the Great Bear Wilderness are loaded with trout. These aren't official fishing waters of the national park, so a Montana fishing license is required. The raft companies listed above do double duty as fishing outfitters.

Bicycling

Rent bikes at **Grizzly Mountain Bike Rentals,** tel. 888-5787. It's right by the park entrance, and charges $5 an hour, or $20 a day.

During the summer, the Forest Service roads and ski trails around Essex are suitable for mountain biking, and the Izaak Walton Inn has bikes for rent, tel. 888-5700.

Cross-country Skiing

Ski trails around the **Izaak Walton Inn** are free to hotel guests, $5 for nonguests. Over 30 km of trails are groomed regularly, and though most of

*cross-country
skiing near
Glacier National Park*

JUDY JEWELL

them are geared toward novice or intermediate skiers, a few runs are studded with face-plant opportunities, even for good skiers. There's usually enough snow for skiing from Thanksgiving through mid-April.

Trail networks are also maintained by the Glacier Wilderness Resort and the Glacier Highland Motel. The Glacier Highland's seven miles (11 km) of trails start right behind this West Glacier motel; stop in the office to get a map.

The 13 miles of trails near the Glacier Wilderness Resort are between West Glacier and Essex. Skiers follow old sections of Hwy. 2 and climb to Garry Lookout.

Golf

Glacier View Golf Club, tel. 888-5471 or 888-9917, is just north of Hwy. 2 on the way into the park. It's a public 18-hole course looking onto the mountains. Greens fees are $18 for 18 holes; $10 for nine holes.

ACCOMMODATIONS

West Glacier Area

The view from the **Vista Motel,** tel. 888-5311, is indeed grand. Perched on a bluff overlooking Hwy. 2 and the peaks of Glacier, with a helicopter in the front yard, this is a hard one to miss on the drive in from Kalispell. The view *is* the best thing about this place, and that, plus convenience and friendliness, makes it a good bet for rooms in the $40 range. Though operations scale down in the winter, the Vista is open all year.

The **River Bend Motel,** 200 Going-To-The-Sun Road, tel. 888-5662, is just off Hwy. 2 toward the park entrance. Its location on the Flathead River makes for easy access to fishing and float trips, which can be arranged by the management. Rooms run about $50, cottages are a few dollars more. The motel season is mid-May through mid-Septmber.

It gets a little more posh at the **Glacier Highland Motel** on Hwy. 2 right near the park entrance. It's the only motel in town with a pool, hot tub, and sauna. Rooms are $40-50, tel. 888-5427 or (800) 766-0811.

Mountain Timbers Bed and Breakfast is seven miles from West Glacier near Columbia Falls at 5385 Rabe Rd., tel. 387-5830. It's a large log house with five guest rooms running $50-75; full breakfast included.

Glacier Wilderness Resort, tel. 888-5664, is peacefully far from the main drag between West Glacier and Essex. The cabins are better appointed than many homes, with hot tubs on each deck. During the summer, lodgings are booked for a minimum five-night stay; once the park season winds down, two-night stays are allowed, though three nights bring a slight price break. A two-bedroom cabin that sleeps six costs $125/night (summer), $95-105 a night (fall, winter, and spring). A one-bedroom cabin is $105 during the summer, $85-95 in the off-season.

Izaak Walton Inn

For those who aren't bent on barreling right down Going-To-The-Sun Road after spending a night near the park entrance, it may be wise to look 30 miles southeast to the **Izaak Walton Inn,** in Essex. The hotel was built by the Great Northern in 1939 to house railroad workers. (Essex was, and is still, an important railroad post; it's where extra engines are added to help trains over Marias Pass.) It's now popular with park visitors, and has gained a cult-like standing among railroad buffs and cross-country skiers.

And well it should. Amtrak's Empire Builder stops a stone's throw from the half-timbered hotel, and groomed ski trails run for miles. Energetic skiers can take a guided tour in the park, or can drive themselves to the unplowed Going-To-The-Sun Road or to East Glacier for a ski trip to Two Medicine Lake.

Rooms in the lodge are $60-80 s, $65-85 d (cheaper rooms have a bath down the hall). The Izaak Walton has also renovated some cabooses and plunked them down on a hillside across the tracks. The cabooses have kitchenettes, sleep four, and cost $350 for a three-night stay, $600 for seven nights. None of the rooms have TV, radio, or telephones, but there is a sauna. Call 888-5700 for reservations.

Campgrounds

All of West Glacier's campgrounds are private, $10-15 a night, RV enterprises, though there is a Forest Service campground, **Big Creek,** at the north end of the Camas Creek Rd. about 20 miles northwest of West Glacier, and there are many coveted campsites in Glacier Park itself (see "Lake McDonald Valley").

San-Suz-Ed serves up waffles and sourdough pancakes in a café alongside the RVs and tents.

It's just off the highway, three miles west of the park entrance, tel. 387-5280, and has a longer season than its neighbors—May 1-Oct. 30. **Lake Five Resort** is on Belton Stage Rd. a little ways north of Hwy. 2. It's a pleasant Montana-style lakeside resort complete with boat rentals and lake swimming. The season runs mid-May through mid-September, tel. 387-5601.

Tent campers may shun the **West Glacier KOA**, tel. 387-5341, but RVers will find it handy (two miles west of the park entrance) well-equipped, and large. Even bigger and closer to the park, **Glacier Campground** is noted for its evening barbecues and a generally high activity level on the sprawling, forested campground. The season for both the KOA and Glacier Campground runs mid-May through September, tel. 387-5689.

FOOD AND DRINK

The **West Glacier Restaurant** at the River Bend Motel, tel. 888-5403, is open May through September for breakfast, lunch, and dinner. This is not an expensive (or fancy) place—it's easy to eat dinner for less than $10 and, as befits a place on the Flathead River, the house specialty is trout.

Casual barbecue dinners are served at the **Glacier Campground**, tel. 387-5689. Steak, chicken, or ribs come with an assortment of picnic-style side dishes—it's a fun place to eat with a family or a group—dinners are about $10, with children's prices available.

The **Dew Drop Inn** is a roadside bar as classic as its name. It's in Coram, just west of West Glacier, tel. 387-5445.

Belton Chalets not only run the Sperry and Granite Park chalets; they also serve up "Health-building Food" in the dining room of their West Glacier headquarters, tel. 888-9964. Even if the

area's best (only?) salad bar doesn't turn your head, it's worth a pause to look at the chalets—they were built in 1912 by the Great Northern Railway and were part of the backcountry accommodations used by horseback travelers before the Going-To-The-Sun Road was built.

The food is kinda health-building at the **Izaak Walton Inn,** too. Lunchtime teriyaki chicken is served on a whole wheat roll at this Essex hotel . . . But there's really more of an emphasis on railroading than on food groups here. Rather than ordering oatmeal, ask for the "Caboose"; the chicken sandwich is a "Brakeman." The dining room looks right out on the tracks, and railroad workers mix with Essex neighbors, railroad buffs, and cross-country skiers in the dining room. It's a great place to stop for a meal, and it'll make most diners want to sign up for a hotel room. Lunches are $5-6; dinners are roughly twice that.

TRANSPORTATION

Amtrak stops at West Glacier's Belton Station daily at 9:30 p.m. (westbound) and 7 a.m. (eastbound).

Park buses shuttle rail passengers from the train station to various destinations within the park: it's $1 to Apgar, $3.25 to Lake McDonald Lodge, $10.75 to Logan Pass, $14.75 to Rising Sun, and $16.50 to St. Mary.

Car rentals are availabe at Glacier Highland Motel, just across from the depot, tel. 888-5427 or (800) 766-0811.

INFORMATION

Rangers at the **Walton Station** on Hwy. 2 near Essex, tel. 888-5628, will offer advice on local hiking trails and dispense information sheets on mountain goats (the goat lick is just up the road).

THE NORTH FORK

The North Fork of the Flathead River forms the western border of Glacier National Park—roads both inside and outside the park run up the valley to the small settlement of Polebridge. Since early in the park's history, the hamlet of Polebridge has been a quiet neighbor just outside Glacier's boundary. Many residents of Polebridge have fought development that would bring them fully into the tourist hubbub. The North Fork Road is still not paved all the way to town, and there's no electricity running up the North Fork.

Don't look for naturalist-led day-hikes or bus tours of this northwest corner of Glacier—it's the park's least developed, though perhaps the most threatened, valley. Curiously, the Inside North Fork Road is the park's oldest, built in 1901 when oil was struck near Kintla Lake.

Threats of road-building, logging, dams, mineral exploration, and general development continue in the non-national park areas of the North Fork. In the late 1980s, environmental groups successfully squelched plans to dig an open-pit coal mine just over the border into Canada. Now, logging and the attendant road networks threaten the area's habitats, and there are fears that Polebridge is all too ripe for development.

SIGHTS

Five miles up Camas Creek Road from Apgar, **McGee Meadows** is a marshy magnet for wildlife. Moose are particularly fond of such boggy areas, and may be spotted by quiet evening visitors. The road, relatively high and exposed here, yields good views of the park's mountains. To the west, there are a couple of hiking trails from Camas Creek Road into the Apgar Mountains. Howe Ridge is to the east, and ridge runners must hike up from the Inside North Fork Road—the trail past shallow Howe Lake crosses moose and beaver habitat.

Bowman Lake is one of the park's prettiest. Long and thin and half-surrounded by mountains, this is a good spot for photography and reflection.

Spend a night up the North Fork and look at the stars. With no electric lights to compete, they're particularly bright. The local café is called the Northern Lights, which are, indeed, commonly visible.

RECREATION

A flat, seven-mile trail edges Bowman Lake's northwest shore, and is a good up-and-back walk for a family. Extend the trip by continuing past the lake on a relatively gentle creekside climb to Brown Pass. (It's another seven miles between the backcountry campground at the head of Bowman Lake and the Brown Pass campground.) From the pass, hikers can cross the divide and continue east to Goat Haunt, on Waterton Lake, or take the high road back west to Kintla Lake.

Or, try this variation: start at **Kintla Lake,** hike 32 miles east to Goat Haunt, and then head south to a terminus at Logan Pass. Cut this trip shorter by taking the boat from Goat Haunt up to Waterton. The country between Upper Kintla Lake and Brown Pass is phenomenal, and one of the places a hiker is most likely to see black bears or grizzlies. The Hole-in-the-Wall Campground, a mile west of the divide along this trail, may be the park's finest, and is certainly one of the most remote.

The **Numa Lookout** trail, five uphill miles to Numa Ridge, is a good place to walk slowly with an eye out for wildlife and good views of Bowman Lake and the Livingston Range. Catch the trail at Bowman Lake Campground.

Also starting at the foot of Bowman Lake, a trail skirts Numa Ridge and runs almost six miles to tiny **Akokala Lake.**

Fishing And Boating
Fish the lakes up the North Fork for magnificent scenery and an occassional Dolly Varden or cutthroat trout. Most anglers take to boats on Bowman Lake—both Bowman and Kintla lakes are open to motorboats with less than 10

WOLVES

Gray wolves have made a comeback to Montana, after being hunted and trapped to near-extinction; in 1991 an estimated 40 to 50 animals were reported to be living in northwestern Montana. Wolves were decimated when white settlers came into the state in the late 1800s. Between 1883 and 1918, 80,730 wolves were bountied. A federal government control program removed another 24,132 animals from 1915 to 1942.

Denning wolves reappeared in 1986 after packs migrated southward from Canada into Glacier Park and the Bob Marshall Wilderness Area. In the park, the North Fork and Two Medicine areas have been hubs for wolves, but a pack's territory can range from 70 to 800 square miles depending upon its prey base and the size of the pack. One animal, radio-collared in Glacier National Park, was spotted 500 miles to the north.

Wolves are protected under the Endangered Species Act. Although classified as endangered, they can be removed by designated agents for preying on livestock. A compensation system for livestock lost to wolves was set up by Defenders of Wildlife in 1987. This "wolf compensation plan" has a fund of $100,000 and has paid out $11,000 during the past three years for 33 animals lost to wolves. Though not perfect, such compensation plans are a first step towards the co-existence of stock-growers and predators. And, since there's no livestock in the national park, and hunting and trapping are prohibited, Glacier seems to be a good place for wolves to regain their foothold.

---

horsepower engines. Canoeists will go nuts over both these lakes—they're long, with miles of animal-sheltering shoreline to explore.

Skiing

The broad North Fork Valley is just as beautiful, and even more isolated, when it's covered with snow. Skiing is generally good here—cold temperatures keep the snow powdery. And it can get *cold*—a 35° below zero morning at the North Fork Hostel may sharply reduce outhouse visits and early-morning ski tours may not be quite so early.

Two ski trails start at the Polebridge Ranger Station: one, suitable for beginners, heads three miles north to Big Prairie; the other follows the six-mile-long unplowed road to Bowman Lake. Stop in at the ranger station before heading out—they'll tell you if it's safe to ski onto Bowman Lake.

ACCOMMODATIONS, FOOD AND DRINK

There isn't much to say about lodgings in the North Fork, except that the **North Fork Hostel** is a *great* place for a budget traveler, or anyone with a relaxed sense of sociability. Lights and kitchen appliances are powered by propane, wood stoves provide the heat, guests come prepared with sleeping bags and food, and the outhouse is plastered with reading material. The hostel's owner is one of the North Fork's leading environmentalists, and has done much to keep prospectors out of town. Reservations are a good idea at the North Fork—call 862-0184. It's open year-round, and beds go for $10 a night.

The other place to stay in Polebridge is not much more expensive, and no fancier than the hostel. **Polebridge Mercantile,** tel. 888-9926, rents one-room cabins for $25 a night. Anyplace else, these propane-powered cabins would be the really *cool* place in town to stay, but here they've got strong competition from the hostel. Either way, bring a sleeping bag or bedding, and don't even bother with the blowdryer or travel iron.

During the summer, the café next to the mercantile is worth a stop for its conviviality as well as its good food. The **Northern Lights** pours beer as well as coffee, and is a comfortable North Fork hangout.

Campgrounds

Bowman Lake Campground is the largest and most popular in the North Fork. Hiking trails wander off in all directions, including an easy one along the lakeshore. The campground at **Kintla Lake** is smaller, with fewer trails to choose from, but equally desirable. Both these campgrounds are fairly developed, though not to the parking-lot degree of those in the more traveled areas of Glacier.

Other roadside campgrounds a notch down in development are **Big Creek,** a Forest Service campground on the Outside North Fork Road near the Camas Creek entrance to the park, **Logging Creek** and **Quartz Creek,** on Inside North Fork Road between Apgar and Polebridge, **Bowman Creek,** near Polebridge, and **River,** on the North Fork River north of Polebridge. These are primitive campgrounds; bring your own water.

INFORMATION

The **Polebridge Ranger Station,** tel. 888-5416, is right near the no-longer-pole-constructed bridge over the North Fork. Stop here for backcountry permits, trail information, or a chat about the local wolf packs.

Transportation

Drive in from the park on Camas Creek or Inside North Fork roads—the Inside North Fork is rougher, but there are some campgrounds along it. From Columbia Falls, the Outside North Fork Road, with good views of the Livingston Range, leads to Polebridge. Blankenship Road connects the Outside North Fork Road with West Glacier. In the winter, the outer North Fork Road and Blankenship Road are plowed.

WATERTON NATIONAL PARK

Waterton National Park is just across the Canadian border from Glacier. Though a much smaller park (it covers only 203 square miles) it's worth visiting for spectacular scenery with a distinctly Canadian flavor.

The two parks are known collectively as the Waterton-Glacier International Peace Park, but are managed separately with separate entry fees. A 24-hour pass to Waterton costs $4.25 per vehicle; a four-day pass is $9.50.

There's actually a town in Waterton Park, with a handful of year-round residents, a number of private summer cottages, and a small tourist strip on the Cameron Creek delta. Development has been kept pretty well in check, though; there are no soaring condominium towers and no McDonald's.

All prices quoted for Waterton are in Canadian dollars. Alberta's **area code** is 403.

THE LAND

Waterton Valley was filled by an enormous glacier during the ice age ending 10,000 years ago. It advanced down the valley until it met resistance from the hard-rock protrusion now called the Bear's Hump (the high ridge overlooking the townsite). The glacier piled up behind the Bear's Paw and Vimy Ridge, digging deep into the ground, and eventually slipped over the top and cut a channel. This Bosporus Channel now links Upper and Middle Waterton lakes. The bowl dug out behind the resisting ridge now contains the nearly 500-foot-deep Upper Waterton Lake.

Once the valley glacier reached the present-day prairies, it began to melt. As ice melted and the glacier shrunk back, piles of debris were dropped, forming long chains of moraines. A huge piece of ice left behind by the retreating glacier formed Middle and Lower Waterton lakes.

Waterton crosses half a dozen ecological zones as it ascends from wetlands through prairie, parkland, montane, subalpine, and alpine zones.

As over most of the east slope of the Rockies, the wind can be persistent and strong in Waterton.

HISTORY

Native people camped in the Waterton Valley some 8,500 years ago; By 500 B.C. a Plains culture based on buffalo hunting was firmly established. By A.D. 500 the locals picked up and moved to the western slopes of the Rockies, and became known as the Kootenai (or, in Canada, the Kootenay). Kootenai hunters continued to travel regularly to the Waterton area for bison until forced from the plains by the Blackfeet, who controlled the southern Alberta plains from the early 1700s until the buffalo disappeared a century later.

Thomas Blakiston, a British military man, was sent to the Canadian West in 1857 to pave the way for settlers. He named Waterton Lakes for an eccentric British naturalist.

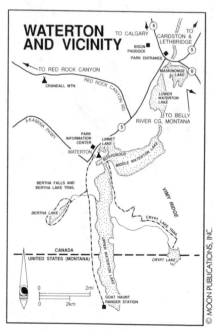

Oil seepages had been noticed by Indians and early white settlers, and in the early 1900s, modest oil strikes were accompanied by major machinery and ruckus. This disruption, and the formation of Glacier National Park in 1910, led to the establishment of Waterton Lakes Dominion Park in 1911. Although hunting and commercial fishing were prohibited within park boundaries, building was not, and a community soon developed on the north shore of Upper Waterton Lake. Kootenai Brown, a well-educated mountain man who'd settled near the lakes, was named the park's first superintendent.

The Prince of Wales Hotel was built by the Great Northern Railway in 1926 as a stopover for tour buses shuttling between Glacier National Park and Jasper, Alberta.

In 1932, the Canadian and U.S. governments agreed to form the Waterton-Glacier International Peace Park as a symbol of friendship between the two countries. Both parks are now designated "Biosphere Reserves."

SIGHTS

The M.V. *International* has cruised Upper Waterton Lake since the Prince of Wales Hotel opened in 1927. The two-hour RT boat ride from the Waterton marina to Goat Haunt, Montana, at the southern end of the lake costs $13 and departs several times daily from mid-May to mid-September, tel. 859-2362. Backpackers and Crypt Lake hikers should let the cruise personnel know of their plans before boarding the boat.

Cameron Falls drops from a hanging valley, where a small glacier came in from the side and was swallowed up by the large Waterton Valley glacier.

A paddle-wheeled boat submerged in Emerald Bay beneath the Prince of Wales Hotel can be seen through the clear water. It holds a particular fascination for divers.

Take the nine-mile-long **Red Rock Canyon Parkway** from town to the canyon. At road's end, there's a short, self-guided walk around the canyon and a picnic area; it's a 20-minute amble to Blakiston Falls.

A **bison paddock** north of the park entrance corrals a small herd of buffalo. There's a driving tour through the paddock.

RECREATION

Hiking
Walkers and bicyclists share the **Townsite Trail,** a two-mile tour along the lakefront to Cameron Falls.

Take off from the park information center and follow the trail up the **Bear's Hump** for a great view of the lakes and town below. It's less than a mile to the top of the ridge, but the climb is steep and views are often accompanied by stiff winds.

The **Bertha Lake Trail** is a three-mile tromp through montane and subalpine forests to a high cirque lake. Waterton is known for its variety of wildflowers, and they're particularly well-displayed along this trail. For hikers not up to the seven-mile roundtrip, **Bertha Falls** is just under two miles up the same trail.

Take the boat to **Goat Haunt** at the south end of Waterton Lake and from there hike a mile to Rainbow Falls and back, or take off on foot back to Waterton townsite. There's an eight-mile trail up the west side of the lake, though the trail passes mostly through lodgepole pine, Engelmann spruce, and some aspen and birch trees with only a few views over the lake.

Debark the tour boat at Crypt Landing for the five-mile hike to **Crypt Lake.** On the way to the lake, hikers pass several waterfalls, sidle along steep trails, creep through a natural tunnel, and climb 3,000 feet. This is a hike to challenge both muscles and nerves . . . it's rather scarier than most day-hikes, but when you get to the lake, you're up there with the mountain goats.

For a longer backpack, try the **Tamarack Tour** towards the northwestern end of the park. Start on the Rowes Lake trail from the trailhead on the Akamina Parkway, and follow north and west past tiny Lone Lake, Twin Lakes, and Lost Lake to Avion Ridge and Goat Lake. (For the best views and a hike through an alpine larch forest, forgo the Bauerman Trail, aka Snowshoe Trail, short-cut and take to the more difficult, less well maintained, Avion Ridge) The last three miles to Red Rock Canyon are on the Bauerman Trail, rounding out an approximately 27-mile trip.

Before setting out on an overnight trek, get a free backcountry permit and trail information from the park information center or administrative office.

Fishing

There's a $5.25 fee for a four-day Canadian National Park fishing permit. Purchase one at the park information center or administrative office if you plan to go after the trout, northern pike, or whitefish of the Waterton Lakes.

Swimming

The lakes are a little too chilly for most swimmers, but there's a public pool on Cameron Falls Dr., tel. 859-2333. It's an outdoor pool, open mid-June through Labor Day, with a $2 fee for adults, $1.25 children.

Divers will want to scout around the paddle-wheel boat submerged in Emerald Bay. Fish gravitate to the rusty, rotting boat, which hauled logs on the Waterton River in the early 1900s, and was subsequently a floating tearoom, until it fell to disuse and was deliberately sunk in 1918.

Bicycling

The townsite trail is perfect for an easy bike ride; for more of a challenge, pedal up to the Prince of Wales Hotel for tea or out the Red Rock Canyon Parkway. **Pat's** rents mountain bikes for $5.50 an hour, $27 a day at the corner of Mountain View Rd. and Windflower Ave., tel. 859-2266.

Golf

The 18-hole **Waterton Golf Course,** tel. 859-2383, is on the Red Rock Canyon Rd. just north of Hwy. 5.

Cross-country Skiing

Though it's not a big winter destination, there's usually good snow around Waterton Lake and several trails are maintained each winter for cross-country skiing. Check at the park administrative office for current trail conditions.

ACCOMMODATIONS

The **Prince of Wales Hotel** is perched on a bluff over town. It's run as part of the Glacier Park, Inc. hotel system, and has a Laura Ashley-British Isles theme overlaid on the Glacier Park hotel chassis. Big wing-backed chairs look out from the lobby over Upper Waterton Lake, and the Garden Court dining room looks out onto neither a garden nor a court. Rooms run $84-99

upper Waterton Lake from the Prince of Wales Hotel lobby

s, $92-108 d—the top-end fees buy an awe-inspiring view onto the lake. Call (403) 236-3400 for reservations—the hotel is open Memorial Day weekend through early September.

A congenial, though not inexpensive, alternative to the Prince of Wales is the **Kilmorey Lodge** at the base of the hill, just on the edge of town, tel. 859-2342 or (800) 661-8069. It's like an overgrown log cabin bed and breakfast, with a homey lounge complete with an oversized atlas of Canada on the coffee table, a tiny bar, and a dining room. Rooms run $63-90. During the winter, cross-country ski packages are offered—two nights' lodging and several meals are included for the $129 per person fee.

Downtown, the **Bayshore Inn,** tel. 850-2211 or (800) 661-8080, is a typically nice AAA type of place, with lake views and a hot tub. Double rooms run $79-89, again, the extra $10 buys the view. A small step down in both price and ambience is the **Aspen Windflower Motel,** tel. 859-2334 or (800) 661-8069.

The **Stanley,** a small downtown hotel, has rooms upstairs from the Dill General Store, a woolen goods store on Waterton Ave. Clean but basic rooms are $45, tel. 859-2345.

Crandell Mountain Lodge, tel. 859-2288, is open April 1-Oct. 31 and has 12 country-inn style rooms starting at $35.

The wind-tossed **Townsite Campground** is of the parking lot variety, but many of the 238 sites are close to the lake, and there are showers. It's immediately south of downtown, and near the Bertha Lake trailhead and the Falls Theatre on Windflower Drive. No reservations are taken, so get there early in the day, especially on summer weekends. Camping fees are $11.75, and the camping season runs mid-May to early October.

Belly River Campground is a cheaper ($6.50), but not necessarily more appealing alternative off Chief Mountain International Highway just north of the international border. It's away from the lakes, can be hot, and is open mid-May through mid-September. The **Crandell Moun**tain **Campground** is a pleasant, though sometimes crowded, spot five miles from town on the Red Rock Parkway. It's open mid-May through Labor Day, and charges $9.50 to camp.

FOOD AND DRINK

Pearl's, Windflower Ave., tel. 859-2284, has soup, salad, and sandwiches ($2-6) with a healthy touch and patio seating that recalls school desks. **Zummmm's,** on the corner of Waterton Ave. and Cameron Falls Dr., tel. 859-2388, is just a shade more expensive, and also has a deck, good sandwiches, and berry pie.

Things get fancier as you head toward the Prince of Wales Hotel. Mid-way between downtown and the hilltop hotel, the **Lamp Post,** Kilmorey Lodge's dining room, strikes a happy medium for a good dinner in comfortable, attractive surroundings. Lunches are about $6, and dinners are $12-15; call 859-2334. After a few dinners in Glacier Park hotels, this may provide a welcome fresh touch. Tucked behind the Kilmorey Lodge, the outdoor **Gazebo Café** is informal and reasonably priced for pasta or salads. For a drink, try the intimate bar inside the Kilmorey.

The dining room at the **Prince of Wales,** tel. 859-2231, puts a British Isles twist on the standard Glacier Park hotel menu—they serve sheperd's pie for $7.95 at lunch; dinners thankfully include British Columbia salmon ($15.25). There's also a quite charming tea room here, serving up delicious scones and other pastries from 2-5 p.m.

If you prefer to focus on eclecticism and economy, try the **New Frank Restaurant,** on Waterton Ave., where a Chinese-Western six-course evening buffet costs $9.95 ($4.95 for children). New Frank is open for breakfast, lunch, and dinner.

INFORMATION AND SERVICES

Just across from the Prince of Wales Hotel, the **Park Information Centre** is open mid-May through Labor Day, tel. (403) 859-2445. The **park administration office** is open year-round on Mountain View Rd., tel. 859-2224. The in-town **Heritage Centre** is run by the Waterton Natural History Association, tel. 859-2267. The friendly staff will help plan hikes, meals, and

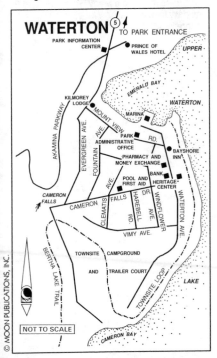

motel stays. A small historical museum and a bookshop operate out of the same Waterton Ave. building.

The **Waterton Natural History Association** runs summer classes, including a one-day "Vision Quest" class, based on Native American spiritual quests, $35. Contact the Waterton Natural History Association, Box 145, Waterton Park, Alberta TDK TOK 2MO, tel. 859-2624 for schedules.

Free interpretive programs are presented each evening in the **Falls Theater** across from Cameron Falls, and in the theatre at **Crandell Campground.** Programs focus on both history and nature studies, and usually include slides or a movie.

First aid is proffered at the swimming pool on Cameron Falls Dr., tel. 859-2333. For **emergency services,** call 859-2636. The **police station** is at the corner of Waterton Ave. and Cameron Falls Dr., tel 859-2244 or Zenith 5000.

There is a **treasury branch authority** upstairs from Caribou Clothing on Waterton Ave., but it closes at 1 p.m. If you need money changed at other times, the pharmacy on Waterton Ave. offers a fair exchange rate. Most businesses will accept U.S. dollars at the current exchange rate, but dispensing foreign currency in change is restricted.

The **Itussiststukiopi Coin-Op Laundrette** is on Windflower Ave., tel. 859-2460.

TRANSPORTATION

The Chief Mountain International Highway (Hwy. 17) connects Glacier and Waterton national parks, but both the highway and the customs stations along it close down mid-Sept. to mid-May, forcing drivers to head north from Montana on Hwy. 89 to Cardston, then west on Hwy. 5 to Waterton.

Citizens of Canada and the U.S. will generally find the border crossing expeditious. Remember not to bring firearms into Canada, or citrus fruits into the States, and you probably won't have any trouble.

Greyhound sends buses to Waterton (via Lethbridge) from late-June until Labor Day. **Red tour buses** leave from Many Glacier Hotel at 9 a.m. daily for a day-trip to Waterton. The round-trip fare is $31.

BOOKLIST

DESCRIPTION AND TRAVEL

Alwin, John A. *Eastern Montana: A Portrait of the Land and its People*. Montana Geographic Series, no. 2. Helena: Montana Magazine, 1982. A broad overview of the people, sights, and regions of eastern Montana, in text and photos.

Federal Writers' Project of the Work Projects Administration for the State of Montana. *Montana: A State Guide Book*. State of Montana: Department of Agriculture, Labor and Industry, 1939. New York: Hastings House, 1949. Long out of print, but it's worth snaring a copy at a used bookstore.

Gildart, R.C., ed. *Glacier Country: Montana's Glacier National Park*. Montana Geographic Series, no. 4. Helena: Montana Magazine, 1990. An introduction to Glacier Park and its natural history, with ample illustrations and intelligent text.

Gildart, R.C. *Montana's Flathead Country*. Montana Geographic Series, no. 14. Helena: Montana Magazine, 1986. Colorful histories, a look at the environment, and splendid photos define the area around Flathead Lake.

Gildart, R.C. *Montana's Missouri River*. Montana Geographic Series, no. 8. Helena: Montana Magazine, 1985. Text and photographs celebrate the Wild and Scenic Missouri.

Meloy, Mark. *Islands on the Prairie: The Mountain Ranges of Eastern Montana*. Montana Geographic Series, no. 13, Helena: Montana Magazine, 1986. Pictures and text about the often-ignored mountains in eastern Montana.

Moore, Rae Ellen. *Just West of Yellowstone*. Laclede, ID: Great Blue Graphics, 1987. Charming illustrations and handwritten text give a real picture of West Yellowstone and surrounding areas.

Mullan, John. *Miners and Travelers' Guide to Oregon, Washington, Idaho, Montana, Wyoming, and Colorado via the Missouri and Columbia Rivers*. 1865. New York: Arno Press, reprinted 1973.

Pringle, Heather. *Waterton Lakes National Park*. Vancouver, B.C.: Douglas and McIntyre, 1986. A comprehensive guide to history, nature, and hikes in Waterton.

Schneider, Bill. *Montana's Yellowstone River*. Montana Geographic Series, no. 10. Helena: Montana Magazine, 1985. An enthusiastic portrait of the Yellowstone River, with a strong conservationist cast.

Tirrell, Norma. *Montana*. Oakland, CA: Compass American Guides, 1991. An easy-reading, coffee-table guide.

Wetzel, Betty. *Missoula: The Town and the People*. Helena: Montana Magazine, 1987. What makes Missoula tick.

HISTORY

Bradshaw, Glenda Clay. *Montana's Historical Highway Markers*. Helena: Montana Historical Society Press, 1989. A complete reference to the roadside historical signs in the state, with special notice taken of early illustrators that conceived the markers.

Brown, Mark H., and W.R. Felton. *Before Barbed Wire*. New York: Bramhall House, 1956. A commemoration of the life of L.A. Huffman, the frontier photographer who captured on film the era of the Indians and the open range.

Cheney, Roberta Carkeek. *Names on the Face of Montana*. Missoula: Mountain Press, 1983. When you must know how Two Dot and Ubet got their names, check this book.

Chesarek, Frank, and Jim Brabeck eds. *Montana: Two Lane Highway in a Four Lane World*. Missoula: Mountain Press, 1978. A western Montana eighth-grade class dedicated themselves to writing a one-volume history of Montana; now out-of-print, it may be the single best overview of the colorful history of the state, told with energy and insight.

Garcia, Andrew. *Tough Trip Through Paradise*. Sausalito, CA: Comstock Editions, 1967. Maybe it's true, maybe only half so, but it's a whale of a story about mountain men and Indian life in 1878.

Howard, Joseph Kinsey. *Montana: High, Wide, and Handsome*. Lincoln: University of Nebraska Press, 1943. A lively and opinionated history.

Lopach, James, ed. *We the People of Montana*. Missoula: Mountain Press, 1983. An historical analysis of the Montana governmental system.

Malone, Michael P., and Richard B. Roeder. *Montana: A History of Two Centuries*. Seattle: University of Washington, 1976. Now the accepted text on Montana's history, it is authoritative, rich in vignette, almost punchy.

Thompson, Larry. *Montana's Explorers*. Montana Geographic Series, no. 9. Helena: Montana Magazine, 1985. It's not *all* explorers; the focus is on naturalists, including Lewis and Clark and Prince Maximilian of Weid.

Vichorek, Daniel N. *Montana's Homestead Era*. Montana Geographic Series, no. 15. Helena: Montana Magazine, 1987. A mix of reminiscence and history, regarding the huge influx of homesteaders during the early 20th century.

West, Carroll Van. *A Traveler's Companion to Montana History*. Helena: Montana Historical Society Press, 1986. An excellent roadside historical companion.

Wilson, Gary. *Honky-Tonk Town: Havre's Bootlegging Days*. Havre: High-Line Books, 1986. Most Montana towns have had *somebody* chronicle their history, and a few of the resulting books are actually pretty good reads. Pick up *Honky-Tonk Town* if you want old-time Havre to come to life.

NATIVE AMERICANS

Bryan, William L. Jr. *Montana's Indians*. Montana Geographic Series, no. 11. Helena: Montana Magazine, 1985. Historical and contemporary sketches.

Eagle/Walking Turtle. *Indian America*. Santa Fe: John Muir Press, 1991. Tribal histories and cultural information for visitors.

Ewers, John C. *The Blackfeet: Raiders on the Northwestern Plains*. Norman: University of Oklahoma Press, 1958. An anthropological study of the Blackfeet, this is fascinating reading for non-anthropologists, too.

Hungry Wolf, Adolf and Beverly, compilers. *Indian Tribes of the Northern Rockies*. Skookumchuck, B.C.: Good Medicine Books, 1989. Tribal histories from Indian and non-Indian sources.

Lowie, Robert H. *Indians of the Plains*. Lincoln: University of Nebraska Press, 1954. An anthropological look at all the Plains tribes.

Miller, David Humphreys. *Custer's Fall: The Indian Side of the Story*. Lincoln: University of Nebraska, 1957. An enthralling retelling of the familiar Custer story based on Indian documentation.

Wilfong, Cheryl. *Following the Nez Percé Trail*. Corvallis, OR: Oregon State University Press, 1990. An absolutely wonderful, well-thought-out, and moving book that will enhance any trip intersecting with the Nez Percé Trail.

LEWIS AND CLARK

Cutright, Paul Russell. *Lewis and Clark: Pioneering Naturalists*. Lincoln: University of Nebraska Press, 1969. Lewis and, to a lesser extent, Clark, were the first to write of Montana's flora and fauna. Cutright's narrative draws their reader in to the observations of prairie dogs and candlefish.

DeVoto, Bernard, ed. *The Journals of Lewis and Clark*. Boston: Houghton Mifflin, 1953. Of the one-volume versions of the journals, this is the best.

Duncan, Dayton. *Out West*. New York; Viking Penguin, 1987. Along the Lewis and Clark Trail in the 1980s.

Lavender, David. *The Way to the Western Sea*. New York: Harper and Row, 1988. One of the West's most noted historians gives the fascinating details of the Lewis and Clark story.

Olmstead, Gerald. *Fielding's Lewis and Clark Trail*. New York: William Morrow and Co., 1986. How to do what Dayton Duncan did.

NATURAL SCIENCES AND THE ENVIRONMENT

Alt, David, and Donald, W. Hyndman, *Roadside Geology of Montana*. Missoula: Mountain Press, 1986. A comprehensive road-by-road guide to Montana's unique geology. For those willing to read slowly, there's a wealth of information.

Anderson, Bob. *Beartooth Country*. Montana Geographic Series, no. 7. Helena: Montana Magazine, 1984. An environmentally-conscious look at Montana's highest country.

Chronic, Halka. *Pages of Stone: Geology of Western National Parks and Monuments*, Vol. 1: Rocky Mountains and Western Great Plains. Seattle: The Mountaineers, 1984. A clearly-written and untechnical geology to the West, including Yellowstone and Glacier parks.

Ferguson, Gary. *Montana National Forests*. Billings and Helena: Falcon Press, 1990. A guide to Montana's 10 national forests, amply illustrated.

Fischer, Carol and Hank. *Montana Wildlife Viewing Guide*. Billings and Helena: Falcon Press, 1990. A guide to 113 designated refuges and habitats where Montana wildlife is most easily viewed.

Gildart, Robert C. and Jan Wassink. *Montana Wildlife*. Montana Geographic Series, no. 3. Helena: Montana Magazine, 1982. An illustrated study of Montana's wildlife heritage and its many ecosystems and species.

Hart, Jeff. *Montana: Native Plants and Early Peoples*. Helena: Montana Historical Society, 1976. Well-illustrated and engagingly written, this is the best book on ceremonial and medicinal plant usage by native Montanans.

Horner, Jack, and James Gorman. *Digging Dinosaurs*. New York: Harper Collins, 1990. Read this before visiting Choteau or the Museum of the Rockies and the you'll be able to keep up with the seven-year-olds.

Manning, Richard. *Last Stand*. Salt Lake City: Gibbs Smith, 1991. Manning went after the story of logging in Montana and lost his position as the *Missoulian's* environmental reporter.

McPhee, John. *Rising From the Plains*. New York: Farrar, Straus, Giroux, 1986. OK, so it's about Wyoming. It's a good read, and the most lucid account of Rocky Mountain geology in print.

Reese, Rick. *Greater Yellowstone*. Montana Geographic Series, no. 6. Helena: Montana Magazine, 1984. One of the best of this series, with a strong focus on environmental issues.

Van Bruggen, Theodore. *Wildflowers, Grasses and Other Plants of the Northern Plains and Black Hills*. Interior, SD: Badlands Natural History Association, 1971. A good guide to the plant life of Montana's arid plains, with photographs.

RECREATION

Bach, Oroville. *Hiking the Yellowstone Backcountry*. San Francisco: Sierra Club Books, 1973. Pick a trail and leave the crowded roads of Yellowstone National Park.

Cogswell, Ted. *Montana Golf Guide*. Great Falls: Art Craft, 1985. A complete listing.

Feldman, Robert. *The Rockhound's Guide to Montana*. Billings: Falcon Press, 1985. Feldman breaks the state into over 50 rock-hunting regions, complete with maps.

Fischer, Hank. *Floater's Guide to Montana*. Billings and Helena: Falcon Press, 1986. A comprehensive guide to floating 26 Montana rivers.

Glacier Natural History Association. *Hiker's Guide to Glacier National Park*. West Glacier: Glacier Natural History Association, 1978. Glacier's greatest hits—details on day-hikes and overnight trips.

Green, Stewart M. *Back Country Byways*. Billings and Helena: Falcon Press, 1991. A guide to BLM-designated scenic backroads throughout the West.

Henkel, Mark. *The Hunter's Guide to Montana*. Billings and Helena: Falcon Press, 1985. A sensitive guide to hunting in Montana, with a focus on the process of becoming acquainted with wildlife.

Kilgore, Gene. *Ranch Vacations*. Sante Fe: John Muir Press, 1991. A comprehensive guide to guest and dude ranches throughout the West.

Konizeski, Dick. *Montanans' Fishing Guide. Vol. II: Montana Waters East of the Continental Divide*. Missoula: Mountain Press, 1982. Out-of-print, but worth looking for in a library for anyone who wants the low-down on every fishing hole in all of Montana's east-flowing rivers.

McCoy, Michael. *Mountain Bike Adventures in the Northern Rockies*. Seattle: Mountaineers, 1989. Some of the West's best trails for the mountain biker.

Rudner, Ruth. *Bitterroot to Beartooth*. San Francisco: Sierra Club Books, 1985. Indispensable for serious hikers in southwest Montana, and good environmental reference for casual hikers or readers.

Sample, Michael S. *Angler's Guide to Montana*. Billings and Helena: Falcon Press, 1984.

Schneider, Bill. *Hiker's Guide to Montana*. Billings and Helena: Falcon Press, 1990. Descriptions and maps of 100 hikes, mostly in western Montana.

Short Hikes and Strolls in Glacier National Park. West Glacier, Glacier Natural History Association, 1978. For those not up to the stiffer hikes in the above book, try these easy jaunts.

Stienstra, Tom. *Rocky Mountain Camping*. San Francisco: Fog Horn Press, 1991. An exhaustive listing of public and private campgrounds in Montana, Wyoming, and Colorado.

Williams, Rebecca, ed. *Roads and Trails of Waterton-Glacier International Peace Park: The Ruhle Handbook*. Billings and Helena: Falcon Press, 1986. An update of George Ruhle's noteworthy logbook of the park.

LITERATURE

Bevis, William W. *Ten Tough Trips: Montana Writers and the West*. Seattle: University of Washington Press, 1990. One of the first works of literary criticism solely on Montana writers.

Blew, Mary Clearman. *All But the Waltz*. New York: Viking Penguin, 1991. Blew's family came to Montana in 1882. These affecting essays trace their lives in the Judith Basin country. Also look for her collections of short stories, *Runaway* and *Lambing Out*.

Cannon, Hal, ed. *Cowboy Poetry: A Gathering*. Salt Lake City: Peregrine Smith, 1985. A historical overview of cowboy poetry.

Cannon, Hal, ed. *New Cowboy Poetry: A Contemporary Gathering*. Salt Lake City: Peregrine Smith, 1990. An anthology of the best of today's cowboy poets.

Crumley, James. *The Last Good Kiss*. New York: Random House, 1978. Follow hard-boiled Montana detectives around the seedy sides of the West in this book and in *Dancing Bear* and *The Wrong Case*.

Ford, Richard. *Wildlife*. New York: Atlantic Monthly Press, 1990. A Great Falls teenager watches his father go off to fight fires and his mother take up with another man.

Frazier, Ian. *Great Plains*. New York: Farrar Straus Giroux, 1989. A wonderful conglomeration of Frazier's rambles across the historical and contemporary plains.

Garcia, Andrew. *Tough Trip Through Paradise*. Sausalito, CA: Comstock Press, 1967. Discovered in 1948, this is the powerfully-written chronicle of the 1878 Montana frontier penned by a white man who lived with Native Americans.

Hugo, Richard. *Making Certain It Goes On*. New York: W.W. Norton, 1984. Hugo's collected poems.

Kittredge, William, and Annick Smith, ed. *The Last Best Place*. Helena: Montana Historical Society Press, 1988. This 1,158-page compendium anchors down every Montanan's bedside table. From Native American myths to Paul Zarzyski's modern cowboy poems, it's all here.

Kittredge, William, ed. *Montana Spaces*. New York: Nick Lyons Books, 1988. Evocative essays by the likes of Thomas McGuane and Gretel Ehrlich with perfect black and white photos by John Smart.

Krakel, Dean. *Downriver: A Yellowstone Journey*. San Francisco: Sierra Club Press, 1987. The eclectic chronicle of a float trip down the full length of the Yellowstone River.

Maclean, Norman. *A River Runs Through It*. Chicago: University of Chicago Press, 1976. The classic novella of fly-fishing and two brothers' love and doomed relationship.

McGuane, Thomas. *Keep the Change*. Boston: Houghton Mifflin, 1989. In this, as in the earlier *Something To Be Desired* and *Nobody's Angel*, tough, sensitive guys try to set their lives straight in Deadrock, Montana (which is a lot like Livingston).

McMurtry, Larry. *Lonesome Dove*. New York: Pocket Books, 1985. A masterfully written epic of the last days of the great Texas cattle drives, told from the point of view of faded but wise-cracking cowboys. Also from McMurtry, *Buffalo Girls* is an engaging saga of Calamity Jane and her gang.

Stegner, Wallace. *Wolf Willow*. New York: Viking Press, 1962. Stegner spent his youth on a homestead *just* north of Montana in Saskatchewan.

Stockton, Bill. *Today I Baled Some Hay to Feed the Sheep the Coyotes Eat*. Billings and Helena: Falcon Press, 1983. Vignettes by a Montana-raised, Paris-educated writer and illustrator on the vicissitudes of sheep ranching.

Van Cleve, Spike. *A Day Late and a Dollar Short*. Kansas City: Lowell Press, 1982. The full-spirited reminiscences of one of Montana's foremost dude ranchers and story-tellers.

Welch, James. *The Indian Lawyer*. New York: W.W. Norton, 1990. A Blackfeet lawyer in Helena finds his life suddenly very complicated . . . it's a pageturner with good insights. Welch's other novels include *Fools Crow, Winter in the Blood*, and *The Death of Jim Loney*.

MAGAZINES

Montana Magazine is published in Helena, and is a good collage of history, photography, travel information, discussion of current issues, and whatnot. You're warned: it can become addictive reading. Call (800) 821-3874 in Montana, or (800) 654-1105 out-of-state for subscription information.

Montana Outdoors is published by the Montana Dept. of Fish, Wildlife, and Parks, and contains the latest information on fishing, hunting, and recreation, and of course, great photography. Call (800) 678-6668 for subscription information.

INDEX

Boldfaced page numbers indicate the primary reference; *italicized* page numbers refer to information found in photos, illustrations, captions, or callouts.

THE METRIC SYSTEM

1 inch = 2.54 centimeters (cm)
1 foot = .304 meters (m)
1 mile = 1.6093 kilometers (km)
1 km = .6214 miles
1 fathom = 1.8288 m
1 chain = 20.1168 m
1 furlong = 201.168 m
1 acre = .4047 hectares (ha)
1 sq km = 100 ha
1 sq mile = 2.59 sq km
1 ounce = 28.35 grams
1 pound = .4536 kilograms (kg)
1 short ton = .90718 metric ton
1 short ton = 2000 pounds
1 long ton = 1.016 metric tons
1 long ton = 2240 pounds
1 metric ton = 1000 kg
1 quart = .94635 liters
1 US gallon = 3.7854 liters
1 Imperial gallon = 4.5459 liters
1 nautical mile = 1.852 km

To compute centigrade temperatures, subtract 32 from Fahrenheit and divide by 1.8. To go the other way, multiply centigrade by 1.8 and add 32.

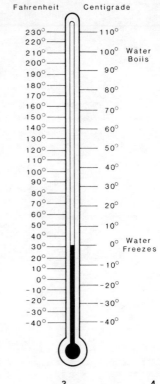

ABOUT THE AUTHORS

William McRae

Bill McRae was born in eastern Montana and grew up on his family's ranch. He used his college years as an excuse to travel, attending universities in the U.S., Canada, Scotland, England, and France. He has taught English language at several universities, worked as a waiter and bartender, was features editor for a community newspaper, and ran a catering company. In his free time he enjoys gardening, playing bridge, house restoration, and buying bargain airline tickets. He now lives in Portland, Oregon, where he works for the Powell's corporation.

Judy Jewell

Judy Jewell grew up in Baltimore and retains an affection for both the Orioles and crab cakes. Since moving west in 1977, she's been a biology major, a pizza cook, a bartender, a crayfish-eyestalk-plucker, a Forest Service grunt, a healthworker, a calligrapher, and a bookseller. She got into both Montana and travel writing through the backdoor, but that's all too long a story.

Moon Handbooks—The Ideal Traveling Companions

Open a Moon Handbook and you're opening your eyes and heart to the world. Thoughtful, sensitive, and provocative, Moon Handbooks encourage an intimate understanding of a region, from its culture and history to essential practicalities. Fun to read and packed with valuable information on accommodations, dining, recreation, plus indispensable travel tips, detailed maps, charts, illustrations, photos, glossaries, and indexes, Moon Handbooks are ideal traveling companions: informative, entertaining, and highly practical.

To locate the bookstore nearest you that carries Moon Travel Handbooks or to order directly from Moon Publications, call: (800) 345-5473, Monday-Friday, 9 a.m.-5 p.m. PST

The Pacific/Asia Series

BALI HANDBOOK by Bill Dalton
Detailed travel information on the most famous island in the world. 12 color pages, 29 b/w photos, 68 illustrations, 42 maps, 7 charts, glossary, booklist, index. 428 pages. **$12.95**

BANGKOK HANDBOOK by Michael Buckley
Your tour guide through this exotic and dynamic city reveals the affordable and accessible possibilities. Thai phrasebook, 16 color pages, 55 b/w photos, 30 maps, 19 illustrations, 9 charts, booklist, index. 214 pages. **$10.95**

BLUEPRINT FOR PARADISE: How to Live on a Tropic Island by Ross Norgrove
This one-of-a-kind guide has everything you need to know about moving to and living comfortably on a tropical island. 8 color pages, 40 b/w photos, 3 maps, 14 charts, appendices, index. 212 pages. **$14.95**

FIJI ISLANDS HANDBOOK by David Stanley
The first and still the best source of information on travel around this 322-island archipelago.
8 color pages, 35 b/w photos, 78 illustrations, 26 maps, 3 charts, Fijian glossary, booklist,
index. 198 pages. **$8.95**

INDONESIA HANDBOOK by Bill Dalton
This one-volume encyclopedia explores island by island the many facets of this sprawling,
kaleidoscopic island nation. 30 b/w photos, 143 illustrations, 250 maps, 17 charts, booklist,
extensive Indonesian vocabulary, index. 1,000 pages. **$19.95**

MICRONESIA HANDBOOK:
Guide to the Caroline, Gilbert, Mariana, and Marshall Islands by David Stanley
Micronesia Handbook guides you on a real Pacific adventure all your own. 8 color pages, 77
b/w photos, 68 illustrations, 69 maps, 18 tables and charts, index. 300 pages. **$11.95**

NEW ZEALAND HANDBOOK by Jane King
Introduces you to the people, places, history, and culture of this extraordinary land. 8 color
pages, 99 b/w photos, 146 illustrations, 82 maps, booklist, index. 546 pages. **$14.95**

OUTBACK AUSTRALIA HANDBOOK by Marael Johnson
Australia is an endlessly fascinating, vast land, and *Outback Australia Handbook* explores the
cities and towns, sheep stations, and wilderness areas of the Northern Territory, Western, and
South Australia. Full of travel tips and cultural information for adventuring, relaxing, or just
getting away from it all. 8 color pages, 39 b/w photos, 63 illustrations, 51 maps, booklist, index.
355 pages. **$15.95**

PHILIPPINES HANDBOOK by Peter Harper and Evelyn Peplow
Crammed with detailed information, *Philippines Handbook* equips the escapist, hedonist, or
business traveler with thorough coverage of the Philippines's colorful history, landscapes, and
culture. 8 color pages, 2 b/w photos, 60 illustrations, 93 maps, 30 charts, index. 587 pages.
$12.95

SOUTHEAST ASIA HANDBOOK by Carl Parkes
Helps the enlightened traveler discover the real Southeast Asia. 16 color pages, 75 b/w photos,
11 illustrations, 169 maps, 140 charts, vocabulary and suggested reading, index. 873 pages.
$16.95

SOUTH KOREA HANDBOOK by Robert Nilsen
Whether you're visiting on business or searching for adventure, *South Korea Handbook* is an
invaluable companion. 8 color pages, 78 b/w photos, 93 illustrations, 109 maps, 10 charts,
Korean glossary with useful notes on speaking and reading the language, booklist, index. 548
pages. **$14.95**

SOUTH PACIFIC HANDBOOK by David Stanley
The original comprehensive guide to the 16 territories in the South Pacific. 20 color pages,
195 b/w photos, 121 illustrations, 35 charts, 138 maps, booklist, glossary, index. 740 pages.
$15.95

TAHITI-POLYNESIA HANDBOOK by David Stanley
All five French-Polynesian archipelagoes are covered in this comprehensive guide by Oce-
ania's best-known travel writer. 12 color pages, 45 b/w photos, 64 illustrations, 33 maps, 7
charts, booklist, glossary, index. 235 pages. **$11.95**

THAILAND HANDBOOK   by Carl Parkes
Presents the richest source of information on travel in Thailand. Color and b/w photos, illustrations, maps, charts, booklist, glossary, index. 600 pages   **$16.95**

TIBET HANDBOOK   by Victor Chan
This remarkable book is both a comprehensive trekking guide and a pilgrimage guide that draws on Tibetan literature and religious history. Color and b/w photos, illustrations, maps, charts, booklist, glossary, index. 1,200 pages.   **$24.95**

The Hawaiian Series

BIG ISLAND OF HAWAII HANDBOOK   by J.D. Bisignani
An entertaining yet informative text packed with insider tips on accommodations, dining, sports and outdoor activities, natural attractions, and must-see sights. 12 color pages, 72 b/w photos, 73 illustrations, 22 maps, 5 charts, booklist, glossary, index. 347 pages.   **$11.95**

HAWAII HANDBOOK   by J.D. Bisignani
Winner of the 1989 Hawaii Visitors Bureau's Best Guide Book Award and the Grand Award for Excellence in Travel Journalism, this guide takes you beyond the glitz and high-priced hype and leads you to a genuine Hawaiian experience. 12 color pages, 86 b/w photos, 132 illustrations, 86 maps, 44 graphs and charts, Hawaiian and pidgin glossaries, appendix, booklist, index. 879 pages.   **$15.95**

KAUAI HANDBOOK   by J.D. Bisignani
Kauai Handbook is the perfect antidote to the workaday world. 8 color pages, 36 b/w photos, 48 illustrations, 19 maps, 10 tables and charts, Hawaiian and pidgin glossaries, booklist, index. 236 pages.   **$9.95**

MAUI HANDBOOK: Including Molokai and Lanai   by J.D. Bisignani
"No fool-'round" advice on accommodations, eateries, and recreation, plus a comprehensive introduction to island ways, geography, and history. 8 color pages, 60 b/w photos, 72 illustrations, 34 maps, 19 charts, booklist, glossary, index. 350 pages.   **$11.95**

OAHU HANDBOOK   by J.D. Bisignani
A handy guide to Honolulu, renowned surfing beaches, and Oahu's countless other diversions. 12 color pages, 93 b/w photos, 67 illustrations, 18 maps, 8 charts, booklist, glossary, index. 354 pages. **$11.95**

The Americas Series

ALASKA-YUKON HANDBOOK   by Deke Castleman and Don Pitcher
Get the inside story, with plenty of well-seasoned advice to help you cover more miles on less money. 8 color pages, 26 b/w photos, 95 illustrations, 92 maps, 10 charts, booklist, glossary, index. 384 pages.   **$13.95**

ARIZONA TRAVELER'S HANDBOOK   by Bill Weir
This meticulously researched guide contains everything necessary to make Arizona accessible and enjoyable. 8 color pages, 194 b/w photos, 74 illustrations, 53 maps, 6 charts, booklist, index. 505 pages.   **$14.95**

BAJA HANDBOOK by Joe Cummings
A comprehensive guide with all the travel information and background on the land, history, and culture of this untamed thousand-mile-long peninsula. 8 color pages, 40 b/w photos, 28 illustrations, 41 maps, 29 charts, booklist, index. 356 pages. **$13.95**

BELIZE HANDBOOK by Chicki Mallan
Complete with detailed maps, practical information, and an overview of the area's flamboyant history, culture, and geographical features, *Belize Handbook* is the only comprehensive guide of its kind to this spectacular region. 8 color pages, 65 b/w photos, 43 illustrations, 25 maps, 30 charts, booklist, index. 212 pages. **$11.95**

BRITISH COLUMBIA HANDBOOK by Jane King
With an emphasis on outdoor adventures, this guide covers mainland British Columbia, Vancouver Island, the Queen Charlotte Islands, and the Canadian Rockies. 8 color pages, 56 b/w photos, 45 illustrations, 66 maps, 4 charts, booklist, index. 381 pages. **$13.95**

CANCUN HANDBOOK and Mexico's Caribbean Coast by Chicki Mallan
Covers the city's luxury scene as well as more modest attractions, plus many side trips to unspoiled beaches and Mayan ruins. 12 color pages, 76 b/w photos, 25 illustrations, 24 maps, 12 charts, Spanish glossary, booklist, index. 257 pages. **$10.95**

CATALINA ISLAND HANDBOOK: A Guide to California's Channel Islands
by Chicki Mallan
A complete guide to these remarkable islands, from the windy solitude of the Channel Islands National Marine Sanctuary to bustling Avalon. 8 color pages, 105 b/w photos, 65 illustrations, 40 maps, 32 charts, booklist, index. 245 pages. **$10.95**

COLORADO HANDBOOK by Stephen Metzger
Essential details to the all-season possibilities in Colorado fill this guide. Practical travel tips combine with recreation—skiing, nightlife, and wilderness exploration—plus entertaining essays. 8 color pages, 92 b/w photos, 15 illustrations, 57 maps, 10 charts, booklist, index. 422 pages. **$15.95**

IDAHO HANDBOOK by Bill Loftus
A year-round guide to everything in this outdoor wonderland, from whitewater adventures to rural hideaways. 8 color pages, 35 b/w photos, 21 illustrations, 42 maps, booklist, index. 275 pages. **$12.95**

JAMAICA HANDBOOK by Karl Luntta
From the sun and surf of Montego Bay and Ocho Rios to the cool slopes of the Blue Mountains, author Karl Luntta offers island-seekers a perceptive, personal view of Jamaica. 8 color pages, 21 b/w photos, 35 illustrations, 16 maps, 7 charts, booklist, glossary, index. 213 pages. **$12.95**

MONTANA HANDBOOK by W.C. McRae and Judy Jewell
The wild West is yours with this extensive guide to the Treasure State, complete with travel practicalities, history, and lively essays on Montana life. 8 color pages, 62 b/w photos, 43 illustrations, 49 maps, 10 charts, booklist, index. 393 pages. **$13.95**

NEVADA HANDBOOK by Deke Castleman
Nevada Handbook puts the Silver State into perspective and makes it manageable and affordable. 34 b/w photos, 43 illustrations, 37 maps, 17 charts, booklist, index. 400 pages. **$12.95**

NEW MEXICO HANDBOOK by Stephen Metzger
A close-up and complete look at every aspect of this wondrous state. 8 color pages, 85 b/w photos, 63 illustrations, 50 maps, 10 charts, booklist, index. 375 pages. **$13.95**

NORTHERN CALIFORNIA HANDBOOK by Kim Weir
An outstanding companion for imaginative travel in the territory north of the Tehachapis. 12 color pages, 200 b/w photos, 54 maps, 36 illustrations, booklist, index. 759 pages. **$16.95**

OREGON HANDBOOK by Stuart Warren and Ted Long Ishikawa
Brimming with travel practicalities and insider views on Oregon's history, culture, arts, and activities. 8 color pages, 113 b/w photos, 26 illustrations, 28 maps, 20 charts, booklist, index. 422 pages. **$12.95**

TEXAS HANDBOOK by Joe Cummings
Seasoned travel writer Joe Cummings brings an insider's perspective to his home state. 8 color pages, 79 b/w photos, 60 maps, 45 illustrations, 18 charts, booklist, index. 483 pages. **$13.95**

UTAH HANDBOOK by Bill Weir
Weir gives you all the carefully researched facts and background to make your visit a success. 8 color pages, 102 b/w photos, 61 illustrations, 30 maps, 9 charts, booklist, index. 452 pages. **$12.95**

WASHINGTON HANDBOOK by Dianne J. Boulerice Lyons and Archie Satterfield
Covers sights, shopping, services, transportation, and outdoor recreation, with complete listings for restaurants and accommodations. 8 color pages, 92 b/w photos, 24 illustrations, 81 maps, 8 charts, booklist, index. 433 pages. **$13.95**

WYOMING HANDBOOK by Don Pitcher
All you need to know to open the doors to this wide and wild state. 16 color pages, 30 b/w photos, 42 illustrations, 64 maps, 19 charts, booklist, index. 427 pages. **$12.95**

YUCATAN HANDBOOK by Chicki Mallan
All the information you'll need to guide you into every corner of this exotic land. 8 color pages, 154 b/w photos, 55 illustrations, 57 maps, 70 charts, appendix, booklist, Mayan and Spanish glossaries, index. 391 pages. **$12.95**

The International Series

EGYPT HANDBOOK by Kathy Hansen
An invaluable resource for intelligent travel in Egypt. 8 color pages, 20 b/w photos, 150 illustrations, 80 detailed maps and plans to museums and archaeological sites, Arabic glossary, booklist, index. 510 pages. **$14.95**

MOSCOW-LENINGRAD HANDBOOK by Masha Nordbye
Provides the visitor with an extensive introduction to the history, culture, and people of these two great cities, as well as practical information on where to stay, eat, and shop. 8 color pages, 36 b/w photos, 20 illustrations, 16 maps, 9 charts, booklist, index. 205 pages. **$12.95**

NEPAL HANDBOOK by Kerry Moran
Whether you're planning a week in Kathmandu or months out on the trail, *Nepal Handbook* will take you into the heart of this Himalayan jewel. 16 color pages, 76 b/w photos, 45 illustrations, 46 maps, 9 charts, booklist, glossary, index. 378 pages. **$12.95**

NEPALI AAMA by Broughton Coburn
A delightful photo-journey into the life of a Gurung tribeswoman of Central Nepal. Having lived with Aama (translated, "mother") for two years, first as an outsider and later as an adopted member of the family, Coburn presents an intimate glimpse into a culture alive with humor, folklore, religion, and ancient rituals. 67 b/w photos. 165 pages. **$13.95**

PAKISTAN HANDBOOK by Isobel Shaw
For armchair travelers and trekkers alike, the most detailed and authoritative guide to Pakistan ever published. 28 color pages, 86 maps, appendices, Urdu glossary, booklist, index. 478 pages. **$15.95**

Moonbelts

Made of heavy-duty Cordura nylon, the Moonbelt offers maximum protection for your money and important papers. This all-weather pouch slips under your shirt or waistband, rendering it virtually undetectable and inaccessible to pickpockets. One-inch-wide nylon webbing, heavy-duty zipper, one-inch quick release buckle. Accommodates traveler's checks, passport, cash, photos. Size 5 x 9 inches. Black. **$8.95**

Travel Matters

Travel Matters is a biannual newsletter for travelers, containing book reviews, practical travel news, articles, and humorous essays. For a free copy, call Moon Publications toll-free at (800) 345-5473.

**New travel handbooks may be available that are not on this list.
To find out more about current or upcoming titles,
call us toll-free at (800) 345-5473.**

IMPORTANT ORDERING INFORMATION

FOR FASTER SERVICE: Call to locate the bookstore nearest you that carries Moon Travel Handbooks or order directly from Moon Publications:

(800) 345-5473 · Monday-Friday · 9 a.m.-5 p.m. PST · fax (916) 345-6751

PRICES: All prices are subject to change. We always ship the most current edition. We will let you know if there is a price increase on the book you ordered.

SHIPPING & HANDLING OPTIONS:
   1) Domestic UPS or USPS first class (allow 10 working days for delivery):
      $3.50 for the first item, 50 cents for each additional item.

Exceptions:
   · **Moonbelt** shipping is $1.50 for one, 50 cents for each additional belt.
   · Add $2.00 for same-day handling.
   2) UPS 2nd Day Air or Printed Airmail requires a special quote.
   3) International Surface Bookrate (8-12 weeks delivery):
      $3.00 for the first item, $1.00 for each additional item. Note: Moon Publications cannot guarantee international surface bookrate shipping.

FOREIGN ORDERS: All orders which originate outside the U.S.A. must be paid for with either an International Money Order or a check in U.S. currency drawn on a major U.S. bank based in the U.S.A.

TELEPHONE ORDERS: We accept Visa or MasterCard payments. Minimum order is US $15.00. Call in your order: 1 (800) 345-5473. 9 a.m.-5 p.m. Pacific Standard Time.

ORDER FORM

Be sure to call (800) 345-5473 for current prices and editions or for the name of the bookstore nearest you that carries Moon Travel Handbooks · 9 a.m.-5 p.m. PST
(See important ordering information on preceding page)

Name:_____Date:_____

Street:_____

City:_____Daytime Phone:_____

State or Country:_____Zip Code:_____

Quantity	Title	Price

Taxable Total

Sales Tax (7.25%) for California Residents

Shipping & Handling

TOTAL

Ship: ☐ 1st class   ☐ UPS (no P.O. Boxes)   ☐ International Surface

Ship to: ☐ address above   ☐ other_____

_____

_____

Make checks payable to:
Moon Publications Inc., 722 Wall Street, Chico, California 95928 U.S.A.
We Accept Visa and MasterCard
To Order: Call in your Visa or MasterCard number, or send a written order with your Visa or MasterCard number and expiration date clearly written.

Card Number: ☐ **Visa** ☐ **MasterCard**

☐ ☐ ☐ ☐   ☐ ☐ ☐ ☐   ☐ ☐ ☐ ☐   ☐ ☐ ☐ ☐

Exact Name on Card: ☐ same as above   expiration date:_____

☐ other_____

signature_____

3-76-X